THE RUGG SOCIAL SCIENCE COURSE

THE READING BOOKS

VOLUME I · An Introduction to American Civilization

VOLUME II · Changing Civilizations in the Modern World

VOLUME III · A History of American Civilization: Economic and Social

VOLUME IV · A History of American Government and Culture

VOLUME V · An Introduction to Problems of American Culture

VOLUME VI · Changing Governments and Changing Cultures

THE WORKBOOKS

VOLUME I · Pupil's Workbook of Directed Study to accompany *An Introduction to American Civilization*

VOLUME II · Pupil's Workbook of Directed Study to accompany *Changing Civilizations in the Modern World*

VOLUME III · Pupil's Workbook of Directed Study to accompany *A History of American Civilization: Economic and Social*

VOLUME IV · Pupil's Workbook of Directed Study to accompany *A History of American Government and Culture*

VOLUME V · Pupil's Workbook of Directed Study to accompany *An Introduction to Problems of American Culture*

VOLUME VI · Pupil's Workbook of Directed Study to accompany *Changing Governments and Changing Cultures*

THE TEACHER'S GUIDES

VOLUME I · Teacher's Guide for *An Introduction to American Civilization*

VOLUME II · Teacher's Guide for *Changing Civilizations in the Modern World*

VOLUME III · Teacher's Guide for *A History of American Civilization: Economic and Social*

VOLUME IV · Teacher's Guide for *A History of American Government and Culture*

VOLUME V · Teacher's Guide for *An Introduction to Problems of American Culture*

VOLUME VI · Teacher's Guide for *Changing Governments and Changing Cultures*

CHANGING GOVERNMENTS AND CHANGING CULTURES

The World's March toward Democracy

BY

HAROLD RUGG

PROFESSOR OF EDUCATION, TEACHERS COLLEGE
COLUMBIA UNIVERSITY

GINN AND COMPANY
BOSTON · NEW YORK · CHICAGO · LONDON
ATLANTA · DALLAS · COLUMBUS · SAN FRANCISCO

PRINTED IN THE UNITED STATES OF AMERICA

832.4

The Athenæum Press
GINN AND COMPANY · PROPRIETORS · BOSTON · U.S.A.

PREFACE

The sixth volume of the Rugg Social-Science Course, *Changing Governments and Changing Cultures: The World's March toward Democracy,* may be used, along with the fifth volume of the series, as a self-contained elementary treatment of world culture. The pupil who may not have studied the previous volumes of the series will suffer no inconvenience. Although reference to these volumes is freely made, the particular fact or principle which is important at the moment is always summarized so that the argument may be followed without embarrassment.

What is this Course in Social Science?

This series of *Reading Books* with their accompanying *Workbooks of Directed Study* introduce the pupil to world civilizations and their history. The first volume, *An Introduction to American Civilization,* concerns chiefly economic life in the United States today. The second volume, *Changing Civilizations in the Modern World,* introduces the pupil to economic and social life in other lands. It considers especially the great industrial nations, the changing agricultural countries, and the interrelation of the two. The third, *A History of American Civilization: Economic and Social,* discusses the land, industrial and commercial history, and their effect upon American society. The fourth, *A History of American Government and Culture,* deals with the experiments in government during America's march toward democracy. Together these last two volumes comprise a comprehensive history of the civilization and culture of the United States in its geographic setting.

The fifth volume, *An Introduction to Problems of American Culture,* completes the description of American society, treating especially the life of the individual in the communities of our changing civilization. It also serves the special purpose of introducing the economic, political, and social problems of American culture — problems the more adequate study of which may well engage the attention of students in the senior high school and the college. This present volume, *Changing Governments and Changing Cultures,* introduces American youth to an understanding of the chief political and social problems of other leading countries of the world.

Thus Volume V rounds out the material of Volume I and Volume VI that of Volume II. The six volumes taken together are designed to provide a comprehensive introduction to modes of living and insistent problems of the modern world.

The Importance of Introducing Youth to an Understanding of Contemporary Civilization

The author firmly believes that young Americans can be given an appreciation of the significant contemporary problems of living together. Current conditions in America throw into sharp relief the critical need of teaching our youth to understand American life and its relation to the modern world. Our schools are confronted with the difficult task of educating pupils to become informed, thinking citizens. During the past 150 years the rapid development of industrial civilization has produced problems of living together that baffle even the keenest adult minds.

It is of the utmost importance that schools bend every effort to introduce our young people to the chief conditions and problems which will confront them as citizens of the world. That is the essential purpose of this new unified course in the social studies.

The Materials are based upon the Findings of Specialists

The foundation of this new course is a series of studies of the basic modes of living and the problems of modern life, the great movements through which institutions and problems have evolved, and the chief concepts and principles which, as history has proved, lie at the roots of living together.

Who knows best what these great institutions, problems, and trends are? Specialists on the frontier of thought who see society from a height, who detect its trends and the long-time movement of its affairs. From the mature thought of established students of modern life and its historical development, therefore, instead of from the single judgments of the textbook-maker, the skeleton of this course has been designed. It is based upon nine years of investigational work. In that time thirteen research studies of what to teach have been made.

A Unified Course in Social Science

Why one general course rather than the separate subjects of history, geography, and civics? Because the chief aim is to understand modern life and how it came to be. To understand any institution or condition of life today the mind must utilize facts, meanings, generalizations, and historical movements that in the past have been set up in separate school subjects. For example, to understand the westward movement of the American people one must see in close relationship the tide of immigration across the continent; the blazing of trails; the evolution of new land and waterways; the rapid development of new types of transportation; constantly changing forms of social life; the rise of cities behind the advancing frontier; the influence of mountains, deserts, climate, rivers, and soil upon travel, transportation, and communication; and where and how people live. All these factors must be tied closely together in their natural relationships. Hence the necessity of combining them into one general course instead of teaching them as separate subjects. In constructing this course one question has constantly been in the foreground: What facts, historical movements, meanings, and principles do young people need to study together to understand the modern world?

In *Changing Governments and Changing Cultures* as in the other volumes of this series, historical, geographic, economic, and other materials are studied *in close relationship*. Whenever history is needed to understand the present, history is presented. If geographic relationships are needed to throw light upon contemporary problems, those geographic relationships are incorporated. The same thing has been done with economic and social facts and principles.

This has *not* caused a reduction in the amount of history or of geography included in the course. Rather, it has produced a sharp increase in the amount of these subjects in the curriculum, and in addition has added to the curriculum a wealth of new material. Comparisons of the amount of history and geography in these six *Reading Books* with that of conventional textbooks in these subjects *should be based on a study of the total series and not on any one book.*

The Use of the Dramatic Episode

The readers of this book will encounter a second novel characteristic: *the frequent use of dramatic episodes.* If young people are to be brought to an understanding of our complicated civilization, it must be chiefly through the medium of words. Hence the imperative need of dramatizing the past and present story of the important modern civilizations and their relations to one another. In this course each topic is illustrated by vivid episodes and by a wealth of maps, graphs, and pictorial material far in excess of their present use in textbooks. The substitution of this vivid episodical treatment for the encyclopedic one which characterizes many of our current school histories and geographies has necessitated a marked increase in the volume of reading material.

"Learning by Doing": the *Pupil's Workbook of Directed Study*

The very center of this course in the social studies is the problem-solving activities of the *Workbook.* The chief goal of the social studies is active and intelligent participation in American civilization and tolerant understanding of other civilizations. To guarantee the attainment of this goal the school must organize its work around a core of dynamic pupil activities. *Young people grow in understanding only by participating actively in the study of the society around them.* Even to the present day the work in the social studies has consisted too much of memoriter recitation from the contents of encyclopedic textbooks in history, geography, and civics.

The essence of this new course in social studies is a succession of pupil activities, dynamic and thought-provoking. Many optional suggestions for these activities are incorporated in the *Workbook* and presented as a series of problems. Each problem of this course is an organized scheme of things for the pupil to do. Each unit compels him to find the answer to one or more important questions. The course, as presented in the *Workbook,* therefore, constantly confronts the pupil with stimulating problems, insight into each of which is important for an adequate understanding of the problems of the modern world. Hence the *Pupil's Workbook of Directed Study* is the very core of the course, and the *Reading Book* has been constructed, unit by unit, in close conjunction with it.

Planned Repetition

The fourth characteristic of this course is the carefully planned recurrence of important concepts, generalizations, and historical themes in varied settings. One of the weaknesses of current school courses in history, geography, and civics is lack of planned repetition. In the present course this defect has been remedied by designing a carefully planned scheme of repetition. In preparing each topic the outstanding concepts, generalizations, and themes that an educated mind should understand have been charted in advance. Episodes, narratives, statistical and graphic exhibits, pictures, and maps have been selected with the need for the illustration of these items clearly in mind. Hence the student will encounter the important meanings, principles, and movements over and over again, but constantly presented in new and varied settings.

Hundreds of Schools have coöperated in the Preparation of this Course, 1922–1929

How can one feel sure that this course is within the comprehension and ability of the pupil?

It has passed through three experimental editions — the first was used in mimeographed form, 1921–1922; the second consisted of printed books used in 1922–1923 in more than 100 school systems; the third consisted of completely reconstructed printed books (known as the *Social Science Pamphlets*) used in more than 300 school systems, 1923–1929.

This series of books could not have been developed successfully without the coöperation of a large number of public and private schools. In more than 40 states, hundreds of schools have purchased and tried out under our direction copies of the experimental editions. Over 600,000 copies of the pamphlets were used by pupils from 1922 to 1929.

Furthermore, the present series has been written with a much simpler vocabulary than was used even in the third experimental edition.

Every kind of community in the United States — small towns, medium-sized cities, large cities — has made experimental use of these books. More than 50,000 tests taken by pupils have been returned to us for examination. The judgments of more than 1000 teachers have been obtained, concerning needed revisions. Many round-table conferences have been held with small groups of teachers using the experimental editions. The theory of the course has been discussed with hundreds of audiences in the past seven years. Debates have been held with specialists in history and geography. Furthermore, careful measurements have proved that several thousand pupils studying the experimental edition achieved a markedly superior understanding of modern life and a distinctly higher ability in thinking about it than a group of 1500 pupils who had studied under similar conditions the conventional history-geography-civics courses.

THE COURSE IS BASED UPON AN ELABORATE PROGRAM OF RESEARCH[1]

Twenty-two thorough investigations have been made dealing with the following topics:

1. Thirteen studies of what to teach of the problems of contemporary life, of the chief trends of civilization, and

[1] The entire nine years' investigational work will be reported in a monograph (in preparation) entitled *American Civilization and the Curriculum of the Social Sciences* (Bureau of Publications, Teachers College, Columbia University). It will also be summarized in *The Psychology and Teaching of the Social Studies* (in preparation). Of the studies upon

of the central concepts and principles which educated minds use in thinking about them.

2. Three scientific studies of grade placement of curriculum materials and of the development of pupil's abilities.
3. Six studies of learning and of the organization of curriculum materials. These have also contributed to the arrangement of the material in this course.

The Need for a Large Allotment of Time for the Social Studies

Finally, no adequate course in the social studies can be developed successfully in the time now allotted to it in most public and private schools. Our elaborate program of research and our seven years of work with experimental editions prove conclusively that *more* than 60 minutes of daily class time must be devoted to the social studies in order that young people may obtain even a partial understanding of modern civilization. The social-studies course should be the intellectual core of the school curriculum. It is earnestly hoped that schools will provide adequately for this central core by allotting to it a large amount of time.

An Important Caution about Accuracy in Using Facts

In this book there are many statements of fact which are necessary for an understanding of the history of our country and its relations to other nations. We have tried to make sure that the facts are stated accurately. One difficulty has been encountered, however: that even the most reliable sources from which

which this course is based the following have already been published: C. O. Matthews, *Grade Placement of Curriculum Materials in the Social Studies* (Bureau of Publications, Teachers College, Columbia University); Harold Rugg and John A. Hockett, *Objective Studies in Map Location* (Bureau of Publications, Teachers College, Columbia University); John A. Hockett's *The Determination of the Major Social Problems of American Life* (Bureau of Publications, Teachers College, Columbia University); Hyman Meltzer, *Children's Social Concepts* (Bureau of Publications, Teachers College, Columbia University); Earle Rugg, *Studies in Curriculum Construction in the Social Studies* (State Teachers College, Greeley, Colorado); "The Social Studies in the Elementary and Secondary School," Part II of the Twenty-second Yearbook of the National Society for the Study of Education (Public School Publishing Company); Neal Billings, *A Determination of Generalizations Basic to the Social Science Curriculum* (Bureau of Publications, Teachers College, Columbia University).

the statistics and other facts have been selected do not always agree. It was necessary, therefore, to choose among them those statements which appear to us to be most accurate.

The reader will note the frequent use of round numbers in statements of number of inhabitants, distances, areas, etc. In most cases it is not important to remember the exact figures; it *is* important, however, to obtain a correct impression from the use of the facts. Hence approximate numbers and estimates have been frequently used. The student should constantly ask himself, How reliable are these facts? He should learn that in the past 100 years the scientific way of doing things has made our records more and more accurate. Nevertheless, much improvement in this matter is still needed. In spite of great care in checking the facts that have been given, the reader may find instances in which correction should be made.

In Acknowledgment

This enterprise could not have been developed without the cooperative support and friendly and critical advice of many persons. First, there are several thousand progressive administrators and teachers who contributed criticisms and suggestions. From 1922 to 1929 inclusive these educational leaders gave unsparingly of their energy to the experimental trial of the tentative editions of these books. By their courage and vision in utilizing novel materials in the social sciences, they have put the children of American schools as well as myself in their debt.

Second, there is the administration of Teachers College, Columbia University, and of the Lincoln School. The American children who will use these materials owe a debt of gratitude to the deans of Teachers College and the directors of the Lincoln School for permitting and encouraging the development of this course by experimental methods.

I have acknowledged with pleasure in the body of the text many instances of coöperation from publishers who permitted quotations from their publications and the reproduction of illustrative materials. Almost without exception requests for coöperation of this character have been cordially granted.

Without the unfailing coöperation of my friends George F. Nugent and R. P. Nugent, Jr., it would have been impossible to carry on this experimental enterprise.

I have listed on a following page the names of the members of the research and editorial staff who contributed studies and materials to the experimental editions of the *Social-Science Pamphlets*.

In addition I wish to express my appreciation for loyal and intelligent assistance in preparing Volume V to Ruth Muriel Aspray and Helen Yorker. For the editing of these volumes to fit the needs of juvenile readers I am deeply indebted to Louise Krueger.

This statement of my indebtedness should not be permitted to close without referring to the unsparing efforts of the staff of Ginn and Company to produce a practicable, attractive, and teachable body of materials. But especially I wish to express my appreciation for the encouragement and support given by Messrs. Charles H. Thurber, Henry H. Hilton, and Burdette R. Buckingham.

HAROLD RUGG

NEW YORK

The following research and editorial staff contributed studies or materials utilized in the various editions of this series of books.

THE FIRST EXPERIMENTAL EDITION
1921–1923

PREPARED BY

HAROLD RUGG

WITH THE ASSISTANCE OF

EARLE RUGG
EMMA SCHWEPPE
MARIE GULBRANSEN

THE SECOND EXPERIMENTAL EDITION
1923–1926

PREPARED BY THE COLLABORATION OF

HAROLD RUGG
ELIZABETH G. WOODS
EMMA SCHWEPPE
JOHN A. HOCKETT

RESEARCH ASSOCIATES

JAMES E. MENDENHALL, 1926–1931
EARLE RUGG, 1921–1923
JOHN A. HOCKETT, 1924–1927
JOHN N. WASHBURNE, 1923–1926
H. MELTZER, 1924–1925
C. O. MATHEWS, 1925–1927
B. R. SHOWALTER, 1924–1925
NEAL BILLINGS, 1924–1927, 1928
HELEN M. LYND, 1926–1927
LAURANCE F. SHAFFER, 1926–1928, 1928–1929

EDITORIAL AND RESEARCH ASSISTANTS

FRANCES M. FOSTER, 1923–1927, 1928–1931
ETHELWYN M. MENDENHALL, 1926–1928
FRANCES YOUTZ, 1927–1929
ELIZABETH MOREY, 1927–1928
JOAN WALKER COYNE, 1929–1930
LOUISE KRUEGER, 1929–1931
RUTH M. ASPRAY, 1930–1931

CONTENTS

UNIT I

INTRODUCING CHANGING GOVERNMENTS AND CHANGING CULTURES

UNIT II

THE BACKGROUND OF WESTERN DEMOCRACY

UNIT III

ENGLAND'S MARCH TOWARD DEMOCRACY

UNIT IV

THE MARCH TOWARD DEMOCRACY IN FRANCE AND GERMANY

UNIT V

CHANGING GOVERNMENTS AND THE WORLD WAR

UNIT VI

RUSSIA: NEW EXPERIMENTS IN GOVERNMENT

UNIT VII

INDUSTRIAL EUROPE PRODUCES A NEW CULTURE

UNIT VIII

THE SPREAD OF EUROPEAN CIVILIZATION AROUND THE WORLD

UNIT IX

HOW THE MODERN WORLD IS GOVERNED

UNIT X

WORLD CONFLICT VERSUS WORLD ORGANIZATION

CHANGING GOVERNMENTS AND CHANGING CULTURES

UNIT I

INTRODUCING CHANGING GOVERNMENTS AND CHANGING CULTURES

CHAPTER I

STORM CENTERS OF THE WORLD: INTRODUCING CHANGING GOVERNMENTS AND CHANGING CULTURES

An epoch-making moment!

Armistice Day, November 11, 1918! The one thought in the minds of the people of all civilized countries was—"The War is over!" The most terrible struggle of history was at an end.

For four long years the peoples of the earth had been thrown into chaos. The prosperous and happy life of the Europeans had been transformed into one of terror and grief. Husbands, fathers, and brothers had marched away from their homes never to return. Mothers had left little children and worked in ammunition factories, tilled fields, driven trucks. Peace-time activities were paralyzed for four years. People had thought of nothing but — War! War! War!

The results of the war were shocking. The whole interdependent trading life of the continent of Europe had crashed. Twenty-six million men, women, and little children were dead, and nearly $200,000,000,000 worth of homes, factories, churches, highways, farms, and schools had been destroyed. Prosperous cities were transformed into dilapidated communities half their former size. Millions of people were starving. Terrifying bread lines crowded the streets of many of the larger European capitals.

On every battle front were terrible scenes of destruction. Twenty thousand factories had been blown up, 500,000 homes were destroyed, 8,000,000 acres of land were covered with the débris of war, and one sixteenth of France was devastated. Coal mines were closed, iron mines and railroad lines ruined, telegraph lines torn down, fine macadam highways gutted, canals well-nigh useless, docks out of repair, and river channels clogged, ... and every European country practically in a debtor's prison! (See figure 1.)

Hate had been unloosed upon the earth. Englishmen hated, Frenchmen hated, Germans hated, Russians and Italians hated. Even Americans, who had had no ill feeling for the peoples of central Europe, had been taught to hate.

Such had been the toll of the World War!

Then came Armistice Day, 1918, and millions of people turned with hope to the tasks of rebuilding their civilizations. Seven months later the ambassadors of the warring countries signed the Treaty of Versailles, officially declaring peace once more. It was a tremendous moment in the world's march toward democracy. New nations came into existence, and oppressed peoples were made independent. Dying monarchies and arrogant empires were destroyed, and republics were set up in their places.

Fig. 1. Humanity locked in a debtor's prison of taxes. Humanity looks for a means of escape and finds that it is war which holds him in. (Harding in the Brooklyn *Daily Eagle*)

Thus the slogan of the war was paraphrased, and echoed round the earth: "The World has been made Safe for Democracy!"

But was it true?

Had the staggering sacrifice been worth while? Had the nations of Europe really learned to coöperate and live together in peace? Had the way been paved for the secure establishment of government "of the people, by the people, for the people" in the countries of the earth?

These are very important questions. Upon the answer to them depends the happiness of hundreds of millions of people. It is, perhaps, still too soon to answer them definitely. But more than a decade has passed since Armistice Day, 1918 — a period long enough to reveal the full results of the war. Within that time important events have taken place and important tendencies begin to stand out. A glimpse of a few of these will help to introduce you to our study of changing governments and changing cultures.

Dramatic Events remind us that the World is still in Upheaval

1. Government by dictators and " terror "

RED, BLACK, WHITE, BROWN TERROR RULES EUROPE

That is the headline of a series of thoughtful articles written in 1930 by a famous American journalist in Europe. In these articles and those of other impartial students, we are told that even within the past few years in many parts of Europe government has been carried on by dictators, and often by "terror" — not by democracy. That is, the people have been ruled autocratically by one man or at most a few men and not by their representatives. Let us consider briefly a few examples of dictators and "terror." Later we shall study them carefully.

1. In Italy Mussolini and the *Black* Fascists marched quickly on Rome and *dictated* the government of Italy.
2. In Russia, in 1917, revolutions succeeded one another rapidly. The *Red* Bolsheviks got rid both of the Czars and of the democratic liberals and *dictated* every detail of living.
3. In Spain Primo de Rivera autocratically took the government, keeping King Alfonso XIII upon the throne as a mere figurehead. He too *dictated* government to the Spanish people.
4. In Bavaria *Brown* Fascists led by Adolf Hitler *dictated* local government in many parts of the new German republic.
5. In Bulgaria, Austria, and Rumania *Green* peasant revolts seized control and *dictated* the government.
6. In Turkey Mustafa Kemal overthrew the long-ruling Sultans and *dictated* government. He dictated what people should wear, their religion, their customs — in fact, their very lives.

7. In Poland, in Hungary, in Yugoslavia, in Albania, in Finland, *dictators* seized control of the government after 1918. Even in France various attempts were made to establish a dictatorship.

Thus in almost every country of central and southern Europe where democratic ideas have made little advance, strong, ambitious leaders seized the power and dictated how people should live.

Dictators have kept control of government by creating terror — fear — among their people. Colors are used as symbols of some outstanding characteristic of the ruling group in each country, as we see by the following:

Red: for the red flag of the Russian communist city workers.
Black: for the black shirts of the Fascists of Italy.
White: for the Czarist aristocrats who oppose the dictatorship of the city workers in Russia.
Brown: for the brown shirts of the Bavarian Fascists of Germany.
Green: for the green fields of the peasant autocracies and terrors of eastern Europe.
Blue: for the terror movements in France.

Although we shall study some of these movements carefully in later chapters, note quickly a few events which illustrate their *undemocratic* character.

1. *The Red Terror of the Russian dictators.* In November, 1917, the Bolshevik city workers seized the government of Russia. A small group of less than 2,000,000 workers led by a mere handful of aggressive leaders — for example, Lenin, Trotsky, and Stalin — dictated completely the government of 140,000,000 people. They decided how land, factories, railroads, telegraphs, and stores were to be owned; what wages and salaries were to be paid; the number of rooms to be assigned to a family; how land was to be farmed; and other aspects of life.

In this book we shall study carefully how it was possible for such a small group to control such a large nation. As we do so, we shall find that one way was by terror. The Bolsheviks, *like all other dictators,* threw their opponents into prison. They exiled tens of thousands, and executed not less than 50,000 of their enemies in the first years of their seizure of the government.

2. *The White Terror of the aristocrats.* These Red Bolsheviks, however, had done only what their White aristocratic czarist rulers had done to them in earlier years. It is estimated that White dictators in Russia, Finland, and Hungary had previously executed more than 50,000 opponents of their governments.

3. *The Brown Terror in Bavaria.* Even in more democratic Germany under the new republican government, a new Fascist dictatorship threatens. Under the leadership of Adolf Hitler an organization of World War soldiers, estimated to be 1,000,000 in number, is forming political groups throughout the German republic. Partly through riots and armed force they won more than 100 seats in the *Reichstag*, which is the German parliament. Riots occur even in staid and orderly German cities when the brown-shirted youths attack the meetings of their opponents. In January and February of 1930 more than 30 of these armed attacks were made upon assembled citizens.

FIG. 2. The downward trend in kingships. Note the "ticker" which Royalty watches so anxiously and the abdication which lies ready to be signed. (Sandusky, Ohio *Star-Journal*, N. E. A. Service)

4. *The Green Terror in Bulgaria, Bavaria, Austria, and Rumania.* In the meantime the common people of the farms also employed terror to enforce their will on their enemies. Peasant uprisings in four central-European regions have used precisely the same means of oppression. In the countries of eastern and central Europe the peasants rise against any group that tries to take their land. For example, in 1929 Rumanian peasants assembled in Bucharest, the leading city of Rumania, caused the defeat of the White aristocrats, and began a Green Terror. People were imprisoned, the press and free speech were suppressed, and other civil rights were abolished.

Thus we see another example of the way in which groups that have been long suppressed turn on their former oppressors when they themselves come into power.

5. *The Italian dictatorship.* Similar conditions existed and still exist, according to impartial foreign observers, under the Fascist government of Mussolini. It is reported on good authority that defenders of democracy have been imprisoned, among them educated writers, lawyers, and independent-minded thinkers. Freedom of speech, freedom of the press, the right of trial by jury,—indeed, all the rights of civil liberty,—are threatened under such a dictator form of government.

FIG. 3. The cartoonist shows us the mailed, or iron, fist of the Kaiser and of Hitler. What is he trying to tell us? (From *The Record*, Glasgow)

6. *Other dictatorships.* The history of government in some of the republics of Latin America, for example, has been little more than the rise and fall of dictatorships. Recall the recent political histories of Mexico, Haiti, Costa Rica, Nicaragua, and Panama. Elections are still frequently won by armed force. Leaders at the head of small national armies rise to power, rule a few years, and then lose control to more powerful dictators.

In these introductory pages we cannot take space for the many other instances of the seizure of the government of a people by daring leaders without the approval of the people themselves. It must be sufficient merely to remind ourselves that in all the continents of the world this is still happening.

These, then, are a few dramatic examples of government in the Western world. Do they not raise serious questions in our mind as to whether the world has really been made "safe for democracy"?

2. Is "all Europe preparing for the biggest war"?

Less dramatic than the seizure of government by dictators, but equally important in the history of world affairs, is the preparation for war. Many students of international affairs declare that the arming of nations is proceeding today more rapidly than ever before in the history of the world. No doubt there is some exaggeration in such statements, but much undeniable evidence of their truth confronts us.

FIG. 4. Civilization adrift and dangerously weighted down. What meaning has the dove in the cartoon? (Macauley in the Brooklyn *Daily Eagle*)

For example, it is estimated by authorities that not less than 3,500,000 trained troops are now ready for action in Europe. There are more than 600,000 active troops in Russia, almost as many in France, almost 400,000 in Italy, and about 200,000 in Great Britain. In addition Russia has 4,528,000 organized reserves, while France has 5,675,000, Italy has 5,551,450, and Great Britain has almost 319,000. It is much the same in the other nations.

In a recent report General Summerall, the former Chief of Staff of the American army, states:

> The past decade has seen no reduction in the mobilization forces of foreign nations . . . the number of men under arms throughout the world is greater than at any previous epoch in the peace-time history of mankind.

The race for the greatest army and navy is revealed in other ways. Scores of warships, cruisers, destroyers, and submarines are being built by France, Italy, England, the United States, Japan, and other countries. Chemical works are being equipped so that on short notice they can be used to manufacture poison gas. Commercial airplanes are being constructed so that they can be swiftly changed into military planes carrying machine guns, bombs, and even small cannon.

Reliable scientific studies have recently come from the press which set forth the enormous expenditures for armaments.[1] A yearbook of the League of Nations presents statistics of moneys spent by six of the leading nations from 1909 to 1928 for military preparation; Table I gives the figures for 1909, 1913, 1926, and 1928. Careful estimates of the Carnegie Endowment for International Peace show that between $4,000,000,000 and $5,000,000,000 was spent for armaments in the year 1930.

TABLE I

Money spent for Military Preparation by Great Britain, France, Japan, the United States, Russia, and Italy	
Before the World War	
1909	$1,602,200,000
1913	2,032,080,000
After the World War	
1926	$2,157,400,000
1928	2,641,000,000

Thus we see that although the world is facing enormous debts for past wars, these debts are being multiplied today in every leading country of the earth. These expenditures, we must remember, are for preparations for *another* war. To get the *total* expenditure for war, the amount spent to pay the debts incurred in *former* wars must be added. When this is done, the amount becomes staggering. It was estimated that in Great Britain, France, and the United States in 1930 approximately three fourths of the huge national expenditures in each country were for war!

These preparations for war are opposed by preparations for world peace

Against this mad rush toward war are the brave struggles of officials and private organizations for the advancement of peace. These we shall also study with care in this book. For example, we shall study the activities of the League of Nations in Geneva, of the International Labor Organization, of the International Institute of Intellectual Co-operation in Paris, and of other international organizations. We shall see how idealists in many

[1] These studies are based upon official figures issued in yearbooks and other documents of the League of Nations, in Geneva.

countries are striving with might and main to build up international understanding through bureaus of education, through schools and colleges, through adult education, and through the work of international educational societies. We shall see the growing movement toward a world peace.

These are but a few conspicuous examples of the peace movements that we shall study in this book. Through these and others we shall review the difficult problems of peace and war.

3. The unrest among the mixed populations of Europe and Asia

Another problem which we shall study carefully is that of the friction between the races, nationalities, and religious groups within most of the countries of Europe and Asia. From Ireland and the British Isles to Siberia, Manchuria, and Korea — a distance of more than 6500 miles — peoples of different races and nations and religions live mixed up together in a score of countries. Not that they live in harmony and good will. Descendants of Irishmen and Scotchmen oppose one another in Ireland. Antagonism exists among Welshmen, Scotchmen, and Englishmen in the United Kingdom. Walloons and Flemings scoff at one another in Belgium. Both Frenchmen and Germans make up the restless and discontented population of Alsace-Lorraine. Czechs, Germans, Poles, Austrians, Hungarians, and others comprise the new little republic of Czechoslovakia; and a dozen nationalities live together in suspicious unrest in Hungary, Austria, Yugoslavia, Rumania, and the other Balkan states.

Scores of differing language and national groups are found throughout the great Union of Socialist Soviet Republics of Russia. India too is made up of a mixture of languages, cultures, and religions. A similar condition keeps parts of China, Mongolia, Manchuria, Indo-China, and the Malay regions in constant turmoil.

Within each of these regions, therefore, there is a lack of understanding among different nationalities and little unity among the population. Differences in language, in traditions, in customs, keep groups in rebellion against those in authority. This problem is a very difficult one, and we must also study it in this volume.

4. Unrest among all the peoples of the industrial world because of unemployment

Once the peace treaty was signed in 1919 the peoples of Europe started vigorously to rebuild their continental system of manufacturing and trade. Mines were opened, and factories were repaired and rebuilt. Rivers and canals became alive with freight and passenger traffic, and radio and aviation service was developed. As time went on, the interdependent scheme of European industry, business, transportation, and communication was put in smooth running order.

© Chicago Tribune

FIG. 5. Here the cartoonist has attempted to show us one of the dangers when millions of people are unemployed. What does the cartoon tell you? (By McCutcheon)

For a few years the tasks of reconstruction kept men busy, but even by the early 1920's many men were out of work. From then on the number of unemployed steadily increased. Indeed, by 1930, there were not less than 10,000,000 idle workers in Europe.

This question of unemployment brings us important problems. Why are there more than 2,600,000 idle workers in England, whose families are living on a "dole," which is a pitifully small sum of money given by the government? Why are the machines and engines of the great textile-manufacturing district of Lancashire silent? Why are there more than 4,700,000 unemployed in Germany? Why do men and women walk the streets of Berlin, Hamburg, Dresden, and other German cities hunting for work?

In Austria, in January, 1931, more than 331,000 people out of work were receiving benefits from compulsory insurance. Why is this true? Even in tiny Denmark, which had stayed out of the war, there were almost 71,000 unemployed. And why do the same conditions prevail in Italy, Czechoslovakia, Spain, Portugal, Belgium, Poland, and other regions of Europe?

The same condition is true even in far-off Japan, which, within the past 50 years, has taken up the machine industrialism of the Western countries. Not less than 500,000 workers are unemployed. Why?

It is clear, then, that distressing problems of unemployment face the people not only of the United States, but of the entire industrial world as well. You have already studied about unemployment in the United States.[1] Do you think that the same factors are responsible for the conditions in other countries? Yes, undoubtedly. In European manufacturing countries men are "hired and fired" in much the same ways as in America. The same changes of seasonal occupations make employment uncertain. But most of all, machines multiply there as here, and millions of men are put out of work by them.

In addition there are serious *international* economic changes which contribute to the growing unemployment in Europe. We shall seek to understand them in our studies this year. For example, we shall learn how the growth of manufacturing in many of the countries which until recently have been largely agricultural has affected England, Germany, and the United States. For many years the latter industrial countries sold their goods to the former. Now those countries manufacture their own goods. Can you see some problems arising as a result?

In this book, then, we shall also study the industrial conditions in these various countries.

So much for storm-torn Europe. In that war-distracted continent, one event after another has revealed nearly 500,000,000 human beings in conflict.

5. Is there a smoldering revolt in Asia?

In Asia, however, the story of a world in ferment is illustrated even more vividly. In our studies we shall see that this vast continent, which for thousands of years lay in quiet isolation

[1] See Volume V, *An Introduction to Problems of American Culture*, Chaps. VIII and IX.

from the changes of the Western world, is now flaring into revolt. From Turkey to the Philippines, from Korea to India, long-oppressed peoples are struggling for greater liberty. The world marches toward democracy in Asia as well as in America and Europe.

Not only against the Europeans, however, but against their own rulers as well, are these Asians in revolt. Note briefly a few examples of the struggles which are taking place in various parts of Asia.

Revolt in Japan and China. In Japan, for example, we are told that revolution against royal rulers is in the air. In great public meetings in the larger cities orators exhort the common people to educate and organize themselves for democracy.

A day and a half westward, across the China Sea, the cities of China — Nanking, Canton, Hong Kong, Shanghai, Peiping, Tientsin — are stirring with exciting events. A nation of 450,000,000 human beings awakens after long isolation from the rest of the world. Young Chinese, educated in Europe and America as engineers, business men, scientists, and democratic statesmen, are arousing the huge masses of their people. Indeed, all China is in an unsettled state. Outside the cities, bandits kidnap wealthy Chinese and occasional Europeans or Americans and hold them for ransom. Military autocrats, who are often generals still in their twenties, conquer whole provinces within a month's time. One revolution succeeds another, and civil war is everywhere.

At the same time, there is also the beginning of a great national movement. In May, 1925, came a violent storm of protest against the continuance of foreign rule over portions of Chinese territory which had been set apart for foreign residents and which had developed into flourishing commercial centers. At Shanghai, for example, a group of Chinese laborers and students gathered in the streets to demonstrate against unfair labor conditions in industries owned by Europeans. Policemen under British officers shot some of them down. Immediately a wave of anti-foreign sentiment swept over China. From the larger Europeanized cities along the coast to the villages far in the interior, "China for the Chinese" has become the new slogan.

Revolt in Indo-China. Similar events are taking place in Indo-China, where the French rule. In Annam, Tongking, Cambodia, and Penang, evidences of the growing friction between the Asians and their European rulers can be seen.

In this region the Chinese are the chief business competitors of the Europeans. They run the little shops, the factories, most of the shipping companies, and the banks. Indeed, the Chinese are the traders of the Far East, and control more than three fourths of the business in the region from Siam to the Philippines.

Already native unrest has burst into open rebellion in Indo-China. Even the long-suffering laborers in the rice fields have risen against their French masters. In the spring of 1930 they started a great strike, as a result of which scores of revolutionaries were executed and hundreds were imprisoned or were exiled. In Yen Bay 200 Tongkingese troops, aided by native civilians, attacked French officers and launched a revolt which spread rapidly into other parts of the country.

New political parties are appearing throughout Indo-China, arousing the people to independence. These parties owe some, at least, of their activity to foreign inspiration: under the leadership of the Russian Soviet government an organization has been launched to develop Asiatic nationalism against European imperialism, and in Indo-China, as elsewhere, agents of this organization have done much to spread unrest among the people.

Revolt in Burma and India. The great peninsula of India also seethes with movements for independence. "Asia for Asians" is the slogan of the All-Indian Nationalist Conference, which meets periodically to assert India's right to rule herself. Mahatma Gandhi, a quiet leader, binds millions of Indians together in passive opposition to Western rule. Although Gandhi is in prison much of the time, his principle of "civil mass disobedience" is followed by millions in India.

Meanwhile there are other evidences of revolt. In the crowded cities white-gowned Indians and Burmese conduct demonstrations against British rule. Parades incite people to boycott European goods, and revolutionary gatherings burn British-made cotton cloth as a sign of their independence. Burmese priests forget their former attentiveness to American and European visitors, shouting roughly at them to remove their stockings as well as their shoes in entering the temples. India too is in revolt.

The Near East begins to adopt Western ways of living but throws off Western control. In Turkey, Persia, Irak, Palestine, Syria, and Egypt the machines, factories, railroads, telegraphs, and telephones, as well as the business methods of the European, are being adopted. Schools are being built, and people are becoming better educated and are learning more about self-government. The movement for independence spreads.

Fig. 6. Gandhi is about to tie firecrackers to the elephant's tail. What will that mean for the British rulers and Indian princes who sit atop the elephant? (From the *Daily Express*, London)

The Arabs, for example, long regarded as indifferent to progressive movements, are beginning to seek ways of expressing themselves and of governing themselves.

Thus, throughout Asia, from Tokyo to Constantinople, revolt is rising against the domination of the European. Japanese leaders in the East work hand in hand with Turkish leaders in the West. The Nationalist leaders of India and of China work together, and commissions of Filipinos seek the support of other Asiatics in their plea for independence from the United States. A new epoch is now being made by this revolt of Asia.

Thus we see that the march of the world toward democracy is producing difficult conflicts

Is there, indeed, any country on earth which is not in upheaval? Are there any places where government is secure and where life goes along peacefully and contentedly? We shall see as we continue our studies.

These Events are the Result of the Startling Economic Changes in Western Europe

It was economic changes which brought about these stirring movements in government. England changed from a tiny country of self-sufficient manors to the modern industrial Great Britain, the center of world trade and of world empire. France, still a country of thrifty shopkeepers and farmers, also built a great industrial system and the second largest empire of the world. Hundreds of quarreling German states slowly unified, and a powerful manufacturing country developed with colonies in Africa and Asia and a remarkable scheme of world trade. Russia, under the autocratic rule of the Czars, conquered all the land between Germany in Europe and the Pacific Ocean, but remained a poverty-stricken country of crude farming villages until after the World War.

These countries and others rapidly built up manufacturing and raced with one another for the trade, land, and markets of Asia, Africa, and America; they conquered and exploited less industrialized peoples; and finally the World War came and dragged them all into armed conflict.

These dramatic events are simply conspicuous examples of deeper movements which the world's march toward democracy has developed

We shall now try to understand the Leading National Cultures of the World

In this book, however, although we shall frequently gather together the chief ideas brought out in the earlier volumes, our work will be concentrated primarily upon the governments and the changing customs and interests of various peoples of the earth. We shall attempt to bring together in closer relationships the threads of historical development, so that we can see as a whole the economic, the political, the social, and the recreational life of different peoples.

As in the preceding volumes of this series, we shall use the single word *culture* to sum up all these ways of living. Because of our frequent use of the term we hope that it does not seem strange and meaningless to you now. Continue to acquire the habit of using it. Remember that *culture simply means the ways in which a people lives, thinks, and feels.* Therefore the culture of the British, French, Italian, Russian, Chinese,— of any people, — is merely what they do and what they are. It is their work life, their play life, and their social life. It is what they think and talk about most, what they enjoy and what they fear, what they appreciate, what they dislike, what they approve, and what they disapprove. Hence our discussions of the culture of each people will bring together all the aspects of their group and individual living.

To understand government and culture in various countries, we must see these countries growing and changing as their civilizations change. Only by seeing them in historical perspective can we form wise conclusions about the advance of democracy around the world. Only thus can we see the insistent problems of today. Hence our study of each country will be historical.

But we shall study history chiefly to understand the problems of today. It is only by perceiving the deep trends and underlying movements of society that we can understand contemporary needs and plan wisely for tomorrow. So in studying each period of the changing government of each country, ask yourself one important question:

What lesson does this teach us that will help solve the world's problem of international coöperation today?

Important Topics and Questions which will Guide our Study

The following topics and questions will guide us as we study the most important governments and cultures in the world today and how these cultures came into being.

1. *The constant struggle of the mass of the people for a larger share in the government.* We shall ask: How democratic was the government? Who could vote and hold office? Who were excluded? Why? Thus the world's march toward democracy will be viewed as was that of America,— namely, as the struggle to

bring "government of the people, by the people, for the people" to the earth.

2. *The continual conflict between groups of people desiring to control the government.* In studying each stage of history we shall be guided constantly by the questions What class or group of people is in control of the government? What classes or groups are opposing them? Why do some groups succeed and others fail?

3. *Changing culture and changing government.* One central theme has appeared in all our studies, — namely, that most of the peoples of the earth live in rapidly changing civilizations. Hence we shall now ask: Did the government of each people change to keep pace with the changing needs of the people? Have all classes and groups of citizens worked together, or have some advocated and others opposed changes in government?

4. *The spread of universal education and the world's march toward democracy.* We shall also inquire: To what extent were the masses of the people educated in each period of their history? Did the spread of universal suffrage parallel the onward march of the people toward universal education?

5. *The rise of nationalism as a stage of the world's march toward democracy.* Why and when did these particular people become a nation? By what means was it brought about?

6. *The rôle of dictatorships in the world's march toward democracy.* We shall see many examples of dictatorships. To understand each one we shall ask such questions as To what extent does the lack of education of the people make this possible? How could a dictatorship be guarded against in this stage of this country's development?

7. *The relation between education and international coöperation.* Do the people of one nation really understand other nations? Are they well informed concerning them? Are they educated sufficiently to discuss how to coöperate effectively and peaceably with them? Can they become educated enough to do that? What is the next step?

8. *The industrializing of agricultural countries and crises of overproduction in the older industrial countries.* Do the leaders plan the production of food, goods, and other things in terms of the needs of their people and of exporting to other people?

What is the next step to bring such plans about in the countries of the world?

9. *The movement toward international control and allotment of the world's basic natural resources.* Should the coal and oil, iron and other metals, be controlled and developed by a central world organization? How could the people of each country be brought into such coöperation?

10. *Increasing interdependence and the trend toward world organization.* Are the countries of all the world becoming more dependent upon one another? How can they be persuaded to coöperate more effectively?

11. *Cultural changes brought about in agricultural countries with the increasing adoption of industrial methods and ways of living.* How is the new industrialism changing the real culture of the people? Are they beginning to feel and think like the people of industrial countries? Or are they keeping their former ways of living, even though they adopt the machines, engines, telegraphs, and trains of the Western nations?

CHAPTER II

EUROPE — THE CENTER OF INDUSTRIAL CIVILIZATION

The New Industrial and Democratic Culture of the World originated in Western Europe

To understand the world's march toward democracy, we must first recall how Europe devised a totally new kind of civilization after 1500 A.D.[1] This, the industrial civilization of power-driven machinery, spread rapidly throughout North America, South America, and parts of Asia, Africa, and Australia. With this new way of producing and exchanging goods, new experiments in government were also tried. Slowly but surely, governments more representative of the people grew up.

But the Industrial Revolution also brought about other changes — changes in the fine arts, changes in ways of thinking and feeling. Indeed, it is not too much to say that a *cultural revolution* was begun that is rapidly transforming the cultures of the entire earth. The result was the development of new *national* languages, new kinds of architecture, new national literatures, original music, painting, sculpture, the dance, and drama. Thus we see that the Industrial Revolution brought in its train wholly new national cultures.

Now, western Europe was the center in which this cultural revolution started. The time was the later Middle Ages. It was from western Europe that the new ways of producing things, the new ways of thinking, the new ways of governing people, and the new fine arts spread to North America and produced the United States. It was from western Europe that the beginnings of the new culture moved outward to Central and South America, changing the Spanish-Indian autocratic states into Latin-

[1] Recall that Europe and Asia, conventionally called by school geographies separate continents, really form one continuous body of land. The single name given to it is "Eurasia." Europe, the western part, totals approximately 3,872,000 square miles; Asia totals approximately 17,206,000 square miles. Thus the land area of Europe is less than one fourth that of Asia.

American republics. It was the descendants of western Europeans who developed Anglo-Saxon democracies in far-off Australia, New Zealand, and southern Africa. And it is from western Europe that the scientific, industrial, and intellectual revolutions are now spreading to Russia, to the Near East, and to centers in India, China, Japan, and the Malay States, where other unique cultures had been established. Thus from western Europe the new industrial and democratic culture spread around the world. This fact is summed up graphically in the map of figure 7.

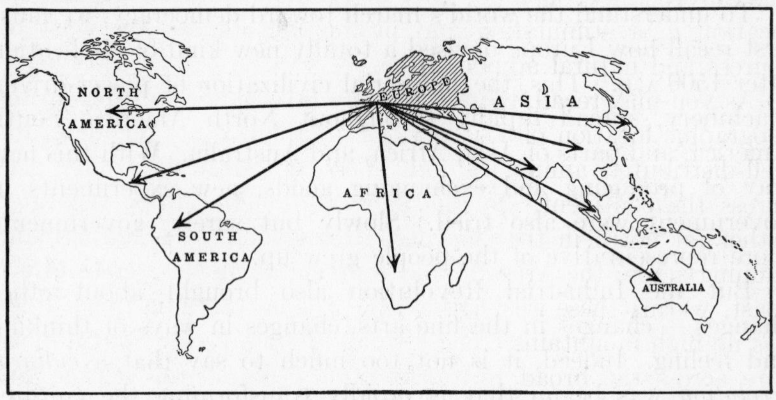

FIG. 7. After the 1500's a new kind of civilization began to develop in western Europe and to spread to every continent of the earth

In emphasizing the fact that the new ways of living spread from Europe, we shall not forget the important part played by earlier civilizations in Asia. Even several thousands of years ago China had developed a remarkable civilization. Europeans learned many ideas and ways of living from the Chinese, as well as from the old civilizations of India and the Near East. We shall discover how these helped to build the modern culture of today.

To understand how Europe became the center of the New World culture we must review the factors which made it possible

How did it happen that Europeans invented such scientific ways of doing things and spread their ideas around the entire earth? Many factors made this possible; some were geographic, others were historical, and still others were psychological. From your earlier studies you may already know much about them. In beginning our study of the rise of democracy in Europe we must first sum up these factors briefly.

1. *The geographic factors which made Europe the greatest industrial and commercial region of the world*

Two geographic factors were of supreme importance in making Europe the economic center of the new culture. These were location in a stimulating and productive climate and vast resources and natural advantages.

As you may recall, there are many favorable conditions in the geographic location of Europe. First: there is an adequate and well-distributed annual rainfall. Second: westerly winds play across the continent. Furthermore, although Europe is located rather far north in the Northern Hemisphere, the Gulf Stream, running across the Atlantic and coursing along the northwestern coast, warms these westerly winds. The northern part of Europe has no high mountains. These winds therefore carry warm moisture across the broad European plain. Third: the seasons are clearly marked out, though the temperature changes frequently. Under such conditions people can work vigorously and crops grow plentifully.

The second geographic factor which helps to make Europe the manufacturing and trading center of the world is her large store of natural resources. Europe is the only continent of the earth which has no deserts and no jungles, and even its mountains occupy only a small proportion of its land area. For contrast examine any map of world vegetation. Note the huge deserts in Africa, Asia Minor, Asia, and Australia. Note the vast tropical jungles of Central Africa, northern South America, and Central America. Even in North America there is a vast desert area. But Europe has neither deserts nor jungles. A large proportion of the continent is a fairly level plain of fertile soil. This plain is approximately 2,660,000 square miles in area — the greatest single food-raising plain in the world. Here more than 200,000,000 farmers produce more than a third of the world's wheat and oats, three fifths of the world's potatoes, nearly nine tenths of the beet sugar, and nine tenths of the rye. They also raise nearly a third of the swine and more than a third of the sheep.

Furthermore, the land of Europe is rich in coal and iron. Enormous resources of coal were discovered and mined in England and in the Ruhr Valley and other parts of Germany. Similarly, great deposits of iron lay on the boundaries between France

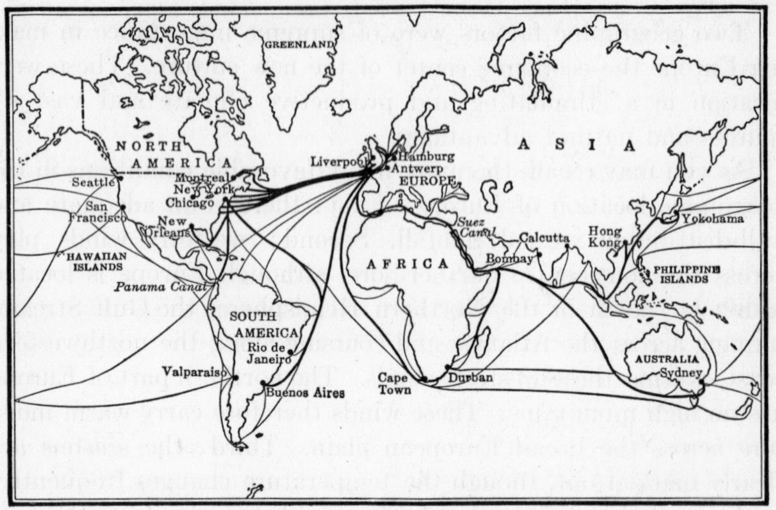

Fig. 8. The lines indicate the world's most important sea paths of trade. Note that they center in Europe

and Germany, in Spain, in Sweden, and in other parts of Europe. Without them Europe could not have become the world's greatest manufacturer.

The very shape of the continent and coast line of Europe was favorable to the development of industrial civilization. The coast line is long and the continent is narrow, and no place in it is far from the sea (see figure 8). A city like Budapest, which is far inland, relatively speaking, is less than 600 miles from a sea. What a favorable condition this is for the development of trade!

Moreover, the coast line is highly indented, the coastal plains being so low that many harbors, bays, and seas have been worn into it by the ocean. Although Europe is less than one fourth as large as Asia, it has approximately half again as many miles of coast line. As a result of these natural advantages, Europe has been a center of sea trade for hundreds of years. Today 12 of the 24 most important ports of the world are on the coasts of Europe.

Thus these basic geographic factors — location in a stimulating and productive climate, the possession of vast natural resources, and a long and highly indented coast line — helped to make Europe the center of a new world civilization.

2. *The psychological factors which help to account for the development of European culture*

But the possession of these favorable geographic conditions alone does not explain the remarkable development and the spread of European culture. Such conditions had existed there for thousands, perhaps tens of thousands, of years without developing industrial civilizations and democratic governments. Somewhat similar conditions have existed in other parts of the earth, also (for example, in central and northern China), without producing the scientific, industrial, and artistic revolution which came from Europe after 1500. So *it was not geography alone which brought about our modern world.*

It was, rather, the combination of these geographic factors with an unusual set of historical and human factors that produced the new culture. This combination of factors we shall consider throughout this book. At this point we can merely outline them briefly.

One was the human factor. In Europe through hundreds of years millions of human beings have been taught the habit of hard work in this northern climate. Even women and children there cultivate the farms, harvest the crops, and work in the factories. The geography of the region is partly responsible for this industriousness. Food must be raised in the warm growing seasons to provide people with their means of sustenance in the cold, unproductive winters, and substantial houses and warm clothing must be provided to protect them against the weather.

Thus these millions of Europeans were driven onward to conquer nature by important human desires and fears. There was the ever-present fear of starvation, the fear of ill health, and the desire for a better and more secure living. These fears and desires urged men to till the fields, cut down the forests, build better houses, and weave better cloth — in short, to build a better civilization.

But of course the Chinese, the East Indians, the Indians of America, and other peoples were also hard workers. They were

FIG. 9. A whole European family in the fields during harvesting time. Geographical and psychological factors account for the hard work these people are willing to do

driven by the same fears and desires. Many of them lived in a fairly severe seasonal climate, which compelled them to work hard. Did they not discover some of the same ways of living which later made the Europeans forge ahead?

Yes, some of them did. In fact, hundreds of years ago some of them taught Europeans many things. But, curiously, they did not invent power-driven machines, and thus they did not produce the industrial way of living. But how did the Europeans happen to learn from them? This question leads us to a third important factor, — namely, the contacts which Europeans had with other peoples.

3. *Europeans traveled the earth and learned new ways of living from other peoples*

Thousands of years ago the Chinese knew how to print and to weave cloth. They knew how to use stone, wood, and other materials to make strong houses, tools, implements, and vehicles. They had a written language and a literature of their own. They had instruments with which to measure. They or their later conquerors, the Mongols, had invented explosives such as gunpowder. In their civilization a calendar of the year, the seasons, the months, and the days was in use.

Similarly, the early peoples of Central and South America — the Mayas and the Incas — knew many of these arts. Besides building huge structures and roads out of stone, the Mayas knew how to read the stars too; they had a well-developed calendar, a written language, and finely developed arts and handicrafts. Other civilized peoples of long ago who lived in the great fertile river valleys of India, Mesopotamia, and Egypt also developed the arts to which we are referring.

Many of the basic ideas, then, from which the modern Europeans developed their civilization were known to earlier peoples. *But the Europeans differed in one respect from other peoples*, as the preceding sentence suggests: *traveling great distances over the earth, they learned many things from the peoples of other lands.* They were great borrowers, and copied other customs and ways of living. More than that, they carried most of these ideas much further than had the originators of them.

Thus, these rich contacts of Europeans with other civilized peoples is an important historical factor. We shall study it carefully in this book. As our studies continue we shall see how knowledge acquired by ancient civilizations was preserved throughout centuries and was carried into medieval Europe principally by European travelers.

4. *The rôle of leaders in the development of European civilization*

We must study carefully one other factor as we learn about the rise of the leading governments and cultures of the world, — namely, the part played by leaders. Even in China, India, and other earlier civilizations it was the leaders who directed the development of culture. In Europe, from the time of the Middle Ages, outstanding leaders appeared — leaders in economic invention, in government, in warfare, in thought, in religion, and in the arts.

The mass of the people merely followed these leaders. From generation to generation they farmed, worked, worshiped, and accepted leadership as their parents had done before them. It was only when unusual men with inventive minds appeared that new ideas were given to civilization. Then new ways of farming and manufacturing came into use, new methods of transportation and communication were introduced, new kinds of government and religion were developed, and new recreations and fine arts were created.

Because of the very great importance of leaders, therefore, we must study carefully their rôle in the development of European culture. We must also find out in what they were most interested. Was it in business, in trade, and in getting money? Was it in inventing machines, in raising the physical standard of living? Was it in science and experiments? Was it in handicrafts? Was it in government? Was it in religion? Or was it in creative writing, in literature, in the theater, in music, in the dance, in painting, sculpture, and architecture?

These are important questions, for the interests of the people of each epoch in a country's history are largely determined by the interests and activities of the talented leaders.

Thus we see in review that *no one factor* caused the Industrial Revolution in Europe and the more democratic ways of living introduced by it. *The new culture of the world was brought about by a favorable combination of several factors working at the same time:* the climate, the soil, and other natural resources, the shape and location of the continent, the need for a more secure living, the contact with other civilized peoples, and the appearance of talented and inventive leaders.

The Europeans introduced their New Civilizations all over the World

Aided by these favorable factors, Europeans produced the new industrial civilization and spread it all over the world. Unlike the other civilized peoples of Asia and America, they sailed ships on all the seas. They built up trade in Asia and Africa, in North and South America, in Australia, and in the larger islands of the world. They emigrated by the millions, establishing European communities on all of these continents. Thus Canada and the United States came into being; thus the combination of Spanish, Portuguese, and Indian civilizations known as Latin-American arose. These and many other facts you already know.

The new European civilization spread, and ways of living changed, even in the ancient, isolated agricultural civilizations of Asia, Africa, and the Americas. When people once learned about mechanical power and how to run machines with it, methods of producing food and of making houses, clothing, and other things were revolutionized. Even perishable food was carried from one continent to another. Finally, the peoples of the entire earth were bound tightly together by means of rapid transportation and communication.

Before all these things happened new kinds of government appeared in Europe, and the fine arts were highly developed. Customs changed as education spread even to the common people. The common man became more important and demanded a greater share in government. The whole outlook upon life changed.

In short, as the industry, agriculture, government, and fine arts of the European peoples gradually changed, the cultures of other parts of the world changed also. This, then, is the background of our study of changing governments and changing cultures. In summary outline we have seen the factors that produced the new culture which is now spreading around the world. To see clearly the great changes that are taking place, however, we must know how they developed.

Next, therefore, we shall go back to the very beginning of the modern world's march toward democracy.

INTERESTING READINGS FROM WHICH YOU CAN GET ADDITIONAL INFORMATION

Blunt, A. W. F. The Ancient World and its Legacy to Us. Oxford University Press, New York. The story of ancient times and peoples simply told.

Clark, Vinnie B. Europe. Silver, Burdett and Company, New York.

Hayward, William R., and Johnson, Gerald W. The Story of Man's Work. Minton, Balch and Company, New York. Part I, Civilization from primitive life through the cultural periods of Egypt, Greece, and Rome. Part II, The evolution of modern industry; invention of machinery; rise of capital and labor.

Hodgdon, Jeannette Rector. The Enchanted Past. Ginn and Company, Boston. Stories of lands where civilization began.

Huntington, Ellsworth, and Cushing, Sumner W. Modern Business Geography. World Book Company, Yonkers, New York. See Chapter XVIII, "The Geographical Conditions of Manufacture," and Chapter XXI, "What Europe Does for a Living."

Parsons, Geoffrey. The Stream of History. Charles Scribner's Sons, New York.

Rugg, Harold. Changing Civilizations in the Modern World. Ginn and Company, Boston.

UNIT II

THE BACKGROUND OF WESTERN DEMOCRACY

CHAPTER III

GOVERNMENT IN THE "DARK AGES" OF UNDEMOCRATIC EUROPE

Europe's march toward democracy can be better understood if we see its origins in earlier times

We must turn back the hands of the history clock and recall conditions of life in western Europe in earlier times. We must go back to, let us say, 1100 A.D., to a time of *undemocratic* government. This brief backward glance is necessary if we are to understand why democratic government has appeared in many parts of the world so recently as the past two centuries.[1]

To comprehend fully why government in 1100 was undemocratic, recall the chief ways of living which we have already studied. Remember that in all the world there were no factories, no manufacturing cities, no railroads. There were no macadamized roads, no automobiles, no telegraphs, no newspapers. Ways of living were simple; in fact, they were almost primitive.

Most people lived in small communities called manors, although here and there traders and craftsmen were already settling towns. These manors, of which there were thousands throughout western Europe, were clusters of thatched peasant cottages surrounding the manor house or the castle of a well-to-do landlord. Each was a complete, self-sufficient community which itself produced nearly all the necessities of life. Craftsmen in iron, wood, and leather made the simpler articles needed. At the lord's mill the peasants ground the community grain; at his smithy they made the cruder tools. Sheep were raised, and wool yarn was spun, woven, and made into clothing.

To see clearly the lack of democracy — the lack of recognition of the common man — call to mind a picture of the crude ways of living.

[1] At this point it will be well to read Chapter II of *Changing Civilizations in the Modern World*, "The Narrow World of the Europeans before the Industrial Revolution."

1. *The inadequate physical standard of living.* Throughout these books we have commented frequently on the comparatively comfortable way of life which has been produced in industrial countries in the past century. Today we take for granted such things as easy ways of producing food in large quantities, many changes of clothing, swift and comfortable means of transportation, ease of communication, and a considerable degree of security.

Fig. 10. A typical manor of about 1100. Close to the well-fortified castle are clustered the peasants' cottages

What a sharp contrast there is between our own high standard of living and the poverty-stricken condition of the common man of 1100! Recall the lack of physical comforts — indeed, of necessities — in the hand-to-mouth existence of the peasants on the manors and the artisans in the towns. Their habitations were crude huts of mud or wood thatched with straw, almost unheated and unlighted even in the cold and cheerless winters. Household utensils and furniture were primitive, table knives and forks unknown. Bedsteads and mattresses, as we know them, were undreamed of. Piles of straw sufficed for beds. Food likewise was simple, the typical peasant's meal consisting of boiled cabbage and salt pork with bread, and occasionally of fish and vegetables other than cabbage.

Even the living conditions of the nobles were not comfortable when compared with modern standards. Their furniture was hard and severe. For lights they depended upon candles; for transportation, upon horses or their own legs. They lacked too our variety of food and our modern systems of heating. Like the peasants, they were also shut in from the outside world.

FIG. 11. If the homes of the wealthy, even long after 1100, were as bare and comfortless as this, one can scarcely imagine in our day what the homes of the peasants could have been. (From Nash, *The Mansions of England in the Olden Time*)

There was no regular postal system; there were no telegraphs, no telephones, no newspapers or magazines.

2. *The lack of knowledge and the narrowness of the world of 1100.* The average European knew little of life outside his own manor, the countryside surrounding it, and perhaps the near-by village or town. His "world" was indeed small. From passing peddlers and entertainers or from strangers at the annual fair he may have heard fantastic tales of Eastern countries — of Cathay (China) and Japan, the Indies (India), or Muscovy (Russia). But even European scholars of that time knew no more of the earth and its inhabitants than is shown in figure 12.

There was an almost complete absence of "book knowledge" and of education as we know it. Schools were only for the well-to-do, and the school subjects as you now know them — reading, writing, arithmetic, history, geography, science, and the like — were not included in the course of study of 1100. Indeed, there were no books as you know them, for the Europeans did not know how to print. Perhaps this will astonish you, for you know that the Chinese had learned how to print from wooden blocks more than 700 years before that time. However, such books as were available in Europe were written laboriously by hand, mostly by monks in monasteries.

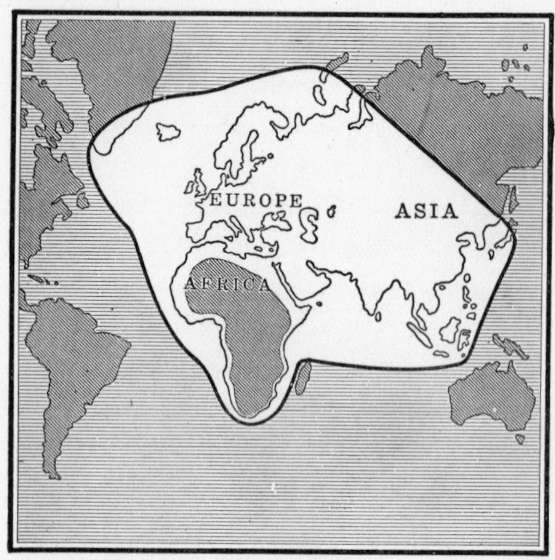

FIG. 12. The line which incloses Europe and parts of Asia and Africa indicates the lands which were known as the "world" in the Middle Ages. The darkened areas within the line had not yet been explored

Even the *spoken* languages were inadequate, compared with our highly expressive languages of today. Thus the very means that people had of communicating with one another were limited. Learning was indeed at a low ebb.

3. *The unprogressive attitude of people generally.* As a result of such conditions the minds of people were slow to change. The world they lived in differed very little from one generation to another. Ways of farming, of weaving, of cooking, and of handicrafts were passed on from fathers to sons, from mothers to daughters. So hundreds of years passed with little change.

As a result people's minds were set, and they were skeptical of new things and new ideas. They were what we call conservative, — even unprogressive.

4. *People accepted everything on faith instead of thinking things out for themselves.* Another result of the low level of civilization and culture in the Middle Ages was the total absence of a scien-

tific attitude. People blindly accepted on the authority of others their beliefs and their rules of conduct. In religion they followed the teachings of the Bible as explained to them by priests and bishops. They never questioned the accuracy of these interpretations, never tried to think things out for themselves. There was only one church — the Catholic Church — which had been in existence ever since the time of Christ. There were no other sects—no Presbyterians, no Congregationalists, no Methodists, no Baptists. Practically every Christian worshiped at the altars of the Catholic Church, and yielded religious obedience to the bishop of Rome, who was called the Pope, and to the hierarchy — that is to say, the archbishops, bishops, abbots, and priests of the Church.

This attitude of living by faith was evident in all worldly ways of living as well as in religious beliefs. There was, for example, little understanding of scientific cultivation of the soil. All physical happenings were traced directly to the anger or good will of a Divine Being. Thus the idea of one event's causing another, of cause and effect, which we learn today in scientific studies in our schools, was unknown. The entire European world was unscientific and unexperimental. Life was regulated, as we have said, by blind acceptance of authority, not by thinking things out for oneself.

How, then, were Europeans Governed?

In this backward way of living were there republics and presidents? Was there a president of France, a president of Germany, a dictator and a king in Italy, as there is today? Were there parliaments, representatives, governors, mayors, and judges?

No; government was a very different thing from government as we know it today. To understand the difference we must remember that there were no national states, or nations, as there are now. There was no England, no France, no Italy, no Germany, no Russia, no Spain. Countries as we know them in the twentieth century did not exist in Europe in 1100.

To make this idea clear let us note what is meant by "nation," or "national state."

What is a national state?

Let us take the United States as an example of a modern national state, and note three of its characteristics.

First, wherever one goes in the United States, north, east, south, or west, the people speak the same language — English. (That is, with the exception of a small proportion of the population who are foreign-born and are still unable to speak our language.)

Second, the people of our country are controlled by one central government under a *national* Constitution. Laws are passed by a *national* Congress. They are executed by a central *national* administration — the president, secretaries of departments, etc. They are interpreted by *national* courts and are enforced by a *national* department of justice. This, then, is a second characteristic of a nation — namely, that all the people are controlled by the same government.

Third, wherever one goes in the United States — in Florida, in Maine, in Georgia, or in Oregon — the people regard themselves as Americans. This is a third characteristic of a national state — namely, that the people consider themselves as of the same nationality, and are loyal to that idea.

These, then, are three tests by which we can judge whether or not a people are a nation: First, do they speak a common language? Second, are they ruled by a single government? Third, do they regard themselves as of the same nationality?

If we apply these three tests, France, for example, is today a nation. Throughout most of the territory of France a single language, French, is spoken, the people are governed by a single central government, and, with very few exceptions, they regard themselves as Frenchmen.

Similarly, Germany is now a nation. Most of the people speak a common language, German, they are governed by a central government, and most of them are proud to be called Germans. So it is, also, in England, Spain, Italy, and in some other countries. There are many nations, or national states, on the earth today, as defined by our three tests.

In 1100 there were no national states in Europe

With this definition of "national state" we can now understand the condition of government in Europe in the later Middle Ages. There was not a single national state as we understand it today.

1. *The lack of national languages.* On the first test the people of each of the regions that are now England, France, Germany, Spain, and Italy did not speak the same language as they do today. In each of these regions many differing dialects, or local languages, were spoken, and no single common language was used. Some of these dialects resembled one another and were the beginnings of uniform languages, but there was no such thing as the English, French, German, Spanish, or Italian language of today. Thus, on the first test the areas which we now know as England, France, Germany, Spain, and Italy were not nations because they did not have national languages.

2. *Single central governments were lacking.* On the second test also there were no national states. There were no presidents, no parliaments, no cabinets. There was no House of Commons in England, no Chamber of Deputies in France, no Reichstag in Germany, no Soviets or Central Committees in Russia. Central national governors, legislatures, courts, and departments of justice or police were lacking. Throughout each great section of the continent, as we shall discover later, were many local groups. One could travel over the regions that are countries now and find not a single central government such as there is today in England, in France, in Germany, in Spain, or in Italy.

3. *People did not recognize their "nationality."* Similarly, there were no loyalties to one's country; there could not be, since, as has been said, there were no countries in the modern sense. People did not recognize themselves as Englishmen, as Frenchmen, as Germans, as Italians, or as Russians.

Thus the three requirements of a nation were lacking: there were no national languages, there were no central national governments, and people did not recognize their nationality. As we can see, there were no national states in Europe.

The Insecurity of Life in Europe in 1100

The disorder of life shows that there was a great need of government to protect people and property. In all Europe hardly a community was safe from attack. Indeed, during the period we are discussing, life for a great proportion of the nobles consisted in making war upon their enemies or in defending themselves from attack.

1. *Constant danger from outside invasions.* In the Middle Ages Europeans who were trying to develop settled communities were attacked from every side by warlike peoples bent upon military conquest and destruction. Sometimes these were marauding bands of barbarians; frequently they were neighbor knights. In the eighth century armies of Mohammedans had pushed through northern Africa, overrun all Spain, and advanced as far as central France, where they were defeated and permanently driven back. In the ninth century they had crossed the Mediterranean from the northern coast of Africa and had conquered Sicily, Italy, and southern France. On the east also, barbarian peoples constantly pressed in upon the communities of what are now Germany, Austria, and France. Among these, for example, were the Hungarians, — bands of savage Asiatics, — who conquered Germany and northern Italy shortly before the period that we are discussing. But finally they were defeated, and were gradually pushed back toward eastern Europe, where they settled in the country we now know as Hungary.

On the north, during the 800's and 900's, there were constant raids from the Northmen, or Norsemen. These highwaymen of the sea sailed down from Sweden, Norway, and Denmark, and made one attack after another upon the British Isles and the west coast of Europe. Some of these Northmen — later called Normans — settled the region called Normandy, on the northwestern coast of France. Other tribes, called Danes, conquered the natives of northern England and eventually became an important element in the British nation. Hardly a section of the region now covered by Holland, Belgium, France, and the British Isles escaped the plundering attacks of these semi-wild pirates.

2. *Europeans also lived in a state of constant neighborhood warfare.* As has been frequently said, "war was the law of the land" in the later Middle Ages. There were no strong central parliaments or national rulers supported by powerful armies to keep order.

For hundreds of years the manors and towns of Europe were in a state of constant bloody fighting. The highways between

FIG. 13. When rival nobles attacked the manor, the serfs rushed within the castle for protection. Can you imagine them anxiously watching the outcome of the battle?

towns and villages were dangerous because of bandits and "robber knights" who made their living by robbing travelers. Each noble was a law unto himself and tried to get more land and power by conquering his neighbors. Indeed, there was little else for the nobility to do. Their serfs cultivated their fields and provided them with the necessities of life, and there were few intellectual pursuits to engage their minds. Hence their chief interest was in fighting, and fight they did — most of the time. They fought their neighbors on the slightest pretext. They fought the more powerful lords, the bishops of the Church, and the heads of near-by monasteries. Sometimes, even, father fought against son, brother against brother. When there was a lull in this warfare, bloody knightly tournaments of daring skill and physical endurance were held. Human life had little value indeed in the later Middle Ages.

How sharply contrasted is the comparative security of life in Western nations today! Now one can walk or ride through England, France, Germany, Scandinavia, Switzerland, Belgium, — in fact, through almost any European country, — with little danger from robbers, murderers, or other public enemies. There is comparative physical security throughout the continent. (As you have learned, there are vastly fewer murders in European countries today than in our own country.) But life and property were not secure in the later Middle Ages because of the lack of strong national governments providing for order within the country and organized defense against attacks from without.

Roads, such as they were, were maintained only by the people in the local community. Each family or group of families provided its own water supply through a well or a spring, and the common man had to be his own practical physician. As for protection against neighbors and outside enemies, except for such help as a man could expect from his lord, everyone had to look out for himself.

The Feudal System of Government of Lords and Vassals

By 1100, therefore, there had grown up a plan of government known as the feudal system. In 870 there were several so-called kingdoms in Europe. There were three large ones: (1) the West Frankish Kingdom, corresponding roughly to the France of today; (2) the Kingdom of Italy; and (3) the East Frankish Kingdom, corresponding to what is today the eastern part of Germany, and Austria, Czechoslovakia, and Holland.

But the kings over these regions were little more than kings in name only. Most of them were not strong leaders. They lacked money, and armies with which to enforce their rule. So the kings of Europe lost their power rapidly until at last they had little more influence than had many of the dukes, bishops, and other landed lords of Europe.

There being no strong central government in any of these regions, a so-called feudal system of lords and vassals had grown up. The kings, unable to give money to the margraves (military commanders), counts, and other nobles in their courts in return for their services, had often granted them large amounts of land. As a result many nobles possessed large estates, some of which included hundreds of manors. Over these estates the nobles ruled.

The larger landowners, unable to keep in close touch with the various districts of their great estates, and also unable to pay money to the vassals under them for their services, in turn granted their vassals smaller tracts of land. These smaller landlords also tended to rule the smaller districts; within each one the landlord made the government.

FIG. 14. After much quarreling, Charlemagne's empire was divided in 870 into these three kingdoms

The very basis of the feudal system was the protection given by the lord and the service given by the vassal. At a formal ceremony of homage (see figure 15), the vassal knelt before his lord, placed his hands between those of the lord, and declared himself to be the lord's man in return for his fief (land). He agreed to be loyal to the lord, to fight in his army, and to do him other services. Thus the vassal swore loyalty to the lord and the lord promised to protect the vassal.

We see, therefore, that a graded system of small and large landlords had grown up during the several hundred years following the decline of Charlemagne's empire. It was, indeed, a kind of pyramid of lords and vassals, at the base of which were many small knights, barons, and abbots governing their little districts. Above them, but less numerous, were wealthier and more powerful counts and bishops ruling over larger districts, and above them, in turn, were still more powerful dukes, earls, margraves, and archbishops ruling still larger regions.

In France, by 1100, some of the most powerful counts and dukes were so strong that they defeated others in open battle and proclaimed themselves rulers of large territories. Among these were the dukes of Normandy, Burgundy, and Aquitaine, and the counts of Flanders, Champagne, and Toulouse, who were

FIG. 15. "I become your man from this day forth, of life and limb, and will hold faith to you for the lands I claim to hold of you"

virtually kings in their own lands. Conspicuous among them was one of whom we shall hear later, William the Conqueror, duke of Normandy, who in 1066 became king of England. In Chapter IV we shall see how, as strong nobles rose to power, kingdoms and national states developed.

In 1100, then, government, like community life, was local and self-sufficient. In place of four powerful national states, as in western Europe today, there were hundreds, even thousands, of small local governments. By 1100 this feudal system was recognized as the established form of government. It was, as one historian has described it, "confusion roughly organized."

Important changes came in European civilization between 1100 and 1500

Recall next from your earlier studies how the isolated manor life of the Middle Ages gradually disappeared after 1100. As workmen learned skill in spinning and weaving, in implement-making, and in the making of tools and weapons, handicrafts developed and labor became more highly specialized. Towns and cities grew. In the city of Florence, for example, craftsmen became renowned for their fine bronzes, glassware, laces, ornamented leather, velvets, satins, and cloths of gold and of silver.

Trade increased, and merchants traveled from one part of Europe to another buying and selling at the fairs which had become well-established institutions. Some of these fairs, such as those at Winchester, London, and Paris, were real international centers of trade. Thus the world of Europeans gradually became larger and larger.

The Influence of Asia upon European Culture

An important factor in these changes, as we know, was the new contact which Europeans were making with the cultured life of the Far East, especially that of China. At the very time when the peoples of western Europe were living in a state of confusion and neighborhood warfare, the people of China had produced an advanced culture. Indeed, for at least 2000 years before that time a well-developed civilization had existed in various sections of Asia. Many of the fine arts were known. Large, prosperous, and orderly cities had grown up, and systematic government was carried on over great areas. The whole order of life contrasted with the confusion, the uncleanliness, and the backwardness of Europe.

Three epoch-making series of events

Shortly after 1100 leading Europeans slowly became aware of this fine Asiatic culture. Knowledge of it helped to rouse them out of the primitive conditions in which they were living and start them on the road toward modern European civilization and culture.

Three series of events helped to bring about the new contacts between western Europe and the Far East.

1. The seven Crusades which Christian Europeans carried on between western Europe and the Holy Land, 1096–1291.
2. The establishment of the vast Mongol Empire by Genghis Khan and his successors, about 1200.
3. The increasing travel of European monks and traders in Asia.

These three movements you have probably already studied.[1] You remember how these seven armed pilgrimages were made by Christian knights, peasants, women, and children to recapture the Holy Land (Palestine) from the Asiatic Turks who had recently taken it. Time after time the region changed hands. It was held first by the Mohammedan Turks; the Christians regained it only to lose it again and again to the Turks.

These famous Crusades are recalled merely to remind us that they helped establish connections between Europeans and Asiatics. Palestine was located in Asia Minor, the region stretching from the Black Sea to the Mediterranean. For hundreds of years this region had been the trading crossroads of the world, and it was directly on the famous trade routes which developed between Europe and Asia. (See map, figure 17.)

A Great Mongol Empire stretched across Asia and Eastern Europe in the 1200's

But by far the most important contact between the civilizations of the Far East and of Europe was brought about by the Asiatic empire of Genghis Khan in the early 1200's. Genghis Khan was a powerful warrior who became the leader of one of the Mongol tribes. The Mongols were nomadic tribes of hunting and pastoral peoples who lived in the region south of Lake Baikal and westward to Lake Balkash in northeastern Asia (see figure 16). They were horsemen with no settled abode, who moved their cattle and meager belongings from north to south with the changing seasons. Like most nomadic peoples, they had a great

[1] You can review them in *Changing Civilizations in the Modern World*, pp. 39–44 and 431–432.

contempt for those who lived in towns and cities. Frequently, when conquering such townspeople, they massacred all of them and destroyed the habitations, irrigation systems, and all other signs of civilization.

During the later 1100's these Mongol tribes had frequent wars with the highly civilized Chinese who lived between them and the Pacific Ocean. It is believed that they learned many

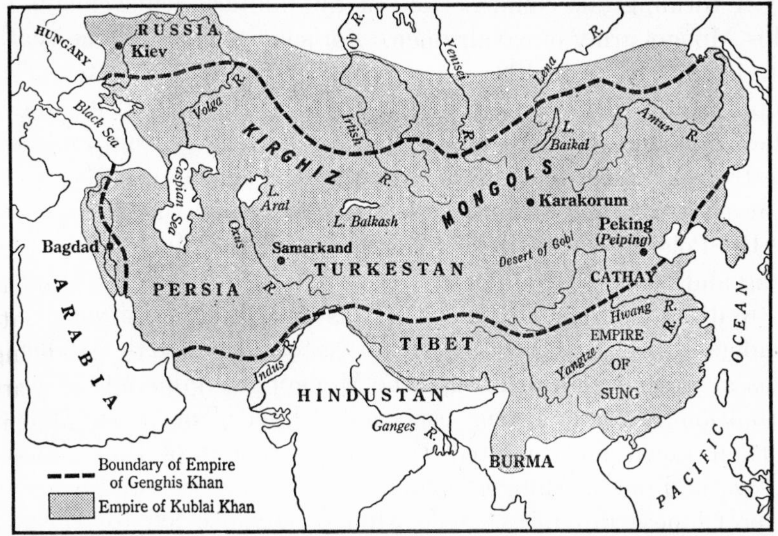

FIG. 16. The empire of the Mongols in the 1200's. Note the boundaries of the empire of Genghis Khan and then how the empire grew during the reign of Kublai Khan

things from the Chinese, including the use of gunpowder and other military arts. By 1200 they were well prepared for a conquest of Asia. All that was needed was a strong, aggressive leader.

This need was filled by Genghis Khan. Within a short time he organized the Mongols into a great army of well-disciplined horsemen warriors. Only thirteen years — 1214 to 1227 — were required for him and his Mongol riders to subdue the settled peoples of most of Asia. Thus he brought together the inhabitants of nearly a whole continent within one great empire. This empire, even larger than that of Alexander the Great or that of Rome at its height, extended from Peking (now called Peiping),

China, on the east, to Russia and the Black Sea on the west (see figure 16). It was not, of course, a national state. There was no single national language, and the peoples within the boundaries of the empire did not claim loyalty to one nationality. Hundreds of different languages were spoken. Indeed, the empire was merely a group of tribes and clans, each of which paid tribute to the central Mongol group under Genghis Khan.

A thrilling tale could be told of the military achievements of this Mongol army of cavalrymen. For some years after the death of Genghis Khan in 1227, they swept westward into eastern Europe. Across Russia they fought their way and in 1240, under the leadership of Ogdai Khan, the son of Genghis, captured and destroyed Kiev. The next year they moved across Hungary, Lower Silesia, and Poland. Then in 1241 came the great stand of the Poles at the battle of Liegnitz, where the Mongols won the long and bloody encounter.

Within the year Ogdai Khan was dead and the princes and leaders returned to the East. The western drive of the Mongols was at an end. From Europe the Mongol chieftains shifted their attention to eastern Asia, especially China. The nomad tribes settled down and adopted the civilized ways of the Chinese. More and more Mongol leaders were appointed as governors over Chinese provinces. One Mongol advance led to another, and in 1260 Kublai became Khan. Nearly twenty years later the southern Sung Empire of the Chinese — a district which had remained independent — surrendered to Kublai's Mongol army. Thus one monarch came to rule over all China and all Mongol territories. The Mongol capital had been moved from Karakorum, south of Lake Baikal, to the Chinese city of Peking. Steadily the wandering Mongols adopted the culture of the Chinese, but they were never thoroughly assimilated by them; and a century later the Mongol element was almost completely expelled from China proper.

Thus for 34 years (1260–1294) Kublai Khan ruled the largest empire in all history, ranging from the Pacific on the east to Hungary on the west, and including Burma and Tibet on the south.

It was the Mongol conquests that kept the trade routes open between Europe and the Far East

This astonishing empire of Asiatic nomadic tribesmen had far-reaching influences upon the changing culture of Europe. Its most important service was to provide a kind of crude government over the entire stretch of 6000 miles from eastern Europe

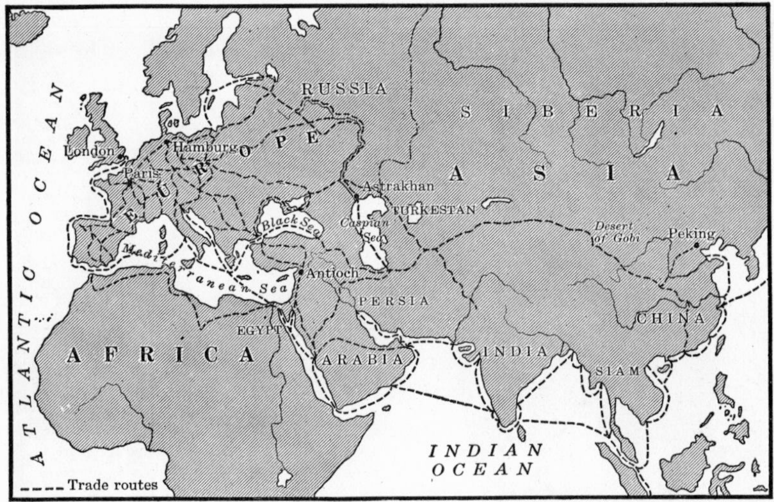

FIG. 17. The principal trade routes of the medieval world

to China. As a result trade routes were kept open and travel was made fairly safe throughout the empire of the Mongol Khans.

It was the Far East to which the eyes of the European business men were turned in the 1200's. (How well named the Far East was from the standpoint of the Europeans!) Now with fairly orderly government established, the trade routes made travel to the East easier. Recall the accounts which you have doubtless already read of the increasing travel of monks and traders between the two regions.[1] It was at this time that Marco Polo and his father and uncle made their astonishing voyage to China, and it was the empire of this very same Kublai Khan

[1] Among these was the Jewish rabbi, Benjamin of Tudela, who traveled in Asia from 1160 to 1173. A second was Friar John of Pian del Carpine (1245–1247). A third was Friar William of Rubruck (1253–1255). A fourth was Marco Polo (1271–1295). A fifth was Friar Odoric (1318–1330).

that is described in the *Travels of Marco Polo.* Although undoubtedly Polo exaggerated, nevertheless the life in China was in the main truthfully described.

The writings of Polo and of other travelers of the 1200's showed Europeans that the Chinese had developed a remarkably fine civilization. Marco describes, for example, the "fine vineyards, fields, and gardens," and "the noble and magnificent city

FIG. 18. The three Polos at the court of Kublai Khan. Marco's father is presenting him to the Khan, saying, "This is your servant, and my son"

of Kin-Sai, . . . an hundred miles in circuit." He refers to its streets and canals, its squares, and its spacious market places. He writes of houses and mansions of great size, of excellent hostelries for travelers, of the elaborate system of exchange of goods, and of the manufacture of "cloth of silk and gold and many fine taffetas." He gives an account also of the remarkable development of India, Burma, and Japan.

Thus in the 1200's and thereafter new ideas and new things were brought into Europe from the East. New foods, such as spices and tea, and fine products were imported. The well-to-do of Europe thrilled over the laces, embroideries, elaborately painted articles made of silk, carved and decorated furniture, rugs, and rich hangings which the returning caravans of trade brought to them.

New ideas and new ways of doing things were also brought into Europe. Among these, for example, was paper-making by improved methods and the art of printing from blocks. These had a tremendous effect upon the minds of inventive persons in Europe, and led somewhat later to the development of printing from movable type and the rapid production of books.

And we must not overlook the destructive invention — gunpowder — which the Mongols and the Chinese had brought to the awakening Europeans.

These, then, were the chief conditions and factors which began to change ways of thinking and living in Europe.

Although Europe was awakening, Democracy was not Possible

In the 1100's there was no sign of the astonishing march toward democracy that was to take place later. There was no such thing as voting. Offices were obtained by inheritance or by the conquest of the weak by the strong.

Education, such as it was, was provided only for the few well-to-do. There were few books and few scholars. There were no national languages and hardly even the beginnings of written literatures.

There was no independence of thought; life was lived by faith alone. There was little intelligent understanding of the physical world. There was a total absence of the scientific way of thinking.

The classes of society were very different from those we know in democratic countries — only the nobles, the clergy, and the common people. There was no middle class of wealthy merchants and bankers. There was little money and no standardized means of exchange of goods among the various regions of Europe.

The common man had no civil and political rights such as he has today in Western countries. Persons were sometimes imprisoned or tortured or executed without respect to law. Indeed, there was no written law as we understand it today. There was, indeed, not a single national state in all Europe.

Thus all the conditions were lacking which are necessary for democratic government to develop. Several hundred years more were to pass before the conditions would be right for the "democratic revolution" to begin.

INTERESTING READINGS FROM WHICH YOU CAN GET ADDITIONAL INFORMATION

Byrne, Donn. Messer Marco Polo. The Century Co., New York. Marco Polo in China.

Davis, William Stearns. Life on a Mediæval Barony. Harper & Brothers, New York. Thirteenth-century life accurately described.

Harding, S. B., and Harding, M. The Story of the Middle Ages. Scott, Foresman and Company, Chicago.

Lamprey, L. In the Days of the Guild. Frederick A. Stokes Company, New York. Children's experiences in the Middle Ages illustrating the guilds and the life and work of craftsmen.

Lansing, Marion. Magic Gold: a Story of the Time of Roger Bacon. Little, Brown and Company, Boston. A good picture of life on a medieval barony.

Salzman, L. F. English Life of the Middle Ages. Oxford University Press, New York. Interesting and lively.

Sherwood, Margaret, and Mantz, Elmer. The Road to Cathay. The Macmillan Company, New York. Travel to the Far East in the Middle Ages.

Stein, Evaleen. Troubadour Tales. L. C. Page & Company, Boston. Short stories of social life in the Middle Ages.

Tappan, Eva March. When Knights were Bold. Houghton Mifflin Company, Boston. Excellent study of life in western Europe from the eighth to the fifteenth century.

Terry, Arthur Guy (Editor). History Stories of Other Lands. Row, Peterson & Company, Chicago. Book IV, "Lord and Vassal, 1066–1485."

Zeitlin, Ida. Gessar Khan. Doubleday, Doran & Company, Inc., Garden City, New York. The Mongolian invasion of Europe and the life and customs of the nomad tribes.

CHAPTER IV

THE FIRST NATIONAL STATES AND ABSOLUTE MONARCHS

What a contrast is shown by the maps of Europe in 1100 and today! In 1100 there was not a single national state in Europe;

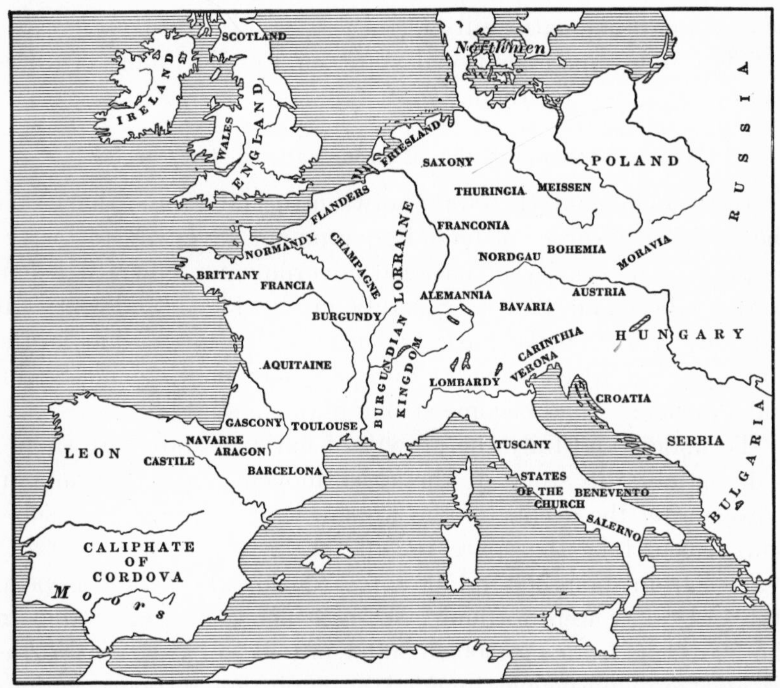

FIG. 19. The principal kingdoms, duchies, and counties of Europe in 1100. Had the less important ones of that time also been shown, the map would have been so crowded as to be unreadable

today there are nearly 30! (See figure 19 and colored map following page 56.) In 1100 thousands of fighting landlords quarreled and conspired for power. Today more than a score of national governments keep order in Europe.

In 1100 there were no *national* languages, and there was little written literature. Today the English, French, German, Spanish, and Italian languages — to name a few — represent an astonishing expansion and improvement in means of communication. With a knowledge of three of these languages one can travel almost anywhere in the Western world.

In 1100 no people recognized themselves as belonging to a definite nationality. There were no patriotic Englishmen, Frenchmen, Spaniards, Germans, Italians, or Russians. Today in more than a score of nations people are proud to be called of British, Danish, German, Russian, Czechoslovakian, Polish, Rumanian, or of some other nationality.

Thus today many national states in Europe fulfill the three tests we have set for them.

When did this formation of strong national states begin?

In the 800 years, therefore, between the 1100's and the 1900's the confused disorder of feudal government gave way to the orderliness and security of national government. Slowly it began in the 1100's and 1200's. Steadily in the 1300's and 1400's it went on. By 1500 the basis had been established; that is, the four westernmost countries of Europe — France, England, Spain, and Portugal — had become strong national states.

To understand fully the growth of national states, we should really study the story of the chief movements and events in Europe after the decline of the Roman Empire. It is impossible, however, to take the space to tell the history of the thousand years — from about 500 to 1500 A.D. — during which the European states of today were forming. We can merely remember that in the 500 years from say 300 to 800 A.D. tribes of barbaric Northern and Germanic peoples invaded the empire and settled at various places, from the British Isles to Italy and the "Germanies." The principal ones and their general locations are shown on the map of figure 20. There were the Britons, Angles, Saxons, Picts, and Scots in the British Isles; the Franks in the general region now covered by France; the Northmen — Vikings — in Scandinavia; and the "Germans" in the general region bounded by Germany, Czechoslovakia, and Austria today.

By about 800 a strong Frankish chieftain named Karl (or

FIG. 20. This map shows where the most important barbarian tribes lived before they invaded western Europe and where they finally settled

Charles) had succeeded in conquering the vast territory shown in figure 14, and had been crowned in Rome as Karl the Great, or Charlemagne, emperor of the Roman Empire.

I. THE RISE OF FRANCE AS A STRONG NATIONAL STATE

The growth of a central government

After the death of Charlemagne in 814 his great empire broke up. By 870, after much quarreling, the empire was divided into the West Frankish Kingdom, the East Frankish Kingdom, and the Kingdom of Italy (see figure 14). After hundreds of years the *West Frankish Kingdom became the national state of France, with boundaries approximately the same as those of France today.* In very brief outline the story is as follows.

For several centuries after Charlemagne the people of this West Frankish Kingdom were governed by scores of little lords, all of whom were themselves the vassals of more powerful dukes ruling large duchies. Each large division was really a small independent state with its own laws, its own ways of collecting revenue, and its own unique customs.

By the 1000's these larger districts had fairly well-marked-out boundaries (see figure 21). Among them were Normandy, Brittany, and the county of Flanders on the west; the county of Champagne and the duchy of Burgundy on the east; the duchies of Aquitaine (later called Guienne) and Gascony, and the county of Toulouse on the south.

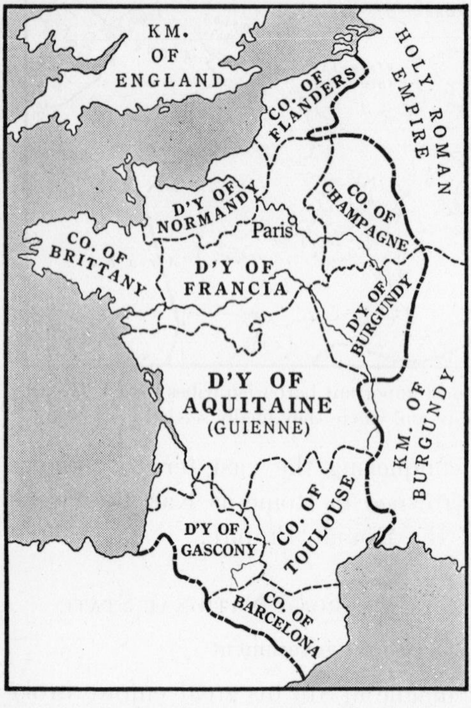

In the north-central region was a little county that was destined to become famous in world history. This was Francia, the capital of which was Paris. The ruler of this territory was first called the count of Paris, and later the duke of Francia. From the latter title came eventually the name of the great modern nation — France. Paris gradually became a great trading center, not only of the French provinces but also of all western Europe, and by the late 1300's numbered 300,000 inhabitants.

FIG. 21. The kingdom of the West Franks about 1000. Note the duchy of Francia and its chief city, Paris

In 987 a strong count of Paris, Hugh Capet, was chosen king of the West Franks. He was a real leader and succeeded in adding to his territory and passing on the throne of his little kingdom to his son. Thus was established the first line of French rulers, the *Capetians* (see Table II). At first the territory *actually ruled over* by these kings was small — little more, in fact, than the immediate neighborhood of Paris. As the centuries passed, however, they slowly achieved more and more power.

Many difficulties had to be overcome by these Capetian kings before they could become really powerful and before France could become a strong nation. In some ways their fairly central position in the kingdom was an advantage; for example, armies could march quickly to other territories. But there were disadvantages too; the duchy of Francia was surrounded on all sides by large counties and duchies ruled by strong lords who owed allegiance to the king but who were unwilling to give it. These lords had to be subdued before safety and power would come to Francia. For that matter, these first Capetian kings did not have very firm control over the smaller lords even on their own estates and manors. Thus their first task was to demand loyalty of their own strongholds — Paris and Orleans. Once that was secured other territories could be conquered and brought under their direct rule.

TABLE II

French Kings from Hugh Capet to Charles VIII (987–1498)
CAPETIAN LINE (987–1328)
Hugh Capet (987–996)
Robert I (996–1031)
Henry I (1031–1060)
Philip I (1060–1108)
Louis VI (1108–1137)
Louis VII (1137–1180)
Philip II (Augustus) (1180–1223)
Louis VIII (1223–1226)
Louis IX (1226–1270)
Philip III (1270–1285)
Philip IV (1285–1314)
Louis X (1314–1316)
Philip V (1316–1322)
Charles IV (1322–1328)
VALOIS LINE (1328–1498)
Philip VI (1328–1350)
John II (1350–1364)
Charles V (1364–1380)
Charles VI (1380–1422)
Charles VII (1422–1461)
Louis XI (1461–1483)
Charles VIII (1483–1498)

So in various ways the kings of France, as they came to be called, added new territories to their realm. Some they conquered from the neighboring lords. Others they acquired by marrying their sons to the daughters of powerful counts, thus bringing more territory into the family. Still other lands they simply took for their own. When certain nobles died without children to inherit their possessions, the kings claimed them for their own. And others they seized by conspiracy.

By such means the Capetian kings gradually gained control over the lands of various feudal lords of France. By the end of the reign of Louis the Fat (1108–1137) they had made good their claims to the lands of the duchy of Francia itself. Then, by force as well as diplomacy, Philip Augustus (1180–1223), Louis's famous grandson, carried on the work. He drove the English kings, who had inherited a great deal of territory in France, out of the valley of the Loire, out of Normandy, and out of Maine and Anjou. He also developed new ways of governing. He established a treasury and a permanent army; he placed *baillis* (bailiffs) in his domains to look out for the king's interests and collect the revenue. He created a council of loyal leaders to help him decide questions of government. Thus Philip did much to make France a real nation and himself the real government.

But the work of another Capetian ruler, Louis IX (1226–1270), or Saint Louis, was also important. Under him government in the modern sense of the word was first established. He extended the institution of the *baillis*, thus keeping his domains closely under control. He divided the council in Paris, which had been established by Philip Augustus, into several bodies. One, the king's council, aided him in the general affairs of the kingdom; the second was the chamber of accounts, attending to matters of revenue; the third was the *parlement*, a court to attend to matters of law. Of the parlement we shall hear much in the later history of France.

Louis IX was recognized throughout all Europe as a wise and just king. One English writer calls him "the king of all earthly kings on account of his [holiness] as also on account of his power and his eminence in chivalry." Thus, under such rulers as Philip and Saint Louis, the kingdom of France steadily expanded and government became more centralized. As this happened the power of the feudal lords decreased.

For 350 years one Capetian son after another inherited the throne of France. Then, in 1328, came a time when there was no son to go on with the work. The throne passed to a cousin, who established the Valois line. By this time a real national state had begun to emerge. In size it had grown from the tiny country of Hugh Capet to a vast territory two thirds as large as France of the present day. Only four isolated "fiefs" remained outside the king's control — Flanders, Brittany, Burgundy, and Guienne.

From 1328 to 1498 seven kings of the Valois line ruled France. During this time the unification of the French nation was hindered by "international" conflicts as well as by local warfare.

Fig. 22. In 1428 the English laid siege to Orleans. The following year Joan of Arc, then only seventeen years old, at the head of a small French army, raised the siege and rescued the city. (From a painting by Lenepveu)

Between 1337 and 1453 the kings of France were almost constantly at war with their rivals across the English Channel, the kings of England. Suffice it to say here that because of the conquest of England in 1066 by William the Conqueror, duke of the French province of Normandy, there ensued in later centuries a prolonged struggle among rival claimants to the thrones of England and of France. These wars of the 1300's and the 1400's were known as the Hundred Years' War. We need not recount here the details of this constant fighting between nobles while the peasants and artisans, mostly ignorant and uninterested, plodded on their ways. It is enough to say that the struggle ended in 1453 with the elimination of the English claimants to the French throne. Calais was the only French territory still occupied by the English at that time.

The names of two kings near the end of the period are worth remembering, because they, more than any of the others, subdued fighting nobles and more firmly established the power of the royal house. The first was Louis XI (1461–1483), a clever diplomat and strong leader, who succeeded in bringing most of the provinces of France under his control. The Duke of Burgundy once called him "the universal spider." One of his outstanding achievements was the defeat of this duke, whose ambition had been to establish a new state between France and Germany. Louis checked the Duke and annexed a part of the Burgundian territory. Anjou, Maine, Provence, and other provinces were also brought under his immediate control. In fact, the only large independent fief remaining outside was Brittany.

Not for long, however, did Brittany remain independent, for Charles VIII (1483–1498), Louis's son, married Anne, the heiress of Brittany, and brought that duchy into the kingdom. Thus all the land between the "Germanies" on the east and the English Channel on the west were now united under one ruling house.

By 1500 "France," therefore, had become a large and fairly strong national state. One government controlled the territory extending from the county of Flanders on the north to the Spanish boundary in the Pyrenees Mountains on the south, from the Rhine on the east to the Atlantic on the west. Within this territory, which is approximately the same as that of France today, the ruling power of dukes and counts and other lords had been destroyed. The King of France was now supreme. There was a strong standing army loyal to the King and a system of government officials who kept order in the kingdom and compelled the common people to pay taxes. Roads had been improved, and officials and troops could travel more rapidly from one part of the realm to another. This enabled the King to put down insurrections and to communicate quickly with his subordinates, even those in distant provinces. Methods of trading and exchanging goods had also been improved, and a fairly uniform system of money under the King's control had been developed.

Accordingly, measured by the first test — a strong central government — France had become a national state.

A national language — French — also developed

A second most important influence in the development of France as a nation was the emergence of a unified national language. To understand this, let us note briefly the rise of national languages in western Europe.

How modern languages developed in Europe

At the height of the Roman Empire, say during the first three centuries after Christ, Latin was widely used throughout western Europe. It was the language used by the Roman soldiers, by the merchants in the Roman garrison towns, and by the traders who traveled from province to province. All treaties, state papers, and other legal documents were drawn up in Latin. Latin was also the language of the Catholic Church,—of its councils as well as its ritual, — of the universities, and of such literature as was considered worth putting into written form. Even after the decline of the Empire, Latin continued to be used for centuries as the only means of written communication among the peoples of Europe.

After the invasions of the various German tribes in the 300's and 400's, however, the rôle of Latin as the spoken language of Europe gradually declined. For quite a while, of course, people in the lands once included in the Empire continued to speak a language which was still in large measure Latin. Then as the power of the German and Frankish chieftains grew, as trade and travel increased, and as a more national spirit developed in each region, new local languages appeared. These were mixtures of spoken Latin and the German dialects brought in by the invaders. As the generations and centuries passed, new and fairly distinctive languages developed in each of the chief national regions.

Although little is definitely known of the steps by which the modern languages of Europe developed, one conclusion is clear. Out of this complex mixing of tribes, races, and nationalities, and of points of view and ways of living, there developed two principal groups of language: (1) the Romance languages and (2) the Germanic languages. The Romance languages developed from the spoken Latin *within* the Roman Empire; the Germanic languages developed generally *outside* the boundaries of the Empire.

Naturally there are close resemblances between many words in each of the great branches of these languages — in the Romance languages, for example, French, Italian, Spanish, and Portuguese. They were all — even English and German — more or less influenced by the common basis, namely, spoken Latin. Consider the following example:

Our word *figure* is ultimately derived from the Latin *figura*. In Italian and Spanish it remained *figura*. In French it became *figure*; in German, *Figur*.

Other striking examples of similarities between the modern European languages and Latin are the following:

English	*German*	*French*	*Latin*
mother	*Mutter*	*mère*	*mater*
father	*Vater*	*père*	*pater*
brother	*Bruder*	*frère*	*frater*

The growing national French language helped to unify the national state

For centuries after the break-up of Charlemagne's empire, many curious mixtures of Latin dialect were spoken in the various parts of France. Gradually, however, these dialects became two fairly distinct languages, each based upon the spoken Latin of the earlier Roman Empire. The first was the language of the northern provinces, which, because of the importance of Paris and the French kings, came to be called French. The second was the language of the southern provinces, called Provençal. The people who lived in the central part of France naturally spoke a mixture of these two.

Then in the 1300's and 1400's, as the French kings extended their control over the entire region and as good roads made trade and communication between distant provinces easier, the language of the northern section became more common. In the border provinces of the south, however, Provençal still predominated as the spoken language, and the influence of the developing Spanish language was plain. On the east the Germanic influence was great. We can see, however, that another of the tests of a national state — that of a national language — was beginning to be met.

National literatures also slowly developed

In the same centuries during which national monarchies were forming, national literatures, made up of poems, songs, plays, and stories, also were slowly beginning to take shape. With education at a low ebb and with national states almost entirely unformed, it was not to be expected that people would write highly perfected literature of the types we know today. There were no great authors, poets, dramatists, or essayists of whom the people could be proud and through whose works national spirit could develop.

In the later Middle Ages — after about 1000 — there did begin to appear in many regions, however, a kind of unwritten literature which was passed on from one generation to another by word of mouth. Verses were recited and sung by poets who lived at the courts of kings and nobles, and by traveling bards and troubadours. Slowly an epic literature grew, which eventually played an important part in the building of national spirit among the various peoples of Europe.

Although many of these epics told of heroes of earlier times and of other lands, — of Troy, of Persia, and of Rome, — many of them were also national. For example, among the West Franks even in the seventh and eighth centuries A.D. there were poets and troubadours who sang and recited long epic poems about the leaders who were considered national heroes. Among these were poems about King Clovis (Louis) and Charles "Martel" (the Hammer). Martel had, in 732, administered a crushing defeat to invading hordes of Moors who had advanced as far as Tours. After 800 Charlemagne and his generals appeared as the leading heroes of these epic poems. One of the best known of these is the *Chanson de Roland* ("Song of Roland"), which tells of the heroic deeds of an officer in one of Charlemagne's armies. This is supposed to have been first written down in the later 1000's — let us say, 200 years after Charlemagne's time.

In the southern French provinces the poetic songs were accounts of the life of knighthood and chivalry. Here lived many famous troubadours, who went from one court to another playing some instrument, usually the lute, and reciting their legendary pieces. They did much to make nobles and commoners enthusiastic over the heroic deeds of national leaders.

The epics were thrilling tales of adventure. As they were passed on from one generation to another, events in them were

Fig. 23. Troubadours were welcome guests in the days when amusements were few. They brought news of distant places, and their songs were stirring and entertaining

more and more exaggerated, until the kings and nobles of whom they told became merely legendary figures. Yet they served the important purpose of developing a national loyalty and of stirring a deep emotional spirit among the people.

Thus in France, in the period between 1100–1300, such songs, epic poems, stories, and prose romances gradually formed a written literature. In the 1200's French began to supplant Provençal as the literary language of France. This written language aided in establishing and spreading French as a national tongue. But it did much more than this. As the literature of their heroes developed, the people of France began to think of themselves somewhat less as members of a province or a duchy and more as members of a nation — as *Frenchmen.*

Indeed, by 1500, according to our three tests of a nation France had reached at least a crude national state: (1) a strong central government ruled the people; (2) a single language was fairly common in various districts; (3) the people had begun to think of themselves as Frenchmen. The whole conception of *democratic* government as we know it in the Western world today was lacking.

II. The Rise of England as a National State

What is known of the earliest history of the British Isles has been pieced together from the relics of the old Celtic and Briton civilizations which preceded the coming of the Angles, Saxons, Danes, and Norsemen.[1]

Our brief story begins with the England of the Anglo-Saxon kings in the period from about 700 to about 900 A.D. In these two centuries England consisted of several small "kingdoms." School histories of England today often refer to the "seven kingdoms" of England, and call them the Heptarchy. However, only three of these were important in the government that afterwards became England — the Kingdom of Northumbria (north of the Humber), called in the 600's the Pirate Kingdom; the Kingdom of Mercia (the region in the Midlands); and the southern Kingdom of Wessex, which later included London. The kings of Northumbria were supreme during the 600's, the kings of Mercia during the 700's, and the kings of Wessex (West Saxons) during the 800's and 900's. On the fringe of these little kingdoms were other peoples — the Welsh in Wales, the Picts in Scotland, and the mixture of Irish and Norsemen in Ireland.

From time to time in these centuries before 1000, certain kings were much more powerful than others. For example, King Offa of Mercia, who reigned from 757 to 796, was so powerful that he was recognized by the Pope as "King of all the English." The Emperor Charlemagne also recognized him, and even married one of his sons to one of King Offa's daughters.

[1] For dramatic accounts of this history see such books as Henrietta E. Marshall's *An Island Story: A Child's History of England* (Frederick A. Stokes Company, New York) and Eleanor Hull's *Northmen in Britain* (Thomas Y. Crowell Company, New York).

Alfred the Great

But the greatest of all these early kings was the Wessex King Alfred (871–900). So strong was he that he was recognized as king by practically all the lords of England. It is said of this

FIG. 24. The division of the British Isles about 800. Note, in particular, the seven kingdoms which later became a national state — England

king that in the whole history of the world no monarch was ever more entitled to be called "the Great." He possessed a rare combination of military strength, true religious spirit, unusual scholarship, and fine administrative ability. Besides being the greatest soldier of his time and a hero because of his success in repelling the invasions of the Danish Northmen, he was also a real intellectual leader. He himself translated many of the outstanding "classics" of his time into the vernacular of Anglo-Saxon England, and had a history of his country written. Furthermore, he demanded that the children of the nobles in his court be educated. We are told that at one time he exclaimed: "God Almighty be thanked that we now have any supply of teachers!"

Fig. 25. A statue of the great king, Alfred

Under Alfred, handicrafts, arts, and architecture flourished as they never had before in that country. Himself a skillful designer of articles in gold and silver, he set an example which attracted to his court clever craftsmen in metals, as well as designers of buildings and writers.

Furthermore, because of tremendous administrative ability, Alfred really *ruled* as well as *reigned.* He planned the expenditures of his government in accordance with a systematic "budget." He personally regulated the finances of the kingdom, *giving half of his revenue to religious and educational purposes*! (That no government does even today.) He codified the laws of the kingdom, making a system which one prominent historian declared was really *national*: "They were not only for his own Kingdom of Wessex, but for all Englishmen." He also reorganized the government of local communities as well as that of the central divisions of the kingdom. In Alfred, therefore, England had the first true English monarch, a ruler regarded by many students as superior to most of the conspicuous figures in world history.

For a hundred years after Alfred's time his successors, the kings of Wessex, ruled as kings of England. As the generations passed, the Anglo-Saxon people slowly became unified with the people of Mercia and Northumbria. Gradually they came to be known as English, rather than by their separate names. Even by the 1060's, however, little real national feeling had developed, and a national language and literature were still lacking. The four main dialects — Northumbrian, Mercian, West Saxon, and Kentish — were still spoken. Furthermore, the people showed little evidence that 800 years later they would become the greatest empire-building nation of the world. Generation after generation when they were not defending their country from invasion they continued to tend their flocks of sheep and to eke out a living on their small farms. Of trade with other countries there was little.

Then came the Norsemen, and British civilization was transformed

After 900 the civilization of the British Isles was greatly changed by the invasions and conquests of the Norsemen, called the Vikings. To understand the manner in which the Norsemen changed English life, let us note briefly their general characteristics and their widespread influence in many other parts of Europe.

The Tremendous Influence of the Norsemen on the Civilization of All Europe

These Norsemen,— the Vikings,— after the decline of the Roman Empire, had brought new customs and new energy into the civilizations of central and western Europe. Southward from Norway, Sweden, and Denmark they had moved in great waves, settling the northwestern districts of Europe and the British Isles. It was they also who helped to found western "German" civilization. And it was they who provided much of the daring, initiative, and organizing ability that developed the Frankish kingdom.

These Vikings combined the traits needed for emigration and settlement, for trade, invention, and government. They were fighters of tremendous ability, as is shown by their repeated invasions of Europe. What vitality and energy they had, too!

What tremendous distances they traveled! They built up the thousand-mile water route from Scandinavia and the Baltic, up the rivers of northern Russia, down the rivers of southern Russia to the trading city of Kiev, and thence to the Black Sea and Constantinople. Far away in eastern Europe this great trading route was being built in the 800's while their brother Vikings on the west were moving southward on other long invading

FIG. 26. The Norsemen displaying their wares to the Russians. What differences do you see between the cultures of the two peoples?

and settling expeditions. The scene of their western conquests ranged from the Norman settlements on the northern coast of France to the Danish settlements in England, Wales, Scotland, and Ireland.

As you can see, these Norsemen were not merely marauding vandals like the Mongol tribes of central Asia. They were settlers and intelligent traders. The water route through Russia, for example, was essentially a *trading* route, inspired by the desire to buy and sell goods with the Eastern Roman Empire and the peoples who came to the trading crossroads of Asia Minor. Similarly, it was the desire for comfortable homes that led them to develop the rich duchy of Normandy on the northwest coast of France. Thus we find these Norsemen traveling and trading all over the known world — indeed, out on the frontiers of the unknown world. They explored Iceland and Greenland, as well as the coast of North America, long before Columbus and the Cabots. They bargained with Arab merchants on the eastern Mediterranean, and received hospitality from and gave armed help to more than one Byzantine emperor in Constantinople. Thus they influenced the entire continent.

It was new groups of these Norsemen who brought about the transformation of the quarreling kingdoms of the British Isles into the truly national state of *England.* England, in turn, became the nucleus of the *Great Britain* we know today. Let us note briefly, therefore, how this first transformation of peoples into the nation — England — took place under the leadership of the Norsemen.

After 900 A.D. waves of invading Norsemen settled in France and the British Isles

To understand what took place in the latter 1000's, we must bear in mind the quiet invasion of groups of Norsemen that had been going on for nearly 200 years. Throughout the 900's and 1000's, groups of Danes and other Norsemen, after raiding the northwest coast of France, had obtained land from the French leaders and, settling there, had developed their own civilization within it. Gradually they had come to be called Normans and, as you know, their land — Normandy — became one of the leading provinces of France. Their leaders, the dukes of Normandy, were among the most daring and powerful of French nobles.

During these same centuries, other groups of Danes swept in upon England, Wales, and Ireland in one invasion after another. After conquering different localities, they settled down in the midst of the Anglo-Saxons, the Welsh, and the Irish, and developed their own ways of living. So many of them came into England that one prominent historian speaks of London as "having become half barbarized at this time by the abundance of its Danish inhabitants." He names various streets in the growing city which were inhabited almost entirely by Norsemen.

These newcomers introduced new blood and a more alert and driving spirit into the civilization of the people. Whereas the English were inclined toward sheep-raising and agriculture, the business-minded Norsemen concentrated in towns and developed trade. Indeed, they were among the first city business men of the new European civilization. Ports were built upon the east coast of Ireland and at Bristol, Chester, and other towns in the west of England, some of which were to become centers of world trade. Under their influence a considerable trade grew up across the Irish Sea.

In the meantime London, York, and other leading cities also developed into important international centers. German merchants began to cross the North Sea to trade with these new Englishmen. A system of trade developed, even as early as 1000, which reached into Asia Minor. When compared with the variety of goods exchanged in our day the articles of trade were, of course, very limited. Raw wool, the hides of animals, and metals were the chief exports from England, and silks, wine, oil, jewels, and other treasures of the East were the principal imports. But, at least, trade did develop which was to help break down the warring spirit between the divisions of the island and create the beginnings of a national state.

We must know one other fact concerning the industry and trade of England before we can understand the important events which took place after 1065 — that is, the relation between England and the county of Flanders on the northern border of France. The Flemish people were of somewhat the same stock as the Anglo-Saxons, who were now becoming English. During these earlier Middle Ages a remarkable wool-weaving industry had developed among them. As the climate and other geographic features of Flanders were not well suited to raising sheep, the Flemings imported wool from England, where sheep-raising had long been an important industry. For many generations English leaders had tried to develop the weaving industry in their country, but they had failed. Even in the 1000's most of England's wool was made into cloth and garments by Flemish weavers.

The Norman Conquest and the New Norman-English Civilization

Then in 1066 an epoch-making event occurred — the overwhelming defeat of the English king, Harold, at the battle of Hastings and the complete conquest of England by a new group of Norsemen. This time, however, they were Normans from the French duchy of Normandy, under the leadership of Duke William, known as the Conqueror.

For many years William and his progressive Normans had eyed enviously the rich lands across the narrow English Channel.[1] But as long as England had as her close ally the Count of Flanders, — William's immediate neighbor and rival on the North, — he hesitated to attack. Finally, however, circumstances enabled him to take England's ally away from her: William married a daughter of the ruling house of Flanders. Now, William was ready for his great opportunity.

At a strategic moment in 1066 when the English king, Harold, was away from his southern lands repulsing an invasion of Danes on the northeast, William sailed across the Channel with a powerful Norman army. He skillfully avoided the English fleet and landed on the defenseless English coast. King Harold, with only a small army, and unaided by his allies from Northumbria and Mercia, rushed southward to battle the Normans at Hastings. His undisciplined troops were no match for the powerful Norman host, however, and in spite of the bravery of the English they were completely routed. One historian says of this battle:

It is an astonishing fact that they repulsed two tremendous assaults; but they, or their leader, were incapable of an organized counter offensive. The territorial levies were even incapable of obeying orders; William was able to decoy them into a pursuit most probably by the old Danish trick of a feigned flight. They were ridden down in the open by cavalry, and the position once being pierced, the Norman archers were able to co-operate with the stormers by searching the rear ranks of the defending line with a shower of dropping arrows, to which the English could not reply. From noon to September twilight the hopeless

[1] It is only twenty miles wide at its narrowest point — one of the roughest of the world's narrow ocean thoroughfares, however.

struggle was maintained, until the King and the flower of his army had fallen at their posts. Only under cover of darkness were the last survivors swallowed in the gloom of the great forest behind.[1]

So England was conquered by the Normans. But William desired to be more than "the Conqueror." He wanted to be truly the king of England, accepted by all English nobles. Within a short time he had secured the loyal approval of some of the leading lords, and on Christmas Day, 1066, was elected king of England and crowned in Westminster Abbey.

FIG. 27. William the Conqueror granting a charter to the citizens of London. (From a painting by Seymour Lucas)

In spite of frequent revolts, which he always put down successfully, William ruled England as king for 21 years (1066–1087). Gradually he brought all the nobles under his control. England was once again at peace. For 200 years his descendants held the throne. Besides England, from time to time they governed much of France also. For example, Henry II (1154–1189), William's great-grandson, claimed and obtained loyalty from the nobles and the people of more of France than did the so-called king of France himself. He, like many other rulers during these centuries, accomplished this by inheritance from both sides of his family and by marriage, rather than by conquest.

[1] Esmé Wingfield-Stratford, *The History of British Civilization*, Vol. I, p. 118. Harcourt, Brace and Company, New York, 1928.

As the great-grandson of William the Conqueror, he inherited the duchy of Normandy and control over Brittany, and by his marriage to Eleanor, heiress of the duchy of Aquitaine, he controlled that region also. Furthermore, from his father, Geoffrey Plantagenet, he received the French provinces of Anjou and Maine. Thus, Henry II, the first Plantagenet king, ruled much of France and all of England for 35 years.

TABLE III

ENGLISH RULERS FROM WILLIAM THE CONQUEROR TO THE TUDORS (1066–1485)
NORMAN LINE (1066–1154)
William I (1066–1087)
William II (1087–1100)
Henry I (1100–1135)
Stephen (1135–1154)
ANGEVIN LINE (1154–1399)
Henry II (1154–1189)
Richard I (1189–1199)
John (1199–1216)
Henry III (1216–1272)
Edward I (1272–1307)
Edward II (1307–1327)
Edward III (1327–1377)
Richard II (1377–1399)
LANCASTRIAN LINE (1399–1461)
Henry IV (1399–1413)
Henry V (1413–1422)
Henry VI (1422–1461)
YORKIST LINE (1461–1485)
Edward IV (1461–1483)
Edward V (1483)
Richard III (1483–1485)

Henry improved the law courts of France and of England, developing local courts and arranging for judges to travel regular circuits. He inaugurated the plan followed today of having a grand jury assembled at regular intervals to hear accusations against lawbreakers. By 1300 it had become standard practice to leave decisions in legal cases to juries of twelve men.

We shall learn in a later chapter of the development of English government under the other ruling houses that followed the descendants of William the Conqueror. Now, however, our chief interest is in the development of England into a national state and in the spread of Norman culture.

4. Effects of the new Norman-English civilization

Under William the Conqueror and his successors Norman civilization spread rapidly through England. It is impossible to state definitely how many Normans emigrated to England at that time, but the number must have been large. At any rate, their ideas of well-organized law and government were introduced and were mixed with established English customs. It is not too much to say that the Norman Conquest brought system into English government. Norman officials were appointed to most of the government posts, both in the central government and in local communities, and a more orderly régime was thus developed.

There were other important results of the Norman Conquest. One was that after the battle of Hastings there were no more successful invasions. It is true that civil war went on for centuries, and that relatives and friends, fathers, sons, and brothers conspired against one another for the throne of England; but attack from outside invaders ceased.

National business life also developed in the next few centuries under Norman leadership. Merchants emigrated from Norman cities in France and built up thriving businesses in London, York, Bristol, and other cities, and Flemish weavers developed the woolen textile trade in various English towns.

Another important result was the adoption of a new style of architecture then being developed in France. Norman architects were brought over from Normandy; in a few decades stone buildings, castles, cathedrals, and monasteries dotted the landscape of England. One writer has said that these "castles and cathedrals are sagas in stone." Furthermore, as the first Norman rulers were European in interests and customs, they brought the French language to England, and new support for the religion of the Roman Catholic Church, which the rulers of the English kingdoms had embraced 400 years earlier. Through them a new national spirit and a thoroughly Catholic religious atmosphere arose in England.

With the danger from outside interference subsiding and feudalism declining, one strong central government succeeded another. A more unified civilization steadily developed. Immediately after the Norman Conquest many a man was heard to say resentfully, "Do you take me for an Englishman?" But the distinctions between Normans and Englishmen gradually ceased to exist. The contempt which the ruling Normans at first had

FIG. 28. Durham Cathedral in England is one of the early buildings designed there by Norman architects

for the English gave way to pride in their own "English" nationality. By 1200 one announced with pride, "I am an Englishman!" Thus long before 1500 England had begun to resemble a national state.

The Unification of the English Language and Literature

As we have just said, when the Normans came to England they brought the Norman-French language with them, and it became the language of the court and of most of the government. As thousands of merchants, artisans, and officers of the Church continued to come into the country from Normandy, French became even more common. Thus a fifth language was added to the confusion of tongues already being spoken in England — the other four being the main dialects of Northumbria, of Mercia, of the West Saxons, and of Kent. These dialects, which had been introduced by the first Anglo-Saxon invaders, were somewhat like the other Germanic languages of northwestern Europe. Furthermore, the Danes who had arrived in the 900's and 1000's spoke still another. In spite of this, each new wave of immigration, although it added new words to the existing languages, was gradually absorbed by the majority of the inhabitants. Even by 1100, however, no common language had been developed.

In the meantime there had been little *written* literature, and hence there was little standardizing of the language. Under King Alfred the Great, however, the classics of that time and the history of England were written in the West Saxon dialect, which for a while became the standard literary language. An example of Anglo-Saxon, written about 1150, will show how unlike our present English it is.

AN EXAMPLE OF ANGLO-SAXON WRITING, ABOUT 1150[1]	TRANSLATION INTO PRESENT ENGLISH
Here on thissum geare Willelm cyng geaf Rodberde eorle thone eorldom on Northymbraland. Da komon tha landes menn togeanes him & hine ofslogen, & ix hund manna mid him.	In this year King William gave the Earl Robert the earldom of Northumberland. Then came the men of the country against him and slew him, and nine hundred men with him.

Later, as in other parts of Europe, traveling bards helped to develop an unwritten epic literature. No doubt they preserved the epic of *Beowulf*, which belongs to the 600's. Bards also sang of the deeds of King Arthur and his Knights of the Round Table,[2] the story of which you probably know.

In the 1100's the upper classes, generally, spoke French, and as one historian puts it "the grand old English of Alfred had now become the patois of boors."

But years passed; one generation succeeded another; the Normans became English; and a new language appeared as a result of the intermixture of peoples. London was becoming the literary and cultural center of England as well as the political and business center, and consequently the East Midland dialect developed most rapidly. But how changed this new language

[1] Adapted from James Harvey Robinson's *Ordeal of Civilization* (Harper & Brothers, New York, 1926), p. 197.

[2] See the collection of them in Malory's *Morte d'Arthur*.

was! Many softer and more musical French words had been added to it. Perhaps you frequently hear the phrase "the King's English" used today to characterize the best English language possible. When you do, remember that English resulted after centuries from the intermixture of the dialects of the Anglo-Saxons, of the Danes, and of the Norman-French.

By 1400 a language had developed which was more like the language of a single nation than the dialects of earlier times had been. This is plain in the writing of England's first great national author, Chaucer (about 1340–1400). Chaucer's great poetry was musical and beautiful. Read aloud the following selection from *The Canterbury Tales*, and see how closely it resembles the English of today.

> A Knight ther was, and that a worthy man,
> That fro the tyme that he first bigan
> To ryden out, he loved chivalrye,
> Trouthe and honour, fredom and curteisye.

Chaucer's influence on the development of the national language was very great. His writing set a standard of excellent form, which was copied all over England. Thus it helped to unify and standardize the national language, — English, — as had King Alfred's fine old West Saxon 400 years earlier.

Another event which greatly aided the improvement and standardization of the English language was John Wycliffe's translation of the Bible into English. His work made it possible for the first time for the English people to read the Bible in their own tongue. We shall have occasion to hear of this great man Wycliffe in another chapter.

By 1400, therefore, the dialects of the various peoples of England had practically disappeared and a national language had developed. Of course, as we saw in the selection from Chaucer, the language still *looked* different from the language of today. There were many letters, including final *e's*, which have since been dropped; and there were other differences in spelling. As one historian described it, however, "It was a language of which any nation might be proud, simple and practical, as befitted the English character, and yet with unlimited possibilities of rich and poetic expression." Less than 200 years later William Shakespeare proved what possibilities for great literature this language had.

England, then, had been transformed from the confusion of Britons, Celts, Angles, Saxons, Danes, Normans, and other tribesmen into a fairly unified national state under a single monarch, with a single language and a growing national literature. It fulfilled in general the requirements of our test of a national state.

FIG. 29. Chaucer reading his tales to the court of Edward III. (From a painting by Ford Madox Brown)

III. Spain also became a National State before 1500

In the meantime, on the Spanish peninsula two more national states had arisen — Spain and Portugal. Three hundred and fifty years before the Norman Conquest of England, warlike Moors had swept across northern Africa, crossed over to Europe, and overrun the region now covered by Spain and Portugal. For several hundred years after 700 they governed the peninsula and made most of its inhabitants conform to the Mohammedan religion. But the Mohammedan religion never reached farther north; all the rest of central and western Europe was Christian.

These Moors were a most enterprising and creative people. At the very time when other parts of Europe were in the Dark Ages of semicivilization, the Arab culture of Spain had advanced rapidly. The agriculture and industry of the peninsula had become most productive, and handicraft had reached a high point of excellence. Art and science were more highly developed there than anywhere else in Europe.

Large, beautifully proportioned palaces and other public buildings had been constructed by this gifted people. Note, for example, the magnificent royal palace — the Alhambra — which was built by the Moorish kings at Granada (see figure 30). This palace has been regarded as one of the great achievements of Arabic culture.

FIG. 30. Most of the Alhambra was built between 1248 and 1354. It covers 35 acres and is inclosed by a wall

The cities of Spain had grown into large metropolises. Even before 1000 Cordova, for example, numbered 500,000 people and had become a great trading and educational center. It had hundreds of mosques (Mohammedan churches), more than 300 public baths, and a university with several thousand students.

All this the Moors had achieved while the rest of Europe was almost totally illiterate and art, science, and literature, as well as handicrafts and trade, were at a low stage of development. Unfortunately, the wonderful civilization of the Moors declined after the eleventh century. The constant warfare into which they were plunged after that date made it impossible for them to maintain their position in the peninsula.

During the 800's and 900's Christian nobles had established

themselves in small provinces in the northern section in Spain and south of the Pyrenees Mountains. The outstanding leaders among them were the king of Castile and Leon, the king of Aragon, and the king of Navarre. As years passed, the story of the rise of kingdoms in France and England was repeated in the Spanish peninsula. Spanish kings gradually asserted their control over larger and larger areas. The armies of Castile, for example, steadily drove the Mohammedans southward, and as early as 1085 captured Toledo and made it once more a Christian city. In the meantime the kings of Aragon had extended their territories to the south and east.

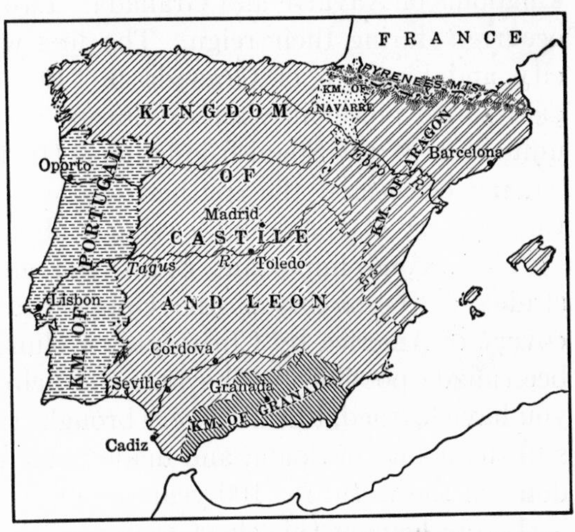

FIG. 31. By 1500 Spain controlled all the land on the peninsula except Portugal

Throughout the next century and a half the Christians steadily drove the Moors toward Africa. By 1250 Castile included all the territory west of Navarre and east of Portugal, except the small mountainous kingdom of Granada, on the Mediterranean. In this southern extension the Castilians had also taken the great port of Cadiz, the prosperous city of Seville, and the university city of Cordova. But for 200 years more the Moors continued to hold the little kingdom of Granada.

So by the late 1400's the peninsula consisted of the large kingdom of Castile and Leon, which occupied about two thirds of all the territory; the smaller kingdom of Aragon; the tiny kingdom of Navarre, which reached across the Pyrenees into France; and the mountain territory of Moorish Granada. On the west coast of the peninsula the small independent kingdom of Portugal had developed. This much had been accomplished by the several hundred years of Christian reconquest.

Queen Isabella and King Ferdinand join Castile and Aragon in 1469

The first important rulers in all these hundreds of years whom we need to remember are Queen Isabella of Castile and King Ferdinand of Aragon. Through the marriage of these two in 1469 all of Spain was brought together except for the little kingdoms of Navarre and Granada. Two other important events occurred during their reign. The first was the conquest of the city and kingdom of Granada in 1492, which marked the end of Moorish power in western Europe and almost completed the unification of the Spanish kingdom. (In 1512 King Ferdinand of Aragon conquered the southern part of Navarre, rounding out the territory of Spain and leaving it about as we know it today.)

The second important event you already know from your studies of the history of the United States. That was the discovery of America by Christopher Columbus, whose voyage had been made possible by the financial help of Queen Isabella. As you have learned, this discovery brought great wealth to the rulers and the nobles of Spain, and made Spain one of the leading kingdoms of the world for 100 years more.

Before leaving this short sketch of the rise of Spain as a national state, we must note the part played by the religious bigotry of the Spanish rulers in wiping out one kind of culture and in developing another. Although Christian kings now ruled the entire peninsula, hundreds of thousands of Moors still lived in the central and southern regions. Jews had settled in many of the cities of Europe and great numbers of them lived in Spain. One historian sums up the situation by saying that the Moors and the Jews "were the most industrious, skillful, and thrifty among the inhabitants in Spain," and that they "well-nigh supported the whole kingdom with the products of their toil." Indeed, the Moors and the Jews brought industry, trade, architecture, the arts, and sciences to a remarkably high state of development.

Nevertheless, the Christian Queen Isabella and her successors were so determined to rid themselves of their Moorish and Jewish subjects that for more than 100 years they persecuted them mercilessly. Religious courts, established by the state, arrested and convicted tens of thousands of persons who were suspected of heresy. No more horrible tale of torture and execution is recorded in the history of Europe than that which took place in Spain at this time. It did indeed achieve the aims of the Christian rulers: it drove the Moors and the Jews out of Spain. But it is the judgment of historians that it also crippled Spain and was the fundamental cause of her later decline as a center of civilization and culture.

Although the marriage of Isabella of Castile and Ferdinand of Aragon had brought most of Spain under a single family, nevertheless Castile and Aragon continued to be practically independent countries. For example, each had a separate parliament called the Cortes; each had its own governing officials; each collected its own taxes; and each continued for hundreds of years to live according to its own customs. Each had its own language and, as in France and England, the people of the various sections of the country had developed fairly different customs and ways of living. Castilian — the language of Castile — was regarded as the finer language, however, and eventually became the Spanish of the written literature as well as that of the more educated and cultured people. The language of Aragon was called Catalan. As Castilian rose in importance, Catalan became more and more the inferior form of speech.

Spain, like France and England, was becoming a national state by 1500. Although they had separate parliaments and separate bodies of officials, the two parts of Spain were united under a single crown, they were gradually adopting a more unified language, and the people were coming to regard themselves as Spaniards.

IV. By 1500 Portugal also became a National State under a King

In the meantime the small kingdom of Portugal on the west coast of the peninsula had also become an independent Christian monarchy, with a continuous line of ruling kings who kept the entire territory under the control of a central government. Indeed, if only the test of government is applied Portugal was a national state even by the middle of the 1200's.

After that time, and especially in the 1400's and 1500's, Portugal became one of the leading sea powers of the European world. You know from your study of history of the remarkable series of discoveries in Africa and in the Far East and of the great world trade developed in the 1500's and 1600's under powerful Portuguese rulers interested in navigation. Prominent in this history is the name of Prince Henry the Navigator.

In Portugal as in England, France, and Spain national feeling and a national language steadily developed. Portuguese, like Spanish, French, and Italian, was one of the Romance languages. Like the others it developed slowly from the spoken Latin used by the inhabitants who resided in the region after the decline of the Roman Empire. By 1500 Portuguese had become a distinctive language. And, as in France and England, a written national literature gradually developed.

V. Other Political Divisions in Northern and Eastern Europe in 1500

These, then, were the four important national states of Europe — England, France, Spain, and Portugal. There were other small independent states in various parts of Europe. In the extreme north, for example, there were the kingdoms of Sweden, Norway, and Denmark, covering in general the same territories that they do today. From time to time these kingdoms had been joined together, but after the reign of Gustavus Vasa (1523–1560) Sweden became an independent kingdom. Norway and Denmark were ruled under Danish rulers as one kingdom until 1814.

There were also other political groups in eastern and northern Europe. The *Slavs*, for example, consisting of the Russian, Polish, and Lithuanian groups, were ruled in several divisions. The leading one was the Grand Duchy of Muscovy, of which Moscow was the capital. (See figure 32.) There were also the kingdom of Poland, the grand principality of Lithuania, and the kingdom of Hungary. Extending over many small states of the Balkans and along the southern coast of the Black Sea down into Asia Minor was the large empire of the Ottoman Turks. These were all scattered principalities, and for several hundred years none of them was destined to play an outstanding part in the development of the world's march toward democracy.

VI. The Holy Roman Empire: Hundreds of Small German States

While the four national monarchies of England, France, Spain, and Portugal were forming, what was happening to Germany? Had it also become a strong national state under a king?

No, Germany was still the "Germanies"— a hodgepodge of no less than 300 states — free cities, baronies, archduchies, margravates, duchies, counties, and other feudal estates, many of them covering a territory of only a few square miles. Almost every one of these divisions governed itself. You will understand conditions fairly accurately if you picture a thoroughly feudal condition existing throughout the "Germanies," even as late as 1500. The larger territories, such as the archduchy of Austria, were ruled by powerful dukes; the smaller ones by bishops, counts, barons, or lesser nobles.

This whole region, called the Holy Roman Empire and shown within the heavy boundary on the map of figure 32, was held together, however, in a kind of loose confederation. It was not an empire in the real sense of the word; that is, it was not a state made up of peoples of various languages and races, paying allegiance to a single ruler. Neither was it Roman, for in 1500 it extended southward only as far as the northern boundary of the Swiss Confederation and the northern Italian city states. A world-renowned French writer of the eighteenth century of whom you will learn later — Voltaire — once said that the Holy Roman Empire was not at all well named: it was not an empire, it had nothing to do with Rome, and it certainly wasn't holy.

There was, however, at least the form of an empire. An emperor was *elected* by seven of the chief rulers of the "Germanies." These "electors" were the archbishops of Mainz, Trier, and Cologne, the king of Bohemia, the duke of Saxony, the margrave of Brandenburg, and the count palatine of the Rhine. On the death of a ruling emperor these electors met and chose the next ruler from one of the German principalities. As a result of the nonhereditary nature of the imperial throne, the power of the smaller nobles continued to be very great. Frequently, for example, the electors agreed upon the emperor elect only after he in turn had promised to leave each of them independent to govern his own state as he wished. Thus, during the very period in which strong kings were unifying England, France, Spain, and Portugal, the "Germanies" continued to be a confused group of independent and quarreling principalities.

In 1273 Rudolph of Hapsburg — member of a family that had originally been located in a small section of Switzerland — was elected emperor of this so-called Holy Roman Empire. Rudolph was a strong leader and soon added the duchies of Austria and Styria to his own possessions. In the next 150 years his successors steadily conquered more land, and by the early 1400's the archduchy of Austria was one of the most powerful political states in central Europe. Hence the German electors tended, generation after generation, to choose the archduke of Austria as the emperor of the Holy Roman Empire. Consequently, the House of Hapsburg became the most important ruling family in central Europe and remained so for several hundred years. Indeed, the Hapsburgs continued in power in Austria until the close of the World War in 1918!

Thus Absolute Monarchs ruled Europe

Our brief sketch of the rise of national states has made one fact clear: in 1500 the Europeans had hardly started on their march toward democracy. It is true that England had made a beginning, but on the continent government was autocratic. It was absolute.

Everywhere government was undemocratic according to modern ideas. The few ruled the masses. A tiny group of kings and nobles governed; the millions of common people supported them. A single person and his favorites decided everything. Even the intelligent scholars and business men were denied a share in government.

There was no voting by the people; there were no parlia-

FIG. 32. Europe in 1500. The darkened areas indicate the four nations which had grown up by this date

ments which really represented the people. There were no elected officials; all were appointed by the king. Government was absolute! This was the condition before Europeans started on their march toward democracy.

And then came epoch-making and world-changing episodes. Then came events of great significance in the development of freedom of thought and speech, of the civil and political rights of men, and of better ways of living. These events dealt with every aspect of civilization and culture: the creation of totally new methods of industry, agriculture, and business; the invention of new kinds of government; the exploration and settlement of strange and hitherto unknown continents; the devising of new and creative arts and new customs and standards of value.

The events themselves were not political; they had nothing to do immediately with government. They had to do with *new ways of thinking*! They ushered in the scientific revolution, the real basis of the march toward democracy.

INTERESTING READINGS FROM WHICH YOU CAN GET ADDITIONAL INFORMATION

BALDWIN, JAMES. The Story of Roland. Charles Scribner's Sons, New York.

BOLTON, IVY MAY. The King's Minstrel. L. C. Page & Company, Boston. Social life in Norman England.

CATHER, KATHERINE DUNLAP. The Castle of the Hawk. The Century Co., New York. Rudolph of Hapsburg; the guilds.

CONVERSE, FLORENCE. Long Will. E. P. Dutton & Co., New York. Medieval England; Chaucer.

GOODENOUGH, LADY. The Boy's Chronicle of Muntaner. D. Appleton and Company, New York. Struggle of the Christians and Moors in Spain and the consolidation of Castile and Aragon.

HUTCHINSON, HORACE G. The Greatest Story in the World (Second Period). D. Appleton and Company, New York. From the dissolution of the Roman Empire through the Middle Ages.

PAINE, ALBERT BIGELOW. The Girl in White Armor. The Macmillan Company, New York. Excellent.

SCOTT, SIR WALTER. Ivanhoe. Saxons and Normans in England.

STEIN, EVALEEN. Pepin. L. C. Page & Company, Boston. Social life in early France.

TAPPAN, EVA MARCH. In the Days of Alfred the Great. Lothrop, Lee & Shepard Co., Boston.

TAPPAN, EVA MARCH. In the Days of William the Conqueror. Lothrop, Lee & Shepard Co., Boston. The early life of the Conqueror and his conquest of England.

WILSON, CALVIN DILL. The Story of the Cid. Lothrop, Lee & Shepard Co., Boston. Spain and the Moors.

CHAPTER V

THE SCIENTIFIC REVOLUTION: NEW WAYS OF THINKING

One day in 1590 a crowd of students and professors from the University of Pisa gathered around the base of the famous leaning tower. (See figure 33.) Eagerly they looked upward to the platform at the top, where several other people were leaning out, straining their eyes to watch the downward course of two balls of lead,—a large 100-pound ball and a little one-pound ball,—which had just been pushed out from the top.

FIG. 33. Galileo's experiment

What was the excitement about? An experiment! One of the first scientific experiments in the modern world—a simple one, but a very important one! Galileo Galilei, professor of mathematics in the university, was testing a hypothesis concerning falling bodies originated by Aristotle (384–322 B.C.), the Greek scientist and philosopher.

Up to this time people had believed Aristotle's hypothesis—namely, that the velocity of two falling bodies would be in proportion to their weights. In other words, they believed that a 100-pound weight dropped from a great height would strike the ground in one one-hundredth of the time that it would take a one-pound weight. Galileo had said that this hypothesis was ridiculous, and that two such bodies would strike the ground together. To test the truth of his *hypothesis* and disprove that of Aristotle he had planned the simple little experiment of dropping the two balls.

Imagine the suspense while everyone watched the descending balls that day! Down they came together, neither gaining on the other, and they struck the ground, as nearly as the critical eyes of doubters could measure, at the same time! Thus an old *hypothesis* which had been held for 1900 years was demolished. A new *hypothesis* (namely, that, allowing for the friction of air, all bodies fall from the same height in equal time) was confirmed.

Galileo's experiment illustrates the new ways of thinking that ushered in the scientific revolution

One central factor has produced the changing governments and changing cultures of modern times — NEW WAYS OF THINKING! After 1500, *men began to think differently.* They thought about making things in new ways; as a result they made power-driven machines. They thought about buying and selling things in new ways; as a result they accumulated vast amounts of capital through corporations. They thought about transporting things and communicating with one another in new ways; as a result they made better ships, trains, and telegraphs, and finally the radio to bind the distant continents of the world tightly together. We call all of these new ways of doing things the Industrial Revolution.

Men also thought about religion in new ways; and new churches and new points of view about worship resulted. They thought about civil and political rights in new ways; and new experiments in government resulted.

Thus the very basis of our changing civilization lies in new ways of thinking. After 1500, *men came to think things out for themselves rather than to accept everything on faith* as their ancestors had done. Instead of accepting the dictates of kings and lords, they began to think about governing themselves. Instead of worshiping as the officers of the established churches told them to do, they began to think out their religion for themselves. Instead of planting, cultivating, and harvesting crops as their forefathers had done for thousands of years, they began to think out new and better ways. Thus in every aspect of life new ways of thinking resulted in new ways of living.[1]

What is the scientific method of thinking?

The new ways of thinking differed in one important respect from those which had characterized men's thought for thousands of years — *they were more scientific.* About the 1500's educated leaders began to think in ways that we call today *scientific.* To appreciate the astonishing changes that came in Europe after 1500, therefore, we must understand clearly what is meant by "the scientific way of thinking," or more briefly expressed — the *scientific method.*

In these books we have referred frequently to the discovery of this scientific method of thinking. But thus far we have defined and discussed it only in a very general way. We have said, for example, that it was "thinking things out from facts," . . . "drawing conclusions from careful observations," etc. We have also said that one of the four fundamental factors that produced both American and European civilizations was the scientific way of doing things. Science led to the successful invention of engines, machines, railroads, telegraphs, airplanes, and radios, and also to the new experiments in government.

But to understand the development of science in the modern world, we must study carefully the steps involved in scientific thinking. Let us consider some practical examples; from them we can learn just what the scientific method is. First, note again Galileo's experiment. Besides being a good story, it illustrates admirably the essential steps in this method.

[1] *An important caution.* In our studies we speak frequently of this new period in the culture of civilization as developing after 1500. This precise dating of the scientific and intellectual awakening of Europe is, of course, merely for convenience. No sudden revolutionary change in attitudes or ways of living occurred in the year 1500 or even in the generation or two immediately after. Some changes had been occurring for several centuries preceding 1500; others occurred soon after that time. For example, we have already learned of the awakening interest in trade in Europe after 1100 and the establishment of new contacts with Asia. Thus gradually during the three or more centuries preceding 1500 the basis had been laid for the more rapid development of new ways of living after that date. However, so many radically new ways of thinking and living actually came about in the 1500's and 1600's that for convenience we can date the scientific revolution and the beginning of the modern world with the year 1500.

First: Think out hypotheses. The first step is to think out a conclusion from all the available facts. Such a conclusion is called a hypothesis. It is not a mere guess; it does not depend on whim, for it is based on careful observations. Nevertheless it needs to be *tested* with further observations; so we call it a *hypothesis.*

Aristotle and Galileo both thought out hypotheses in the case of falling bodies. But the two men arrived at very different hypotheses. One (Galileo) said the velocities of bodies falling from the same height would be equal; the other (Aristotle) said the velocities would be proportional to their weights. Each man *reasoned* from his observations and stated his hypothesis.

FIG. 34. Aristotle (384–322 B.C.)

Second: Observe accurately. Hypotheses must be based upon careful *observations.* Both Aristotle and Galileo based their hypotheses upon observation of falling bodies. We know that Aristotle was one of the first scientists to practice the art of observing carefully the world about him and to urge others to do so. Galileo too was famous as an acute observer. Evidently Galileo's observations were more accurate than Aristotle's; for his hypothesis was proved to be correct, and Aristotle's wrong.

Third: Experiment to test the truth of the hypothesis. In the problem of falling bodies Aristotle ignored this step, as most earlier scientists did. But Galileo, having reasoned out a hypothesis by observing the speed at which bodies fell, prepared a careful *experiment* in which to *test* his hypothesis. He pushed two balls of very different weights from the top of the leaning tower of Pisa and observed very carefully the time which each required to fall to the base. Thus Galileo *experimented to test the truth of his hypothesis.* As we shall learn more fully later, the testing of hypotheses under practical conditions, observing as accurately as possible the happenings during the experiment, was an aspect of the scientific method which developed chiefly after 1500.

Fourth: Measure exactly. But to observe accurately the changes which occur during an experiment one must *measure* accurately. For example, Galileo needed apparatus (1) to be sure that the balls left their height at exactly the same moment; (2) to be sure that they struck the base at exactly the same moment; (3) to measure accurately the time of their fall. When he performed this experiment there were no mechanical or electrical timepieces or other kinds of exact measuring apparatus like those we have now. He was compelled to improvise a "water clock," which was, of course, exceedingly inaccurate. In another experiment Galileo needed to measure the time of each swing of a lamp swaying in a church tower. Having no accurate timepiece, he was compelled to count his pulse to determine the number of seconds required for each swing of the lamp. Not a very accurate way to measure, no doubt you are thinking. To arrive at a sound conclusion from an experiment, therefore, one must be able to *measure* with great exactness the facts observed.[1]

FIG. 35. Galileo Galilei (1564–1642). (From a painting by Sustermans)

Fifth: Collect many measured facts. Modern scientists do not depend upon a *single* experiment for their conclusions. They must have many observations. For example, William Harvey, physician to both James I and Charles I of England, spent years in making painstaking experiments on the circulation of the blood. Like Galileo, he tested his hypotheses by many practical experiments and observations. To do this he dissected many animals

[1] On this important point see Volume V, *An Introduction to Problems of American Culture,* Chap. XVI, pp. 383–388, "Reasoned Conclusions versus Unreasoned Opinions."

— snakes, dogs, cats, — in all *87 different species*, before he was willing to publish his conclusion. After twelve years he gave his conclusion to the world (1628), having proved that, propelled by the beat of the heart, the blood circulates through the body continuously.

Sixth: Tabulate and classify the measured facts systematically. Another difference between modern science and earlier ways of thinking is that in a truly scientific experiment facts were carefully classified. For example, as just stated, Harvey made experiments and measured observations upon 87 different species of animals. To keep all these facts systematically in mind, he was compelled to tabulate and classify them in orderly arrangements.

Seventh: Drawing conclusions, finding scientific laws, and making predictions. Now we come to the last step of the scientific method — namely, drawing a conclusion from the facts which will confirm or refute the hypothesis made at the beginning of the experiment. In a general way this can be done as Galileo and his observers did it — *by observation.* But to do it accurately, the scientist makes elaborate algebraic and geometric calculations. He is not content to depend even upon systematically tabulated facts. He plots them in graphs, writes equations, and treats them in other mathematical ways. As a result he may succeed in finding such a general truth that it can be called a scientific law, from which predictions can be made of future happenings.

These, then, are the steps of the scientific method of thinking. These are the new ways of thinking that produced the Industrial Revolution with its power-driven machines. These are the ideas that gave the Western nations, especially America, the world's highest physical standard of living.

Modern Science was helped by Knowledge acquired in Earlier Civilizations

The practical knowledge of the ancient civilizations

Were all these ways of thinking invented after 1500? Some were, but not all. Indeed, some were the product of thousands of years of human study by the thinking men of many countries, for the scientific way of thinking is international and universal.

In every country and in every age of man's history upon earth some addition has been made to scientific knowledge.

Much of the practical knowledge upon which our modern civilization is based goes back to the people who lived in Asia and Africa 5000 and 6000 years ago. The recent excavations of archæologists and the translations of long-hidden mysteries in

FIG. 36. The slab of painted stone shown in the picture is part of a building erected in Egypt more than 3000 years ago. It still bears the name of the overseer of public works

ancient books have proved that from 2000 to 4000 years before Christ highly developed civilizations existed in several fertile river valleys. Among them were the Babylonian civilization of the Euphrates River valley; the Egyptian, of the Nile valley; the Assyrian, of the valley of the Tigris River; the Chinese, of the Hwang and Yangtze rivers; and the civilizations along the valleys of the Indus and Ganges rivers in India.

In each of these five river-valley civilizations a vast amount of practical knowledge was acquired. Much of it was passed on to other peoples living at that time; some of it was passed on to later civilizations. Some of it was lost. As we shall see, this civilization was on a higher level than the Europeans attained several thousand years later, in the Middle Ages.

The chief differences between ancient "science" and modern science

To perceive clearly the additions to the world's knowledge that have been made by modern science since 1500, let us note which of the elements of the scientific method and which sciences the ancients knew and utilized. We shall see that they utilized two of our elements of scientific thinking. That is, (1) they observed certain phenomena and drew hypotheses from them, and (2) they knew that hypotheses should not be based upon a single observation but upon many observations.

Most of the ancient peoples had a practical sort of astronomical knowledge. As early as 3800 B.C. Babylonian priests — and about the same time Egyptians also — had observed with considerable exactness the movement of the heavenly bodies. This knowledge was acquired to satisfy *a practical need* — namely, that of telling time. As a result of their observations of the sun, the moon, the stars, and the planets, they had a well-worked-out calendar. They also knew the four cardinal points of the compass — north, east, south, and west — and laid out their temples, palaces, and public buildings (and in Egypt their pyramids) with respect to them. Furthermore, they had well-developed star maps and had succeeded in constructing star clocks, somewhat like the sundials of later civilizations.

These ancient peoples had also accumulated many practical observations concerning animal and human life. Physical need had developed the practice of medicine and had begun the study of anatomy, physiology, botany, and chemistry. Records of physicians are found in Egypt as far back as 4500 B.C., and of surgical operations as early as 2500 B.C. In the time of King Hammurabi (about 2100 B.C.) Babylonian surgeons had such technical knowledge and such delicate instruments that they could remove cataracts from the eye.[1]

[1] But the unscientific attitude of those who made the laws of the land was revealed in one which stipulated that if the patient lost his life or his sight the hands of the surgeon should be amputated!

Thus we see that these ancient peoples — the Egyptians, Babylonians, and Chinese — made many observations and drew hypotheses from them. But did they go further? Did they experiment? measure accurately? tabulate? treat their observations mathematically? Did they know geometry, algebra, and what we call higher mathematics?

Yes — and no. They had a very elementary knowledge of arithmetic, algebra, and geometry. As early as 2300 B.C. the Babylonians had developed multiplication tables from 1 to 1350, and tables of squares and cubes. They weighed, measured, and counted, but they did so with great inaccuracy in comparison to our modern standards. For example, among the ancient Chinese the unit of linear measurement was the grain of millet. Ten millets laid end to end made an "inch"; ten inches made a "foot." (Note that they used the decimal system.) Considering the variation in the length of seeds and other natural objects which were used in measuring, the inaccuracy of this method is plain.

However, there is little evidence of an interest in *abstract science*, and there were few general scientific laws or mathematical principles. The knowledge was *practical*, suited to the needs of getting a living in a moderately well-developed civilization.

Just what, then, was the state of science in those times?

First, the people accumulated many practical observations.

Second, the results of these observations were utilized in the development of agriculture, handicrafts, building construction, architecture, and medicine.

Third, this knowledge was mixed up with naïve superstitions.

Fourth, there were no *precise* methods of measuring. There were no *exact* scales, balances, transits and levels, sextants, telescopes, or microscopes, such as we have today.

Fifth, there was no knowledge of advanced mathematics of the abstract type; almost nothing was known of algebra and demonstrational geometry. Even the scholars of the times knew little trigonometry, and the analytical geometry, the calculus, and other forms of higher mathematics were quite undiscovered.

The beginnings of abstract science among the Greeks

It was the Greeks and their students — especially Thales (640–546 B.C.), Pythagoras (sixth century B.C.), Plato (about 427–347 B.C.), Euclid (about 300 B.C.), and Aristotle (384–322 B.C.) — who first discovered the bases of *abstract* mathematics and science. Whereas the thinking men of the earlier civilizations were

FIG. 37. The school of Athens. Beside the aged Plato stands Aristotle, who was his pupil for twenty years. (From a painting by Raphael, in the Vatican)

essentially practical-minded, primarily interested in riches and comfort, Greek scholars were interested in *abstract* ways of thinking.

For example, the Egyptians studied geometry to determine how to build barns, stairways, roofs, and the like; but Thales, Pythagoras, Euclid, and Aristotle were interested in the *relations between lines, angles, and numbers* — in short, in scientific principles. Thales perceived that the angles at the base of an isosceles triangle are equal. Pythagoras and his followers discovered many of the propositions of geometry which now comprise the first, second, and fourth books of Euclid. These propositions are still taught in plane-geometry courses in high school.

The famous Greek geometrician Euclid taught mathematics in his native city, Alexandria, about 300 B.C. Influenced by Pythagoras and Plato, he developed the basis of demonstrational geometry as it was known throughout the Middle Ages. Indeed, his work *Elements* is the basis of even modern textbooks on geometry. Euclid was not interested in the *practical* applications of science with which he was surrounded in Egypt, as the following anecdote shows. A practical-minded Egyptian student, rebelling against learning the abstract propositions of Euclid's *Elements*, asked, "What does one profit by learning these things?" Euclid called an assistant to him and said, "Give him money, since he studies for gain." We are also told that a famous saying originated in Euclid's reply to the King of Egypt, who had asked for an easier explanation of certain propositions of geometry. "*There is no royal road to geometry*," he answered.

The beginnings of natural science among the Greeks are credited to Aristotle, who is frequently called *the first scientist.* Whereas Thales, Pythagoras, and Euclid were interested in abstract mathematics, Aristotle devoted himself to the development of natural science. He was the first great systematizer and classifier of human knowledge, and his influence was felt all over Europe, the Near East, and northern Africa for nearly 2000 years.

There was hardly a subject that was discussed in his day about which Aristotle did not write or study. For example, he wrote a practical book on mechanics, called *The Problems*, in which he explained the principles of the lever, the balance, the wheel and axle, and the rudder. He wrote a description of 500 forms of animals and plants, as a result of which he is sometimes called the first biologist. For this work, it is reported that he dissected animals of 50 species.

Lack of space prevents us from multiplying examples. Enough has been said, however, to show that the work of the Greeks and of their students who collected at the Egyptian city of Alexandria after 300 B.C. laid the foundation for the development of *abstract* mathematics and science.

There is, however, a sharp contrast between the Greek science of 2000 years ago and the modern science which developed after 1500. This is due partly to the fact that the Greek scientists lacked several necessary things, as did the Egyptians, Babylonians, and Chinese. First, they lacked accurate measuring instruments. Second, their mathematical methods of treating facts were very limited. Third, they lacked the modern idea of *repeated* experimentation. These deficiencies alone were sufficient to account for their failure to develop natural and physical science more highly. Correspondingly these would account for their failure to produce industrial civilization.

Then came the Dark Ages, and science seemed lost

For nearly 1900 years, from Aristotle and Euclid (about 300 B.C.) to Galileo and his contemporaries (about 1600 A.D.), little that was new was added to the scientific knowledge of the world. The chief political movements of this long interval were (1) the decline of Greece, and its conquest by Rome in 146 B.C.; (2) the rise of Rome to a position of tremendous imperial power during the next 400 years; (3) the decline of the Roman Empire in the 300's and 400's A.D.; (4) the migrations of the Germanic tribes and the Northmen; and (5) the thousand years of the building of new national states in Europe. From the standpoint of science this great medieval period was well named the Dark Ages.

During the rule of the practical-minded Romans abstract science was encouraged very little; it was even hindered. For instance, in the rule of Julius Cæsar the largest Alexandrian library was destroyed, and hundreds of thousands of precious rolls of manuscript were lost. Naturally, the barbarians of the North did not understand the value of scientific learning. Furthermore, the Christian Church, which rose to power after the 300's, had little interest in science. Most of the bishops believed that science was opposed to religion. Only a few scholarly monks were interested in the old manuscripts. Hence, in frequent raids upon centers of learning, libraries and important scientific records were destroyed.

Two influences, however, preserved much of the scientific knowledge

To go back for a moment in our story, we should remind ourselves that civilizations and cultures have always developed through contact between different peoples. Important examples of this are shown in the way in which the Babylonians, Assyrians, Egyptians, Chinese, and Indians influenced one another. We know, for example, that Indian, Babylonian, and possibly Egyptian goods and ideas had found their way across Central Asia to China as early as 300 B.C., and that these contacts with the outside world led to important changes in Chinese scientific thought. About 130 B.C. the Chinese Empire began to extend its power westward into Turkestan, and this resulted in greatly increased intercourse with India and with the countries around the Mediterranean.

Even earlier the Babylonians and the Egyptians had also borrowed ideas of culture from each other. The Buddhist religion was introduced into China from India some time during the 100 years preceding the birth of Christ, and not long afterwards the Japanese began to borrow from the culture of the Chinese. These are merely a few examples of the fact that knowledge was passed on from generation to generation and from old declining civilizations to young rising ones.

Two important groups helped preserve the scientific knowledge of the ancients during the Dark Ages: (1) the Arabs, who rose to power in Western Asia in the 600's; (2) certain monks and scholars of the Catholic Church. Just a brief word concerning each.

1. *The important services of the Arabs.* In the centuries following Aristotle and the brilliant Alexandrian scholars, the new learning developed steadily throughout Western Asia. The knowledge of the Greeks had been brought into Syria, and Hindu arithmetic and astronomy had been brought in through Persia. Among the Mohammedans of Western Asia after 600, therefore, the Greek science found a rich soil for growth. By 800, in the time of Harun-al-Rashid, the Mohammedan capital of Bagdad was a brilliant center of scientific learning, especially of mathematics and astronomy. An astronomical observatory was built, and very accurate measuring instruments and scientific apparatus constructed. Sextants and quadrants, with which to measure the angular position of heavenly bodies, and surveying instruments were perfected. The Arabs had also constructed new mathematical and astronomical tables, some of which were indispensable to the later development of modern European science.

Furthermore, the works of Aristotle, Euclid, and other Mediterranean scientists had been translated into the Arabic language, and the system of so-called "Arabic" numerals which we, in common with all Western nations, use today was introduced from India and Persia. The records lead us to believe also that the first book called *Algebra* was produced by an Arab mathematician, as were the elements of trigonometry. All this was accomplished by Arab culture before 1300.

The name of one Arab scholar is worth remembering — that of a physician and philosopher, Averröes (1126–1198), who translated and commented on many of Aristotle's works. It was primarily through him that these scientific works of Aristotle became known to Europeans in the 1100's and 1200's.

We have no space here to tell how this knowledge of the Arabs was spread over Europe. Suffice it to repeat that during the more than 300 years when they held Spain and Portugal, such cities as Cordova, Granada, Toledo, Barcelona, and others became brilliant centers of a highly developed Moorish civilization.

Thus the science of the Greeks and the Alexandrians was preserved for the Europe of 2000 years later, and was also added to by talented Arabic mathematicians and scientists.

2. *Some scholars of the Catholic Church also devoted themselves to science.* In the meantime, in the isolated monasteries and towns of Italy, France, Spain, England, Ireland, and the "Germanies," scholarly monks of the Catholic Church devoted themselves to the preservation and development of scientific ideas. They laboriously copied manuscripts dealing with arithmetic, geometry, astronomy, and other studies, and translated Arabic scientific works into Latin, the only written language which was understood by all the scholars of Europe. They traveled about between the western monasteries of Ireland and the churches of the Eastern Roman Empire, slowly spreading scientific ideas over all Europe.

Roger Bacon: medieval devotee of the scientific method

One name that is of historic importance in this connection is that of Roger Bacon (1214–1294). Bacon was an English Franciscan monk, a highly educated and widely traveled Oxford

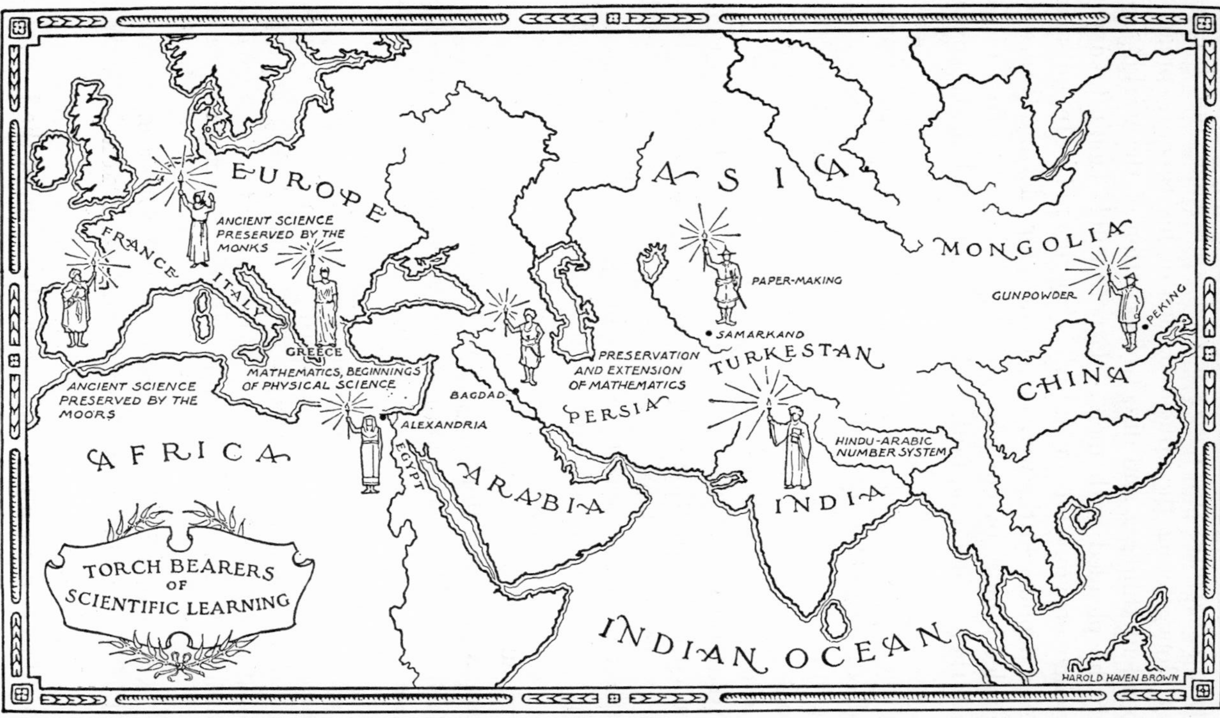

FIG. 38. A picture map which illustrates where some of the ancient scientific knowledge began and where it was preserved

scholar. He stands out in the history of science not for his own scientific discoveries or mathematical knowledge, but because, almost alone among the educated men of his time, he preached independent thinking and direct observation of the world. Constantly he pleaded with men: "Experiment! Don't take your knowledge or your life on faith! Experiment!" In his many books he denounced the weakness of men for allowing themselves to be ruled blindly by custom. He ridiculed the tendency of men to base their religion on faith and to accept docilely the government of "accidentally born" kings. He was a rebel against authority in the Church, and dogma in business, in government, — indeed, in practically every aspect of life.

He himself translated and commented upon the works of Aristotle, making available to the navigators and explorers of later centuries Aristotle's idea of another continent close by in the Atlantic Ocean. (It is said that Christopher Columbus was influenced by this writing of Roger Bacon.) Nevertheless Bacon never ceased to denounce the unthinking acceptance of Aristotle and the inaccurate translations and interpretations of him.

That Bacon had vision of what might be accomplished by science is shown by the manner in which he predicted the invention of such things as telescopes, steamships, trains, and airplanes. Note, for example, an extract from one of his writings:

> Machines for navigating are possible without rowers, so that great ships suited to river or ocean, guided by one man, may be borne with greater speed than if they were full of men. Likewise cars may be made so that without a draught animal they may be moved *cum impetu inaestimabili* ["with undreamt-of speed"] as we deem the scythed chariots to have been from which antiquity fought. And flying machines are possible, so that a man may sit in the middle turning some device by which artificial wings may beat the air in the manner of a flying bird.

New Inventions and Contacts with the Outside World in the 1300's and 1400's prepared the Way for New Ways of Thinking

Recall from our earlier studies how the world of the Europeans broadened after 1100. The Mongol empire of Genghis Khan and his successors kept open routes of travel between Europe and the

Far East, and Asia Minor became the real trading crossroads of the world. Italian commercial travelers, and monks bent upon converting the heathen, tramped the fatiguing highways to Cathay, and brought back many new ideas and ways of living.

1. The mariner's compass, more accurate geographical knowledge, and epoch-making explorations

It was in the 1300's and 1400's, for example, that men began to venture farther and farther upon the sea. Among several of the ancient peoples it had been observed that lodestone, or a piece of iron which had been touched by it, would point to the north. Rude compasses based on this knowledge had been constructed which made it possible to go farther from the sight of land. In the 1300's, using these devices, navigators from the Portuguese port of Lisbon dared the unknown Atlantic, and sailed westward and southward, exploring farther each year. By 1350 they had discovered the Canary Islands, Madeira, and the Azores Islands. A glance at the map of figure 39 gives us an idea of the courage and perhaps the desire for gain which were needed to take these bold navigators hundreds of miles from the European mainland.

Prince Henry of Portugal, known in history as the Navigator, until his death in 1460 fostered exploration to enrich his country and founded a school of navigation. Due to the interest which he aroused and the knowledge of navigation which was spread through his efforts, these later explorations were made possible.

By 1445 the Portuguese had ventured along the coast of Africa south of the Sahara region and had discovered the western cape which, because of the luxuriant greenness of its tropical vegetation, they named Cape Verde. As the years passed, other Portuguese ships sailed farther and farther south along the coast of Africa, and in 1488 Bartholomew Diaz wrote his name into history by rounding the southern tip at the Cape of Good Hope. Vasco da Gama sailed around this cape, crossed the Indian Ocean with the aid of Arab pilots, and in 1498 reached Calicut in Hindustan, or India as we call it today. Year after year Portuguese trade developed, extending to such a degree that it finally included the whole eastern coast of Asia. First (1509) Sumatra and the port of Malacca, at the northern extremity of the Malay

Peninsula, were reached; then the traders found their way (1512) to Java and the Moluccas; next the mainland, the region covered by the Malay States. Eventually Portuguese ships sailed into the long isolated Chinese and Japanese harbors. Thus at last direct ocean trade was established between western Europe and eastern Asia. Cathay and the famous Spice Islands were a part of the European world.

In the meantime mariners of other countries had been sailing the Atlantic, exploring the northern coasts and hunting for the Spice Islands, for Cathay, and for other rich lands of the Far East, which they guessed could be found by sailing westward. Long before this time they had become convinced that the earth was round and that *one could eventually find the east by sailing west.*

You know the story of the other epoch-making explorations and discoveries which extended the world of the European to include the entire earth: the four famous trips of Columbus, the circumnavigation of the world by Magellan, the discovery of the northern coast of North America by the Cabots, of the St. Lawrence region by the Frenchman, Cartier, and of the Hudson River and Manhattan Island by the Englishman, Henry Hudson, sailing under the flag of Holland.

These dramatic events in the world's history must be borne in mind to understand the startling advances which were being made in every field of human endeavor after 1500.

2. Independent thinking and discussion developed by the increased use of paper-making and printing

It was difficult for new ideas to spread through Europe before 1400. The chief reason was the lack of printed pamphlets and books. Even in the early 1400's the only books were *written* by hand on parchment or papyrus, as there were no printing presses and little paper, as we know it.

Throughout Egyptian, Greek, and Roman history manuscripts had always been written upon papyrus or parchment. Papyrus (from which we obtain our word *paper*) was a heavy material prepared from the fiber of a reed which grew abundantly in the Nile River valley, while parchment was the prepared skin of sheep or other animals. These two materials were both very

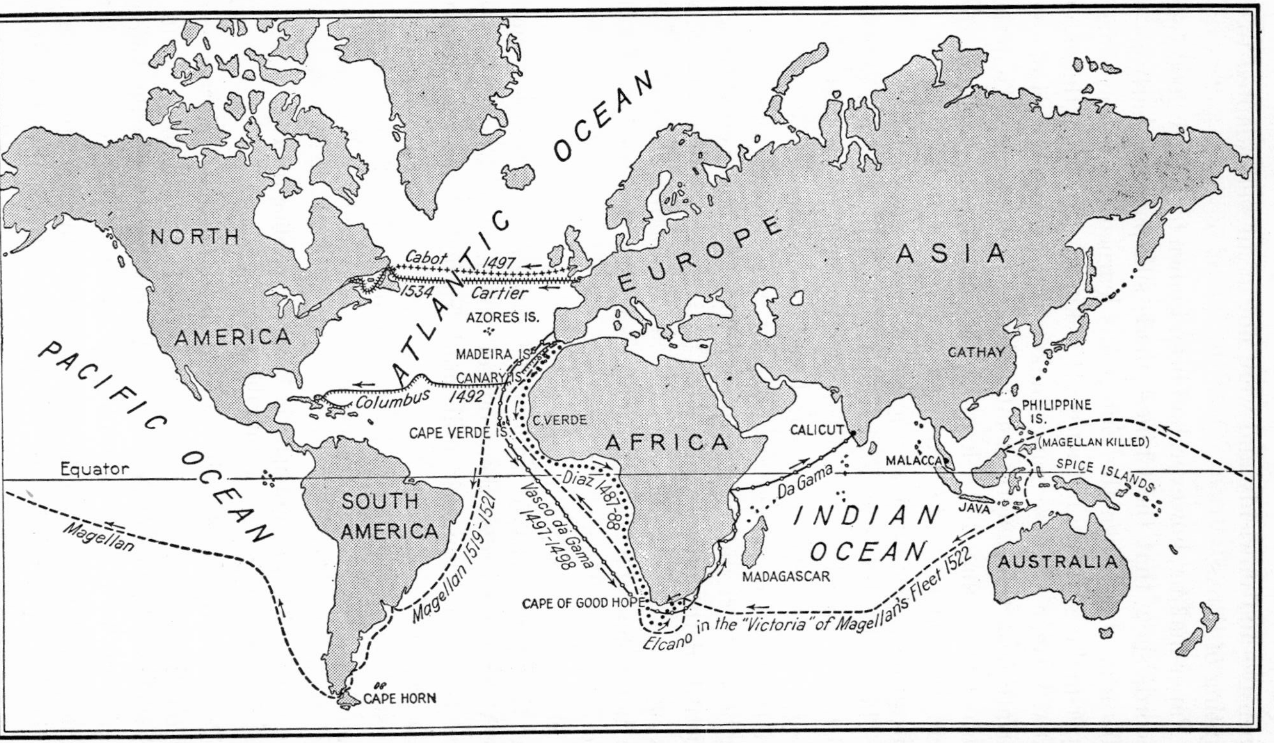

FIG. 39. The scientific revolution made possible these long voyages of exploration between 1492 and 1522

expensive and unwieldy and were not at all well adapted to the printing of books.

Paper-making, however, had been known for nearly 2000 years. Records show that the Chinese made silk paper as early as the 100's B.C. Just when the Europeans learned the Chinese art of paper-making we are not sure. It is known, however, that about 750 A.D. some Chinese paper-makers were taken as prisoners in warfare near the eastern Asiatic city of Samarkand. That their Arab captors may have learned the art of paper-making from them is shown by the existence today of Arabic manuscripts written on paper made in the 800's.

The Arabs, however, substituted cotton for silk and made, in Western Asia, what was called "Damascus" paper. The use of this Damascus paper was introduced into Europe through Greece and Italy and in a more roundabout way through the Moors of northern Africa and Spain. In each country, however, the people substituted the fibers which were native to their land for either silk or cotton. Thus in Spain the art of making fine paper from the hemp and flax which were grown in that region was developed by the Moors.

All of this took place before 1100. You will recall that after that time the Christian princes of Castile and Aragon conquered the Moors and drove them out of Spain. The Christians took over the Moorish paper mills and learned the art of making linen paper. It is said, however, that the paper made in the Christian mills was decidedly poorer in quality than that made formerly by the Moors of Spain and by the Arabs of Western Asia.

The first examples of European printing from movable type

Paper-making gradually spread into northern Europe — on the one hand from Italy and on the other hand from Spain — and was well known after 800. However, there was little demand for paper until men began to print from movable type. As long as books were made by laboriously copying manuscripts by hand, publication was limited and expensive and the demand for paper slight. As we have seen, for thousands of years all books had been made in that way, and copying manuscripts had become an important occupation. Great skill was developed, and many manuscripts more than 1000 years old today compare well in beauty with fine books printed much more recently.

Nevertheless the lack of mechanical printing made the cost of books so great that only the well-to-do could own them. For example, the library of one Italian ruler, consisting of 200 volumes, required 45 copyists working two years to complete it.

FIG. 40. The first printed book in England being presented to Edward IV by the author, Lord Rivers. Caxton, who printed it, kneels in the foreground. (From an old print)

In the 1400's, however, Europeans began to print with movable type. Exactly who should have the credit in Europe for the introduction of this method of printing is still a matter of some uncertainty; but various authorities assert that the credit should go to a Dutch printer named Laurens Coster, who died in 1440. We can be certain, however, that Johann (or John) Gutenberg printed from movable type in Mainz, Germany, in 1450. Once the first presses were made, they spread swiftly over Europe. In 1466, presses were in operation in Italy; in 1477, Caxton's press in Westminster, England, issued its first book; in the early 1500's, the Aldine Press of Venice had an international reputation. Styles of type, arrangement of page, and binding were vastly improved as time went on.

Almost overnight there was a tremendous increase in the volume of books in Europe; for instance, in one year in the early 1500's, 24,000 copies of one well-known classic were printed on these crude hand presses. When one remembers that hand power only was used and that every page had to be printed separately, the significance of this number becomes clear. You should remember, furthermore, that not until more than 300 years after that time was this hand method of printing improved upon! The first steam-driven rotary printing press in the United States was invented in 1845 by Richard Hoe.

Thus, even though books were still printed by hand, they had become more numerous by 1500. As their cost was small compared with that of hand-written manuscripts, the demand for books spread rapidly among the less well-to-do. At last the people of the middle economic classes, as well as kings, bankers, and bishops, could afford to own books.

Then, after 1500, came the Scientific Revolution

By 1500, therefore, conditions were favorable for the rapid spread of more exact scientific ways of thinking and working. Thus it came about that in 200 years — from about 1500 to about 1700 — a truly scientific "revolution" developed in various centers of Europe. As we have seen, the way had been well prepared for it. Within a short time the movement became international. Men of genius appeared in almost every country of western Europe, all contributing to the new science. New measuring instruments and new methods of thinking were applied to every aspect of life. Theories 2000 years old were discarded and were replaced by the new ones which were born in this fermenting age of genius. The old "sciences" were entirely remade.

There were so many important events in this new revolution in thinking that it is necessary to organize them systematically in order to understand them clearly. Let us note briefly five outstanding ways in which the scientific revolution developed: first, the invention of more exact measuring instruments; second, the development of higher mathematics — for example, algebra, geometry, trigonometry, analytic geometry, and the calculus; third, new scientific discoveries; fourth, the classification of the sciences and the development of the scientific method of thinking; and fifth, the increase in discussion among learned scholars of all nations.

1. The invention of more accurate measuring instruments

As we have seen, the ancients — the Greeks and the Arabs — lacked instruments with which to measure the events of the physical and natural world. They had no powerful lenses with which to see the distant stars or the tiny microörganisms; they lacked micrometers, barometers, thermometers, timepieces, what not. This lack alone helps to account for their limited scientific knowledge.

But this need for measuring-instruments was satisfied in the astonishing inventive work of the 1500's and the 1600's. It was at this time, for example, that such instruments as the following were either invented or else markedly improved:

1. The thermometer.
2. The pendulum clock.
3. The telescope.
4. The micrometer.
5. The barometer.
6. The thermoscope.
7. The simple microscope.
8. The compound microscope.
9. The quadrant.
10. The sextant.
11. The astrolabe.

Note the wide range of activities opened up to investigators by these instruments. With the pendulum clock, time could be recorded with much precision in units of minutes and seconds. With the thermometer, heat could be measured in units of degrees, and with the barometer, elevation above sea level could be recorded in units of feet. With the quadrant and the sextant, the angular position of bodies in space could be measured in units of degrees, minutes, and seconds. Without such instruments, physical science could not be quantitatively stated. Thus the importance of the invention of exact measuring instruments in these remarkable centuries is clear. Let us note a few names of the men who gave these instruments to the world. As we do so, note also that men from almost every western European country contributed to the work.

1. *The quadrant and the sextant.* The Danish astronomer Tycho Brahe (1546–1601) greatly improved the quadrant and the sextant. Tycho, called "the Magnificent," partly because of his glowing appreciation of his own abilities, is renowned for his construction of large and accurate astronomical instruments at the

Observatory of Uraniborg. With these instruments he accumulated many hitherto unknown facts about the heavenly bodies and published new star tables.

2. *The telescope and Galileo.* These two, the instrument and the man, are associated in the history of astronomy. Indeed, the instrument was frequently referred to in the 1600's as the "Galilean telescope." The Italian professor had combined two lenses made by the Dutch spectacle-makers, Zacharias and Lippershey, to form a powerful telescope, with which he could see the spots on the sun, the rotating satellites of Jupiter, mountains on the moon, and other hitherto unseen details of the heavenly bodies. These discoveries gave the world definite knowledge about the movement of these bodies, and consequently a whole new theory of the universe was formulated.

FIG. 41. The astrolabe, forerunner of the quadrant

3. *The microscope and discoveries of unknown forms of animal life.* The same Dutch spectacle-makers to whom we have referred also constructed powerful microscopes, using the principle of the convex lens, which had been known for hundreds, perhaps thousands, of years. With a simple microscope, Leeuwenhoek discovered bacteria and also tiny animal organisms. Then, in 1661, with the compound microscope which magnified objects very much better, the Italian investigator Malpighi was able to observe the circulation of blood in arteries and veins, and thus confirmed Harvey's hypothesis made in earlier years from the dissection of animals.

4. *The pendulum clock.* In 1657 Christian Huygens (1629–1695), of Holland, succeeded in constructing a practicable pendulum clock. Clocks had been known in Europe in the 1200's — indeed, had been invented even earlier. But these first clocks were very inaccurate. Huygens, in his observations of the heavenly bodies, found that he needed a more exact means of measuring time. Therefore he set himself the task of making a correct timepiece, and consequently evolved the pendulum clock.

The most famous of the old clock-makers was Thomas Tompion, often called the father of English watchmaking. Many beautiful watches and clocks were made in his shop in the latter part of the 1600's.

5. *The thermometer.* A crude thermometer had been suggested by Galileo and was constructed in 1603. However, it was not until about 1641 that a reasonably accurate thermometer was

Fig. 42. An early clock-maker's shop, probably during the 1600's. Clocks were then made of iron, and the forge is shown in the background. (From an old print)

constructed. Still another generation passed before a successful mercury thermometer was devised — the first appearing in 1670.

6. *The barometer.* About the same time, Blaise Pascal (1623–1662) and Torricelli (1608–1647) were independently striving to develop an instrument for the measurement of elevations by determining the weight or pressure of the atmosphere. The experiments of both were successful. The barometer was devised, and many old prejudices were broken down. Furthermore, in 1650 Otto von Guericke, a German (1602–1686), invented the air pump, which was improved later by Robert Hooke. Thus

the way was paved for Robert Boyle (1627–1691) to perform his epoch-making experiments on the pressures of gases.

These are a few examples of the additions to man's measuring instruments which were produced in this astonishing age of invention. More than any other one single factor, these instruments made possible the development of exact science. With them, distant heavenly bodies as well as minute animal organisms came within man's vision, and scientific observations could be made quantitatively. For the first time in history men now had instruments by which they could *observe and measure* the exact relation between the objects of their physical world. But they still lacked adequate means of *expressing* these relationships in an orderly manner.

2. The invention of the higher mathematics: ways of expressing relationship

We have seen that for thousands of years the scientific knowledge of the world had been hampered by the lack of mathematics. Even the Greeks (the Alexandrian as well as the ancient Greeks) and the Arabs had known only demonstrative geometry, the rudiments of algebra (simple equations), and the barest elements of trigonometry.

Why were higher mathematics necessary for the development of science? For the simple reason that some way was needed of arranging facts in an orderly manner so that the *relation* between them could be determined. Knowledge of the heavenly bodies, plant and animal life, the physical world, and the human world was increasing with great rapidity. But what was to be done with all this knowledge? How could it be arranged in orderly fashion so that *relationships* could be seen and conclusions drawn?

For example, Galileo noted, with his strong telescope, that a number of small bodies seemed to be moving *with* Jupiter. Now, was there a definite *relation* between the movement of these bodies and that of Jupiter? To discover this *relationship*, Galileo needed mathematical methods by which curves could be drawn of the paths of these bodies, and algebraic methods by which equations could be written describing them. But methods by which the relationships could be treated mathematically were not available until long after Galileo had died.

Examples of the *relationship* between facts surround us on every hand today. There is, for instance, a direct *relationship* between the cost of a railroad ticket and the number of miles traveled. A stated number of cents is added to the cost for each additional mile.

Similarly, automobile and airplane motors are made powerful enough to carry the loads which they are to pull. That is, in an airplane there is a *relation* between the power in the motor and the load which the plane is to carry. This is shown in the way transatlantic fliers carefully determine how much gasoline and how many passengers, added to the weight of the plane itself, the motor can lift and can propel through the air. Similarly, there is a definite *relation* between the motor and the number of miles traveled per gallon of gasoline. No doubt you have heard your parents discuss this relationship in comparing your car with others.

Furthermore, the physical world around us abounds in illustrations of *relationship*. Water is composed of certain elements — hydrogen and oxygen — combined in a definite *relationship*. Similarly, there are definite *relationships* between one's health and the kinds of food one eats. Furthermore, although not so much is known about social life, there are definite *relationships* which determine how well people get along together.

Thus we have seen that the physical world, the plant and animal world, and human societies exist and progress because the elements that compose them are arranged in orderly *relationships*. We need not multiply illustrations to see the tremendous importance of having exact ways of measuring these *relationships*.

Throughout ancient time and well into the Middle Ages only the simplest mathematical ways of expressing *relationships* were known. In Euclid's time algebraic equations in one unknown could be worked, and the relations between lines and angles were discovered and written down in geometry. But beyond this men could not go until the remarkable discoveries in mathematics in the 1600's.

By this time mathematicians and scientists, such as Galileo,

Descartes, Newton, and Leibnitz, had recognized the importance of ways of measuring and describing the *relationships* between things that change together. They devoted themselves to supplying this need, and, in a century marked by mathematical genius, invented analytic geometry and the calculus.

After Descartes, still more elaborate and remarkable mathematical methods were devised. Sir Isaac Newton (1642–1727), a prominent leader in scientific work in England, and Gottfried von Leibnitz (1646–1716), a German, developed another useful system of mathematics — the calculus — combining arithmetical, algebraic, and geometric ideas. There were other mathematicians who also contributed new ideas. Accordingly scientists working on many different kinds of problems had mathematical methods of arranging their facts and of detecting hitherto unknown *relations*.

Descartes (1596–1650), in addition to being a distinguished philosopher, was the founder of analytic geometry — a brilliant application of algebra and geometry. For example, a circle or an ellipse is completely described by an equation such as you are familiar with.

Today even a high-school boy or girl has three ways of describing the *relation* between things that change together. There is (1) an arithmetical way, (2) an algebraic way, and (3) a geometric way.[1]

3. A few examples of the new scientific discoveries

With the new ways of thinking, the more exact measuring instruments, and the new mathematical methods, scientific knowledge about the physical and natural world increased rapidly. Whole volumes could be written about the dramatic discoveries of these astonishing years; we have space to note briefly only a few outstanding ones.

1. *The Copernican theory of the universe confirmed by Galileo and Kepler.* Perhaps the most revolutionary discovery was the law of heavenly bodies stated by the Polish astronomer and physician Koppernigk, known in history under the Latin form of

[1] For a simple illustration of these three ways of describing relationship, see Harold Rugg and John R. Clark's *Fundamentals of High School Mathematics* (World Book Company, Yonkers, New York), pp. 147–162.

his name, Copernicus (1473–1543). For more than 1400 years people had believed that the earth did not move, that it was the center of the universe, and that around it revolved the sun and stars, the moon and the planets. This view was called the Ptolemaic system, because the Alexandrian scholar Claudius Ptolemy had formulated it (about 140 A.D.).

In the year of his death, 1543, Copernicus, after more than 35 years of study, published a radically different theory. He said that the earth rotated once every day and that the earth, as well as all the other planets, revolved around the sun. This theory was of course opposed by the Church, which believed that its religious teachings depended upon the conception that the earth was the center of the universe.

An interesting illustration of intolerance is shown by the treatment of Galileo. After Copernicus died, Galileo and Kepler, a German astronomer, showed by means of improved telescopes that the sun did revolve on its own axis, and also that Jupiter was accompanied by "revolving moons." The officials of the Church, however, compelled Galileo to recant publicly his declaration that the earth revolves about the sun. When he arose from his knees, however, he is supposed to have muttered, "But it does just the same."

4. Francis Bacon and Descartes classified the sciences and developed the scientific method

In these exciting years men were not only inventing new instruments and new mathematical methods and piling up one discovery after another; they were also beginning to inquire into the scientific method of thinking. These new ways of thinking, about which we are talking in this chapter, needed to be clarified, described, and analyzed, and the increasing number of sciences needed to be classified.

This task was undertaken by Francis Bacon, Lord Verulam (1561–1626), whose elaborate classification of learning was a kind of inventory of all human knowledge. He dealt with philosophy, including natural philosophy, and natural and civil history. Natural history, Bacon said, supplies the facts that we need in studying life, and is, indeed, a sort of scientific description of life. He included no less than 130 separate kinds of history dealing with such subjects as the heavenly bodies, hail and snow, the seasons, the earth and the sea, flame, air and water, metals, fossils, stones, plants, vegetables and fishes, the parts of the human body, the animal species, disease, what not.

Bacon himself was not a scientist in the strict sense of the word; he neither developed new mathematical methods, invented new measuring instruments, nor made original scientific

Fig. 43. Francis Bacon, Lord Verulam (1561–1626)

Fig. 44. René Descartes (1596–1650)

discoveries. Instead, he was a government official, lord chancellor of England under James I, a philosopher, and a student of the scientific method of thinking. His ideas on the development of science he put into two famous books. In these, *The Advancement of Learning* (1605) and *Novum Organum* (or *New Method*) (1620), he pointed out the shortcomings of the methods of scientific work among the ancients and formulated the modern scientific methods. Like his earlier namesake, Roger Bacon, he denounced the blind acceptance of authority. Like Roger he demanded that the world "Experiment!" "Collect facts under controlled conditions!" "Measure exactly!" "Draw conclusions from classifications of facts."

Descartes, whom we have already mentioned as the founder of analytical geometry, extended Bacon's analysis of the scientific method. He also denounced living by blind faith in authority alone. He wrote (in French) an important book called *Discourse on Method* (1637), intended for people not educated in the classics who were interested in a better understanding of the modern world. In this and in *The Principles of Philosophy* (1644) he discussed the steps necessary to clear thinking. He placed his trust only in known and recorded observations and hoped to show how the various worlds in which we live can be arranged in orderly fashion. Above all, he was a mathematician, using algebraic and geometric methods of explaining natural phenomena. Furthermore, he was the supreme student of the relationships which exist between phenomena. He says in one of his writings that the reasonings of the geometers led him to believe that "everything which might fall under the cognizance of the human mind might be *connected* together in the same manner." That is, that *relationships* exist in the world which the human mind, with sufficient care, can discover. Hence the importance of a clear method of thinking.

We need not take the space to amplify our discussion of the work of these great leaders. Enough has been said to show that through the work of Copernicus, Galileo, Francis Bacon, Descartes, Isaac Newton, Leibnitz, and others the scientific method of thinking as we know it today was established in the world. Is it any wonder that the seventeenth century is called the "century of genius"?

5. The Royal Society and other organizations of scientists spread the scientific movement

In one of Francis Bacon's books, *The New Atlantis*, published in 1627, a plan was devised for a College of Fellows. It was an imaginative utopia, in which the chief institution was a sort of "research institute" called the "House of Solomon." Bacon's book was read widely, and showed thinkers all over Europe the need for scientific societies through which discussion of scientific achievements, methods, and discoveries could go on. Such societies sprang up first in Italy, and later in England and France. The most prominent of them was the Royal Society, founded in

London in 1662, with the King of England, Charles II, as patron. Among its Fellows were some of the most important men in European history. To name only a few, there were Sir Isaac Newton, the discoverer of the principle of gravitation; Robert Boyle and Robert Hooke, physicists; Sir Christopher Wren, the architect of famous buildings; Abraham Cowley, the poet; and Samuel Pepys and John Evelyn, whose descriptions of life in their time have come down to us in their famous diaries — all of them interested in the new sciences. Many leading scientists of other countries were also Fellows of the Society in the first few years of its existence, among them Huygens of Holland, Leibnitz of Germany, and Malpighi of Italy.

Fig. 45. Sir Isaac Newton (1642–1727)

One of the most important contributions of the Society was its series of publications. Since 1664 it has printed the scientific and philosophical researches of its members. In these publications, therefore, some of the most famous scientific discoveries in all history have been reported. To consider a single one — Sir Isaac Newton's *Principia*, in which he set forth his great theory of gravitation, was published by the Society.

Newton, already mentioned as sharing with Leibnitz the honor of discovering the calculus, was born in a small English village in 1642. Even as a youth of fourteen he showed more interest in mathematics than in the farm work that he was supposed to do. At eighteen he was sent to Cambridge University, from which he was graduated. He eventually became the greatest scientist of his age — indeed, one of the greatest of any age. He died in 1727.

Newton's theory of gravitation was his greatest contribution to science. By his time it had been proved, as we have seen, that the earth is but one of many bodies revolving around the sun.

The sun itself is really only one of countless suns; other stars have satellite bodies moving around them. How all these stars and suns were kept in place was a baffling question. Newton studied this problem for a long, long time. One day, it is said, he observed an apple falling to the ground, and reasoned thus: Some force made that apple fall to the ground. The same force must control the moon, the sun, and the stars. Thus the earth is pulled toward the sun, but it is also pulled toward other stars; therefore, it does not fall to the sun or any other star but revolves around the sun. In other words, the same force which makes the apple fall toward the earth keeps the moon — indeed, all the bodies of the universe — in their orbits. Newton succeeded in stating the principle in a fairly simple, but definite, mathematical formula.

This Illustrates the Scientific Revolution Which Brought Many Changes to the World After 1500

At last, then, after thousands of years, the new ways of thinking which we call scientific were discovered. The thinkers of many countries and many generations had contributed to their ultimate perfection. Facts and relationships had been uncovered by the invention of measuring instruments and by the tireless observation of nature, of the heavenly bodies, of the working of the human mind, and of human societies. New methods of mathematical arrangement put the countless facts together in clear order. At last men began to see relationships between various aspects of living. At last order began to replace chaos.

This orderly way of thinking and arranging facts, called the scientific method, eventually enabled James Watt and other inventors after him to make power-driven machines and to transmit power over long distances. It produced our industrial civilization. It developed new ways of transportation and communication, and of exchange of goods. It markedly raised the standard of living in the western world of Europe and America.

But for our purpose in this book, it is more important to see how these new ways of thinking led to new experiments in government and started the world upon its march toward democracy.

Furthermore, this critical, independent way of thinking made men question the authority of the Church and eventually led to radical changes in men's views about religion.

INTERESTING READINGS FROM WHICH YOU CAN GET ADDITIONAL INFORMATION

BLUNT, ALFRED W. F. The Ancient World and its Legacy to Us. Oxford University Press, New York.

BRIDGES, T. C. The Young Folk's Book of Invention. Little, Brown and Company, Boston. Story of inventions from prehistoric to modern times.

COLLINS, A. FREDERICK. A Bird's-Eye View of Invention. Thomas Y. Crowell Company, New York. The invention of units of measurement, printing-presses, etc.

DARROW, FLOYD L. Masters of Science and Invention. Harcourt, Brace and Company, New York.

HOLLAND, RUPERT S. Historic Inventions. Macrae Smith Company, Philadelphia. Interesting and valuable.

LANSING, MARION FLORENCE. Great Moments in Science. Doubleday, Doran & Company, Inc., Garden City, New York. Man's victories in the field of science and invention.

LANSING, MARION FLORENCE. Magic Gold: a Story of the Time of Roger Bacon. Little, Brown and Company, Boston.

NOYES, ALFRED. The Watchers of the Sky. Frederick A. Stokes Company, New York. A verse story of astronomers through the ages.

PROCTOR, MARY. The Young Folk's Book of the Heavens. Little, Brown and Company, Boston.

SMITH, DAVID EUGENE. Number Stories of Long Ago. Ginn and Company, Boston. Arithmetic long ago.

VAN LOON, HENDRIK W. The Story of Mankind. Horace Liveright, New York. See pages 402–432.

WELLS, MARGARET E. How the Present came from the Past, Vol. II. The Macmillan Company, New York. The contributions of the ancient world to us.

CHAPTER VI

THE REVOLUTION IN THE ARTS OF LIFE

Accepting things on authority versus thinking things out for yourself

One central theme was illustrated in the last chapter — new ways of thinking! New ways of thinking about the stars, about measuring, about the physical world. Scholars and scientists urged people to look at the world, observe carefully, experiment, think things out for themselves, and not to take ideas merely on authority from other people.

This command of the new scientists to "think things out for yourself" ran counter to every traditional way of life. Generation after generation people had followed their way of living as had been the custom of the people around them for generations. Most of them, in fact, never asked if a different method of life were possible. They lived in every way just as their ancestors had lived. There were no experiments! They farmed as their fathers had farmed. There were no experiments in farming! They accepted government as it was given to them. There were no experiments in government!

Superstition played an important part in every aspect of life. For example, if one's forefathers had planted crops "in the light of the moon," then one also planted in "the light of the moon." If one's elders taught that "needfire," or "wildfire," made by rubbing two pieces of wood together, would ward off disease from flocks and herds, one assiduously made "wildfire" instead of thinking and experimenting to find out what really *caused* the disease. One placed holly and evergreens in houses during the winter months as "a refuge for sylvan spirits from the inclemency of winter." Amulets were worn to ward off "spirits." Superstition rather than thinking controlled much of the conduct of the mass of the people.

Furthermore, government was accepted on the authority of others. Loyalty to the lord and master was the chief idea for thousands of years, and the common man never thought out ways of government which would give him a share in it. He paid taxes and rendered laborious service to his lord, even asking permission to regulate his personal life and that of his family. Thus there were no experiments in government that would include the common people. Loyalty and submission to authority were the supreme ideas. The vassal was submissive to his lord. Women were submissive to their husbands. Children were submissive to their elders and lived as their parents had lived. There was little or no thinking things out for oneself. There were no experiments.

There is, therefore, an important contrast between the new way in which scientific men thought and the old way in which the masses thought.

We must remember, indeed, that the scientific revolution of which we have just read touched only a minute fraction of the inhabitants of Europe. The Royal Society, for example, consisted of a few score of Fellows; its total membership did not make up a thousandth of 1 per cent of the population of Europe. Let us not forget, as we thrill over the dramatic episodes of these centuries of discovery, that two hundred years more were to pass before the rank and file of the people would reap the benefits of the new ideas. Two hundred years more were to pass before the common man himself would learn to read and acquire the knowledge of either the ancients or the moderns. Two hundred years were to pass before he would be able to "think things out for himself."

When the revolution in thinking began, however, it was not restricted to physical science and invention. It influenced every aspect of life — religion, art, family life, and government. Let us see now, therefore, how the independent ways of thinking developed in religion and in the arts. An understanding of these two will help our study of the world's march toward democracy in government.

The Organized Catholic Church

In all Europe in the year 1500 there was only one recognized religion and one organized church — the Christian religion and the Catholic Church. Almost everybody accepted the teachings of that religion and was a member of that church. Every child on receiving baptism became a member of the Church, and later was taught its beliefs and its code of conduct. Practically everyone accepted its authority and gave a tithe (a tenth of his yearly income) for its support. As the Catholic Church was the official one in each country, the religious and ecclesiastical life of the continent was governed by one church and one doctrine.

In 1500, after more than a thousand years, the Church had become a continental organization of enormous wealth and political and spiritual power. It was a great religious organization with an elaborate system of officials. At the head was the Pope, the chief bishop of Rome, who ruled the entire Church. Under the Pope was a graded system of officials, or secular clergy.

First, all Western Christendom was divided into provinces, ruled by archbishops, the headquarters of each being in a large city, such as Canterbury and York in England; Cologne, in Germany; Seville, in Spain; Lisbon in Portugal; Upsala, in Sweden; and Lyon, in France.

Second, each province was divided into dioceses governed by bishops. These were the larger local divisions of the Church, consisting generally of a town or a city and the surrounding countryside.

Third, each diocese was divided into small local parishes, usually composed of a village or a part of a city. Each of these had a separate church building under the control of a priest and his assistant, the deacon.

In addition to the secular clergy there were the regular clergy — the monks and nuns who lived in monasteries and convents, the great missionaries of the Church. Many of the orders, as the various organizations of monks were called, were famous. Among them were the Order of Saint Benedict (the Benedictines), the Knights Templars, the Franciscans, and the Dominicans, the two latter being wandering, or preaching, friars. Thus, the Catholic

Church was indeed a vast organization, ranging from the Pope and the cardinals to the priests and the monks.

As we have said, this organization was very rich and powerful. During the 1000 years that had passed since the Church was organized, the Popes and their officials had drawn up rules of conduct to be followed by all its members. The Pope was the supreme maker of religious laws, and even the other chief officials of the Church could not veto his decrees. He had political and financial power over the Church, and even claimed that it was superior to that of kings and dukes. From time to time the Pope had insisted on the right of crowning the Holy Roman Emperor, and even of putting emperors and kings out of office. Finally, he levied certain dues on all members of the Church — practically all the people of Europe.

The Protestant Revolt against the Catholic Church

Against such conditions there came about an active and widespread revolt. Throughout the later Middle Ages many kings and nobles strove to reduce the political power of the Church and tried to take much of their wealth away from the Popes, archbishops, and bishops. The conflict with the Church grew more bitter during the 1300's and 1400's, and finally, in the 50 years between 1520 and 1570, there came open rebellion. During those years three outstanding religious leaders appeared, who *protested* publicly against the abuses of the Church. These *protestants* aroused kings and nobles on the one hand and the common people on the other into widespread revolt. In less than half a century every country in northern Europe was affected by the uprising. When the rebellion was over, Protestant churches had been set up in England, Scotland, Germany, Scandinavia, northern France, and Holland, and drastic reforms were coming about within the Church itself.

Three phases of this Protestant revolt are worth remembering: (1) that of religious reformers, such as Martin Luther, John Calvin, and Huldreich Zwingli; (2) that of the kings in national states and the nobles in feudal regions; and (3) that of the common people. Let us note briefly each of these three phases.

FIG. 46. The Pope receiving the ambassadors of the English king, Henry V. With the rise of the Catholic Church, kings sought its powerful support, especially when their own security was threatened

1. The revolt of protesting reformers

a. Early protests against the Catholic Church. Even as early as the 1300's leaders had appeared who protested against the abuses of the Church. One of these was John Wycliffe, regarded as the "Father of English Prose," who, as you already know, translated the Bible into English. He was not only a famous scholar; he was also one of the first independent thinkers to urge that each person should think out his religion for himself.

About 1370 the Pope and his council issued decrees against Wycliffe because of his criticisms of the organization and of the leaders of the Church. In making his criticisms, Wycliffe defended the right of the national government to take over the property of the Church whenever the latter abused its power. He denied that the Pope's power extended beyond the interpretation of the Gospels.

Another early reformer was John Huss, a rector in the Czech University of Prague, who had been influenced by the doctrines of Wycliffe. He too criticized the scandalous abuses of the Church, and as a result was excommunicated in 1412. When the officers of the Catholic Church met at the Council of Constance, Huss attended under a guarantee of safety given by the Emperor. Once in the power of the council, however, he was ordered to recant his heretical views. He refused and was burned alive in the city of Constance (1415). This act aroused the people, and four years later Huss's followers in Bohemia rose in armed insurrection. In the following year the Pope, Martin V, issued a proclamation calling for a crusade against Hussites, Wycliffites, and all other "heretics." One group after another of Catholic loyalists attacked Bohemia between 1420 and 1436, but the Czechs repulsed practically all of them.

b. Later protests — Luther, Zwingli, and Calvin. In Germany the revolt was led by Martin Luther, who, although a son of peasants, had achieved a university education, had entered the Augustinian monastic order, and shortly after 1510 had become a professor of theology at the University of Wittenberg. Through his studies and through observations during a visit to Rome, Luther became convinced that a reform of the Church was necessary.

In 1517, aroused by the methods in the preaching of indulgences used by Tetzel, a prominent papal officer in Germany, he openly protested against the conditions in the Church in 95 theses (statements) which he nailed on the church door in Wittenberg. In 1520 he published pamphlets in which he defended such revolutionary ideas as the following: (1) that the Catholic clergy

FIG. 47. Luther, the Augustinian monk, being examined regarding his doctrines before Charles V of the Holy Roman Empire and his council. (From an old print)

should be deprived of their special privileges; (2) that the political control of the Church should be abolished and that much of its wealth should be taken away; (3) that much of the formality and ritual of the sacramental system should be abolished; and (4) that man's conduct should depend upon his own religious faith and not upon the formal creed and system of an ecclesiastical organization.

Luther's protests amounted to an open declaration of war upon the Church. However, when told to recant his opinions, Luther answered that his conscience would not allow this.

The Pope banned Luther from the Church, and he was outlawed by the Diet of the Holy Roman Empire. However,

Lutheranism, as his ideas were called, caught the popular approval of both nobles and peasants and made steady progress throughout northern Europe. Furthermore, Luther's tremendous energy and tact bound the German princes and peasants together in a common cause.

In the meantime Huldreich Zwingli, a Catholic priest in Switzerland, also proclaimed that men must base their religious life upon the original Scriptures themselves and not on the creeds of the Church. He too attacked the Church for what he declared to be its mercenary politics, its abuses, its financial greed, and its hypocritical practices. As a result civil war broke out, which ended in the death of Zwingli and in the division of Switzerland — part of it remaining Catholic and part becoming Protestant.

While these events were taking place, John Calvin, a French law student, influenced by the Lutheran revolt and the growing criticism of the Church, also became a leading Protestant. Fleeing royal and papal disapproval in France, he went to Switzerland and published his religious views in a book called *The Institutes of the Christian Religion* (1536).

In Geneva, Calvin became a political as well as religious leader, establishing rigid codes of life which were in direct opposition to the practice of many members of the Catholic Church. Consequently the city became a center for religious rebels from England, Scotland, Holland, France, and Germany. Later many of these people returned to their own countries and spread Calvin's ideas among their people. In France, Calvin's followers became known as Huguenots. In Scotland, John Knox (1505–1572), who had been associated with Calvin in Geneva, returned to his native country and established the Presbyterian Church. In England, Calvin's ideas were the basis for Puritanism, a movement which helped to bring about the establishment of the American colony at Massachusetts Bay in the 1630's.

Within 50 years (1520–1570), therefore, the work of these tireless reformers set up new church organizations in Germany, Holland, Scandinavia, France, Switzerland, England, and Scotland. Thus, in general, the northern half of Europe had become Protestant while the southern half remained Catholic.

The Protestant revolt showed that many leaders were breaking away from the idea of one church. To that extent they were thinking independently, and their revolt could hardly fail to encourage

Fig. 48. Hugh Latimer, a leader of the Reformation in England, preaching before Edward VI. Latimer was burned at the stake in 1555. (From a painting by Ernest Beard, in the House of Lords. Courtesy of the Fine Arts Publishing Company, London)

freedom of thought in a still wider sense. Yet it is a fact that most of the leaders of the new churches were themselves intolerant. They allowed their followers little personal independence.

In England the King and the national state seized control of the Church

In England the revolt was almost purely political. It affected the actual conduct of the people very little indeed. Henry VIII, king of England in 1509–1547, was determined to rule England as an absolute monarch. A few years after his accession to the throne, he determined to break with the Pope and to take control of the Church as well as of the government. We need not go into the details of the story except to say that the immediate cause of his action was a personal one. Henry wanted to divorce his wife, Catherine of Aragon, and marry Anne Boleyn, a maid of honor in his court. Up to this time (1531–1534) he had been a stanch supporter of the Pope, from whom he received the title of "Defender of the Faith." At last he asked for papal annulment of his marriage. There was prolonged delay, and Henry decided to take action himself.

In 1534 Parliament, entirely subservient to him, passed a number of laws separating the Church of England from the Catholic Church. One of them declared that the King of England was the "only supreme head on earth of the Church of England." Catholics who rebelled were tortured and beheaded by Henry's orders, and the property of Catholic monasteries was confiscated by the King.

Thus the whole revolt of the English branch of the Church was mainly a political and personal transaction of the King. Henry had no sincere religious reasons for it; he was swayed merely by his greed for wealth and political power, and his determination to handle his personal affairs as he saw fit. The form of worship was not changed by this so-called "English Reformation." Nothing was reformed. In fact, the new Church of England, or the Anglican Church, as it came to be called, retained much of the creed and many of the ceremonies of the Catholic Church.

We cannot tell here the bloody story of the religious and political intrigue in England during the next century and a half as Henry's successors upon the throne alternated between Catholicism and Anglicanism. But the new Anglican Church remained nearly as formal and ceremonial as the Catholic Church had been. An elaborate organization was built up, with an Archbishop of Canterbury at the head. All this was done by the government, by the King and his nobles. The Church in England had become a *state* church. But it is doubtful whether these *political* changes brought the English Church in any way closer to the idea of the brotherhood of men that Christ had proclaimed centuries before.

As the Church of England itself remained unchanged, free-thinking, "dissenting" groups arose, — for example, the Independents, the Puritans, the Quakers, and the Separatists, — some of which are already well known to us. As you know, some of these free-thinking people, because of persecutions, left England in the early 1600's and eventually settled at Massachusetts — at Plymouth under William Bradford and others, and at Massachusetts Bay under Winthrop. Somewhat later, Quakers under William Penn settled the prosperous colony that grew into the state of Pennsylvania.

The revolt of the common people

A third phase of the Protestant revolt was the armed insurrection of the miserable peasants. In Germany, Martin Luther had advised the nobles to seize the lands of the Catholic Church and to put out all immoral and grasping officials. But once the movement of revolt was started by the leaders, the masses of the poor people carried it much further than Luther had intended. Long oppressed and discontented, they were easily persuaded by fanatical leaders to take up arms not only against the Church officials but against the nobles as well. The revolt soon became a general economic rebellion. The peasant leaders demanded that serfdom be abolished, that the people be paid wages for their labor, and that they be given the civil rights which were due to every human being in the world.

By 1524 the revolt had spread over central and southern Germany and had become a general political insurrection. Frightened at the result of his own deeds, Luther himself forsook the people and took sides with the nobles. He encouraged the latter to put down the revolt, saying, "Whoever can, should smite, strangle, or stab, secretly or publicly." Acting upon his advice, the lords ruthlessly exterminated the peasants. The latter were untrained in the arts of war. They were badly equipped for fighting. They lacked skilled military leaders and were unorganized.

As a result the revolt was easily crushed. But how murderously! It is estimated that probably 50,000 were killed. Thus the whole revolt, instead of bettering the condition of the masses of European people, had made it much worse. Indeed, records lead us to believe that the living conditions of the common people of Germany during the 1500's and 1600's were worse than those of the people of any other country of Europe.

Some Catholic Leaders also brought about Reforms within the Church

The Protestant revolt succeeded in arousing sincere Catholics to reform the Church itself. We must not forget that there were many honest churchmen, especially in southern Europe, — Italy, Austria, France, and Spain, — who agreed with the criticisms of Luther, Calvin, Zwingli, and their associates. In these countries a *steady reformation within the Church itself* went on.

For example, under Paul III (1534–1549) and other Popes of the next century really honest and superior officials were placed in high positions in the Church. Successive councils of Church officers attempted to smooth out the differences between the factions within the Church. They also did away with the worst abuses; for example, the selling of offices and filling them with relatives and friends of officials.

One of the most important factors in the reform within the Church was the work done by the Society of Jesus, an order established in 1534 by Ignatius Loyola. This order of priests developed into a powerful world-wide missionary organization of the Catholic Church. It was devoted to the preservation of the power of the Pope and to the systematic extension of the Catholic religion throughout the world. In the next 200 years Jesuit priests established missions in every continent. Some of these leaders you have already heard about in American history. Father Marquette was famous as one of those who explored the unknown continent of North America. Jesuit priests established outposts of the Church in Canada, throughout the Mississippi Valley, and even in the northwestern part of what is now the United States. Others penetrated to the jungles of Brazil and to the inner districts of Paraguay in South America, while still others went to India, China, and other parts of the Far East.

Summing up the Religious Revolt

These, then, were the chief events of that epoch-making movement, the great religious revolt that swept all civilized Europe after 1500. It showed very clearly that educated men were beginning to think things out for themselves. They were not merely taking their religion on the authority of others.

What changes came about in Europe? Did the revolt advance Europe's march toward democracy? Did it improve the living and spiritual conditions of the people? Did it bring the Church closer to the spiritual brotherhood which Christ had advocated?

Summed up briefly these are the chief outcomes.

1. New church organizations came into existence. In place of one church there were now several. In northern Europe, from northern Germany and Scandinavia to England and Scotland, there were Lutherans, Puritans, Independents, Huguenots, Presbyterians, Anglicans, and other sects. In most of southern Europe, however, — in Italy, Austria, southern Germany, France, and Spain,— the Roman Catholic Church still held the allegiance of the people. But the religious conditions, as well as the inefficient organization of churches, had been much improved.

2. The national states and the political rulers had gained in power at the expense of the Pope and his officials. In England complete separation had come, and the State controlled the Church. Throughout most of northern Europe also religion was coming under the control of the State.

3. Many kings and nobles had increased their wealth at the expense of the Church leaders. Great Church estates had been confiscated, and the rising middle class of business men in the towns had profited greatly, as we shall see later.

4. A régime of rigid morality had been instituted in many parts of Europe. In England this was the beginning of the later Puritan régime which influenced the general outlook upon life in the United States until almost our own time.

5. But perhaps the most important result, although it was not immediately felt, was the spread of freedom of thought concerning religion and the rise of dissenting groups in England,

Holland, and other parts of Europe. The example of Wycliffe and Huss had borne its fruit. So also had the independence of Calvin, Knox, and other leaders. It is true that these men were intolerant of opinions which differed from their own. But the fact that they set up new systems, combined with the amazing development in science that began shortly after, laid the foundation for freedom of thought in the modern sense.

Moreover, the religious persecutions in Holland, in France, and in other parts of Europe led to the frequent emigration of skilled craftsmen to other countries, especially to England. In the 1600's thousands of weavers, jewelers, watchmakers, engravers, bookbinders, and artisans skilled in the manufacture of plate glass, parchment, hats, and other articles, settled there. Largely as a result of this, England's handicrafts expanded rapidly.

Did the Protestant revolt help to bring about Europe's march toward democracy?

The Protestant revolt brought little immediate benefit to the civilization of Europe. Devastating wars continued. Monarchs and nobles became more oppressive, and the living conditions of peasants and artisans were worse than ever before. There were few signs of any march toward government "of the people, by the people, for the people." There was no real advance in education, and historians of the time say that the rank and file of the people sank into "deeper and deeper ignorance." Although reformers within as well as outside the Catholic Church had urged the development of education, there was little increase in the popular schooling of the masses.

The Renaissance in the Arts Paralleled the Scientific and Religious Reformations

The new ways of thinking that produced the remarkable scientific revolution were accompanied by new ways of feeling in the arts — architecture, literature, painting, and sculpture. From about 1300 such a wonderful development in all these arts occurred that the period is generally called the *Renaissance* —

that is, the "rebirth." The spirit of creative expression seemed literally to be born again.

The way for it had been well paved by the remarkable beauty of earlier medieval architecture. After 1100 vast, beautifully ornamented cathedrals were constructed. A glimpse of their grandeur and the engineering skill necessary to build them is given by the pictures in figures 49 and 50. Compare them with the churches you have seen in American cities. Notice especially the heights and proportions of these cathedrals, the beautifully arched doorways and windows, and the carved towers that pierce the sky. We think of the hundreds of years these buildings have endured, and we realize how well the architects of the Middle Ages built.

The beauty and dignity of the high, vaulted roofs and arches and the long, quiet aisles of the interiors match the exteriors. One cannot walk through them without feeling the religious spirit itself. In each niche is a statue of a saint carved or sculptured to fit its space. Light filters through stained-glass windows that have never been surpassed in beauty. Design of building, sculptured decoration, and stained glass form a harmonious whole. The medieval cathedral was truly a work of creative art.

In addition to planning churches, medieval architects also built great castles for feudal nobles, and town houses for merchant princes. In these, and in a few town halls and royal palaces, the artists created unique and beautiful designs. Thus they prepared the way for the tremendous outburst of creative energy and interest in the arts that appeared first in Italy after 1300 and spread to every country in Europe.

How the wealthy nobles and clergy made the renaissance in the arts possible

History has harsh things to say about many of the kings and princes, Popes and cardinals, nobles and clergy of those days. It scores not a few of them for their greed, their conspiracies and their murders, their extravagances, and their oppressive rule of the people. But one thing many of them did — they used some of their wealth to support the creative artists of their time. Without their support it is doubtful if the Renaissance could have occurred. They built beautiful churches, cathedrals, and palaces, and employed painters to decorate the walls and ceilings. They financed sculptors to ornament the buildings as buildings had never been ornamented before and have seldom been equaled since. They supported and encouraged poets and writers. Thus the greatest renaissance of creative art that the world had ever known was made possible.

Fig. 49. The cathedral built at Amiens, France, between 1220 and 1288

The Italian renaissance in letters began in the 1300's

Under the patronage of the wealthy and famous Medici family, scholars, painters, musicians, architects, and sculptors were encouraged. Lorenzo de' Medici accumulated a great library in his palace in Florence and employed scholars to translate the old Greek and Roman classics. Under his endowment a group of scholars called Humanists grew up, of whom Petrarch (1304–1374) was the most famous. The Humanists searched monasteries for ancient manuscripts and discovered many that had been lost for more than a thousand years. Furthermore, they built schools in Florence and in other Italian cities.

Lorenzo de' Medici's son became Pope under the name Leo X. With his encouragement, interest in painting, sculpture, poetry, music, and the theater grew rapidly. From Italy the new learning spread into other countries of Europe. By 1450 Greek had been reëstablished in schools in England and in France as well as in Italy. New universities were established in the German countries. French armies invading and plundering Italy took the classical learning back to France. Great scholars appeared in other countries too. For example, Erasmus (1466–1536), a Dutch churchman, became one of the greatest classical students of all Europe.

FIG. 50. The cathedral at Cologne, Germany, which was started in the 1300's. What similarities do you find between figures 49 and 50?

The new creative writing laid the foundations for *national* languages and literatures

In addition to this renewed interest in the Greek and Roman classics, creative writers in the various countries of Europe were at work developing their own *national* literatures. It is important to remember that until about this time (1300 and after) there had been no really *national* languages. There was no standard English, no standard French, Spanish, or Italian. As has already been intimated, these new writers, therefore, did much to *standardize* languages — that is, to set up a form of writing that others after them would follow. Their work led also to the establishment of *national* literatures. Let us note briefly merely a few of these great creative artists.

In Italy, as early as 1300, Dante (1265–1321) laid the foundations for modern Italian. He used the Florentine dialect, thus making it the literary language of Italy. His great epic, *The Divine*

Comedy, in which he drew vivid pictures of hell, purgatory, and heaven, is still regarded as one of the world's great writings. Later Petrarch, whom we have already mentioned, wrote many famous odes, sonnets, and lyrics in Italian instead of in Latin. *The Decameron* of Boccaccio (1313–1375) is another of the early works in Italian prose that has become famous in the world's literature. Nor should we overlook Machiavelli (1469–1527), who added to the increasing Italian literature a book called *The Prince.* This work was long regarded as one of the basic writings on the science of politics. It defended the idea that a ruler has the right to use *any* means to carry out his aims. More than one haughty and oppressive king defended his actions on the theories of Machiavelli. Thus such writers as Dante, Petrarch, Boccaccio, and Machiavelli standardized the Italian language and laid the foundations of the national Italian literature.

FIG. 51. A portrait of Dante holding his copy of *The Divine Comedy.* (From a painting by Domenico di Francesco, in the cathedral at Florence)

We have already spoken of the beginnings of modern English through the writings of John Wycliffe and Geoffrey Chaucer. In the 1400's another great book was produced — Sir Thomas Malory's *Morte d'Arthur.* The 1500's, however, is the time when some of the greatest English literature, indeed, some of the world's greatest literature, was written. In 1516 Sir Thomas More published his world-famous *Utopia.* Late in the century Christopher Marlowe (1564–1593) produced his plays. Still later

William Shakespeare (1564–1616) wrote *Hamlet, The Merchant of Venice, Richard III, Henry IV, Macbeth,* and other plays. Taken together, these writings make Shakespeare one of the world's greatest dramatists. The first three books of Edmund Spenser's *Faerie Queene* appeared about the same time (1590). Other well-known writers were also at work; English literature was indeed developing rapidly.

Meanwhile the French language and French literature had begun to develop. We have already learned of that first French masterpiece — the *Chanson de Roland.* Among other early works is the *Roman de la Rose,* written in the 1200's. There were many writers in the several centuries that followed; of the names in this period one stands out — that of Rabelais (about 1490–1553). His work provided a sort of mirror of the social life of the 1500's in France. His tales combined biting satire, a poetical imagination, and keen observation. Thus in France too a national literature was beginning to emerge.

In Germany a national language was slower in developing than in other countries. By the close of the 1400's some progress had been made, stimulated largely by the religious movement of the Reformation. The writings of Martin Luther helped to establish a standardized German, and his translation of the Bible (1522–1534) was an important document in German literary history. Even in the 1500's, however, Germany was still far from having a unified language. Geographical and political conditions were important obstacles. Nevertheless there were the crude beginnings of a national literature. *The Nibelungenlied,* a powerful epic, was written about the end of the 1100's, and much lyric poetry was produced a century or so later. Furthermore, in the 1500's several dramatists appeared. Thus Germany too was developing a standardized language and a national literature.

In Spain also a national literature began to form about the same time. Under the patronage of Alfonso X (1252–1282), King of Castile and Leon, many literary works appeared. In the period that followed, one name stands out — Cervantes (1547–1616), whose masterpiece was *Don Quixote,* the famous satire on the romances of chivalry of sixteenth-century Spain.

FIG. 52. William Shakespeare

Records in Stratford on Avon, England, show that an infant, William Shakespeare, was baptized on April 26, 1564. His father's hitherto comfortable living taking a bad turn, the boy left the Stratford free grammar school at the age of fourteen and was probably apprenticed to a local trade. Four years later he married Anne Hathaway. Presently he left home, apparently in disrepute for killing game on a neighbor's property. About ten years later he went to London, where, according to tradition, he became a flunky around London theaters, later acting minor parts. When we hear of him again he has written some poetry and plays, works destined to endure through 300 years to our own day and undoubtedly to enrich the world's literature for centuries to come. He died in 1616, at the age of 52. Thirty-seven plays are ordinarily attributed to Shakespeare, although we know that other men worked on some of the less important ones. Among those best known and still produced today are *The Merchant of Venice*, *Romeo and Juliet*, *Julius Cæsar*, *Hamlet*, and *Macbeth*. Shakespeare, who so vividly portrayed the drama of human life, is the greatest figure in English literature

Have you heard of Don Quixote and his fight with the windmill? Cervantes' novel about a crazy knight with a brass bowl on his head is one of the world's six greatest books. Its author, Miguel de Cervantes Saavedra (1547–1616), was a dashing soldier in the Spanish army until he was captured by pirates. After five years of slavery he went back to Spain and became a purchasing agent for the Spanish navy, in which rôle he wandered about through the south of Spain for a number of years. Difficulties with his superiors and with the peasants, from whom he requisitioned wheat and oil; losses; irregularities of one sort and another; imprisonments — all show how unfitted Cervantes was for this type of work. Between times he wrote, making use of his rich experiences as captive and traveler. In *Don Quixote*, which Cervantes tells us he wrote to poke fun at the extravagant romances of chivalry, he persuades us to see life as it is. In this book all society in sixteenth-century Spain passes in diverting review: nobles, priests, farmers, scullions, barbers, traders, kitchen maids, country girls, ladies, convicts, and poets. *Don Quixote* is perhaps even more popular today than it was three centuries ago

FIG. 53. Miguel de Cervantes Saavedra

Thus we see that in the various countries of Europe national languages were beginning to take form, and, stimulated by the Renaissance, national literatures were emerging.

The renaissance in painting and sculpture

In painting and sculpture the renaissance in the arts went forward, along with the increased enthusiasm for creative writing. Some of the greatest artists in all history appeared during the 1300's and 1400's. Let us note a few of them.

Giotto (Giotto di Bondone, 1267(?)–1337). One great creative painter led the way for the astonishing revolution that developed in painting — Giotto, son of an Italian peasant. Above scores, even hundreds of contemporary workers, his name is remembered. A legend, the truth of which we cannot verify, has it that Cimabue (an Italian painter of the 1200's) saw Giotto, when a young boy, drawing a picture of one of his father's sheep with a sharp stone on another smooth, large stone. Astonished at his skill, he carried him off to be his apprentice. Other stories attribute his discovery and training to prominent sculptors of the time. Regardless of which one is the true account, one fact we know: Giotto became one of the greatest painters of all time — some critics say "the very greatest." Many stories are told of his skill. One tells that Pope Benedict XI asked for proof of his great ability. Giotto submitted as a sample merely a large letter "O," which he painted at a single sweep of his brush. But it convinced the Pope.

What did he paint? Mostly frescoes on the walls and ceilings of churches. Painters and sculptors of the times usually took religious themes. The Popes and the dukes paid royal commissions to those who would ornament their churches, cathedrals, and palaces. So Giotto, like his successors, painted scenes from Christian history. Perhaps most famous among his works are the four great paintings at Assisi in honor of Saint Francis. (See figure 54.) He also contributed frescoes to buildings in Padua, Ravenna, Rome, Naples, and other Italian cities. At the age of 68 he planned and began the famous campanile, or bell tower, at Florence.

Giotto was always a popular hero. Petrarch and the historian Villani wrote of him, and Boccaccio made him the subject of tales and anecdotes. Today he remains the "great man of painting."

Lorenzo Ghiberti (1378–1455). Today in Florence, Italy, the ancient baptistery still stands opposite the cathedral. Two of its bronze gates are very beautifully decorated with sculptured scenes from the Bible. This work, completed only after many

Fig. 54. "The Marriage of Saint Francis to Poverty," one of the four allegorical frescoes painted by Giotto in honor of Saint Francis of Assisi

years, was done by Lorenzo Ghiberti, one of the first of the Renaissance sculptors. It is said that Ghiberti labored for fully twenty years over his first gate! The magnificence of these gates was such that Michelangelo, himself one of the greatest artists of the Renaissance, declared them "worthy to be the gates of Paradise." Ghiberti also executed statues of several of the saints, and was an architect of the Florence cathedral.

Albrecht Dürer (1471–1528). Occasional painters appeared in Germany also, although Italy was the great center. In Nuremberg, Albrecht Dürer achieved an international reputation as the leader in the development of engraving and etching. Even today his

Fig. 55. Leonardo da Vinci

More than 400 years ago, in Florence, Leonardo da Vinci (1452–1519) painted one of the most famous of all portraits, the *Mona Lisa*, and the familiar picture of *The Last Supper*. But this most extraordinary man did other creative things. He designed airplanes — designs that are considered practical by engineers of this day. As a scholar he anticipated Darwin's hypothesis of evolution. He was painter, engineer, architect, sculptor, poet, composer, athlete, mathematician, organizer — many say as perfect in each rôle as if it had been his only occupation. He possessed an amazingly encyclopedic mind which he applied to all aspects of the world. In the 5000 pages of scientific and speculative observations left by him are revealed the foundations of many sciences and arts which came later. These discoveries he kept to himself, possibly because he was afraid that the Church would object to them. The manuscripts lay concealed for centuries, while men were laboriously learning what Leonardo could have told them. He knew something of what, years later, Galileo, Bacon, Newton, and Harvey were to discover

One of the greatest achievements in art is the decoration of the dome of the Sistine Chapel in Rome — a set of frescoes illustrating the Bible story of the Creation. The most famous single painting in the world, perhaps, is the *Last Judgment*. And the dome of St. Peter's Cathedral in Rome is one of the finest architectural creations yet achieved by man. Any one of these three works would be a vast contribution from one man to civilization, but Michelangelo (1475–1564), the immortal Florentine, produced all three — and much more. Tremendous strength of character, as well as genius, was necessary for the completion of some of these masterpieces. For example, Michelangelo worked four years on the Sistine Chapel paintings, much of the time lying on his back on a scaffold. When the task was done he wrote his father: "Today I finished the chapel I was painting. The Pope is very well satisfied." The statue of David is evidence of his ability as a sculptor. He was also an engineer, a poet, and a student of anatomy

Fig. 56. Michelangelo Buonarroti

Saint Jerome in the Wilderness ranks among the greatest engravings of all time. Dürer was also a painter of considerable importance.

Painters also appeared in Holland and Spain. The development of painting in Holland and Spain was slower than in Italy, but in the 1500's and 1600's several artists of note appeared in both of these countries. In Holland, Rubens (1577–1640) and Van Dyck (1599–1641) became famous; in Spain, Velásquez (1599–1660) and Murillo (1618–1682) also achieved eminence.

FIG. 57. The picture of this painting by Raphael can give us no idea of its exquisite colors, but it does show the harmony and balance of Raphael's work

The development of music and musical instruments in the Italian Renaissance

In the Middle Ages musical instruments had been crude, and music itself had been a rudimentary art. However, in the 1500's delicate instruments were perfected which made possible the later development of great music. This development we will discuss in a later chapter. It is sufficient here to state that composers began to create beautiful music, especially music for use in the Church Mass.

Thus life in Europe began to change after 1500

We therefore see that, by about 1500, changes had come about in the development of national languages and national feeling.

Fig. 58. Titian

Titian, the central figure of a group of painters known as the Venetian school, painted pictures for wealthy persons who would pay high prices for them. Because of this he has been called "the first professional painter." A highly intelligent, educated man, ambitious for personal gain, he aimed his extraordinary genius at the richest markets for his wares, painting his way to fame and fortune. As he employed a clever man to promote his patronage, he had, like many modern celebrities, a "press agent." Titian's outstanding talent was his use of color. He was also one of the first to appreciate nature, especially mountains, as subjects for pictures. It is reported that Michelangelo, after inspecting Titian's picture *Danaë in the Rain of Gold*, said of him, "That man would have had no equal if art had done as much for him as nature." Among his well-known pictures are *The Man with the Glove* and *Charles V*. Titian died in 1576, at the age of 99, enriched by commissions from the princes and the wealthy of Europe

Raphael was born in 1483, the son of a hard-working artist who taught his boy the principles of drawing and color. In addition to his great natural talent, Raphael was a hard worker. It was perhaps because he was so devoted to his work that he never married. His charming manner and good looks endeared him to all who knew him. When he died, at the height of his powers, only 37 years old, he had painted pictures that will live forever. There has probably never been a more universally popular painter than he. Like the other Italian painters of his time, Raphael selected his subjects largely from the principal events of Biblical history. Among his best-known pictures are the *Crowning of the Virgin*, the *Marriage of the Virgin* (see figure 57), and the *Entombment of Christ*. His brush decorated a suite of magnificent rooms for the Pope Julius II, and his designs helped to beautify the Vatican. For many years he superintended the construction of St. Peter's Cathedral, the dome of which was designed by Michelangelo

Fig. 59. Raphael

Furthermore, science, religion, and the arts had changed, too. A real rebirth of thought and creative effort had taken place. As a result experiments were launched in all the fields of thought and action. Indeed the period following 1300 was increasingly a time of revolution in all the arts of life.

INTERESTING READINGS FROM WHICH YOU CAN GET ADDITIONAL INFORMATION

BARTON, GEORGE A. Jesus of Nazareth. The Macmillan Company, New York. The story of Jesus.

CATHER, KATHERINE D. Boyhood Stories of Famous Men. The Century Co., New York. Includes sketches of Titian, Murillo, and Giotto.

CERVANTES SAAVEDRA, MIGUEL DE. Don Quixote de la Mancha. Dodd, Mead & Company, New York. Retold by Judge Parry.

DAVIS, WILLIAM S. The Friar of Wittenberg. The Macmillan Company, New York. Luther, the Reformation, and the religious wars.

HUMPHREY, GRACE. The Story of the Williams. The Penn Publishing Company, Philadelphia. Includes the story of William Shakespeare.

JEWETT, SOPHIE. God's Troubadour. Thomas Y. Crowell Company, New York. Medieval church and St. Francis of Assisi.

MACY, JOHN A. The Story of the World's Literature. Horace Liveright, New York.

MARTIN, MRS. GEORGE. A Warwickshire Lad. D. Appleton and Company, New York. Shakespeare's boyhood.

READE, CHARLES. The Cloister and the Hearth. Thomas Y. Crowell Company, New York. Conditions in Italy, Germany, France, and the Netherlands during the Renaissance.

VAN LOON, HENDRIK W. The Story of Mankind. Horace Liveright, New York.

WHITCOMB, IDA PRENTICE. The Young People's Story of Art. Dodd, Mead & Company, New York. Stories of famous artists and their work in architecture, sculpture, and painting.

UNIT III

ENGLAND'S MARCH TOWARD DEMOCRACY

ENGLAND'S MARCH TOWARD DEMOCRACY

For the beginnings of Europe's march toward democracy we turn to England. It was there that the middle class of traders and well-to-do townspeople first developed. It was there that charters of liberty were first wrung from absolute kings by determined merchants. Hence in Chapter VII we trace England's first steps toward democracy — a long, slow evolution paralleling the rise of England as a nation. Chapter VII, therefore, will carry the story up to about 1700.

To understand how Great Britain evolved the first representative government after 1700, we must study the rôle of the new ways of thinking which were applied to government as well as to the physical world. Thus in Chapters VIII and IX we shall see how "frontier thinkers" directed the world's march toward democracy. In Chapter VIII will be considered the application of their ideas to the ownership of property and to the control of government until the late 1700's. In Chapter IX we shall see especially how the rise of the Industrial Revolution produced, in the nineteenth century, a new group of frontier thinkers who changed the world's thinking about government.

With this background of understanding we shall see, in Chapter X, how these new ways of thinking were applied to the building of the first representative government, that of Great Britain after 1800.

CHAPTER VII

ENGLAND'S FIRST STEPS TOWARD DEMOCRACY

As we have seen, Roger Bacon had commanded: "Look at the world! Experiment! Think out your ways of living; don't take them merely on the authority of other people!" And new ways of thinking appeared — in science, in religion, in the arts!

Slowly but surely government in every country of Europe changed. Slowly kings lost their autocratic powers and the common people secured more political rights. But not for 500 years after Roger Bacon's time were real experiments in *democratic* government begun.

The change took place earlier in some countries than in others. In Germany and in Russia, for instance, it was long postponed; in some countries, indeed, it has come only in our own time. But in England the march toward democracy began much earlier than in others,— a long, slow, and rather steady evolution toward representative government. Hence it is to England that we turn for our first study of modern European governments and how they grew up.

The rôle played in government by the private capitalist

One group of people, more than any other, brought about the increase in representative government in England. This was, in general, the business class — the landowners, manufacturers, shipowners, and merchants. To understand Europe's march toward democracy, therefore, we must first understand the emergence of this group, especially after 1500.

The group has been known in modern history by various names. Sometimes it is called the middle class — the kings, nobles, and other wealthy landlords being the upper class, and the great mass of common people the lower class. Sometimes it is known as the third estate — the first and second estates being the clergy and the nobles. Sometimes, because these people lived chiefly in the towns, they are called the bourgeoisie, from the French word *bourg*, meaning "town." The group is also referred to as the private capitalist or merely the capitalist class, meaning the people who possess capital.

As you doubtless know, it was this class that, especially after 1750, built up the new industrial system of England. It came to own the factories and the business enterprises, the mines, the transportation and communication systems, even most of the land; eventually it took control of the government. Hence, to understand the way in which Europeans developed their experiments in democratic government, we must see clearly how this middle class rose to power after 1500, and how they developed what we call today representative and parliamentary government.

To do that we must first glance back at the economic happenings in England.[1] For a long time before 1500 the landowners had slowly been taking the "common land" away from the peasants and "inclosing" it — fencing it in to provide a grazing place for their growing herds of sheep. Facing ever-increasing hardships in getting a living from their tiny plots of land, the peasants had turned more and more to handicrafts in order to eke out a living. Some had left their cottages and had gone to live in towns; others had become skilled spinners, weavers, or shoemakers, and carried on their crafts in their rural cottages.

Thus, by 1700 cloth-making, cabinetmaking, the manufacture of knives and other kinds of hardware, and the production of fine pottery were flourishing handicrafts in English homes. Wool from the English flocks, raw silk from China, and cotton from Egypt and India were being woven into fine textiles on English looms. In the towns paper-making, printing, bookbinding, and the manufacture of tools, glassware, soap, and other articles rapidly developed.

But to supply the raw materials and the wages for these growing crafts required capital, especially money and credit. In this period, therefore, capitalists — the forerunners of our modern capitalists — appeared in England. In the cloth-making

[1] At this point it would be well to read Chapters V–VIII of *Changing Civilizations in the Modern World*.

industry, for example, men of ambition, thrift, and cleverness saw that they could make more money by buying wool and other raw materials and hiring workmen to spin and to weave them into cloth than by laboriously manufacturing cloth themselves. These clothiers, or traders in cloth, steadily increased the volume of their business as their orders in England and in other countries grew. Hence they accumulated ever larger amounts of capital.

Fig. 60. Many English homes of the 1700's were factories in which the handicrafts flourished. In this family the women carded and spun wool while the man wove the yarn into cloth. (From the *Universal Magazine*, 1750)

England became the pivot of world trade. As the crafts developed, British trade mounted by leaps and bounds, and Bristol and other English ports became thriving centers. British merchants formed great trading companies under charters from the crown which gave them a monopoly of trade between England and other countries. Recall the fabulous sums made by the British East India Company through importing the products of the Far East and selling them for large profits in England and on the Continent. Recall also that in the early 1600's the Plymouth and London Companies were chartered, the American colonies were established in Virginia and Massachusetts, and commerce increased between England and the New World.

Two important ideas: (1) private capitalism; (2) private ownership

Thus a new economic class — capitalists — developed in England and in the other countries of western Europe about the same time. Since we shall use the term *capitalist* many times let us illustrate it very carefully.

Manufacturers, for example, are capitalists. Owners of railroads and shipping companies are capitalists. Owners of houses and of apartments which are rented for profit, bankers and owners of stocks and bonds, farmers who hire "hands," and storekeepers who hire clerks are capitalists. In general, then, anyone who makes a profit from the labor of others or from income derived from rent or the use of money is a capitalist. Thus today in most countries of the world a very considerable number of the inhabitants are capitalists. We shall note later the increase in this class in various countries.

But back of this idea of capitalism is another important idea — namely, that of private ownership of property. This is perhaps the most important single idea underlying civilization in most countries of the world. Therefore we must understand it also. In the United States, England, France, Germany, China, Japan, and India — in fact, in almost every civilized nation — *things are owned and produced by private individuals.* For example, farms are owned privately and food is produced by the individual farmer *for profit.* Coal lands are owned and coal is mined by private citizens *for profit.* Oil fields, iron mines, and other natural resources are owned and worked by private citizens *for profit.* Even railroads, telegraphs, telephones, the radio, and most forms of entertainment are owned and operated in this way.

Thus, in these countries, all food, shelter, and clothing and most services needed by the people are provided by private individuals. Very little is produced by the state — that is, by the government. It owns little property, produces few goods, and carries on very few services. It operates the postal system, supplies water in most communities, and provides certain other services of government. But beyond these, *nearly everything upon which our lives depend is carried on by capitalists for private profit.* Thus we speak of our civilization as a *system of private capitalism.* It is a capitalist civilization.

Back of this idea is the belief that all these things will be done most efficiently if they are left to the desires and ambitions of individual citizens. This has been held by practically all modern nations and is the economic basis for practically all government. As we shall learn in later chapters, there is one important exception — the present experiment in state ownership and operation of property which is now being carried on in Russia.

In beginning the study of the development of representative government in England, therefore, it is most important to keep in mind the rise of this middle class of private capitalists after 1500. These owners of farm land, of herds of sheep, of coal and iron mines, of warehouses, of docks, and of banks took more and more control of both local and national government, especially after 1600. This capitalist class ousted the kings, the princelets, the dukes, the archbishops, and the abbots from political rule and developed what we know today as parliamentary and representative government.

One other important question: What is meant by "parliament"?

Before considering the steps by which England and other countries built up the parliamentary government which we have in the world today, one other important idea must be made clear —*parliament.* In Great Britain, in France, in Germany, and in some other countries, government today is spoken of as "parliamentary." To understand what the term means let us note how it developed.

The English word "parliament" comes from the French word *parlement,* which was the name applied to any meeting held for discussion. This word, in turn, came from the French *parler,* meaning "to speak." The French word *parlement* was first given to annual councils which the Capetian kings called together on the occasion of certain festivals (about 1000 A.D.). To these council meetings the leading lords and officials of the Church were invited, and the kings secured their advice on various problems of the kingdom. The kings also decided various legal controversies which came up for decision.

When William the Conqueror and his Norman successors introduced French customs into England after 1066, they continued to call together nobles and clergy in a Great Council to advise the king. One reference in the Anglo-Saxon Chronicle,[1] for example, states that William the Conqueror had "very deep speech with his Witan." (*Witenagemot* was the name applied at that time to this council, or meeting, of landowners and prelates who were known as the *witan*, or "wise men.")

By the early 1200's the French word *parlement* was in frequent use in England as a name given to debates and discussions; shortly after that it was applied formally to the Great Council of the king. Thus, the Statute of Westminster of 1275 speaks of the Great Council in England as the *parlement*. As the standard English language slowly evolved out of the mixture of the West Saxon, Danish, Kentish, and other dialects and the new Norman tongue, the English term "parliament" finally emerged as the official name of the legislative body of the English government. Today the British Parliament includes the king and two legislative houses — the House of Lords and the House of Commons. Although the king is a constituent part of Parliament, yet in the ordinary use of the term only the Lords and Commons are included. In the remainder of this chapter and in Chapter VIII we shall describe and illustrate parliamentary government.

Three Declarations of Rights upon which the British Constitution is Based

Today the rights of a British subject, which are essentially the same as those of an American citizen, are protected by a written constitution, as in the United States. But the British

[1] The Anglo-Saxon Chronicle is a contemporary record of events covering the years from the reign of Alfred the Great until 1154.

Constitution is unlike the American Constitution in one very important respect — it was not made in the same way. The seven articles of the American Constitution were written at one time, in the summer of 1787, by leaders of the thirteen American colonies. In the century and a half since that time nineteen amendments have been added. The British Constitution, however, was not written at one time. It evolved very slowly, item by item, during a period of nearly 700 years.

Three charters of British liberties comprise the heart of the Constitution.

1. Magna Carta (the Great Charter), 1215.
2. The Petition of Right, 1628.
3. The Bill of Rights, 1689.

These three declarations of rights are justly famous in the history of parliamentary government. The American Declaration of Independence, the American Constitution, and, in a large part, the French Declaration of the Rights of Man, 1789, were based upon them. Indeed, the parliamentary government which evolved in England was the basis for most of the experiments in parliamentary government in various parts of the world. Let us note briefly the circumstances under which these three documents were prepared, and the civil and political rights which they guaranteed.

1. Magna Carta, 1215—the first charter of English liberties

Nearly a thousand years passed from the time of the kings of Northumbria, Mercia, and Wessex to the time when government in England became representative. Nearly 1000 years were required to substitute for the absolute rule of a single hereditary king the representative House of Commons of the capitalist class.

About midway in this long period came the first great written document in the history of representative government in England. This was the so-called "Great Charter," *Magna Carta*, which the more well-to-do land barons and Church officials compelled King John (1199–1216) to sign in the year 1215. As one eminent historian says, the Magna Carta was "the first, clearest, most united and historically the most important enunciation [of English liberties]." It marked the beginning of the checks upon royal authority and laid a foundation for the development of representative government in England and in western Europe as well. It shows that at least a few of the Englishmen of that time — the large landowners and the clergy — had achieved enough power to deny the king the right of absolute or autocratic government.

Included in the list of 63 fundamental rights of the leading property-owners were the following: the King promised not to levy taxes upon the owners of land and other property without the consent of the Great Council; the Church was left free to choose its own officials and otherwise administer its business; London and other cities were guaranteed certain rights to carry on their collective affairs. Furthermore, the Charter said that "no freeman shall be arrested, or detained in prison or deprived of his freehold, or outlawed, or banished, or in any way molested . . . unless by the lawful judgment of his peers and by the law of the land." Thus, government was to be only "by the consent of the governed."

FIG. 61. In England before 1215 anyone might be imprisoned without trial

But we must note carefully that the Magna Carta did not guarantee self-government to the English people as a whole. "The governed," in the foregoing phrase, meant only the large property-owners, the land barons, the bishops and abbots of the Church — in short, it meant only the nobility and the clergy. These made up, certainly, less than 1 per cent of the population. Those who owned no property — more than 99 per cent of the English people — were still without a written guarantee of liberty.

The House of Commons also began in the 1200's

In 1254 came the next step in the evolution of a government which would be representative of more of the British people. In that year, in summoning the nobles and prelates to meet in the Parliament, the King also called two lesser knights from every shire or county. That is, the "gentleman" landlords of each rural district elected two representatives. In this election only the owners of property were permitted a voice. It is said that the King added these lesser landowners to the Great Council not from any desire to let more of the people have a deciding voice in government, but to obtain directly from the rural landlords information concerning the amount of taxes which each district could pay into the royal treasury.

Eleven years later, in 1265, another event took place which increased very slightly the representativeness of English government. Simon de Montfort, a wealthy land baron who objected to the autocratic ways of King Henry III, took matters into his own hands and called a parliament. Not only were the chief nobles and Church officers and two lesser knights from each shire included, but also *two burgesses from each of 21 towns* were summoned. These knights of the shire and burgesses of the towns were generally owners of small amounts of property and were regarded as "commoners."

In subsequent years the Parliaments continued the practice. Thus in 1295 Edward I summoned a "complete parliament," including not only archbishops, bishops, abbots, earls, and barons, but also *two knights from every shire and two citizens from every city and borough* which satisfied certain requirements. By the early 1300's the representatives met separately in two bodies: (1) the House of "Lords, Spiritual and Temporal," including the archbishops, bishops, abbots, earls, and other chief barons; and (2) the House of Commons, including the knights of the shires and the burgesses of the cities and towns. During most of the six centuries that have since passed the British Parliament has been made up of these two bodies—the House of Lords and the House of Commons.

As the story of representative government in England unfolds, we shall see two steady changes: (1) the step-by-step decline in the power of the House of Lords; (2) the inclusion in the House of Commons of representatives of a larger and larger proportion of the British common people.

But let us note carefully that at the time of the formation of the House of Commons and for 500 years thereafter, this so-called House of Commons still represented only owners of property. The great mass of peasants, craftsmen, and other wage-earners — and these made up the vast preponderance of

FIG. 62. The distribution of the English people in the year 1300 according to their right to vote. The upper bar represents the per cent of people who were entitled to vote. The lower bar represents the per cent who had no vote

the people — were not yet represented. A beginning had been made, however, in building up a government of the British people; for now the small capitalists of the towns and villages, as well as the hereditary landlords, were represented in Parliament.

THEN BEGAN THE LONG STRUGGLE BETWEEN THE KING AND THE PARLIAMENT FOR THE CONTROL OF GOVERNMENT

As we have already seen, the political history of England was essentially the story of the rise and fall of kings — of the attempt of one family to keep the throne and of others to take it away by intrigue or by force, by conspiracy or by murder, by any means, fair or foul. "The king is dead! Long live the king!" Generation after generation, when British kings died the throne passed to their sons, their daughters, or to younger brothers and sisters, or lacking those, to cousins. As the chart of Table III showed us, the descendants of William the Conqueror and of the Plantagenets of France ruled until nearly 1300. Then for almost 200 years the rival families of Lancaster and York conspired, intrigued, even murdered one another, in their eagerness for the throne. In 1485 Henry VII started a new line — the Tudors (Table IV). This family — Henry VII, Henry VIII, Edward VI,

Mary, and Elizabeth — kept the throne until 1603. The story of the reigns of many of these earlier monarchs is, indeed, a tale of riotous and extravagant living by the rulers and their favorites. Huge sums of money were squandered upon elaborately furnished palaces. Other stupendous sums were wasted in useless wars: wars of aggression and spite against other kings — the King of France, the King of Spain, and the rulers of Holland and other parts of Europe; wars conducted by the rulers to put down the insurrections of rival nobles who rose in rebellion to secure the throne or to wrest greater privileges from their kings.

TABLE IV

English Rulers from the Tudors to the Present
TUDOR LINE (1485–1603)
Henry VII (1485–1509)
Henry VIII (1509–1547)
Edward VI (1547–1553)
Mary (1553–1558)
Elizabeth (1558–1603)
STUART LINE (1603–1714)
James I (1603–1625)
Charles I (1625–1649)
Oliver Cromwell, Lord Protector (1653–1658)
Richard Cromwell (1658–1660)
Charles II (1660–1685)
James II (1685–1688)
William and Mary (1689–1702)
Anne (1702–1714)
HANOVERIAN LINE (1714–)
George I (1714–1727)
George II (1727–1760)
George III (1760–1820)
George IV (1820–1830)
William IV (1830–1837)
Victoria (1837–1901)
Edward VII (1901–1910)
George V (1910–)

But regardless of who occupied the throne the story of government in the centuries in which England was forming as a national state is essentially the story of the long struggle of the property-owners of the shires and the towns to take the control of government away from the king and to make him financially dependent upon them. This was the political history in those centuries — the story of conflict over the control of government.

"He who controls the army, controls the government!"

Perhaps you wonder why millions of people permitted a tiny group of so-called royal leaders — kings, princes, earls, and dukes — to squander their wealth and to govern them so autocratically. There are several reasons. One was the long-established tradition of reverence for the king. The royal ruler became a symbol of the nation itself, and of the power and the glory of the people as a group.

But there was a far more important practical reason than that — the king controlled the army. He appointed the officers, paying them and the soldiers from the royal treasury. He saw to it that the army was well paid, well fed, and, in general, contented. Hence the loyalty of the army was to the king, not to the people. The king knew that he governed so long as the army did his bidding. The moment he lost the army he lost the government. Note carefully, therefore, as you continue your studies of Europe's march toward democracy, how frequently this maxim of earlier governments is borne out — "He who controls the army, controls the government."

The chief cause of conflict over government — control of taxation

But who really paid the army? Who really paid for the devastating wars that went on year after year, generation after generation, between the kings and princes of England and France, Spain and Holland, and other countries? The farmers grubbing a meager living out of the soil of England, Scotland, and Wales; the weavers and spinners, shoemakers, carpenters, tool and implement makers, and other artisans of the towns and cities. Everybody, except those exempted by the king, had to help pay the costs of government. Taxation fell most heavily upon the common people.

Now from the 1200's on the more powerful landowners and merchants were in almost constant conflict with the kings over the control of taxation. In the Magna Carta the leaders in the Parliament had shown the kings their growing power. From then on, one English king after another was compelled to reaffirm the Great Charter of liberties in order to secure the approval of the Parliament and get necessary subsidies of money.

Then, in the 1500's, England fell under the Sway of Absolute Monarchs

There came a time, however,— in the 1500's,— when it seemed that the march of the lesser nobles toward control of the government had been stopped. Several clever, energetic kings and queens of the Tudor family followed one another on the throne of England and succeeded in obtaining almost absolute power. These were Henry VII (1485–1509), Henry VIII (1509–1547), Edward VI (1547–1553), Mary (1553–1558), and Elizabeth (1558–1603). Of these, Henry VII, Henry VIII, and Elizabeth had the most ability and built up control over the British government.

Fig. 63. Queen Elizabeth, last and greatest of the reigning Tudor family. (From a painting by Schrader)

These monarchs succeeded in this where earlier ones had failed, for several reasons. First, they kept rigid control of the army. Second, they secured great wealth without burdening the people generally with heavy taxes. For example, they confiscated valuable properties of the Catholic Church. It was in Henry VIII's reign, you will remember, that the control of the Pope and his officials was thrown off and the king made himself head of the

Church. As a result millions of dollars' worth of properties were seized by the throne, and the revenue of the royal family was increased without working a hardship on the nobles or the mass of the people. Third, Henry and, after him, his son and daughters economized carefully and kept strict control of the finances of the kingdom.

As a result of these factors, there was little conflict between the king and Parliament. The House of Lords and the House of Commons met only a few weeks in each year and generally approved the king's requests without much discussion. Thus as time went on the government of England became nearly an absolute monarchy. That is, the king settled most political questions without asking the consent or advice of Parliament or any other representatives of the people.

James I proclaims the "divine right" of kings

When Elizabeth died in 1603 without an heir to the throne the Tudor line of kings and queens came to an end. Elizabeth, a few days before her death, had expressed a preference for James VI, king of Scotland, as her successor. James was the son of Mary Stuart, Queen of Scots, who was the grandniece of Henry VIII and was therefore a logical candidate for the English throne. Thus James VI of Scotland became also James I of England.

There are two important facts to remember concerning this event. First, the landowners of Parliament were glad to accept James as king, because coming from outside the realm he would have little following in England and it would be easier for them to build up their own power at royal expense. As our narrative continues, we shall note that twice more in a little over 100 years Parliament chose a foreigner to reign over England.

The second fact is perhaps even more important. King James proclaimed that he ruled England by "divine right." He declared boldly:

> It is atheism and blasphemy to dispute what God can do; . . . so it is presumption and high contempt in a subject to dispute what a king can do or say that a king cannot do this or that.

Not only was King James to rule absolutely, but it was to be definitely agreed by all that he ruled by divine right. He was to be regarded as God's representative in England, and *not as the choice of the people of England.*

James attempted to carry his proclamation into practice, passing laws without consulting Parliament, assuming the power of absolute master of the fate of every one of his subjects, and demanding that huge sums of money be raised by taxation. His acts as well as his proclamations angered the earls and barons and the lesser representatives in the House of Commons. Their irritation was greatly increased by the extravagance and foolhardiness of the King in entangling England in foreign wars with France and Spain and in living in a wasteful and lavish manner.

Trouble started early in his reign. When James asked for large subsidies of money with which to finance his needs, Parliament refused. The King retaliated by attempting to force some of his wealthy subjects to make loans to him. Presumably these loans were to be paid back. Actually they rarely were — hence the term *forced loan.* Such a practice amounted to confiscation of property — taking something by force without payment of any kind.

King James used other illegal methods to get money. He sold noble titles (many kings of Europe did this) to well-to-do persons in return for money or gifts paid into his treasury. He imposed royal duties on certain imported goods, which means that a tax had to be paid to him on certain articles brought into England from another country. He granted monopolies to certain clever leaders in return for a percentage of their profits; for example, he granted lands in North America to the London Company and to others in return for a share of the profits.

Steadily members of the House of Parliament rebelled against these high-handed methods. Matters came to a head in 1621, when the members of the House of Commons solemnly inscribed in their records a Great Protestation against King James's illegal assumption of power. In high rage James tore the Protestation out of the Journal of the House and sent the members of Parliament to their various homes.

Many Important Advances and Changes were Made in England during the Early 1600's

To understand why members of Parliament even dared to draw up such a protestation against a king who had proclaimed himself ruler by "divine right" we must recall the stirring events of the times. Men were beginning to think for themselves about government as well as about every other phase of life. As we have seen, this was the period of the scientific revolution. Galileo was making observations and experiments in Italy. In England, Harvey was discovering new facts about the human body, and Francis Bacon was classifying scientific knowledge and was inciting men to think independently. In France, Descartes was inventing the new mathematics and was supplementing Francis Bacon in the study of the sciences. Many new measuring instruments were being invented, and many new facts about the physical and the human world were being piled up.

Great changes had also been made in religious beliefs. Only two generations before, the great Reformation had swept over Europe, and many people had been led to think out their beliefs for themselves. In England and Scotland new sects of independent-minded persons were appearing who insisted on worshiping as they saw fit — the Puritans, the Independents, the Separatists, the Quakers, the Presbyterians, and others.

Remember, moreover, that this seventeenth century was the period in which extensive explorations of North America were being followed by settlements in the New World. In the early 1600's colonies appeared near every important harbor on the Atlantic coast. Sir Walter Raleigh and Sir Humphrey Gilbert had led their ill-fated expeditions to Virginia in the late 1500's; Captain John Smith had taken his to Jamestown in 1607. Recall others: Plymouth, 1620; Massachusetts Bay, 1628–1630; the Dutch colony of New Amsterdam, 1624; Roger Williams, 1635–1636, and Anne Hutchinson, 1638, in Rhode Island; Thomas Hooker in Connecticut, 1635–1636.

This was also a period of great literature in England. Shakespeare was writing *Othello* and *The Tempest* in the reign of James I. Francis Bacon was writing his great book *The Advance-*

ment of Learning (1605), dedicating it to King James I. Furthermore, the authorized translation of the Bible into English was made — the King James Bible, which is used even today in many Protestant churches in English-speaking countries.

Thus, these earlier years of the 1600's were a period of dramatic change in European life. Hence it is easy to understand that in

FIG. 64. The Pilgrims land at Plymouth. Breaking away as they did from almost all that was familiar to them illustrates both the changes that were taking place during the early 1600's and the independence of thought that made some of these changes possible. (From a painting by Henry Sargent, in Pilgrim Hall, Plymouth)

such free-thinking times men of ambition and intelligence who had accumulated wealth would insist on having their proper share in the governing of their collective affairs. That is exactly what took place under leadership within the capitalist class.

The important part played by the Puritans in English life in the 1600's

In these stirring times one group took the lead in opposing the absolute "divine right" assertions of the kings — the Puritan capitalists. They were, in fact, the same Puritans of whom we learned in American history, members of the various Protestant churches which had sprung from the teachings of "protestants" against the abuses of the Catholic Church. Thousands of them emigrated to America in the great migration of the 1630's under the leadership of John Winthrop, Endicott, Cotton, and others.

The name *Puritans* came from their desire to "purify" the Church practices and from the stern code of life which the followers of this faith preached and practiced. To understand it, recall the characteristics of the Puritans who settled in Massachusetts. Recall their plain manner of living, their strict observance of the Sabbath, the formality of their speech, their dress, their houses. These were the people, remember, who thought dancing around the Maypole a sin, and who drove Roger Williams and Anne Hutchinson out of Massachusetts Bay Colony for disagreeing with them. These were the men who hanged "witches."

Now these Puritans were leaders in the life of England. They were among the rising business men and factory-owners of the cities and towns, the shipowners and the merchants who were building up foreign trade. They were the wool-growers and the well-to-do gentlemen farmers of the shires. They were leaders in scientific undertakings as well as in religion. They were also the men who refused to take orders from "divine right" kings in England in the 1600's.

The struggle for the control of government between the King and the Puritan leaders

Now we have an illustration of a principle that was revealed so many times in the history of American government — namely, that the strongest economic group tends to control the government. From your study of American history you will recall that this happened in every generation from the landing of the Puritans to the rise of the great industrial corporations of our own day.

On the other side of the Atlantic, in England, the same thing took place. It was the Puritan business men who acquired more wealth than other men and who, as they did so, increasingly asserted their control over government. It was they who rose in the House of Commons and recorded the Great Protestation against the King; it was these same Puritan leaders who succeeded in obtaining two more great charters of liberty.

The conflict between the King and the representatives of the middle-class property-owners in Parliament was a quarrel over every kind of right. It was a quarrel over *economic* rights, to determine who should pay taxes and duties, who should have monopolies, and the like. It was a quarrel over *civil* rights. The rising middle class demanded the right of free speech, of protection against unfair imprisonment, and the like. It was a quarrel over *religious* rights also, the same business leaders demanding of the King freedom to worship as they pleased. Thus, this astonishing seventeenth century was indeed historic in the world's march toward democracy. Let us see some of the significant events.

The Petition of Right, 1628 — the Second Charter of British Liberties

James I succeeded in living out his life and dying a natural death without further open rupture with the Puritans, and his son, Charles I, came to the throne in 1625. From the moment of his succession Charles continued the same policy of arrogant, absolute government established by his father. He embroiled England in expensive wars and demanded great sums of money from the people to finance his extravagant court.

One dramatic event followed another in swift succession. Within three years the controversy between the King and the leaders in Parliament came to a head. Charles demanded vast subsidies, to be supplied by heavy taxes upon the people. When the House of Commons refused to approve his request, Charles did as his father had done — sold titles of nobility for money, forced large loans from wealthy subjects, imposed duties upon imports, and sold monopolies in return for a share of the profit. Persons who objected, he punished by imprisonment without trial. Soldiers and sailors were quartered in houses of subjects who had incurred his disapproval.

Still he lacked sufficient money to provide for his extravagant needs, and in 1628 he was compelled to accede to the demands of the House of Commons in return for the desired subsidies. These demands were embodied in the second great charter of British liberties — the Petition of Right. This document was in a sense a restatement of the essential rights guaranteed in the Magna Carta — the first charter of liberties — 413 years before. Indeed, the Great Charter was actually referred to in the Petition of Right. The civil right of fair trial was exacted again, and the control of Parliament over taxation was asserted.

From a list of the promises by the King, four should be remembered:

1. No Englishman could be taxed *without the consent of Parliament.* (A new political right)
2. No free man could be imprisoned or otherwise punished without being tried and due cause of imprisonment proved. (A renewed civil right)
3. No one could be compelled to quarter soldiers and sailors in his house. (A new civil right)
4. No one could be tried by military courts in times of peace. (A new civil right)

Note that one significant gain seemed to have been made for representative government. The Petition of Right stated that *no Englishman* could be taxed without the consent of Parliament. No Englishman — not merely the landlords.

The quarrel between the King and the Puritan business men in Parliament continued

But the treacherous Charles had barely signed the Petition of Right when he began to violate it. The very practices against which Parliament had objected were continued. As a result, the House of Commons started investigations of the acts of the King's ministers. They were beginning with the affairs of the unscrupulous Lord Buckingham, when the latter was assassinated. The House of Commons then investigated the illegal collection of customs by the King's officers and the introduction of Roman Catholic practices into the Anglican Church. Incensed at this, Charles sent the members of Parliament home. The King of England was still permitted to do that!

For eleven years (1629–1640) Charles ruled England as *an absolute king without Parliament.* For eleven years he levied fines and taxes, collected duties, and forced loans from his British subjects. He granted monopolies in the sale of wine, salt, and other commodities in return for a payment of a large amount of "graft" to him. He compelled the shipping towns to contribute money to his treasury for a navy.

Out of this last form of royal tyranny grew the famous case of John Hampden, a member of the House of Commons, who refused to pay a tax of twenty shillings for ship money. Hampden was arrested, tried before a court made up of king's judges and convicted — but only by a bare majority. This case became famous in the history of English liberty, because it revealed the marked increase in the independence of the people, and showed very clearly that the property-owners of England would shortly take the government into their own hands. For, although the judges, as favorites of the King, were under his influence, nevertheless almost half of them refused to convict Hampden.

While this conflict over taxation and the raising of money went on, the leaders of Parliament were also greatly incensed at Charles's attitude toward the Catholic Church. He appointed William Laud Archbishop of Canterbury — that is, head of the Church of England. Much to the anger of the strict Puritans, the English Church, under Laud, became much more like the Roman Catholic Church. "High church" formalities were introduced. Catholics were favored all over the country, and the exactions on the Puritans increased. It was in this decade of the 1630's that thousands of Puritans emigrated to America and settled at Massachusetts Bay.

But Charles went too far. He tried to introduce the ritual and organization of the Anglican Church into Scotland, and in 1638 the Scotch Presbyterians rose against him and his bishops. Troops which Charles ordered to advance against them mutinied. The situation of the King became worse and worse. For two years his armies were defeated at home and abroad. At last, in 1640, he was compelled to summon a Parliament. Three times in that year the King tried to deal with Parliament, which openly denounced him and his favorites. The Short Parliament assembled, wrangled three weeks, and was dismissed. A council of lords was then called together to advise Charles. Finally, in November, 1640, he summoned the last Parliament of his reign. This was known as the Long Parliament — well named, for it lasted from 1640 to 1653. During these years famous events happened and important history was written for England.

The Puritan Revolution

More and more insistently the Puritan leaders boldly demanded the democratic control over government which the charters of liberty had implied. Daring middle-class gentlemen like John Hampden, John Pym, and Oliver Cromwell rose in their seats in the House of Commons and defied the tricky king. In fiery speeches they maintained that government of England could be only by the consent of the governed and that the supreme authority lay only in the House of Commons.

Step by step they took the power they asserted. First they impeached Archbishop Laud and Thomas Wentworth, the Earl of Strafford, King Charles's close friend and minister. To save his friend, Charles plotted to seize London by means of the army. Discovering these plots, the Puritan leaders hastened the preparations for Strafford's trial. Fearing an acquittal by the House of Lords, the House of Commons changed the impeachment charge to a bill of attainder; that is, a general argument against Strafford's misdeeds was presented instead of specific proof of definite charges. This was successful, and King Charles was ordered to sign the execution warrant. Crowds gathered everywhere in London demanding the head of the English minister, as they did later that of Archbishop Laud. The King, who was, as one English historian says, "probably one of the meanest and most treacherous occupants the English throne has ever known," was badly frightened by the menacing mobs and signed his friend's death warrant. In 1641 Thomas Wentworth, Earl of Strafford, the confidant and the personal minister of the King, was beheaded. Four years later, Archbishop Laud was tried for high treason against the people and was likewise beheaded.

One dramatic event followed another. Steadily the leaders of Parliament became bolder. At one stage of the controversy Charles tried to bluff. At the head of an armed force, he went to the House of Commons to arrest the ringleaders of the Puritans. These, however, having been informed of his plans, had left the House and had gone to a safe place in London. Charles demanded that they be handed over to him. The Londoners refused. For a

FIG. 65. Charles I in the House of Commons, autocratically demanding that five of its members be delivered to him on a charge of treason. This was the first and only time in history that a British ruler invaded the House of Commons. (From a painting by John Singleton Copley)

week there was intense excitement in the city. Finally the King, who was steadily losing followers, left the city, and the Puritan leaders were reëstablished in Parliament with great acclaim.

England moved swiftly toward civil war. Two groups lined up against each other. On one side were the King, a few favorite nobles, the Church leaders who were inclined toward Roman Catholic practices, and occasional loyal country squires. Against them were arrayed the so-called middle classes, led by a few of the great landowners, most of the small country gentry, and the business men, manufacturers, and merchants of the towns. Thus it was "divine right" aristocrats against middle-class business men. For the first time in English history the middle class was powerful enough to fight a king openly.

Thus the Great Rebellion of 1642–1652 developed. In 1644 Charles and his Royalist armies were defeated in battle at Marston Moor by a combined army of Parliamentary and Scotch-Presbyterian forces. Throughout Scotland the High Church formalities which had been introduced into the Church by the Anglicans were abolished.

Oliver Cromwell and his army take control of England

A man destined to make important changes in English government now entered the scene. This was Oliver Cromwell, a country squire, a member of Parliament, and an Independent in religion. Cromwell had organized a regiment of cavalrymen, who had become the most efficient soldiers among the Puritan troops. He was a stern, God-fearing taskmaster, who had gathered together a regiment of like-minded soldiers, "honest, sober Christians." These soldiers of Cromwell's, who were fined a shilling if they swore, represented well the stern Puritan way of living. For example, they went into battle singing psalms! They earned the name of "Ironsides" because of their strength in battle. Cromwell's Ironsides set such an example that they served as the New Model on which the whole Independent army was reorganized. Gradually Oliver Cromwell himself became the leader of the opposition to Charles, and by 1646 the New Model army had thoroughly defeated Charles's troops and had made the king a captive.

Then followed two years of indecision and quarreling among the various religious and economic groups of Parliament. Some wanted to put Charles back on the throne with restricted powers. Others — extremists — demanded that he be tried for treason to the English people. Others, equally dissatisfied with the king but believing in his authority, asked themselves: Can a "divine right" king commit treason?

The crisis came in December, 1648, when the Presbyterian members of the House of Commons declared they were willing to receive Charles back again on the throne. Thereupon Colonel Pride, an Independent army officer, stationed his soldiers at the door of the House, arrested 143 Presbyterians, and excluded them from the deliberations of the Parliament. This high-handed act has been known throughout English history as "Pride's Purge"; that is, he purged the House of the adherents of the "divine right" kings.

FIG. 66. Mean and treacherous though Charles I was, he met his end with dignity. "He nothing common did or mean Upon that memorable scene." (After a painting by William Fisk)

Sixty Independent opponents of King Charles were left. This remnant is known as the Rump Parliament. These immediately appointed a High Court of Justice to try King Charles for treason. The court, made up of his enemies, tried him and convicted him of treason to the English nation. On January 30, 1649, Charles I mounted the scaffold in front of his own palace of Whitehall in London, and his head was cut off.

Thus a small group of middle-class property-owners quarreled with an absolute "divine right" king and asserted that the power of government lay in the hands of the larger propertied class. Democracy moved forward a little in England.

But let us not forget that more than nine tenths of the English people were unconcerned with all this quarreling over civil and political rights. Most of the people went on harvesting their fields, weaving at their looms, buying and selling in their shops, and loading and unloading their ships. They thought much about their daily bread and little about government. Probably not more than a tiny fraction knew of the striking events which led to the beheading of an English king, and certainly only the few who were close to the scene of action in the larger cities had an inkling of the root of the controversy. But through the work of a few leaders — selfish though their motives may have been — the cause of all the people was promoted, and autocratic rule by English kings ceased.

The Commonwealth: England a Republic for a Few Years

Then for several years out of its long history England had neither king nor House of Lords. Parliament — this same "Rump" of the total Parliament — ruled England without even a figurehead on the throne.

Let us not think for a moment that democracy had come to England. An absolute oligarchy, centered in a Council of State of 41 persons, had merely taken the place of an absolute monarchy. The mainstay of the oligarchy was Oliver Cromwell's army; again we see the principle which is especially true in unsettled times, that "he who controls the army, controls the government."

Almost immediately this army faced rebellion in every section of the kingdom. Royalists, as the defenders of the King were called, arose in Ireland and Scotland. But Cromwell, the efficient military leader, quickly marched against his enemies. He slaughtered thousands of Royalists in Ireland, defeating the opposition in one battle after another. Other thousands he sold as slaves or exiled to the West Indies. When the rebellion against the Commonwealth had been put down in Ireland, he turned to Scotland and butchered the opposing armies which in the meantime had risen in support of Charles II, the son of the beheaded Charles I. As a result Charles II was compelled to flee from the British Isles and hide in France.

In the meantime the Rump Parliament, once in power, had begun to "graft," as had its royal predecessors. But when Cromwell's wars were won, he marched his troops back to London and took charge of government himself. In 1653 he sent the members of the Rump Parliament to their homes, saying to them, "Your hour is come; the Lord hath done with you!"

For five years, 1653–1658, Oliver Cromwell ruled England as the Lord Protector, with a small Council of State.

Cromwell, the most efficient leader of his time, the most masterful military and political man of his era, ruled wisely though sternly. In religion he was an Independent, a democrat as far as religious organization of the Church was concerned. He was known to be interested in art and music.

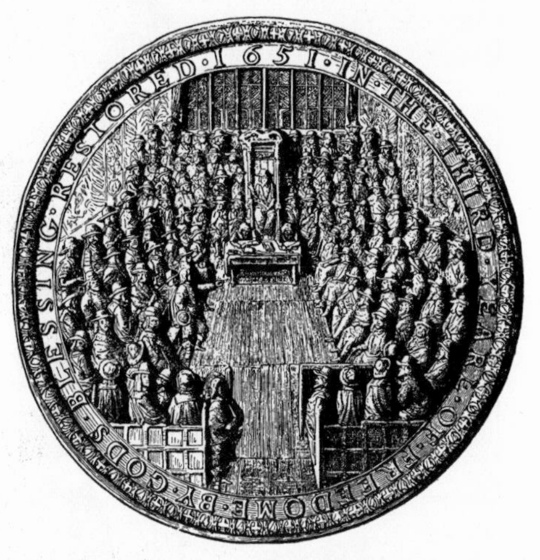

Fig. 67. The Great Seal of the Commonwealth. It shows Parliament once more in session. Read the lettering and note the date

With the establishment of the Protectorate — as Cromwell's first government was called — what is believed to be the first written constitution of modern times was prepared. This, the Instrument of Government, provided that Parliament was to meet at least every three years, that it had the sole power to make laws and to levy taxes upon the people. The Lord Protector — who was really a constitutional monarch — was forbidden the right to veto laws passed by the Parliament. Also, there was to be one religion for the entire country — namely, the Puritan religion.

Other reforms were made. Parliament was to consist of only one house and was to be the "Parliament of Great Britain and Ireland"— not merely of England. Furthermore, members of Parliament were apportioned on a new basis of representation. The larger towns were given more representatives, and the many small places which had had an unduly large proportion of the representation now lost it.

For the last three years of his life (1655–1658) Cromwell ruled England as military dictator, his army enforcing order throughout the country. For three years the nation carried on its business, agriculture, and foreign trade in prosperity. Skilled artisans, irrespective of race and religion, were permitted to settle in England. The sea was made safe for merchantmen by the punishment of Barbary pirates. Spain was defeated by the English navy, which

Fig. 68. Cromwell (on horseback) and his Ironsides at Marston Moor during the Great Rebellion. It was in the battle fought here that Cromwell scored his first great victory over the Royalist forces of Charles I. (After a painting by Ernest Crofts)

strengthened England's claim to be mistress of the seas. Treaties were signed with Holland and France. It was indeed a time of prosperity for England.

But it was not *democracy*; it was *autocracy* — absolute government. Cromwell was a military dictator, ruling England because he controlled the army. For the time being, representative Parliamentary government was dead. Government was not by the consent of the governed.

Then, in 1658, Oliver Cromwell died. Again England was left without a head — even a figurehead! For a short time Richard Cromwell, the dictator's son, tried to carry on the government. But, lacking his father's remarkable powers, he soon lost the army and the control of the Parliament. For two years the government of England was disorganized.

In this interval the soldiers of Cromwell's armies really ruled the country. No single leader appeared among them strong enough to seize the power. No single person appeared among the Puritans or the various Independent groups strong enough to receive the support of a majority of the leaders. Finally, it became clear that rather than continue the anarchy of the soldiers' government, most people preferred a Stuart king. Thus, public opinion grew in favor of restoring the Stuart kings to the throne of England.

The Restoration of a King, — but without Divine Right, — 1660

Now there happened in England what has so frequently happened throughout the history of civilization. The leaders put back on the throne again the very family — the Stuarts — which only a few years before they had ousted. You will note in the history of our own country and in the history of other countries that the attitudes of people change. First they put one group in control of government. Becoming discontented with that group, they put it out. But perhaps in a very short time they swear allegiance to the very group that they have put out of power. Note how frequently this happened in the history of France and of other countries. Such examples will teach us how important it is to study the psychology of such attitudes — how opinions and loyalties are formed and what changes them.

Thus in 1660, Charles II, who had been in exile in France, was welcomed back to England as king. The House of Lords and the House of Commons convened once more and passed a resolution that "according to the ancient and fundamental laws of this kingdom, the government is and ought to be, by King, Lords, and Commons." So it was that the republic of England came to an end and the kingdom of England was restored. From that day to this the same form of government has been maintained.

But note that Charles ruled as *king by permission of the leaders of Parliament, not by divine right.* Representative government, that is, government as representative as it had ever been during the reign of former kings, was established once more in England.

Fig. 69. The people forgot what they had suffered at the hands of their earlier kings and enthusiastically welcomed Charles II back to England. (After a painting by Benjamin West)

We need not recount in detail the happenings of the reign of Charles II. He succeeded in ruling England for twenty-five years and died a natural death. Yet, like his father, he was crafty and hypocritical, constantly conspiring to advance himself. It was later discovered that he had signed a secret treaty with Louis XIV of France by which he was to receive approximately $1,000,000 annually and aid from French armies in case of need. He, in his turn, was to help Louis against his enemies, Holland and Spain, and was to announce himself as a Roman Catholic.

The government of Charles II looked little different from that of James I or Charles I. The King revived the very practices for which Charles I had been beheaded. The old Royalist clique went into power again — the earls and barons, the bishops and abbots. There were the same demands for money; there were the same forced loans. In one case, for example, Charles refused to pay back approximately $7,000,000 worth of gold which London goldsmiths had lent to him. A forced loan indeed!

In the meantime the religious controversy continued. Members of the Anglican Church controlled Parliament, established one uniform church, and decreed that no one should hold an office who was not a member of the Established Church of England. They passed an Act of Uniformity in 1662, debarring every clergyman of the Church who refused to accept every item in the Book of Common Prayer.

Throughout the 1670's and 1680's, Charles himself, however, leaned toward the Catholic religion. Steadily he urged legislation which would favor Catholicism. In 1672 he issued a Declaration of Indulgence, which tended to give freedom of worship to all Dissenters, including Catholics. Furthermore, his brother, James, heir to the throne, was a Catholic.

Fear spread among Puritan leaders in Parliament that Catholicism would increase throughout the realm. Hence the House of Commons assumed more power than ever before. It passed an Exclusion Bill in 1680, which, if agreed to by the House of Lords, would debar James from the throne at the death of Charles II. After a long fight, however, the House of Lords refused to pass the bill.

The Complete Establishment of Parliamentary Government, 1688

When Charles II died in 1685 and his Catholic brother, James II, was placed upon the throne, Parliament was prepared to assert its power. Within three years it did so, for in that short time James II had so antagonized the leaders of Parliament that he was forced to flee from the country.

Once more England was without a royal head. Once more Parliament was confronted by the problem of choosing a leader. We must note, however, the real significance of the next event; for there has been none more important in English history — perhaps in Europe's march toward democracy.

Parliament had now (1688) achieved such power that it could choose the king! In doing so, it stated the conditions to which he must subscribe in order to be king of England. That is, it compelled him to recognize the fundamental civil and political rights of the British people in the world-famous Bill of Rights.

The Bill of Rights, 1689, the third great charter of British liberties

So in 1688 Parliament invited a royal couple — Prince William of Orange (Holland) and Princess Mary — to become king and queen of England. Princess Mary was the daughter of James II and Prince William was his nephew. In inviting them to become rulers Parliament stipulated very carefully the conditions of the invitation in a famous document — the Declaration of Rights. After these conditions had been accepted and the new king and queen had been duly crowned, this Declaration of Rights was made a part of the statute law of the kingdom in the form of a Bill of Rights, which is the third great charter of British liberties, the first two being the Magna Carta, 1215, and the Petition of Right, 1628. Its thirteen articles make clear that the British Parliament had invited William and Mary to take the throne only with the understanding that certain enumerated evils of government should be eliminated. The Declaration stated, for example, that James II had assumed many illegal powers such as taxation, quartering soldiers upon civilians, discriminating against Protestants in favor of Catholics, prohibiting freedom of election and speech, imprisoning persons illegally, imposing excessive bail and fines, and inflicting illegal and cruel punishments.[1]

The Bill of Rights stipulates that there shall be freedom of election to Parliament and freedom of speech within it; that Parliament shall be assembled frequently; that laws cannot be suspended, taxes levied, or an army maintained *without the consent of Parliament*; that English subjects shall be tried by impartial juries; that excessive bail shall not be required, or excessive fines and cruel or unusual punishments be inflicted.

[1] You will recall that Jefferson and the American colonists, in preparing the American Declaration of Independence, recited a similar list of evil and illegal practices of which King George III had been guilty. Compare what follows to find other similarities between the two documents.

"But these are like articles and amendments in the American Constitution!" perhaps you exclaim. They are, in essentials at least. For the British Bill of Rights became famous in world history and was copied into the constitutions of many other countries. It was the basis of the Bill of Rights in the Constitution of the United States.[1] It also definitely influenced the leaders of the French Revolution in their famous Declaration of Rights exactly 100 years later, 1789. Thus, the British Bill of Rights has justly become a famous document in the history of written constitutions in the modern world.

Other civil liberties which are today dear to people in democratic countries were also protected in this period of advance in democratic government. In 1689, for example, the Act of Toleration was passed, permitting freedom of worship to the dissenting religious sects of England; that is, to all but Unitarians — those who denied the idea of the Trinity — and Catholics. A bill was then passed establishing comparative freedom of the press and revoking all the former laws by which the government censored and licensed the publishing of books. Thirty years before that time, John Milton, the famous poet, had written an eloquent denunciation of government censorship of books in his *Areopagitica,* but nothing had been done. Thus, this new act of Parliament was another forward step in the freedom of thought and speech.

There is little more of importance in England's slow march toward democracy to tell at this time. William and Mary reigned together until the death of Mary in 1694. Then William reigned alone until his death in 1702. After that, Mary's sister Anne reigned as Queen of England, 1702–1714.

One political event is perhaps worth remembering — the Act of Union of 1707. This *legally* united England and Scotland in what was known as the Kingdom of Great Britain. Although from the time that James had ruled Scotland as King James VI and England as King James I (1603–1625) there had been a kind of personal union between the two countries, they had never

[1] At this point you might re-read the first ten Amendments to the American Constitution.

been a really united nation. For hundreds of years the English and the Scotch had quarreled. Gradually, however, old hatreds had died down; in 1707 the two peoples legally became one. Steadily the loyalty of people to England or to Scotland has been

FIG. 70. On the top row are shown St. George's Cross and St. Andrew's Cross, the emblems used on the early flags of England and Scotland, respectively. The first drawing on the second line shows how these two crosses were combined into one flag under James I to signify the union of the two countries. When Ireland was made part of the kingdom St. Patrick's Cross (lower center figure) was added, and the final drawing shows how the symbols of the three countries are combined today in the Union Jack

replaced by loyalty to Great Britain. Little by little, as generations have passed, Scotchmen, Englishmen, and Welshmen have come to regard themselves as British. Figure 70 shows how this union is set forth in the Union Jack — the British flag.

How far then had England marched toward democracy in 1700?

Looking back now we see that the idea of government by divine right had been supplanted by the idea of government by a small group of property-owners. A small, wealthy upper class had developed a government representative of itself. Step by step the middle-class landowners and business men had increased their wealth and had taken the control of government away from the king and his small circle of noble favorites. Thus the foundations of parliamentary government had been laid, and three great charters of liberty had been written and accepted by the kings. All this had been accomplished before 1700.

But government was by no means representative of the British people. Not more than 3 per cent of the total population of England had representation in the national government, for at least 97 per cent were still without the right to vote and hold office. Thus it could not be said that the English people had political liberty in 1700.

Similarly, some gains had been made in the attempt to guarantee civil liberty to the people as has been shown by the Bill of Rights. People could no longer be taxed at the whim of a king; no one could be imprisoned or otherwise punished without fair trial. Thus, by 1700 definite gains had been made in both civil and political liberties. They revealed very clearly that the foundations of England's march toward democracy had been laid.

INTERESTING READINGS FROM WHICH YOU CAN GET ADDITIONAL INFORMATION

Dix, Beulah M. Hugh Gwyeth. The Macmillan Company, New York. Cavaliers and Roundheads.

Dumas, Alexandre. The Black Tulip. Little, Brown and Company, Boston. William of Orange.

Gilman, Arthur. Magna Charta Stories. Lothrop, Lee & Shepard, Boston. Stories of struggles for liberty.

Hawes, C. B. The Dark Frigate. Little, Brown and Company, Boston. The days of Cromwell.

Marshall, Bernard. The Torch Bearers. D. Appleton and Company, New York. Story of Cromwell's time.

Marshall, Henrietta Elizabeth. Our Island Story: a Child's History of England. Frederick A. Stokes Company, New York.

Masefield, John. Martin Hyde, the Duke's Messenger. Little, Brown and Company, Boston. James II and the rebellion of 1685.

Quennell, Marjorie and C. H. B. The History of Everyday Things in England. Charles Scribner's Sons, New York. See Part II, 1500–1799.

Quiller-Couch, Arthur T. The Splendid Spur. Doubleday, Doran & Company, Inc., Garden City, New York. Interesting account of the time of Charles I.

Stevenson, Robert Louis. The Black Arrow. Charles Scribner's Sons, New York. The Wars of the Roses.

CHAPTER VIII

HOW "FRONTIER THINKERS" DIRECTED THE WORLD'S MARCH TOWARD DEMOCRACY

We must turn aside for a moment from our study of the development of British parliamentary government and note what was happening among the thinking men of western Europe. It will aid us in understanding the stirring events of the next two centuries.

In the 1600's the scientific revolution had been centered about the facts of the natural and physical world. In the 1700's, however, it began to affect people's ways of thinking about industry, government, and the social world as well. The idea held by the two Bacons, by Galileo, and by the other physical scientists that men should observe the problems of the world carefully and think them through clearly was being seriously considered. A few thinking men began to speculate and draw hypotheses about economic life and government as well as about the physical world.

It was high time they did so. Vast changes were taking place in Europe — changes in the way men worked, in the way they worshiped, and in their living conditions. As a result of these far-reaching changes, difficult and immediate problems were demanding thought. There was, first and foremost, the problem of providing every man with a job and a decent income. There was the problem of making government efficient and economical. There was the problem of safeguarding the health of the people. And there was the problem of guaranteeing civil and political liberty — making government truly of, by, and for the people. Do you not recognize these as the chief problems of today?

In the midst of those stirring changes and insistent social problems, most people of intelligence and initiative devoted themselves to seeking personal prestige or to building up their personal fortunes. Some physically daring men went exploring new lands — witness Columbus, the Cabots, Cartier, Pizarro, and Magellan.

Other adventurers took charters from ambitious kings and financed or settled colonies — as, for example, Walter Raleigh, John Winthrop, and William Penn. Still others sailed the high seas either in merchant ships, buying goods in Asia and selling them at great profit in Europe, or in pirate vessels, making fortunes for themselves by the capture of a single Spanish galleon or a shipload of Oriental spices and teas.

Many of those who remained at home became kings' ministers of war or tax collectors, using their energy and intelligence to fill the royal coffers and incidentally to enrich themselves. The world was muddling along, while the leaders in business, industry, and government secured most of the wealth. In the meantime the mass of the people, less intelligent or less fortunate or both, submissively accepted their poverty-stricken fate, knowing nothing about the management of their collective affairs.

A few clear-minded "frontier thinkers," however, in France, England, Germany, America, and other countries, began to apply their minds to the solution of the difficult social problems. A very small company of students undertook to think through the baffling problems of human living together. It was these first "social scientists" who really redirected Europe's march toward democracy. It was this little band of hard thinkers who saw what lay beneath the surface of the new civilization which Europe was producing. It was these adventurers in creative thinking who gave the world new and important hypotheses about government.

Therefore to understand the experiments in government which have come in recent times we must understand the ideas of these thinkers. To a brief consideration of them we turn next.

The Fundamental Problem: How should Property be owned?

Throughout the recorded history of the world, problems of government have been closely tied up to questions of owning property. Perhaps the simplest example to us is the fact that until very recent times, even in the United States, in order to vote or to hold office one was required to own a stated amount of property. Indeed, political liberty in America, even three generations ago, was given only to those who owned property. In the previous chapter we saw that the same thing was true in England. In later chapters we shall see similar examples of the relation between government and property in still other countries. This important topic of property and its ownership is the fundamental question upon which the plans and experiments in democratic government have been carried out in the Western world. Indeed, the basic question which every political philosopher of the past 200 years has been compelled to face, sooner or later, is, *How should property be owned?*

We have already seen the long struggle of western Europeans for the control of property. We have seen kings fighting kings to satisfy their desire for more property. We have seen son pitted against father, brother against brother, family against family, in the attempt to secure more land, money, ships, trade, horses, cows, factories, houses — in short, more property.

Adventurous explorers dared the dangers of the Atlantic to accumulate property. Drake and Hawkins — bold highwaymen of the sea — plundered the Spanish Main in the mad race for property. Merchant companies of England, Holland, France, Spain, and Sweden founded colonies in America, essentially to increase their property. The triangular trade in molasses, rum, and human slavery which grew up in the 1700's is another example of what men will do to secure more property.

Were this a history of the ancient world, we should record examples in every age of that time and in every continent of how men fought to secure slaves, raw materials, and other possessions, even as the animals in the jungles, forests, and plains about them fought for food. Indeed, in viewing the history of advancing civilizations we can see it as the story of men settling the age-old question *How should property be owned?*

Furthermore, had we the space for a long historical view of this problem, we should see how most men, for tens of thousands of years, answered the question in just one way — namely, that property shall be owned by the strongest or the cleverest. They said: "You can own whatever you can take by force or by ingenuity. Might makes right." This idea was put into practice in the age-long armed struggle for thrones, in the enslaving of millions

FIG. 71. The age-long struggle for property

of men conquered in battle. It was revealed in the cruel devastating wars of the "absolutist" kings. It was shown in the exploits of the pirates of the seaways and the robber knights of the land highways. Even today it is illustrated in the organized gangs of our cities and in the dishonest practices of some of our politicians.

For tens of thousands of years the private ownership of property, established by force and cleverness, even included the

FIG. 72. A middle-class family of property in the 1700's. Compare with figure 60. What differences do you see between these two families? (From a painting by Hogarth. Courtesy of the National Gallery, London)

ownership of human beings. Until the nineteenth century — in fact, until within the past three quarters of a century — human beings were regarded as property. They were bought and sold as were horses and cows, land and trees, houses and implements. Recall to mind the enslaving of the Negro in America until 1863, as well as the enslaving of millions of white men, women, and children as serfs on the landed estates of Russia. Thus ages passed while man was evolving an idea that to us, who are accustomed to it, seems to be obvious — namely, that human beings are not property.

But in the meantime there has been much hard thinking, much controversial debate, indeed, much shedding of blood and much human suffering, over the question *How shall property be owned?* Most owners of property themselves have been inclined to answer, "Privately" . . . "For private profit." Some impartial frontier thinkers have drawn the same conclusion. But among other scientific students of society there has been an increasing tendency to propose that many things should be owned publicly, communally.

What is meant by "public ownership"?

To understand the long struggle over the control of property we must comprehend clearly what is meant by "private ownership" and "public ownership." To do so look about you in your own community. What kinds of property are owned and operated publicly — that is, by the community as a whole?

Several very important things are so owned. Consider, for example, the water-supply system. In most communities of the United States and of England, France, Germany, and other Western countries, reservoirs, pipe lines, pumping stations — the water works as a whole — are owned and operated by the community. Each house-owner or house-renter pays a certain amount for water supplied from the public reservoir to his home. The amounts charged are supposed to cover merely the actual cost of storing, purifying, and delivering the water. Thus a community's water supply is a good example of communal or public ownership. No private profit is expected to be made from its management.

The public streets, parks, and playgrounds are also owned by the community as a whole. Every man, woman, and child has the right to walk or drive upon the streets, or play upon the playgrounds. Similarly, public libraries, museums, town or city halls, police and fire stations, and the like are owned by the community as a whole, and operated in the interest of the people. The people of the community, through taxes of one kind or another, contribute to the establishment and upkeep of these public enterprises, but no individual is supposed to make a profit out of their maintenance.

In the same way a state or a whole nation owns and operates

some things. The postal system is an example of national ownership. In the United States, England, France, Germany, and other countries the postal service is owned and operated publicly. This is carried on by officials who are servants of the people as a whole. Their office buildings and their work facilities, such as automobiles, trucks, and clerical equipment, are owned by the nation as a whole.

The examples given illustrate collective, or communal, ownership. Each of these enterprises is supposed to be carried on at a minimum cost to all the people. No single person is supposed to make a private profit from them.

Most things are still owned privately

We have named but a few examples of public ownership. As you have learned, most things and most services are owned privately and carried on for private profit. In the United States, for example, although water is owned publicly, in most communities the land, either farm land or city land for residence, trade, or manufacturing, is owned privately. Farming, mining, manufacturing, and trade are also owned privately. Although the postal system is owned publicly, transportation and other communication systems — railroads, ships, telegraphs, telephones, and radio — are owned privately. Thus *the means of production and distribution of food, shelter, and clothing are owned privately* in the United States.

In some European countries, notably in France and Germany, railroads, telegraphs, and telephones are owned by the national governments. Thus there are differences among countries with respect to the ownership of some of the public utilities.

We need not multiply cases further. Enough of them have been presented to illustrate the meaning of public ownership and operation as contrasted with private ownership for private profit. It is important to understand this distinction clearly, because it has been the chief problem of controversy among frontier thinkers and political leaders for several hundred years. It is not an exaggeration to say that Europe's march toward democracy has depended upon the settlement of the questions Which things should be owned publicly? Which should be owned privately?

How Leading Frontier Thinkers proposed to solve the Difficult Problems of Government

They began to use the scientific method

In the 300 years that have passed since Galileo and Francis Bacon, many talented minds have attempted to devise more effective schemes of government for the modern nations. These minds have tried to apply the scientific method to problems of political and social life as Copernicus, Galileo, Descartes, Isaac Newton, and a host of other men were doing in the study of the physical world.

Fig. 73. Physical scientists of the 1700's paved the way for the conquest of the air. (Courtesy of the Smithsonian Institution)

After 1700 these students were inspired and aided by the growing group of clear-thinking physical scientists. We must not forget that no sooner had Newton, Descartes, and Leibnitz invented their clever schemes of mathematics and physical science than successors appeared who carried their discoveries much further.

For example, this was the infancy of the age of electricity. The American, Benjamin Franklin (1706–1790), was discovering that lightning is a manifestation of electricity. Alessandro Volta (1745–1827) and Luigi Galvani (1737–1798) were making their great discoveries in electricity. Perhaps you have heard electricians speak of "voltaic cells," which are named for this same Volta, or tinsmiths refer to "galvanized iron," named for Galvani. It was at this time that Joseph Priestley (1733–1804), Antoine L. Lavoisier (1743–1794), and others were discovering oxygen and other chemical elements, and building up the foundations of our modern science of chemistry. Explorers were also adding to our knowledge of the earth. The voyages of Captain James Cook (1728–1779), both in the Arctic and in the South Seas, were revealing regions about which little had been known in Europe.

We must bear in mind that once the scientific method was adopted (about 1600) it began to be applied to every aspect of the physical and human world. First the physical universe was studied by means of it. Then the plant and animal worlds were brought under its scrutiny. And after 1700, students began to think scientifically about the problems of government, industry, business, and social life generally.

François Quesnay and the Philosophy of *Laissez Faire*

About the middle of the 1700's there emerged in France and England men who proposed new solutions for the difficult problems of government. The movement started in the court of the French king, Louis XV, under the leadership of a middle-class physician named François Quesnay. Quesnay was investigating the general conditions under which a nation's wealth could become greatest. He and others were debating to what extent the government of a country should control what private capitalists did. They asked such questions as Who should be taxed — farmers? owners of land? manufacturers? merchants? artisans?

As a result of their inquiries Quesnay and his associates advanced a new idea about taxation; namely, that it is only the farmers and miners who produce real goods and thereby add to a nation's wealth. Manufacturers and merchants merely buy and sell, transport and exchange goods; they do not produce new "real" things. Hence, these new political economists said, tax only the farmers and the miners. Leave manufacturers and merchants free to compete with one another as they please. The authors of the new idea coined a simple slogan which epitomized their philosophy,— *laissez faire,*— which, being freely translated, means "Let them do as they will."

Adam Smith's *Wealth of Nations* presented a more complete statement of the philosophy of *laissez faire*

The work of these new political economists was given widespread recognition in an epoch-making book that was to be read throughout the entire intellectual world of Europe and America, a book heralded by politicians and business men alike as a political classic. This was Adam Smith's *Inquiry into the Nature and Causes of the Wealth of Nations,* known more generally as *The Wealth of Nations.*

Fig. 74. Adam Smith (1723–1790). (After a medallion by Tassiel)

Smith was a professor of moral philosophy in the University of Glasgow, Scotland. He had studied the ideas of Quesnay and the new political economists, accepted many of the essential ones, and presented them, together with his own theories, in his systematic and historic book. One historian, commenting on the fact that *The Wealth of Nations* appeared in 1776, the same year as the American Declaration of Independence, described it as a "declaration of independence for industry."

"Leave every person free to compete with every other person in taking all the land, coal, iron, oil, forests, and other natural resources which his initiative and intelligence permit him to take," was the basic idea of Smith's book. Let business, industry, and agriculture be unrestricted by government, said Smith, and the greatest wealth will be produced for the nation. In this way, he said, the collective life of a people can be carried on most effectively. Upon this principle high standards of living for a people will result.

As you can readily understand, this idea was eagerly taken up by the merchants and manufacturers in England and on the continents of Europe and North America. If adopted it would give them a free hand to develop their business. To make a short story of a long one, it was adopted generally. It became the basic economic principle upon which the westward settlement of American land developed in the 1700's and 1800's. Upon this fundamental principle coal, iron, and other mineral land was taken and exploited by the first discoverers. This idea of unrestricted competition of private owners was the one upon which hundreds of millions of acres of forests were cut down. It was the basic idea upon which oil was squandered in America, in the Near East, and in Asia. With this slogan English business men, French business men, Italian business men,—in fact, the business men of every European country (except Russia today) and of the industrialized countries of Asia, Africa, and Latin America,—developed their modern enterprises.

Can you not see the very great importance of the idea in developing modern industry, business, agriculture — and government?

In the 1700's Talented Writers attacked the Inequalities among Men

In the discussion and theorizing of Quesnay, Smith, and their followers, there was little questioning of the idea of private ownership. That principle was accepted — indeed, assumed implicitly. Land, mines, factories, means of transport, selling agencies — all were to be owned by individuals, by private citizens who were to be left free and unrestricted to compete with one another for the world's goods.

But Adam Smith and the new political economists represented only one group among the thinking men of the period. Opposed to them was a steadily increasing group of more radical thinkers. Their minds were grappling with the two problems which we have been considering: (1) How should property be owned? (2) What form of government will best represent all the people?

These more independent critics comprised a twofold group. On the one hand there were literary men — essayists, novelists, satirists — who lashed out at the evils and the unfair practices of the times; and on the other, scholarly students of government and economics.

Again came the slogan "Think things out for yourself"

In the 1600's and repeatedly in the 1700's the clarion call of the earlier physical scientists was sounded for the study of government and social life. Two writers stood out above all the others for their courageous attack upon the idea of people living without some share in solving the problems of their collective affairs.

John Locke, English student of government psychology and education

The first was the Englishman John Locke (1632–1704), son of a soldier in Oliver Cromwell's army. He was well-educated, a graduate of the English university of Oxford. He was brought up in the midst of the most revolutionary period in England's long history — the period of the Commonwealth. After the collapse of the republic in 1660, being an advocate of democratic ideas he was compelled to live in exile in Holland for some years.

Locke influenced thinking in those strenuous times by means of several important books. The most famous are his *Two Treatises on Civil Government* and his psychological and educational books, especially the essay *On the Conduct of the Understanding*.

In his scholarly studies of government Locke advanced a revolutionary idea, — an idea which has recurred again and again in the march of the peoples of the world toward democracy. This was the principle that sound and progressive government can be developed only by the consent of those who are governed. Government will fail, said Locke, unless it is so designed that the will of the people as a whole is represented.

Here, then, is the principle of consent, upon which the American government has been built. This idea of Locke's is the same principle of consent that lay behind the struggle of the backwoodsmen of the North American colonies for 150 years. It was the guiding idea of the revolt of the common people against the captains of industry who controlled the government after 1870. This is the same idea that Abraham Lincoln had in mind when he wrote his famous phrase "government of the people, by the people, for the people." And here, indeed, is the basic idea of those who brought about the French Revolution in 1789 with the slogan "Liberty, Equality, Fraternity."

Locke was more than a creative student of government. He was also a student of psychology and education. Some, indeed, have regarded him as the first modern psychologist. For Locke broke definitely with the teachings of the Church about human understanding and was one of the first to apply the scientific method to the study of the human mind. The Church had taught that man's capacity to see with his eyes, hear with his ears, feel with his sense of touch, think with his mind, was bestowed on him by God; that he could think thoughts and achieve acts only through the grace of God. The new psychological scientists (notably Locke and a bishop, William Berkeley) maintained, however, that we inherit our capacity to see, hear, feel, touch, and think from our elders, and that we develop these capacities through contact with our environment. They described the "psychology of growth" as the response of a human being to the world about him. Two hundred years later experimental psychologists were to prove the essential truth of Locke's contention.

Fig. 75. John Locke (1632–1704)

Thus even before 1700, under the leadership of John Locke, men began to apply to the study of human behavior the scientific method of observing the world and thinking principles out for oneself. The idea, also, of experimenting rather than of accepting one's fate on the mere say-so of persons in official authority was again applied to government and to social behavior. And thus was laid a little more of the groundwork for the world's march toward democracy.

Then in the 1700's came Voltaire, urging allegiance to "him who masters our minds by the force of truth, not to those who enslave men by violence"

In almost every age the world has produced powerful thinkers who have helped to destroy the abuses, the useless ceremonials, and vicious class distinctions of their time. Such a creator of discontent with the authority of absolute monarchs was François Marie Arouet (1694–1778), known in his later years and throughout history by the name he gave himself — Voltaire.

Voltaire was not a *constructive* political economist, nor a careful student of government or business. He was a destructive antagonist of every aspect of life which seemed to him to enslave man. In a long lifetime of prodigious work he produced "a hundred volumes." In comedies and in tragedies, in epic poems, in "histories of civilization," with biting sarcasm he satirized the luxurious extravagances and the scandalous behavior of the kings and nobles of Europe. He was a determined opponent of the Church, which he regarded as an enemy of social welfare and human progress. Year after year he ridiculed the ceremonial of the Church and urged men to think out their religion for themselves, not to take it on authority.

As a result Voltaire was constantly in danger of imprisonment and bodily attack, even of exile. Like many another critic of government and of the Church in those times, he lived close to the frontier, where he could slip quickly across the border in case his attacks upon the kings and bishops should provoke retaliation. Thus he was constantly on the move. When things became too unpleasant for him in France, he moved to Prussia. There he lived in Berlin for a time as the protected friend of the Prussian despot, Frederick the Great. Even there, however, his tongue got the better of his discretion, and after a short time he left. Even in Switzerland he incurred the enmity of the magistrates of Geneva.

There was one government in Europe that he admired most of all — the parliamentary government which he saw evolving in England during his three years' stay there. There it was that he became greatly attracted to Isaac Newton and the ideas of the physical scientists. Indeed, he said that he worshiped Newton for the independent thinking which had brought about his discovery of the law of gravitation. The three years in England also built up in him a great respect for the business middle class which had then risen to power. His disdain of the idling nobles of

FIG. 76. A noonday meal at the palace of Frederick the Great during Voltaire's visit to that despot. Frederick is facing you, and Voltaire is second at his right. (From a painting by Adolph Menzel)

Europe and his admiration for the business man of England and elsewhere is shown in the following quotation from his writings:

> I am not sure that the merchant who enriches his country, gives orders from his countinghouse at Surat or Cairo, and contributes to the happiness of the globe is not more useful to a state than the thickly bepowdered lord who knows exactly what time the king rises and what time he goes to bed, and gives himself mighty airs of greatness while he plays the part of a slave in the minister's anteroom.

Through his vitriolic satire Voltaire spread discontent among the reading classes of Europe for many years. Although he preached the substitution of scientific thinking for reverence for authority, not once did he offer constructive suggestions for rebuilding society; his task seemed to be to destroy the evils of the old, dying one.

At the age of 84 this international scoffer returned to Paris. He was received by the populace with cheers of flattering admiration. By that time (1778) he had become known as the intellectual dictator of Europe,—hated, feared, and admired more, perhaps, than any other single man on the Continent.

Rousseau offers constructive suggestions for government and ownership of property

Then came Jean Jacques Rousseau (1712–1778), the man who may be said to have influenced Europe's march toward democracy more than any other single person of modern times.

The recital of the bare facts of Rousseau's personal life gives little indication of the powerful influence which the man exerted through his writing. He was a wandering ne'er-do-well, a failure at every occupation he followed. In Switzerland, France, Italy, Prussia, England, he wandered from place to place, working as household servant, as liveried footman, as tutor for youthful noble heirs and heiresses, as secretary to lords, as a copier of musical notation.

Scarcely any fine qualities can be revealed in his personal life. He was notorious for his unfaithfulness and his immorality. One might comment, too, on his inconsistency in deserting his own five children and permitting them to be brought up in a foundling asylum while he wrote one of the greatest educational books in modern history.

Nevertheless, through several books he brought to the modern world a new outlook on life, new insight into psychology and education, and a clearer and sounder understanding of the ownership of property and of government among men.

It was in two books that Rousseau's stimulating ideas about government and the ownership of property were presented to the intelligent reading public of the Western world. The first was an important essay, *What is the Origin of Inequality among Men?* (1753); the second was *The Social Contract* (1761). In these he turned his pen to the analysis of government and the organization of society. In the first he stated the principle of the tremendous individual differences among men. Some are strong and others are weak; some are talented and have great intellectual ability, others are mediocre in power of thought; still others are dull, unable to solve even simple problems.

Furthermore, some of those who are strong and very intelligent are also ambitious and greedy. It was these intelligent, ambitious, greedy men who had developed society as it was then organized in Europe. That society was based upon the principles that might makes right. Rousseau said that, in a society like that of Europe, the strong tyrannized over the weak. Greed "for the profit of a few ambitious men" had "subjected thenceforth all the human race to labor, servitude, and misery." Therefore, said Rousseau, society must find some way of controlling the strong, some way of restricting their ambitions so that they will not oppress the weak. In this little essay, then, is a statement of one of our most fundamental democratic theories.

That essay appeared in 1753. Eight years passed, filled with more wandering, more living close to nature, much discussion of government, law, and the reorganization of society. Then, in 1761, came *The Social Contract*, which has become famous in political history. The essay begins with these words:

> Man is born free and yet is now everywhere in chains. One man believes himself the master of others and yet is after all more of a slave than they. How did this change come about? I do not know. What can render it legitimate? I believe that I can answer that question.

Rousseau answers it by declaring that government can rightly be based only upon the will of all the people. He presents a theory that a social contract had been made among peoples in early civilizations in which they bound themselves to be governed "only by their own consent." *The only true sovereign* in any country *is the will of the people.* Every act of government, therefore, must be for the people, in the interest of the people, and not "for the profit of a few ambitious men."

What kind of government will tend to bring that about? Certainly not absolute monarchy, said Rousseau. A republic appealed to him as giving the best chance for the people to make their own laws by popular vote. Rousseau, like Voltaire, was also attracted to the experiment in parliamentary government which was then developing in England. A republic, he said, would respond more easily to the will of the people than any other imaginable form of government.

In Rousseau's writings can be found a development of the central ideas of Locke's principle of government by the *consent* of the governed. Here we find Rousseau advocating even a larger popular share in the government — government by the *will* of the people, the people being conceived as the true sovereigns.

Fig. 77. The last days of Rousseau. Here he is shown with his wife at his home in Montmorency

Rousseau's books were printed and reprinted, read and reread, by a curious mixture of people. They were read by the lords and ladies of the courts, by the intellectuals of the universities and the churches, and by the rising leaders of the middle class. They directly influenced the young group of city leaders who shortly were to rise and throw off the autocratic rule of the French court.

Let us add one word concerning Rousseau's influence on other aspects of social life. He played as important a part in the development of modern ideas of education as of government and economic life. In a great educational treatise, *Émile,* issued about the same time as *The Social Contract,* he set forth his ideas of "natural" education. Instead of imposing education artificially upon children, as the schools of Europe did at that time, and as many schools in the modern world still continue to do, he would fit education to the child's nature. In this sense Rousseau was the great forerunner of John Dewey and other pioneers who are developing progressive schools today.[1]

Thus, along with the development of scientific ways of thinking about the natural and physical world, the attention of thinking men was turning to the problems of political and social life. Not until the great Industrial Revolution, however, did the ideas of these frontier thinkers permeate the masses. We shall see in the next chapter how these changes took place.

INTERESTING READINGS FROM WHICH YOU CAN GET ADDITIONAL INFORMATION

BRIDGES, T. C. The Young Folk's Book of Discovery. Little, Brown and Company, Boston. The age of exploration and discovery.

HOLLAND, RUPERT S. Drake's Lad. The Century Co., New York. The adventures of a lad who sailed with Drake.

KELLY, MARGARET D. The Story of Sir Walter Raleigh (Children's Heroes Series). E. P. Dutton & Co., New York.

KINGSLEY, CHARLES. Westward Ho! The Macmillan Company, New York. The spirit of adventure and exploration.

LANG, JOHN. The Story of Captain Cook (Children's Heroes Series). E. P. Dutton & Co., New York.

MACY, JOHN A. The Story of the World's Literature. Horace Liveright, New York. See Chapter XIX.

ROBINSON, JAMES HARVEY, and BEARD, CHARLES A. The Development of Modern Europe (Completely Revised and Enlarged Edition). Ginn and Company, Boston. See Volume I, Chapter VIII.

[1] In considering only Locke, Voltaire, and Rousseau as leaders who paved the way for more democratic experiments, we must not forget that other constructive thinkers also helped uproot the evils of European society and absolutism in government. Were there space at least two other constructive thinkers would be discussed. The first is Montesquieu (1689–1755), a French noble who made important studies of the law. In two famous books, *Persian Letters* (1721) and *The Spirit of the Laws* (1748), he insisted that government must be designed to fit the peculiar needs of each nation. Many of Montesquieu's ideas were incorporated later into the Constitution of the United States.

The other was Denis Diderot (1713–1784), the director and editor of the great *Encyclopedia.* This was a seventeen-volume monument of learning, written by the most scholarly Europeans in the fields of science, mathematics, philosophy, and government. It was more than a storehouse of knowledge; it was also a courageous and honest criticism of existing institutions. It went far toward helping men to dispel their superstitions and misconceptions of the world by giving them "scientifically established" facts about it. The *Encyclopedia* was suppressed by the French government of Louis XV because of its frank criticism of the Church, of government, and of social life. Diderot and his associates were known as the Encyclopedists.

CHAPTER IX

HOW "FRONTIER THINKERS" DIRECTED THE WORLD'S MARCH TOWARD DEMOCRACY (CONTINUED)

THE BEGINNINGS OF THE INDUSTRIAL REVOLUTION

As the years of the eighteenth century passed, the criticism of government and of the inequalities among men increased, and plans for alleviating the evils began to be proposed. To understand these changes, let us review what was happening during this period of the Industrial Revolution.

The first step was the invention of practicable machines and engines.[1] As early as 1690 the Frenchman Denis Papin had discovered the principle of the piston and the cylinder, which is the basis of the modern engine. In 1698 Captain Thomas Savery had constructed a crude steam engine. In 1705 this had been much improved by Thomas Newcomen's "fire engine," a machine that would pump water from the iron and coal mines of England effectively and cheaply. But the real Industrial Revolution started 60 years later, after the Scotch instrument-maker James Watt, while repairing a Newcomen engine, succeeded in producing the first really practicable steam engine.

In the meantime effective machines were being invented to do the work of human muscles in manufacturing goods. John Kay invented the fly shuttle in 1733. Richard Arkwright patented his "waterpower-driven spinning frame" in 1769, and Hargreaves his spinning jenny in 1770. Samuel Crompton combined these earlier inventions in the so-called Crompton "spinning mule" in 1779, and in 1785 Edmund C. Cartwright succeeded in driving a loom by water power. Shortly after, in 1793, on the other side of the Atlantic, Eli Whitney, an American school-

[1] At this point it would be well to read Chapters III and IV of *Changing Civilizations in the Modern World*; also Chapters VII and XII of *An Introduction to American Civilization.*

teacher, produced a practicable cotton gin with which raw cotton could be cleaned with great rapidity. Thus the Industrial Revolution got under way.

You know the story of these events and the swift transformation in the production of all kinds of goods which took place especially after 1800. You know that British spinners, weavers, shoemakers, and ironworkers left their spinning wheels, hand looms, shoemakers' benches, and iron forges, and went to work for wages in factories. Fourteen to sixteen hours a day they huddled together in noisy, filthy workrooms, little children and women as well as able-bodied men working at exhausting labor. Day in, day out, week in, week out, with few holidays, they slaved for a miserable pittance.

As these things happened the population of cities grew by leaps and bounds. Hamlets and villages disappeared as the people drifted into the manufacturing towns. Even by 1800 Leeds, Birmingham, Liverpool, and Manchester had become large cities ranging from 50,000 to 100,000 inhabitants. As industry grew, railroads and canals were built and the steam locomotive was made practicable. The whole face of the countryside changed. Coal-mining cities grew up near rich deposits of coal. Little iron forges became the iron and steel mills of great industrial centers.

Recall also the social changes that were brought about by this Industrial Revolution. The people of England were divided more sharply than ever into economic and social classes. The capitalist system had begun even before 1500, but the industrial capitalist who appeared in the late 1700's and the 1800's was more important than ever before. Consider Richard Arkwright, for example, the man who started the first modern textile factory. No sooner had he built one successful factory, using his water frame, than he started others, hiring foremen and managers for his various mills. Within a few years he had become a millionaire and had considerable influence in politics. Then George III made him a knight — "Sir" Richard Arkwright.

Arkwright was merely a single example of the hundreds of capitalists who organized the new industrial enterprises. To understand what took place in England in the late 1700's and throughout the 1800's, one needs merely to recall the corresponding industrial expansion in the United States. A few energetic, intelligent business leaders built up vast fortunes, while the mass of the people remained in comparative poverty.

Other distressing economic problems were brought about by the Industrial Revolution. One of these was the problem of unemployment. In the first years of machine invention thousands of craftsmen were thrown out of work. Rioting was common in the growing towns and cities. Starving weavers and other craftsmen smashed the new machines which were taking away their means of a livelihood. Thousands of paupers lived on government help. Poor people who could not pay their bills were imprisoned in workhouses, and their children were compelled to work as slaves in factories. Laws were so inhumane that until the early 1800's more than 200 offenses, many of them of a minor character, were still punishable by death.

These, then, were the new industrial conditions that developed about the turn of the nineteenth century. These are the conditions which must be borne in mind in considering the proposals of the frontier thinkers for the development of more democratic kinds of government.

Poverty of the Masses led to Philanthropic Experiments in Socialized Government

Then, about 1800, came experiments in community government. For more than a century frontier thinkers had theorized, talked, and written books about the ownership of property and how to set up more democratic kinds of government. For more than a century humanitarian leaders in the wealthier classes had increasingly questioned the unequal distribution of wealth. But it was not until the early 1800's, when the new power-driven machines had produced the foul tenement slums and the filthy and noisy factories, that men began to act upon the ideas of these leaders. Then theories were actually tried out, even though slowly and only in isolated experimental communities.

It was to be expected that the first experiments would be little more than benevolent business philanthropies. They were experiments of the masters rather than of the workmen. That the workmen were muttering among themselves is well known. But they were uneducated and did not understand even the rudiments of government. Furthermore, they were unorganized and lacked the means of bargaining collectively with the masters. Indeed, they were prevented from doing so by the very laws of the land. A few wealthy business men, however, began the experiments with new communities.

1. Robert Owen's experimental communities

The first of the philanthropists to experiment actively with more socialized ways of owning property was the British inventor and factory-owner, Robert Owen (1771–1858). While still a young man, Owen had made successful improvements for cotton-spinning machinery, had built and managed factories, and had accumulated a small fortune. While working shoulder to shoulder with his employees, he became impressed with the need for vast improvement in working conditions and for a more equitable division of the returns from industry and business. He saw that the owners and the managers of factories and farms received most of the financial returns, while the workers did not receive even enough to enable them to live decently.

Determined to try out some new ideas, he and several other small capitalists built an experimental mill community of about 2000 workers at New Lanark, Scotland.

Within a few years New Lanark became famous all over Europe as a model industrial community. Owen's experiment seized the minds of thinking people everywhere. Dukes and princes, lords and ladies, theorists, factory-owners, and new industrialists visited the community. Many went away loud in their admiration of results. Even conservative newspapers like *The Times* and the *Morning Post*, of London, supported Owen in his proposal that industries should be developed all over Europe in small communities patterned after New Lanark.

Owen and other socializers of property foresaw that industrial civilization would spread rapidly over Europe and America, and perhaps into other continents. Unless the movement was forestalled very soon, the condition of the great factory cities of

England would be duplicated elsewhere. He believed that New Lanark could be used as a model for the setting up of thousands of *little* communities, of about 1200 inhabitants each, practically self-supporting, with farm land, buildings, implements, factories, machines, engines, and the like being owned "communally," that is, by the community. He believed that if this were done, the evils of the growing factory cities could be done away with. He cites the fine results obtained at New Lanark, summing them up in these words:

FIG. 78. Robert Owen. (1771–1858)

> For 29 years we did without the necessity for magistrates or lawyers; without a single legal punishment; without any known poor rates; without intemperance or religious animosities. We reduced the hours of labor, well educated all the children from infancy, greatly improved the condition of the adults, diminished their daily labour, paid interest on capital, and cleared upwards of £300,000 of profit.

Robert Owen threw himself into the campaign to extend his model-community idea around the world. He wrote pamphlets, made speeches, and helped establish other socialized communities at Orbiston, Scotland, at Tytherley, England, and at Ralahine, Ireland. He even founded a community in America. Gathering a considerable group of workers together, he crossed the Atlantic to the United States, joined some westward-bound immigrants, and established a settlement at New Harmony, Indiana.

In the meantime, under the forceful campaign of Owen and his associates and in spite of the selfish opposition of factory-owners generally, the British Parliament finally passed the first Factory Act, 1819. This law was a pioneer step in the regulation of the way in which industrial capitalists might manage their property. Compared with the laws upon the statute books of

England and other countries today, it was feeble, indeed; but it was important because it was a first step in what was to be more than a century of new social legislation.

Especially was it important because it was the first attempt to control child labor by law. Let us not forget that up to 1819 little children worked in factories as wage slaves, often fourteen or sixteen hours a day. The Factory Act of 1819 prohibited *children under nine years of age from working more than twelve hours a day*! A feeble beginning, indeed! But it was the beginning of a continuous effort to free the children of the poor from industrial slavery and ignorance. As one historian has said, it was the "Magna Carta of childhood."

Owen's experiment at New Lanark succeeded as long as he remained on the spot to guide it. But as success came to him, he became interested in other social problems. Among other things he made severe attacks upon the evils of the organized church and radical suggestions for changing marriage relations and other social conventions. As the years passed he made enemies on every hand. Conservatives in every walk of life — factory-owners, outraged churchmen, and citizens — joined hands to discredit the experimenter and his socialized communities.

In 1828 Owen's partners in the New Lanark community bought out his share. For a time this and the other experimental communities survived. But misunderstandings and jealousies gradually arose among the settlers. There was lack of clear thinking about the questions of what should be owned communally and what personally. Social difficulties of various types arose, and so, one by one, Owen's communal experiments failed.

But Robert Owen and his socialized communities had builded better than they knew. Though they failed ultimately, they had provided the Western world with concrete materials for thinking about the public ownership of property. They had achieved beginnings in the practical working out of coöperative ownership. Out of their experiments developed later the movement for coöperative stores, a plan which spread through England and other countries with great steadiness and stability. Beginnings had also been achieved in more humane legislation for the improving of conditions of work. Courage to carry on the march toward democracy had been given to the leaders of industrial workers everywhere. And last, but by no means least, social experiments were actually being launched. Roger Bacon's command "Look at the world! Experiment!" was being carried out 600 years after his time.[1]

2. Other experimental communities

At the same time other plans for model communities were being developed in France and new experiments were being tried in America. In France there were the somewhat visionary theorists, Count Henri de Saint-Simon (1760–1825) and François Marie Fourier (1772–1837). Saint-Simon tried to get Louis XVIII to support a movement to build a new industrial society with scientific thinkers in charge. Fourier devised another plan for the joint ownership of property. His plan, like Owen's, was to set up small farming and manufacturing communities of from 1500 to 2000 persons, with buildings, machinery, tools, land, and the like owned jointly. Profits were to be divided, the largest share going to labor, the next largest to capital, and a smaller proportion to the organizing and managing minds of the community.

In America as well as in Europe many thinking people were influenced by these plans of Owen, Saint-Simon, Fourier, and others. You have probably read of the communist experiments of the Massachusetts group — Bronson Alcott, George Ripley, and others. These unpractical people tried several times to establish communal settlements, but their attempts also failed.

One community experiment, however, succeeded in a rather unusual manner. This was the Oneida Community (1845–1881), at Oneida, New York. It illustrated the importance of having a clear-thinking, hard-working dynamic leader in charge. The Oneida community lasted for 36 years, largely because of the intelligence and industry of John Humphrey Noyes. Under his leadership Oneida became prosperous, accumulated large amounts of property, and developed into a strong business corporation. It paid large dividends and became respected in the business world. But in 1881 it too was dissolved.

[1] It is not too much to say that the model communities which exist in various countries today are the descendants of Robert Owen's experiments.

Thus, sooner or later, all these socialized communities failed. Many factors contributed to their lack of success. Jealousies and friction arose among their members; there was lack of careful planning; but, probably more than anything else, there was inability to think through the complicated problems of public and private ownership of property. Not enough insight had come to the Western world in the 1830's and 1840's to answer the ever-pressing questions What should be owned privately? What should be owned publicly? How can all the people be given a full share in carrying on government?

Fig. 79. Louis Blanc (1811–1882)

3. Louis Blanc and his social workshops: his proposals for government ownership

By the 1840's still other proposals for the socialization of the ownership of property and of government were being made. One of the most important came from Louis Blanc (1811–1882), a talented Parisian journalist, who proposed a kind of government ownership of industry. He suggested that the national government should go into the manufacturing business, creating many little social workshops. The employees of each shop should select their own managers, organize their factory, and receive their wages in the form of a division of profits. The scheme was the forerunner of many later proposals for state capitalism. In this plan the state, rather than any private owner, becomes a capitalist, building plants, railroads, warehouses, and the like, and letting the workers of each community organize their own enterprises.

Blanc's influence among the workingmen of northern France was very great. His writings and his leadership among the trade-unions of the 1840's played a large part in bringing about the widespread revolutionary movement of 1848. Others regard his proposals as the beginning of the movement which eventually led to the government ownership of public utilities in some European countries.

Out of these experiments and other movements grew socialism

Those who originated or defended these communal experiments were often attacked and derided as visionary dreamers whose plans were quite impracticable. Robert Owen and his associates were frequently called by their opponents "Utopians"[1] or "Utopian socialists." As years passed such plans for reorganizing society were called indiscriminately socialism. As we continue our studies, however, we must distinguish their proposals from what is known as socialism today. These early plans were paternal, built up by rich or moderately well-to-do capitalists in the interest of helping the workers. They were masters' movements, not workers' movements.

Need increasingly recognized for the universal education of workers

To build up a permanent and truly democratic society required something the world had never yet provided, namely, *universal education* — education not merely in "reading, writing, and reckoning," of which there was a little even in the years from 1825 to 1850, but *education in thinking* about industry, about government, about the ownership of property, about community life. Historians, looking back over the past century of struggles over problems of democracy, can see that the people in the experimental communities and the labor unions of the early 1800's were not ready for democracy. They lacked the education necessary even to *understand* their current problems, let alone to *solve* them. Not one in ten could read and write well. Even elementary education was far from universal, and such as there was had little to do with the real lives of the people.

[1] Visionaries or idealists, so called from Sir Thomas More's book *Utopia*. Utopia is the name of an imaginary island where a state of ideal perfection existed.

The Workers began to Organize: the First Trade Unions

In one sense the education of adult workers was actually developing in the early 1800's. This took place not in formal schools, but in workingmen's associations. The new industrial conditions of the larger cities were bringing this about. In the growing manufacturing cities of the United States, in the period between 1800 and 1825, mechanics in the various trades were forming clubs. It was in these same years that similar organizations were formed in England, to be followed soon after by others in France and Germany.

The great need of the workers was to join together for the purpose of bargaining collectively with their employers. As we have already learned, when the craftsman left his home craft and went to work in the factories, he lost his power of deciding independently the conditions under which he would work. The individual workman was completely at the mercy of the capitalist employer, who dictated hours of labor, wages, and working conditions in the factory. The worker had to take what the employer offered him or starve.

But manufacturing cities grew in England, France, and Germany as they did in the United States — in England even more rapidly than elsewhere. As they did so, the same conditions of social discontent arose. As workmen were herded together in factories and tenements, they talked together about their grievances. More and more they began to demand their rights.

The Declaration of Rights in the British, American, and French constitutions helped them to phrase their desires. Educated and intelligent leaders developed among them and organized them into clubs, societies, or associations. These leaders saw that one man alone was unable to obtain what he regarded as his rights, but that many together could bargain effectively. *United* they could obtain short hours of labor, decently high wages, and healthful working conditions. And, at first, that was practically all that they demanded; there was little thought of the right to vote or to hold office in government. The demand for political liberty came somewhat later.

In the early 1800's, even in England, laborers were prevented by law from combining in order "to raise prices or wages." So, for many years, workmen organized secret societies, social clubs, and the like, masking the real trade-union purposes of their organizations. As employers became even more harsh in their handling of labor, as they attacked these societies, and as many timid workers refused to join them, the conflict sharpened between employers and employees.

Robert Owen and other leaders took sides with the workers, demanding changes in legislation which would permit trade-unions. Largely as a result of their efforts, the British Parliament repealed the law which prohibited workmen from joining together. A year later a new law was passed which definitely allowed the formation of unions "to determine the scale of wages or hours of labor." But even that law hampered the labor organizations, for it was still an offense against society to strike. Thus workers could only organize, talk, hold meetings, confer with owners, and ask for changes. They still lacked the real power needed to obtain what they regarded as their rights. They still lacked the power to vote and to control government.

From this time on, however, trade-unions developed rapidly in England and somewhat later spread to France, Germany, and all other countries which had adopted machine manufacturing.

Karl Marx, Friedrich Engels, and Modern Socialism

This was the condition of the working classes in Europe when important leaders arose who not only helped to organize unions, but who also thought hard about the basic problems beneath these signs of workers' distress. Outstanding among them were two western Europeans, Karl Marx (1818–1883) and Friedrich Engels (1820–1895).

Karl Marx was the son of a lawyer who lived at Trier, near the border between France and Germany. He was a brilliant youth, educated in the classics and in modern literature, trained at the universities of Bonn and Berlin. In 1841 he received a degree of doctor of philosophy in history and philosophy from the University of Jena. Through the influence of Georg Wilhelm Friedrich Hegel, professor of philosophy and a world-renowned writer upon the philosophy of history, Marx became very much interested in the history of civilization. Through studying with Hegel, Marx became convinced that a clear understanding of current problems could be obtained only by the study of the history of man's institutions; for example, in order to understand how to plan better governments, one should study the history of government in the rise and fall of civilizations. One central idea of Hegel's helped him especially to formulate his

FIG. 80. Friedrich Engels (1820–1895)

FIG. 81. Karl Marx (1818–1883)

later theory of socialism. This was the idea that the history of the world shows men slowly but steadily advancing from a condition of unintelligent slavery under despotic rulers to one where they controlled, by reason, their own destiny.

On leaving the university Marx plunged into journalism and edited the *Rheinische Zeitung*. He made it a frankly liberal newspaper and openly criticized the Prussian government. In 1843 the government suspended the journal, prevented Marx from getting the university position to which he aspired, and, because of his campaign for freedom of speech, compelled him to leave the country.

Marx turned to Paris, long the cosmopolitan center of culture and now the haven of exiled liberals. For two years, 1843–1845, he made a meager living by writing and editing the journal *Vorwärts*. It was in Paris that Marx met Louis Blanc, who was then organizing mechanics and laborers and agitating for his social workshops. He became acquainted with Proudhon and Bakunin, of whom we shall hear shortly as the founders of another school of thinking about government and property. In Paris Marx studied Robert Owen's plans for experimental communities. There too he met Goethe, the great poet, and joined a group of creative literary men. In Paris, also, Marx came into first-hand contact with labor problems. He went into factories and studied working conditions. He helped organize the workers, wrote pamphlets and editorials, and spoke at meetings.

And it was in Paris that Marx met Friedrich Engels. Engels was the son of a German cotton-spinner who owned a factory at Manchester, England. He had become a socialistic critic of industrial conditions in 1842 and 1843 through his work as manager of his father's cotton-spinning factory. In 1844 Engels issued a book, *The Condition of the Working Class in England in 1844*. It was the reading of this book that made Marx the close friend and associate of Engels. From that time on the two men worked together, developing the ideas known later as modern socialism.

Wherever Marx went, however, the eyes of the Prussian government followed him. In 1845 Prussia succeeded in persuading the French government to suppress his newspaper *Vorwärts* and banish Marx from France. He fled to Belgium and lived in Brussels from 1845 to 1848. There he developed his theories of government, of the social classes, and of the ownership of property. There, also, he threw himself into the trade-union movement, organizing associations, lecturing, and writing.

Steadily Marx was evolving a new theory of government. In 1847 he and Engels attended a meeting of the International Alliance, at London. This organization was an outgrowth of the Communist League, which had been created in France eleven years before by other exiled Germans. At the meeting Marx and Engels entered into the discussions of the place of the workers in society, of the redivision of property, and of the reconstruction of government.

Marx and Engels issue *The Communist Manifesto*, 1847

Then in 1847 came one of the epoch-making documents in the history of government — *The Communist Manifesto.* It was a little pamphlet and, at the time it was published, created no stir at all. Indeed, its publication was known only to a small group who were in the centers of economic and political ferment. Gradually, however, as the socialistic movement spread in western Europe, more and more people turned to the pamphlet as a basic statement of the workers' creed. In our own day, because of the present Russian experiment, it has again become a theme of discussion.

Marx's later history can be told in a few sentences. The Prussian government again compelled him to move on by persuading the Belgian officials to ask him to leave. He returned to Paris at the very beginning of another revolution in France and the establishment of the Second Republic. Then, as revolutions swept western Germany in 1848, Marx returned to his native land. But his stay there was short-lived. In 1849 he was exiled again. This time he moved to the more stable and quiet circumstances of London, where he lived for 34 years.

Always a student, Marx spent most of those years in London in the musty alcoves of the library of the British Museum, writing a philosophy of history and economics which he called *Das Kapital* (*Capital*). It is in this volume that Marx attempted to base his plan for the reorganization of society upon a careful historical study.

One other important event is remembered in connection with Marx's name — the organization of an international society of workingmen, 1864. Of that we shall speak soon.

What were the Chief Ideas of Marx and Engels?

The main ideas upon which modern socialism has grown in the past three quarters of a century are to be found succinctly stated in *The Communist Manifesto.* They are developed in greater fullness in Marx's *Das Kapital.* And they have been written about, interpreted, and criticized by literally thousands of writers. For our brief summary, however, let us go back to the original writings themselves.

In order not to become confused with too many details, let us take only a few main ideas, — namely, the class war, the public ownership of the means of production, the elimination of differences in opportunity among people, compulsory useful labor, the public control of credit, the redistribution of population, and free public education for every child. The last of these ideas has long been accepted by most people in Europe and the United States. As the others have been the center of intense controversy, we should study them a little now.

1. *The idea of the constant struggle for power over government by economic classes.* The very basis of Marx's plan for a more democratic society lay in his years of study of the historical records in the British Museum. From that study he developed the theory that in each civilization fortunate people — fortunate because of their position, their wealth, or their abilities — seize land and trade and acquire most of the wealth, and that with it they control the armed force of the group and thus the government.

The history of society was viewed as a continual struggle between class-conscious groups.

Marx maintained that in recent times a new and powerful economic class had arisen — namely, the industrial capitalists. These ambitious men, he said, had seized the coal, iron, and other raw materials, as well as the land, had secured trade concessions and monopolies from kings and other governors, and had succeeded in getting control of governments everywhere.

Furthermore, Marx said, in setting up the new industrial system, a new economic class had been brought into existence. These were the city workers, whom Marx called the proletarians.[1] These city workers and the farm workers with them, Marx maintained, had been and were exploited by the capitalists, who had seized the ownership of property and the control of government.

At that point Marx forsook history and ventured a prediction, namely, that this proletarian class of city workers would organize

[1] This comes from the Latin word *proletarius*, from *proles*, "offspring." In ancient Rome a *proletarius* was "a citizen of the lowest class, without property and regarded as capable of serving the state only by having children."

itself, secure the ballot, rise to power, and by means of its political power supplant the capitalist class. Thus would be established the true communist state.

2. *How should property be owned?* The second idea in Marxian socialism deals with the difficult question of the ownership of property. The question, according to Marx, is to be settled by organizing the workers everywhere. They will secure the vote and, because of their superior numbers, will eventually wrest political power from the few owners. It may be a peaceful way or it may develop into a violent way.

Once in power the proletariat will pass laws which will abolish the private ownership of certain kinds of property. *The means of production will become the property of the entire community.* Neither Marx, Engels, nor their followers were exactly clear concerning what was included under "means of production." In general, however, they included factories, mines, farm land, and banks and treasuries controlling credit. Such things as these, they said, should be owned and operated by the national state and its local communities. Means of transportation and communication, they maintained, should be operated under the supervisory control of the state.

Thus Marx and his followers proposed to substitute the public ownership of all basic means of producing food, shelter, and clothing for the system of private ownership which was then in force in every civilized country on the earth. Thus this second idea of Marx's would set up state capitalism in place of private capitalism, public ownership instead of private ownership.

3. *The elimination of unequal economic advantages at birth.* Marx proposed to abolish all inheritances; each child should start life without an economic advantage over any other child.

4. *The idea of compulsory useful labor.* So far as his physical and mental abilities permitted, each human being must work; each must contribute to the common good, either with physical work, with mental work, or with artistic achievement.

5. *The control of credit.* All capital should be owned publicly; that is, the control of credit should be taken away from private bankers and centralized in a single national bank.

6. *The redistribution of population.* The rapid concentration of population in towns and cities should be broken down by the settlement of people in villages and towns.

7. *Free public education.* The most fundamental provision of all was the education of every child at public expense. The crucial importance of this latter point is recognized when we recall the insistence of a great body of Marxian socialists upon using peaceful means to socialize society. Throughout three quarters of a century they have opposed those extremists who advocate armed violence, military revolution, as the way to establish government by all the people. Most modern socialists have followed Marx's slogan, "Educate. Give every individual a fundamental knowledge of society."

Thus class war meant to Marx and many of his followers the peaceful use of the ballot, not the warlike use of guns. No government would be permanent, they maintained, that did not rest upon the intelligent understanding and approval of the vast majority of the people. Hence, educate!

Briefly summed up, these are the central ideas of Marxian socialism; we see in them an attempt to think through the complicated problems of economic, political, and social life. That they have influenced leaders in every walk of life since that time cannot be doubted. As we continue our studies we shall see how these ideas played a most important rôle in the redirection of Europe's march toward democracy.

The International Workingmen's Association, 1864: the First International

With the idea of putting his views into practice, Marx spent many years helping to organize workingmen's associations. In France, in Belgium, in England, he devoted himself to this work with trade-unions. The principal idea behind the work was that of a world-wide brotherhood of man, with all the world conceived as one society. Thus Marx's message was international in character.

At the London Exposition (1862) a gathering of workingmen was tentatively organized through the union of workers from France, England, and Belgium. Two years later, under the leadership of Marx, a permanent organization was created called the International Workingmen's Association. Gradually this came to be known in various countries as the International and later, as successors to it appeared, as the First International.

For several years the First International spread slowly in France, Belgium, England, the United States, Italy, Germany, Holland, and Switzerland. It lasted for twelve years — years

FIG. 82. The spread of the influence of the International Workingmen's Association is illustrated in this procession, which took place in 1871 in New York. The procession commemorated members of this organization who had been executed in France in that year. (From *Leslie's Illustrated Newspaper*, 1872)

marked by internal disagreements as to policies and programs, and by attacks which were made by its capitalist opponents.

European trade-unions went into politics

In the meantime, however, as we shall see in the later chapters, workingmen went into politics in each of the leading industrial countries. In Germany, during the years between 1863 and 1875, the Social Democratic movement gained headway under such leaders as Ferdinand Lassalle, Wilhelm Liebknecht, and August Bebel. Although not all these Social Democrats subscribed to every proposal of Marx and Engels, they all sought the right to vote so as to secure their share in the German government. In the minds of many was the hope of getting control of government affairs, as Marx predicted they would, and putting into practice many of the socialist proposals.

Several socialist organizations also developed in England, all playing an increasing part in government. We shall learn in Chapter X how in 1867 the English laboring men finally achieved the right to vote, and how they finally came in our own time to secure a plurality of the votes in the House of Commons.

The Labor party of England today arose as a result of the activities of several groups. Chief among them was the Social Democratic Federation, an organization favoring Marx's ideas. In 1883 a group of brilliant thinkers formed the Fabian Society in London, which today includes such prominent leaders in Great Britain as Sidney and Beatrice Webb, George Bernard Shaw, Graham Wallas, Arthur Henderson, and Ramsay Macdonald. The Fabian Society was devoted primarily to the discussion of economic, political, and social problems, and to educating the public generally in the principles of socialism.

Then, in 1893, the Independent Labor party appeared, under the leadership of a miner, Keir Hardie. Eventually these various groups representing different varieties of socialism combined in a general, working political party known as the Labor party. It is this party which, under the leadership of Ramsay Macdonald, twice secured control of the British government in the 1920's.

In the meantime, as you have already learned, the socialist movement also developed in the United States. It grew steadily until, in the national election of 1912, that party polled nearly 900,000 votes. At present one can find it in most countries of the Western world.

Only one more fact should we remember about the development of Marxian socialism. That was the split among the followers of Marx after his death in 1883. The split came over questions of how socialists should organize themselves to secure control of the government. Most socialists were agreed upon the fundamental Marxian principles which we have enumerated. But they divided on the question of how to put them into practice. One group was called "strict Marxians" or "Marxists." The other group was called "Reformists" or "Revisionists." As we shall see later, in the discussion of the development of government in France, Germany, and Russia, these two groups came to form separate political organizations. Each took a separate position on questions of religion, how trade-unions should be used, ownership of farm lands, and problems of internationalism.

All Marxian socialists believe in government. They make no attempt to abolish it. They recognize clearly that in our modern civilizations of villages, towns, and cities there must be a central

FIG. 83. Sidney Webb (see page 223), English statesmen, socialist, and analyst of industrial and political problems

FIG. 84. George Bernard Shaw (see page 223), Irish dramatist, essayist, socialist, and crusader against social evils

government to carry on the life of the community in a quiet, orderly way. Thus Marxian socialists have always recognized the need for orderly social control.

Anarchism — another theory of social living

There were extremists, however, working at the same time as Marx and his associates, who proposed the abolition of all government. There were, for example, the Frenchman Pierre Joseph Proudhon (1809–1865) and the Russian Mikhail Bakunin (1814–1876), who proposed to carry on social life without government. Neither of them ever showed clearly how any single country, let alone our interdependent and industrial world society, could be carried on without central government. Each was listened to and followed by only a minute fraction of the people.

In Conclusion

This, then, must bring to a close our very short outline. We have seen how certain outstanding frontier thinkers on social conditions laid the basis for important changes in the 1700's and 1800's.

One fact can be seen clearly from the vantage point of the 1930's: a people could not make substantial progress toward a more democratic way of living *until thinkers had pointed the way.* Clear thinking about the basis of living together was what the people of the world needed. But this was rarely forthcoming in the 2000 years from Aristotle and Plato to the social scientists of the eighteenth century. A few thinking men, students of the scientific method, stood out above the mass. But until the time of John Locke, Montesquieu, Diderot, Rousseau, and Marx the intelligence of the Western world was applied principally to the study of the physical and natural world and preparation for a new world after death. Then slowly appeared social scientists, students of government, of property ownership, of wages and hours of labor, of city and town life — of social life generally.

Our next task, therefore, is to see what influence these leaders have exerted on the development of government in the past 200 years. What *was* the condition of government and social life?

INTERESTING READINGS FROM WHICH YOU CAN GET ADDITIONAL INFORMATION

Bridges, T. C. The Young Folk's Book of Invention. Little, Brown and Company, Boston. See Chapters IV and VI.

Craik, Mrs. Dinah M. John Halifax, Gentleman. Harper & Brothers, New York. Early years of the Industrial Revolution.

Gibson, Charles R. Heroes of Science. J. B. Lippincott Company, Philadelphia. The dramatic stories of scientific leaders.

Holland, Rupert S. Historic Inventions. Macrae Smith Company, Philadelphia. See Chapter IV, "Watt and the Steam Engine," and Chapter V, "Arkwright and the Spinning Jenny."

Osgood, Ellen L. A History of Industry. Ginn and Company, Boston. The industrial development of England.

Rugg, Harold. Changing Civilizations in the Modern World. Ginn and Company, Boston.

Van Loon, Hendrik W. Man, the Miracle Maker. Horace Liveright, New York. This book tells of many inventions that broadened the world of Europeans.

Van Loon, Hendrik W. The Story of Mankind. Horace Liveright, New York.

CHAPTER X

GREAT BRITAIN: THE FIRST REPRESENTATIVE GOVERNMENT

The history of government in the countries of the world is essentially the story of the conflict between groups. Recall the struggles in American history: colonial aristocratic merchants and planters against poor, back-country farmers; merchants, shippers, and manufacturers of the North against slave-owning planters of the South; bankers and captains of industry against farmers and laborers. *Each group tried to control the government to get what it wanted, rather than by expert or scientific plans to give all the people what they needed.* This was the history in America. But it was likewise the story of other governments before North America was discovered.

The beginnings of democracy in England illustrate the same conflict of groups. Duke fought against duke; prince against prince; king against king; landowners against kings; merchants and capitalists against peasants and artisans — each trying to control government in order to have wealth, comfort, and power. After a thousand years of struggle the landowners, merchants, and small capitalists had sheared the "divine right" kings and their courtiers of their power. By 1688 government had become parliamentary and representative of property-owners; that is, government was "representative" of, let us say, 3 per cent of the people.

England's Experiment in Representative Government first produced Political Parties

But the little group of lords and merchants that now controlled England's affairs did not agree perfectly as to the government of England. Having succeeded in reducing the power of the king, they differed among themselves on many issues. They differed about religion, about taxation, about the kind of government which would be best for England. So, as happened later in America, France, Germany, and other modern countries, they split into factions — that is, into political parties. Those who wanted relatively the same things and believed in the same general ways of getting them tended to clique together, to gather together socially, and to vote together on matters of government.

Fig. 85. In the early 1700's two Whigs, Joseph Addison and Richard Steele, through their writings influenced landowners to be more kindly and considerate to their tenants. (After a painting by C. R. Leslie)

This brought political parties into existence in England before it did in other countries. Indeed, after 1775 the United States, France, Germany, and other modern nations tended to pattern their governments on that which England had developed before them. Hence the importance of understanding the first political parties in the modern world.

In the reign of Charles II (1660–1685) Parliament had split into two parties — called Whigs and Tories — over the question of the exclusion of the Catholic James from the throne. The Whigs were the more liberal faction. Many of them were Dissenters in religion, whose elders had been Presbyterians in Scotland. As such dissenting groups in Scotland had been called Whigs, this nickname was given to the new party and clung to it for a century and a half.

Persons of varying wealth and social position gathered in the Whig party. There were the merchants and the other business men of towns and cities who wanted greater power in government. There were also certain leading earls and barons who, jealous of the king, were eager to assert their own authority. This mixed group was held together by a common desire to reduce the king's power and increase its own. Furthermore, the Whigs disliked both the Catholic and the Anglican Church, favoring instead the more liberal nonconformist sects.

The name "Tory," given to the other party, had been the nickname applied to certain Irish outlaws, professedly Royalists. This party was made up of country squires and clergymen and members of the Anglican Church. These people were true conservatives — they disliked change, they feared experiments, they shunned new ways of thinking. Many of them lived in little communities where changes came slowly. They disliked the rising business men of the towns and cities, regarding them as upstarts and interlopers. Most of all, they feared civil war, turmoil, and political and social disorder of any kind. Consequently they said about government: "Keep a hereditary king. Any kind of king is better than civil war and hard times."

Into these two parties, in the 1700's and early 1800's, the English people who could vote grouped themselves. The division shows two differing attitudes: the more progressive attitude of the Whigs and the more conservative outlook of the Tories, who wanted things left as they were. Later, in the 1830's, the names, though not the principles, of these two parties gradually changed. The Whigs became the Liberal party, and the Tories the Conservative party, of today.

In the later 1600's the Whigs gradually increased their power and succeeded in passing important laws. One, which really constitutes an important document in the British written constitution, was the *Habeas Corpus Act of 1679*. This act provided that no individual could be imprisoned for an indefinite period without being given an opportunity of a hearing before a court. It is the basis for similar *habeas corpus* provisions in our own constitution and in those of other countries.

In the "Glorious Revolution" of 1688 the Tories, fearing Catholicism, joined the Whigs in offering the throne to the foreign Prince William of Orange. During the reign of William and Mary the Whigs further increased their power. As the king was a foreigner, more interested in other matters than in English government, they succeeded in passing the *Toleration Act of 1689*, giving all Dissenters except Unitarians freedom of worship. They also passed other laws repealing the censorship of books and allowing greater freedom of speech.

Thus by the early 1700's the government of England was not only parliamentary but, generally speaking, it was also carried on by two clearly divided political parties.

A New Family of Kings for England: the German Hanoverians, 1714 to Today

Nothing the members of Parliament could have done would have increased their power more than having another foreigner for a king.

Anne, queen of England, died in 1714 — without an heir. Parliament had provided for that very possibility by an Act of Settlement in 1701, which named another foreign ruler — Sophia of Hanover (a German state), a granddaughter of James I — or her children as successors to the throne. Thus in 1714 George, a German elector, son of Sophia and great-grandson of James I, became King George I of England.

Since the accession of George I, in 1714, eight sons and daughters of the House of Hanover have been sovereigns of Great Britain. Notice their reigns as given in the chart of Table IV, page 161. The first four Georges were kings during the 1700's and early 1800's. After William IV, who served for only seven years (1830–1837), Victoria was queen for nearly two thirds of a century (1837–1901). Two other members of the House of Hanover (now called House of Windsor) have followed her — Edward VII and the present ruler, George V, whose eldest son, Edward, Prince of Wales, will presumably succeed him as king some day.

For 200 years these German-English sovereigns (now wholly English, of course) have been generally content merely to *reign*, letting Parliament *rule*. In that time there has not been a single instance of armed revolution in England. While other countries have been the scenes of civil war and revolt, England has gone steadily onward to an increasingly democratic government.

About 1700 the British Government became the First Cabinet Government

During this period, when foreign kings occupied the throne, and Parliament really ruled, the so-called *cabinet* government of England was evolved. Let us see how it developed.

Even before 1500 the king had been aided by a small Privy Council of advisers selected from the Great Council of earls, barons, bishops, and abbots. As the Great Council became the ever-larger British Parliament, the Privy Council also grew. Finally it also was too large for effective discussion and decision. Hence it was gradually supplanted by a little inside ring which was called a Cabinet Council because it met secretly with the king in a private room called a "cabinet."

The importance of the Cabinet Council grew steadily during the rule of William and Mary and during the reigns of the first Georges. As you know, these kings were foreigners. William of Orange, for example, was much more interested in the success of Holland and in defeating the ambitions of Louis XIV of France than he was in matters of state in England. Consequently he relied more and more on the council of ministers for decisions on questions of government.

The Cabinet was composed of Leaders of the Majority Party in Parliament

When William III first began to use the cabinet to aid him in discussing and directing government, he included leaders of both political parties — Whigs and Tories. This plan did not work very well. When the Whigs were in the majority in Parliament, Tory ministers were constantly criticized and were sometimes in danger of impeachment, and vice versa.

Hence the king learned that *government was carried on more smoothly if his cabinet was composed altogether of ministers from the political party that was in power.* Thus when the Whigs had a majority in Parliament the cabinet came to be made up of Whigs. When the Tories secured a majority the king replaced the Whigs by a Tory cabinet. Thus the *majority party,* through the members of the *cabinet,* virtually governed England. This practice of changing the cabinet when the party in power changed, begun in the late 1600's and early 1700's, has continued from that time on. It is the practice today.

FIG. 86. A session of the House of Lords during the reign of George II. The King is facing you, seated on his throne. (From an old print)

George I (1714–1727) was as uninterested in English matters of state as was William III. One English historian said that he was "ideally fitted to be an incompetent king of England." In every way he was German rather than English; he could not even speak the English language. When he came to England he was accompanied by a retinue of German attendants, and the court became a center of German culture.

George knew nothing about English politics or about the English people. Hence he too left most of the decisions of government to the Cabinet Council, made up of the leaders of the majority party — the Whigs. Indeed, he did not even attend cabinet meetings! The king became more and more a ceremonial figurehead. He presided at social functions, signed state papers, and became a *symbol* of royalty which the people respected and to which they were loyal.

THE CABINET MEMBERS WERE HEADS OF GOVERNMENT DEPARTMENTS

Another step in the development of modern government was accomplished when the members of the cabinet became also the heads of government departments. For example, one member of the cabinet became the *secretary of state for foreign affairs*, or foreign minister, dealing with international problems. Another member became *chancellor of the exchequer*, handling certain financial matters; another, the *first lord of the treasury*, managing other finances. Similarly, the *secretary of state for war* was responsible for the army, and the *first lord of the admiralty* for the navy. As the duties of government multiplied with the growth of the British Empire, the departments were still further subdivided. Eventually the cabinet was made up of nineteen of these chief officials. There were even more department heads, however, not all of them being members of the cabinet.

The leader of the majority party became the prime minister, replacing the king as the real head of government

As the kings of England continued to stay away from cabinet meetings, a chief minister gradually became the leader. He and the other ministers of the cabinet were also members of Parliament. As today, each attended meetings of the House of Lords or the House of Commons, personally presented his proposals for bills to his house, and was available on the floor of his house to answer questions and to defend his ideas. This is another difference between the British form of government and the American form. In the United States, although the heads of departments are members of the president's cabinet, they are not members of the Senate or the House of Representatives.

Thus, in the years from the accession of William and Mary to the middle of George I's reign, the *leader of the majority party* gradually came to be regarded as the *chief minister*. He presided at cabinet meetings and, if strong enough, dictated the policies of government. Eventually, during the times of George I and George II, this leader was called the "prime" minister — that is, the first minister, the real head of the government.

FIG. 87. A scene in the House of Commons in Sir Robert Walpole's day. Sir Robert is seen at the extreme left. (After a painting by Hogarth and Thornhill)

The position of the prime minister in England, indeed in all modern countries, was really established in the years between 1721 and 1742 by Sir Robert Walpole, earl of Orford. Walpole was a master of debate, a man of prodigious industry, and a calm and patient politician. Furthermore, he knew trade and finance; it was said that he was the best "master of figures" of his time. He was secretary of war at one time and was later treasurer of the navy. By 1721 he was recognized as the leader of the Whig party, which position he held for twenty-one years. He it was who first came to be regarded as the prime minister.

Cabinet Government proved to be very Responsive to the People Represented

What does it mean to say that a government is *responsive* to the people? It means that as the desires of the people change, laws and the actions of government change with them. Thus government really fits the needs of the people; the representatives conduct it as would the people as a whole.

Now students of government agree that the parliamentary cabinet form, which was developed in England during the 1700's, is really more responsive to the popular will than are the forms in other countries. Indeed, it has been said by one prominent historian that this form "is the most perfect which has yet been devised for speedily and peacefully voicing the will of the people."

FIG. 88. When Parliament refused to support the measures advocated by David Lloyd George in 1922, he tendered his resignation as prime minister. That necessitated a general election in Great Britain. Here we see Lloyd George appealing to the people during his campaign for reëlection

How? By being arranged so that the government changes whenever Parliament as a whole refuses to approve the policies of the prime minister and his cabinet. The cabinet, of course, is made up of ministers chosen from the majority party. As time goes on, however, members of the House of Commons, representing the people who elected them, change their views about various political matters. As this happens — for example, as the Liberals lose seats in Parliament and the Conservatives gain them (or vice versa) — the majority changes. The Conservatives rather than the Liberals then constitute a majority. Thus the proposals of a Liberal cabinet are defeated in the House of Commons. When that happens one of two things occurs: either (1) the ministry resigns and the king asks the leader of the opposition party to form a new cabinet; or (2) Parliament is dissolved, the members return to their homes, and a general election is held all over Great Britain.

As a result of this general election the party or temporary combination of parties totaling the majority of members of the House of Commons then forms a new cabinet. The leader of the new majority party becomes the prime minister and appoints new heads of departments. These officials make new plans for the government of the country and present them to the new Parliament. If they are approved, the cabinet stays in power; if not, the government changes again.

Thus the government changes as frequently as the members of Parliament and, behind them, the points of view of the people who elected them change. This is what is meant by saying that the British form of parliamentary cabinet government is *responsive to the people.*

But did this Government really represent All the British People?

In the 1700's and early 1800's was this the representative government it was heralded to be by such contemporary students of government as the French writer Voltaire? Was this government of all the people? No, it was government representative of a very small proportion. *Not more than 3 per cent of all the people* were represented.

During the 1700's and early 1800's the members of Parliament included (1) the wealthy bishops of the Anglican Church; (2) the "peers" (nobles who held hereditary seats in the House of Lords); (3) the newly rich tradesmen who, because of their financial favors to the kings, had been given titles; (4) the knights of the shire, or smaller landlords of the rural districts; and (5) the representatives of the trading towns and cities. We see, therefore, that these members represented the Church, the aristocracy, and those who controlled land or money. The mass of the people — *97 per cent of the population* — was unrepresented. Even the two knights from each shire were elected by the relatively well-to-do. To vote, a man was required to own an estate from which he obtained a yearly rent of 40 shillings ($10), a very considerable sum in the 1700's. Furthermore, all women, no matter of what wealth or ability, were debarred from voting.

Thus, historians have estimated that not more than 1500 men out of a population of several millions actually controlled a majority in the House of Commons. Hence 1500 men really controlled the government of England.

The Real British Government

To understand the real character of government in the 1700's we need merely recall what we have learned about the real government of America and of other modern countries today.[1] We found that in American communities there are three groups, each one wanting something from government:

1. The rank and file of the people.
2. The interested groups.
3. The politicians.

In England the communities of the nation divided themselves for two centuries in the same political way, and do so still. First there were the mass of the *people*, who until recently were not allowed to vote. Second, there were the *interested groups* of rich landlords, millionaire merchants, shipowners, manufacturers, owners of monopolies, and the like, who, because of their wealth or social position, secured favors from the government. Third, there were the *politicians*, the leaders in the House of Lords and in the House of Commons and the ministers in the cabinet.

Furthermore, then, even more than now, the mass of the people had no means of exercising their will upon government or of getting what they wanted. Thus, government in England in the 1700's and 1800's, as in America today, was controlled by the interested groups and by professional politicians — those

[1] An interesting comparison between the present discussion and that in Chapter XI of *An Introduction to Problems of American Culture* can be made at this point.

Fig. 89. Election day in a village during Sir Robert Walpole's time. Members of two rival parties are trying to buy the vote of an enfranchised citizen. (After a painting by Hogarth)

who made a job of governing. In those days, however, politics was regarded as a "gentleman's game." In a recent book Hayes describes the condition of real government as follows:

> The nobleman who sat in the upper house [the House of Lords] had his dummies in the lower chamber [the House of Commons]. A certain Sir James Lowther had nine protégés in the lower house, who were commonly called "Lowther's Ninepins." A distinguished statesman of the time described the position of such a protégé: "He is sent here by the lord of this or the duke of that, and if he does not obey the instructions which he receives, he is held to be a dishonest man." [1]

Thus at this time a system of politics developed in England which was imitated in nearly all civilized countries. It first achieved prominence under the leadership of Sir Robert Walpole and the Whig party. Under it the well-to-do people, working

[1] Carlton J. H. Hayes, *A Political and Social History of Modern Europe*, Vol. I, p. 435. By permission of The Macmillan Company, publishers, New York, 1920.

closely with professional politicians, controlled government and ran it in their own interest.

The evils of the system are clear. First, voting was public, — not secret, as today. In any community of England any freeman had the right to examine the poll books and see what any other voter had done. Hence fear of disapproval compelled the less well-to-do to vote as the most well-to-do wished them to vote.

Second, votes were openly bought and sold. Politicians went among the people bidding for votes, the standard price being about £5 ($25) at that time. However, prices differed in various localities. "By long-established custom the price of a vote at Hull was two guineas [over $10]; at Stafford, seven." When rival politicians were competing for a seat in Parliament, the price sometimes went as high as £25 ($125) or even more. Not only were individual voters bribed, but politics was so played that the votes of whole boroughs were sold to the highest bidder. It is said on good authority that to secure the vote of a borough cost about $25,000.

George III openly bribed people to vote for candidates to the House of Commons who he knew would do his bidding. Anecdotes recount that he used to go out into the towns and villages, giving money to the shopkeepers, artisans, and farmers to vote for his candidates.

Third, politicians appointed their political associates and their friends to government posts at fat salaries. This practice was openly carried on by Walpole as the Whig prime minister. As we have already seen, these political associates decided the policies of the government in secret cabinet meetings.

Fourth, the various districts of England were not represented in Parliament in proportion to population. Some sections with almost no population at all had more representation than had large towns and cities. In the 1700's and early 1800's people left the villages and moved into the growing manufacturing towns and cities, thus redistributing the population, but the plan of representation remained the same. A quotation from Hayes will illustrate the problem:

. . . Old Sarum had once been a prosperous village and had been accorded representation, but after the village had disappeared, leaving to view but a lonely hill, no one in England could have told why two members should still sit for Old Sarum. Nor, for that matter, could there have been much need of representation in Parliament for the sea-coast town of Dunwich. Long ago the coast had sunk and the salt-sea waves now washed the remains of a ruined town. Bosseney in Cornwall was a hamlet of three cottages, but its citizens were entitled to send two men to Parliament.[1]

Thus Lord Macaulay, a famous English historian, could say that the English government was "a mass of represented ruins and unrepresented cities." And a political leader of the times, William Pitt the Younger, could say of the House of Commons in the 1700's:

> This House is not a representative of the people of Great Britain; it is the representation of nominal boroughs, of ruined and exterminated towns, of noble families, of wealthy individuals, of foreign potentates.

Indeed, corruption was so prevalent in those days that these so-called "rotten boroughs" were also called "pocket boroughs" — that is, they were in the pockets of the politicians who had sufficient money to purchase their votes and thereby control their seats in Parliament.

This, then, was the system of British cabinet government and the degree to which it represented the British people throughout the 1700's.

The Industrial Capitalists began to play an Increasingly Important Part in British Government

We see, therefore, that while the introduction of machines pauperized and enslaved the masses of the people, it produced a rich, powerful section of the middle class — namely, the industrial capitalists. A group of several thousand owners of factories, banks, coal and iron mines, steel mills, machine shops, railways, canals, ships, wholesale and retail stores, and exporting and importing companies rose to power. It was a new group of the *bourgeoisie* — the leading people of the manufacturing towns.

[1] Carlton J. H. Hayes, *A Political and Social History of Modern Europe*, Vol. I, pp. 434–435. By permission of The Macmillan Company, publishers, New York, 1920.

For two hundred years this class had been slowly growing stronger because of its ownership of land and its control over craftsmen. Now, as the new business promoters accumulated wealth, the capitalist class grew rapidly in numbers. After 1800 these captains of industry — like the captains of industry in the United States, France, Germany, Italy, Japan, and other countries — worked with the politicians for the control of government. They saw that thus they could control the production and prices of goods and the costs of labor (or wages), and thereby control profits.

© Detroit Publishing Company

FIG. 90. William Pitt, the Younger (1759–1806). (From a painting by William Hoppner in the Pennsylvania Academy of Fine Arts)

Not until 1832 did the new industrial capitalists secure much representation in the government

Until after 1800, however, Parliament was largely under the control of the descendants of the old nobility—rich landlords and merchants of the older type. With this inner ring that controlled government, the rising industrial middle classes at first had little influence. Great towns like Manchester and Birmingham still lacked actual representation in either the House of Commons or the House of Lords. Thus the industrial captains were excluded.

In the meantime, in the later 1700's, the conditions of the masses of the people had become so bad that liberal people had joined together under the leadership of William Pitt the Younger (1759–1806) to improve them. The forces of reform gained adherents rapidly. Bills were proposed in Parliament which would take representation from the rotten boroughs and give it to the growing towns and cities more directly in proportion to the number of inhabitants in each. Newspapers were established in London and in the larger cities and, by reporting the discussion of debates in Parliament, did much to inform the rising middle classes of the condition of affairs. They also stimulated discussion among the people of the towns and cities and increased their desire for change.

It was the well-to-do manufacturing capitalists, however, who led the demand for reform in government. They were intelligent, wealthy, and therefore of growing authority in the country. Moreover, they were organized and felt most keenly the lack of representation in Parliament. They therefore led the general movement for reform.

In the 1820's three important improvements were made in the laws of England. The first was the revision of the criminal laws, 1824. You will remember that more than 200 offenses were punishable by death. Among them were many "crimes," such as petty thieving in stores and shooting game upon the lord's land, which did not warrant such a severe penalty. The criminal act of 1824 changed this cruel system of punishment, making such petty offenses punishable by fines and imprisonment but not by death.

The second improvement was a law passed in 1824 which repealed earlier laws prohibiting the organization of workingmen's unions. Thus laboring men could organize unions "to determine the scale of wages or hours of labor." Even then, however, laborers could not strike in the attempt to enforce their demands upon employers. But democracy had marched forward a little. Those in political power had yielded more rights to the common people.

The third improvement was aimed at the existing religious intolerance. Although those who differed with the Anglican Church were no longer persecuted for their beliefs, yet not all of them were permitted representation in Parliament. An act passed more than 100 years before (1678) compelled all members of Parliament to declare that the Catholic form of religion was "idolatry." This, of course, Catholics would not do. Hence they were not represented in Parliament.

In the early 1800's vigorous movements to give Catholics equal rights in Parliament started in Ireland, then as now largely a Catholic country. In 1828, in a defiant uprising of 50,000 Irish Catholic farmers, Daniel O'Connell, a popular lawyer, was elected to a seat in the House of Commons. Parliament refused to seat him because he would not declare that the Catholic religion was idolatrous. Three times between 1821 and 1828 the House of Lords vetoed measures proposed by the House of Commons to remove the discrimination against Catholics. Finally the movement toward rebellion in Ireland became so strong that the House of Lords passed a Catholic Emancipation Bill, 1829. This permitted approximately a quarter of a million small property-owners in Ireland real representation in Parliament.

Then the Reform Bill of 1832 gave the rising business aristocracy a larger share in government

After the Catholic Emancipation Bill had been passed, events moved swiftly toward greater reform in government. Even conservative Tories and cautious Whig leaders in the House of Commons, such as Lord John Russell, Earl Grey, and Lord Macaulay, urged a change in the unfair representation in Parliament. The conservative House of Lords, however, fearing the increasing power of the manufacturers and business men, were deaf to all proposals.

In 1831 a reform bill proposed by the Whigs was defeated by the House of Lords. A general election held the same year gave the Whigs a new majority in the House of Commons, but of course this did not affect the House of Lords. A second reform bill was passed by the House of Commons, but was again defeated in the House of Lords.

Riots broke out in several of the manufacturing centers of England where the disappointed workingmen believed that the passage of the Reform Bill would have given them the right to vote. Leaders even urged their constituents to refuse to pay taxes, to withdraw their deposits from the banks, and thereby to create a financial revolution and eventually a military revolution. For the first time in nearly 200 years England seemed near civil war.

Seeing the turmoil they had brought about, however, the Tory lords gave in. The Reform Bill was passed in 1832.

Did democracy gain by the Reform Bill of 1832?

Three changes were made in the government of England by this new law — three additions to the British Constitution. First, representation in Parliament was changed, all seats being taken away from each borough having less than 2000 inhabitants and only one seat being allowed each borough having a population between 2000 and 4000. Most of these seats were given to the larger towns which until this time had not been represented in the Parliament — for example, Birmingham, Manchester, Leeds, Sheffield, and others. The larger rural shires also received new seats, and a few were given to the people of Scotland and Ireland.

Second, in the new towns which had just secured representation, all persons renting property at £10 a year (about $50) or over were allowed to vote. Some gains were also made in the rural districts.

Third, all voting in a general election was to be completed within two days. At one time an election had extended over forty days; later it had been reduced to fifteen days. Even then, however, there had been time enough for buying and selling votes and for much social disorder.

Did the Reform Bill of 1832 really bring about true representation of all the people?

It did not. It increased the number of voters from 3 per cent to approximately 5 per cent, and gave representation to the industrial capitalists and to all who owned or rented property valued at a certain amount. But still only the comparatively well-to-do could vote. For example, only 6700 of the 187,000 inhabitants of the manufacturing city of Manchester could vote under the new act. Thus the increase in the representativeness of British government was slight. Before the Reform Bill of 1832 was passed, 3 per cent of the people could vote; after that, approximately 5 per cent could vote. *But 95 per cent of the British people were still without a direct share in the government of their own affairs.*

We must remember, furthermore, that the communities which obtained representation by the new bill were essentially factory towns. Thus at last the industrial capitalists had obtained a real place in the House of Commons, and hence in the government of Great Britain.

THE INFANCY OF DEMOCRACY IN EUROPE, 1800–1850

It could hardly be concluded, therefore, that in 1832 government in England was democratic. In the 600 years that had passed since the signing of the Great Charter by King John, England's march toward democracy had been slow indeed. It took more than 400 years to secure the Petition of Right and the Bill of Rights, giving the control of government to noble landowners, country squires, and city merchant princes. Almost another 200 years were necessary before the manufacturing princes and the banker princes had an equal share. But 95 per cent of the people were still without a voice in government.

Of course we must not forget that most of this slow, sure advance had taken place without civil war and revolution. With the exception of the stirring times (1625–1660) of Charles I and Oliver Cromwell and the Commonwealth, the drama of British government was staged in comparative physical peace. In this respect it was a sharp contrast to the revolutionary history of France, Germany, Italy, Russia, and other countries.

However, in the 1830's it must have been clear to the true students of democracy — men like Thomas Carlyle in England and Ralph Waldo Emerson in America — that the world still had far to go in its march toward democracy.

But the Industrial Revolution changed conditions and made greater democracy inevitable

After 1800 the rising machine industry, the new international trade, and the ever swifter transportation and communication brought about conditions which increased the democratic character of government in the Western world. This was done in ways of which you have already learned. Let us summarize them.

First, millions of workers left rural cottages and herded in crowded city tenements near factories, mines, and stores. Intolerable working and living conditions in mills and mines, sweat shops, and slum tenements were created. Great bitterness and social unrest grew among the workers.

Second, by the crowding of people into cities and towns, by the invention of modern printing presses, and by better means of communication there was a great increase in the *discussion* of social, political, and economic conditions. The development of trade-unions and of other organizations of workingmen also promoted the exchange of ideas among the common people. Thus increasingly in the 1800's men of the working classes discussed their wrongs and the evils of their living and working conditions. As they did so their leaders instilled in them more and more the desire for a direct voice in the government.

Fig. 91. How would industrial conditions such as this help to make "greater democracy inevitable"? (From Cobden's *White Slaves of England*, 1853)

Third, while the rising middle classes steadily received more education many children of the poor were also taught to read and write. Newspapers reporting current problems were read by a slowly growing educated class. The better educated among the well-to-do read the multiplying books of the social philosophers. Thus through the 1800's education and the Industrial Revolution advanced together.

Fourth, as conditions in industrial cities and towns became worse and worse, a growing body of social philosophers and philanthropists appeared. They denounced the inequalities of the existing régime and proposed new plans of government and community life. We discussed some of their ideas in the previous chapter.

The conditions which had been brought about and the development of discussion concerning them made the onward march toward more democratic government inevitable. Thus the period of the first half of the nineteenth century was that of the infancy of democracy in Europe.

Democracy opposed by the selfish upper classes of the Victorian Era (1837-1901)

Working against the growing demands of the people for better wages, healthier working and living conditions, and a larger share in government, was the selfish opposition of members of the two powerful upper classes — the wealthy dukes, marquises, earls, etc.; and the manufacturers, bankers, merchants, captains of industry, and their representatives in Parliament. Throughout the whole era of Queen Victoria's reign (1837–1901), nearly two thirds of a century long, the conservative wealthy classes were in control. They fought every proposal by the liberal leaders for improvements in the living conditions of the mass of the people and extension of the vote. This conservative attitude was reflected in the home life, the recreations, and the arts of the people. It was a time of conservatism in most aspects of life. "Keep things as they are. Don't change" was the slogan of those who controlled government. And this in the very period of the world's history in which industrial changes came about most swiftly!

The failure of the Chartists (1838-1848) to bring about reform

The agitation for more complete democracy continued because of the failure of Parliament to give all the people the suffrage and to make other reforms. Year after year liberal leaders reiterated their demands for more rights—for a charter of liberties for the common people. The upper classes, five in each 100 people, were now protected by written documents, but 95 per cent of the people were not. The Magna Carta, the Petition of Right, and the Bill of Rights had helped in the main only the rich land barons and the older merchants. The Reform Bill of 1832 had aided only the owners of the new industries.

The demands of liberal leaders now consisted of six points:

1. All adult males should have the right to vote.
2. Voting for all offices should be secret.
3. Election districts should be represented strictly on a basis of the number of people in them.
4. To be a member of Parliament one should not have to own property.
5. Members of Parliament should be paid a salary.
6. Parliament should be elected each year.

Fig. 92. A peaceful procession of the Chartists. Such processions as these were intended to show the strength of the movement and to gain supporters. (From the *Illustrated London News*, 1848)

These democratic ideas seized the imaginations of the workingmen. Beginning in 1838, the so-called Chartist movement spread rapidly through the large factory towns and cities, especially among the trade-unions. Mass meetings and conventions were held. Discussion spread from section to section.

In 1839, representatives of the laboring classes met in London in a Workingmen's Parliament. A petition demanding votes for all adult males was presented to Parliament, but was emphatically refused by that conservative body. Working conditions steadily became worse, and in 1842 another petition was presented. Again it was refused. In the next six years, in spite of disunion among the members of the Chartist movement themselves, agitation increased. Leaders went about preaching armed revolution if Parliament refused to give the people their rights. The climax came in 1848, when a giant petition with 2,000,000 names was prepared for presentation to Parliament. It was rumored that 500,000 men would present it and that some of them would be armed, ready to enforce their demands.

It looked as if revolution were going to be necessary in England to bring about changes in government. Parliament got ready for the coming struggle by enlisting the aid — as special constables — of the well-to-do people of London. Then suddenly the whole demonstration collapsed, and the Chartist agitation died down.

The Second Reform Bill (1867)

Thirty-five years passed after the Reform Bill of 1832, which gave the industrial capitalists their desired power, before another clear sign of advance in democracy was revealed. Then came the Second Reform Bill, which extended the vote to 1,000,000 more people, mostly factory workers in the cities.

During this period, agitation for reform had continued under liberal leaders. One of these, influential in the 1840's and 1850's, was John Bright (1811–1889). Bright, a Quaker nonconformist, was a popular leader of the masses. He worked for the restriction of hours of labor in the mines and factories. For years he gave himself without stint to bringing about the reform of Parliament. He also opposed capital punishment and urged further reforms of the criminal code and the prison system.

Furthermore, during these 35 years the Whig and Tory parties had definitely changed into the *Liberal* and *Conservative* parties. In this period also two famous political leaders rose to power and were important figures in the advance toward democracy. The leader of the Liberals was William Ewart Gladstone (1809–1898). Gladstone was an aristocrat, the son of a wealthy Liverpool merchant, and originally a Conservative. He became a Liberal after seeing the conditions under absolute government in Italy. In 1859 he became a member of the Liberal cabinet as chancellor of the exchequer. In that position he made a world reputation for himself as the leader of the free-traders; that is, those who would abolish import and export duties.

We need not rehearse the details of tariff history in England except to remind ourselves that before 1850 the heavy tax levied upon hundreds of articles manufactured in other countries and imported into England was removed. Thus sale prices of articles used by the common man were lowered. National plans were devised by which the expenses of government could be met by inheritance and income taxes, taxes on liquor sales, and the like. Finally, under the financial guidance of Gladstone, although income taxes were reduced several times, and although many additional articles were put on the free tariff list, England became more prosperous than she had ever been before.

FIG. 93. Gladstone addressing the House of Commons

Meanwhile the Conservative party gradually came under the leadership of a brilliant English Jew — Benjamin Disraeli (1804–1881), later Earl of Beaconsfield. He was a shrewd politician, a powerful public speaker, and a strong leader. He openly favored laws which would improve the working and living conditions of the masses and which would extend the right to vote to a much larger proportion of the population.

Although the leaders of the two parties represented very different political points of view, they both helped to advance the cause of democratic government in England. Because Disraeli and Gladstone both wanted to maintain their political power, they vied with one another in making concessions to the voters. In 1867, as a result of this competition to win votes, Parliament passed the famous Second Reform Bill. This extended the redistribution of the seats of Parliament which had been begun in 1832, giving to the growing manufacturing towns and cities 58 more seats in the House of Commons, formerly held by thinly populated rural districts.

FIG. 94. Benjamin Disraeli (1804–1881)

But, more important still, this act increased by over 1,000,000 the number of persons permitted to vote. In the cities the suffrage was given to every householder and renter of a separate dwelling, whether he owned property or not, and to every lodger who paid a rent equal to $50 annually. In the rural districts the vote was given to all tenants of property worth $60 a year.

At last democracy had really begun to march forward. Two and one-half million voters now had a voice in the government of Great Britain—2,500,000 out of a population of 32,000,000. Nevertheless government was still far from representative of all the people. Agricultural laborers — and there were many of them — were still unfranchised.

So the fight for more democracy went on under Gladstone's leadership. In 1872, in the *Ballot Act,* public voting, one of the worst evils of English politics, was done away with. The Australian ballot scheme (so called because it was first used by British colonists in the province of Victoria, in Australia) was adopted. Voting was thus made *secret*: a person could drop his vote in a ballot box without others' knowing how he voted. This made it impossible for persons of prominence in a community to intimidate others so that they would vote contrary to their convictions.

The Australian method is now used in the United States and in many other countries.

Twelve years later, in 1884, Gladstone brought about the passage of the first *Representation of the People Act.* This gave the vote to 2,000,000 agricultural laborers, increasing the number of those who could vote by 40 per cent. Other measures slowly increased the number of voters until at the outbreak of the World War it is estimated that about four out of every five adult males in England could vote. At that time approximately 8,000,000 men were eligible out of a total population of 45,000,000.

In 1885, under Gladstone, Parliament passed another bill, again redistributing the seats in the House of Commons. This bill provided that each member of the House of Commons should represent a definite number of people. Thus the British Parliament became still more representative of the masses.

One Important Obstacle to Democratic Government still remained — the Power of the House of Lords

All the reforms in Parliament which we have discussed applied only to the House of Commons. Throughout the centuries of steady march toward representative government, the House of Lords remained untouched.

Most of the 600 members of the House of Lords were "hereditary peers," and so entitled by birth to membership. Many of them rarely attended the meetings of Parliament — except when it was necessary for them to vote to protect their own interests. Many, indeed, showed no political ability whatsoever. The only reason for their position in the British government was the fact of their birth.

Although the House of Commons had long been the chief lawmaking body because of its control over finances, legislation had to be agreed to by the House of Lords. We have seen that the House of Lords frequently defeated progressive legislation which had been passed by the Liberal party in the House of Commons. Thus for nearly a century liberal leaders had recognized that as long as the House of Lords had the power of vetoing the legislation of the House of Commons, a tiny group comprising less than a fraction of 1 per cent of the population could prevent more than 99 per cent from expressing their real will.

Furthermore, Liberals wanted to shear the House of Lords of its powers because the presence in that body of the bishops of the Anglican Church gave the Established Church an unfair advantage over all other religious denominations of the kingdom.

Thus in the later 1800's the movement to restrict the power of the House of Lords steadily advanced. Matters came to a head in 1909, when the Lords broke their long-established custom of approving budget bills passed by the House of Commons and rejected the Finance Bill. This created such a storm of opposition from the Liberals that the ministry resigned and a general election was held. When the Liberals were overwhelmingly returned to office, they immediately made plans to pass legislation which would still further restrict the power of the House of Lords. Again they were blocked. Another election was held. Once more the Liberals were in the majority. This time the House of Lords submitted to the expressed will of the people, passing the Parliament Act in 1911. This act provided that financial bills passed by the House of Commons would become the law of the land one month after being sent to the House of Lords, whether or not they were approved by the Lords. All other bills would become law even if rejected by the Lords, provided they were passed by the House of Commons in three successive sessions, and provided also that two years had elapsed between the first proposal of the bill and its final passage. Thus the House of Commons was given complete charge over national finances and virtually over government. It left only one control still in the hands of the House of Lords, namely, that it could *postpone legislation for two years* by vetoing acts passed by the House of Commons.

British Women were Enfranchised, and All Property Restrictions to Suffrage were Removed

But in all these centuries what about the women? They were still without voting privileges — still without representation in Parliament. The agitation for "votes for women" started three quarters of a century ago both in America and in England. For many years it was met by ridicule and severe opposition. During the past twenty years, however, the woman's suffrage movement, led in England by Mrs. Emmeline Pankhurst, became very militant. A great campaign was put on by the women leaders and their men sympathizers, with parades, conventions, pamphlets, and books. Hunger strikes were resorted to when women were thrown into prison. Steadily these methods attracted adherents, and gradually most men became convinced that women could use the power to vote as intelligently as they. Then the active and able work of women in the World War swung political leaders to their support all over the world. In 1918 the Equal Franchise Act was passed, giving the vote to every woman over 30 years of age; thus at one stroke millions more voters were enfranchised in England. Ten years later (1928) this age restriction was lowered, and today women over 21 are permitted to vote. About the same time another act gave women the right to hold seats in the House of Commons. However, even now they cannot sit in the House of Lords.

FIG. 95. Mrs. Emmeline Pankhurst, leader of the woman's suffrage movement in England

The Representation of the People Act of 1918 redistributed the seats of Parliament again and *abolished all property qualifications.* Today men and women 21 years of age and over have the privilege of the vote in England.

SUMMING UP GREAT BRITAIN'S MARCH TOWARD DEMOCRACY

This must complete our brief outline of Great Britain's march toward democracy. She was first among the nations of Europe to experiment with representative government. A century before those in France and two centuries before those in Germany, the property-owners of Great Britain defied the authority of arrogant "divine right" kings to rule them absolutely. Thus the people of Great Britain had the beginnings of a democracy a century before the French or the Americans and more than two centuries before the Germans, the Russians, and most other European peoples.

What, then, have been the gains in democracy in Great Britain? To answer this question let us sum up the civil and political rights of the people:

1. *The gains in civil liberty.* Step by step, after King John signed the Magna Carta in 1215, the British people were guaranteed certain civil rights dear to all democratic peoples. Seven hundred years of struggle among the various classes achieved this, and to it we owe much of our own Constitution, including the Bill of Rights. Note that these civil liberties are essentially the ones that have been written into the Constitution of the United States.

a. The right of free speech — that is, the right to speak what one believes to be true.

b. The right of a free press — that is, the right to state one's thoughts, beliefs, or criticisms in writing.

c. The right of free assembly — that is, the right to meet with other persons in public places and to discuss matters of public or private interest.

d. The right to petition the government on any matter.

e. The right to religious freedom — to worship according to one's beliefs.

f. The right to a fair trial in court and to protection against illegal confinement.

2. *The gains in political liberty.* But, as we have learned in our earlier studies, civil liberty can be guaranteed to each citizen only by giving him political liberty — that is, the right to share in the government by voting and holding office.

In Great Britain this has been achieved in large measure by the steady evolution of a written constitution. Dramatic events have passed before our eyes which illustrate the way in which this was done — for example, the signing of the Magna Carta

(1215); the acceptance of the Petition of Right (1628); the acceptance of the Bill of Rights (1689); the development of political parties; the rise of cabinet government under the leadership of a prime minister; the more adequate representation of the cities, towns, and other districts of England; the extension of the right to vote; the development of secret voting; the frequent election of Parliaments; and the control of the government by the people as represented in the House of Commons.

Note, therefore, the gains in political liberty:

a. Political liberty and religion. In earlier times only members of recognized churches could vote and hold offices. Now there are no religious restrictions.

b. Political liberty and the ownership of property. Formerly only persons owning a stated amount of property could vote and hold office. Now there are no such bars.

c. Political liberty with respect to sex. Formerly only men had the right of suffrage. Now women as well as men can vote.

In these great civil and political rights we see the long road that the British people have traveled in their experiment with representative government.

INTERESTING READINGS FROM WHICH YOU CAN GET ADDITIONAL INFORMATION

MARSHALL, HENRIETTA E. An Island Story. Frederick A. Stokes Company, New York. A child's history of England.

ROSEBERY, EARL OF. Life of Pitt. The Macmillan Company, New York. Pitt and the political life of England during his time.

TAPPAN, EVA M. In the Days of Queen Victoria. Lothrop, Lee & Shepard Co., Boston.

TERRY, A. G. New Liberty (History Stories of Other Lands). Row, Peterson & Company, Evanston, Illinois.

WARREN, HENRY P. Stories from English History. D. C. Heath and Company, Boston. See pages 406–417.

UNIT IV

THE MARCH TOWARD DEMOCRACY IN FRANCE AND GERMANY

THE MARCH TOWARD DEMOCRACY IN FRANCE AND GERMANY

We turn now to two more examples of the world's experiments in representative government, those of France and Germany. The story of the march toward democracy in each of these countries is very different from that in England. "Divine right" government continued in France long after it disappeared in England, and in Germany it lasted for more than a century after it had died out in France. The long story of the revolutionary overthrow of absolute monarchy in France will be told in Chapter XI.

In Chapter XII we shall then show democracy's difficult march under many changing governments from the French Revolution to the present day.

In Chapter XIII we shall trace the advance toward democracy in Germany. Here empire by divine right held on much longer than it did in the other leading European nations. Indeed, not until the end of the World War did the democratic movement triumph in Germany.

CHAPTER XI

FROM ABSOLUTISM TO REPRESENTATIVE GOVERNMENT IN FRANCE

Liberté, Égalité, Fraternité!

Emblazoned over the entrances to public buildings, carved on monuments, stamped on coins, chorused in national songs, — in fact, everywhere in France, — one finds this slogan of the French Revolution: Liberty, Equality, Fraternity!

It was phrased first during the democratic uprising of the Parisian workers in the 1790's. Then it radiated swiftly over France, arousing the desire for freedom among the downtrodden peasants and artisans of distant provinces. Ten years passed, and Napoleon Bonaparte, that false "Son of the Revolution," led his armies, spreading the message of democracy north, south, and eastward over Europe.

Decade after decade the catchword stirred men who were oppressed and dulled by the new industrialism. By 1850 it had reached the workers in far-off Vienna and Budapest, the artisans in the growing cities of northern Italy and in the new manufacturing centers of Germany. In the meantime the flaming fire of the democratic idea had leaped even the broad Atlantic. In the Spanish colonies of America it stimulated peoples to throw off their oppressive rulers and to form a score of Latin-American republics.

Thus in the 1800's *Liberté, Égalité, Fraternité* became not merely the epitome of the hopes of the French common people: it became the clarion call of advancing democracy around the world. It became the cry of long-oppressed and harassed commoners. The leaders of the people were beginning to embody the scientific ideas of the philosopher John Locke in their demands for a share in the government. They were beginning to consider seriously the emotional denunciations of the scoffer Voltaire and the ringing message of the revolutionary Rousseau.

In Democracy the French People had lagged far behind the British

In studying the rise of representative government in England it was necessary to trace its origin in earlier centuries. The story is one of long evolution, with various upper classes taking the control of government away from others who happened to be holding it. As we have seen, by 1700 the rulers had been shorn of much of their power, and the government was in the hands of a Parliament which represented the well-to-do property-owners.

Fig. 96. Claude Rouget de Lisle singing his own composition, *La Marseillaise.* He filled the need of the French revolutionists for a stirring marching song. (From a painting by I. A. Pils)

That is not the story of France, however. There the one-man idea continued in force until almost 1800. There government was absolute, not by the consent of the governed. At the very moment that the British landowners were exacting from their kings written guaranties of civil rights and political liberties, the cardinals of the Church in France were building up for their sovereign the most autocratic kingly government in Europe.

It was Cardinal Richelieu, especially, who made himself the true ruler of France as the chief minister of Louis XIII. A bishop of the Catholic Church at the age of 21, a cardinal when he was 37, this suave master of political intrigue had, before his death in 1642, built up the absolute power of the king. Ignoring the nobles, Richelieu made a small royal council of favorites the lawmaking and executive body of France. He centralized the machinery of the French government, taking away from the nobles and clergy the right to levy taxes. He transferred the powers of local provincial governments to tyrannical royal officials who policed their districts and forced amazingly large taxes out of the peasants and artisans.

FIG. 97. Armand Jean du Plessis, Cardinal de Richelieu (1585–1642). (From a painting by Philippe de Champagne)

Richelieu also knew the principle that he who controls the army controls the government. So he built up a large standing army which, being paid directly from the royal treasury, was loyal only to the king. By clever intrigue at home he pitted one noble courtier against another, and at the same time he conspired in foreign politics by setting one ruling house of Europe against another. Thus through his diplomacy and intrigue Richelieu not only made the king of France an absolute monarch among his people, but also laid the foundation upon which France soon became the leading government of all Europe.

Louis XIII died in 1643, and upon the accession of the five-year-old boy king, Louis XIV, another cardinal, Mazarin, became the chief minister until 1661. Mazarin continued Richelieu's policies. He schemed and planned, put down all revolts with a harsh hand, and ruled directly from Versailles as Richelieu had done. In 1661, at his death, he passed on to Louis XIV an unexcelled position as absolute ruler of France. There were no visible signs of democracy. The Estates-General, which was a consultative and advisory body, had not met since 1614. There were no elections, no local government. All was done from the royal center near Paris.

As you can readily understand, in the building of this absolute centralized government grave abuses had developed. We can best understand the revolution that shook first France and then the entire Western world after 1789 if we first study some of the abuses which brought it about. It was during the reigns of Louis XIV and his successors, Louis XV and Louis XVI, that these abuses became so conspicuous as to cause the complete destruction of this autocratic society.

Louis XIV, the Perfect Example of the "Divine Right" King

Of the four Louis who ruled over France during the 1600's and the 1700's, only the second, Louis XIV, can really be credited with a capacity for hard work. He rose early in the morning and delved deeply into the problems of state. He actually *worked* at his job of king, which to him was a real trade. "One reigns by work and for work," he told his great-grandson, who reigned after him as Louis XV. And he practiced what he preached, keeping in direct touch with his provincial officers as well as his personal ministers, watching every detail of the administration of his realm.

Louis XIV applied his ideas to his personal life and the development of his court as well as to the management of government affairs. He was a handsome man, a regal and elegant courtier and diplomat. It was said of him that even while playing billiards "he retained an air of world master." In him we see the Grand Monarch, the perfect example of the "divine right" king. Thus a century and a half after James I had pronounced the doctrine of divine right in England, Louis XIV of France carried it to its highest point.

Fig. 98. At the dinner table are Louis XIV (left) and Molière. Even for such an ordinary occurrence Louis XIV surrounded himself with pomp and ceremony. Cardinal Mazarin and a group of courtiers attend the king. (Painting by J. L. Gérôme)

"I am the State" fittingly described the attitude of this "enlightened despot," this paternal king. Louis maintained that he was the representative of God on earth and that attacks upon him and his sacred image were blasphemy and sacrilege.

From the billions of francs exacted from the poor peasants Louis built a magnificent court, a center of pleasure

Europe had seen fine royal palaces before, but never of such inspiring magnificence as was revealed in those which Louis XIV built. Twelve miles out from Paris was the palace of Versailles, a collection of massive, spreading structures with a town surrounding them. For more than 100 years after its construction Versailles supplanted Paris as the center of French government.

Versailles still stands, with much of its later furnishings and equipment preserved for sight-seers. One can walk in imagination with elegantly costumed nobles and ladies of Louis's court through miles of broad corridors, acres of great rooms. In imagination, in richly draped banquet halls, seated at tables laden with deliciously prepared viands and the most delicate wines and liqueurs, one can toast again the glories of Louis XIV. From winding stairways above broad courtyards or from heavily draped windows one can look out upon rich, green terraces.

To this palace were brought furnishings from the handicraft centers of the entire world. Walls were covered with rich tapestries; furniture was hand-carved in styles which are still models of excellence. And surrounding the buildings were vast, well-kept forest preserves and parks and beautifully sculptured fountains. This was, indeed, a palace appropriate for the Grand Monarch.

Here a great pleasure center developed during the long reign of Louis XIV (1643–1715). By far the most dazzling court of all Europe, it was heralded far and wide, attracting the luxury-loving nobles of France and a constant flow of visitors from other countries. Here, in these great suites of apartments, Louis's courtiers lived with him. Eagerly they waited upon the monarch, quick to serve his slightest wish. From the very moment of his awakening in the morning until the time for bed at night they attended him. Only a noble could comb the king's hair or attend him at the bath. Never did a king have such lordly servants.

Louis XIV's court became a world center of art and letters

There was perhaps one redeeming feature in this extravagant use of money wrung from the peasants and artisans of France. Not all the money was wasted, for some of it was used to foster the arts. Under Louis XIV, Versailles became a great center of writing, art, science, and handicraft. He gathered around him a group of brilliant writers, dramatists, artists, craftsmen, and scholars, some of whom became internationally famous.

Especially in the drama and in letters did these French creative writers of Louis XIV's era excel. The great "father of French tragedy," Corneille (1606–1684), lived his most mature years in Louis's reign. One of his plays, *Le Cid*, has achieved a secure place in the history of drama. Like his other plays, it is a portrayal, in heroic proportions and style, of the conflict between impulse and duty; it depicts, with oratorical eloquence, men as they ought to be.

Of equal rank with Corneille stands Molière, the creator of

Fig. 99. Pierre Corneille (1606–1684). (After a painting by Le Brun)

Fig. 100. Molière (1622–1673). (From a painting by Mignard)

Fig. 101. Jean de La Fontaine (1621–1695)

Fig. 102. Jean Racine (1639–1699)

comedy in France. His keen eye for sham in all walks of life, his passion for sanity and balance, are attested by such plays among the long list of his masterpieces as *L'École des Femmes*, *Tartuffe*, *Le Misanthrope*, *Le Bourgeois Gentilhomme*. Without malice and without bitterness he challenges in these plays the intolerances and the humbuggery of his contemporaries.

At the same time Jean Racine, a brilliant young dramatist, was coming into prominence. At first he showed, as was natural, the influence of the great Corneille, but soon his insistence on simplicity of action and his interest in the passions of the human heart led him into original fields. His *Andromaque*, *Phèdre*, *Britannicus*, and *Athalie* are masterpieces of classical tragedy. They depict men as they are. Not only was Racine a great dramatist: he is also in the first rank of French poets.

From these dramatists came an influence which spread far and wide in Europe. Steadily it affected the stage in other countries as well as in France. Here was a new style, which served as an inspiring model for later writers.

The literary minds of the court of Louis XIV are also remembered for other types of writing than the drama. La Fontaine (1621–1695) was the author of gay, graceful fables. Saint-Simon (1675–1755) was a courtier at Versailles and had ample opportunity to observe the inner workings of Louis's brilliant court, which he analyzed toward the end of his life in his famous *Mémoires*. In spite of the fact that the *Mémoires* contain errors of judgment and fact, as well as distortions due to prejudices, nevertheless they are remarkable for their keen observation and vivid portraiture and are of great historical value. Mme. de Sévigné (1626–1696) wrote with more fairness than did Saint-Simon, but her canvas was smaller. Her letters from Paris to her daughter in Provence — published after her death — touched intimately on every topic of the times. Brilliantly, simply, and frankly she wrote her estimate of contemporary social and literary manners, and the wit and intelligence of her letters have put her among the world's most distinguished letter-writers.

Not only was some of Louis's enormous wealth used for letters and art: science and scholarship were also supported. The scientific magazine *Journal des Savants* was established and has been in existence almost continuously to the present day. Louis built libraries and astronomical observatories, his own royal library being regarded as one of the most important in the world. He stimulated many nobles to build scientific laboratories on their own estates. In fact, it was in one of these that Voltaire spent much of his time, dabbling with science. Cardinal Richelieu had founded the French Academy, an organization including men of unusual talent in science, politics, letters, and art. The Academy still carries on today — a limited little group of 40 men who have the approval and patronage of the French government. Louis XIV encouraged this organization during his reign.

The interest in handicrafts paralleled the brilliant development of the arts. Never before had Europe seen the art of weaving fine fabrics, of furniture-making, and of costume-designing carried to such a high point. Working with metal and leather, paper-making, book-printing and bookbinding, wood-carving, gilt ornamentation, and alabaster sculpture were encouraged. This was the period, too, in which elegant Chinese lacquer ware, tapestries, rugs, and other interior decorations were imported, setting a new standard of beauty and costliness for the courts of Europe.

Versailles became the model for other courts. Lesser kings, as well as dukes, counts, and petty nobles, had to have their centers of pleasure and culture patterned on the lines of the palaces of the Grand Monarch himself. That there were some splendid results in the development of a higher level of culture cannot be denied. This autocratic government had, indeed, produced new standards of excellence in architecture, had improved the French language and literature, and had stimulated the development of science and the pursuit of fine handicrafts.

The Ambitious and Greedy Louis nearly Ruined France by his Wars of Aggression

But Louis XIV was not satisfied to be merely the absolute ruler of his own realm. He was ambitious to extend the territory of France and to put his relatives into positions of power in other parts of Europe. In this respect, of course, he was but doing what every other strong ruler had done and was trying to do. Apparently each was consumed by a driving ambition to accumulate more wealth, more territory, and to bring an ever-larger number of human beings under his absolute power.

This greed for wealth and power was illustrated in the lives of the earlier English kings and of the dukes and other petty monarchs who developed the various national states prior to 1500. It was present as well in all earlier empires built on conquest — those of the Roman emperors, of the Mohammedan conquerors, of Genghis Khan and other Mongol chieftains. The desire for wealth and power has driven every strong leader on to ever-greater conquest.

The inevitable outcome in each case was devastating wars of aggression — the killing and enslaving of peaceful human beings, the destruction of the results of civilization. Nothing can condone these wars of aggression, which have torn mankind since the earliest days of recorded history.

Throughout the later 1600's Louis XIV launched one aggressive war after another, keeping the leading nations of Europe constantly in turmoil. French rulers had long believed that there were certain "natural boundaries" for France. These were the Rhine on the north and east, the Pyrenees Mountains and the Mediterranean on the south, and the Atlantic on the west. So for half a century Louis's armies tried to satisfy his ambitions.

We must not use valuable space to rehearse the details of these personal conquests of an arrogant, selfish king. If the military details are desired they can be read in books devoted to military history. They form a very unimportant part of the great march of the world toward democracy. Let it suffice merely to enumerate examples of the destructive effect of absolute government on a continent.

There were, to name outstanding examples, (1) the War of Devolution (1667–1668), in which Louis tried to conquer the Belgian Netherlands; (2) the Dutch War (1672–1678), in which he extended the frontier of France a little nearer the Rhine; (3) the War of the League of Augsburg (1688–1697), in which the rulers of England, Spain, Sweden, and several German states fought for nine years to keep Louis out of the Holy Roman Empire; (4) the War of the Spanish Succession (1701–1713), which resulted from Louis's conspiracies to put his grandson Philip on the throne of Spain and which involved most of the nations of Europe. For twelve years the armies fought over this attempt of a king at further aggrandizement. Louis was defeated on every hand, and at the settlement after the slaughter he had lost all his conquered gains.[1]

As you can see, Louis XIV's ambitions kept the French nation almost continuously at war. Millions of francs were needed to feed, clothe, and equip the thousands of soldiers sent off each year to fight Louis's battles. Millions more were needed to build and keep up his extravagant palaces. Year after year the tax collectors came and took away most of the meager income of the peasants and artisans. Thus the hard-earned income of the people was wasted in useless destruction and in the gay living of their masters. Steadily the national treasury approached bankruptcy. That it did not actually become bankrupt was owing in part to the clever schemes of Louis's ministers of finance. It was also owing to the ability of the people to give ever-larger sums in response to the increasing demands of the tyrannical officials.

In the Meantime what was the Attitude of Peasants and Workers?

Was there enthusiasm in France for these imperial conquests of Louis XIV? No, indeed. The great mass of humanity throughout Europe was relatively unconcerned with these wars which its absolute rulers waged with one another. In fact, until the 1800's political history was little more than the story of conflict among a few ruthless rulers. The common people provided the money, but had not the slightest knowledge of why their respective armies were at war.

During the time of Louis XIV, for example, except for those who lived near international frontiers the common people of one nation knew little about the common people of another. There

[1] Louis died in 1715, but his successors kept up the aggressive wars with other ambitious, grasping rulers of Europe. Hence there followed the War of the Austrian Succession (1740–1748) and the Seven Years' War (1756–1763). The latter, you will remember, finally drove France out of America and left Great Britain master of most of the colonial possessions of North America.

were no newspapers, telegraphs, telephones, or radios. There were no macadam highways and swiftly speeding automobiles. There was little or no understanding of the ways of living among other peoples. Nor did the common people of France hate the common people of England, Germany, Holland, and other countries of which they were supposed to be enemies. It was only the kings and their courtiers and generals who hated, and they hated in little more than the economic sense; that is, they wanted the wealth and the power that their opponents possessed.

In France the condition of the people was perhaps a little better than elsewhere on the Continent. By the middle of the 1700's, for example, English and American travelers reported that French peasants seemed to have food enough to keep body and soul together, although in some districts they were in actual destitution. But in spite of the poverty of the 19,000,000 common people and the luxury of 200,000 nobles, there was no open rebellion.

Several factors contributed, no doubt, to this attitude of submissiveness to their condition, among which two deserve mention here: (1) owing to the increase in trade with other parts of the world, the rise of handicrafts, the discovery of new methods of agriculture, and the like, most of the peasants did not face actual starvation; (2) the common people lacked education. There were few schools — indeed, almost none — for the common people, and a total lack, for them, of such means of communication as newspapers, magazines, and books. The ruling classes organized the universities, the royal societies, and the academies. With splendid buildings, academic pomp and ceremonial, education merely helped to make the ruling classes seem more powerful and more wonderful. Scholars and artists lived on royal pensions, and few of them dared risk offending the rulers by appeals for the common people.

Did the common people gain any rights in the reign of Louis XIV?

From what has been said, it is clear that many of the rights which the Englishmen across the Channel had acquired were denied the French. They had no *political rights*. Nobody could hold office except by appointment from the king. Government was absolute. There was no voting by the people.

Did the French have *civil rights* — freedom of worship, speech, and the press, the right of petitioning the government and of protection from unfair punishment? No, indeed. All these civil rights were lacking in the France of 1700. Anyone who dared to criticize the king or his officials could be thrown into prison without trial. Against such independent-minded people the king issued *lettres de cachet* ("sealed letters"). Armed with these letters, police officials arrested thousands of lovers of liberty and threw them into prison without trial. Many died miserable deaths, forgotten even by the people who had put them there. Such warrants were actually issued to government officials in blank form, with authority to fill in the names of any individuals who in their judgment ought to be disposed of. Thus there was no right of trial by jury, no habeas corpus, no right of petition.

There was, furthermore, the greatest religious intolerance. Freedom of worship was totally lacking. It was the day of strife between Catholics and Protestants, and quite generally throughout Europe whichever of the two religious groups was in power persecuted the other. France was officially a Catholic nation, and yet, at this time, in a total population of about 19,000,000, there were not less than 1,000,000 Protestants. Most of these Protestants were called Huguenots. They were a thrifty people, skilled in manufacturing and trading. In spite of continued oppression they had become the most prosperous single group in France. A common saying of the times illustrated this fact: "He is as rich as a Huguenot."

In the reign of Louis XIV these Huguenots were subjected to the most brutal persecution. Their own churches were destroyed, and they were required to attend the official church and to take part in its service. Parents were compelled to teach their little children a faith which they did not believe. At the same time their business enterprises were restricted. They were compelled to take the dragoons — the mounted soldiers of the king's army — into their homes to live. Inevitably, as a result of generations of this sort of treatment, many French people, although outwardly conforming to the requirements of the Catholic Church, became unbelievers, skeptics, and inwardly sneered at the dishonest practices which they saw about them.

Can you see how little democracy there was in France in 1700?

Under the Incompetent Louis XV the Old Aristocratic Régime neared its End

Louis XIV died in 1715 at the age of 77. In the meantime his son and his grandson had died, and now his five-year-old great-grandson became Louis XV, king of France. For 59 years longer, absolute government was to continue in France under this new king. But it was a depleted and almost ruined France, very different from the conquering nation of Louis XIV's earlier years.

Louis XV was an "incompetent imitator" of his great-grandfather. During his reign more destructive wars were fought. Whole provinces were ruined. Tens of thousands of French people were killed. Increasingly larger sums of money were taken from the artisans and peasants of France to keep up the luxuries of the courts. The search for pleasure dominated the nobles. The courts of Europe combined to plot against one another as they had in reigns gone by.

In this way government went on well through the 1700's under the absolute rule of despotic kings. Men were imprisoned without trial, and the population was taxed without being represented in the government. Serfdom still existed. Freedom of worship was not permitted. No political or civil liberties were gained by the people.

Louis XVI; the End of "Divine Right" Monarchy

But the end of absolute monarchy and wasteful aristocracy was close at hand when Louis XVI, the grandson of Louis XV, came to the throne. He was a well-meaning but unintelligent prince, utterly lacking in administrative ability. He was also an idler, spending his time pottering with locks in his workshop or lolling at the palace windows or shooting the deer in his forest preserves. From time to time he did his best to put his mind to the problems of government, but he was the tool both of shrewd ministers and of his silly young wife, Marie Antoinette, the daughter of Maria Theresa of Austria. This thoughtless young woman surrounded herself with the gayest and most brilliant of lords and ladies in Europe. She was little more than an overgrown child, acting always upon whim and demanding that her every desire for pleasure be satisfied.

And the extravagances continued to mount. It has been estimated that in the 1770's the households maintained by the King, the Queen, and the other members of the royal family cost not less than $12,000,000 a year. Another equally great sum was consumed each year in the reckless grants and pensions which the King made to his favorites.

Desperate Attempts to save the Government by Financial Reforms

In the meantime several ministers in turn tried to adjust the finances of the nation. One of these was Turgot, a friend of Voltaire and Diderot, and an intelligent, experienced student of government. He tried to effect economies and arrange the finances on a sound basis. He tried to lighten the tax burden on the peasants and artisans and to increase the burden on the nobles, the clergy, and the King's favorites. He abolished taxes on food and salt and did away with monopolies. He punished scoundrels who were robbing the people.

But these reforms were exactly what the privileged classes did not want, and at every turn Turgot encountered crafty opponents who whispered against him to the King. Within two years he was dismissed.

Jacques Necker, the minister who succeeded Turgot, was a banker. At first he was popular with the court, for he borrowed hundreds of millions of francs, piling one new loan upon another. It is interesting to know that some of this money was given to the struggling colonies in America to aid them in their revolution against England, Louis XVI's enemy.

Necker did one thing which hastened the end of this period. He published a financial report in 1781 which laid bare to the bankers of the world the bankrupt condition of the royal French treasury. As a result, too, he incurred the enmity of the selfish nobles and of Marie Antoinette. They demanded his dismissal, and Louis, the willing and complacent husband of a spendthrift queen, yielded to their demand and dismissed him.

Then followed Calonne, another controller-general, and more reckless borrowings. Higher and higher mounted the deficit in the national treasury. In spite of the danger Marie Antoinette and her friends continued to dazzle the courtiers of Europe with masked balls at which millions were spent on jewels, silks, satins, and expensive food. By 1786 the national debt amounted to $600,000,000, and it was increasing at the rate of $25,000,000 a year. Now the bankers were shaking their heads. No more loans to a bankrupt government! A crisis was imminent.

In August, 1786, the controller-general informed his king and queen, to their astonishment, that they confronted a national emergency. The government must be completely changed to save it from absolute ruin. "Everything vicious in the state" must be reformed — taxes, customs, financial expenditures, administration of government — or revolution would come.

What could be done? First, assemble the Notables and have a conference about the whole problem.

The Real Beginning of the French Revolution: the Assembly of the Notables in 1787

A hundred and forty-five bishops, dukes, judges, and other government officials met in conference with Calonne and the central government. In no sense did this assembly represent the people of France. Of the 25,000,000 people in France the conference probably represented a small fraction of 1 per cent of all the people.

Calonne told the Assembly of the Notables frankly that to raise the necessary revenue for the government nothing would satisfy but the elimination of the "abuses." These abuses were the special privileges which were enjoyed by the nobles and the clergy. Among them the exemption from taxation was perhaps the most significant. It was this abuse especially which Calonne was attacking.

"Yes, gentlemen," he exclaimed, "the abuses offer a source of wealth which the state should appropriate . . . the abuses must now be destroyed for the welfare of the people."

But the Assembly of the Notables would not listen to such attacks upon their privileges. After voting for a few minor reforms which would not affect them, they asked and secured from the King the dismissal of Calonne.

A new minister was appointed, and plans for a new loan were made. This time the *parlement* of Paris refused to register the act.[1] Instead it drew up a truly revolutionary declaration of rights. Then it made what was to be a historic pronouncement:

> Only the nation assembled in the Estates General can give the consent necessary to the establishment of a permanent tax. Only the nation after it has learned the true state of the finances can destroy the great evils and open up important resources.

Here was rebellion — a call for the assembling of the Estates General. The Estates General had not met since 1614 — 173 years before. Rebellion, indeed, thought the King and his courtiers, and Louis dismissed the *parlement*.

But now Paris and the other cities of France seethed with rebellious mobs. Orators played upon the emotions of the crowds. Indignant protests arose all over France. The King ordered his troops to arrest the rebellious officials. The soldiers refused. At last Louis, thoroughly frightened, decided to call the Estates General together.

So little was known about this ancient lawmaking body that scholars had to conduct researches to discover how the members were chosen and what the powers and duties were. A growing interest spread over France as to the best form of organization for the Estates General. A plan was drawn up giving the third estate — that is, the middle classes — as many deputies as the nobles and clergy together.

In August, 1788, the plan was finished. Louis XVI, no longer able to govern alone, sent a summons far and wide over his

[1] The *parlement* of Paris, unlike the English Parliament, was a judicial body. Before a new law could be enforced it had to be recorded or registered in the statute books of this court. On frequent occasions before this the *parlement* had refused to register laws which it regarded as unenforceable.

kingdom, calling for the election of representatives to the Estates General. In preparing for the meeting, a real expression of public opinion was obtained. Statements of grievances and plans of reform were submitted from many villages and towns. The people demanded a "really national constitution, which shall define the rights of all and provide the laws to maintain them." Note that they did not ask for the establishment of a republic. There was no request that the office of king be abolished. What they wanted was a limited, or constitutional, monarchy, perhaps a "crowned republic," a parliamentary government like that of England across the Channel.

At last we are to see the influence of 200 years of using more scientific ways of thinking. Now are to appear the results of the work of the political economists, of the sentimental Rousseau, of the novelists, of the destructive Voltaire, of the scholarly Diderot and the Encyclopedists.

The Peaceful Revolution continues: the Work of the Estates General, 1789

On May 5, 1789, the Estates General assembled in Versailles. It was not much like its predecessor, the Assembly of the Notables, or its ancient forerunner, the Estates General of 1614. The Estates General of 1789 was predominantly an assembly of representatives of the middle classes, consisting of small and large property-owners.

From the beginning this middle-class group took charge of affairs. The nobles and the clergy refused to sit with them to form a truly national lawmaking body. The middle-class deputies refused to meet separately. After six weeks of delay the latter declared themselves a "National Assembly." Rebellion, indeed!

The National Assembly claimed to represent the peasants and workers of the towns as well as their own middle-class group. "We represent," they said, "more than 95 per cent of the French people." This step indicated that the members of the third estate were determined *to take into their own hands the task of reforming the government.*

A short time afterwards the "commons," who had been locked

out of their usual place of meeting, assembled in a building called the Tennis Court and there took the *Tennis Court Oath*, in which they declared that they would assemble whenever the needs of France demanded it and "until the constitution of the kingdom shall be established."

One dramatic event followed another. The King threatened armed force; but the deputies, firm under the leadership of the

Fig. 103. Members of the National Assembly taking the oath in the Tennis Court. (From a painting by Couder)

distinguished Mirabeau and the Abbé Sieyès, refused to be dismissed. At last the nobles and clergy were ordered by the King to join the third estate in a real National Assembly.

The Workers of Paris rise against their Masters

Two striking events in the summer and autumn of 1789 showed clearly that the end of the old régime was near. On July 11 the suffering hordes of commoners in Paris, led by Camille Desmoulins (1760–1794) and other emotional orators, armed themselves with whatever implements were at hand. Within three days they had taken the great city into their own power. Stores and warehouses were looted; government offices were seized; and on the fourth day, July 14, 1789, the royal prison known as the Bastille was destroyed. The slumbering hatreds of centuries had burst into armed violence.

In the meantime leading citizens had elected representatives from the various districts of Paris and formed a new city government called the *commune*. The capital of France now had popular

FIG. 104. The revolutionists storming the Bastille. In a few hours the fortress-prison which had stood for over 400 years yielded, and its prisoners were freed

government. Knowing the need of armed force, this new people's government organized its own volunteer troops, 48,000 strong.

During this interval the bewildered King and the disdainful Queen were continuing their luxurious living at Versailles, only twelve miles from the turmoil and suffering of the capital. Either from stupidity or indifference the Queen regarded the whole matter as an awful bore. It is reported that when one of the more humane nobles said to her that the people were starving for lack of bread, she replied with an air of astonishment, "Then why don't they eat cake?"

So the summer passed, and the cold of autumn came. Conditions in the city grew worse. While banquets for richly gowned lords and ladies were held in Versailles, hordes of starving and shivering people muttered together in Paris.

Then came the historic March of the Women on Versailles. Angered beyond endurance by the reports of the feasts and parties of the care-free nobles at the court and by a rumor that the King was about to dismiss the Assembly, a horde of poverty-stricken, starving women began the long twelve-mile tramp from Paris to Versailles. They believed that great stores of food were secreted at the palace, and they still retained a childlike confidence in their King, regardless of what they might think of his advisers. The King would hear them and feed them.

What a picture that was! Hundreds of ragged women tramping through a drizzling rain to ask bread from their king!

When they finally crowded before the great gates of the palace the royal guard faced them from within. What would happen? The members of the mob (men had joined the women by now) were either unarmed or armed with the crudest sort of weapons. The guard was half in sympathy. The rain was pouring down by now. What did they want? "Bread and speech with the King," they shouted. Nothing else would suffice. They gained the courtyard. They insisted on seeing the King and the Queen. They demanded food. Finally the rulers yielded and showed themselves on a balcony, and the King promised to do all in his power to find food for "his children."

After a night of rioting, when only the presence of Lafayette and his soldiers saved the palace from utter ruin and the Queen from bodily harm, the mob, believing that the mere presence of the King in Paris would assure them of prosperity, demanded that he, the Queen, and their small son return to the capital.

So in the midst of a shouting, milling mob Louis XVI, Marie Antoinette, and the little Prince Louis returned to Paris.

But the news of the taking of the Bastille and the March of the Women showed clearly that a real crisis had been reached.

Rebellion spread throughout France

Swiftly word spread throughout the provinces that Paris was in the hands of the people. Rebellion began to break out in one center after another. In the towns and cities royal officers were dismissed, new popular governments were elected, and National Guards were recruited.

The contagion spread to the rural districts. Peasants, armed with clubs and whatever other weapons they could find, drove nobles out of their castles, burned their buildings, and took possession of their other property. In many places they took great care to secure and destroy the legal documents which gave the nobles title by inheritance to these vast estates.

By the autumn of 1789 the worst of the old aristocratic régime was ended forever in France.

The Great Achievements of the National Assembly, 1789–1791

While these dramatic events were taking place, legislative changes were being brought about that have resounded in history even to the present time. The Estates General had been transformed into the National Assembly. Within two years, from August, 1789, to September, 1791, this body of men, more representative of the people of France than any previous assembly, laid the foundations for popular government.

First and foremost, they destroyed all the vestiges of feudalism and serfdom. They abolished the old courts of the manors, the game laws, the tithes paid to the clergy, and the right to obtain offices by purchase. When the work was over, the entire French feudal system, which had outlived its English counterpart by 200 years, was gone.

Liberty, Equality, Fraternity: the Declaration of the Rights of Man

Then the National Assembly drew up a historic statement of rights for the masses called the Declaration of the Rights of Man and of the Citizen. This document was based in part upon

Fig. 105. Honoré Gabriel Victor Riquetti, Count Mirabeau (1749–1791)

Fig. 106. Jean Paul Marat (1744–1793)

Fig. 107. Maximilien François Marie Isidore de Robespierre (1758–1794)

Fig. 108. Georges Jacques Danton (1759–1794)

Four Leaders of the French Revolution

the phrasings of the English Bill of Rights, but for the most part it incorporated the ideas of Locke, Montesquieu, Rousseau, and other frontier thinkers.

In fact, the influence of Rousseau was revealed very clearly in many of the revolutionary acts of that period. Such books as the *Social Contract* put phrases into the mouths of the French leaders. Note how the demand for political and civil rights was phrased:

> Men are born and remain free and equal in rights.
>
> Law is the expression of the general will.
>
> No person shall be accused, arrested, or imprisoned except in the cases and according to the forms prescribed by law.

But *there was no suggestion of abolishing the ownership of private property.* On the contrary the right to property was definitely recognized as one of the rights of man, along with freedom of speech, of the press, and of worship.

Thus the Declaration of the Rights of Man and of the Citizen became another historic charter of liberties. Thus also democracy marched on, this time on the mainland of Europe. The groundwork was being laid for the overthrow of absolute government everywhere.

For a year France went on as a constitutional monarchy

Space is lacking to describe all the other remarkable acts of this National Assembly. For example, it brought order out of chaos in local and provincial administration. The old abuses were wiped out. France was divided into 83 departments and subdivided into districts and local divisions. Government and the administration of law was made subject to *popular election of the people in each local district.*

The National Assembly also confiscated the property of the Church, the institution which then owned between a fifth and a fourth of all the land of the country. With this newly acquired wealth the government was able to issue a new kind of paper currency with which to carry on its affairs. In this way the financial administration of the nation was straightened out.

Finally, a systematic, written constitution was prepared. This was based in part upon the ideas of the theorists whom we have studied in previous chapters, especially upon those of Montesquieu. It was also based in part upon the English and American constitutions. Since this constitution was but the first of nearly a dozen that were to be made within the next few decades, we shall not study its details at this time. Suffice it to say that the French government, under this new constitution, became essentially a republic. For the first time in the history of France government represented the mass of the people. In the meantime the king had lost all his power. France was, for the time being, a constitutional monarchy.

The First Republic, 1792–1795

But conditions were such that France could not long remain a constitutional monarchy. You can readily understand that the rulers of Europe were opposed to the revolutionary movement in France. Every king, duke, and count, every petty autocrat in Europe, was swayed by one thought as he witnessed the terrifying developments south and west of the Rhine: "How long will it be before my power will be taken away as has that of Louis XVI?" For a time the rulers forgot their selfish quarrels and joined their armies together against the common enemy, the armed force of the rising spirit of democracy that was spreading among the peoples of Europe.

At the same time the treacherous Marie Antoinette and her weak husband were conspiring with the nobles who had fled from France. This group was concentrated near Coblenz, on the border between France and Germany, conspiring with the rulers of Europe. Marie Antoinette had urged her brother, the Emperor of the Holy Roman Empire, to intervene in French affairs.

Then on a dark night in June, 1791, the King and Queen, disguised as common citizens, slipped out of their Paris palace and drove quietly through the city. Once beyond its walls, they turned their horses toward the royal armies on the Rhine. They had almost arrived; but at Varennes, near the frontier, a too-curious guard looked into their carriage and recognized the royal pair. The guard arrested them and took them back to their palace. From that day they were kept as prisoners.

Then it was that the Austrian emperor and the Prussian king joined hands against the French popular government. With the exception of one party the National Assembly (the legislature which had now come into operation) was enthusiastically in favor of a foreign war as a means of consolidating national sentiment behind the new government. War was declared in April, 1792. At the very beginning the leader of the Austro-Prussian allies openly proclaimed that the war was to end the anarchy in France. Its purpose, he said, was "to check the attacks upon the throne and the altar, to establish the legal power, and to restore to the King the security and liberty of which he is now deprived."

More than any other fact, this showed the popular leaders of the French Revolution what they must do. They must not only fight against the rest of Europe to maintain their independence, but put an end at once to the monarchy. In the meantime the commune, which had begun as a workers' group, was being controlled by the semi-aristocratic business class. They must abolish this also, thought the leaders.

On August 9 and 10, 1792, the workers of Paris, under the leadership of Danton, Marat, and Robespierre (see figures 106, 107, and 108), seized control of the city government and organized a mob attack upon the Tuileries, the royal palace. The King and the royal family took refuge in the Hall of the Assembly, where they were protected against physical violence. But the Assembly, intimidated by the threats of the mob, voted to suspend the King, to dismiss the ministers, and to summon a new national convention which should determine the future form of the national government. Representatives to this convention were to be chosen by "universal manhood suffrage." Every man was to have the right to vote. Thus the French leaders proposed to establish completely representative government at one blow. Democracy seemed, indeed, to be marching on.

In the meantime tens of thousands of loyal French youth had responded with great enthusiasm to the defense of their country. Nationality became a living thing to the people of France. Men went to war singing the new national hymn, the "Marseillaise" (named from Marseille, where it was composed and first sung).

Surprisingly enough, these gallant, untrained youths held back the Prussian and Austrian armies at Valmy, in northeastern France.

In September, 1792, the National Convention[1] abolished all royal forms of government. Three months later it placed Louis XVI on trial for treason and condemned him to death. The death vote was passed by a slight majority of the Convention. A month later, January, 1793, the guillotine[2] received the King of France as its most noted victim. Danton roared to the crowd as the head fell: "The kings of Europe would challenge us? We throw them the head of a king!" A few months later the Queen, Marie Antoinette, followed him to the same death.

FIG. 109. The widowed and imprisoned queen of France — Marie Antoinette

Then came dictators and the Terror

The new National Convention consisted of almost 700 members. It was soon recognized that this number was too large to administer the affairs of state efficiently. So a Committee of Public Safety, composed of nine members, was appointed. It was this committee, led by such persons as Danton and Robespierre, that for the time being turned the Republic into an absolute dictatorship ruled by terror. For almost a year following the summer of 1793, France was governed by fear — fear of the guillotine. It

[1] The earlier National Assembly became the Legislative Assembly, which in turn had now become the National Convention.

[2] Named for Dr. Guillotin, who suggested the instrument as a more humane way of execution than that of beheading with an ax. The guillotine consists of a wooden frame containing upright posts between which falls a huge knife which cuts off instantly the head of the person held beneath it on a board.

is estimated that not less than 2500 persons were guillotined in Paris alone. The Convention decreed that every noble, every office-holder of the earlier governments, every person who did not have written evidence of his loyalty, was to be placed under suspicion.

The Terror was more than local; it was national. In every center of any size the local Revolutionary Tribunal arrested,

FIG. 110. Robespierre, one of the most extreme of the revolutionaries, lies wounded on a stretcher. He has been brought before the Tribunal, where, after being identified, he was ordered to be executed without further trial. (After a painting by François Flameng)

convicted, and guillotined its suspected enemies. The entire number thus disposed of is unknown, but it is believed to have been more than 10,000.

As the hysteria of blood mounted higher and higher, suspicion spread even to the revolutionaries themselves. When Danton advised them to be more moderate, he himself was accused of disloyalty to the Revolution, taken to the guillotine, and beheaded. Marat was murdered in his bath by Charlotte Corday, a young woman of an opposite faction. Finally Robespierre himself, the most extreme of the leaders, was beheaded, and the Revolution was over.

For a very short time France became a socialistic state

While the Revolutionary Tribunal and the Committee of Public Safety were spilling the blood of their enemies, the National Convention was instituting what amounted to a really socialistic régime. It set prices for farm products; it confiscated the property of all the Royalists who had fled from France. The great estates of the nobles and clergy were divided and sold on easy payments to the peasants. Note, however, that even the National Convention did not adopt the public ownership of property: they merely took property from one group and gave it to another.

Other important changes were made by this body. An improved system of weights and measures was established. This was the metric system, which has now come into use in nearly every country of Europe.[1]

An elaborate system of education at the expense of the state was created. This became the very foundation of the modern system which is now in force. A beginning was made at recodifying and simplifying the laws of the country.

These revolutionaries were so determined to wipe out everything which pertained to royalty that they went to ridiculous extremes. In place of the title *Monsieur* (Mr.) every person was to be called Citizen or Citizeness. (Louis XVI was referred to as Citizen Capet.) Almost no one would permit himself to wear the knee breeches and silk stockings which were conspicuous parts of the dress of the upper classes.

Then came the Directory, 1795–1799

Smaller and smaller became the group that ruled France in these revolutionary days. Slowly the bloody extremists passed out of power, and upper-middle-class business men increased their hold over the government.

In 1795 still another constitution went into effect. In the new

[1] In this respect the United States and England are regarded as backward countries, for they still continue to use the pound-foot system of measuring weight and length. This is done in spite of the attempts of engineers in both countries for nearly a century to bring about a change.

legislative body which was created, it was discovered that the middle-class property-owners had secured control. The central administration was now turned over to a board of five Directors — the Little Directory, as it was called.

Then followed conspiracies and counter-conspiracies. Royalists were quietly coming back into France. Some were elected to the assemblies. These conspired constantly to take back the control over local and national government.

At the same time, leaders of the city workers saw the government slipping back into the hands of the new well-to-do class and tried to keep it for the masses. One leader, named Babeuf (1760–1797), said of the miserable condition of the city workers of Paris:

> When I see the poor without the clothing and shoes which they themselves are engaged in making, and contemplate the small minority who do not work and yet want for nothing, I am convinced that government is still the old conspiracy of the few against the many, only it has taken a new form.

Under the leadership of Babeuf the workers rose in rebellion against the *bourgeois* Directors. They were a badly equipped and unorganized band, however, and their rebellion was soon put down. Babeuf, their humanitarian leader, was executed.

Other difficulties arose. In handling the huge finances of the nation the Directors began to take some of the money for themselves. Quarrels and plots continued. At the very moment that the people of Paris were starving for want of food, the Directors were secretly seizing larger and larger amounts of gold. Furthermore, they were running the new government by issuing huge amounts of paper money. The very thing happened that has happened in the history of the United States and of other countries. Faster and faster the printing presses moved, and lower and lower went the value of French money. By 1798 it was clear that the new government faced bankruptcy, unable to extricate itself from its financial difficulties.

So in 1799 the Time was Favorable for the Rise of a Powerful Military Dictator

In the short space of ten years France had swayed first in one direction, then in another. How totally unlike England's slow but sure onward march to representative government!

Then came one of the most astonishing turns in the fortunes of France. A successful young military leader arose unexpectedly, won the loyalty of "young France," seized control, and soon made himself dictator. To the story of this unknown youth's astonishing rise to world power, his unwitting scattering of revolution throughout all Europe, and the frequent changes of government in France for another century, we turn in the next chapter.

INTERESTING READINGS FROM WHICH YOU CAN GET ADDITIONAL INFORMATION

Adams, Katherine. Red Caps and Lilies. The Macmillan Company, New York. Story of the French Revolution.

Bill, Alfred H. The Red Prior's Legacy. Longmans, Green & Co., New York. The French Revolution.

Dark, Sidney. The Book of France for Young People. Doubleday, Doran & Company, Inc., Garden City, New York.

Doyle, A. Conan. The Refugees: a Tale of Two Continents. Harper & Brothers, New York. The Huguenots in the time of Louis XIV.

Dumas, Alexander. The Three Musketeers. E. P. Dutton & Co., New York. Gives a good picture of the court of France and Richelieu.

Gras, Felix. The Reds of the Midi: an Episode of the French Revolution. D. Appleton and Company, New York.

Haynes, Herbert. The Red Caps of Lyons. D. Appleton and Company, New York. The French provinces during the French Revolution.

Major, Charles. The Little King. The Macmillan Company, New York. The childhood of Louis XIV.

Marshall, Henrietta E. The History of France. Doubleday, Doran & Company, Inc., Garden City, New York. An interesting history.

Martineau, Harriet. The Peasant and the Prince. Ginn and Company, Boston. Describes Louis XVI, France before the Revolution, and the conditions that led to the Revolution.

Pitman, Leila W. Stories of Old France. American Book Company, New York. Covers the period from Charles VII to the French Revolution.

Price, Eleanor C. Stories from French History. Dodd, Mead & Company, New York.

Sabatini, Rafael. Bardelys the Magnificent. Houghton Mifflin Company, Boston. Louis XIII and Richelieu.

Seaman, Augusta H. When a Cobbler ruled the King. The Macmillan Company, New York. The French Revolution and the Reign of Terror.

CHAPTER XII

DEMOCRACY'S DIFFICULT MARCH UNDER CHANGING GOVERNMENTS IN FRANCE, 1800–1914

The changeable government of France

For nearly a century, 1789–1870, the political fortunes of France swung from one extreme to another. From absolute monarchy to Republic . . . from Republic to dictatorship and Terror . . . from dictatorship and Terror to the absolutism of Empire . . . from Empire to constitutional monarchy. Then more swings of the political pendulum: from middle-class monarchy to short-lived Republic again . . . back again to Empire . . . then the final reëstablishment of the present Republic.

"How changeable!" perhaps you exclaim. How unlike England and America, which, once started on their experiments with representative democracy, went slowly and steadily on their way. Yes, different indeed. But through all the shifts, through all the changes in masters, the French common people established more and more securely the civil rights for which they had overthrown the "divine right" government. And, as we shall see, they, like their English and American brothers, were finally guaranteed these in the more fundamental political rights of voting and sharing in the government.

To tell fully even the major events of this century of swift political changes would require a whole volume. At best our account can be but an outline.

I. 1799–1814: Dictatorship, Napoleon I, and the First Empire
II. 1814–1830: France a constitutional monarchy
III. 1830–1848: Revolution — France a middle-class monarchy
IV. 1848–1852: Revolution — the Second Republic
V. 1852–1870: Napoleon III and the Second Empire
VI. 1871 to the present: Revolution — the Third Republic; the business men in power

I. Napoleon Bonaparte and Imperial France, 1799–1814

In Paris, in 1797, the five dictators of the Directory were quarreling among themselves, each striving to gain what he could for himself. The guillotine had stopped cutting off heads, and France was outwardly quiet. Inwardly the people were bewildered by the sharp turns of events. Nobody saw clearly what should be done to establish orderly and democratic government.

Fig. 111. General Bonaparte during the Italian campaign at Arcola, where he defeated an army almost twice the size of his own. (From a painting by Gros)

The country needed one thing — a leader! The people needed someone to follow enthusiastically, someone who would bind them together in a great national program, someone to create the spirit of patriotism expressed in the slogan "Fraternity," a leader to work out the governing machinery which would make real the other two great ideas of the Revolution — Equality and Liberty.

In the lull of this situation came startling news — General Napoleon Bonaparte had defeated five Austrian armies in Italy, and France had gained great territories and great glory. Every important military post in Italy was in French hands.

Here, then, was the long-awaited leader — Napoleon Bonaparte. What mattered it if he was a Corsican whose family was of Italian origin? Wasn't Corsica a French territory? Had he not been brought up in France? Had he not fought in the Revolution, been a Jacobin — indeed, been almost guillotined under the suspicion that he had disclosed some government secrets? Was he not "a son of the Revolution," as he had already announced? The Directory knew him well. Had he not helped to keep them in office with his artillery? And they had given him command of the French armies in Italy.

With the success of his army General Bonaparte became the most-talked-of man in France. The Directory praised and flattered him, really afraid to do otherwise. The people generally adored him. From his Italian headquarters went "generals, officials, purveyors, as well as the highest nobility and most distinguished men of Italy, who had come to solicit the favor of a glance or a moment's conversation."

Bonaparte, a man of enormous conceit believed himself that he was "the Man of Destiny." He had a vision of a victorious empire of France leading the whole world. Although he repeated glibly enough the slogans of the Republic, he had no idea of helping France to establish one. Witness the statement that he made in Italy at the very beginning of his success:

> Do you think either that my object is to establish a republic? What a notion! . . . What the French want is glory and the satisfaction of their vanity . . . The nation must have a head [himself, of course], a head who is rendered illustrious by glory and not by theories of government, fine phrases, or the talk of idealists.

Was this not a clear enough statement of a practical man who proposed to take charge of things in France? And he took charge of them in the most spectacular career of modern times.

He waited two years. In the meantime he led an ill-fated expedition to Egypt with the idea of making that country a stepping-stone for an attack upon Great Britain's Indian possessions. We cannot pause to tell of the disastrous Egyptian campaign. Suffice it to say that in the summer of 1799 he deserted his army in Egypt and had the good fortune to reach the coast of France in October without the French people's learning of his losses.

General Bonaparte returned to Paris to find that the Directory had practically destroyed orderly government. The people were in a ferment of excitement, demanding that the Directors be ousted. Furthermore, foreign armies had won back all that Bonaparte had captured and were about to invade France on every side.

It was a moment for a daring adventurer. Bonaparte seized it. Conspiring with a few leaders to overthrow the Directory, he led troops into the Assembly on November 9, 1799, and forcibly expelled the members who refused to accept him as leader. This unexpected political move, or *coup d'état*, as it is called, established Bonaparte as military dictator of France.

Napoleon and his fellow conspirators, the most prominent of whom was Abbé Sieyès, now proceeded to draw up a new constitution. They placed the government of France under three consuls, of whom Bonaparte was to be First Consul. In taking this title, Napoleon was putting into practice his dream of reviving the Roman imperial government.

As First Consul, 1799–1804, Bonaparte brings administrative order and military success

We see, then, this astonishing situation — a nation of nearly 28,000,000 people, including noble families, business men of wealth and influence, and millions of hard-working peasants and artisans, acclaiming a little man of 30 years as "the Man of Destiny." Napoleon, selfish and conceited, accepted their plaudits as his due. He saw himself as another Cæsar, mastering all Europe. In this quest of power he was aided by his lack of scruples, always playing with the group that offered him most at the moment. And with these traits he had the remarkable ability to act quickly and directly. He moved swiftly, putting his plans into action while his opponents were deliberating. He was a "direct actionist" — in no sense a deep thinker.

It was especially this last trait that led to two outstanding achievements in the five years from 1799 to 1804. The first was an efficient internal reconstruction of his country; the second was the complete defeat of all her enemies in battle.

As First Consul, Bonaparte announced a new constitution which gave him virtually a dictatorship over France. This constitution was submitted to the vote of the people. The result was 3,000,000 for acceptance and 1500 against. We must remember that such a vote represented really the willingness of the French people to follow and be ruled by any leader who seemed to guarantee them peace and prosperity. Witness what a foreign diplomat in Paris wrote at the time:

> The people are so sick and weary of revolutionary horrors and folly that they believe any change cannot fail to be for the better. . . . [They] prefer to see a single man of talent possess himself of the power than a club of intriguers.

So Bonaparte got the power of a dictator and set about reorganizing the national and local governments. He created a centralized scheme of major and minor officials called prefects and subprefects to govern the departments and smaller districts. As First Consul all were appointed by him, worked under his direction, and reported to him. These officials in turn appointed the mayors of the communes. There were locally elected bodies chosen by the voters of the communes, but they had merely advisory power. Thus government was as autocratic as under the absolute monarch Louis XIV. Republic, indeed! Bonaparte's plans for imperial personal power were being realized.

Then the finances of the nation were put in order. Bonaparte reorganized the system of taxation so that increased amounts of money were available for his government. He set up an efficient and economical administration which saved large sums of money. He confirmed the earlier confiscation of the lands of the Church, making the clergy salaried employees of the state. He established a central bank, called the Bank of France, which from the date of its founding in 1800 has had an enviable reputation for maintaining the financial security of the country.

He appointed legal experts to simplify and codify the laws of the country. The laws were assembled under the name *Code Napoléon,* and this code, because of the great improvement it effected in judicial practice in France, brought to Bonaparte great personal renown.

In public works he accomplished important improvements also. He built not less than 200 well-paved roads with great trunk highways leading from every direction to Paris as the center. In this way his armies could be moved swiftly from one part of the land to another, meeting invaders on every side. He built bridges, dredged rivers, and improved harbors.

Bonaparte also restored and improved the ancient palaces, built and endowed art museums and libraries, and provided for the establishment of a national system of schools. This school system was to include an elementary school in every commune of the country, *lycées* (high schools) in the larger towns, and hundreds of technical, engineering, and military schools. The system was completed by a central normal school, in which teachers were to be trained.

Thus, for a time, through Bonaparte's energetic efforts life in France became quieter than it had been for many years. The turmoil of Revolution and Terror gave way to a degree of security which the people had not felt for a long time. And government went on with an efficiency in administration hitherto unknown.

In the meantime the First Consul and his generals had saved France from foreign armies. Early in 1800 Great Britain, Austria, and Russia had joined together and threatened France on every frontier. Acting with his accustomed swiftness, Bonaparte himself led an army over the Alps and in June, 1800, smashed the Austrians at Marengo, in the valley of the river Po. Almost at the same time another French army defeated other Austrian troops in southern Germany.

Against her maritime enemies, the British, France was not so successful. By the beginning of 1802 both France and England were weary of war, and in March the representatives of the two governments signed a treaty of peace at Amiens.

Napoleon I, Emperor of the French, 1804–1814

It is little wonder, therefore, that in 1802 Napoleon Bonaparte, First Consul of France, had so bound the people to him that they authorized his election as consul for life. In addition they gave him the power to appoint his successor. Democracy had indeed marched backward in France! Government had become a hereditary dictatorship. Once more it had become absolute, — as absolute as that of the "divine right" kings.

Bonaparte now had everything but the title that symbolizes imperial power. And in 1804 he determined to add that to his name. In the cathedral of Notre Dame in Paris he was proclaimed Emperor Napoleon I. To bless the coronation and give it the approval of the Church of Rome, the Pope (Pius VII) had been brought from Rome to Paris. As Pius was about to place the crown upon his head, Napoleon "seized the crown, waved the Pope aside, and crowned himself."

From this point on, Napoleon's imperial ambitions knew no bounds. He saw himself as the head of a family of ruling monarchs,

Fig. 112. The coronation of Napoleon I, Emperor of the French. Napoleon is about to place the crown upon his head. (From a painting by David)

governing the entire Western world. Not merely France but all Europe was to be the scene of his exploits and his dictatorship. To further his plans he put his brothers on various thrones. In 1806 his brother Louis became king of Holland, and his brother Joseph, king of Naples (later he became king of Spain). Napoleon himself ruled the so-called Kingdom of Italy, and his stepson, Eugène de Beauharnais, was viceroy over these partially unified Italian states. Another brother, Jerome, was made king of Westphalia, which was formed by joining together various little states of western German territory.

Furthermore, the *form* of empire came into French life again. Titles of the old nobility came back. *Monsieur* began to be heard again in place of the revolutionary *citoyen.* Silks and satins marked once more the new aristocracy. In fact, most of the old monarchical forms came back.

Pretending to be "a son of the Revolution," Napoleon spread democracy over Europe by military conquest

We must note one important fact, however. Throughout his career Napoleon, always behaving as an autocrat, talked the language of democracy. He called himself "a son of the Revolution," and wherever he went he proclaimed the magic catchwords *Liberty, Equality, Fraternity.* With respect to the second and third words he was probably sincere. He tried in various ways to provide for a certain degree of equality, and he certainly exemplified the idea of fraternity, the brotherhood of Frenchmen. Under Napoleon national patriotism grew as it never had before. But liberty he did not give the French people. As we have seen, he set up a completely centralized government in which popular sovereignty was totally lacking. He said disdainfully, "What the French people want is equality, not liberty."

Without knowing that he was doing so, Napoleon paved the way for revolution which 50 years later spread throughout the industrial centers of Europe. From Italy to Hungary, from Vienna to Berlin, he laid the foundation for this new movement in four years of military success. In October, 1805, he defeated the Austrians at Ulm, in Württemberg, and, in December, both the Austrians and Russians at Austerlitz. As a result he took vast territories from his enemies and carved more kingdoms for his relatives. In 1806 he invaded Prussia and routed an army of more than 100,000 men at the battle of Jena. Napoleon then marched into Berlin, the victorious master of most of Prussia. Following that he arranged a remarkable treaty with the Czar of Russia, securing the latter's help against Great Britain and the northern kingdoms of Europe. But we shall see later how this very conquest spread the ideas of democracy throughout the regions which were conquered.

But Napoleon Overreached himself and Destroyed his Own Empire

By 1808 this young man of 39 had most of Europe at his feet. A Charlemagne indeed! Emperor of the French, king of Italy, and lord to whom the kings of Europe paid respectful homage.

Fig. 113. Europe in 1808. Either by conquest or through alliance Napoleon controlled most of the Continent, as the map indicates

For nine years (1799–1808) the world had seen the most daring and able adventurer in modern history rise to imperial power. Had Napoleon Bonaparte been a truly great man he could have helped the world's march to democracy more than any man before him. He could have brought peace and order to Europe. He could have given real significance to the words *Liberty*, *Equality*, and *Fraternity* that he spoke so glibly.

But at the height of his position, in 1808, Napoleon's greed for power was still not satisfied. One great rival, Great Britain, had not been humbled. Although Napoleon was master of the lands of Europe, England was still mistress of the seas. With her remarkable navy and her growing merchant marine, Great Britain was developing an enormous trade with Asia and America and was becoming a rich world empire.

To destroy England's trade, Napoleon tried to establish the "Continental System"

It was in the attempt to defeat his one powerful rival that Napoleon lost all. Within six years he had toppled from his position as the leading emperor of the world and become an exile on a rocky island off the southwest coast of Africa.

To more than any other single factor, Napoleon's fall can be ascribed to the failure of his plan to unite all Europe against Great Britain. The plan itself was a simple one. The governments of the Continent were to be leagued together in a rigid boycott of England's goods. This plan was called the Continental System.

"Let us refuse to buy from Great Britain," said Napoleon to the Czar of Russia and the kings of the other states of Europe. "Close your ports to every British merchantman. Then England will sue for peace." What he really meant was that if England's trade were ruined she would humble herself before him — Napoleon the Great; for if England's trade were ruined, what would it profit this "nation of shopkeepers" if it did have the world's greatest navy?

The economic war had already been begun in 1806 with Napoleon's declaration that a state of blockade existed around the British Isles. In a series of decrees he announced that all ports of France and of every country allied with her would refuse to receive British merchantmen. Even neutral vessels, if they sailed from British ports, would be seized by France.

In 1807 Great Britain retaliated with similar decrees. All ships bound for the ports of France were to be seized and the goods confiscated. The influence of these proclamations was immediately felt in all neutral countries, including America. Do you recall the depression and unrest in the United States occasioned by President Jefferson's Embargo Act? The merchants and manufacturers of the Northern states vigorously opposed this limitation on trade with France and England. In fact, the ill feeling that developed between the United States and England led, only a few years later, to the War of 1812.

With this plan, however, Napoleon had overstepped his bounds. He was unable either to compel or persuade the trading countries of Europe to close their ports to British merchantmen. Even his own brother Louis, king of Holland, refused to do so. In Spain and Portugal also Napoleon met with defiance. Hitherto he had interfered little in the affairs of those countries, but now he sent armies against them in the attempt to prevent trade with Great Britain. For a short time he was successful, but not for long. The British landed troops in Portugal and steadily drove the French back.

At the same time the Spanish patriots took part in the fighting. By 1812, with the aid of the British armies, they had forced the French as far north as Valencia. Napoleon's brother Joseph, who occupied the throne, was driven out. Then the patriots drafted their own new constitution, based in part upon those of the French and the Americans and definitely reflecting the spirit of the French Revolution. Thus we see more imperial conquests providing the conditions for democracy.

The disastrous Russian campaign of 1812, however, provided the final blow to Napoleon's empire. Until that time Napoleon and the Czar Alexander had conspired together to divide the Western world between them. Alexander had said to Napoleon at one of their meetings, "We are the world!" — a statement not unlike the reported declaration of Louis XIV, "I am the State." But the Czar had no desire to play a secondary part to Europe's new Charlemagne. He saw what it would mean to Russia to boycott Great Britain's trade. Russia, as a farming country, depended on Great Britain and other manufacturing countries for many goods. To cut off these goods would harm his merchants and himself. So Alexander, Czar of all the Russias, broke his relations with Napoleon.

It became clear to Napoleon that Russia would not help to maintain the Continental System against Great Britain. Consequently in June, 1812, Napoleon invaded Russia at the head of a Grand Army of nearly 500,000 men. We have no space for the details of this historic and disastrous campaign. Suffice it to say that the retreat of the Russian armies drew Napoleon farther and farther across the vast plains of Russia, farther and farther away from the food supplies which his army so sadly needed. Finally Napoleon entered Moscow, only to have it burst into flames two days later under his very eyes. From the middle of September until October 19 Napoleon, hoping that the Czar would sign a new treaty, remained in the half-ruined city.

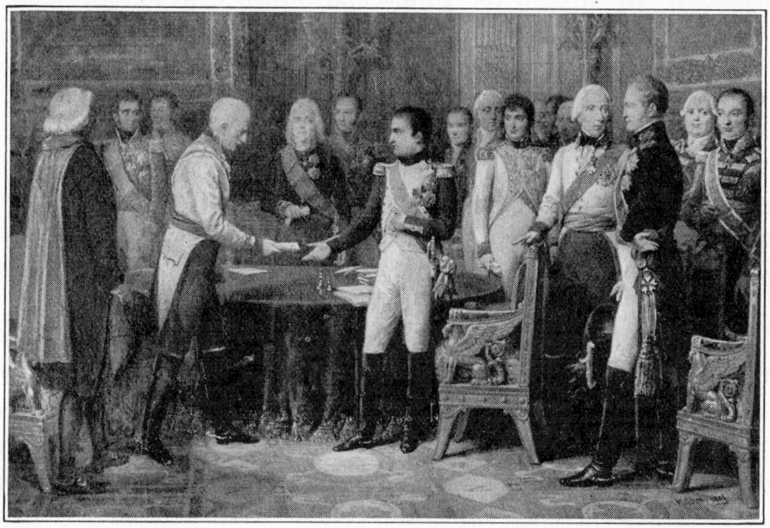

Fig. 114. A meeting of Alexander I and Napoleon I in 1808, which resulted in a short-lived treaty between Russia and France. (From a painting by N. L. Gosse)

Then, after the first frosts of winter had already set in, he began his retreat westward. Under the most horrible conditions an army ever experienced, the retreat became a historic disaster. In the cold of early December a mere fragment of the Grand Army, perhaps 20,000 men, succeeded in getting back to Poland. Indeed, it was only by using many horse-drawn sleighs in swift relays that Napoleon himself returned to Paris.

From that moment the leading rulers of Europe — Prussia, Russia, Great Britain, and Sweden — knew that Napoleon was near the end of his power. They joined hands to destroy him and his empire completely. In one battle after another they fought their way, the Prussian armies reëstablishing their ancient military glory. But despite rumbles of discontent from the people, Napoleon conscripted more of the youth of France. By October, 1813, he was again in command of a great army of 400,000 men. For a time he won a few minor and spectacular victories. But the end of all was foreshadowed in the three-day battle of Leipzig, known in history as "the Battle of the Nations." There, on October 19, 1813, Napoleon was completely defeated. He crossed the Rhine and returned to Paris.

From that time the empire dwindled quickly. One by one Napoleon's brothers, whom he had seated on various thrones, were ousted. On March 31, 1814, in spite of all that Napoleon was able to do, he was forced to surrender Paris to the armies of Great Britain, Russia, Austria, and Prussia. Then he abdicated his throne and was given the little island of Elba, in the Mediterranean Sea, just east of Corsica, to govern. There he remained for ten months, his tiny "empire" in sharp contrast to the pan-European empire to which he had aspired.

Suddenly, on the night of February 26, 1815, Napoleon escaped from Elba at the head of a small body of troops. After landing on the Mediterranean coast of France, he marched northward, gathering a growing army as he went. Even the troops sent to arrest him responded to the magnetic personality of the man and began to march back under his banner. On March 20, 1815, Napoleon entered Paris, claimed again the throne of France, and issued a proclamation that he had returned to save the country from her oppressors.

For 100 days he played his last scene in the drama of European politics and war. Then in June, 1815, all was over. Facing him were the combined armies of the British under the Duke of Wellington, the Prussians under Blücher, the Austrians under Schwarzenberg — 300,000 soldiers. There, on the field of Waterloo, in Belgium, June 18, 1815, he fought his last battle. The allies won decisively; and since that day, in speaking of someone's downfall, the world has made frequent use of the phrase "He met his Waterloo."

Soon afterwards Napoleon again was forced to abdicate the throne of France and on July 15, 1815, sailed away to begin his last exile, a prisoner of the British on the rocky island of St. Helena, in the Atlantic Ocean, off the west coast of Africa. There he lived for five and a half years, writing his memoirs, in which he tried to explain and defend to posterity his meteoric and destructive career.

What had Napoleon contributed to the March toward Democracy?

The period of Napoleon's career, which covered the fifteen years from 1799 to 1814, is one of the most dramatic in all history. Was it important in the world's march toward democracy?

Undoubtedly, it was — very important. Not that Napoleon himself was a sincere democrat or a devout defender of liberty. As we have seen, he crushed liberty, seizing upon the loyalty to the idea of fraternity, the brotherhood of Frenchmen, to secure power for himself.

1. Napoleon's influence in developing national patriotism in Europe

But his conquests, both in France and in the other countries of Europe, helped democrats everywhere to spread the idea of liberty, as well as the ideas of equality and fraternity. It happened in this way. Central and eastern Europe were divided into some 300 small states. In many cases small provinces, cities, and bishoprics were states, with counts, dukes, or bishops ruling the small territories. Most of these states quarreled among themselves, each in turn wishing for more power.

As Napoleon conquered the territory he unified many of these states under one government and himself appointed a ruler.

In 1803 the Diet of the Holy Roman Empire abolished nearly 200 tiny independent free states, free cities, and the like. Out of these little states a few large ones were formed, such as Bavaria, Württemberg, and Baden. Three years later (1806), under the demands of Napoleon, the rulers of these states, together with those of a dozen other smaller ones, broke up the Holy Roman Empire and established a new union — the Confederation of the Rhine, with Napoleon as Protector. The Hapsburg emperor,

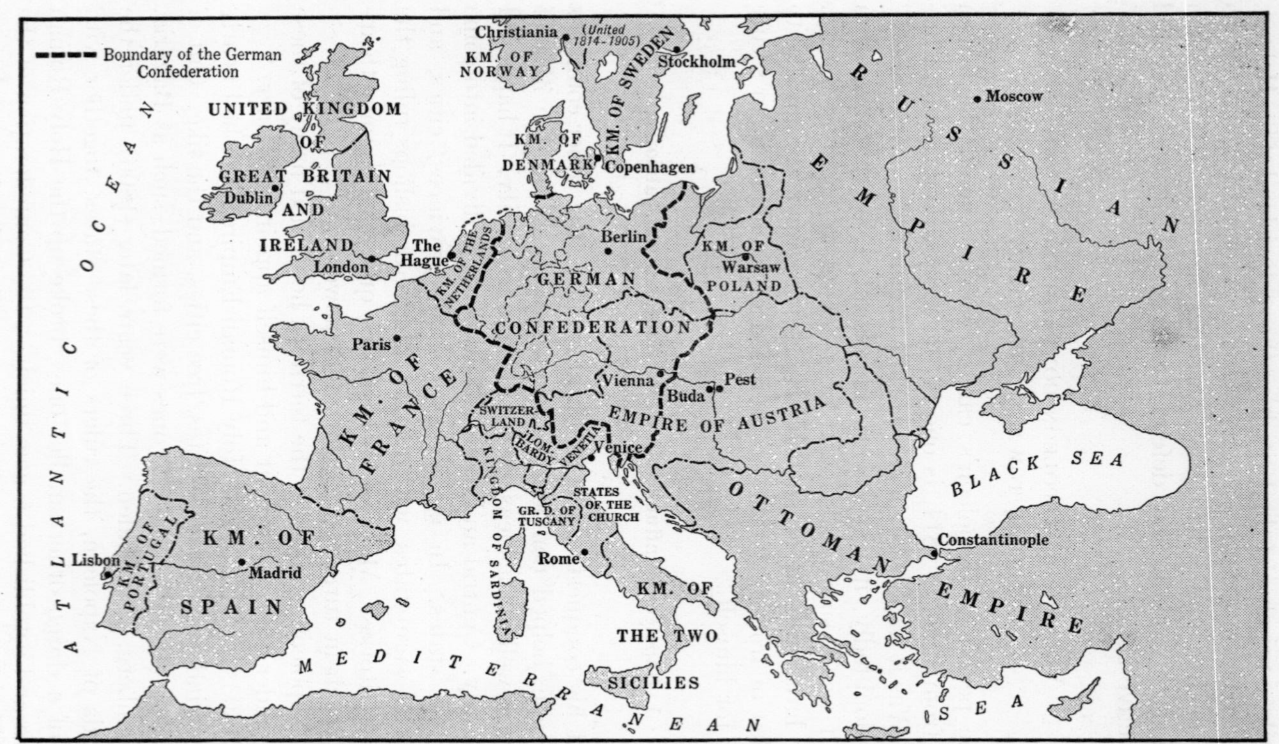

FIG. 115. Europe after the Congress of Vienna (1815). Note particularly the German Confederation and the two new kingdoms of Poland and the Netherlands

Francis I, gave up his title of "Holy Roman Emperor" and contented himself with that of "Emperor of Austria."

This unification into larger districts helped to create in the various peoples feelings of *national loyalty*. This patriotism was aided and increased by the reforms brought about by Baron vom Stein and Chancellor von Hardenberg. In 1807 the former secured in Prussia the formal abolition of feudal serfdom, giving peasants the right to own land. Under the latter, in 1811, other reforms were made; for example, towns and cities were granted self-government. Thus, although Napoleon himself actually opposed some of these reforms, his very conquests helped to bring them about.

In Italy similar events took place. For nearly 1500 years the peninsula had been broken up into many city states, Papal States, and the like. For centuries they had been torn by rivalries and wars of conquest. At one time various northern states were under Austrian control. Rome and the land around it was controlled by the Pope. The people of Naples, Sicily, and Sardinia, and other small territories, although of similar stock and speaking similar languages, had never felt a national patriotism. Under Napoleon, however, who ruled the territory as king of Italy, the various parts were somewhat unified, and a definitely national spirit began to grow. We shall see later that by 1870 this was to result in a genuine unification of all Italy into a nation.

Similar national loyalties arose at this time on the north, in Holland and Belgium, and on the east, in Austria, Hungary, and Poland. It is clear, therefore, that Napoleon's activities had brought about a marked advance in nationalistic feeling.

2. Napoleon's influence in advancing the civil rights of the people

Although political liberty was denied the common people of Europe during this era, marked advances were made toward guaranteeing them civil rights. First and foremost a radical transformation was made in the ownership of land in Europe. Remember that until the French Revolution millions of peasants did not own their land. They were still serfs in the feudal sense.

Most European farm land was owned in great estates, and the people were rigidly bound to the land as in earlier feudal days.

Under the influence of the French Revolution and of Napoleon's conquests serfdom was abolished from the Atlantic Ocean to the Russian border (not in Russia, however). Huge estates owned by the nobles and the clergy were confiscated, divided into small holdings and sold to peasant owners. Thus the principles of (1) private ownership of land and (2) inheritance of land were extended to the common people almost throughout the Continent. In that sense it could be fairly said that Napoleon exerted an influence in helping to establish equality among men.

As you can see, although political liberty was denied people generally, civil liberties were somewhat better protected. To this extent democracy did march on in Europe.

II. France again a Constitutional Monarchy, 1814–1830

Louis XVIII (reigned from 1814 to 1824). Less than a month after the battle of Waterloo, Louis XVIII,[1] a brother of Louis XVI, began again (after the interrupt on occasioned by Napoleon's return from Elba) his reign as king of France. To be sure, he was not a "divine right" monarch; on the contrary he was a constitutional monarch, definitely limited in his powers.

During the first year of his reign still another constitution was announced to the French. This one created a parliament, the upper house consisting of lords named by the king, the lower house (Chamber of Deputies) being composed of representatives of property-owners. Only those could vote who paid at least 1000 francs (about $200) in taxes each year. Since only the well-to-do paid as much as $200 a year, even the lower house represented but a small proportion of the French people. Nevertheless a beginning had been made in granting suffrage to the people.

The constitution provided for other important changes. For example, it restricted the lawmaking power of the king. The French parliament was not permitted to pass laws, but neither

[1] After the death of Louis XVI and Marie Antoinette their son was looked upon by the Royalists as Louis XVII. He was imprisoned with his parents and is believed to have died from the effects of ill-treatment at the hands of his jailers. Although he takes his place in the line of the French kings, Louis XVII never reigned.

could the king and his ministers do so without its consent. In addition various civil rights which had been established by the Revolution were confirmed. Among these were the right to own land, freedom to worship according to one's beliefs, and freedom of speech.

Not for long, however, was this liberalism practiced. There was a short and bloody White Terror, in which radicals were executed, imprisoned, and exiled. At this time extreme monarchists got control of the legislature and in 1820 wiped out the gains in civil liberty that had been made. They censored speech and the press. They passed new laws which prevented any but the very well-to-do from holding office.

Charles X (reigned from 1824 to 1830). Louis XVIII died in 1824, and a second brother of Louis XVI ruled for six short years as Charles X. These years also marked the continuation of a conservative monarchist rule. The Catholic Church reassumed much of its influence in government, and the old aristocratic society of privileged nobles came back and reëstablished itself.

The *Bourgeois* Capitalists now began to assert their Power in France

It was at this point that the Industrial Revolution began to take hold in France. In 1825 England repealed a ban it had laid upon the export of new machines. With Napoleon finally disposed of and a semblance of order established in Europe, the new power-driven machinery was introduced into the northern cities of France, into the manufacturing districts of western Germany, even into the factories of Vienna, Budapest, Warsaw, and other European cities. Thus in the 1820's and the 1830's France's Industrial Revolution got under way, 40 years behind England's, which had been unhampered by revolution and Napoleon.

Note the startling advance in both manufacturing and farming after 1789, as shown in Tables V to IX.

These figures reveal, among other things, that, as manufacturing and trade increased, thousands of capitalists were made wealthy. As time went on, this new *bourgeois* class demanded and obtained a larger and larger share of the control of the French government. In the 1820's it was they who coöperated with the workingmen in the demand for a liberalizing of the government. It was they who resented most the return to France of the aristocratic group under Louis XVIII and Charles X. Many of the new manufacturers and merchants were Protestants, and they were much disturbed by the return of the Catholics to power. Especially were they discontented with the action of the monarchist government in paying indemnities to the returned Royalists to reimburse them for the confiscation of their property during the Revolution. These indemnities, which totaled 1,000,000,000 francs, were paid largely out of a refunding of the national debt and took from the *bourgeois* bondholders a large share of their income. No wonder that they disapproved!

TABLE V

Production of Wheat and Potatoes in 1789 and 1848		
Year	Million Bushels of Wheat Grown	Million Bushels of Potatoes Grown
1789	93	5
1848	152	275

TABLE VI

Value of Woolen Goods exported from France in 1788 and 1838	
Year	Value
1788	24,000,000 francs
1838	80,000,000 francs

In France, therefore, we are now to witness a duplication of the struggle between the town and city capitalists and the monarch and his favorites that had been enacted in England a century and a half before. Matters came to a head in the spring and summer of 1830. In the June and July elections the Liberals defeated the Monarchists for control of the Chamber. In retaliation the king established a rigid censorship of the press, took the right to vote away from the majority of the people who had been entitled to vote, and dissolved the parliament. In this way Charles X attempted to reëstablish "divine right" monarchy.

TABLE VII

Silk Production in 1822 and 1847	
Year	Value
1822	99,000,000 francs
1847	165,000,000 francs

But the seeds of liberty had by this time sprouted strong

democratic roots. In July, 1830, the Parisian workingmen, led by journalists and other publicists, rose in revolt, defeated the royal troops, and seized control of the city. Charles X thereupon abdicated the throne.

TABLE VIII

Production of Pig and Bar Iron, 1789, 1830, and 1850	
Year	Number of Tons of Pig and Bar Iron
1789	69,000
1830	266,000
1850	416,000

In his place Louis Philippe, duke of Orleans, and a member of the younger branch of the Bourbon family, which had occupied the throne for over 200 years, was invited by the Chamber of Deputies to become "King of the French." His selection was a victory for the rising capitalists, the merchants and manufacturers of the towns and cities. As we have seen, from the time of the French Revolution they had steadily intrenched themselves in the government. As new constitutions were made in successive overturns of government, the provision was almost always inserted that to vote one must pay a stated amount of taxes; that is, one must own property. And it was the *bourgeoisie* who owned property. So it came about that they secured a growing representation in the government. Furthermore, as their wealth increased, governing officials became more subservient to them. We shall see later that this was exactly what happened in each of the other countries of the world that were becoming industrialized.

TABLE IX

Coal Production in 1789, 1830, and 1860	
Year	Tons of Coal Mined
1789	250,000
1830	1,800,000
1860	8,000,000

The Parisian revolt of 1830 furthered rebellion in other countries

The change of government in France almost immediately affected other centers in Europe. No sooner had the Parisians risen than the Belgians did the same thing, rebelling against the Dutch king, William I, and proclaiming their independence in October, 1830.

Popular uprisings on a smaller scale developed in Hanover, Saxony, and other German states. Governments were not actually overthrown, but the insurrectionists in each instance secured promises that they would be given more liberal constitutions — greater civil and political liberty.

In Italy also the idea of rebellion spread. Certain radicals in the central part of the peninsula rose against their foreign

Fig. 116. Louis Philippe welcomed by the citizens of Paris after the three-day revolution of July, 1830. By August 7 he was proclaimed "King of the French by the grace of God and the will of the people." (After a painting by Horace Vernet)

rulers; but Austrian troops were hurried to the scene of conflict, and by this means open rebellion was crushed for some years.

Even in distant Poland the tremors of the revolution that put Louis Philippe on the throne were felt. Groups of rebels rose in Warsaw in November. Russian autocrats were expelled, and the Poles declared their independence. But their rebellion was short-lived. Russian forces were too strong for them, and after an eight months' war the Poles were defeated. Hundreds of patriotic leaders were executed, and others were exiled from their homeland.

Thus, although the uprisings were successful only in France and in Belgium, it was becoming increasingly clear that democracy was marching slowly forward in Europe.

III. France, a Middle-Class Monarchy, 1830–1848

The Revolution of 1830 definitely ousted "divine right" monarchy. The power of the new king, Louis Philippe, was restricted. The French constitution was modified, and the right to vote was extended to another small group — namely, all who paid 200 francs (about $40) in annual taxes. With this act the right to vote was granted to a large proportion of the middle-class landowners and shopkeepers, as well as to the larger industrialists and merchants.

Other political reforms were brought about at this time. Membership in municipal councils was won by election (instead of by appointment). Elementary schools were also provided for the smaller communes in a new law of 1833. It has been estimated that within the next fifteen years the number of children who attended primary school nearly doubled. Thus you can see that the French *bourgeois* capitalists received an important place in government during the very same years that their brothers the business-men politicians of England were winning an important place in their government. But note that in 1832, exactly as in England, the masses of the French farm laborers, mechanics, unskilled city workers, and the smallest property-owners were still without the vote. Although the exact proportion is not known, certainly in 1833 in France less than 5 per cent of the population was allowed to vote.

The rise of trade-unions and of the socialists in France

As time went on, agitation continued among the workingmen for the right to vote and hold office and for shorter hours of work, higher wages, and better working conditions. In the city of Lyon, for example, silk weavers were working from fourteen to sixteen hours a day for a wage of ten to twelve sous (cents). Conditions in the industries in Paris and other large cities were no better. As the royalists and the larger merchants and manufacturers became more powerful, the workingmen definitely organized themselves for the battle for political liberty.

It was at this time that Louis Blanc advanced his plan for social workshops. It was in these years of the 1840's that Karl Marx and Engels and other social reformers were organizing the workingmen and writing their theories of government. In his newspaper, *The Reform*, Blanc proclaimed the right of the workingman to a job. He said:

> To the able-bodied citizen the state owes work; to the aged and infirm it owes aid and protection. This result cannot be obtained unless by the action of a democratic power.

Seizing the slogan of the Revolution, Blanc proclaimed the rule of the people through universal suffrage.

IV. Another Revolution — the Second Republic, 1848–1852

With almost all the political groups of France demanding change, it was clear before the end of 1847 that the monarchy could not last long. Meetings at which were discussed the rights of the people were being held publicly in the winter of 1847. Matters came to a head on February 22 and 23, 1848. Workingmen, writers, students in the colleges, and National Guardsmen came to an open clash with the royal troops in the Place de la Concorde in Paris. A score of citizens were killed, and the revolt spread rapidly through the city. Streets were barricaded, and the usual fighting characteristic of city rebellions went on.

Almost at once Louis Philippe abdicated as king of the French. Then, for a time, two separate governments claimed control — the *bourgeois* republicans and the working-class republicans. Later the two merged in a joint provisional government.

Gradually, however, the capitalist leaders again secured control, putting Blanc and the socialists in the background. More minor revolts of the workmen occurred. Several more days of street fighting followed, in which many workers were killed. Eventually the *bourgeois* troops subdued the revolutionaries by shooting some and exiling 4000 others to colonial prisons. From that time on, the socialistic workmen of the lower classes learned to hate their *bourgeois* masters as they had formerly hated their noble landlords.

For four years, from 1848 to 1852, these capitalist republicans controlled France. They too adopted the slogan of the Revolution — Liberty, Equality, Fraternity. In the new constitution of the Second Republic they established freedom of speech and of the press and granted universal manhood suffrage. In December, 1848, a presidential election was held, and Louis Napoleon Bonaparte, nephew of Napoleon I, was elected president of the Second Republic.

More revolutions in Europe!

Once more we note the swift communication of revolution from France to other centers of discontent. In other countries leaders of the trade-union and socialist movements had been carrying on agitation similar to that conducted in Paris. On receipt of the news of the establishment of the Second Republic, there were outbreaks in other centers.

Austria was still in control in Italy. When Italian patriots heard of the setting up of the new French Republic, they rose in revolt against the Austrian troops. From Milan and Venice to Naples and Sardinia national enthusiasm spread, and armed revolt developed against the foreign rulers.

Parallel uprisings took place in the attempt to set up republics in Baden, Bavaria, Saxony, Württemberg, Nassau, Hesse-Cassel, and Mecklenburg-Schwerin. In none of these small states did the people succeed in overthrowing the government, but, as before, they succeeded in securing added constitutional liberties.

In Berlin, street fighting developed in March, 1848, and hundreds were killed in a nationalist movement which demanded a unified Germany and a liberal constitution. A constitutional convention was called, one representative being included for every 50,000 persons in the so-called German Confederation.

Likewise, in Vienna, a constitution was granted by the Emperor in April, 1848, and a constitutional assembly, which was to be elected by universal manhood suffrage, was called.

In the meantime the Hungarians were seceding from Austria and setting up their own government, in which more democratic provisions were made. The Hungarian constitution was also a result of the movement of national patriotism. Freedom of the press and speech was guaranteed, national legislatures were to be elected by all persons who owned $150 worth of property, and feudal serfdom was abolished. Democracy marched forward again, even in eastern Europe.

V. Napoleon III and the Second Empire, 1852–1870

For four years Louis Napoleon gave promise of being a really democratic president of France. We must remember that he had been born in 1808 in the palace of the Tuileries, at Paris, during the height of the power of his uncle Napoleon I. Thus he was brought up in the midst of revolution. Throughout his youth he was frequently aligned with liberal, even socialistic, movements. He had connections with Louis Blanc, the socialist, and he wrote socialistic books himself — one, for example, which was called *The Extinction of Pauperism.* In every way he gave promise of being a democratic leader.

Louis Napoleon's democratic connections, along with the fact that the great Napoleon had by this time become a legendary hero to the French people, had enabled him to win the election as the president of France; he received 5,400,000 votes. The other candidates received 1,400,000 votes, 370,000 votes, and 17,000 votes respectively. At first he did all that he could to obtain popular support by encouraging industry and trade, securing old-age insurance for the workers, getting the support of the Catholic Church, and ingratiating himself with all classes.

Now, however, was revealed another sign of the growing struggle between the industrial middle-class leaders and the workers. In the Revolution of 1848 all adult males had been given the right to vote. This made it possible for the workers to play a considerable part in the political life of France. When the more well-to-do town and city people saw this happening, they passed a new electoral law in 1850 to prevent the rise to power of the lower classes. The law stated that no person could vote unless he had lived and paid taxes in the commune in which he was to vote. It was an amazingly bold attempt to take the suffrage away from the masses. It deprived at least one third of the voting population of France of the right to vote.

At this action Louis Napoleon, pretending to favor the common people, dismissed the Assembly and seized control of the government by proclaiming himself in sole authority. In December, 1851, he held throughout France a plebiscite, or special vote of the people, at which he secured popular support for the drawing up of a new constitution. His success was probably due to the fact that he had previously proclaimed universal suffrage as the right of all adult males. Out of about 8,300,000 votes which were cast, Louis Napoleon received 7,700,000.

Thereupon Louis Napoleon showed his real hand. He announced a new constitution which gave him practically supreme power over France. It made him president for ten years and gave him the power to appoint a cabinet, a council of state, and a senate, the command of the army and navy, and the right to appoint all governing officials. Always preaching democracy, Louis Napoleon prepared the way for a proclamation in December, 1852, which made him Napoleon III,[1] Emperor of the French. Even at this time he went through the pretense of holding an election. So great was the faith of the mass of the people in Louis Napoleon that even at this election he received the votes of nearly 8,000,000 citizens, confirming him in the right to set up a new imperial constitution.

This Napoleon seemed to be living up well to the tradition of the Bonaparte family. Although he too was an adventurer, he held the throne of France as emperor for nineteen years. His ability as a clever politician enabled him to do so. He devoted himself to making friends with the leaders of all classes. He established his position with mechanics and laborers and called himself "the Emperor of the Workmen." In the drawing-room he was a polished courtier. He had married a Spanish princess (Eugénie), who helped him to maintain a brilliant court which aristocrats found to be a center of culture. He succeeded also in securing the friendship of the Catholic leaders.

At the same time Louis Napoleon developed many public works, built up trade, and made many internal improvements.

[1] Napoleon II was the son of Napoleon Bonaparte. Like Louis XVII, he never reigned.

This was the time when railways and factories were appearing rapidly. Harbors were dredged and docks were built to receive the larger seagoing vessels. Louis Napoleon also improved on his uncle's plans in beautifying the city of Paris. It was during his reign that two world expositions (1855 and 1867) were held. The French people came and saw with their own eyes the magnificence which their capital had attained under this new emperor.

It was at this time also that the French government launched more vigorously upon its conquest of colonies. It acquired territory in Africa, in Indo-China, and in the islands of the Pacific. It also obtained trade privileges in China.

As we have said, for nineteen years this second Bonaparte emperor maintained himself in power as the magnificent Emperor of the French. But his story is somewhat like that of his uncle, Napoleon I. Not through internal opposition but through foreign wars was his downfall brought about. He had scarcely taken office in 1852 when he prepared for war against Russia. In this war, which is known as the Crimean War, he was aided by the British. It began in 1854, lasted two years, and cost nearly 500,000 lives and $2,000,000,000. It is estimated that not less than 75,000 young Frenchmen met death and $500,000,000 were spent — all for practically nothing. You can readily see that this would make Louis Napoleon decidedly unpopular in France.

Three years later Napoleon III interfered in another foreign situation; namely, that of forcing the Austrian rulers out of Italy and helping the Italians to declare their independence and unify themselves into a national state. In 1859 he declared war against Austria.

This is not the place to tell how the revolution spread and the Austrian rulers were expelled. Suffice it to say that within two years, from 1859 to 1861, the people of the various little Italian states joined together and formed the kingdom of Italy — a nation of 22,000,000 people under Victor Emmanuel as king. Five years later (1866) Venice, which was still outside the kingdom, was also brought in, when, by a public vote, with more than 99 per cent of the people voting, the Venetians declared that they wished to join the kingdom of Italy. Four years later (1870) the city of Rome, which had been controlled by troops loyal to the

Pope, was captured, and in 1871 Rome was named as the capital of the completely unified kingdom of Italy.

To go back once more to the story of Napoleon III, the war against Austria had hardly helped to increase his popularity in France. As the 1860's went on, various enemies rose against him.

Grandiose plans for world conquest filled the mind of this dabbler in militarism. In 1862 he intervened in Mexico. Mexico City was captured, and in 1864 Louis Napoleon placed Archduke Maximilian of Austria on the throne as Emperor of Mexico. But the success of this excursion into foreign affairs was short-lived, for within three years the Mexicans rose against their foreign conquerors and captured and executed Maximilian. He had already been deserted by Napoleon III for two reasons — the demand of the United States that France respect the Monroe Doctrine and retire from Mexican politics, and the threatening war between Prussia and Austria, which might embroil France.

FIG. 117. By 1870 all the political divisions of the Italian peninsula as far north as the dashed and dotted line had joined to form the Kingdom of Italy

This adventure brought Napoleon III more enemies. One faction after another rose against him. In the elections of 1869 his doom was foretold by the return to the national legislature of a very large number of liberals and republicans. In a last effort to retain the confidence of the people of France, he made many democratic reforms in the government. But it was to no avail. The socialists and those who wanted to restore the Republic became steadily more audacious. In May, 1870, in a public vote for a new constitution, 2,000,000 people refused to vote, and 1,500,000 were definitely against Napoleon's proposed constitution. Opposition to the empire was increasing, although in this instance Napoleon was upheld.

It was at this point that he ventured once more to unite the factions of France behind him. He allowed himself — perhaps willingly — to be drawn into a conflict with the armies of the newly unified German nation. In Chapter XIII we shall read

FIG. 118. Maximilian of Austria arriving in Mexico, 1864. After three years of turmoil France withdrew her troops from Mexico, and the Emperor was besieged, captured, and executed by the Mexican republicans. (From a painting by J. A. Beaucé)

of the swift dispatch with which German troops swept down upon France in the Franco-Prussian War of 1870–1871. They defeated Napoleon's armies at Sedan in September, 1870, capturing Napoleon himself and 80,000 men after a short six weeks' campaign. Then the Germans captured Paris and proclaimed the new "German Empire" at Versailles, the very palace of the French kings.

While Napoleon was a prisoner a government of national defense had been set up. A National Assembly was elected to deal with the victorious enemy; and in February, since Paris was in the hands of the enemy, the Assembly held its first session in the city of Bordeaux.

VI. The Final Establishment of the French Republic, 1871 to the Present

The people divided into three groups

For 80 years the middle and lower classes had tried to set up a permanent democratic kind of government in France. Each time that they asserted themselves, however, military leaders had made *coups d'état*, overturning their republics and establishing imperial dictatorships or constitutional monarchies. Now, near the close of the disastrous Franco-Prussian War, came another interval of disorder and uncertainty. For five years (1870–1875) struggling factions fought one another for the control of government.

By this time it was clear that the struggle for power in modern France lay among three groups: (1) the royalists, or monarchists, who wanted a king with limited power; (2) the *bourgeois* republicans, who steadily inclined toward some form of republic; (3) the workingmen, consisting either of Marxian socialists, of more radical socialists, or of anarchists, who were not clear as to the kind of government which they wished to set up.

The revolt of the Parisian workingmen

During the year following the overthrow of Napoleon III thousands of people were starving in the city of Paris. Tens of thousands were out of work. The suffering exceeded perhaps that of the starving time of 1789. Paris, the ancient capital, again became the scene of a terrible but short-lived revolution. The workers of Paris attempted to set up an independent local government known as the Commune. Then, during April and May, 1871, troops of the National Assembly and of the angry populace outside of Paris marched against these workers and slowly conquered the barricaded city. Every day marked the death of hundreds of citizens. The total number killed or exiled has been variously estimated at from 15,000 to 25,000. Finally, at the end of May, the suffering city capitulated, and the last military revolt in the history of the French government was over.

A new constitution and the permanent establishment of the Republic

For four years more the National Assembly carried on, while the factions strove to come to an agreement as to the form of government which would best fit the needs of the French people. The Commune had put the socialists in a discreditable light with the country at large. Thus one of the three groups was practically eliminated from real power. The contest remained for the monarchists and the republicans. In the election of 1871 the sentiment of the nation seemed to favor a limited monarchy, a sort of "crowned republic," somewhat like that of Great Britain.

Gradually, however, sentiment began to swing toward setting up a republic. In 1873 a definite step was taken in that direction. An act was passed which created the office of President of the Republic, with a seven-year term. A complete constitution was not written at that time, however, as in previous changes of government. Instead, one by one, a series of constitutional laws were passed. During the four years between the defeat of the Commune in 1871 and the proclamation of the constitutional laws of 1875, the basis of the Third Republic of France was laid.

Now let us note two points. First, the government organized in 1875 has lasted essentially in the same form to the present day. Second, it resembled other governments which had come into existence by that time, especially those of Great Britain and the United States.

In addition to a president, a national legislature was created, which was called the National Assembly. This was organized into two chambers: (1) the Chamber of Deputies, consisting of approximately 600 members, *elected by universal manhood suffrage* for a term of four years; (2) the Senate, of 300 members, elected by officials in the various departments and districts of the country for a term of nine years. Thus the deputies are elected *directly* by all males over 21 years of age; the senators indirectly by officials appointed by the central government. The president is elected by the Senate and the Chamber of Deputies, meeting together.

France resembles the United States in that it is nominally a republic, under a president and a national legislature. However, as in England, the government is run by the ministry (resembling the British cabinet), which consists of the heads of various government departments. Each minister also has a seat in the Chamber. Thus the government is "responsive to the people" in much the same way as Great Britain's. New ministries are formed whenever the one in office fails to receive a majority support in the Chamber of Deputies. Provision was made for the Chamber to be dissolved and a general election held in approximately the same way as in Great Britain.

Thus, at last, France had come to substantial parliamentary government. The chief executive officer, — the president of the Republic, — like the king in England, had little power. The real power lay in the parliament, especially in the Chamber of Deputies — "the Commons."

Final establishment of civil liberties for the French people

This period of the Third Republic recorded still another success of the people in their march toward democracy. In a series of historic laws, passed between 1881 and 1901, the civil rights of the people were recognized more definitely than in most European countries. One act definitely protected the right of the people to public assemblage and guaranteed complete freedom of discussion of economic, political, and social matters. Another guaranteed freedom of the press, leaving the decision in controverted cases to a jury. Still another guaranteed the right to form labor organizations.

As you can see, both political and civil rights were assured. There is, however, one important item of political liberty that is still lacking, even today. All men can vote, but women are still denied the right. Half the adult population still has no share in the French government.

The Great Industrial Expansion

To understand who has controlled the French government from 1870 to the present day, we must bear in mind that this was the great period of the industrial development of France. At the very moment that each of the other leading industrial countries — the United States, Great Britain, and Germany — was entering upon a period of great industrial expansion, France was doing likewise.

TABLE X

Tons of Coal mined and Pig Iron produced, 1865 and 1913		
Year	Coal	Pig Iron
1865	11,840,000	1,290,000
1913	45,020,000	5,126,000

Under the stable government and the comparative peace of the Third Republic, machine industry, agriculture, and world trade developed rapidly in France. How rapidly can be noted in the adjoining tables (X–XII) and graphs (figures 119 and 120). In 1913 more than three times as much coal and four times as much pig iron were mined as in 1865. Note the steady growth in the number of industrial establishments in France between 1872 and 1912. Note also the sharp rise in the amount of steam power used in French manufacturing plants.

TABLE XI

Number of Farm Machines used in One District of France			
Year	Mowing Machines	Reapers	Reapers and Binders
1892	450	180	60
1908	15,000	25,000	1,200

Agriculture also felt the impact of the industrial expansion, especially after 1890. In one district of France the number of mowing machines increased thirtyfold between 1892 and 1908, and the number of reapers more than a hundredfold.

TABLE XII

Value of All Farm Products in 1860 and 1913	
Year	Value
1860	6,000,000 francs
1913	11,000,000 francs

The new government itself had much to do with this swift economic advance. Within a quarter of a century (1879–1904) it built 200,000 kilometers of modern highways and 30,000 kilometers of railroad, vastly extended the canals of France, and improved the harbors. Agriculture was also definitely benefited by public aid. Growers of grapes and producers of silk, flax, and hemp were given financial support by the government. Coöperative societies, similar to those which had developed on

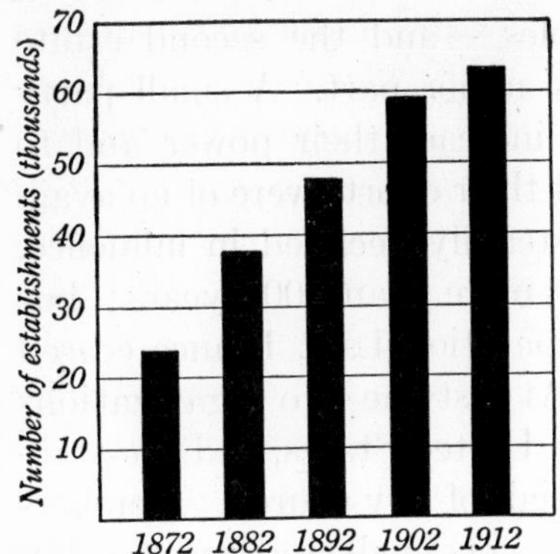

FIG. 119. Increase in the number of industrial establishments in France, 1872–1912

such a large scale in Denmark and in the United States, spread among the farmers. Banks and insurance companies were established to help them. Table XII sums up the remarkable agricultural growth from 1860 to the outbreak of the World War.

Inevitably, as a result of this enormous expansion of manufacturing agriculture, and trade, the wealth of France grew swiftly. A startling illustration of the industry, thrift, and perseverance of the French people is provided in the astonishing way in which they paid off the indemnity demanded by the victorious Germans after the Franco-Prussian War, in 1871. Within three years, instead of the five years promised, the entire indemnity of 5,000,000,000 francs (or $1,000,000,000) had been repaid, largely through the loans made by millions of thrifty French peasants. It was in this period, also, that French peasants purchased many billions of francs' worth of the bonds of foreign governments. Other billions were invested in the mines, railways, public utilities, and industrial enterprises of other countries, as well as in similar undertakings in France itself.

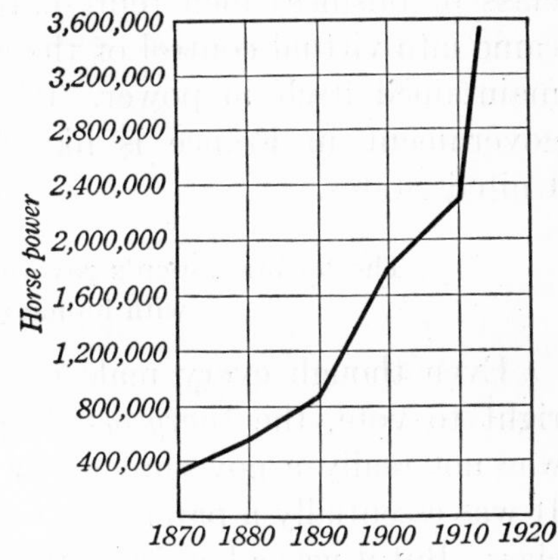

FIG. 120. Increase in steam power used in industry in France, 1870–1920

THE THIRD REPUBLIC RULED BY THE BUSINESS MEN

We are now in a position to understand that the *bourgeoisie*, the small and large capitalists of the towns and cities, became the real masters of French government. From 1880 to the present day the first estate — the nobles — and the second estate — the clergy — have played a very minor part. A small party of monarchists tried repeatedly to increase their power and to place a royalist on the "throne," but their efforts were of no avail.

Similarly, the Catholic Church steadily declined in influence. Church and State had been one for more than 1000 years; but in 1905, with the passage of the Separation Law, France ceased *officially* to be a Catholic country. At last the two organizations were completely separated, as in the United States, and the state ceased paying the salaries of the officials of any church. Members of all religious denominations and believers in all creeds were given equal recognition — all being allowed to form independent church organizations.

With monarchists, clericalists (leaders of the Church), and socialists in the background, the republicans, the upper middle class of business men representing essentially the third estate, came into virtual control of the government. For 50 years it has maintained itself in power. In this respect also the history of government in France is like that in Great Britain and the United States.

The business men's government protected the people with humane legislation

Even though every male over 21 years of age did have the right to vote, the *bourgeois* government of the Third Republic was not really a government by the common people of France. It was essentially a paternalistic government of the upper middle class. But it was a benevolently inclined government, as is shown by the advanced laws passed for the protection of the workers.

In 1884, laws were passed protecting, even encouraging, trade-unions of workingmen. At the outbreak of the World War more than 2,000,000 skilled workers belonged to the trade-unions. An act of 1892 and later laws reduced the hours of labor for women and otherwise regulated their work. It also prohibited the employment of children under thirteen and established the ten-hour working day and the six-day working week.

In the following year other acts guaranteed workers' health and safety and gave them free medical attendance for injuries incurred while at work. In 1898 a law was passed compelling employers to compensate laborers for injuries received at work. Further legislation was enacted in the interest of workers when, in 1910, France passed an act granting old-age pensions to all wage-earners, except those already provided for. Other bills passed in the last half-century reformed the criminal code of the nation.

It was in this period also that the present universal system of elementary education was introduced. Attendance at school was required of all children, and provision was made for public elementary schools in every commune of the nation.

These illustrations suffice to show, therefore, the extensive advance in democratic legislation that came under the paternal middle-class government of France.

Summing up France's March toward Democracy

Here we must close our brief synopsis of the rise of parliamentary government in France. The people of France lagged far behind the people of Great Britain in throwing off absolute rulers. To achieve freedom required many revolutions and *coups d'état*. But once it had begun, the march toward democracy really did not stop until extensive civil and political liberty was given to the people.

At this point let us sum up the civil and political liberties of the French people.

1. *The gains in civil liberty.* First and foremost, feudal serfdom was completely abolished. The peasants of France secured the right to own land. As a result millions of peasant proprietors came into existence. These made France practically a self-supporting agricultural nation while she was also becoming one of the world's leading industrial and trading nations.

Furthermore, the French constitutional laws now guarantee the people the civil liberties which are prized so highly in Great Britain and America. Summed up briefly, they are

The right of free speech.
The right of a free press.
The right of free assembly.

The right to petition the government on any matter.
The right to religious freedom.
The right to habeas corpus and trial by jury — in brief, to fair treatment by the government in legal matters.

2. *The gains in political liberty.* But in France, as in Great Britain and in America, the people knew that civil liberty could be guaranteed to each citizen only by assuring him political liberty as well. Therefore all French males over 21 years of age have been given the right to vote and to hold office without restrictions as to religion or ownership of property.

In only one respect do the people of France lack the political liberties granted to the people of Great Britain and the United States. The women of France cannot vote. Thus half the adults are still without the franchise.

In the attainment of these great civil and political rights, therefore, we see that the French people, like those of Great Britain and America, have marched far toward democracy.

INTERESTING READINGS FROM WHICH YOU CAN GET ADDITIONAL INFORMATION

BILL, ALFRED H. The Clutch of the Corsican. Little, Brown and Company, Boston. Tells of Napoleon's rise and fall.

BROOKS, ELBRIDGE S. A Boy of the First Empire. The Century Co., New York. Tells of the domestic life of Napoleon.

CASTLE, AGNES. The Wind's Will. D. Appleton and Company, New York. France about 1815–1820, after Napoleon's downfall.

JOHNSTON, ROBERT M. Napoleon. Henry Holt and Company, New York.

MARSHALL, HENRIETTA E. The History of France. Doubleday, Doran & Company, Inc., Garden City, New York.

MARSHALL, HENRIETTA E. The Story of Napoleon (Children's Heroes Series). E. P. Dutton & Co., New York.

SIMPSON, FREDERICK A. The Rise of Louis Napoleon. Longmans, Green & Co., New York.

TAPPAN, EVA M. Hero Stories of France. Houghton Mifflin Company, Boston. Short biographies of outstanding Frenchmen from the early times to Marshal Foch.

VAN LOON, HENDRIK. The Story of Mankind. Horace Liveright, New York.

CHAPTER XIII

EMPIRE BY DIVINE RIGHT: GERMANY UNTIL 1918

In Europe, as the democratic movement spread, one after the other "divine right" monarchies disappeared. Step by step, in country after country, as the one-man idea was given up, government of the people, by the people, for the people, took its place.

As we have seen, this happened first in England. Isolated and protected from the feudal and aggressive wars of Europe, England could throw off the absolute régime earlier than the other countries. By 1700 an increasing number of people disbelieved that kings ruled by divine right. Property-owners were beginning to rule instead. France followed England's lead, but not until a century later. The English had had their Bill of Rights and a parliamentary government for 100 years before the French phrased their Declaration of the Rights of Man and set up their first National Assembly. Unlike the English, the French were constantly in danger of invasion, owing to the predatory activities of their greedy and ambitious kings. There were other important reasons, too, which prevented the advance of representative government.

In Germany, however, a kind of government by divine right existed until the 1900's. It was 1918 before the German people threw off the control of a divine-right monarch. Thus democratic constitution-making in Germany lagged more than 100 years behind that in France and 200 years behind similar happenings in England. We have tried to picture this fact simply and graphically in figure 121.

The Industrial Revolution also developed much more slowly in France and Germany than in England (see figure 122). As you know, English inventors and business men first launched power-driven machine manufacturing in the period 1765–1785. Frenchmen did not take up the machine until after 1825. The Germans began to adopt it slowly in the 1830's and 1840's, but

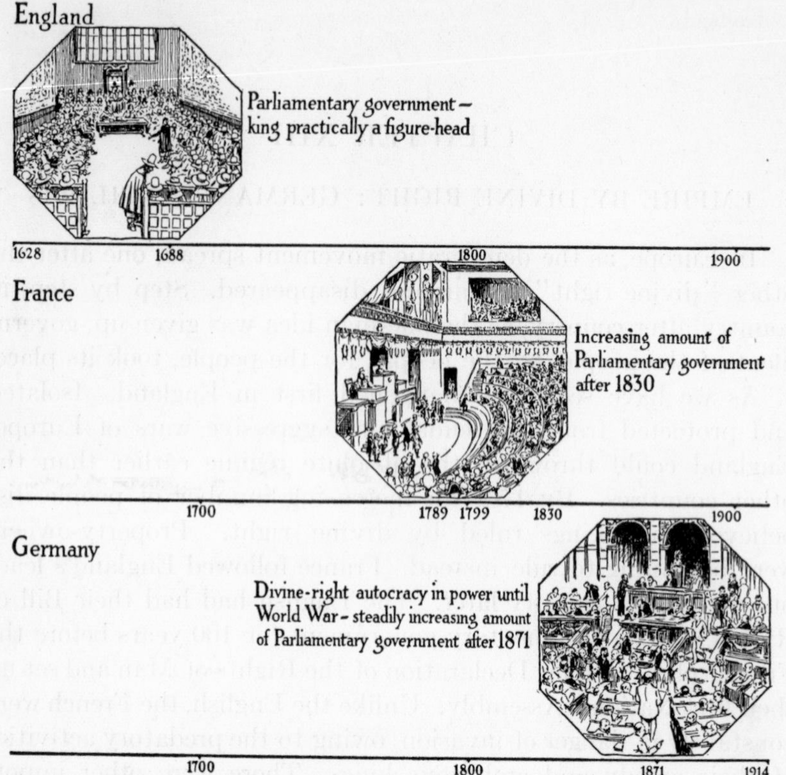

Fig. 121. The growth of representative government in England, France, and Germany

it was not common in Germany until 1870. Thus we see a very interesting parallel between the invention and spread of the *industrial way of living* and the invention and spread of *representative* government.

It is also interesting to note that in Europe the democratic movement spread from west to east. It arose in Great Britain. It appeared next in France and, a little later, in Bavaria, Belgium, Switzerland, and other regions of *western* Europe. Then it spread slowly *eastward,* to Austria, Hungary, and Germany in the middle and later 1800's. There the movement rested for some forty years until we find it achieving its final destruction of "divine right" monarchs in the 1900's in Russia and in parts of the Balkans and the East and the Near East.

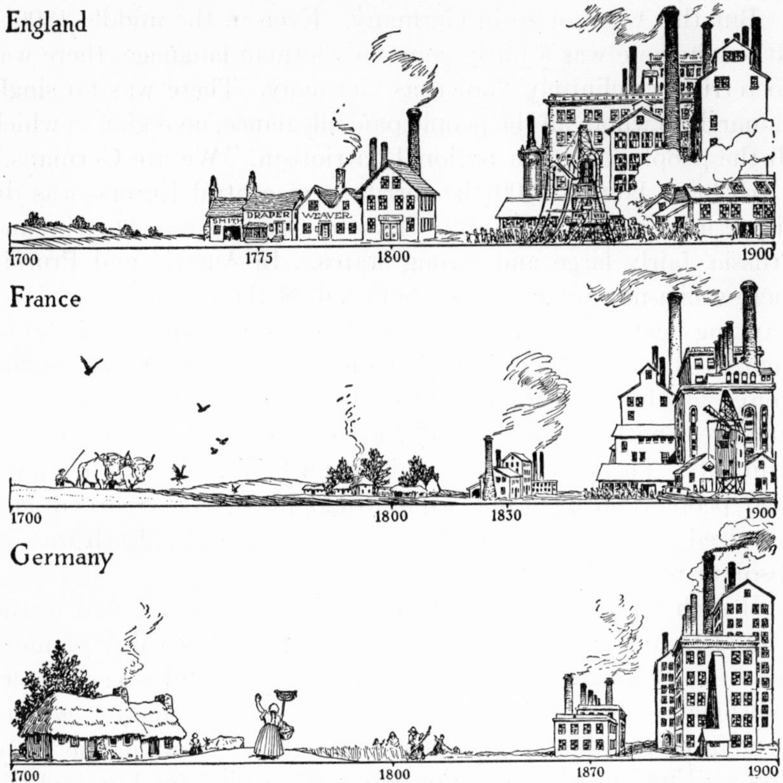

Fig. 122. The growth of the Industrial Revolution in England, France, and Germany

One Reason why Democracy came so Late in Germany

How did it happen that representative government came so late to the German people?

There are several factors which explain its delay, but one is more important than the others: there was a lack of unity among the German peoples. There was no German nation until the late 1800's. France and England, as you know, had achieved a kind of nationality even in the 1500's. Even then each had attained about the same boundaries that it has today. Most of the people within each country spoke the same language. Each people as a whole recognized the same central government and spoke of themselves as being English or French.

But this was not so in Germany. Even in the middle 1800's, although there was a fairly common German language, there was no territory definitely known as Germany. There was no single monarch to whom all the people paid allegiance, no region in which all the people said with national patriotism, "We are Germans."

Even as late as 1800 the territory of central Europe was divided into some 300 units. Two of these were Austria and Prussia, fairly large and strong states. In Austria and Prussia there was a mixture of races, about half of the people being Slavs. Ranking next in importance were about 30 medium-sized states, such as Bavaria, Baden, and Saxony, whose population ranged from a few hundred thousand to a million or so. Following these 30 states, both in size and influence, came about 250 petty governments. These were very small, some totaling only a few hundred people and including what would have been regarded as a fair-sized estate; others numbering 10,000 people. Each was an absolute monarchy, ruled by a duke or a count.

If such a hodgepodge, within a territory one tenth that of the United States, was not confusion enough, try to think of more hundreds of knights, each of whom ruled over still fewer people. In England these men would have been merely country gentlemen, fathering their less well-to-do neighbors; but in the Holy Roman Empire, as this region had been called for hundreds of years, they were *monarchs*. Each of these little monarchs had his own little court, his courtiers, and his obsequious officials. Each collected taxes in his own way and charged other "monarchs" tariffs for the privilege of trading within his domain. And each ruler had his own little army. Historians were certainly justified in speaking, not of Germany, but of the "Germanies."

Thus instead of the country Germany, there were in 1800 some 300 quarreling units, — kingdoms, grand duchies, duchies, principalities, and free cities, — all bound together loosely in the so-called German Confederation. So uncertain were the boundaries and so indefinite was the feeling of nationality, however, that we can certainly say that in the early nineteenth century there was no such thing as the German nation.

We must see how the German nation was formed out of this loose confederation.

Hapsburgs versus Hohenzollerns

The story of Germany is the story of how two powerful families slowly acquired control over all the German states. These families were the Hapsburgs of Austria and the Hohenzollerns of Prussia. As you know, the Hapsburgs became so strong that the successive heads of their family — their dukes — gradually got control of the duchy of Austria and for hundreds of years were elected emperors of the Holy Roman Empire.

In the 1600's, however, the Hohenzollerns began to stand out as real rivals to the Hapsburgs of Austria. Indeed, the story of the building of the German nation is essentially the story of the rise of the Hohenzollern family. It covers 1000 years, from the time when they were counts, ruling over a single little valley, to the time when, having been successively the dukes of this and the margraves of that, they finally became kings in Prussia and emperors of Germany.

Thus the history of the *German nation* goes back 1000 years to about 900 A.D., when a certain feudal count ruled the hamlets about a hilltop castle (whence the name of the family, *Hohen-Zollern*, "high castle") in southern Bavaria. During the next 300 years his successors fought with the neighboring feudal lords and steadily added more territory to their little principality.

They not only conquered territory: they married into it as well. Their sons married the daughters of other feudal nobles, thus gradually bringing more territory under the Hohenzollern rule. For example, in the 1200's marriage made one of the counts of Hohenzollern a burgrave (commander) of the fine trading city of Nuremberg. There were many such instances.

Two hundred years passed, and then, at one stroke, came a large addition to their territory. In 1415 the Hapsburg emperor of the Holy Roman Empire gave to the count of Hohenzollern the *mark*, or margraviate, of Brandenburg, a northern territory some 500 miles from his ancestral home. That this territory was regarded as important is shown by the fact that the margrave of Brandenburg was one of the seven electors — one of the seven princes who chose the emperor of the Holy Roman Empire.

Another 100 years passed. The rise of the Hohenzollerns continued steadily. During the Reformation in Germany — after 1520 — the Elector of Brandenburg and the other northern German princes followed Martin Luther out of the Catholic Church and adopted Protestant Lutheranism as the official state religion. This too increased the strength of the Hohenzollern family by making enormous additions to their wealth. The Elector merely helped himself to the vast lands and other properties of the Catholic Church in Brandenburg, as did other German

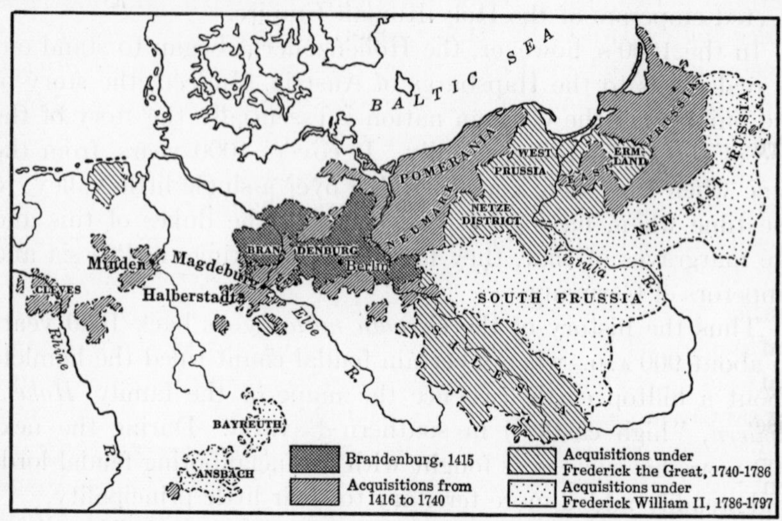

Fig. 123. A graphic map telling the story of the rise of the House of Hohenzollern from 1415 to 1797

rulers and as Henry VIII did in England. Since not less than one fourth of the German territories had been owned and governed by bishops and abbots of the Catholic Church, the electors of Brandenburg became many times richer than they had formerly been.

This newly acquired wealth made it possible for them not only to conquer still more territory but also to continue to marry their sons to the daughters of more important rulers. A hundred years later they were gathering in more and more lands and people by that method. In 1609 the Elector claimed and occupied about half of Cleves, after the death of its duke, on grounds of kinship. By 1614 he had the entire duchy. Cleves lay away to the west of Brandenburg, on the Rhine. In 1618 East Prussia, a large duchy north of Poland, on the Baltic (see figure 123), became the property of the Brandenburg line of the Hohenzollern family.

Then, after the bloody Thirty Years' War (1618–1648), the Hohenzollerns acquired Magdeburg, Minden, Halberstadt, and half of Pomerania.

By the time the monarch Frederick William, the Great Elector (ruled from 1640 to 1688), came to rule these northern German states, the nucleus of a large, powerful kingdom was under the control of the Hohenzollern family. It was the Great Elector who completed the conquest of the duchy of East Prussia and united Brandenburg, East Prussia, and Cleves under a single government controlled by a strong army.

At the same time, more than all his predecessors, he developed profitable farming and stimulated varied handicrafts and industries. During his rule the little town of Berlin became a thriving city of 20,000 people. Huguenots who had been exiled from France by the edict of Louis XIV settled there. They were skilled craftsmen and helped to lay the foundation for the fine German crafts of modern times. Upon Frederick's death only one reigning family in Germany— the Hapsburgs —was stronger than his.

Although the Hohenzollerns held many titles, Elector of Brandenburg, Duke of Prussia, Duke of Cleves, as well as a long string of minor ones, yet Frederick III of Brandenburg, son of the Great Elector, desired to be a *king*. He gained the title in 1701, when he made a bargain with the Emperor of the Holy Roman Empire whereby, in return for Hohenzollern assistance in the coming War of the Spanish Succession, the Emperor permitted him to crown himself Frederick I, King of Prussia. His territories, though not unbroken, stretched from East Prussia to Cleves, on the lower Rhine, and included scattered possessions in other parts of Germany. Much empire-building had been accomplished by the Hohenzollerns during the 300 years since the Count of Hohenzollern became Elector of Brandenburg.

Frederick I (reigned as *king* 1701–1713) was followed by Frederick William I (reigned 1713–1740), and he, in turn, by the most famous of all the Hohenzollerns, Frederick (II) the Great (reigned 1740–1786).

By 1740 the Hohenzollern family of Prussia had become the leading rival of the Hapsburg family of Austria for control among the German states. In that year Frederick, the Hohenzollern, and Maria Theresa, the Hapsburg, came to the respective thrones of Prussia and Austria. For years, under these absolute monarchs, the two families fought out the quarrel over power, land, imperial titles, thrones, and money. It was during that time that the Hohenzollerns definitely defeated the Hapsburgs and added the rich province of Silesia to the Prussian kingdom.

Twenty-three years of almost constant warfare were required to change definitely the ownership of that valuable territory. There was the War of the Austrian Succession (1740–1748), a quarrel among rulers about who should occupy the throne of Austria. There was the Seven Years' War (1756–1763), which Frederick the Great finally won, thereby establishing his claim to Silesia. During these wars countless thousands of men were killed, the labor of millions of farmers and artisans was destroyed; but the King of Prussia got his Silesia, attained greater renown in the society of kings and princes, and made Prussia a reorganized power in European affairs.

Did the people have anything to say about it? Not at all. Frederick and Maria Theresa were absolute monarchs, like Louis XIV of France shortly before them. While their armies were killing each other, millions of peasants were living in the misery of feudal serfs. They did not own their land. They had no civil or political rights. Travelers of the time tell us that their living conditions were miserable indeed — far worse than those of the farmers of England and of France.

Frederick the Great, the "benevolent despot"

In the meantime Frederick the Great set up a splendid court near Berlin and made it a center of pleasure and culture, as Louis XIV had done in France. In many respects this German Hohenzollern is to be compared to the French Bourbon, Louis. He too worked at his trade of being king. He was a true "benevolent despot." Like Louis XIV he rose early in the morning and worked at matters of state all day long. He personally supervised the administration of the provinces of his realm; he reviewed the decisions of his judges. He abolished the "third degree," that is, the practice of torturing suspected criminals in order to make them confess. He granted freedom of worship and established elementary schools in many communities of the kingdom.

He encouraged industry and agriculture, stimulating farmers to use more scientific methods. He developed water transportation by connecting rivers with canals. He developed new industries, such as the weaving of silk. And he did try to protect the people by keeping down taxes to a minimum and using the money which he received from the peasants and artisans of the nation in efficient and economical ways.

Fig. 124. Frederick the Great. (From a painting by Antoine Pesne)

This was the practice of the enlightened despot. While ruling with an iron hand, he devoted himself vigorously to economical and efficient administration. In a book which he wrote on government he said, "The monarch is not the absolute master, but only the first servant of the state." Yet he really conceived himself and all kings as the fathers of their people. He did not want the masses to think about government; he wanted to do the thinking and directing himself. He said, "The prince is to the nation he governs what the head is to the man; it is his duty to see, think, and act for the whole community."

Do you think that political liberty advanced at this time? No, indeed. The nobility and Frederick were the only ones considered necessary to making plans and carrying them out. And Frederick held his power by means of an army which at one time reached 200,000 men.

At the very moment of the meeting of the Constitutional Convention in the United States, at the time of the outbreak of the

French Revolution, and 100 years after the signing of the Bill of Rights in England, government in Prussia and the German states was by divine right.

Then came Napoleon, the Humiliation of German Monarchs, and the Spreading of Democratic Ideas

When Frederick the Great died in 1786, Prussia was recognized as the leading state of central Europe. It was unified and seemingly prosperous, and the people were apparently contented under the benevolent though autocratic rule.

Within the next 25 years, under weak kings, all this was changed. One after another the armies of Prussia (and Austria too) were defeated. The Hohenzollern king lost his prestige. The states which made up Prussia lost their feeling of unity, and the *democratic spirit spread rapidly* in the towns and cities. What happened to cause such a reversal?

You already know the story. Napoleon I, the dictator of Europe, rose to military power in France after 1797, made himself Emperor of the French, King of Italy, and Protector of the Confederation of the Rhine (a combination of Bavaria, Württemberg, Baden, and several other states). In 1805 he defeated the Russians and Austrians at Austerlitz. In 1806 he invaded Prussia, destroyed a Prussian army of 65,000 men at the battle of Jena, and marched into Berlin as the master of Prussia. Changed, indeed, were the fortunes both of the rulers and of the people in Prussia.

The King of Prussia, Frederick William III (reigned 1797–1840), had now lost all his territory west of the river Elbe — about half of his entire kingdom. At the same time Napoleon combined many of the smaller German states and made his relatives the rulers.

Serfdom was abolished; the peasants could now own the land

Although Prussia was subjugated, the war had brought into Prussia the seeds of democracy. A storm of criticism rose all over the German states, and there was much discussion among the advisers of Frederick William III as to the unrest among the people and the need for reforming Prussia from within.

Two leaders were chiefly responsible for the reorganization of the country between 1807 and 1813. They were Baron vom Stein (1757–1831) and Chancellor (Prime Minister) von Hardenberg (1750–1822). Although of the noble class, Stein had decidedly democratic leanings. He had read Rousseau and the other French revolutionary philosophers. He had studied the parliamentary government of England and admired many things about it.

As a result of Stein's effort, in 1807 the King of Prussia issued the renowned *Edict of Emancipation* abolishing serfdom. At last millions of peasants who had been rigidly bound to the great landed estates were freed and were given the right to own land in their own names. At last land could be bought and sold and owned privately by any citizen of the kingdom. At the same time members of the lower economic and social classes were given the right to enter any occupation or profession in which their abilities enabled them to work. It was a signal victory for democracy.

The liberal minister also attempted to obtain a written constitution for the common people of the kingdom, but in this he was defeated by the great landowners. Stein succeeded, however, in making important changes in city governments: from 1808 every property-owning burgher had a voice in the election of the councilors and other officials who administered the local affairs of the towns and cities.

Education and national patriotism advanced

At the same time another movement was launched for the purpose of unifying the German peoples. *Education instead of armed force!* Teach the masses to understand and to love the Fatherland, to respect the king and the government, instead of commanding loyalty from submissive herds of human beings by armed force. This was the new method of the leaders.

Throughout the kingdom a common-school system was set up under the minister of education, Karl Wilhelm von Humboldt (1767–1835). Schools soon sprang up in practically every village and town. Every child was to be taught to read and write, so that national patriotism could be developed. Every child must learn the thrilling history of the German peoples so that the unification of the German nation would be furthered. Singing was also taught in the schools. Patriotic singing societies were

FIG. 125. Germany, 1815–1914. Note the changes in boundary between 1866 and 1871. What did Germany gain? What did she lose?

organized, and the love of the Fatherland was enhanced through national festivals. Systematic physical training was introduced; the people were to be made strong and healthy in order to create a strong nation.

Thus you see that the leaders instituted their reforms largely to build up the German nation, to increase national patriotism, and to develop love of Fatherland. Germany was still a hodgepodge of little states, and the new Prussian leaders, under their Hohenzollern king, were visualizing a completely unified Germany.

The purpose of education, then, was loyalty to the *state.* Children were not taught to think, to learn how to solve their country's problems; they were taught to obey. But it was to be an intelligent obedience, not a stupid one. The state was to become *a strong national state* by developing an obedient, loyal, intelligent common people. For 100 years, even to the World War, this was the goal of the Prussian leaders. Thus democracy, though marching on in Germany, was advancing very slowly.

At the same time that these partially democratic changes were taking place, Chancellor von Hardenberg was making the Prussian army into a highly efficient machine. It was under him (1811) that compulsory military service for all men was developed in Prussia. Prior to the French Revolution the armies of the kings of Europe had been made up of hired professional soldiers. After the French Revolution and the dismemberment of the royal army, compulsory military service was instituted to provide an army for France. Napoleon's conquests with such armies popularized the idea. So in Prussia the "draft" came into existence. Each year those young men who attained a certain age were sent to training camps and military schools and taught the art of war. People who hated war called this training in the art of murder.

So it was that a national state began to develop in Germany. So it was that love of country and forced military service in defense of one's country began to spread throughout Europe as well.

The Congress of Vienna, 1815, put down Democratic Movements Everywhere in Europe

You remember that Napoleon, the disturber of European peace, was finally disposed of in 1815. In the same year emperors, kings, ministers, princes, electors, dukes, counts, and generals met in Vienna in a spectacular international conference to reconstruct Europe. The Czar of Russia, Alexander I, was there; the Emperor of Austria, Francis I, was there; the King of Prussia, Frederick William III, and Chancellor von Hardenberg were there, as well as the kings of various little states, the electors of the former Holy Roman Empire, the Duke of Wellington of England, and the wily Talleyrand of France.

Suavely guiding the whole aristocratic convention was the Austrian chief minister, Count Metternich. The assembly was dominated by reaction and conservatism; liberal democrats were either entirely missing or unable to get a hearing for their proposals.

Fig. 126. Clemens Wenzel Metternich-Winneburg (1773–1859)

For nine months these nobles conspired, exchanged favors, and put over their schemes for the defeat of every sign of liberal tendencies. They finally arranged the boundaries of Europe and the occupancy of thrones to suit their desires.

As for the German states, the princes did their best to stop the movement toward the unification of Germany under the Prussian king. All the German states excepting East Prussia and Posen joined the western part of the Austrian Empire in setting up a new German Confederation. The legislature of this Confederation, called the Diet, contained no representatives either of the common people or of the rising *bourgeois* class. It consisted solely of ruling princes, primarily under the leadership of Austria, and its principal function was the organization of defense against foreign invasion.

For fifteen years democratic movements everywhere were suppressed. The old ruling houses, the nobility, controlled the governments. In France it was the period of Louis XVIII and the White Terror, of Charles X and the extreme monarchists. In Spain members of the Bourbon family were put back upon the throne. In Portugal the ruling house, which had fled to Brazil in order to escape from the armies of Napoleon, returned to power. Even in more democratic Great Britain the Tories were in power, and the business men of the cities and the workingmen generally were excluded from the government. In Russia the government, which earlier had tried liberal experiments, became harsh and oppressive. Autocracy was maintained everywhere in central Europe.

After 1830 the Industrial Revolution began to develop in Germany

In the meantime, as you know, far-reaching industrial changes were taking place in the West, especially in England. Machines had been invented and perfected, and English manufacturers and merchants were taking trade away from French and German competitors.

In 1825 England passed a law permitting machines to be exported to other countries. Almost immediately, both in France and in Germany, beginnings were made in the introduction of power-driven machinery. As long as central Europe was upset by Napoleon's armies, there was little opportunity to develop the new industry in German states; but with the strict quiet enforced by the new autocratic régime, this could be done.

In the 1820's and 1830's power-driven machinery was introduced into the growing manufacturing towns, especially in Prussia and the other North German states. A little later the manufacturers of Vienna, Budapest, and other central cities of the Austrian Empire followed their lead.

Industry grew swiftly from that time on. In 1840 the German textile mills spun and wove only approximately 9000 tons of raw cotton; in 1855 the total reached 25,000 tons. By 1865 approximately 1,000,000 tons of pig iron were being produced each year. The mining of coal rose rapidly. In 1830 the rich coal mines of the Ruhr valley, in Westphalia, had hardly been touched. In 1865 about 28,000,000 tons were mined. At that time Germany had actually surpassed France in the production of coal. It was still far behind England, however.

As machines improved, factories increased, and roads improved, workers left the farms of Germany and became machine-tenders in the towns and cities. The working class grew and grew, and the foul tenement slums of the cities grew too. As the workers lived closer together they began to organize. Trade-unions sprang up, especially in the western German states. In the meantime the upper middle class of industrial owners (the German *bourgeoisie*) increased their wealth and aspired to political power. Thus the history of the Industrial Revolution in other countries was being repeated in Germany.

The Prussian customs union and the new railroads unified the German states

Very soon the Prussian business men began to realize that the English could manufacture and sell goods more cheaply than they. Under the leadership of their government they worked out plans for unifying and protecting the industries of the German states against the more efficient ones of England.

Again we see the importance of economic changes in bringing about changes in government. During the twenty-five years that followed the Congress of Vienna two things happened which did more than all the wars of ambitious kings to tie the scattered German states together in national unity. The first was the formation of a *Zollverein* ("customs union") under the leadership of Prussia.

This had an immediate influence on the ways of living in the German states, as well as on trade. People began to exchange goods with one another as though they were citizens of the same country, not as quarreling members of enemy states. The business men of Prussia in the north traded with those of Bavaria in the south much as those of New York traded with others of Pennsylvania in the United States.

Through the *Zollverein* the protective tariffs which each little state had placed on goods imported from other German states were now abolished. The people of any German state in the *Zollverein* could trade with those of another member state freely, without paying customs duties. At the same time a tariff was placed on all goods imported into the German states from foreign countries, or states outside the union. In this way the *Zollverein* served to tie together the hitherto unfriendly states. The only large political body to remain outside was Austria, and Austria was soon to lose all her control over German life.

The second economic change also served to bind the German states together. This was the rapid building of railroads. The first railroads were laid down in Prussia in 1835. By 1844 there were 500 miles of track in operation in that single state alone. In 1860 the number was 3500 miles. In the meantime railways extended out into Saxony, Hanover, and Baden, and joined Bavaria in the south with Prussia in the far north.

Thus unity through mutual economic interests took the place of attempted unity by the "mailed fist" of armed force. Is it not clear that mutual gain through trade will do more to bind people together in coöperation than the sworn oaths of princes to love and help one another? Was there a more effective way to make the people of Catholic Bavaria and those of Protestant Prussia feel that they were citizens of the same country?

As industrialism spread, democracy spread with it

As time went on, the *bourgeois* merchants and manufacturers, on the one hand, and the workingmen and peasants, on the other, kept demanding a larger share in the government. They were encouraged and helped in their demands by the professors and students in the universities of Berlin, Vienna, and other cities.

Not only was this true in Germany and Austria. In every oppressed country of Europe, as well as in the rising republics of Latin America, it was in the colleges and universities that democratic ideas were most vigorously discussed. Here they were thinking about the age-long problems: How shall property be owned? How can government be truly of the people, by the people, for the people? How can the income of a people be equitably divided among them?

This was the period in which Karl Marx was studying the history and philosophy of civilization. Later he was to be driven from country to country by the autocratic Prussian government, which feared the influence of his democratic and socialistic ideas. It was the time, also, of Friedrich Engels and the organization of workingmen's unions.

The Revolution of 1848 in the German States

Scarcely a year passed in the larger cities of Germany without demonstrations by students and workingmen who demanded reforms.

There was a growing feeling that the German states should be united in political bonds more strong than those afforded by the Confederation. Political parties began to spring up advocating different solutions. The democratic group favored a united German republic, to take the place of the many separate governments of the Confederation. All favored reforms of one kind or another.

Then, early in 1848, came the news that Louis Philippe had been forced to abdicate the throne of France. Almost at once democratic groups in Italy, in the German states, and in Austria revolted against their autocratic masters. So rapidly did the revolutionary movement sweep over Europe that before the end of the summer half the lesser monarchs had either been put off their thrones or had been forced to give their subjects charters of liberty in the form of written constitutions.

In March, 1848, workers and students rose in armed rebellion in Berlin. Streets were barricaded, and bloody fighting ensued. More than 200 citizens were killed, and the frightened king, Frederick William IV, promised to call a national conference and give the people a written charter of liberties.

Swiftly the democratic movement spread throughout other parts of Germany. As a result, in May, 1848, a constitutional convention was assembled at Frankfurt, bringing together representatives from every member state in the German Confederation, including the provinces of Austria within the Confederation. For nearly a year the delegates conferred. On the whole some gains were achieved for democracy. Certain civil rights, such as freedom of speech, freedom of the press, freedom of assembly, and the right to petition the government were granted, and certain declarations of equality were made. But almost no advance in political liberty came to the people.

In the spring and summer of 1849 "Republican" clubs were formed in various cities. Largely as a result of their work provincial governments in the form of republics were set up in the western states of Saxony, Baden, and the Rhenish Palatinate. But these movements, too, soon failed. Order was restored by the armies of the Prussian king, and by July, 1849, the revolutionists were suppressed once more. It was at this time that thousands of German patriots left Germany and settled in the United States, which to them was the nearest approach to the republic of their dreams. These people, as you know from your study of American history, became patriotic American citizens. Not long after, many of them fought in the Civil War to preserve the union of American states.

In the meantime the Frankfurt assembly, now almost a year old, had completed a plan for the formation of the German states into a German Empire with Frederick William IV, king of Prussia, as emperor. But it was impossible to form any real union in which both Austria and Prussia should be included, for neither would be subordinate to the other. Twenty-eight small states agreed to the plan, but Austria, Bavaria, Saxony, Württemberg, and Hanover refused it. Frederick William IV did not believe that the assembly had the right to offer him the emperorship, and he was also friendly to Austria. His acceptance of the offer would mean war with Austria, and so he declined. In April, 1849, the Frankfurt assembly closed without having achieved a closer unification of the German people.

In the reaction which followed, a conservative constitution was granted, 1850

But the people of Prussia obtained at least one thing from the revolutions of 1848–1849. This was a partially liberal constitution. Although it granted certain civil liberties to the people, the king still ruled by divine right.

In the constitution a legislature was provided for, but both the upper and the lower house represented chiefly the large property-owners of the kingdom. A kind of manhood suffrage was granted, but the representatives in the legislature were so proportioned that the control was entirely in the hands of the well-to-do. Thus it could hardly be said that democracy had advanced much in Germany, even by 1850.

Under William I, Another "Divine Right" Hohenzollern King, Prussia strengthened her Military Organization

In 1861 William I (reigned 1861–1888) became king of Prussia. He was the most courageous and able Hohenzollern that the country had had in three quarters of a century. Under William I and his two iron-handed leaders — the war minister Von Roon and Von Moltke, the commander in chief of his army — Prussia strengthened her military organization. Compulsory military service was demanded, and increasingly heavy taxes were laid upon the people to finance the government.

The parliament of Prussia vigorously opposed this policy. The members wanted peace and quiet and business prosperity. They had little interest in strengthening the military organization. But wars threatened; and, under compulsion, parliament did agree to continue the period of three years' military service for all men, but declined to tax the people to the extent that the King and his militaristic ministers desired.

It was during this conflict that the war party discovered the man of destiny who would lead Prussia in the unification of the German states and the final humbling of the Austrian Hapsburgs.

Otto von Bismarck, Cunning Diplomat of "Blood and Iron," created a Unified, Warlike German Empire (1862–1871)

In 1862 Otto Eduard Leopold von Bismarck (1815–1898) was appointed Minister-President (chief minister) of Prussia over the protest of the liberals. It was little wonder that the democrats did not want him, for he was a conservative of the conservatives.

At the time of the Revolution of 1848 Bismarck was a young count and the leader of the "Junkers" in East Prussia. The Junkers were the landed aristocrats of Prussia. They had long played a most important part in German politics, controlling the offices of the government and favoring in all matters the king and his ministers.

Bismarck had made himself useful to the Hohenzollerns and had had valuable diplomatic experience in France and Russia.

In addition to being a shrewd diplomat, he was a believer in the divine right of kings. During his ministry the principles of free speech and a free press gave way to the most reactionary kind of suppression. Editors were jailed for criticizing the government, and their papers were suppressed. When the liberal legislature refused to vote the taxes demanded by the King and his ministers, Bismarck proceeded to collect them by force. Liberals in return threatened to hang Bismarck, but the Junkers controlled the army and all administrative positions in the government.

FIG. 127. Otto Eduard Leopold von Bismarck (1815–1898)

It was by such methods as these that Bismarck kept order at home and made all Germans obedient servants of the Fatherland. The schools were teaching obedience and patriotic self-sacrifice to the state, the aristocrats were developing the strongest army in Europe, and thousands of independent liberals were emigrating from Germany. Hence there was little chance for the overthrow of the monarchy and the establishment of representative government.

In the 1860's and 1870's Bismarck created the German Empire as a result of three wars among the peoples of Europe: (1) the war with Denmark, 1864; (2) the war with Austria, 1866; (3) the Franco-Prussian War, 1870–1871

1. *The war with Denmark, 1864*

The war with Denmark was brought on by the troublesome question of the status of the duchies of Schleswig and Holstein, which had for centuries belonged to the king of Denmark although populated mainly by German people. In 1848, when the spirit of revolution was sweeping over central Europe, the Danish king, fearing an uprising in the duchies, announced his intention of incorporating them as an integral part of the kingdom of Denmark.

There was much indignation in Germany over this proposed step, and some attempt was made to prevent the duchies from becoming Danish possessions. But the controversy continued, and finally, in 1863, Schleswig was definitely joined to the Danish realm.

Thereupon the Diet of the Confederation declared war upon Denmark with the enthusiastic support of German public opinion. This was Bismarck's opportunity. At once he arranged with Austria that she and Prussia should act as the executors of the Diet's decree. Denmark had hoped for the support of England, France, and Russia; but those countries were not favorable to intervention, and eight months later Denmark, utterly defeated, was forced to cede Schleswig and Holstein to Austria and Prussia jointly, to be disposed of as those two powers should see fit.

2. *The war with Austria, 1866*

In 1865 and 1866 Bismarck deliberately instigated a war with Austria over the division of the spoils. We shall not stop to tell the details. There appears to be no justification for the way in which it was brought about, but within seven weeks Germany had defeated her enemy decisively. This was known, therefore, as the Seven Weeks' War (1866).

By the use of armed force great strides were being made toward a unified *German Empire* under a Prussian king. As a result of the Austrian war the North German states of Hanover, Hesse, and Nassau, and Frankfurt (one of the most important free cities) were annexed to Prussia. Austria was excluded from this North German Federation. Prussia had now become the largest German state, with a population totaling about 25,000,000.

We should pause to note here that the mass of the people did not know of the schemes by which Bismarck had provoked the two wars. They went on with their daily work, trying to get a living and occasionally wondering what the warring was really all about.

3. *The Franco-Prussian War, 1870–1871*

By 1866 Bismarck had succeeded in lining up all the North German peoples behind his militaristic policies. Even many liberals and progressives joined hands to extol the glories of the great Bismarck. There was no doubt about the fact that North Germany was unified.

But South Germany was still out of the union, and the creation of the German Empire would not be complete until it was brought in. So Bismarck's schemes went on, this time drawing France into the net of diplomacy and war.

Napoleon III hoped to annex the Rhineland as a reward for his neutrality in the Austro-Prussian War. About this time he talked over his proposal with Bismarck when the latter visited him. Bismarck, with his usual policy of playing one group against another, went to the leaders of the South German states and told them of Napoleon's plans.

Then he published a hitherto secret offensive and defensive alliance that had been made between Prussia and the South German states. Bismarck now felt sure that if a successful war could be fought with France the South German princes would join with the Hohenzollerns to form a united imperial Germany. Furthermore, he felt confident that they would proclaim the King of Prussia as Emperor of Germany.

But Bismarck had to have a pretext for war. It would never do to force war on France, so that other people would think Prussia had started it. The occasion came in 1870. Napoleon III was disturbed because the Spaniards proposed to take as their king a relative of King William of Prussia. This would compel Napoleon to live between two Hohenzollerns, a very uncomfortable position, indeed. So he tried to persuade King William to prevail upon his relative to refuse the crown. He went too far in his demands, however, and William declined.

It was at this point that Bismarck tricked the French. King William sent Bismarck a 200-word telegram telling him to make public the decision and the reasons for it. Instead of giving this telegram or even a true version of it to the newspapers, Bismarck wrote from it a 20-word telegram which made it appear that the king of Prussia had been insulted by the French ambassador and that the latter had been rebuffed. This short telegram went to the German newspapers and was copied in the French press. Immediately the French press became violently excited. It soon began to influence the people, and the government, on July 19, 1870, declared war on Prussia.

This is an important illustration of the way wars of conquest can be brought about by the secret conspiracies of the diplomats.

FIG. 128. Europe in 1871. A comparison of this map with that of figure 115 will illustrate some interesting changes that came about in a little more than fifty years

There was little pretense of morality in this method. Bismarck sought his ends by fraud and violence. Nothing was to be allowed to stand in the way of Prussian power.

The campaign of the Franco-Prussian War was short. Within a few months the German armies overwhelmed the French in a series of startling victories. On September 2, 1870, after the decisive defeat of Sedan, the French general, Marshal MacMahon, and the Emperor Napoleon III himself were captured with 80,000 men.

The Germans pressed on and laid siege to Paris that same month. The city held out until January, when, starving and freezing, it surrendered. The Franco-Prussian War was over.

As a result of this war Bismarck's plans were completely successful. Even before Paris had surrendered, treaties of union were made between the North German Federation and four southern states,— Bavaria, Württemberg, Hesse, and Baden,— and the German Empire was formed. While the Germans were still besieging Paris, Bismarck journeyed to the French palace of Versailles and there proclaimed King William of Prussia Emperor of Germany.

One more of Bismarck's conquests we must mention because of its international importance from 1871 to the World War. In the terms of peace Germany took from France Alsace and part of Lorraine, two rich boundary provinces, even as the French had earlier taken them from the Germans. For nearly 50 years this angered not only the people of Alsace-Lorraine, who had been taken from their beloved France, but also the leaders and people of France itself. Not until the World War was over, in 1918, and Germany had been defeated was this territory returned to France. In the meantime it was a constant source of friction between the two peoples and the two governments.

How the Government of Germany was Organized, 1871–1914

In 1871 a new constitution was formed. In no sense was the new constitution a written guaranty of the civil and political rights of the people. It was a sort of treaty of union between the northern and southern divisions of the empire. At the head of the government was the emperor of Germany, who was in general charge of all government matters in the empire and who had the power to appoint the prime minister, called the imperial chancellor.

There was a legislature, which consisted of two houses. The lower house was called the *Reichstag*. Its members were elected by all adult males over 25 years of age. The *Bundesrat* was the upper house. It consisted merely of the representatives of the 22 rulers and the three free cities which composed the empire.

Each state was apportioned a definite number of votes somewhat in proportion to its size. For example, Prussia, which totaled nearly two thirds of the entire population, was given about one third of the votes. The five states next in size were given, together, one third of the votes, and the remaining small states had one or two votes each in the total of 61 in the Bundesrat and 397 in the Reichstag.

FIG. 129. The ceremony in the Hall of Mirrors, at Versailles, at which King William of Prussia was proclaimed Emperor William I of Germany. (From a painting by Anton von Werner)

The imperial constitution, although apparently liberal in form and granting suffrage to adult males, proved really to be one of the most undemocratic in Europe. It turned Germany over to a "divine right" government, practically under the control of the king of Prussia and the imperial chancellor whom he appointed.

The chancellor (Bismarck, from 1871 to 1890) was indeed the leading power in the empire. He appointed the ministers, proposed most of the laws, controlled Prussia's seventeen votes in the Bundesrat, and presided over the meetings of the Bundesrat. In actual practice this upper house really ran the government. It initiated laws and decided on their constitutionality. Things were so arranged that Prussia, acting through the chancellor, could defeat any proposal to amend the constitution, to reduce taxes, or to regulate the army and navy. Thus the representatives of the princes and the noble landowners ran the German imperial government from 1871 until the end of the World War.

In no sense was the Reichstag a powerful lawmaking body. In no sense did its power compare with that of the House of Representatives in America, the House of Commons in Great Britain, or the Chamber of Deputies in France. Furthermore, as industrial cities grew in Germany, as people crowded together in great manufacturing centers, the landed estates in rural districts came to have a far greater proportion of the seats of the Reichstag than was their due.

Within the separate states themselves, however, there were fairly important gains for democracy. Between 1871 and 1914 all but one of the 26 German states obtained written constitutions. In Prussia local government was made more democratic even before 1890. In Bavaria a written constitution set up parliamentary government in charge of a ministry responsible to the people, somewhat as in Great Britain and in France. In 1906 the method of voting was changed, and the secret ballot, based upon the Australian plan, was adopted. One by one other political liberties were achieved in the smaller states in the early 1900's. In 1904, for example, state and local offices were made elective, and all adult males were given the right to vote for them. Thus throughout this period democracy marched slowly onward.

Between 1871 and 1914 Germany became a Leading Manufacturing Nation

It was in the half-century following Bismarck's rise to power that Germany became the chief commercial rival of Great Britain and one of the four leading manufacturing nations of the world. In Germany, as in the United States, Great Britain, and France, the great industrial expansion took place after 1870.

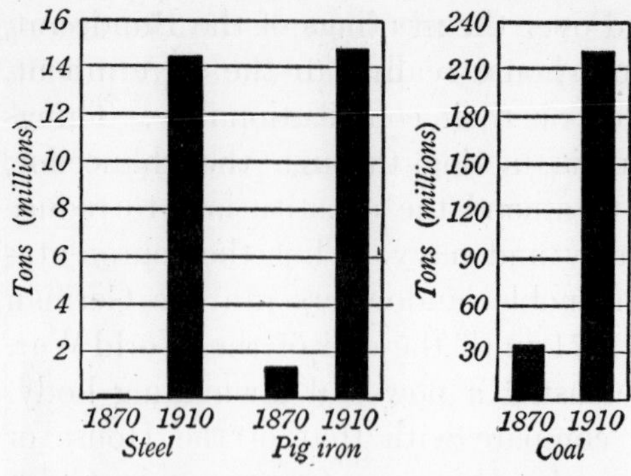

FIG. 130. These graphs illustrate the rapidity with which Germany industrialized after 1870. Steel, pig iron, and coal are the foundations on which an industrial civilization is built

Note the transformation recorded in figure 130. In 1870 more than 1,000,000 tons of pig iron were produced; in 1910 production reached approximately 15,000,000 tons — fifteen times as much. The increase in the production of steel was even more rapid, and in the same interval the amount of coal mined increased nearly sevenfold.

In 1882 the approximate number of workers employed in German manufacturing and trade was 20,000,000; in 1910 it was 35,000,000. The textile industry doubled its output. The goods shipped in German merchant ships more than doubled, and the export trade almost tripled.

In the meantime population grew rapidly. In 1870 it was 40,000,000; in 1911 it was 65,000,000. But the city population grew more rapidly. In 1871 only 36 per cent of the German people lived in cities; in 1910, 60 per cent lived there. At that time there were 45 cities, each having more than 100,000 people.

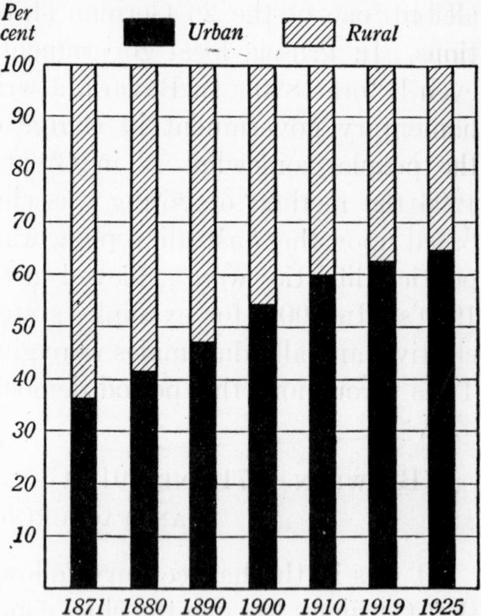

FIG. 131. In 1871 about 36 per cent of Germany's population were living in cities; by 1925 the urban population had grown to a little more than 64 per cent

It was in this period also that Germany built her tremendous system of world trade. We shall see in the following chapter how her trade, which in 1870 was largely local,— that is, among the German states and communities,— in 1914 was world-wide. Encouraged by the imperialistic central government, German commercial travelers competed with Englishmen, Americans, and Frenchmen in the remotest corners of the globe. Long before 1900, articles marked "Made in Germany" were seen in the homes of natives of twoscore countries. There was no more efficient system of trade on the earth than that which Germany built up during this period.

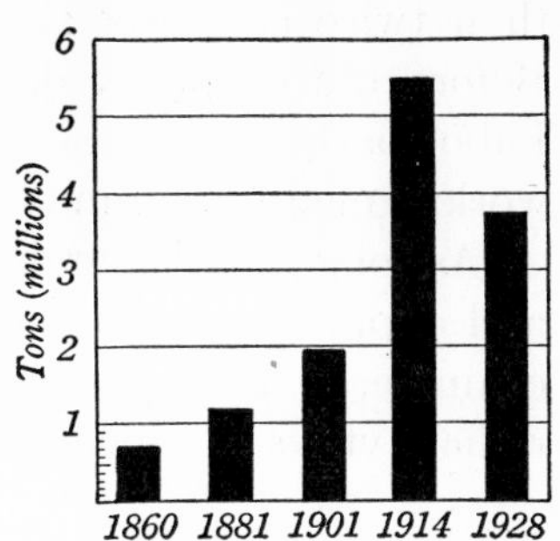

FIG. 132. Growth in Germany's shipping tonnage, 1860–1928

A glimpse can be had of this astonishing growth in the graph of figure 132. This shows the stupendous increase in German shipping. In 1860 the total tonnage of Germany's merchant ships was about 700,000; in 1914 it was 5,400,000 — nearly eight times as much. In 1910 Germany bought from other countries and sold to them three times as much as in 1870.

In the next chapter we shall see more clearly this rapid expansion of the German industrial nation around the world, and the dangerous competition which was developing among the chief industrial nations.

THE RAPID DEVELOPMENT OF SOCIALISM IN GERMANY, 1875–1914

As modern industry developed, German cities became centers of socialist agitation. The ideas of Karl Marx and Friedrich Engels had slowly made their way among the workingmen of the German states. Various groups of socialists had formed the Social Democratic Labor party as early as 1875. Even as scattered groups they had already secured nine representatives in the Reichstag at that time. Two years later (1877) the Social Democratic Labor party secured more than 500,000 votes in the national elections and placed twelve members in the Reichstag.

Table XIII shows the swift growth in the influence of the Social Democratic Labor party from 1874 to the World War. In 1912 it had more than twelve times as many representatives in the Reichstag as in 1874. In 1912 it polled 4,250,000 votes, more than twice as many as were polled by any other single party. Before the outbreak of the World War the Social Democratic Labor party had gathered a large membership not only from the workingmen but from students and upper-class radicals.

As long as Bismarck was chancellor he conducted a drastic and oppressive war upon socialists of every stamp. In 1878, for example, a law aimed at them prohibited the publication of radical views in newspapers or books. Imperial police interfered with legally held public meetings. They arrested and imprisoned socialist critics of the government.

TABLE XIII

Number of Seats in the Reichstag held by Socialists in Various Years, 1874–1912

Year	Number of Seats
1874	9
1881	12
1890	35
1898	56
1903	81
1912	110

After Bismarck's resignation in 1890 the Emperor, William II, carried on his policy. Free speech, free press, and free assemblage were suppressed by the Emperor and his officials. In spite of obstacles, however, the Social Democratic Labor party continued to hold the workingmen — the proletariat of Germany — and to increase its membership.

There were four other major parties in the German Reichstag. There were the *Conservatives*, made up mostly of the Junkers — the large landholders of Prussia — and their followers. There were the *National Liberals*, a group which included most of the business men of the cities and towns. These tended to support the Emperor and the chancellor in their desire to build up a strong central national government at the expense of the smaller princes and the workingmen and the peasants. Third, there were the *Progressives*, the real advocates of democracy. This group was the smallest of the parties and included many of the teachers in universities and other schools, intellectual radicals, and some professional men.

Fourth, there were the *Catholics*, or *Center*, so named because their representatives occupied seats in the center of the Reichstag. This party represented the various Catholic interests in the country. Unlike the people of Great Britain and France, in general the German people were divided in their political life by their religious views. The people of Prussia and the North German states were predominantly Lutherans; those of Bavaria, Württemberg, Baden, and other South German states were still devoted to the Catholic Church.

FIG. 133. This cartoon appeared in an English publication in 1890, upon Bismarck's resignation. It was entitled "Dropping the Pilot," and indicates Bismarck's political importance. (By Tenniel in *Punch*)

Throughout the 1870's there developed a conflict between these two groups which was somewhat similar to the religious conflict in France. But whereas in France the government ousted the Church from all share in matters of the state, in Germany the Catholic party continued to increase its representation. In the election of 1912 it polled 2,000,000 votes. This was more than either the Conservatives, the Liberals, or the Progressives polled, but less than half as many as did the Social Democrats.

In Germany, as in Great Britain, France, and America, much Legislation was passed protecting Workingmen

Although political liberty lagged in Germany, there was marked gain in civil rights. Owing in part to the fear of socialistic revolution and in part to the militaristic desire to insure the health of the young men of the nation, Bismarck himself led the way in suggesting social legislation.

In the 1880's laws similar to the French and English laws were passed protecting the health and security of the German workers in industry. There were laws insuring workingmen against illness and accidents, laws limiting the amount of labor performed by women and children, laws restricting hours of work and prohibiting labor on Sunday, and laws enforcing insurance against incapacity due to old age. In this latter respect the laws of the German Empire in 1890 protected the workers of Germany better than American laws protect our workers today.

FIG. 134. William II (1859–), last of the German monarchs

Moreover, the laws were actually *enforced*. Surveys in 1907 showed that from 13,000,000 to 20,000,000 people had been insured against either accident, illness, or incapacity due to old age, and in the 22 years preceding 1907 more than $1,500,000,000 had been paid out by the state in insurance to workingmen.

Thus under Bismarck and William II Government was Centralized in Germany

So it was that in this period of swift transformation from many small farming states to a unified industrial nation, government was changed to meet the new conditions. As in France, laws were made uniform. Banking was also made uniform throughout the empire, with the great imperial bank — the *Reichsbank* — at the head of the system. This bank matched the Bank of France and the Bank of England in its power. In the two leading industrial nations of continental Europe,

France and Germany, banking was placed definitely under the control of the state.

State ownership of certain public utilities was also developed under the central imperial government. In 1873 the railways of the various states were organized under a central railway bureau. Telegraphs, postal system, and other utilities were also brought under the control and operation of the government.

INTERESTING READINGS FROM WHICH YOU CAN GET ADDITIONAL INFORMATION

BOYLAN, GRACE D. The Pipes of Clovis. Little, Brown and Company, Boston. Tells of the early days of the Holy Roman Empire.

HEADLAM-MORLEY, JAMES W. Bismarck and the Foundation of the German Empire (Heroes of the Nations). G. P. Putnam's Sons, New York.

HENTY, GEORGE A. With Frederick the Great. Blackie & Son, London. The Seven Years' War.

MADDEN, E. A. Two Royal Foes. McClure & Co., New York. Prussia in 1810; Louise of Prussia and Napoleon.

MAJOR, CHARLES. A Gentle Knight of Old Brandenburg. The Macmillan Company, New York.

PYLE, HOWARD. Otto of the Silver Hand. Charles Scribner's Sons, New York. Tells of robber barons.

ROTH, RICHARD. King Otto's Crown. Concordia Publishing House, St. Louis. Germany in the 900's.

SEAWELL, MOLLY E. Lively Adventures of Gavin Hamilton. Harper & Brothers, New York. Frederick the Great and Maria Theresa.

SHEPPARD, A. T. The Red Cravat. The Macmillan Company, New York. Frederick William I of Prussia.

SIDGWICK, C. U. Germany. The Macmillan Company, New York. Home life in Germany.

VAN LOON, HENDRIK W. The Story of Mankind. Horace Liveright, New York.

WILE, F. W. Men around the Kaiser (The Makers of Modern Germany). The Bobbs-Merrill Company, Indianapolis.

UNIT V

CHANGING GOVERNMENTS AND THE WORLD WAR

CHANGING GOVERNMENTS AND THE WORLD WAR

We have now seen how the new ways of thinking produced a new type of industrial civilization in the three leading European nations. Especially have we noted how they made three different experiments in representative democracy. As these dramatic changes took place, others, equally important for the world, began to appear. The most important was the development of world trade — Great Britain, France, and Germany began to trade with remote parts of the earth and to spread in distant continents their industrial ways of living.

As that happened each of the three countries — and with them others, such as Belgium, Holland, and Italy — conquered lands and peoples in Asia, Africa, and America. There began then a fierce race between these industrializing nations for the rich prize of foreign trade.

But this race, in turn, brought other dramatic developments, among which were grave dangers to the peace of the world. In Chapter XIV we shall bring together our knowledge of this empire-building, and we shall see in what world disasters it resulted.

CHAPTER XIV

INDUSTRIAL COUNTRIES EUROPEANIZE THE EARTH AND PRODUCE THE WORLD WAR

So it was that the scientific revolution which spread over Europe after 1600 produced the Industrial Revolution and the march toward democracy. At last the new ways of thinking were bringing forth both power-driven machinery and parliamentary government in the leading industrial nations. The scientific method of thought was being applied to economic, social, and political matters as well as to the physical world.

In the meantime kingdoms and empires were in the making. Dukes and counts had fought and married their way into power over ever-larger territories. First in England and France, then in Spain and Portugal, in Russia and the Scandinavian countries, and later in the "Germanies" and Italy, duchies and counties, electorates and margraviates, free cities and other principalities, were merged by some means into kingdoms and empires.

Sooner or later most of these kingdoms and empires became nations. The people in each were ruled by a uniform system of central and local government. Most of the people in each spoke the same language, and they came to recognize their common nationality. That is, they said proudly: "We are French," "We are German." Increasingly this spirit of national patriotism, this love of country, grew in European countries.

We have seen, then, three very important developments in Europe:

First, the formation of large and powerful nations out of many small, weak, and scattered groups.

Second, the adoption of power-driven machines and the industrialization of Great Britain, France, and Germany. At the same time there was a steady increase in the wealth of the captains of the new industry.

Third, the gradual invention of various kinds of representative government under the control of the industrial capitalists and other property-owners, but with marked extension of civil and political rights to all the people. Although government was not really *by* the people, it was much more *for* the people than ever before in the world's history.

These Movements resulted in a New European Civilization

These three movements have produced a totally new kind of civilization — one new in physical ways of living, new in govern-

Fig. 135. In 1853 ships laid down the cable for a submarine telegraph connecting England and Holland. A new idea in communication began to spread. (From the *Illustrated London News*, June, 1853)

ment, new in its art life and its leisure occupations, new in its social spirit and its outlook upon most of the phases of life.

It is a civilization in which power-driven machines have begun to replace sweating, tired bodies. Swift transportation brings the goods of distant continents to the remotest hamlets, and instantaneous communication binds separated peoples together in an interdependent world. It is a civilization of large corporations, of a few enormously rich property-owners, and of a great mass of comparatively poor mechanics, clerks, and peasant

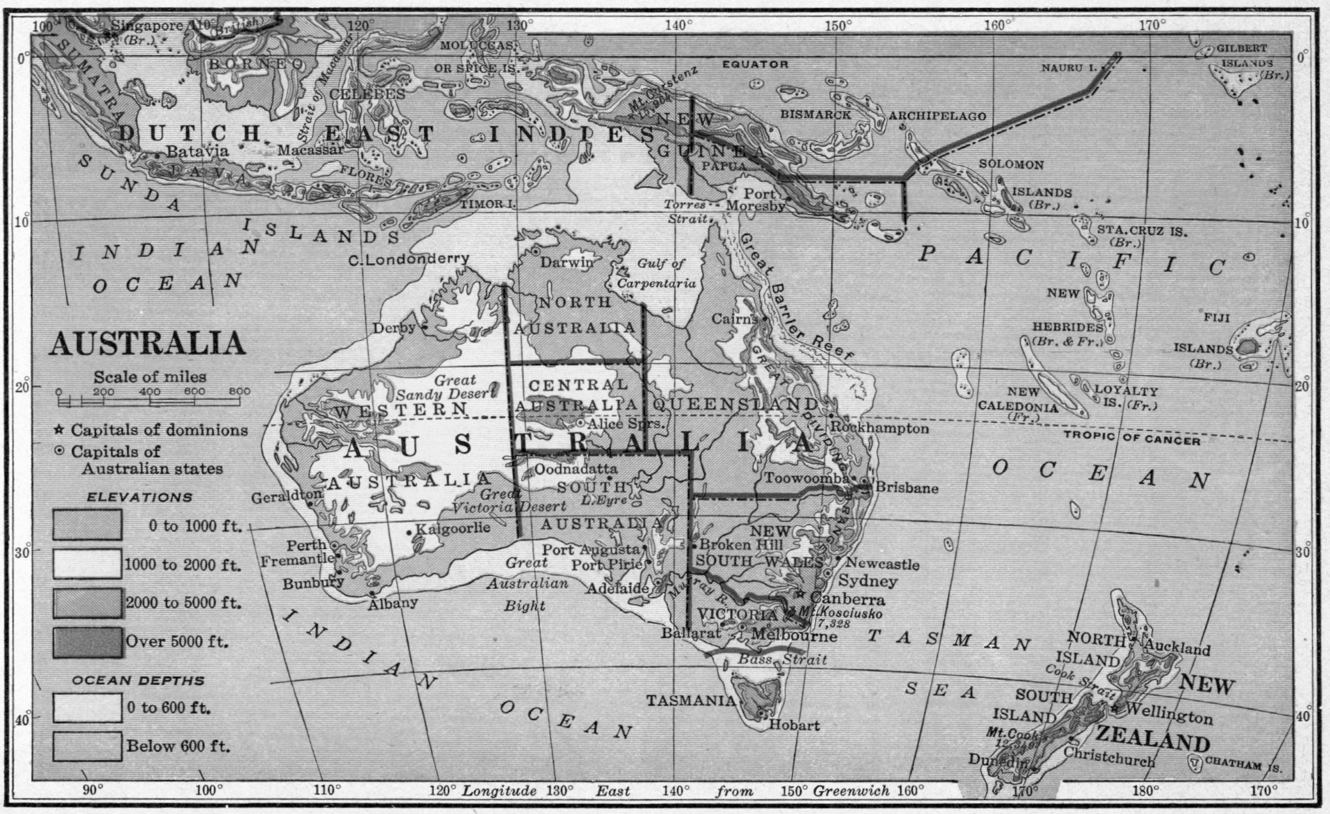
AUSTRALIA
Scale of miles
0 200 400 600 800
★ Capitals of dominions
⊙ Capitals of Australian states
ELEVATIONS
0 to 1000 ft.
1000 to 2000 ft.
2000 to 5000 ft.
Over 5000 ft.
OCEAN DEPTHS
0 to 600 ft.
Below 600 ft.
Singapore (Br.)
SUMATRA
BORNEO
CELEBES
Strait of Macassar
MOLUCCAS OR SPICE IS.
DUTCH EAST INDIES
Batavia
Macassar
JAVA
FLORES
TIMOR I.
SUNDA ISLANDS
INDIAN OCEAN
EQUATOR
NEW GUINEA
PAPUA
BISMARCK ARCHIPELAGO
NAURU I.
GILBERT ISLANDS (Br.)
SOLOMON ISLANDS (Br.)
STA. CRUZ IS. (Br.)
Port Moresby
Torres Strait
PACIFIC
NEW HEBRIDES (Br. & Fr.)
FIJI ISLANDS (Br.)
NEW CALEDONIA (Fr.)
LOYALTY IS. (Fr.)
TROPIC OF CANCER
OCEAN
C. Londonderry
Darwin
Gulf of Carpentaria
Great Barrier Reef
Cairns
NORTH AUSTRALIA
Derby
Great Sandy Desert
CENTRAL AUSTRALIA
Alice Sprs.
QUEENSLAND
GREAT DIVIDING RANGE
Rockhampton
WESTERN AUSTRALIA
AUSTRALIA
Oodnadatta
SOUTH AUSTRALIA
L. Eyre
Toowoomba
Brisbane
Geraldton
Great Victoria Desert
Kalgoorlie
Perth
Fremantle
Bunbury
Albany
Port Augusta
Port Pirie
Great Australian Bight
Adelaide
Broken Hill
NEW SOUTH WALES
Newcastle
Sydney
Canberra
Murray R.
VICTORIA
Mt. Kosciusko 7,328
Ballarat
Melbourne
Bass Strait
TASMANIA
Hobart
INDIAN OCEAN
TASMAN SEA
NORTH ISLAND
Auckland
Cook Strait
NEW ZEALAND
Wellington
SOUTH ISLAND
Mt. Cook 12,349
Christchurch
Dunedin
CHATHAM IS.
Longitude East from Greenwich

farmers. But it is a civilization in which even the lowliest have a better standard of living than their comrades in most nonindustrialized civilizations.

It is a civilization in which nearly all children go to school and most people learn to read and write and to understand something of the scientific knowledge of the modern world. It is a civilization in which the paper governments at least are parliamentary, partially democratic rather than absolute. The legislative bodies are chosen by universal manhood suffrage, and civil liberty is generally protected by written constitutions.

It is a civilization in which the arts of writing, painting, architecture, music and the dance, and the theater have reached a very high point.

There are other characteristics of this new civilization which we shall note as we continue, but these are sufficient to define it clearly. Since it was developed first in Europe we call it *European civilization.*

After 1800 European Civilization spread around the World

Within the past 100 years the chief industrial countries that produced this new civilization have begun to Europeanize the earth. That is, traders, missionaries, and government officials of Great Britain, France, Germany, and other European countries have gone among other peoples of the world and have taught them, in many cases forced them, to adopt the European ways of living. They have gone to China, Japan, India, the Malay States and other parts of Asia, as well as to Africa, Central and South America, and Australia.

Some of this Europeanizing was begun through "peaceful penetration" — that is, by going into a country, building factories and railroads, opening up mines, and taking out the rubber, oil, wood, and other products. At the same time the Europeans would sell goods to the natives, thus introducing them to European ways. In other cases the Europeanizing was accomplished by conquering the natives, seizing control of their government, and taking possession of their territory. These two methods of empire-building by the leading industrial countries spread European civilization in every continent.

The Europeanizing of the earth, then, is the fourth great movement of the modern world. To understand the difficult situation of the industrial countries today we must comprehend clearly this building of great empires by Great Britain, France, Germany, and Russia, and the formation of smaller ones by Italy, the United States, Belgium, and Holland.

Let us review briefly the empire-building of the leading nations.

The Race for Empire

Kings and trading companies established colonies

Recall the years of vigorous exploration after the discovery of America in 1492. In the 1500's and 1600's came permanent colonies. Within 150 years England and France had established colonies in North America, and Spain and Portugal had divided practically all Central and South America between them.[1]

Then came the great period of empire-building

1. *England built the vast British Empire*

In the 1600's and 1700's the English East India Company not only secured control of the trade of the millions of Indian peoples, but also came to govern them as well. At the great rebellion of 1857, however, England stepped in and brought India directly under the control of the British government. In 1877 Queen Victoria was proclaimed Empress of India.

In order to protect her merchant ships in their journey from the British Isles to India, England acquired many strategic points in the Mediterranean Sea and the Red Sea. Even as early as 1713 she possessed the fortress of Gibraltar.

[1] By 1783 the English colonies had become an independent country, — the United States of America, — and even before that time the English, having ousted the French from the New World, had cleared the way for what was to become the Dominion of Canada. In the years from 1810 to 1826 the colonies founded by Spain revolted from the mother country and established a score of Latin-American republics. Even Brazil gained its independence from Portugal.

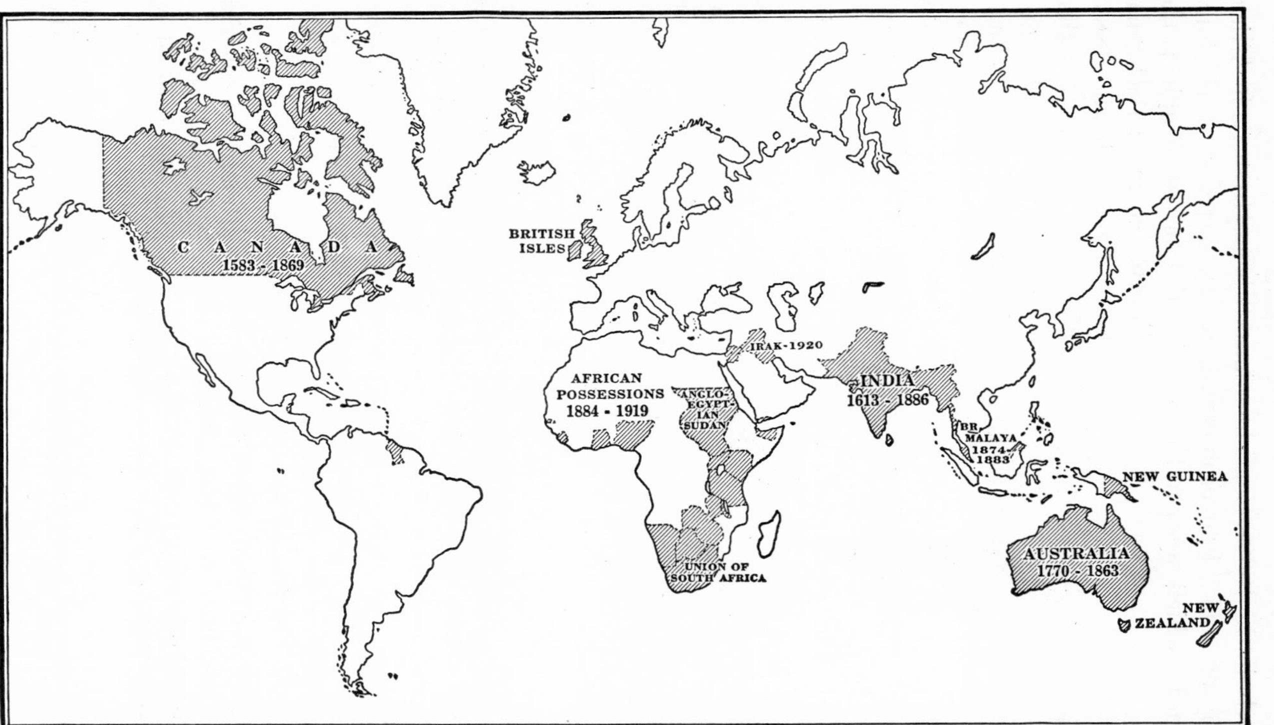

FIG. 136. Lands in every continent of the earth are included within the British Empire. The principal ones and the dates when they became a part of the Empire are given in the map

Early in the 1800's English emigrants began to settle in Africa. One by one official governments were established over the huge provinces, which were made parts of the British Empire: the Gold Coast, 1871; Bechuanaland, 1885; Nigeria, 1886; Kenya Colony, 1887; Rhodesia, 1889; British East Africa, 1890; Uganda Colony, 1894: Tanganyika Territory, 1918; and, in 1910, the Union of South Africa, formed from territory annexed between 1843 and 1885.[1] One can travel today from Anglo-Egyptian Sudan on the north to Cape Town at the southern tip of Africa and remain in British territory all the time.

FIG. 137. A cartoon of Cecil Rhodes, British empire-builder, upon beginning his project of connecting by telegraph the extremities of British Africa. (From *Punch*, 1892)

By 1919 the British Empire included lands in every continent (see figure 136). In 1800 the Empire had totaled less than 2,000,000 square miles; in 1919 it was almost 14,000,000 square miles. At that date more than 400,000,000 people were ruled by the government of Great Britain.

2. *France built the second-largest empire*

As you know, the British defeated French attempts at colonial expansion in the New World and in India. You recall that for more than 100 years France was submerged by the turmoil of revolution. During this time she did not engage in empire-building. But when the industrial capitalists began to need markets, raw material, and places for investment outside of the homeland, the French began to add imperial possessions to their territory.

[1] Gambia had been taken as early as 1618; Sierra Leone, in 1788.

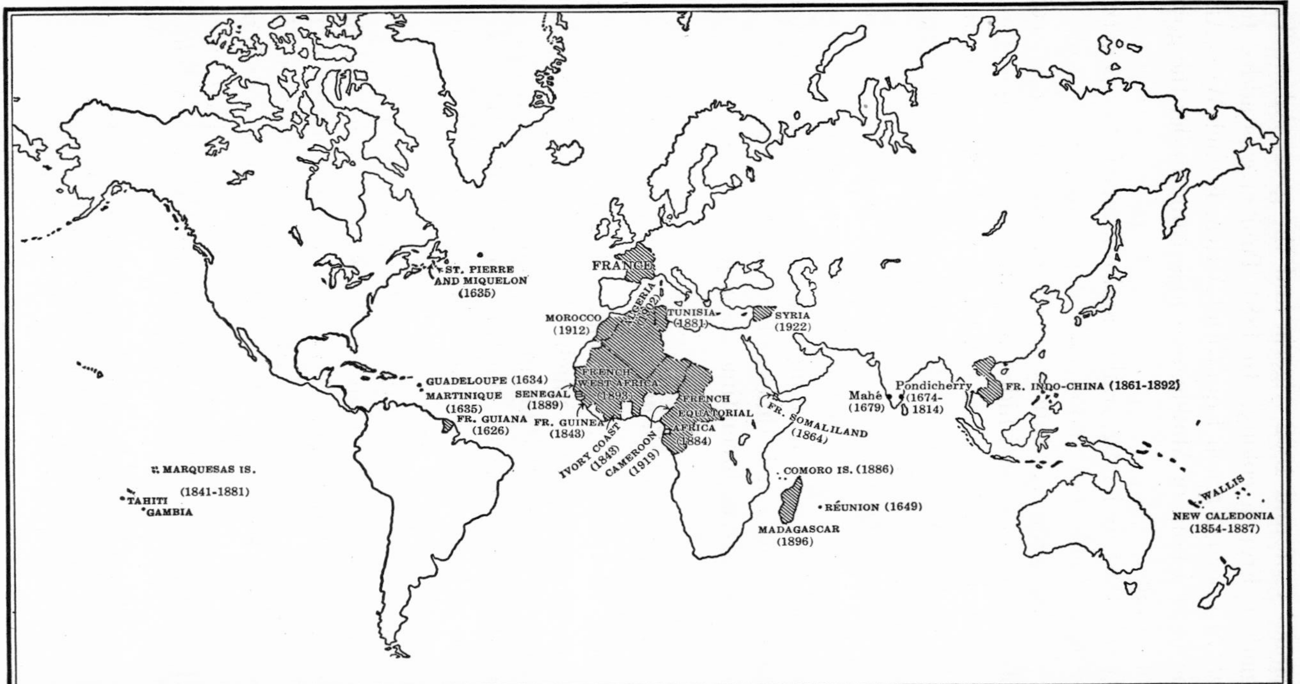

FIG. 138. The lands which belong to the French empire or over which it has a certain amount of control are indicated on the map

Between 1830 and 1902 Algeria and the great Sahara Desert were made a French colony. In 1881 Tunisia was added to the empire. Morocco, French Equatorial Africa, French West Africa, and the large island of Madagascar also came under the government of France.

Between 1861 and 1892, traders and military forces penetrated the region of Siam and Indo-China and made Indo-China part of the French empire. Indo-China grew cotton, sugar, coffee, and tobacco; it produced hides and silks; it had large stores of copper, coal, iron, gold, zinc, tin, all of which were valuable to France. Many other scattered regions were also taken by the French.

By 1919 the French flag waved over the second largest empire of the world, which had a population of over 104,000,000 people and covered 4,000,000 square miles of territory. This population was about two and a half times as large as the home country, and the area was almost eighteen times as large.

3. Germany also built an empire of foreign possessions

Although the industrial development and the political unification of Germany came much later than the corresponding movements in Great Britain and France, Germany too took foreign possessions. But by the time the German business men were ready to begin their empire-building, most of the favorable spots of the world had been taken. Only a part of Africa and some islands in the Pacific remained for German conquest.

Germany took these regions in the same way as the British and the French had done. Traders and missionaries went in first. The former developed trade with the natives; the latter tried to convert them to Christianity. Trouble soon ensued between the Europeans and the native peoples. Then, step by step, the German government took control of the regions and made them colonies in the empire. In this way Togo (1884), Cameroon (1884), German Southwest Africa (1884–1890), and German East Africa (1885–1890) were taken over. In 1897 about 117 square miles of territory in the Shantung peninsula in China were controlled by leases. They included two port

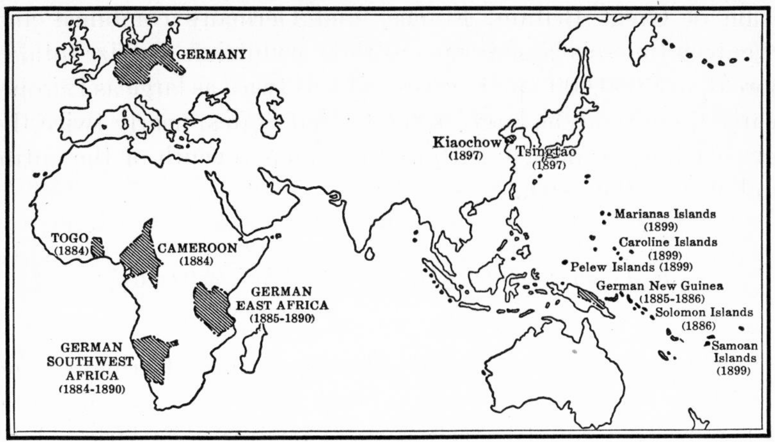

FIG. 139. The darkened areas show Germany's foreign possessions until after the World War

towns, Kiaochow and Tsingtao. Other scattered regions were also taken among the islands of the Pacific. In figure 139 you can see what Germany had acquired before 1914.

4. *Russia built a great inland empire across two continents*

While England, France, and Germany were dividing the world among themselves, Russia was also building an empire. This was done in two ways: first, by military conquest; second, by the emigration of the Russian peoples southward and eastward across Asia.

Russia wanted "warm water" ports — ports which would be open to ships in winter as well as in summer. So in the 1700's and 1800's the Russian armies conquered lands to the west and south, including a large portion of Poland, Lithuania, and the regions bordering the Black Sea.

At the same time emigrants pushed out across the Urals, down the Volga River to the Caspian Sea, and southward into Turkestan. Then slowly the empire expanded across Siberia. Eventually the great migration moved 5000 miles.

By 1900 the Russian Empire reached from Germany, Austria, and the Black Sea on the west to the Pacific Ocean on the east. It was a huge empire, as large in population as the total population of Great Britain, France, and Germany combined and seventeen times as large in area as those countries. Its size totaled more than 8,000,000 square miles. It was twice as large as Europe, nearly three times as large as the United States, nearly twice the size of China, and included practically one seventh of the entire land area of the earth.

5. *As other countries became industrialized they too took lands in other continents*

In the expansion of Great Britain, France, Germany, and Russia we see the chief empire-building of the modern world. Although other countries seized small territories in Africa, Asia, and the Pacific islands, on the whole they were of little consequence. They played little part in the swift Europeanization of the earth or in bringing on serious international crises. We shall merely mention some of them briefly.

Italy's possessions in Africa. Italian trading companies began to buy their way into various regions in Africa as early as 1869. In that year the port of Assab, on the Red Sea, was bought outright by an Italian shipping company. In 1882 the Italian government took control of Assab and developed about it the colony of Eritrea.

In 1889 what is now Italian Somaliland, south of Ethiopia (Abyssinia), was developed as an Italian colony. From the map of figure 140 we see that this region is larger than the entire Italian peninsula. During the following few years the Italians did their best to take Ethiopia itself. But the people of Ethiopia defeated the Italian armies sent against them. Even to the present day they have maintained their independence.

Italy had long wanted the large African province around Tripoli, which, as you see from figure 140, lies directly south across the Mediterranean. In 1911, after negotiations with France, which in the meantime had taken Algeria, Morocco, and Tunisia, near by, Italian armies invaded Tripoli. This region was then in the power of Turkey. In a year of warfare the Turks were defeated, and the entire region called Libya, with Tripoli as the leading city, was made an Italian colony. It is so today.

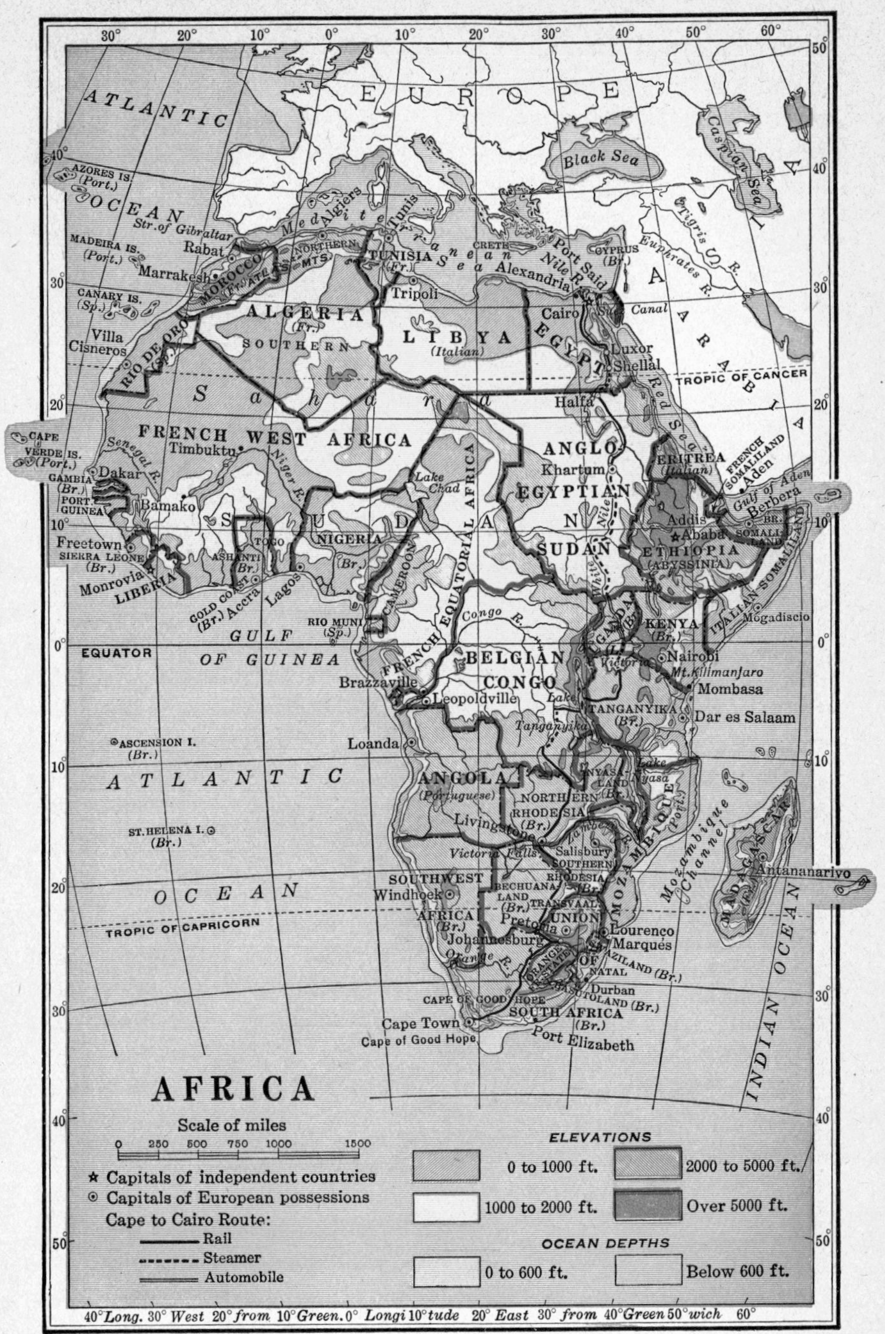
AFRICA
Scale of miles
0 250 500 750 1000 1500
★ Capitals of independent countries
⊙ Capitals of European possessions
Cape to Cairo Route:
Rail
Steamer
Automobile
ELEVATIONS
0 to 1000 ft.
1000 to 2000 ft.
2000 to 5000 ft.
Over 5000 ft.
OCEAN DEPTHS
0 to 600 ft.
Below 600 ft.
40° Long. 30° West 20° from 10° Green. 0° Longi 10° tude 20° East 30° from 40° Green 50° wich 60°
EUROPE
ATLANTIC OCEAN
AZORES IS. (Port.)
MADEIRA IS. (Port.)
CANARY IS. (Sp.)
CAPE VERDE IS. (Port.)
Str. of Gibraltar
Mediterranean Sea
Black Sea
Caspian Sea
ASIA
ARABIA
Rabat
Marrakesh
MOROCCO
ATLAS MTS.
Algiers
Tunis
TUNISIA (Fr.)
Tripoli
ALGERIA (Fr.)
LIBYA (Italian)
EGYPT
Cairo
Alexandria
Port Said
Suez Canal
CRETE
CYPRUS (Br.)
Euphrates R.
Tigris R.
Luxor
Shellal
Halfa
Red Sea
TROPIC OF CANCER
Villa Cisneros
RIO DE ORO (Sp.)
SOUTHERN Sahara
FRENCH WEST AFRICA
Timbuktu
Senegal R.
Niger R.
Dakar
GAMBIA (Br.)
PORT. GUINEA
Bamako
Freetown
SIERRA LEONE (Br.)
Monrovia
LIBERIA
SUDAN
TOGO
ASHANTI (Br.)
GOLD COAST (Br.)
Accra
Lagos
NIGERIA (Br.)
Lake Chad
CAMEROON
FRENCH EQUATORIAL AFRICA
ANGLO EGYPTIAN SUDAN
Khartum
White Nile
ERITREA (Italian)
FRENCH SOMALILAND
Aden
Gulf of Aden
Berbera
BR. SOMALILAND
Addis Ababa
ETHIOPIA (ABYSSINIA)
ITALIAN SOMALILAND
Mogadiscio
KENYA (Br.)
UGANDA (Br.)
Nairobi
Mt. Kilimanjaro
Mombasa
Lake Victoria
RIO MUNI (Sp.)
GULF OF GUINEA
EQUATOR
Congo R.
BELGIAN CONGO
FRENCH
Brazzaville
Leopoldville
Lake Tanganyika
TANGANYIKA (Br.)
Dar es Salaam
ASCENSION I. (Br.)
Loanda
ATLANTIC OCEAN
ANGOLA (Portuguese)
NORTHERN RHODESIA (Br.)
NYASALAND (Br.)
Lake Nyasa
MOZAMBIQUE (Port.)
Mozambique Channel
MADAGASCAR (Fr.)
Antananarivo
ST. HELENA I. (Br.)
Livingstone
Victoria Falls
Zambezi R.
Salisbury
SOUTHERN RHODESIA (Br.)
SOUTHWEST AFRICA (Br.)
Windhoek
BECHUANALAND (Br.)
TRANSVAAL
UNION OF SOUTH AFRICA (Br.)
Pretoria
Johannesburg
Lourenço Marques
Orange R.
ORANGE FREE STATE
SWAZILAND (Br.)
NATAL
Durban
BASUTOLAND (Br.)
CAPE OF GOOD HOPE
Cape Town
Cape of Good Hope
Port Elizabeth
TROPIC OF CAPRICORN
INDIAN OCEAN

In the meantime Belgium also seized territory in Africa. Around the Congo River her traders subdued and cruelly enslaved the people of the rich rubber region. In the Belgian Congo developed the worst examples of exploitation of native peoples in all this

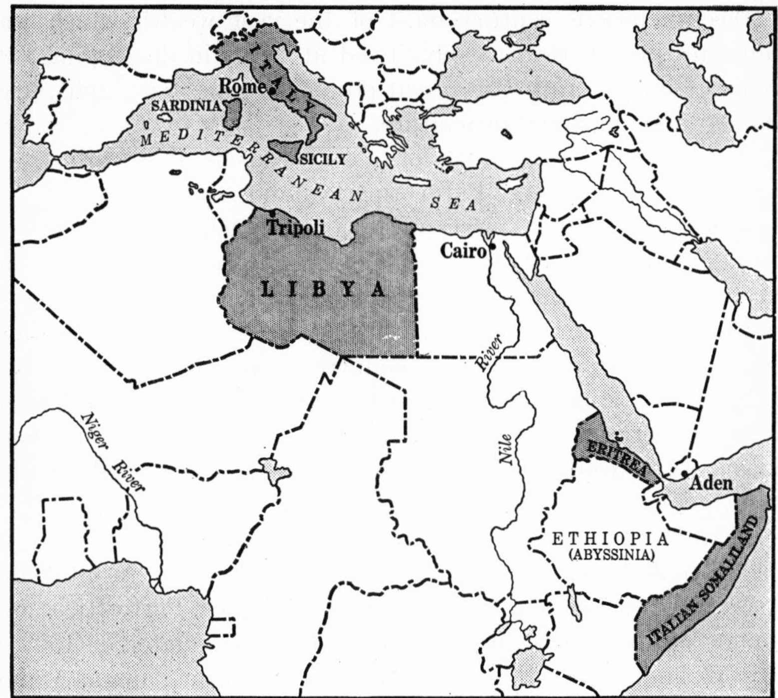

FIG. 140. Italy and her foreign possessions. Compared with the empire of England or France, Italy's empire is a very small one

ruthless empire-building by European peoples. Vast riches in rubber, copper, palm oil, and cotton were taken out of the Congo by Belgian business men.

There were other examples of European empire-building: Spain and Portugal in Africa, and Holland in Latin America and in the East Indies. But the chief examples are those which we have cited. It was through these — especially those of Great Britain, France, and Germany — that the new industrial civilization of Europe was being spread around the earth about 1900.

6. *The United States too was slowly acquiring small foreign possessions*

Alone of the leading powers of the world the United States took little part in empire-building until about 1900. To the end of the nineteenth century most of the vast wealth which was piling up in America was employed at home in developing rich mines, factories, railroads, great power stations, telegraphs, telephones, and machine agriculture.

Even in the 1800's, however, a very considerable world trade developed with Europe, Latin America, and Asia.

During this time American missionaries and traders went out in increasing numbers to the various islands of the Pacific. Increasingly they began to play a larger and larger part in the political life of the regions to which they went. They, like the missionaries and traders of other countries, came into conflict with the natives. Armed uprisings occurred, and eventually the United States government sent naval vessels and troops to put them down. As a result several of these islands were brought under the American flag.

In 1898 the United States annexed the Hawaiian Islands; in 1899 it took Tutuila, one of the Samoa Islands. As a result of the Spanish-American War, in 1898, the Philippines, Porto Rico, and Guam became American possessions. Five years later, in 1903, a strip of land across Panama, known now as the Panama Canal Zone, was ceded to the United States in exchange for a sum of money and certain yearly payments. In 1917 three of the largest of the Virgin Islands — St. John, St. Thomas, and St. Croix — were purchased from Denmark. In the meantime the United States had extended its commercial and political influence in other Caribbean countries, especially in Haiti, Cuba, Nicaragua, and the Dominican Republic.

The First Factor in Empire-Building: Economic Development

Why did industrial countries take colonies? First and foremost, empires were built in the 1800's by industrial countries for economic reasons. These reasons were chiefly three: first, the desire of the business men to sell goods abroad; second, the need of raw materials which are not supplied by the home country; third, the need of a place to invest the surplus money that was accumulating in each country. We will give just a brief review of each of these.

1. *The desire to sell goods abroad.* Industrial peoples easily manufacture more goods than they can use. They therefore need additional markets. The outlying parts of their empires afford such markets. For example, as a result of taking Algeria, French cotton-manufacturers in a recent year sold one third of their goods in that colony. Similarly, Madagascar, French Indo-China, Tunisia, and Morocco purchase millions of dollars' worth of French manufactured goods each year.

So also today the value of the exports of British products to India amounts to more than $380,700,000. This is more than the amount of Britain's trade with any other single country, even with the United States, Germany, France, or with any of her dominions other than India. British machinery, engines, wagons, implements, and other products are sold among the hundreds of millions of people of India.

Until the World War, German business men sold their products among the islands of the Pacific, in the province of Shantung, and among the natives of the four territories which had been taken in Africa. In these examples, therefore, we have brief illustrations of the first economic reason, namely, the desire for profit in foreign trade.

2. *The desire for raw materials.* There was a second economic reason which led each industrial country to want colonies under its own government; namely, the need of raw materials which it could not produce itself. For example, France gets sheep and oxen, animal products, metals, and wine from Algeria; rice, cotton, corn, oxen, rubber, pepper, fish, vegetable oil, silver, zinc, and leather from Indo-China; hides, rice, vegetables, minerals, and other things from Madagascar.

Similarly, Great Britain receives huge shipments of raw cotton, wheat, tea, rice, wool, leather, and jute from India and huge quantities of things from Canada, Australia, and her many other possessions.

Germany took out of Togo large supplies of palm oil and mahogany. From Cameroon it brought out large amounts of rubber, together with ivory, ebony, and mahogany. Its traders developed large rubber plantations. From the grazing plains of German Southwest Africa came cattle, and from the mines came copper, tin, and diamonds.

Similarly, Holland took vast quantities of rubber and other products from Java and the Dutch East Indies; and Italy and Belgium obtained important raw materials from Africa.

Thus raw materials were the second economic reason for imperialism.

3. *The desire to invest surplus wealth.* In time the industrial countries found that their people were purchasing practically all the goods they could. The capitalists had been investing their surplus wealth at home in more factories, more warehouses, more railroads, more shipping companies, more stores. This was no longer profitable. So they looked abroad for other places in which to invest their money. They sent agents to India, to Canada, to Australia, the Malay States, and Africa. There they set up factories, developed cotton, rubber, and rice plantations, opened up mines, and built railroads and telephone and telegraph lines. Indeed, they set up in many of these undeveloped regions much the same kind of civilization that they had developed at home.

TABLE XIV[1]

British Foreign Long-Term Investment	
Period	Millions of Pounds
1870–74	61.0
1875–79	1.7
1880–84	23.9
1885–89	61.1
1890–94	45.6
1894–99	26.8
1900–04	21.3
1904–09	109.5
1910–13	185.0

Note how clearly Tables XIV–XVI show this rapid investment of European wealth in other countries. So rapid was the investment of British money abroad that by the outbreak of the World War it is roughly estimated that $20,000,000,000, or practically one fourth of the entire national wealth of the United Kingdom, was so used!

[1] Herbert Feis, *Europe the World's Banker, 1870–1914*, p. 11. Yale University Press, New Haven, 1930.

French investments abroad increased at the same rapid rate. In 1870 the foreign investments totaled about $2,500,000,000. In 1914 they had reached the grand total of almost $9,000,000,000. The latter sum was estimated to be one sixth of the entire national wealth of France.

TABLE XV[1]

Total French Foreign Investment	
Year	Billions of Francs
1870	12–14
1880	15
1890	20
1900	28
1905	34
1910	40
1912	42
1914	45

German investments, while less than British or French, nevertheless reached the vast total of nearly $6,000,000,000 in 1914, growing after 1895 at the rate of $150,000,000 a year. In 1914, foreign investments were approximately one fifteenth of the entire national wealth of the German people.[2]

It is not an exaggeration to say that in 1914 one fifth of the wealth of the leading industrial nations was invested in foreign lands. This is, indeed, a striking illustration of the way in which economic imperialism developed after 1870.

TABLE XVI[3]

German Foreign Investment	
Year	Billions of Marks
1883	5
1893	10–13
1905	15–18
1914	22–25

A hundred years after Napoleon's time the British had justified his remark that they were "a nation of shopkeepers." British traders were found all over the world dealing in commodities from their home industries and also in commodities from industries which they had established or which they controlled abroad. But Napoleon's own people had become "shopkeepers" too, and so had the sons of the German *bourgeoisie*, both groups being busy with their home and foreign trade.

[1] Herbert Feis, *Europe the World's Banker, 1870–1914*, p. 47. Yale University Press, New Haven, 1930.

[2] In 1914 the pound was worth approximately $4.86, the franc 19 cents, and the mark 25 cents.

[3] Herbert Feis, *Europe the World's Banker, 1870–1914*, p. 71. Yale University Press, New Haven, 1930.

A Second Factor in Empire-Building: the Desire to convert the World to Christianity

The economic reasons for gathering undeveloped lands into empires appealed in the main to business men, manufacturers, bankers, and others financially able to own stock in imperialistic enterprises. Such made up only a very small proportion of all the people. There were other motives which secured the support of much larger groups of people.

One was the missionary motive — the desire to convert the "heathen" of Asia, Africa, and other regions to the Christian religion. This motive had had a long history, dating almost from the establishment of the Church. After 1500 the officials of the Catholic Church aided the exploration and settlement of the world, partly because it would add to their wealth and power and partly because of an honest zeal to convert the "backward" natives of these foreign regions. We have seen, for example, the rôle of the Jesuits in exploring the New World and in establishing missions in foreign lands. They carried on their work in other parts of the world as well.

After the Reformation and the discovery and exploration of hitherto unknown continents, the Protestant churches of Europe also established missions among non-Christian people. The Baptists, the Presbyterians, the Methodists, the Congregationalists, and others developed missionary societies.

Zealous missionaries explored Africa, determined to teach the Christian religion to black-skinned natives of that "Dark Continent," determined to bring new membership into their churches. Missionaries often prepared the way for the business men and the government in German Southwest Africa and in Kiaochow, China.

So frequently has the history of imperialism repeated itself in different parts of the world that one would not be far wrong in summing it up thus: first, the missionaries, then the traders, and then the soldiers. Owing to these three groups scores of regions of Asia, Africa, Australasia, and the Americas were added to the European empires.

A Third Factor: National Patriotism and Helping "Backward" Peoples

As love of country was instilled into the mass of the people, this nationalistic spirit was seized upon to enlist their support for empire-building. In each of the leading countries statesmen, politicians, even educators, became missionaries for the increasing "glory of the empire."

Various reasons were invented for this policy. Europeans and Americans began to feel that the white race, and the people of one's own country in particular, were the superior people of the world. The natives of Asia, Africa, and the islands were in their eyes "backward," "uncivilized," "inferior" people. Hence because people of the white race had invented the new European civilization, they thought it their duty to educate and convert all the other races to this "higher," "better" way of living.

So, along with patriotic reasons for building ever-greater empires, there was this duty of improving the other peoples of the world. In such ways the leaders of each industrial country began to explain and justify their conquests abroad.

The seizure of India by Great Britain was justified in that way. It was claimed that the improvement of the conditions of the Indian people was an obligation upon Great Britain. Poets, novelists, journalists, and political writers built up a growing literature of "the white man's burden" of uplifting the "backward" races.

At the same time patriotic enthusiasm for the Empire grew. Sons of British noble families were brought up with the idea of working in the colonial service. The rank and file of the people were constantly reminded of the glorious achievements of the British armies in foreign lands. The man on the street thrilled over the growth of the Empire. Thus the people of Great Britain began to regard themselves as a great cultural force in the world.

Many other people, of poorer economic conditions, regarded colonies as a place to which to emigrate and get a better living. After 1870, millions of people left England and went to the various colonies.

In the meantime the German people were also taught, in school and out, to believe, as one of their statesmen said, that "the German race is called to bind the earth under its control." The Emperor, William II, said in one of his speeches: "The German people will be the block of granite on which our Lord will be able to elevate and achieve the civilization of the world." And again, in another speech: "God has called us to civilize the world; we are the missionaries of human progress." Again: "We are the superior race in the fields of science and of art; we are the best colonists, the best sailors, the best merchants."

Before the World War a leading German author wrote: "Domination belongs to Germany because it is a superior nation, a noble race, and it is fitting that it should control its neighbors."

Hundreds of such statements could be quoted from the writings of German politicians in the years before the World War. Even educators and scientific writers aided in building up the idea among the mass of the people that the German was the superior type of man upon earth. He it was who was called by God to civilize the earth — but it must be done under his rule.

We must remember, therefore, that in England and France and Germany, in Italy and other countries as well, the schools and books, newspapers and magazines, political speeches and proclamations, steadily increased the spirit of national patriotism. As this took place the support of the common people was enlisted for empire-building.

Summing up, then, we see three sets of factors which led industrial countries to take colonies: first, the economic factors — the desire for profitable markets, for raw materials, and for a place to invest surplus wealth; second, the missionary factor — the desire of Christians to convert non-Christian peoples to their religion, even though these peoples may have had well-developed religions of their own; third, the patriotic factor — the desire to extend the scope of one's empire, to spread one's own culture around the world, and to lift "backward" people up to the level of one's own civilization.[1]

[1] What the so-called "backward" peoples thought about all this we shall study in later chapters.

FIG. 141. In less than 100 years the competition for trade among industrial nations created a revolution in shipbuilding. Besides changing from wind power to steam or electric power, from wooden hulls to hulls of steel, ships have grown steadily larger and heavier so that they may carry more merchandise safely. The following ships are shown in the picture: (1) *Spartan*, built in 1834 — 475 tons, about 135 feet long; (2) *Trident*, built in 1841 — 875 tons, 206 feet long; (3) *Oceanic*, built in 1870 — 3808 tons, 420 feet long; (4) *Campania*, built in 1892 — 12,950 tons, 625 feet long; (5) *Bremen*, built in 1929 — 51,656 tons, 938 feet long. Note how the merchant ships have grown in length and tonnage since 1834

How Empire-Building (1870–1914) finally led to the World War

The dangerous race between industrial nations for trade

After 1870 the race between the industrial nations for the trade of the earth became fiercer. In the years just before and after 1900 the world witnessed the fiercest economic competition in all history.

Merchants and manufacturers in every machine-using country, with the active support of their governments, sent salesmen into

China, Japan, India, and other regions of Asia, into the Latin-American republics, among the natives of Africa and of the islands of the Pacific. Thousands of ships flying the Union Jack traversed the great sea paths of the world. Other thousands, flying the German, French, Italian, Japanese, and American flags, lay beside the British at the docks of Calcutta, Singapore, Manila, Hong Kong, Port Said, and Rio de Janeiro. Merchant marines grew by leaps and bounds. Larger and larger became the vessels; sailing ships gave way later to steamships (see figure 141).

As the slow sailing ships of pre-industrial days changed in the 1870's and 1880's to the steam-propelled liners, the imperial policies of governments also changed. Each one of them saw that it must have coaling stations scattered round the world where huge quantities of coal could be stored, from which their merchant and passenger ships and warships could refill their bunkers. England took island after island, port after port, in the Mediterranean, the Atlantic, the Pacific, and other seas. In this development Germany and France were her close rivals.

The development of larger and more expensive navies

Colonies located thousands of miles from the home country needed protection. Scattered island coaling stations needed protection. The coast line of the homeland must be protected. So reasoned the ministers in the government of each industrial country. The fear of attack from economic rivals spread among the parliamentary and business leaders of each country, and they in turn spread the fear among their respective peoples.

With this feeling of fear, the demand for bigger navies began to grow. In the shipyards of the world, after 1870, new cruisers, battleships, dreadnaughts, and submarines were constructed. Thicker and thicker became the steel armor, bigger and bigger the engines and guns. The cost of a single battleship mounted into millions of dollars.

Heavier and heavier became the taxes; for *the people* had to pay the bills, just as in the days of absolute kings. By 1914 staggering sums were being spent upon the newest instruments of warfare (see Table XVII).

In the ten years preceding 1914 Great Britain alone spent $1,750,000,000 on her navy; France spent $800,000,000; Russia, $700,000,000; Germany, $900,000,000. Together the four leading world powers spent on naval armament more than $4,000,000,000 of the savings and income of their people. Many people began to wonder if democracy had changed things much after all. *Nine tenths of their taxes were still being used for war.*

TABLE XVII

Amount spent for Navies in 1878 and 1914		
	1878	1914
Great Britain	$53,000,000	$244,000,000
Germany	14,000,000	117,000,000
Italy	8,000,000	—[1]

Armies also became bigger and bigger

In the meantime most of the leading countries had adopted universal military service. With certain exceptions every able-bodied young man was compelled to spend a stated number of years in rigorous military training. Conscription, you will remember, had first been used in France and Germany during the time of Napoleon. In the 1870's both the French and the German government extended the requirements.

TABLE XVIII [2]

Number of Men in Peace-Time Armies		
	1899	1914
Germany	604,000	806,000
Austria	346,000	370,000
Italy	258,000	305,000
France	574,000	818,000
Russia	896,000	1,284,000

So, decade by decade, the armies of Germany, France, Russia, Austria, and Italy became bigger and bigger. Table XVIII shows to what size they had grown in 1899 and 1914. Great Britain spent most of her money on her navy and kept only a small standing army. By 1914 France and Germany each had more than 800,000 men in her peace-time army; Russia had more than 1,250,000. Each country also had more than 1,000,000 trained men in reserve.

[1] In 1920 Italy spent $44,000,000.

[2] H. E. Barnes, *The Genesis of the World War*, p. 55. By permission of the publisher, Alfred A. Knopf, New York, 1926.

In the ten years preceding 1914 each of four European countries spent more than $1,000,000,000 for the training, support, and equipment of armies (Table XIX).

Tables XVII–XIX present conclusive proof that *all the leading nations* were anticipating war — building larger and larger navies and armies. Great Britain, an isolated island kingdom and *absolutely dependent on the rest of the world for food,* spent the largest sums on her navy. Her leaders knew that the great merchant fleet must be protected at any cost; otherwise England's millions of city workers would starve. Germany, shut in between Russia and France, devoted most of her expenditures to her army. But *all the leading powers were taxing their people and imposing staggering burdens upon their peasants and artisans in preparation for the war that might come.*

TABLE XIX[1]

Amount spent for Armies, 1905–1914	
Russia	$2,406,402,863
France	1,688,112,539
Germany	2,177,404,139
Austria	1,140,488,458

Fear and suspicion grew; secret alliances were made between the leading governments

As the race for trade grew swifter, as armies and navies grew greater, each government sought to protect itself by alliances with certain other governments. Between 1878 and 1914 one secret treaty after another was drawn up by the ministries of the six powers — Great Britain, France, Germany, Russia, Austria-Hungary, and Italy. Viewed from the 1930's, the making of these secret counter-alliances was one of the most important factors in bringing on the World War. *All the six powers were engaged in secret treaty-making; no one was more responsible than another.*[2]

[1] Adapted from H. E. Barnes's *Genesis of the World War* (Alfred A. Knopf, New York, 1926), p. 56. By permission of the publishers.

[2] This chapter is based upon such standard works as S. B. Fay's *Origins of the World War*, J. S. Ewart's *Roots and Causes of the Wars, 1914–1918*, C. J. H. Hayes's *Essays in Nationalism* and *A Political and Social History of Modern Europe*, and G. T. Gooch's *History of Modern Europe*.

As early as 1879 Austria-Hungary and Germany had secretly formed an alliance, and in 1882 they were joined by Italy. The alliance was essentially an agreement for a kind of mutual defense. Each party agreed that if any other country attacked one of them, the others would remain neutral. Later the agreement stated that if one party were attacked, the others would come to its aid with armed force.

After 1890 the Russian and French governments, each regarding the other as a natural ally, signed secret agreements. Each confronted Germany on a border; neither had anything to fear from the other. If Germany should attack France, Russia could distract her attention by making war on Germany's eastern frontier. If Germany should attack Russia, the case would be reversed.

Not only did the Russian and French ministries sign secret agreements binding the two nations to defend each other, but the *French peasants and artisans lent more than two billions of dollars to the Russian government after 1880.* The Industrial Revolution did not begin to develop in Russia until after 1890. The Russian people were so poor that, in spite of oppressive taxes, the Russian government could not build a navy and an army or construct railroads and factories without loans from abroad.

Even England, protected by the seas and remote from land attack by most of these powers, entered into secret agreements. She concluded a treaty with Japan in 1902, with France in 1904, with Russia in 1907. One of the leading ministers said frankly in defending one of these treaties:

> What do we see on all sides? We observe a tendency to ever increasing naval and military armaments . . . in these days war breaks out with a suddenness which was unknown in former days, when nations were not as they are now, armed to the teeth and ready to enter upon hostilities at any moment. . . . The country which has the good fortune to possess allies is more to be envied than the country which is without them.

The "Concert of Europe"

This practice of forming alliances among the leading European powers was the result of two points of view. On the one hand were the attempts to guarantee the peace of Europe by coöperation; on the other were the attempts of sovereigns and governments to conquer their enemies. During the 100 years from the Congress of Vienna, in 1815, to the World War, in 1914, the leading governments tried to maintain a "balance of power" and so keep peace in Europe. At the close of each war they tried to arrange things so that no one government could become strong enough to conquer the others. Each one thought, "We must ally with other strong nations."

Thus, after 1870, France and England, watching Germany's rise to industrial power, feared her as a disturbing factor. England saw with anxiety that Germany was building railroads through the Balkans and the Near East, aiming to capture her trade with India and the Far East. Russia was fearfully watching Austria seize lands in the Balkans and build up leadership there which would be hostile to her interests.

As a consequence, throughout the 1800's there came alliance after alliance and war after war. In the *Crimean War*, 1854–1856, Great Britain and France fought against Russia; in the *Seven Weeks' War*, 1866, Prussia fought against Austria; in the *Franco-Prussian War*, 1870–1871, Prussia fought against France. In one crisis after another the powers combated one another both on the battlefield and in their treaty-making foreign offices.

Although these alliances were made secretly by the foreign offices, information gradually leaked out concerning them. Members of each of the national legislatures then began to ask their foreign minister if it was true that the government had bound the country in a secret treaty to defend other countries in case of war. In 1896, for example, members of the French Chamber of Deputies attempted to find out if secret treaties had been made with Russia. The minister of foreign affairs either declined to answer or answered falsely. Similarly, on several occasions in the British House of Commons members asked the prime minister whether there was a secret defensive alliance with France, and in each case the minister either evaded the question or gave a false answer. Thus the people of democratic countries were being denied information concerning the acts of their governments in binding them to go to war.

We must remember, furthermore, that although these "understandings" were not legally binding on parliaments, they were practically so. Whenever a crisis came and the foreign minister appealed to the "honor" of the country to fulfill the pledges he had made, both the legislature and the credulous public supported him in war on the enemy country.

In the meantime there was growth in popular demand for permanent peace

After 1870 there was a marked advance in international coöperation leading toward permanent peace. The invention of the telegraph, the telephone, and the rotary printing press, together with swift means of land and ocean transportation, made it possible for ideas to spread quickly among the countries of the West. International unions, economic and social societies, organizations of various kinds, grew swiftly. For example, 30 nations joined together in the Universal Telegraph Union in 1875; 60 nations joined in the Universal Postal Union in 1874; 20 nations in 1883 adopted standard patent laws; 12 nations adopted uniform copyright laws in 1887; 23 nations adopted the metric system of weights and measures in 1875. These economic unions all helped to develop international understanding and coöperation.

The work of the peace societies also helped by developing into strong antimilitaristic movements. As education spread, more and more people in Western countries demanded *openly made treaties* which would bind nations together to prevent wars in the future. Wealthy men, such as Alfred Nobel, the Swedish philanthropist, endowed prizes to reward those who had performed notable work in establishing peace or had promoted better understanding among nations. There was a great gain in the movement toward international arbitration.

Governments responded to the popular demand for peace by accepting the suggestion of Nicholas II, Czar of Russia, that a conference be held at the Hague, in Holland, in 1899 to discuss the means of continuing the existing state of peace and of reducing the excessive cost of increasing armaments. A second conference was held in 1907, at which 44 nations met to discuss again the limitation of armaments and other phases of war and war preparation. A proposal was made for a world organization which should have its central government at the Hague, and for permanent courts and congresses as well as international laws and other means of regulating world affairs.

In spite of these movements for peace the leading governments were drifting into war

By 1914 the six strongest governments of Europe were sharply divided against one another in two powerful groups under secret agreement.

THE TRIPLE ALLIANCE		THE TRIPLE ENTENTE
Germany Austria-Hungary Italy	*against*	Great Britain France Russia

From 1900 to 1914 one political crisis after another confronted the contending groups. The Balkans were seething with revolts and wars. Friction among industrial nations was increasing. Germany and England were struggling for control of trade in the Near East. Russia was ready to go to war any moment to keep Austria out of the Balkans, and Germany from expanding in any direction. The French people were a unit in demanding that Alsace-Lorraine should be returned to them, even if a war had to be fought to get it. There was fear, suspicion, and increasing tension.

The spark that set off the world explosion

On June 28, 1914, the Austrian archduke Franz Ferdinand, heir to the Austro-Hungarian throne, and his wife were assassinated in Sarajevo, Bosnia. This brought on the World War, 1914–1918.

For four years the people of almost the entire earth suspended the normal activities of life and devoted themselves to mass killing. In four years 26,000,000 human beings were wiped out, the goods of tens of millions of others were destroyed, and millions of people were thrown out of work.

We cannot tell here the details of the world's worst war. No doubt you have already read and studied about them.[1] If so, you have learned of the terrible destruction and of how the entire interdependent scheme of trade and international coöperation in Europe was smashed. Then you have seen how, after the war, the key industries of Europe were slowly rebuilt and how international coöperation helped Europeans to renew fairly peaceful relations. In order to understand clearly the grave difficulties which Europe — indeed, the entire earth — still confronts, you have only to consider the serious economic conditions of recent days.

FIG. 142. In 1930 this cartoon appeared. It seems to show that the world has not yet learned the lesson of 1914

WE MUST TURN NOW TO OTHER NEW EXPERIMENTS IN GOVERNMENT

But our chief task in this book is to study changing governments and changing cultures. Hence we must now turn to a nation which provides the clearest contrast with those which we have been considering — Russia. In that vast Eurasian country is now being tried the world's most spectacular experiment in government and culture. Because of the interdependence of the world, the changes in Russia affect us vitally even here in the United States, 5000 miles away. For that reason it is very important for each of us to attempt to understand the present-day Russian experiment.

[1] A treatment in some detail is contained in *Changing Civilizations in the Modern World*, Chap. XV.

INTERESTING READINGS FROM WHICH YOU CAN GET ADDITIONAL INFORMATION

ATKINSON, ELEANOR. "Poilu," a Dog of Roubaix. Harper & Brothers, New York. The World War.

BENEZET, LOUIS PAUL. The World War and what was Behind It. Scott, Foresman and Company, Chicago.

GILMAN, BRADLEY. Son of the Desert. The Century Co., New York. Tells of Great Britain's expansion in Egypt.

MILLER, WARREN H. Sahara Sands. Harper & Brothers, New York. The expansion of Europe.

ROLT-WHEELER, FRANCIS. The Boys' Book of the World War. Lothrop, Lee & Shepard Co., Boston.

VAN LOON, HENDRIK W. The Story of Mankind. Horace Liveright, New York.

UNIT VI

RUSSIA: NEW EXPERIMENTS IN GOVERNMENT

RUSSIA: NEW EXPERIMENTS IN GOVERNMENT

We turn now to a very different kind of political experiment, that of the Russian people. We have learned of the early evolution of representative government in England, of its later development in revolutionary France, and of its still later emergence in Germany. Thus for two centuries the democratic way of government spread slowly eastward.

Finally, in the midst of the World War the smoldering fires of rebellion blazed up in European Russia and soon produced one of the most novel experiments in government the world has ever seen. It is this dramatic overturn of the government of 140,000,000 people that we shall study next.

To understand it we must comprehend the conditions of autocratic one-man rule in the old Russia which brought it about. These we shall study in Chapter XV.

In Chapter XVI we shall consider how a new Russia, a modern industrial nation, is being produced out of a backward agricultural and poverty-stricken old Russia. Furthermore, we shall see the rise of one of the most spectacular dictatorships in all history, that of the Russian Communist party. Thus, taken together, Chapters XV and XVI will introduce us to the story of one of the world's most important experiments in government.

CHAPTER XV

THE OLD RUSSIA: FROM IMPERIAL AUTOCRACY TO PROLETARIAN DICTATORSHIP

The astonishing happenings of the past fifteen years in Russia can only be understood if we comprehend the racial make-up of the people, the geography of their land, and their long history of oppression. Let us discuss, first, the people themselves.

The Russian People

In the region known today as Russia there are almost 160,000,000 people divided into about 200 nationalities, speaking some 150 different languages and dialects. This mass of humanity lives scattered over a territory which extends across the great continent of Asia and, in Europe, reaches from the Ural Mountains westward to Poland and Hungary. Three fourths of these people live in Europe, west of the Ural Mountains. One fourth, about 40,000,000 of them, live in the vast area of Asia from Turkestan to Vladivostok. As a whole the Russians are more Asian than European. For 1000 years and more they have looked *eastward* rather than westward for their ways of living.

About 1500 years ago three groups of Slavic-speaking people lived between the Carpathian Mountains and the Dnieper River. The eastern group, which eventually acquired the name "Russians,"[1] moved northeastward and spread out over the vast plain stretching toward the Ural Mountains.

Centuries passed. In the 800's these primitive Slavic agriculturists were conquered for a while by bands of adventurous Norse traders called Varangians. No doubt you can recall the long water routes through the lakes and rivers of Russia which these world travelers and traders followed from the Baltic to the Black Sea while their brothers were settling in the British Isles

[1] Scholars disagree concerning the origin of the name "Russia."

and on the west coast of Europe. As a result the trading city of Kiev developed into an important capital.

More centuries passed. During the first half of the thirteenth century the Mongol hordes, under the descendants of Genghis Khan, came sweeping across Russia, conquering the land and exacting tribute from the people. For 200 years these European Slavs paid allegiance to Asiatic warrior rulers. For 200 years

Press Cliché

FIG. 143. A Siberian tribe gathered for a religious celebration. Does this scene remind you more of Asia than of Europe? Why?

they were accustomed to looking eastward toward Asia for their orders and the models for their civilization. It was during this time, the 1200's and 1300's, that the foundation was laid for a gigantic *Eurasian* empire.

As time went on, a group of strong fighting men around Moscow gradually rose against the Mongol rulers. By 1400 these so-called Princes of Moscow had gathered strength enough to drive out their last remaining Mongol governors. Then slowly the Muscovites, as these men of Moscow were called, extended their realm southward. Shortly before the time that the Turks conquered Constantinople (1453) and brought the ancient Eastern

Roman Empire (the so-called Byzantine Empire) to an end, one of these Princes of Moscow, Ivan III, became prominent enough to marry a niece of the last of the Roman emperors. Later Ivan IV started the custom of calling the Muscovite ruler Czar — a modification of the Roman *caesar*.

Great conquests and migrations were made after 1450, when the wide plains of Asia had captured the imagination of the Princes of Moscow and their rich landowning nobles. For 400 years armies and pioneer settlers pressed outward in every direction. During the 1700's and 1800's conquest and migration continued eastward from Moscow. Whole villages migrated, southward into Turkestan and eastward across Siberia. By 1721 they had reached to the Baltic; by 1793, to the Black Sea.

As this great movement took place, more and more Russian villages were established in Asia. Settlements had appeared around Lake Baikal as early as 1652. By 1800 a range of farming communities stretched almost continuously halfway across Siberia, and scattered outposts continued to the Pacific. It was another tremendous conquest of a continent, and it produced the greatest inland empire in the world.

As you can well imagine, peoples of many races and languages were intermingled during these conquests and migrations. In a few pages of description it is impossible to give an adequate understanding of the mixture of peoples and temperaments that are revealed by the Russians today. A library would be required to give a full account of the Asiatic mixtures that have been produced by the intermingling of Slavs and people of the Turcoman Republic, the Uzbek Republic, the Kirghiz Republic, the Kazak area, the Siberian and Yakutsk areas, to name only a few of the territorial groups.

Students who have lived in Russia for many years shake their heads and give the same answer that is so frequently heard there when one asks a native for an explanation of certain happenings in his strange land: "I don't know." One finds it almost impossible really to know the Russians. But from a few significant facts concerning their geography and their history we can at least get a hint as to the temperament of the people and the conditions under which they live. Perhaps from these we can understand better the difficult conditions under which they are making the world's most comprehensive experiment in government and social life.

This brings us to the second factor that must be studied carefully if one is to understand the temperament of the Russian people and their present startling experiment in government and social life. That is the geography of their land.

Geography Again!

Three geographic factors help to explain the Russian way of life: (1) the tremendous size of the territory, (2) the relative scarcity of high mountains, (3) the climate.

The land of the Russians is for the most part a tremendous continental plain more than 5000 miles from east to west and more than 2000 miles from north to south. Over 8,300,000 square miles of relatively level land are comprised in this one country. On the Trans-Siberian Railway one rides for twelve days from Moscow to Harbin, Manchuria — across, for the most part, a flat plain. One gets far to the east before this plain is broken by mountain ranges, by deep and winding river valleys, or by seas and lakes.

In European Russia, as well as in the Asiatic territories, one can ride for weeks in the stiff, crude oxcarts of the natives as upon a level ocean of land. From village to village one gropes along the "traces" that pass for roads, trying to find one's way. Occasionally the spire of a church can be discerned over the horizon, and an hour or two later one bumps one's way over muddy roads into another Russian village of log and mud huts. There are 300,000 such villages scattered over the continental plain, varying in size but looking very much alike.

In these villages have lived nine tenths of the people of Russia. Generation after generation most of them have been isolated from one another and from the cities, unconnected by railroads, by telegraphs, telephones, or radio. Shut in away from the Western world, they have been looking toward the primitive uniformity of the Asian plain rather than to the varied, stimulating, changing world of western Europe and America.

Then we must not forget the part played by their unusual climate. Owing to the vast range of their country, which reaches from the arctic zone on the north to the warm Black Sea on the south, the range of temperature is twice as large as that of any other country, even of the United States. At one place in the north the average January temperature is nearly 60 degrees below zero (Fahrenheit). In the south, in Turkestan and the Caspian region, there is a short, intensely hot summer. Between these the Russian people experience many variations in degrees of summer heat and winter cold. The seasons change swiftly — winter going out suddenly within a few days and summer coming in almost before one is aware that even spring has arrived.

The intense cold, the long nights, the huddling together of large peasant families in small huts — all this has helped to produce passive, submissive temperaments. And it has also played a part in producing the loquaciousness of the Russian peasant. As one American who has spent several years in Russia says:

> No people in the world talk so much as the Russians. They have behind them centuries of long winter nights around the samovar. Russian friends have kept me up all night to convince me on some point in metaphysics, and when I, in weariness, would be convinced, they would switch positions and attack me with the very arguments I had used ten hours before. That's why so many Russians are political prisoners on the island of Solovetsky in the White Sea. They just *must* talk. . . . Foreigners in Russia get that way, too.[1]

Paralleling these long, dark nights of winter are the "white nights of summer." In these there is no real darkness, at most a twilight; the sun circles the heavens day and night, practically without setting, as we understand it.

This astonishing climate has worked its effect upon the personality of the Russian. In the summer he works eighteen hours a day, but he does very little work in winter. He cannot change the climate; so he learns to live with it and to accept it and the hardship the winter brings. Many students think that it produces the general attitude of "No matter!" which characterizes his conduct in so many situations. Constantly one gets the response *Nitchevo* ("It doesn't matter") from the taxi-driver of the city, the clerk in the government office, the railway guard, or the peasant

[1] Bruce Hopper, *Pan-Sovietism: the Issue before America and the World*, p. 23. Houghton Mifflin Company, Boston, 1931.

in the village. It reflects a sort of fatalistic attitude of accepting what comes.

So for many centuries this long-suffering, melancholy people clung to their plains, enduring life, living a semicommunal existence. For centuries most of them knew few comforts — indeed, scarcely knew even the idea of property. Therefore, in studying the experiment in halfway communism that is being forced on them today, we must keep in mind the living conditions in the making of which their geography has played such an important part.

Centuries of Oppression by Autocrats

From the days of the first Muscovite Czars the Russian people had been governed by autocratic rulers. In fact, in the late 1400's Ivan III had taken the title of "Autokrator"; that is, "one who rules in his own right."

One ruling house, the Romanovs, held the throne for 300 years — from 1613, when Michael Romanov was elected Czar by the national assembly of nobles, until Nicholas II and his entire family were killed by the Bolsheviks in 1917. It was under this family of rulers that the Western world saw one of its worst examples of tyranny. But it was not until about 1700 that all restrictions upon the power of the Czar were removed. From that time on, the government was known for its absolutism, its oppression, and its iron discipline.

It was the grandson of the original Michael Romanov, Peter the Great (ruled 1682–1725), who really laid the foundation for the autocratic rule of the Czars. Peter was a man of great ability who, like Louis XIV of France and Frederick the Great of Prussia, worked at his task of being Czar. As a young man he had traveled incognito to France, England, and other Western countries, studying their advanced ways of living.

When Peter returned to Russia in 1698 he was determined to "modernize" his backward people. By royal edict he compelled them to adopt Western instead of Oriental ways of living. With his own hands he cut off the beards and mustaches of many of the leading nobles and officers of the empire. He compelled them to wear western-European clothing. He made them follow the new custom of smoking tobacco. He removed all restrictions upon women and had the two sexes associate together in his court.

He took control of the Russian Church, making the patriarch subservient to the Czar from that time on. He abolished the law-making rights of the assembly of nobles and decided that the Czar should appoint his own council of state.

It is important to remember that from the middle 1600's to their emancipation in 1861 more than 90 per cent of the Russian

FIG. 144. Peter the Great and his son in the palace study

people were serfs. They had not always been serfs, for until the 1600's Russia had never adopted feudalism. Before that time the Muscovite princes had ruled over the nobles, and even the mass of the peasants had owned small amounts of land. But about the time that feudalism passed out of existence in England, France, and other parts of western Europe, it was introduced into Russia.

For example, under the law of 1649, peasants were ordered to remain with the owners of the land which they occupied. Even the nobles were "enserfed" in the sense that they held land directly from the Czar and must give him military service as long as they lived. So in Russia the Czar enslaved the nobles, and the nobles enslaved the peasants.

A century and a half of feudal slavery passed. Then in 1861 came the emancipation of the serfs. By the decrees of Czar Alexander II, 46,000,000 people were freed; that is, they were given permission to buy and sell land, to move from one district to another, to leave the country and go to the city, or to move from the city to the country.

Soon it was seen, however, that the condition of the peasants was worse than before. They were compelled to pay the government for their land, and they had little or no money with which to do it. They were in much the same plight as the Negroes in the United States at about the same time (1865). They were "free as birds"; yet they had no place to live. In fact, they became slaves to the government, as before they had been slaves to the nobles.

Russian Farms became Smaller and Smaller

Another difficulty soon made itself felt. As Table XX shows, the farms were small in 1861. But as time went on they became even smaller, for the reason that when the owners of estates died the land was divided up among their heirs. In fact, the farms became so small that individual families were unable to get a living from them. Observe the startling decrease in the size of farms from 1861 to 1905, as shown in Table XX. At the same time estimates showed that to support a Russian peasant family 30 acres were required — and that on the meager Russian standard of living. Even in the rich black-earth district an average family cleared only $40 a year over and above food expenses and taxes. Is it any wonder that the Russian peasant was always poor and often hungry?

TABLE XX

Number of Acres of Farm Land per Male Peasant, 1861–1905	
1861	13.0
1880	9.5
1905	7.0

This problem of the dwindling size of farms was made more serious by the use of the strip system that was followed so widely over eastern and central Europe. This system assigned to each individual strips of land in various sections of the countryside around the village. As you can see, this was a wasteful arrangement. Not less than one seventh of all the farming land was lying unused in the ridges or fences between the strips. The strip system was especially disastrous in that it made impossible the use of power-driven tractors, cultivators, and other farm machines. This was one factor which delayed the coming of machine agriculture to Russia.

TABLE XXI

Average Number of Quintels[1] of Wheat raised per Hectare[2] of Land in Various Countries from 1901 to 1915	
England	21.8
France	13.6
United States	9.9
Russia	6.6

Naturally, then, farming was done in the most primitive ways. Despite this the soil was so fertile that Russia produced about two thirds as much wheat as did the United States on the same amount of land. (See Table XXI.)

Remember the ingrained Russian attitude toward property

To understand changing Russia today bear in mind that for centuries most of the people owned no property. The state owned nearly everything. As has been said, until recent times even the nobles did not legally own the land: they merely held it as a fief from the Czar, paying him service for it. As one historian says, "In the eighteenth century the supposed owner could not chop down an oak tree on his land without becoming liable to the death penalty."

This helps to account for the lack of a *bourgeois*, or middle, class like that which appeared in England even in the 1600's and in France and Germany in the 1800's. The possession of other basic civil rights also came very much later to the Russians than to the other peoples of Europe. They dared not criticize the government; indeed, they could not even petition the government. There were no such rights as trial by jury, habeas corpus, or other civil rights of the type that had been established 200 years before in England and 100 years before in the United States and France.

[1] 3.674 bushels. [2] 2.471 acres.

Although farms grew smaller, population increased

The living conditions of the Russian masses were made still worse by the rapid increase in population. As Table XXII shows, the number of people nearly doubled in the last half of the nineteenth century. At the outbreak of the World War it was nearly two and a half times as large as in 1851.

TABLE XXII

Estimate of Number of People in Russia, 1851, 1897, and 1914	
1851	67,000,000
1897	129,000,000
1914	140,000,000

The multiplication of these peasants is astounding when one considers that millions of Russians died because of the lack of knowledge of sanitation and prevention of disease.

The Late Development of Machine Manufacturing

Not until after 1890 did the Industrial Revolution really get under way in Russia, and not until nearly 1900 did it become at all widespread. By that time, however, railways were being built, and manufacturers of the northern cities were bringing out the rich coal and iron from the fields around the Caspian Sea.

TABLE XXIII[1]

Tons of Iron produced in Russia, 1900 and 1914	
1900	1,467,000
1914	3,606,000

In 1913 the railways of Russia totaled 36,000 miles. The Trans-Siberian Railway alone measured 6312 miles from the Polish-Russian frontier to Vladivostok and was built at a cost of more than $200,000,000. But it was only a single-track line.[2]

After 1895, factories began to be constructed. Swiftly the industrial idea took hold. On the warm plains of Turkestan and Transcaucasia it was found that cotton would thrive. By 1914

[1] The statistics for iron and oil production, for the textile industry, and for urban population are taken from G. V. Vernadsky's *History of Russia* (Yale University Press, New Haven, 1930). Units of weight (poods) have been converted into tons.

[2] In recent years it has been improved and is now double-tracked. In 1930 the Turkestan-Siberian Railway, joining the Trans-Siberian with the main line through Turkestan, was completed. At last the great Asiatic regions of Russian territory are being opened up to rapid transportation and communication.

more than 1,500,000 acres of land were under cultivation in cotton, and planters in southern United States, India, and Egypt were anxiously watching their new competitor. Correspondingly, in the cities the textile industry grew rapidly. By 1911 more than 8,000,000 spindles were spinning yarn, and more than 200,000 looms were weaving cloth. The Russian people began to use more goods. For example, in 1910 the consumption of cotton cloth per person was twice as great as in 1890.

TABLE XXIV

Number and Per Cent of People in Russian Towns, 1851, 1897, 1914, and 1930

	Number	Per Cent
1851	3,500,000	8
1897	16,300,000	13
1914	26,300,000	17.5
1930	31,000,000	20

Valuable coal deposits were found and opened up in the Donetz basin, where, in the year before the World War (1913), 25,000,000 tons of coal were mined. From this region came more than half the coal used in Russia. Including coal from other local deposits, more than 85 per cent of all coal used in Russia was produced within the empire.

In the same years the oil fields of Baku were exploited with great rapidity. By the year 1905 the annual production of oil was 7,294,000 tons. Russia produced 27 per cent of the world's supply in that year.

As industrialism at last took hold in Russia, there was the same drift to the cities as in other countries. In 1851 only 8 per cent of the people lived in cities; in 1930 the per cent had risen to 20.

The Czarist Government began to control Industry

Once industry got under way the government, autocratic in all things, played a leading part in its development. By 1900 the state owned three fifths of all the railroads and many of the factories. It controlled the credit of the entire nation. By establishing the powerful State Bank it became autocratic in economic life as well as in political life.

By 1900 the conditions of the common people employed in the factories and mines had become as bad as those of England 100 years earlier. Workers slaved under wretched conditions, working fifteen and sixteen hours a day for wages of $1.50 to $3 a week. Social legislation, which had developed early in England, France, and Germany, was almost lacking in Russia. Labor unions were prohibited. To strike brought long imprisonment or exile.

Factory-owners and government officials worked hand in hand to oppress the growing proletariat of the larger cities as well as the

FIG. 145. Not all Russians were poor. A small class of rich and cultured people enjoyed the opera, theater, and other luxuries which the wealthy elsewhere enjoyed

peasants on the farms. The Russian worker of the city began to hate the industrial masters, and especially the government which controlled them.

At the same time the property of the Czar, of his family, and of the government which he controlled grew to staggering amounts, while more than 90 per cent of the people lacked a decent living wage. Peasants and machine-workers paid huge taxes which were used for palaces, battleships, amusements, and the like. Peasants were compelled to deliver their hard-earned bushels of wheat, rye, and other grains to the tax-collectors, to be exported to Germany and other countries. The income went to the government — not to the people.

Yet, decade after decade, even in the 1800's, when democracy had marched far in western Europe, the Russian peasant dumbly admired the "Little Father," grubbed the soil to maintain him in his splendor, and — occasionally wondered what it was all about.

Long ago Creative Writers laid the Foundation for Future Revolution

Long before the Industrial Revolution, however, a background of future revolt was being laid by a group of brilliant poets, novelists, and playwrights. Indeed, in no country was there a more important group of creative writers in the nineteenth century than in Russia. While Karl Marx and Engels were organizing workingmen in western Europe and writing theoretical treatises on the history of society, Pushkin, Gogol, Turgeniev, Dostoievsky, Chekhov, and Tolstoy were portraying the Russian character and Russian economic, social, and political life in books that have become famous. In the 50 years following 1825 there came from the pens of these men studies of human life that stand high among the world's classics.

Alexander Pushkin (1799–1837) is regarded by many as the greatest of all the Russian poets. He has been called "the Sun of Russian Poetry." His poems picture with rare feeling the moods, despairs, and hopes of the "dark people" of Russia. Interested in the social life of the various classes in Russia, as well as in the individual human soul, he served as a great interpreter of the culture of the nation, and he helped to pave the way for a liberal understanding of the needs of the people.

Like Marx, Pushkin was interested in the history of civilization and in the improvement of the political and civil rights of the people. He lived near enough to Russian society to see clearly the conspiracies and plots of the bureaucracy that had grown up in the court and the government. Pushkin died at the early age of 37, in a duel. He left behind him writings which many years later were to help students in schools and universities to grope their way toward an understanding of the culture of the Russian people.

Nikolay Gogol (1809–1852), a Ukrainian novelist, did much the same sort of thing for southern Russia. His chief novel,

FIG. 146. Fyodor Dostoievsky

"The people are seeking eagerly for truth. . . . After the liberation of the serfs, the great longing for truth appeared among the people — for truth perfect and entire, and with it the resurrection of civic life." So wrote Fyodor Dostoievsky (1821–1881), whose sympathy with the poor and the unfortunate led him to join the meetings of a group of young writers who were studying the French philosophers and discussing means of reform in Russia. Suddenly the members of this group were arrested and sentenced to death. Just at the moment when they were to be executed, a reprieve came, and Dostoievsky's sentence was changed to four years in prison. Out of this experience came his most widely read novel, *The House of the Dead*, depicting prison life in Siberia. Then followed such others as *Crime and Punishment*, *The Idiot*, and *The Brothers Karamazov*, whose power and truthfulness to life in Russia during his day have placed him among the novelists of all time

During the early years of the 1900's people from countries scattered all over the world made pilgrimages to an estate in Russia to talk with an old man who dressed in peasant's garb, ate the simplest of food, and often worked long hours in the fields. This was Count Leo Nikolayevich Tolstoy (1828–1910), dramatist, novelist, and philosopher — pleader against all forms of violence and against the false standards, the greed, and the corruption which he saw in the life of his time; pleader for simpler living and for human brotherhood. His young manhood had been spent largely in social gayety, and his earlier writings exalted the idle rich. Gradually, through travel, and through civic work performed when the serfs were emancipated, his eyes were opened to evils he had never noted before. From then on, in such essays as *A Confession* and *What I Believe In* and in such stories as *War and Peace*, *Master and Man*, and *The Death of Ivan Ilyich*, he spread his gospel, and millions were influenced by it

FIG. 147. Count Leo Nikolayevich Tolstoy

Dead Souls, paints a vivid portrait of peasant life in the Ukraine. In other books Gogol revealed many scenes of the life of the rich landlords and contrasted their conditions with those of the common people on the farms. He too was a student of the ills of society, unhappy at the intrigue and the distressing inequalities among men. It was also through the works of Gogol that the standard Russian language came to include many Ukrainian words.

The Rise of the First Revolutionary Movements

The relatively liberal acts of the Czar Alexander II in his freeing of the serfs in the early 1860's had been followed, ten years later, by a period of harsh oppression. The local village councils based on popular election were restricted, and the press was rigidly censored. An infamous detective organization of the Czar's officials was established. Suspects were seized by these secret police and thrown into jail or exiled to Siberia without hearing. The slightest criticism of the government resulted in drastic punishment. Schools were censored, and the new scientific movement which had been well launched by 1860 was sternly suppressed.

As this happened a revolutionary movement developed among the intelligent, thinking men of the universities and the professions. These people were students of the democratic ideas which were sweeping over England, France, and other Western countries. They believed in education as the real means of advancing the world's march toward democracy.

In a novel of the great writer Ivan Turgeniev (1818–1883), called *Fathers and Sons* (1862), these students of modern science and democracy were called *nihilists.* The name soon attained wide adoption. The so-called nihilists were peaceful students of society. They opposed the intrigue of the courts and the inequality of the classes. They denounced the abuses of the Church and the ignorance that it had fastened upon the Russian people. They preached a new creative life for the people, based upon scientific knowledge and the education of all the people. They urged Russians to join the movement toward democracy which was then sweeping over the Western countries. This was nihilism in the 1870's — essentially a peaceful democratic movement.

In the meantime, however, two more violent revolutionary movements were spreading. One was the anarchism of the Russian socialist, Mikhail Bakunin; the other was the terrorist movement, advocating assassination of autocrats and forcible seizure of the government.

Secret societies were organized in Petrograd, and a widespread campaign of educating the masses against their masters developed.

FIG. 148. A meeting of the Nihilists. Gatherings of this sort often took place in abandoned cellars and were conducted with the greatest secrecy. (From a painting by Ilja Repin)

Secret printing offices turned out pamphlets, bulletins, and handbills and distributed them among soldiers, artisans, and peasants. Between 1878 and 1881 the terrorists assassinated six leading officers of the government and many secret police.

At the same time the government itself employed drastic measures. It executed nearly 40 terrorists, exiled many others to Siberia, and imprisoned large numbers. And in 1881, just as Alexander II was about to institute reforms, he was killed by a bomb. His son, Alexander III (ruled 1881–1894), came to the throne determined to put down the revolutionary movement. In the 1880's and 1890's the government was centralized, strengthened, and made more oppressive than ever.

Education was at such a low ebb that from 50 to 90 per cent of the people in rural districts and approximately half of those in the cities were unable to read and write.

Here, then, was a small, educated, and compactly organized class, loyal to the imperial Romanov family. This group controlled the army and maintained itself in autocratic domination over 100,000,000 illiterate peasants and proletarian workers. These masses of common people were scattered, uninformed, and unorganized, lacking both the understanding and the organized force with which to take matters into their own hands. If we can keep these conditions in mind, we shall see why democracy advanced so slowly in autocratic, isolated Russia.

Enter Karl Marx and Communism again

We must now bring together the several revolutionary factors which we have seen at work in western Europe that we may understand the transformation of Russia since 1917. Especially must we bear in mind the work of the socialist reformers. Recall, first, Robert Owen and the Utopian philanthropists who experimented with ideal communities.

Remember, second, the revolt of the workingmen of Paris under Babeuf in 1797. Babeuf proposed a *dictatorship of the workers and an equalization of property among all the people.* This proposal is important for us to remember if we are to understand the Russian experiment in communism which was launched in 1917.

Fifty years passed, and then Karl Marx, Friedrich Engels, and their *Communist Manifesto* of 1847 were written into European history. *The Communist Manifesto* and Marx's *Das Kapital* were to become the Bible of the revolutionary movement in Russia. We must remember also that many eminent economists who believe thoroughly in our capitalistic way of living and have little sympathy for Marxian socialism respect Marx himself as one of the most influential writers of all time. For example, Professor E. R. A. Seligman says that with one or two exceptions "there has been no more original, no more powerful, and no more acute intellect in the entire history of economic science."

The writings of Marx and other founders of socialism made their way slowly into Russia in the 1880's and 1890's. The young intellectuals of the universities and the scientific men generally read them eagerly. The idea which they saw in them of the struggle of the oppressed classes against tyrannical masters became the keynote of the program of action of the rising socialist group in Russia. Other writers, such as Maxim Gorky (1868–), spread the socialist teachings through novels and plays as well as through pamphlets and other literature.

The Workers form Political Parties

By 1898 the organization of workers into a political party, called the Workers' Social Democratic party, was well under way. In factories and mines, railroads and other industries, branches of the party, called "cells," were organized. They were secret clubs, for such organizations were still prohibited by the government. These cells held meetings and read and discussed especially the writings and interpretations of Marx and Engels.

By 1900 the influence of these groups had spread among the peasants, who in turn organized the Social Revolutionary party. This political party also kept its plans as secret as possible. The special aim of the movement was the confiscation of the large estates of the nobles and the division of the land into small holdings among the peasants.

There was still another liberal movement, which was less secret than the others — that of the growing upper middle class itself. It included a few especially liberal merchants and owners of factories and a small number of nobles and professors of the universities. In 1905 this group also organized a political party called the Constitutional Democratic party.

Of all these groups, however, it was the Workers' Social Democratic party that was to make Russian history. At its congress in 1903 it was divided into two groups — one, the Bolsheviks (the Majority), and the other, the Mensheviks (the Minority). The leader of the Bolsheviks was Vladimir Ulianov, who wrote socialist pamphlets, interpretations of Karl Marx, and the like under the pen name "Lenin," by which he has become famous round the world.

Lenin (1870–1924) was the son of a schoolmaster. He was well educated, and early in his youth came into contact with socialist ideas. He and his brother joined secret revolutionary organizations while they were still young. The brother, who advocated violence, was arrested in connection with a plot against the life of Czar Alexander III and was executed in 1891. From that time Lenin became an avowed Marxist and a determined enemy of the propertied classes. From 1900 to 1917 he lived in exile most of the time.

Press Cliché

FIG. 149. Vladimir Ilyich Ulianov Lenin (1870–1924)

All these parties agreed on one aim; namely, to get rid of the autocratic control of the Czar and his government. But they disagreed among themselves as to further details of a program. The Social Democrats — who were later called communists — wanted the city workers to rule. The Social Revolutionaries wanted all land to be taken over by the government and divided among the peasants. The Constitutional Democrats wanted parliamentary government, built on the lines of the government of Great Britain or of France.

THE FIRST RUSSIAN REVOLUTION, 1905

These revolutionary movements, partly peaceful and partly violent, brought about a crisis early in 1905. The defeat of the Russian armies in the war with Japan (1904–1905), which came as a great shock to the self-confidence of the nobility of Russia, greatly increased the criticism of the government.

Petitions were sent to the Czar to reform the government, to guarantee liberty, and to establish a representative assembly with a written constitution. But the Czar vacillated, and more violent demonstrations resulted. Finally, workers began to strike in the various factories of Moscow, Riga, Petrograd, and other cities. The climax came on January 22, 1905 ("Red Sunday"), when the Czar's soldiers dispersed the crowds of unarmed striking workmen in Petrograd by volleys from their rifles.

Then the revolutionary history of France, Germany, and other countries repeated itself. Rebellion spread rapidly among the city workers and then to the peasants in the Social Revolutionary party. The latter burned and looted the homes of well-to-do land-owners. Disorder became general throughout European Russia.

At last the smoldering resentment of the people broke through the restraint of centuries. The Grand Duke Sergius was assassinated in Moscow, and various other members of the government were killed. Martial law was proclaimed in Petrograd; the universities were closed; city streets were patrolled by troops.

The rebellion spread from civilians to the army and from the army to the navy. In June, 1905, the sailors on the battleship *Potemkin* mutinied against their officers. In the autumn of 1905 Czar Nicholas II, alarmed at the extent of the discontent, issued a manifesto promising freedom of speech, popular election of a *Duma* (House of Commons), and manhood suffrage. In March, 1906, he issued a decree providing for a national assembly with two houses. The lower (the Duma) was to be elective; half the upper house was to be appointed by the Czar and half to be elected by the Church, the universities and learned societies, certain commercial bodies, and the nobility.

For the first time in Russian history a Czar's decree omitted the statement that he was an autocratic and absolute monarch.

The granting of a constitution soon proved to be a mere gesture, for it was found that real political control was not to be given to the representatives of the people. Members of the Duma were elected on the plan shown in Table XXV, a scheme which gave the upper classes complete control. Yet more than half the members were firmly opposed to the ruling bureaucracy.

We must note the leadership of two groups in this first revolution of 1905, for it was these groups which afterwards came to play the leading part in the present communist government of

Russia. One was the Soviet of Workers' Deputies, led by one Bronstein, who wrote under the pen name of "Leon Trotsky." Trotsky, like Lenin and the other revolutionary leaders, assumed a pen name as a means of hiding his identity from the Czar's secret police. The other was the Bolshevik group of the Workers' Social Democratic party, under the leadership of Lenin. Thus twelve years before the final revolution Lenin and Trotsky were in command of the rebelling groups.

TABLE XXV

Number of Inhabitants per Elector in Various Russian Social Classes	
Gentry	1 elector for 230 people
Peasants	1 elector for 60,000 people
Workmen . . .	1 elector for 125,000 people

Gradually the revolutionary movement was suppressed, although not until thousands of people had been killed on both sides. Leaders of the Social Democratic party were arrested and tried for treason, and 31 were exiled to Siberia. Trotsky was included in this group. He escaped almost immediately, lived in various countries of Europe, and finally came to the United States. In his wanderings he never ceased active work in behalf of the socialist cause. Lenin left Russia and worked in Switzerland and other countries, organizing the socialist movement.

Order was finally restored. In 1909 the Duma was recognized as a part of the national assembly, "advising" the Czar and his ministers. Other slight reforms were made. The ownership of land by the *mir* (village) had been practically abolished. Tentative laws for workingmen's insurance were made, and education by the Church was extended. Thus democracy had marched forward, even if only a little. As one of the official reports of the Russian government announced in 1914, the government had become "a constitutional monarchy under an autocratic Czar." In both civil and political rights the Russian people still lagged far behind the peoples of the other leading nations of the Western world.

Russia and the World War

In 1914, with the declaration of war against Germany and Austria, the people of Russia were bound together for a time in a great nationalistic wave of "Pan-Slavism." The Czar and his ministers tried to unify the great mass of the people in support of the war. They promised reforms, and even for a time ceased religious persecution, which for many years had been directed especially against the Jews.

But not for long did the enthusiasm last. As you know, in spite of enormous expenditures for armaments, the Russian government was utterly unprepared for war. The peasants were untrained. Highways were bad; railroads were inadequate to transport troops. There was insufficient clothing, food, and even arms and ammunition. And so millions of young Russians — peasants and city youth — fought, almost totally ignorant of what they were fighting for.

A year after the outbreak of the war, in August, 1915, practically one third of the Russian troops had no guns. Had the Germans been able to move their food supplies fast enough to keep pace with the advancing German lines, Russia would have been defeated early in the war. But again the vast plains helped the Russians, even as they had 100 years before in Napoleon's advance upon Moscow.

As the war went on, however, the people in the local communities and the leaders in the larger cities alike became dissatisfied with the inefficiency of the government. This was revealed in a division between the Duma and the Czar's government. The former demanded that the Czar appoint a cabinet of advisers which would reorganize the army and carry on the war efficiently. In September, 1915, Nicholas II made himself commander in chief of the Russian army; but he surrounded himself with incompetent assistants, and matters went from bad to worse.

Weaker and weaker grew the government

Unrest pervaded the entire country, and socialist leaders — some in exile and others within Russia — secretly took advantage of the situation to spread propaganda against the war and to urge revolution. The Bolsheviks were the most active of all. Lenin, from his exile in Switzerland, carried on a world-wide campaign. In 1919 he was influential in forming a Third International, with headquarters at Moscow. He urged civil war in all the warring nations and revealed that he was now leader of the socialists.

Each year more millions of Russian youth were called to battle, and each year more millions of men were wounded or died from wounds and disease. Early in 1917 the total number enrolled had reached 12,000,000. There was hardly an able-bodied man of military age in Russia who had not been called to the colors. A large proportion of these soldiers were inactive, encamped behind the lines, unequipped and lacking supplies. Disease spread among them, killing them by the thousands. Between 1914 and 1917 some 9,000,000 of the best of Russian manhood were dead, wounded, prisoners, or missing. The vast proportion of the 1,800,000 who died, died from disease and were not in action at all.

Such was the state of backwardness that an autocratic militaristic government had produced. Was it any wonder, then, that the pamphlets, books, and whispered words of the socialist agitators gripped the imaginations of these millions of idle soldiers? So propaganda spread among the troops in 1916 and 1917.

Week by week in 1916 it became increasingly clear that the Czar and his ministers could no longer handle the situation. Expenditures mounted swiftly. Many millions of dollars were required each day to finance the enormous number of troops in the service. But the money was no longer forthcoming. The government had taken over three quarters of all the industrial plants to manufacture military supplies. The income of the Russian people was dwindling steadily. The government had requisitioned the grain supplies of the peasants. Taxes were left unpaid, because there was no money or crops or goods with which to pay them.

Then history repeated itself in another way: paper money was issued, and the credit of the nation became worthless. The printing presses of the imperial treasury ran faster and faster, turning out the paper bills. By 1916 more than 5,000,000,000 rubles ($2,500,000,000) were in circulation in paper money. Fear of a financial crash spread.

Among the soldiers the propaganda of the socialists was having its effect, and the determination grew to take things into their own hands and stop the war. Steadily the struggle for control increased between the Czar and the Duma. By November, 1916, opposition against the royal family was expressed in public addresses.

The Second Russian Revolution, March–November, 1917

Within three months the Czar practically ceased to rule. With money gone, with the army disorganized and in open mutiny, with socialists coming out into the open, the aristocrats made one last desperate effort to meet the emergency. They promised a new cabinet which would include representatives satisfactory to the Duma and to the mass of the people.

But before action could be taken the second and final revolution broke out. On March 12, 1917, mobs of workmen rioted in the streets of Petrograd, hunting for food and killing police who tried to maintain order. They opened jails and released prisoners; they set fire to public buildings. Finally they made their way to the Tauride Palace and demanded action from the Duma.

Then it was that the Duma acted. It appointed a temporary committee to take charge of affairs. On this committee was Alexander Kerensky, who soon afterwards organized the first Provisional Government.

On March 15 the Provisional Government demanded that Nicholas II abdicate the throne. He and his entire family were arrested and exiled to Siberia. A year later, July 16, 1918, they were murdered in Ekaterinburg. About the same time the Grand Duke Michael was arrested. It is assumed that he too was murdered, for he has never been seen since. After reigning 300 years the Romanovs were no more; the last of the Czars had ruled.

For a few months the Provisional Government tried to carry on, but it soon showed that it was nonsocialist in character. Its decrees promised the civil and political liberties common to democratic countries — freedom of speech, of the press, and of organization, as well as a representative assembly based on popular election. It was a thoroughly parliamentary program, like that in operation in England and in France.

This, however, did not satisfy the socialists, who, in the meantime, had quietly organized another government — the Petrograd Soviet (or Council) of Workers' and Soldiers' Deputies. This organization ignored the Provisional Government and gave orders directly to the soldiers of the army to organize themselves into units, take control of all weapons, and report only to the Soviet.

The Provisional Government tried to revoke this order, but the soldiers quickly organized themselves and deposed their officers. By this time vast numbers of soldiers had left the front and returned home.

So it was that two opposing governments developed during the spring and summer of 1917: (1) the Provisional Government, a weak parliamentary organization without strong leaders, but

Press Cliché

FIG. 150. Lenin addressing a May Day gathering. Since the International Socialist Congress met in 1889, May 1 has been considered the international labor holiday

still regarded as the legal government; (2) the Soviet of Workers' and Soldiers' Deputies, working behind the scenes and steadily growing in sureness of organization and power.

The Provisional Government still held the legal power, and under it new local governments were set up based upon universal suffrage, the secret ballot, and equal representation. In the meantime the Socialist Democratic party was organizing soviets (local councils) all over the country, in cities and in villages. In June the Central Executive Committee, which consisted almost wholly of the socialist leaders, called a meeting of the party (which they named the All-Russian Soviet Congress) in Petrograd. Even in this congress, however, the more moderate and democratic Mensheviks were in the majority. The radical Bolsheviks were still in the minority.

At the congress the Bolsheviks maintained that their soviets were the only true representatives of the Russian people, and they demanded that the Provisional Government be overthrown and that the soviets take charge.

In the meantime the Russian army had completely collapsed. Soviets had been formed in every unit, and these were openly opposing their officers. Russian and German soldiers hobnobbed with one another on the front. For all practical purposes the war was over.

During the summer and autumn of 1917 the Bolsheviks became increasingly strong. Lenin arrived from Switzerland, after passing through Germany into Sweden under the protection of the German government, which believed that if he were permitted to go to Russia he would help to break down the Russian government, demoralize the army, and thus make war impossible on the Eastern Front. Trotsky arrived about the same time from the United States. By this time he had become an extreme defender of world revolution and the right-hand man of Lenin.

Under the leadership of these two men the Bolsheviks drew together the workmen of Petrograd and Moscow. The rapidity of the Bolsheviks' rise to power is shown by the fact that in a city election in Petrograd in July they received 11 per cent of the votes; in September they had a majority in the city council. The same thing was happening in other cities. Tens of thousands of the proletariat were aligning themselves with the extreme socialists, known generally now as the communists. Marxian arguments and slogans were heard on every side. Pamphlets, handbills, and speeches increased the enrollment of the people in the soviets.

The Communists take over the Government of Russia, November, 1918

Between November 4 and November 8 the final overthrow of the Provisional Government under Kerensky was completed. The communists, under Lenin and Trotsky, took command of the army, seized the government offices, and set up a completely socialist government. It was all done quickly and almost without opposition. The *coup d'état* illustrated again the fact that "he who controls the army controls the government." Another government had tumbled down in Europe. But this time it was not democracy that was supplanting the old autocracy: it was an unknown kind of socialism.

From that day to this the entire Russian land from Poland to the Pacific Ocean has been ruled by a small group of Bolsheviks representing the Communist party. This group comprises less than 3 per cent of all the people. Since November, 1917, Russia has been ruled by a dictatorship of the proletariat. The dictatorship of autocratic Czars has given way to the dictatorship of *leaders* of the city workers.

INTERESTING READINGS FROM WHICH YOU CAN GET ADDITIONAL INFORMATION

Aksakov, Sergiei Timofieevich. The Chronicles of a Russian Family. E. P. Dutton & Co., New York. Russian home and school life at the end of the 1700's and the first half of the 1800's.

Breshkovsky, Catherine. The Little Grandmother of the Russian Revolution. Little, Brown and Company, Boston.

Charskaya, Lidïya A. Fledglings. Henry Holt and Company, New York. Life in a boarding school in Petrograd.

Charskaya, Lidïya A. Little Princess Nina. Henry Holt and Company, New York. Story of a little Russian girl who lives in the Caucasus.

Lustig, Sonia. Roses of the Wind. Doubleday, Doran & Company, Inc., Garden City, New York. Life in Russia about the middle of the 1800's.

Underwood, Edna W. The Penitent. Houghton Mifflin Company, Boston. Alexander I of Russia.

Van Bergen, Robert. The Story of Russia. American Book Company, New York. To the end of the Russo-Japanese War.

Verne, Jules. Michael Strogoff; or, The Courier of the Czar. Charles Scribner's Sons, New York. Russia in Siberia in the early 1800's.

Walpole, Hugh. The Secret City. George H. Doran Company, New York. Petrograd during the revolution.

CHAPTER XVI

THE NEW RUSSIA: TRANSFORMING A "BACKWARD" NATION

"The Bolsheviks won't stay in power one year!"

"They'll be out in six months! The peasants outnumber them eight to one. A little group like that can't dictate to 140,000,000 people. They are surrounded by enemies on every side. That dictatorship will be short-lived!"

So went the comment everywhere at the world-wide announcement that the Bolshevik branch of the Socialist Democratic party had seized the Russian government.

A tiny group of men controlling small contingents of troops had seized the government offices in Petrograd and were attempting to compel a vast nation to become socialists. It seemed preposterous, indeed. "Surely they cannot succeed!" was the thought of most people both inside and outside of Russia.

Years passed . . . Famine came . . . Suffering people starved to death . . . Factories and mines stopped running . . . Trains stood still . . . Stores closed, as they had no goods to sell . . . The population of Petrograd and Moscow dwindled by hundreds of thousands as starving people rushed out to the countryside in the vain hope of finding food . . . Civil war broke out, and foreign countries attacked the new Russian government on every side . . . More and more frequently came predictions of early failure.

But month after month, year after year, the dictators held on. More firmly they began to control the people. Then they began to cope with the overwhelming problems that confronted them.

Gradually living became a little easier in Russia and government a little more orderly. Slowly agriculture and industry revived, crops were raised, factories began to open again, and trains ran once more. Coal mines began to pour forth fuel, and the iron mines and steel mills began to produce metals. In spite of terrific odds against them the communist dictators continued to control all Russia from Petrograd to Vladivostok, from Archangel to Baku. It was one of the most astonishing feats in the world's history.

A decade passed, and then a stupendous Five-Year Plan was announced. This was a proposal to plan scientifically every aspect of living for the entire nation. Never before had such changes been proposed for a people. Never before were changes to be put into operation on such a vast scale. Changes in government . . . changes in farming . . . changes in manufacturing . . . changes in health . . . changes in the ownership of land . . . changes in education . . . changes in family life. A new social order began to arise in the largest national territory on the earth.

The attempt stunned the world; rumors concerning the astounding plan spread in every capital. Premiers considered together what it would mean for international relations, and business men all over the world began to wonder how it might affect them.

As the years have passed one fact has become increasingly clear — the happenings in Russia are so important to the entire world that every citizen of every nation must do his best to understand them. In this chapter, therefore, we shall attempt to comprehend the unusual experiment in government and social life that is taking place. First, let us note how the scattered nationalities and races of the great territory are bound together under one government.

What is included in the Union of Soviet Socialist Republics of Russia?

After the revolution of 1917 the former Russian Empire gradually broke up into various republics and regions. In 1929 there were seven so-called republics:

1. The Russian Socialist Federated Soviet Republic
2. The Ukrainian Socialist Soviet Republic
3. The White Russian Socialist Soviet Republic
4. The Transcaucasian Socialist Federated Soviet Republic
5. The Uzbek Socialist Soviet Republic
6. The Turcoman Socialist Soviet Republic
7. The Tadzhik Socialist Soviet Republic

In each of these republics (see figure 151), the people were closely enough united in language and nationality to join together in a separate government. In addition to these there were various large areas that were permitted to organize their own governments,— as, for example, the Siberian area and the Yakutsk area.

FIG. 151. The seven republics of Russia

To understand how each of these republics and areas is governed, let us consider the government of the Russian Socialist Federated Soviet Republic (R. S. F. S. R.).

There is one outstanding fact about the form of the new government. It is a sort of pyramid of political control. At the base are the millions of peasants and city workers, organized in local branches called soviets. These soviets are local councils, or committees, elected every three months, with one representative to every 100 workers in the city and one representative to every 1000 peasants. As you can see, the city workers have ten times as much representation as the peasants. The well-known older classes — nobles, clergy, business men, property-owners, and the like — have no share whatever in the government.

The next step of the pyramid is the Rural District Congress, made up of deputies elected by the village soviets, with one deputy for every ten members of each soviet.

The third step is the County Congress. This Congress consists of not more than 300 members, who are selected by the deputies of the local soviets, with one member for each 1000 people.

Press Cliché

Fig. 152. A gathering of representatives of a village soviet from a farming district. They have just pledged themselves to enter into a competition for bumper crops

The fourth step is the Provincial Congress, made up of not more than 300 deputies. In this congress each city deputy represents 2000 electors, while each rural deputy represents 10,000 inhabitants.

The fifth step is the Regional Congress, made up of not more than 500 deputies, one deputy to each 5000 electors in the city and one to each 25,000 people in the country.

The sixth step is the All-Russian Congress of Soviets. This is the supreme representative body, which meets once a year and is made up of more than 2000 members selected from either the regional or the lower congresses.

The All-Russian Congress is so large that it delegates its executive power to the *Central Executive Committee.* But this group is also too large (386 members) to work effectively; hence it delegates the control to the *Presidium* (27 members).

But even this group is not the real governing power. At the top of the whole scheme there is a small *Council of People's Commissars,* which is the cabinet and the real administrative body. This group consists of nearly a score of administrative heads of departments, responsible to the Central Executive Committee. The chairman of this council has authority equivalent perhaps to that of the chief executive officer (president, prime minister, etc.) in other countries. The chart of figure 224 shows the chief departments administered by the members of the Council of People's Commissars and their associates.

This, in brief, is the organization of the Russian Socialist Federated Soviet Republic — the chief area of the entire territory. Each of the other six republics and of the areas not called republics is organized on approximately the same plan.

These Seven Republics are bound together in a Union

To understand how this entire area of Russia from Leningrad to Vladivostok is centrally governed, let us think of these seven republics, shown on the map of figure 151, as leagued together in a federation called the Union of Soviet Socialist Republics (the administrative plan also provides for some slight representation of the regions that have not been made into republics). Figure 224 shows us that these seven divisions choose deputies who meet together in a Union Congress of Soviets. These deputies are elected by the provincial congresses in the individual republics. This Union Congress, being very large, delegates its work to the Union Central Executive Committee, made up altogether of nearly 600 members. Thus the committee corresponds to the Central Executive Committee of the All-Russian Congress. This committee, also being too large for effective work, delegates its administrative duties to a Union Council of Commissars.

Thus Russia today is a gigantic federation of supposedly independent states. Actually, as we shall see, all the people are governed by the edicts that go out from Moscow.

The Communist Party — the Real Government of All Russia

But this vast territory and mixture of races, nationalities, and governments is held together by the Communist party, which, as such, has no constitutional status. But the group of Communists at the head of the Russian government *have*, as individuals, the legal power which comes from having been elected to their offices. It was the communists (then called the Bolshevik branch of the Workmen's Socialist Democratic party) who carried through the revolution in November, 1917. They were aided by the peasant groups, namely, the Socialist Revolutionary party and the Peasants' party.

In 1918 the Bolsheviks merged the loyal members of these groups into a closely unified party. From that time they dropped the name "Socialist Democrats" and were known as the Russian Communist party. It is organized much as any political party. Small local branches, called "cells," are organized in villages, in factories, in government bureaus. The members of the local cells elect representatives to meet in a higher committee representing a larger district. These representatives, in turn, elect others to meet in a still higher committee. Finally, the party as a whole, for all Russia, is represented in the committee at the top, called the All-Union Party Congress. This meets generally less than once a year. Thus the party is organized in the same general way as the Soviet government itself.

The work of the party is carried on by the central committee, which consists of 71 members. But the real control is held by a little group of twelve determined men at the top of the party pyramid. This group, called the *Politbureau* (political bureau), really runs the party.

Thus this new socialist government is not democratic. *It is autocratic. It is a one-man government.* During the past few years one man by his ability and force has succeeded in persuading his associates in his Politbureau to support his plans for government. Together they *run* the affairs of Russia. No peasant, mechanic, clerk, professional person, or any group of these has a direct voice in the selection of the central power which governs this vast land. The government is in the hands of the leaders of the Communist party. Leading this little group is one man, Joseph Stalin. Stalin — "the man of steel" — is the real dictator of Russia. As long as he controls his associates in the Politbureau he will continue to be dictator over the lives of almost 160,000,000 Russian people.

TABLE XXVI

Membership in Russian Communist Party, 1930	
	Per Cent
Industrial workers	68.2
Peasants	18.8
Others	13.0

Furthermore, the Communist party itself is very small. Belonging to it are only 1,500,000 people out of a total population of about 160,000,000. As Table XXVI shows, more than two thirds of these are industrial workers. Less than one fifth are peasants. All other classes, including the professional and clerical groups, make up little more than one eighth of the membership. In short, the party controls the government, and the proletariat — the industrial workers — control the party. Thus Karl Marx's idea of government under the control of the industrial workers is being tried out.

The dictatorship is made possible partly by the pyramid form of indirect representative government

This new Soviet government contrasts sharply with our American form. In America each citizen votes directly for most of his officials — for the mayor and council members in his local community, for the governor, the lieutenant governor, representatives and senators in his state legislature, and for Representatives and Senators in the Federal Congress. He votes for the higher officials directly, as he does for the local officials. Therefore we call our American form of government direct representative government.

But, as you can see, the Soviet plan is indirect. The individual citizen votes only for the local soviet. He does not vote for representatives in the Rural District Congress, in the County Congress, in the Provincial Congress, in the Regional Congress, in the All-Russian Congress, in the Central Executive Committee, or in the Council of People's Commissars. Even if he lives in the city he is not permitted to vote directly for the upper four levels of this scheme of government. This Soviet plan, then, is an example of indirect representation.

Furthermore, this indirect form of representative government makes it easier for the little group of dictators to keep the control.

The dictatorship is made possible partly by the armed force and iron discipline of the party

But there are other reasons why the little Communist party has kept control over Russia. One is, of course, that it keeps control over the army and the police — the armed force of the government. Another is that it demands absolute obedience from every member of the party. In the discussions of local soviets (see figure 152) or of any of the higher legislatures every member is permitted to say what he thinks; but once a vote has been taken and the majority has decided things, support of the decision is required of all.

No factions are permitted within the party. If an opposition to the group in power develops, it is ruthlessly crushed. Independent plans and thinking are not wanted. Because of their opposition many influential leaders have been expelled from the party and exiled from the country. Even Leon Trotsky, who opposed Stalin and his associates, was driven out.

After Lenin's death in 1924 Stalin succeeded in defeating every opposition group in the higher committees and either imprisoning these leaders or expelling them from office. So determined to continue the dictatorship have Stalin and his associates in the Politbureau been that in the fifteen months following January, 1928, they expelled 170,000 members from the party.

This demand for absolute conformity with the orders of the leaders goes far, indeed. For example, a member of the party must accept any task that is required of him, no matter how distasteful it may be to him or how much it interferes with his personal life. He may be required to leave his trade, profession, or department and go to live in another part of the country. He is absolutely at the command of his superiors. To refuse means expulsion from the party, loss of job, and possible starvation. The control of the leaders over the members of the party is absolute.

To understand how completely a true communist must conform to the dictates of the party, consider *what he cannot do.* He dare not marry outside of his class. He dare not dress like a capitalist. He cannot engage in trade for profit. He dare not hire laborers with a view to making profit from their work. He must not be seen with persons of another class, or he will be under

Press Cliché

FIG. 153. A meeting of the Pioneers. These young people are discussing questions regarding the sowing of the new spring crops

suspicion. Habitual drunkenness or inefficiency in work brings drastic punishment. Thus the party tends to control the thoughts and feelings as well as the actions of the individual members.

The leaders of the Communist party have carefully built up their political organization so as to obtain absolute loyalty. For example, one must *prove* his qualifications for membership by passing through a long probation period, ranging from six months to two years. During this time his every word and act is weighed by his superiors. The consequence is that most of those who are eventually admitted to membership are truly loyal.

The leaders of the party are also planning for the years to come by carefully training the young people to believe in communism. They have organized three large groups: (1) the *Communist Youth,* called *Komsomols*; (2) the *Pioneers*; (3) the *Little Octobrists.*

The Communist Youth is a sort of junior auxiliary to the party itself. It includes 3,000,000 young people between the ages of sixteen and twenty-three, organized in more than 70,000 cells. These young people, like their elders, are held together under iron discipline. They are taught constantly to serve the state.

Younger than the Komsomols are the Pioneers — 2,000,000 of them, ranging between the ages of ten and sixteen. And even the little boys and girls — the Little Octobrists — up to the age of ten receive special training. This training of the youth of Russia is putting into practice another of Lenin's preachings: "Give me four years to teach the children, and the seed I have sown shall never be uprooted."

Thus more than 5,000,000 young people and children are now being actively trained to become communists. Already one fourth of the 1,500,000 communists are young men and women who formerly belonged to these youth organizations.

In Russia, as in other countries, a political party is the real government behind the scenes

It is through such a carefully developed organization and such rigid discipline as this that a small political party, representing not more than 5 or 6 per cent of the entire population of Russia, succeeds in imposing its will upon the people. The party has no legal power. Nevertheless, because the leaders who control the party also occupy the chief positions in the government, *the party is really the government.*

The Third International was organized by the Russian Communist Party

Before leaving the question of the organization of the Communist party and the government, we must note its *international* activities. Recall that in 1864 Karl Marx himself had helped to organize an international workingmen's association known as the *First International.* It struggled along, and finally died in 1876.

In 1889 the Second International was organized. During the World War, one by one, most of the socialist leaders in the various warring countries dropped their international interests and supported their respective governments. Then the Second International collapsed also.

During the war Lenin tried repeatedly to launch a Third International. Not until 1919, however, when the Russian communists had been in power for more than a year, did they succeed in organizing it. It is known as the *Comintern* or Communist International, and more popularly as the Third International. Its object is to create a "World Federation of Soviet Republics" under its own leadership. The leaders regard the Union of Soviet Socialist Republics of Russia only as an important beginning. They wish to include the whole world in their plan.

We must remember that three fourths of all the communists in the world today are in Russia, and the leaders of the Russian Communist party control this new International. Although Stalin and his co-workers insist that the Third International is entirely independent of the Russian government, it is only on paper that this is true. Actually the same men run the Communist party, the Russian government, and the Third International.

The Present Russian Experiment has passed through Three Stages since 1917

To comprehend the situation today in Russia one must study the recent history of the Russian experiment in government. Since 1917 it has passed through three different stages: first, from 1917 to 1921, the attempt to make a completely communist state; second, from 1921 to 1928, the period of the New Economic Policy ("Nep"), in which some of the communistic ideas were given up and some of those of capitalist countries were tried; third, from 1928 to date, a new attempt, now going on, to set up a truly communist, or collective, state.

The First Stage, 1917–1921

The central problem: public ownership of property versus private ownership

When the communists seized the government in Russia in November, 1917, they attempted to set up public ownership of all the means of production; that is, farms, factories, mines, power plants, railroads, telegraphs, and the like were to be owned by the state. No one was to be permitted to hire labor for profit. No one could obtain dividends from stocks and bonds, for there were to be no stocks and bonds. All individual ownership was to be wiped out. Capitalism, as it was known in every other country of the world, was to be killed. This, in brief, was the first aim of the communists, and for nearly four years they tried to carry out this aim.

Fig. 154. The cartoonist has tried to show the great difference between the number of peasants and the number of those who tried to convert them. (From the *Evening Express*, Cardiff)

The overwhelming difficulties which confronted the government, 1917–1921

The new government attempted to set up this totally new system under grave difficulties. First, the leaders were stanchly opposed by the peasants—100,000,000 strong. Even before the communists set up their government, the peasants had already seized the lands of the nobles and of the *kulaks*, the richer peasants, and had divided these lands among themselves. Each peasant felt, therefore, that his little plot of ground, his house, animals, and implements, were his own. Almost to a man they refused to recognize the right of the communist leaders in the cities to claim ownership of their land. This was a difficulty, indeed, since the peasants controlled the food of the nation. Without their support the city people would starve.

Second, even if the communists succeeded in persuading the peasants to deliver to them the grain, dairy products, and other agricultural supplies with which to feed the city workers, there was almost no means of transporting these products to the cities. The railroads were practically in ruins.

To meet the emergency the new government seized all food supplies in the cities and issued food cards to the people. Only those who worked were assured of food, and they only on working days. Members of the Communist party were fed first; other workers second; and if anything was left over, the nonworkers could have it. Most of these received very little.

Third, in 1920 and 1921 there came the worst series of droughts in Russian history. Crops failed and famine spread.

> At one time 20 million were starving. Between 1920 and 1922, 10 million died of starvation. Then came the epidemics. There were 35 million cases of typhus and relapsing fever in Russia after the war. On the heels of these came tuberculosis, which took off almost all the chronic cases. Malaria was next, with 18 million cases, some as far north as Archangel and Murmansk on the Arctic, spread by the enormous mass movement of the people, and aggravated by the lack of quinine and medical personnel.[1]

This terrible condition spread over the country at the very beginning of the new government.

Fourth, to make matters still worse, civil war broke out in several parts of the country. When the new government tried to take food from the peasants by force, the latter resisted. A general uprising against the government developed among them.

Early in 1918 the returning armies from the German front, and Cossack troops in the south, also rose in civil war against the communists. Other forces rose against them in Siberia. Czechoslovaks who had been serving against their will in the Austrian armies had been made prisoners of war by the Russians, and had been organized later into Russian regiments for service against their former Austrian oppressors. They now joined the attack upon the communist forces, or Red Army.

[1] Bruce Hopper, *Pan-Sovietism: the Issue before America and the World,* pp. 36–37. Houghton Mifflin Company, Boston, 1931.

In the meantime, in 1918 and 1919, foreign armies attacked on the north, on the west, and on the south. By October, 1920, the Red Army had succeeded in putting down insurrections and in defeating invaders on all sides.

These, then, were the conditions under which the communists attempted to set up a completely socialized government. By 1921 people were dying by the thousands; peasants were refusing to coöperate in giving up food and other supplies; factories and railroads were at a standstill. Then it was that Lenin, Trotsky, Stalin, and the other leaders recognized that a new policy must be instituted to save the situation.

The Second Stage — "Nep": Individual Capitalism permitted, 1921–1928

Under these circumstances the communists had to give up their attempt to impose socialism on the nation. They saw that they must get the help of the peasants by permitting them much more individual liberty.

Fig. 155. In this cartoon we see that the old horse, Private Enterprise, has been called into service to tow the automobile, Bolshevism. What does the cartoon imply? (From the *Western Mail*, Cardiff)

In 1922 they issued a new land code which guaranteed to the peasants the land which they held. Individual ownership and private enterprise were permitted. Persons were allowed to rent land and to hire laborers for profit. This return to private capitalism pleased the peasants, who soon resumed the cultivation of their fields.

From Table XXVII we can see that in 1928 communism had made almost no advance among the farmers of Russia. It is true that small experiments had been launched on state farms, but these were not considered by the peasants to be of any significance.

The return to capitalism brought almost immediate results

The "Nep" revived agriculture, industry, and trade almost immediately. Once the peasants were assured of their land they quickly began to produce crops (see Tables XXVIII and XXIX).

TABLE XXVII

Per Cent of Russian Farm Land owned Privately and Publicly in 1928	
Privately owned	98
Publicly owned	2

By 1927 farm production had been so increased that although there were fewer peasants than there had been in 1913, nevertheless they produced exactly the same value of farm products (Table XXX).

The New Economic Policy also served to revive industry and trade in the cities and villages, but differently from the way in which it revived agriculture. Although private citizens were allowed to go into business for themselves and to compete with the state industries, the state rapidly took over control of factories, mines, warehouses, and stores.

TABLE XXVIII

Number of Dessiatines[1] of Land under Cultivation in Russia, 1922, 1923, 1927	
1922	49,000,000
1923	59,000,000
1927	83,000,000

TABLE XXIX

Tons of Grain collected in Russia, 1924, 1926	
1924	35,600,000
1926	72,000,000

During the previous period, that of complete communism, 1917–1921, industrial production had fallen to a point at which it represented only a small proportion of the goods that had been produced in 1913. For example, in 1920 the amount produced per worker in the textile industry was only 22 per cent of that produced before the World War; in the mining of coal, only 25 per cent. So demoralized had industry become by 1920 that the value of all manufactured goods was only 13 per cent of that produced in 1913.

TABLE XXX

Total Value of Agricultural Products in Russia, 1913, 1927	
1913	$6,400,000,000
1927	6,400,000,000

[1] 2.7 acres.

Transportation also had declined. In 1920 only one third as many freight cars were unloaded as in 1916, in the midst of the war.

Then came the "Nep," and industrial production began to increase. Table XXXI shows that in 1927 the value of all goods produced by Russian industries had passed that produced in 1913.

TABLE XXXI

Value of All Goods produced by Russian Industries, 1913 and 1927	
1913	$3,200,000,000
1927	3,300,000,000

New power plants were constructed on the rivers; pipe lines were laid down to transport oil from the fields of the Caucasus to the Black Sea ports; new railroads were built. The Turkestan-Siberian Railway, for example, known as the "Turksib," was undertaken during these same years. It was not completed until the year 1931.

New roads were built from the few main highways to many isolated districts. Remember that in the building of roads Russia had been almost as backward as the isolated regions of China. One person described the highways as a series of tracks 100 yards wide. In spring and autumn they were "troughs of mud." Then, after 1922, came the race to build roads and introduce automobiles. By 1928 a marked beginning had been made.

TABLE XXXII

Millions of Metric Tons of Coal produced in Russia, 1913, 1927	
1913	29,000,000
1927	30,000,000

TABLE XXXIII

	Metric Tons of Oil Produced	Meters of Cotton Cloth Produced
1913	9,000,000	2,238,000,000
1927	10,000,000	2,342,000,000

Wholesale and retail trade also picked up. When the New Economic Policy went into effect, nine tenths of the 500,000 buying and selling agencies were privately owned. Although at first these were permitted to continue, as the years passed they were gradually suppressed. In 1928 *nine tenths of all the trade of Russia was carried on by the state.* This was one of the most important changes in the direction of public ownership.

THE THIRD STAGE OF THE RUSSIAN EXPERIMENT, 1928 TO DATE: A NEW ATTEMPT TO ESTABLISH THE SOCIALIST STATE

The communists saw that so far as industry and trade were concerned they were succeeding in establishing their socialistic state, but they still lacked control of the most important thing, namely, the food supply. Only 2 per cent of the products of Russian farms were produced on "socialized" land; 98 per cent of the farm land was still owned privately by the kulaks, by the middle peasants, and by the poor peasants.

Press Cliché

FIG. 156. The dam of the power plant on the Dnieper, which, when completed, will be the largest hydroelectric plant in the world

Then in December, 1927, at its Fifteenth Congress, the Communist party announced a momentous resolution: "We must strive in the shortest possible historical period to overtake and surpass the most advanced capitalistic countries." As the United States is, perhaps, regarded as "the most advanced capitalistic country," this resolution really meant, "We must beat America."

A vast national Five-Year Plan was developed

This time Stalin and his associates bore in mind the failure of their first attempt to set up the communist state during the years 1917 to 1921. This time they prepared very carefully. A State Planning Commission, called the *Gosplan*, was established, and a so-called *Five-Year Plan* was drawn up.

The Five-Year Plan is nothing less than a gigantic attempt to plan the economic and cultural life of the whole Russian people. Every aspect is included within it: industry, trade, agriculture, education, social life — everything. It is the most daring and at the same time the most scientific attempt that a large nation has ever made *to plan its ways of living.*

In most countries in which farming, manufacturing, and trade are carried on by individual persons for private profit, the government as a whole has never *planned* how much food shall be raised, how much coal and iron shall be mined or how much goods shall be manufactured. This is not done today in America, France, Germany, or any other country. As a result the amount produced has often not been the amount that was needed. Whenever that has happened, serious economic difficulties have occurred.

The new Russian government, then, having secured control of industry, trade, transportation, — in fact, of everything but agriculture, — decided in 1928 to try the experiment of *planning* everything in advance.

There were two aims behind the plan. The first was to transform a backward farming country into a rich industrial one — one in which all wastes in the production and distribution of physical goods would be eliminated, one which would be even more efficient than America. The second was to do away entirely with private capitalism, to set up the completely socialized state.

The Five-Year Plan was adopted by the Russian Communist party in April, 1929, and by the All-Russian Congress of Soviets in May, 1929. To describe it somewhat in detail, we can say that it proposes to achieve the following results:

1. *Increases in industry.* The graphs of figure 157 sum up the bold plan to start Russia, a farming country, on the road to being a leading *industrial* nation. The Russian leaders propose to *more than double* the production of factories in five years.

2. *A modern transportation system in five years.* The Five-Year Plan proposes to more than triple the amount spent on transportation — from 3,000,000,000 rubles to 10,000,000,000. This will be used to build more than 10,000 miles of railroad and to develop the Volga-Don Canal, uniting the two great rivers and tying together the coal and grain regions with important southern ports.

One billion rubles is to be spent on new roads alone. It is proposed to increase the number of automobiles from 25,000 to 300,000, and 100,000,000 rubles are to be spent on airplanes.

3. *Increased national income.* At the top of the whole scheme is a gigantic *Finplan* providing for the raising of the enormous sums of money with which to carry on these enterprises. In 1922 Lenin himself announced that the state had "earned this year

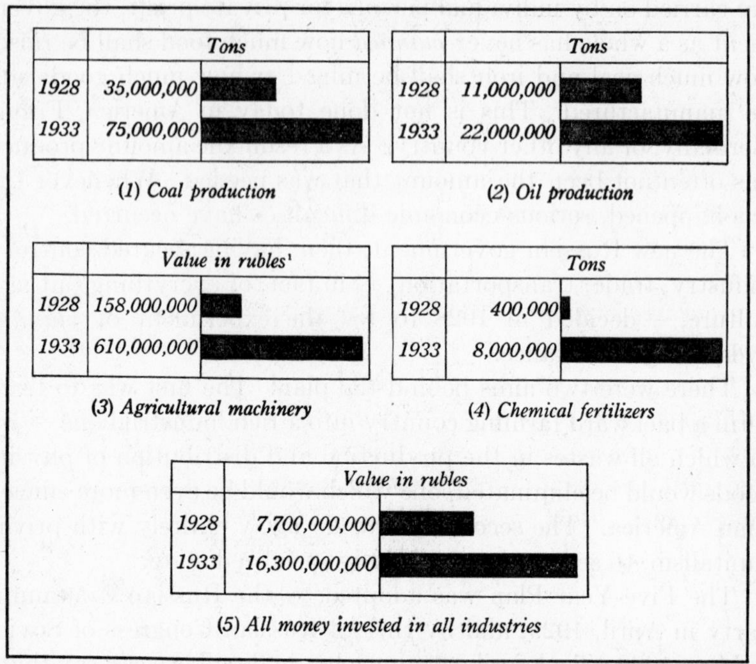

Tons
1928 35,000,000
1933 75,000,000
(1) Coal production
Tons
1928 11,000,000
1933 22,000,000
(2) Oil production
Value in rubles[1]
1928 158,000,000
1933 610,000,000
(3) Agricultural machinery
Tons
1928 400,000
1933 8,000,000
(4) Chemical fertilizers
Value in rubles
1928 7,700,000,000
1933 16,300,000,000
(5) All money invested in all industries

FIG. 157. Increases in production and investment according to the Five-Year Plan

but very little, a trifle more than 20,000,000 gold rubles" (or $10,000,000). The Five-Year Plan proposed to put 65,000,000,000 rubles into circulation — 3250 times as much! In order to do this, enormous amounts of wheat, cotton, coal, oil, manufactured goods, and other products must be sold to other countries to bring in the gold with which to finance the tremendous plan. It is indeed a breath-taking proposal.

4. *The transformation of agriculture by increasing the land under cultivation by nearly one fourth.* Thirty-seven million acres of land

[1] Approximately 50 cents.

for new cultivation are to be provided. Within five years the entire value of agricultural products is expected to rise from 11.2 billion rubles, which it was in 1928, to 16.7 billion in 1933. Not only will the amount of wheat, rye, and other grains be increased, but that of various special agricultural products will also be greater in ever-increasing proportion.

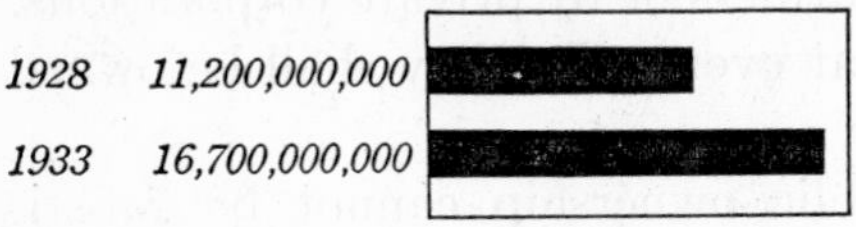

1928	*11,200,000,000*	▬▬▬▬
1933	*16,700,000,000*	▬▬▬▬▬▬

FIG. 158. The value in rubles of all agricultural products raised in 1928, and the planned production for 1933

In five years power-driven machines must be doing the work of human muscles all over the level plains of Russia. Cows and other stock will be improved, and soil will be treated scientifically, orchards developed, and a great variety of new crops raised.

TABLE XXXIV

SOVIET NATIONAL INCOME (RUBLES)	
In 1922	20,000,000
Proposed amount to be put into circulation, 1928–1933	65,000,000,000

But how are these things to be done under existing conditions, with 25,000,000 little farms and almost no farm machinery, tools, fertilizers, or scientific knowledge of farming? By a drastic change in the whole agricultural enterprise of the nation, answer the Soviet leaders.

THE SOVIET GOVERNMENT PROPOSES TO FARM THE LAND OF RUSSIA COLLECTIVELY

To do these things the small farms must be given up. All land, horses, cows, farm implements, and fertilizers are to be put into a common pool and used collectively. Fences and other barriers between existing little private plots of ground are to be taken out. Plowing, cultivating, harvesting, and the like will be done by gasoline machines — tractors, harvesters, etc.

Vast cow barns, piggeries, dairies, and other farm plants are to be built in every section of the wide land. Farms will extend thousands of acres, instead of being ten acres or less, as many of them are at present. In short, mass production is to come to Russian farms, as it has already come to the farms of America.

But there is a sharp difference between American mass farming and the proposed Russian plan. In America these great farms are owned by individual farmers or by private corporations. In Russia the plan provides that eventually they shall be owned by the state.

The leaders know that public ownership cannot be substituted for private ownership all at once; so they have devised three plans of running the farms collectively. One is that of the *sovhoz*, or state farm, owned and managed directly by the central government. Giant tractors and other machines do much of the work on these farms, and the products raised go directly to the government.

The second is that of the *kolhoz*, of which there are various types. The most common is the *artel*. In the artel, peasants pool such of their belongings as land, farm buildings, and accumulations or savings, in money or in kind; but they may own their individual homes and may keep a cow, hens, geese, and the like. Their personal possessions, however, must bear a fair proportion to their needs.

The third plan to collectivize Russian farms is that of the *tractor service station*, which is owned and operated by the government. Many of these stations are now being developed in various districts of the country. They are equipped with modern farm machinery which is rented to villages and artels so that they can plow, sow, cultivate, and harvest their crops.

How did the Soviet government get the peasants to join the "collectives"?

In the summer of 1929 the peasants produced one of the largest crops in the history of the country. No sooner was it harvested than the government started a vast campaign to get the peasants to stop their wasteful small-scale farming and work together in "collectives," or *kolhozy*. They launched a widespread attack upon the kulaks.

Brigades of workers were sent into thousands of villages to educate the peasants. They held meetings, gave lectures, showed lantern slides, maps, motion pictures, and placards. They enthusiastically tried to convince the peasants of the great gains which would come to their villages if they would pool their resources, throw their lands together in great collective farms, introduce tractors and other farm machinery, build collective cow barns and other animal stations, and harvest their crops together and sell them together.

TABLE XXXV[1]

The Individual Peasant Farms embraced by the Collective Farms		
Date	Number of Individual Farms Collectivized	Per Cent of Total Individual Farms Collectivized
October 1, 1927 . .	286,000	1.1
October 1, 1928 . . .	595,000	2.3
October 1, 1929 . . .	2,131,000	8.1
October 1, 1930 . . .	5,565,000	22.2
March 1, 1931 . . .	8,830,000	35.3

The attack succeeded far beyond all expectations. On October 1, 1929, as Table XXXV shows, only 8 per cent of the 25,000,000 farms in Russia were owned and operated collectively. So swiftly did the new drive of the communists succeed, however, that on October 1, 1930, more than 22 per cent were owned collectively. In March, 1931, the percentage had risen to more than 35. Within this short time more than 6,500,000 individual peasant households have been persuaded to put their little farms, animals, and implements into a common pool with those of their neighbors. They keep for private use only their crude houses, their gardens, and one cow. Fences and other barriers between separate plots have been destroyed, making vast open fields on which tractors and other farm machinery can operate.

Force as well as persuasion brought the peasants into the collectives

Naturally the poor peasants, who owned little land, joined the collectives first. The middle peasants, who owned, say, from 10 to 35 acres, felt less willingness to join. Nevertheless they also began to join the coöperative enterprises.

It was the despised kulaks, however, who held out. So in the drive of 1929–1930 the Soviet organizers began to use armed

[1] Adapted from V. M. Molotov's *Success of the Five-Year Plan* (International Publishers, New York, 1931), p. 45.

force. When three quarters of the peasants of a district had joined a collective, government agents then took possession of all other farms. They confiscated animals and tools and machinery and exiled the kulak to one of the various prison stations of the new government. Members of families were separated from one another. If a building was needed by the *kolhoz*, agents took the house of a kulak. He and his family were compelled to find a new place to live.

Maurice Hindus, an American citizen born and brought up in Russia who has been there recently to study conditions, gives us an example:

> The agent confiscated the hidden rye, the man's best horse, his best cow, his best calf, a mowing machine, ten sheep, seventeen geese, and even the fiddle which the poor fellow had inherited from his grandfather. Not only that, but he was expelled from the village coöperative [collective] — not an ounce of salt, not a drop of kerosene, not an inch of dry goods can he buy there. Everything he needs he must obtain in open market, where the prices are from two to four times as much as in the coöperative.[1]

The son of another kulak was a student in a university, studying to be an engineer. One day the Soviet authorities learned that his father had refused to join a *kolhoz*. They immediately dismissed the son from the university.

So it is by education and by force that the small Communist party is actually succeeding in getting tens of millions of farmers to join with them in setting up a state in which the means of production are owned and operated publicly. So it is that the theories of Karl Marx and Friedrich Engels are being tried out on a large scale.

The Social Reconstruction of the Village

The Five-Year Plan is not merely a scheme for economic development. Those who made it are even more concerned with the rebuilding of the whole culture of the people. Since about 80 per cent of the population of Russia live in villages, the re-

[1] Maurice Hindus, *Red Bread*, p. 51. Jonathan Cape & Harrison Smith, New York, 1931.

construction of the village is a basic aim of the communists. To bring new ways of living to the backward, isolated people of several hundred thousand villages is the purpose.

And the purpose is beginning to be realized. The whole world of these *muzhiks*, or peasants, is being changed, and they themselves are changing. Clubhouses are being built, radios are being provided, and distant villages which have been isolated for centuries are "tuning in" on Moscow and other sending stations (see figure 164). Telephone and telegraph lines are being built, connecting the scattered villages with the cities. New schoolhouses are rising spick and span with whitewashed walls. Nurseries for little children and health stations are being established.

New kinds of Western clothing are being adopted; for example, modern hats, collars, ties, and underwear. The girls are beginning to use rouge and lip stick as in other European nations and in the United States. A recent visitor tells us of watching young villagers preparing for a dance:

> I was impressed by the vast improvement in the dress of these peasant youths since my previous visit five years before. Not one, boy or girl, any longer wore *lapti*, the age-old bast sandals of the *muzhik*. Not one was barefooted. The boys wore finely made boots of soft leather, the girls' feet were neat in factory-made shoes, their coarse hand-knit stockings replaced by machine-woven ones. . . . Finger rings, too — mostly of tin and brass — gleamed in the sun as hands moved one way or another, and handkerchiefs, previously unknown, were as common as boots and shoes. . . . Scarcely any wore dresses of homespun fabrics, now considered inferior; cottons, satins, city fashion, replaced them.[1]

The plan to educate a whole nation

A fundamental part of the Five-Year Plan is the stupendous proposal to educate 160,000,000 people. That this is an overwhelming problem can be seen from the facts of illiteracy. In 1920 approximately *63 per cent* of the people of all the Russias were *unable to read or write*. There was no more illiterate nation in the Western world than Russia. Remember that in the United

[1] Maurice Hindus, *Red Bread*, pp. 52–53. Jonathan Cape & Harrison Smith, New York, 1931.

States and other modern nations all but 5 to 10 per cent of the people can read and write.

The Five-Year Plan proposes to reduce illiteracy from 63 per cent to 18 per cent by 1933. More than 3500 schools are to be specially established for the purpose of teaching *adults*. In five years it is expected that these new schools will teach 18,000,000 persons between the ages of 18 and 35 to read and write.

Press Cliché

FIG. 159. Schools for teaching grown-ups to read and write have already made progress in cutting down the percentage of illiteracy in Russia

In addition, for the first time in Russian history, there is a nation-wide plan for the development of elementary, secondary, and higher education and for special technical studies. It is proposed that in every section, except the distant, isolated parts of Asia, every child between the ages of eight and eleven years shall be in school by 1933. The number of children in the four-year primary school is to increase from 10,000,000 to 17,000,000, and 43,000 new teachers are to be trained.

High schools will be similarly increased, and engineering and vocational schools are to be set up. Enrollment in peasant universities will be increased from 130,000 students (1927) to 393,000 in 1933. Enrollment in workers' universities in the cities will increase from 14,000 to 56,000. Furthermore, young men and women are to be paid while going to the higher schools.

The number of cottage reading rooms in villages is to increase from 21,000 to 38,000; libraries, from 23,000 to 34,000; peasant clubs, from 6100 to 7600; workers' clubs, from 3700 to 4500.

The motion picture, the radio, and newspapers are regarded by the communists as a most effective means of educating the mass of the people. Hence they have inaugurated a mighty program of development. In 1928 the entire Soviet Union had 8521 motion-picture theaters and stations, attended by about 300,000,000 people in that year. The number is to be increased to 34,700 in 1933, and 25,000 of these are to be in villages. Half of the latter will be traveling theaters. Schools and clubs are likewise to be equipped with motion-picture apparatus.

The number of radios will also be greatly increased. In 1928, in the entire Soviet Union, there were only 350,000 sets and approximately 2,000,000 people listening to them. It is proposed that in 1933 there shall be more than 6,000,000 sets, listened to by 40,000,000 people.

Already great advances have been made in the development of the press. In 1913 all Russia, including Poland and the other western sections, issued only 119,000,000 separate copies of books; in 1928, under the Soviet Union, almost twice that number were published. It is proposed that in 1933 more than 600,000,000 books shall be issued. Whereas 2,000,000,000 newspapers were issued in 1928, it is proposed that there shall be 6,300,000,000 in 1933.

This, in brief statistical form, is the famous Five-Year Plan, which is being talked about around the world. It is a plan to make a backward nation into one of the most advanced nations of the earth, and to do so in an incredibly short period. The present Russian leaders propose to do in a generation what England, France, Germany, and the United States have taken 100 years to do. When the first Five-Year Plan is finished, another is to take its place. That will be followed by another and another — no one knows how many.

Is the Plan Succeeding?

No one except the Soviet officials knows exactly how well the plan is succeeding. They alone have the figures with which to answer the question. According to their figures they are succeeding beyond their expectations, and they are now talking of completing parts of the Five-Year Plan in four or even three and a half years.

Even if their statistics are exaggerated it cannot be denied that in many aspects their campaign is succeeding. Note the summary figures of Table XXXVI.

TABLE XXXVI[1]

The Russian Government's Own Report of the Results of the First Two Years of the Five-Year Plan, 1928–1930

	Proposed Increase for First Two Years	Absolute Increase	Per Cent of Set Tasks Achieved
National income (in billion rubles) .	58.3	59.5	102
State budget (in billion rubles) . .	17.0	21.0	124
Capital investments in the basic capital of the socialist sector (in billion rubles)	12.7	13.8	124
Total production of the socialist sector of industry, including the food and drink trades, on a 1926–1927 price basis (in billion rubles) . . .	29.3	30.5	104
Area under seed (in million hectares)	239.0	245.8	103
Production of market grain (in millions of double hundredweights) .	221.2	267.3	121
Goods traffic (in millions of tons) .	350.9	409.2	117

In their reports the authorities grant frankly that there are many weaknesses which must be corrected. For example, they lack engineers, scientists, and skilled industrial workers. In spite of their vast scheme of education the *quality* of skilled factory production has not kept pace with its quantity. The leaders are now campaigning hard to raise the quality of the product.

In the rural districts, as well as in the industrial cities, the plan seems to be succeeding. In 1930 nearly two fifths of the peasants had become a part of the socialist state. There were

[1] Adapted from V. M. Molotov's *Success of the Five-Year Plan* (International Publishers, New York, 1931), p. 41.

142 state farms cultivating approximately 23,000,000 acres of land. In 1930 they produced 1,000,000 tons of grain, practically as much as the kulaks had formerly produced and exported.

Visitors to Russia agree that, whether or not the plan is being achieved, there is a growing enthusiasm among the mass of the people for the possibility of making a modern state out of Russia.

Here is what one student of the new system says:

> Life is moving at high speed in Russia, . . . great power plants are being built, steel mills are springing up, factories are turning out tractors and combines, oil is flowing at a tremendous rate, new railroads are tying up the industrial centers with the sources of raw materials, unemployment has disappeared, and the Russian land, which today has one-fifth of the total cultivated area of the globe, is being tractorized and motorized.[1]

This, in outline, is the story of the dramatic transformation of Russia. This is the way in which the third largest nation in the world has overturned absolute monarchical government. And this is the way in which a few socialist leaders seized the government, turned their backs on democracy, and experimented with socialism.

INTERESTING READING FROM WHICH YOU CAN GET ADDITIONAL INFORMATION

Ilin, M. New Russia's Primer. Houghton Mifflin Company, Boston. What the Soviets are doing in new Russia.

[1] Bruce Hopper, *Pan-Sovietism: the Issue before America and the World*, p. 86. Houghton Mifflin Company, Boston, 1931.

UNIT VII

INDUSTRIAL EUROPE PRODUCES A NEW CULTURE

INDUSTRIAL EUROPE PRODUCES A NEW CULTURE

The new ways of thinking which developed in Europe after 1500 affected every aspect of modern culture. Two of these aspects have already been studied: economic life and new experiments in government. We turn now to the third aspect of European life which was changed by the new ways of thinking,— to the "lively arts" and the fine arts. This new European civilization produced more than science, machine industry, and a high material standard of living: it produced also increased leisure and more interesting arts with which to enjoy it. It gave the common man many new ways of entertaining himself — the use of the automobile, the motion picture, the radio, and the widespread reading of magazines, newspapers, and books. These we shall study in Chapter XVII.

In Chapter XVIII we shall learn something about Europe's contribution to the fine arts — her architecture and sculpture, her beautiful music and painting, her literature, the dance and the theater.

CHAPTER XVII

THE "LIVELY ARTS" AND THE CHANGING CULTURES IN EUROPE

In 1900 the people of hundreds of little British villages were carrying on their quiet lives in much the same way as had their great-great-grandfathers 100 years before in the same little villages. For years the English countryside and its villages had changed but little. Winding lanes, hedge-lined, along them cottages bowered in roses . . . occasional fishing hamlets, their steep, rocky streets connected by stone steps . . . rambling village streets, shaded by ancient, spreading trees, along which jogged horses drawing phaëtons and carts . . . villagers gossiping together over hedges or outside the shops . . . a village shop itself "with its green-bottle windows and the assortment of licorice, note paper, shoe laces, and soap."

Not only in England but in France and Germany — indeed, in all Europe — most people lived their threescore and ten years in villages. They cultivated their fields, tended their gardens, did their daily work, worshiped in their little stone churches. How quiet and leisurely life was! There were no motor cars with loud horns and screeching brakes, no radios barking from open windows, few trains, no telephones. Occupations, means of transportation and communication, and recreation — all were marked by the quietness of the natural countryside itself.

Of course such ways of living had their disadvantages too. Life was often uniform, even monotonous, and surely isolated. There was little contact with other parts of the world, even with the near-by cities of one's own country. One seldom saw new people or discussed new ideas. Physical life was made difficult by the lack of conveniences and comforts.

Nevertheless, in the late 1800's life for most people in the villages of western Europe was leisurely and uneventful. Their wants were few and easily satisfied.

Then, as in America, came the New Industrial Revolution

Today much of the countryside has changed. Telephone and telegraph wires appear on the landscape between village and city. Railroads draw more and more communities within national transportation systems. Billboards advertising soap, tires, automobiles, hotels, and the latest millinery and hosiery line the roads.

FIG. 160. An unchanged village. Were the two men not shown in this picture, one might almost believe that this little English village had gone to sleep in the 1600's and was yet unaware of the Industrial Revolution which has taken place

How different, too, is life in many of the villages! Power stations, belching forth smoke, light them with incandescent lamps. Down the once quiet streets whiz automobiles and motor cycles. Gasoline stations and garages line the main streets; drug stores as varied as department stores stand on the corners. Cinema theaters — as motion-picture theaters are called in Europe — display colored posters. Even the little villages already show pictures once a week; "soon it will be twice a week, and after that 'the talkers,' as they are called." In the evenings families go to the cinema, or else gather about radio sets, listening to jazz bands playing in London, Liverpool, or perhaps even in America.

Thus the New Industrial Revolution, which swept the United States after 1890, changing all its ways of living, is now rolling back over Europe. As you know, in the 1800's England and other countries invented power-driven machines and European-

Fig. 161. A changing village. In the days of the Tudors, English earls and squires stopped here to quench their thirst for ale and to gossip of crops and politics. Today, to the same place, motorists bring their "thirsty" automobiles, and the talk centers about the merits of competing cars and oils

ized other continents. Today, in the 1900's, the United States, which has carried the Industrial Revolution farther than other countries, is Americanizing Europe — indeed, the earth. So, at least, declare European leaders, most of whom fear the changes that are coming.

You already know the chief characteristics of this New Industrial Revolution:[1]

[1] See *An Introduction to Problems of American Culture*, Vol. V of this series, Chaps. VIII–IX.

1. The ever-increasing invention of power-driven machines to do the work of men.

2. The invention of practicable and cheap automobiles.

3. The widespread use of the telephone.

4. The improvement of the motion picture and its adoption as the chief form of recreation by the mass of the people.

5. The invention and widespread use of the radio.

6. The rapid increase in the number and kinds of organizations — fraternal societies, neighborhood clubs, business and labor organizations, memorial, patriotic, and charitable societies.

7. The changing attitudes of and toward women — their work, their play, their rapid entrance into occupations outside of the home.

8. The movement toward universal elementary education and an increase in the amount of education received by all.

9. The result of these important changes and developments showing itself in the most astonishing growth of cities that the world has ever known.

Recall that populations had grown swiftly

As in the United States, so also in other countries, population had increased with astonishing rapidity in the 1800's and early 1900's. Figure 162 shows the increase in the larger European nations. Between 1820 and 1920 the Russian population grew from about 45,000,000 to 134,000,000; the population of Germany, from 24,000,000 to 60,000,000; of the United Kingdom, from 21,000,000 to 43,000,000; of Italy, from 18,000,000 to about 39,000,000. Only France grew slowly, as French families continued to be small.

Not only in Europe and America has this growth in population occurred. It is a *world* development. In 1845, it is estimated, the population of the entire earth, in round numbers, was 1,000,000,000; in 1930 it was estimated at approximately 1,900,000,000. The number of people on the earth has almost doubled in 85 years. Why? For many reasons which you have already studied. The chief reason was the world-wide use of scientific knowledge in improving human health conditions. As a result, water supplies were improved, dairies and other centers of food production and distribution were made more sanitary, centers of pestilence were eliminated, and knowledge of surgery, preventive medicine, and the like was spread through the world.

The rapid drift to the cities

But no change that is coming about in European culture is causing more anxiety than the increasing size of cities. In 1800 few of the people of the British Isles lived in the cities; today almost 80 per cent are crowded together in such communities. Only 6 per cent of the people are occupied in the production of food. Of the rest four out of every five work in factories, offices, and schools, on trains and boats, or at like occupations.

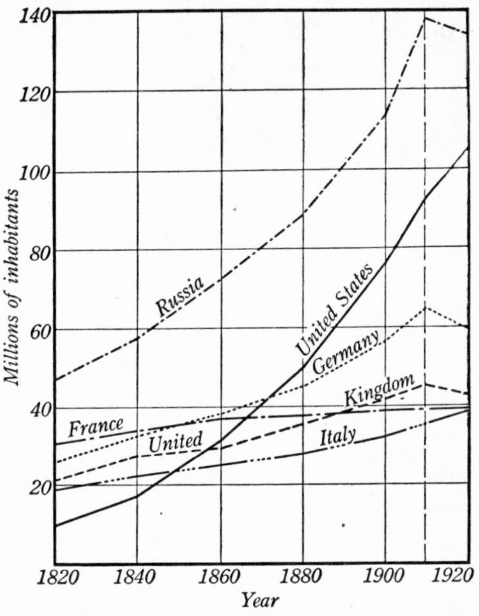

Fig. 162. Increase of population in the principal countries of Europe and in the United States, 1820–1920. (Adapted from *Mankind at the Crossroads*, by Edward M. East. Courtesy of Charles Scribner's Sons)

In France a somewhat similar transformation is taking place, particularly in the northern industrial sections. In 1872 approximately 70 per cent of the French people were living in towns and rural villages which contained less than 2000 inhabitants; in 1926, only 51 per cent. Furthermore, Table XXXVII indicates that all sizes of towns and cities are now growing.

That the same thing happened in Germany is clearly illustrated by figure 131. In 1871 about 36 per cent of the German

TABLE XXXVII

Growth of Cities in France, 1921 and 1926		
	1921	1926
Number of communes with 5001–10,000 inhabitants . .	394	429
Number of communes with 10,001–20,000 inhabitants .	175	207
Number of communes with 20,001 inhabitants and over	140	159
Number of towns with over 100,000 inhabitants	15	17

people were living in towns and cities of over 2000 inhabitants; in 1925, about 64 per cent.

Table XXXVIII presents the most recent estimate of this astonishing drift to the cities. It is clear that the countries which have introduced power-driven machinery most completely are the ones in which the most people have left the farms to live in cities.

TABLE XXXVIII[1]

Per Cent of Inhabitants of Various Countries living in Urban Districts (generally of 2000 People or More)	
England and Wales	79.3
Scotland	77.3
Germany	64.4
Belgium	57.1
France	46.4
Denmark	43.4
Czechoslovakia	43.3
Sweden	30.7
Ukraine	19.9
Japan	18.7
Portugal	17.4
Finland	16.1
India	10.2

This, then, is an important fact which we must keep in mind in considering cultural changes in Europe. As the people of England, France, Germany, Belgium, Czechoslovakia, and other countries are crowding into cities as fast as, or even faster than, the people of the United States, we must expect to find somewhat the same changes in ways of working and playing as in our own country.

And that is what we do find. Let us consider some aspects of this dramatic change that is taking place in countries as they adopt industrial civilization.

The Increasing Use of the Automobile

In our earlier studies we found that the basis of the changes that were taking place in the family, neighborhood, and community life of America was the automobile. America played an important part in the invention of the automobile. Here huge factories were constructed to produce automobiles. In 1930 more than 75 per cent of all the automobiles in the world were in use in America. Nearly 9,000,000 were in use in other countries, mostly in Europe. Interestingly enough, after the United

[1] Based on the most recent census figures.

States, it is the other English-speaking countries (the United Kingdom and its dominions) that have made the most use of the automobile if the ratio of automobiles to population is considered. France has adopted it almost as much as England. However, Germany lags behind, with one car to each 99 people. What a contrast to the United States, which has one car to each 5 people!

TABLE XXXIX

Number of Passenger Automobiles in Use in some of the Leading Countries, January 1, 1930	
United States	23,181,000
United Kingdom	1,054,000
Canada	1,018,000
France	930,000
Germany	475,000
Australia	461,000
Argentina	296,000
Union of South Africa	130,000
Brazil	128,000
Spain	127,000

In England and in the neighborhoods of large cities in France and Germany, one sees lines of automobiles on the highways on holidays and week-ends, as in the United States. In many parts of England traffic conditions are indeed very much like those in America. But, except in the very largest cities, other European countries have not yet adopted the automobile so generally. The chief reason is, perhaps, that the people have less money and cannot afford automobiles. Nevertheless, leading students are very much troubled by the rate at which this aspect of Americanization — this whizzing through the country in motor cars — is taking up the leisure time of the people.

With the automobile came the swift improvement of paved roads. Although somewhat more slowly than in the United States, macadamized, asphalt, and concrete roads have been built throughout western Europe. Except for Russia, few have been constructed in eastern Europe. Today there are more paved roads in Europe than in any other continent, even in North America.

One can ride through the British Isles, through France, Belgium, Holland, Germany, and much of Italy and Austria, on fine macadamized roads. And in increasing numbers people are turning to automobile riding for recreation, as well as for speed in conducting their business.

The Cinema — revolutionizing the Wants and Interests of the People

After the automobile as an influence in changing ways of living comes the motion picture — the cinema. Utterly unknown in 1890, it is today a leading form of entertainment in western Europe. In the four outstanding countries — Great Britain, France, Germany, and Russia — there are today almost 20,000 motion-picture houses, seating more than 8,000,000 people.

TABLE XL

Estimated Number of Motion-Picture Theaters and their Seating Capacity in Several Countries, 1930

	Number of Theaters	Number of Seats
United States	21,000	12,000,000
Germany	5,267	1,876,000
Russia	5,200	2,200,000
Great Britain	4,226	2,200,000
France	4,221	2,100,000
Spain	3,000	1,468,000
Italy	2,800	1,800,000
Belgium	930	300,000
Poland	631	203,000
Turkey	104	37,000
Albania	3	1,400

The statistics that are given in Table XL afford a glimpse of the speed with which the new American enterprise is Americanizing Europe. For the cinema is essentially an American institution. The chief inventions which led to the perfection of the motion-picture camera and of other apparatus were made by Americans, and American producers developed the enterprise to its present tremendous size. As a result, today 80 per cent of all the feature plays shown in England are made in the United States. Although German "movies" have achieved international reputation for their creative excellence, more than 60 per cent of all pictures shown in German theaters are made in America. Indeed, it is estimated that 90 per cent of all "movies" made and displayed in the world today are made in the United States. These pictures are shown in more than 60 countries, and their subtitles are now translated into no less than 37 languages.

Note carefully the tremendous influence of the motion picture in transforming the culture of the world. Men, women, and children now sit in darkened rooms in little villages in England, Germany, Norway, Lithuania, Russia, Turkey, South Africa,

Argentina, India, China, Japan; in short, in practically every country of the globe. They see the drama of current events in distant sections of their own country, as well as in America and other lands. By way of contrast to the monotony of the life in their own villages, they see the variety of life in great cities and other ways of living. They are bedazzled by new styles of clothing, houses, motor cars, and the like. They witness the breath-taking wonders of totally different civilizations and the greater comfort of the peoples of industrial nations. They note the ease with which goods are produced and distributed. They see broad, well-paved streets, clean, substantial houses, happy youth in schools and on playgrounds, and so on.

FIG. 163. Through this billboard on wheels a French movie is advertised in Morocco

And more and more they imitate American customs. As one student of the problem says:

> Chinese girls are abandoning pantaloons for short skirts, long hair for boyish bobs. American manners and morals are spreading throughout the world. Peruvians are demanding player pianos and athletic underwear. Yorkshire manufacturers of boots and clothing complain that they have been obliged to alter their plants because the Near East wants vests like Valentino's and [clothes] like Clara Bow's.[1]

Thus we see again that the East is being affected by the West and that movies are playing a part in the change.

[1] Peter Odegard, *The American Public Mind*, p. 208. Columbia University Press, New York, 1930.

Is Listening to the Radio becoming a Popular Means of Recreation?

In 1920 there was not a radio broadcasting station in Europe. At the beginning of 1928 there were 200 stations. This increase indicates the rapidity with which the radio is seizing the time and interest of western Europeans. Indeed, if we add the 500

Press Cliché

Fig. 164. Russian peasants listening to a radio program. For those who cannot read, the radio is a particularly important means of instruction and entertainment

stations (at the beginning of 1928) in the United States, we can see that listening to the radio is becoming a leisure-time activity for the entire Western world.

So swiftly did radio broadcasting spring up in the leading countries of Europe that by 1925 it was recognized that there was grave need for international control of the air. Announcers in French, German, and English sent their words out over the boundaries of 30 countries, mixing them with those of Spanish, Italian, Portuguese, Danish, Swedish, and the various Slavic tongues. The air represented a confusion of tongues indeed.

It was necessary, therefore, for European broadcasters to agree upon rules of international control. This they did at conferences in 1925 and 1926. Within a year and a half a pan-European radio scheme was in operation — *another step toward international coöperation.*

While most of the radio sets in Europe are owned by individual families, as they are in the United States, there is also a definite movement to install radios in community centers. Loud-speakers are being set up in hospitals, hotels, cafés, moving-picture houses, and other public places. In many small communities the public squares are now the centers of attraction at various hours of the day because of the loud-speaker, which broadcasts world events, opera music, and lectures. Is it not clear that such an innovation must radically transform the isolated, self-sufficient villages and towns of Europe?

Of what are European programs composed? Mostly of music, as in the United States. Approximately 70 per cent of the radio programs of Great Britain are devoted to music. In the early days, 1923–1925, almost no classical music — symphonies, operas, and the like — were put on the air. Only the lightest and most trivial kind of music was presented.

Then in 1924 and thereafter came sharp changes. Even more than in the United States the public demanded good programs. The result was that more fine singing, instrumental chamber music, and orchestral and choral music were carried into the homes of the British people. As in the United States, the larger symphony orchestras now broadcast their principal performances. Thus at the present time a considerable proportion of the radio programs in Great Britain is devoted to fine music. Indeed, American experts have declared, after comparing radio programs in Great Britain with those in America, that the British programs are distinctly superior to most of the programs given here.

The People of Industrial and Democratic Countries are now Able to Read

No fact of the changing culture of Europe is more important than *the increasing ability of the people to read.* Steadily during the past 150 years literacy has spread. In the Middle Ages even many ruling kings and dukes and counts were unable to read and write. Alfred the Great of England, as you have learned, was a notable exception to the rule. In 1500 not one tenth of all the people could read. In 1700 the fraction was only a little larger. But after 1800, as machine manufacturing was taken up in the western-European countries and as democratic movements spread swiftly, the demand for education also increased. As attendance at elementary school was made compulsory for all children, more and more people learned reading, writing, and simple arithmetic.

TABLE XLI

Per Cent of Population Unable to read and write (according to Recent Censuses and Estimates)

Industrial Countries		Nonindustrial Countries	
United Kingdom	Less than 1	Spain	54
Germany	Less than 1	Russia (changing in industrialism and in literacy)	49
Japan	Less than 1	China	80
United States	6	Syria	80
France	8	India, more than	90
Belgium	9		

As a result, by 1870 about three fourths of all the people of Great Britain, France, and Germany could read and write. In Germany 90 per cent of the people were literate even as early as 1841; 97 per cent, by 1881; and 99.7 per cent, by 1895. A remarkable achievement, indeed, when we consider that even today in the United States only 94 per cent of the total population can read and write.

But note, in Table XLI, the sharp contrast between industrial and nonindustrial countries. Six industrialized countries with well-developed educational systems have almost no people unable to read and write. In five nonindustrial countries from half to nine tenths of the people are illiterate. Is it not clear that the ability to communicate with other people through reading and writing is markedly higher in the countries that have developed or are developing the new industrial civilization?

Increased Reading of Newspapers, Magazines, and Books marked the Changing Culture of Western Europeans

As industrial civilization spread from England after 1800 and as literacy increased, reading became more and more universal among the masses. As early as 1600, newspapers had been in existence in England and in western-European countries. But printing was laboriously done by hand, newspapers were expensive, and circulations were very small.[1] Then, about the middle of the 1800's, the new rotary printing presses were developed in the United States. The linotype and other machines were also invented. As these were used and improved in western Europe the manufacturing of newspapers, magazines, and books became easier and less expensive, and circulations increased. Later the use of the telegraph, the telephone, and railroad express trains increased the facilities with which news could be carried from every spot of the earth into the growing newspaper offices of European cities. The demand of the literate people for better and larger newspapers grew hand in hand with these advances in the method of gathering news.

Let us consider newspapers in the three leading industrial nations of Europe — Great Britain, France, and Germany. Circulations increased greatly in each of these countries, especially after 1875. Great metropolitan newspapers developed. In London were the London *Times*, the *Morning Post*, and the *Daily Mail*; in Paris were the *Matin*, the *Petit Journal*, the *Figaro*, the *Écho de Paris*, and the *Journal des Débats*; in Germany were the *Deutsche Allgemeine Zeitung*, the *Frankfurter Zeitung*, and the *Berliner Tageblatt*. In France, indeed, the circulation of such metropolitan newspapers as the *Petit Journal* and the *Petit Parisien* exceeded 1,000,000 before similar papers in the United States had reached such numbers.

As circulations increased, newspapers became Big Business, as the American papers had. Great chains were developed, especially after 1920. Consider, for example, the Rothermere chain of newspapers in England, which includes the *Daily Mail*, the *Evening News*, the *Sunday Dispatch*, the *Overseas Mail*, the *Daily Mirror*, and others. This chain has a total capitalization of about $35,000,000. There are also the Beaverbrook chain and the *Daily Chronicle* chain.

But the largest English chain is that of the two Berrys. This enormous concern, which owns newspapers in the larger cities and in smaller communities all over England, has a capitalization of more than $160,000,000. It controls three daily and two Sunday

[1] See Volume V, *An Introduction to Problems of American Culture*, Chap. XIV.

newspapers in London; eight morning, eight evening, and three Sunday newspapers outside of London; and fourteen weekly newspapers. In addition it controls two morning, two evening, and two weekly newspapers and one Sunday newspaper in Scotland.

In France this amalgamation of separate newspapers into great corporate chains has not developed to the same extent. In

Fig. 165. A newspaper stand in Bucharest, Rumania. The various piles of newspapers which you can see indicate that even in this comparatively small country enough people know how to read and are sufficiently interested in daily happenings to support several newspapers

1928, in Paris alone, there were 337 general newspapers and 127 sporting newspapers. In all France, outside of Paris, more than 3000 separate newspapers were published.

However, in Germany a few people tend to control the newspapers as they do in England and in the United States. One owner, Alfred Hugenberg, through his control of the ideas published in newspapers, has become almost a dictator. He supplies no fewer than 1600 journals with telegraphic news, and some of the smaller papers which are unable to maintain editorial staffs of their own he supplies with editorial matter. He also owns the leading moving-picture company and an important advertising agency.

Think of the influence over public opinion exerted in Germany by this one man and his few wealthy associates! Hugenberg controls 1600 newspapers, 150 "movie" houses, and the leading news and editorial services of the nation. Will this help the growth of democracy? Will government become really expressive of the will of the people? Will the people form their own opinions or will Hugenberg tell them what to think?

In the smaller European countries also newspapers increased, especially after 1880. Today newspapers in Belgium are published in both French and Flemish. In Brussels alone there are seventeen daily papers; in Antwerp, nine. Newspapers have also developed in the Netherlands. The eight daily newspapers in Amsterdam, the seven in the Hague, and the five in Rotterdam are distributed all over the little country.

In Austria there is a wealthy newspaper press which is concentrated in Vienna. Such leading newspapers as the *Neue Freie Presse* and the *Neues Wiener Journal* are distributed throughout Austria and much of Hungary. In Budapest, Hungary, are ten daily newspapers which have large circulations in the provinces outside the city. In Czechoslovakia newspapers developed rapidly after the World War. Every political party — and there are many of them — has its newspaper; but although freedom of the press is guaranteed by the constitution, government censorship is practiced.

The New Revolution in Outdoor Sports

Recently a schoolboy in a southern province of France was asked by a foreign traveler to tell who, in his opinion, was the greatest hero in France.

"Jean Bovet," he replied.

Who do you suppose Jean Bovet was? The champion football-player of the local school!

This little episode illustrates a revolutionary change in the attitude of European people, especially of the younger ones, toward sport. Football, bicycling, hockey, cricket, tennis, golf, and hiking are rapidly becoming popular outdoor recreations.

1. *Sports in England.* In England sport has long been a leading activity of the well-to-do. But now Playing Fields Societies for the less well-to-do are springing up in the larger communities. There are, for example, the London Playing Fields Society and the Manchester Playing Fields Society. These societies are building new grounds, providing equipment, and encouraging football, cricket, and other sports among the working classes of British cities.

The extent to which this movement has developed in the British Isles is shown by recent reports of these societies. In London, for example, there are, under the auspices of the London Playing Fields Society, "187 cricket pitches, 104 football grounds, 5 hockey grounds, and 145 lawn-tennis courts." This means that a private organization has provided playing space for more than 10,000 players. Under public auspices there are even more provisions for sports. London alone has provided playing space for tens of thousands of players.

In addition to these agencies, there is the National Playing Fields Association. This has developed football grounds, cricket, hockey, tennis, and other playgrounds in all the leading cities of England and Scotland. On these playing fields, in the late afternoon, the evening, and during week-ends, millions of young Britishers are engaging in sports.

2. *Sports in France.* In France athletic sports and games are a more recent development than in England. However, since the World War the lure of outdoor athletics and competitive games has been felt by the French people more and more. Here too, although not so well developed, are societies for athletic sports, gymnastic societies, and the like. Altogether there are more than 8000 of these, representing football, tennis, hockey, swimming, skating, cricket, gymnastics, winter sports, and rugby. Although it is difficult to estimate the total membership of these societies, it is believed that more than 500,000 people belong to them.

Thus the organized athletic and sports associations provide for a vast amount of outdoor recreation. Increasingly the younger French people spend their leisure time in sports. There is also increasing interest in bicycling, hunting, fishing, and hiking.

3. *Sports in Germany.* In Germany a great change has come since 1914 and the World War. Before that time relatively few

boys and girls engaged in outdoor sports. Students in the universities occasionally played tennis and football; they swam in summer and skated in winter. Army officers hunted and rode horseback. However, there were almost no golf courses and few tennis courts or playing fields. There was little interest in track and field athletics or in boxing. Military drill and exercise in indoor gymnasiums were the chief kinds of athletics.

But now all is changed. With great enthusiasm millions of German youth have taken up outdoor sports. Throughout Germany football fields, tennis courts, and even golf courses are being developed, and playing fields are crowded with people. So swiftly has the demand grown for physical development that almost no child is now allowed to leave school in Germany without having learned to swim.

Organizations have been started in most of the leading cities to develop playing fields. Laws are being proposed and passed providing state and national aid in securing city land for parks and playgrounds. This is necessary because, with the growth of cities, land for leisure-time activities is increasingly difficult to get. It has been estimated that more than 5,000,000 people in Germany belong to athletic organizations, more than 1,500,000 of whom are women and 2,500,000 of whom are over twenty years of age.

A fine example of German public spirit in developing municipal playgrounds is illustrated in the Frankfurt Stadium. This is a public pleasure resort, sometimes known as the "People's Versailles." In the very heart of the great city this play place provides recreation for 500,000 people. Here, surrounded by beautiful public forests, are a stadium for athletics, a swimming pool, bicycle and running tracks, and provisions for skating in winter. Here are large play spaces for little children. Here also are fine clubhouses, broad lawns on which *Turnvereine* (gymnastic clubs) go through their exercises, several football fields, a field on which handball can be played, and a large indoor gymnasium. In this way a great city provides splendidly for public recreation.

Other German cities, notably Berlin, Bremen, Hamburg, Dresden, and Leipzig, although not duplicating the Frankfurt plan, are developing municipal playgrounds of similar types.

The Youth Movement

Of all the swift changes in ways of living that have come in Western nations since the close of the World War, none is more important than the changes in the lives of young people. In our earlier studies we have already seen how these changes took

Fig. 166. A hiking club of German boys in the mountains of Switzerland. So popular has the Youth Movement become in Germany that German boys are seen hiking all over eastern and central Europe during the summer months

place in America as family life changed sharply, influenced by the automobile, the increase in the size of cities, and other phases of the New Industrial Revolution.[1]

Even more drastically than in America, the lives of the youth of Germany have been changed by the Youth Movement. This movement was really started a century ago by the wandering, or hiking, clubs that sprang up among young Germans. Throughout the 1800's there were also scattered groups of nature-lovers who spent their leisure time outdoors, away from the towns.

[1] See Volume V, *An Introduction to Problems of American Culture*, Chaps. V and VI.

But the real Youth Movement did not begin until after the World War, under the leadership of young soldiers who had returned. The terrible experiences through which these young people had passed turned them away from the hurry and artificialities of city life to the simplicity of life "close to nature." Thus they were in a sense followers of Rousseau.

Young people's societies and clubs were formed, resembling in some ways the various youth associations in this country. The members were trained in the simple life. They were urged to avoid smoking, strong drink, and heavy foods. Sports were developed and walking tours were organized. Groups of German young people tramped from place to place, living out of doors in a healthful, moral atmosphere.

Frequently these societies allied themselves with political groups; for example, one joined the socialist group, another the Protestant group, another the communist group, others the pacifist group or the Catholic group.

In 1927 a national Youth Exposition held in Berlin showed how great the development of the movement had been. For example, handicraft products made by the members of the Youth Societies were displayed — woven fabrics, metal work, and cabinetwork. The way in which interest in music, literature, the dance, and dramatics has been increased was also shown. There were samples of magazines, journals, bulletins, and books published by more than 40 houses, which, through these societies, were educating and broadening the culture of young people.

The Youth Movement has helped to revive folk-dancing as it existed in Germany prior to the coming of great factory cities. Folk-song societies have sprung up, as well as clubs for the development of simple handicrafts. Other organizations of young people have developed amateur dramatics; still others, choral singing. In these ways the Youth Movement has been influential in the rebuilding of German culture.

Thus we see that the industrial nations of Europe have come under the same changing influences as has the United States. The New Industrial Revolution in England, France, Germany, and other countries is influencing the culture of the people in many ways, as it is here. It is true that the changes are on a smaller scale than in America. There are fewer pleasure automobiles owned and driven in European countries. Fewer communities and homes are equipped with electric appliances and with the telephone. Then, too, the motion picture and the radio have not made such great inroads upon family and neighborhood life. Because, to date, these new devices are far more characteristic of American culture, this widespread change in the culture of Western peoples is increasingly called Americanization.

INTERESTING READINGS FROM WHICH YOU CAN GET ADDITIONAL INFORMATION

ADAMS, KATHARINE. Midsummer. The Macmillan Company, New York. Life in Sweden. See also the author's *Midwinter*.

BENSON, EDWARD F. David Blaize. Doubleday, Doran & Company, Inc., Garden City, New York. Also *David Blaize of King's*. Education and sports in English schools and universities.

CHARSKAYA, LIDÏYA A. The Tartar Princess. Henry Holt and Company, New York. Life in Russia.

CREW, HELEN COALE. Saturday's Children. Little, Brown and Company, Boston. Thirteen stories of European children in thirteen European cities.

HASKELL, HELEN E. Katrinka; the Story of a Russian Child (Little Schoolmate Series). E. P. Dutton & Co., New York.

MARSHALL, ARCHIBALD. Jimmie, the New Boy. Frederick A. Stokes Company, New York. Story of English school life.

WILLIAMSON, MARGARET. John and Betty's English History Visit. Lothrop, Lee & Shepard Co., Boston.

Peeps at Many Lands Series. The Macmillan Company, New York.

CHAPTER XVIII

MODERN EUROPEAN CULTURE AND THE FINE ARTS

Was Art, as well as Science, highly developed by Western Europe?

Has Europe given the world art as well as science and government? It has, indeed. During the very centuries in which scientists were inventing the new ways of thinking and applying them to manufacturing, trade, and government, artists were creating beauty, to make life more worth living.

They developed music the like of which mankind had hitherto not imagined. In literature their achievement is the equal of that of any other time and place in man's history. They learned how to build masterpieces of architecture. They carried dramatic art in the theater and in the dance far beyond the attainments of most earlier peoples.

Thus European culture is distinguished from all others by its twofold success in developing both science and art. Really to understand European culture, therefore, we must study its arts, as well as its industry, trade, and government. We turn briefly to that task now.

How Western Europe developed the World's Finest Music

The modern orchestra and its music

Today, since Western scientists have invented and made usable the radio, tens of millions of families can listen to beautiful music. No longer are such things given only to kings and nobles. The common man can now enjoy one of the finest of the arts.

Consider, first, the wonder of the modern symphony orchestra. There is no finer example of the art of western Europe. In the symphony orchestra from 50 to 100 persons play about twenty different instruments and produce very different kinds of tones. Yet all are artistically woven together by the conductor into the world's most beautiful music.

No doubt you have heard over the radio some great symphony orchestra. Study for a moment the seating plan of such an orchestra in figure 167, noting the kinds of instruments and how they are played. The score of different instruments are grouped

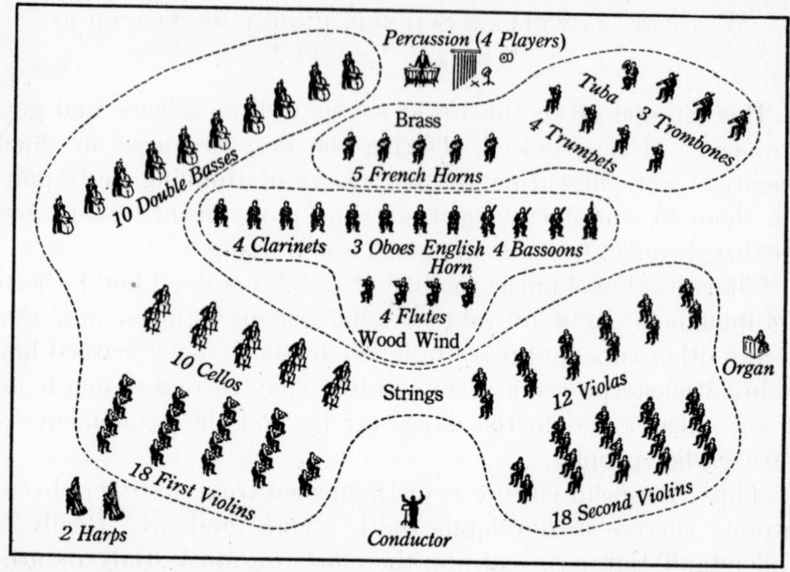

FIG. 167. Note how skillfully the various instruments of the symphony orchestra are arranged. By this arrangement the music of the loud instruments does not drown the others. To provide against this still further there are also definite ratios between the numbers of the various kinds of instruments in the orchestra

in four chief divisions. First, most of them in front, are the stringed instruments — violins, violas, violoncellos (commonly called cellos), and double-basses. Second, in the center, are the wood-wind instruments, in the form of tubes of various sizes — flutes, an English horn, clarinets, oboes, and bassoons. Third, behind and beside the wood wind, are the brass instruments — French horns, trumpets, trombones, and tubas. Fourth, at the rear, are the instruments of percussion — kettledrums (or tympani), bass drums and snare drums, cymbals, triangles, tambourines, castanets, gongs, the glockenspiel, the xylophone, the celesta, and the bells (or chimes). Often one or two harps are included in the orchestra, and sometimes even an organ.

Before such an orchestra could play for you, five difficult tasks had to be accomplished. Thousands of years of effort were necessary to achieve them. Let us note what had to be done. First, instruments had to be invented and perfected. Second, a system of writing music had to be devised. Third, musicians had to be trained to play different instruments correctly. Fourth, knowledge of harmony had to be attained — a knowledge of how to put tones together. Fifth, genius was necessary in composers who, writing for these different instruments, could create fine music.

Difficult tasks, indeed, — tasks not to be mastered in one generation or in one century. The foundation of modern music was not laid until about 1500. Back of that was a long, steady evolution covering several thousand years. In those "Dark Ages" of music a few simple, basic instruments — string, wood-wind, percussion, and brass — were invented, and the art of writing music was slowly devised. To understand later developments let us turn back a moment to this earlier period.

A Brief Glance at Music before Modern Times

The music of the earlier peoples

Music among the Egyptians, Assyrians, Hebrews, East Indians, and Chinese 3000 and 4000 years ago was primitive indeed. Their instruments were very simple. However, they knew something of all four of the principal types known today. For example, they had stringed instruments, such as the lyre and the harp (see figure 168), to which large choruses chanted and dancers danced. They had wood-wind instruments, such as flutes and "pipes"; and brasses, such as trumpets and horns. And they had many percussion instruments — drums, tom-toms, cymbals, gongs, and bells.

But remember that these instruments were not complex, as ours are today. The ancient peoples knew no such intricate and finished stringed instruments as the violin, the viola, the violoncello, or the bass viol (double-bass). They had no knowledge of the piano or of its predecessors, the clavichord and the harpsichord. They knew nothing of such wood-wind instruments as the clarinet or oboe or of such delicate percussion instruments as the kettledrums. Simplicity, even crudeness, marked their instruments.

Similarly, they knew almost nothing of harmony — that is, of putting various tones together in different arrangements. Nor did they know how to write down music. It could be passed on only directly, one person teaching another.

FIG. 168. Two ancient instruments, the lyre and harp. (Drawn from Egyptian wall paintings)

Though most of the instruments that we have named were known in one form or another to all these ancient peoples, different races had their favorite kinds. Whereas the agricultural Egyptians, for example, made greatest use of the lyre and the harp, the warlike Assyrians turned to the horns and trumpets. The Chinese were especially proficient in the making and use of percussion instruments. Perhaps the most important of these was the "king," known almost 4000 years ago. This consisted of sixteen stones hung from bamboo sticks, and was played by hitting the stones with a mallet. Combinations of large bells were also used. In India gongs and cymbals were used among the early Hindus, while religious songs were chanted to the accompaniment of the tambourine.

We see, therefore, that although musical history goes back beyond recorded history, early music was simple and undeveloped. Only the crudest of instruments and the simplest of melodies existed.

Among the Greeks music was the basis of all education

Then came that remarkable civilization of the Greek city-states, especially of Athens. The cultured people among the Greeks were very sensitive to beauty. And they made music the very basis of all education. Music meant not only the playing of instruments and singing but also the dance, poetry, and gymnastics. Indeed, they even used music in their work. It is said, for example, that while temples and other public buildings were being erected, musicians "accompanied" the workers on their lyres.

Although small contributions were made, it cannot be said that the Greeks gave much to modern music. They too used stringed instruments — the lyre and the harp — as well as simple wood wind. They developed choral singing for religious and patriotic celebrations.

Pythagoras, the mathematician and musician, devised a new instrument known as the "monochord" — a single string tightly stretched over a sounding board. In the later history of music this instrument was developed into more complicated stringed instruments. Moreover, the Greeks experimented with *writing* music. Although they lacked clear means of showing pitch and meter, they recorded melodies by writing letters of their alphabet over the words of the songs.

In this way Pythagoras and other Greeks helped to build up the *scientific* basis of music. And, as a result, even 2000 years ago advances were made in instruments, in the intellectual study of music, in choral singing, and in the use of music in connection with other activities.

For more than 1000 years the Catholic Church preserved and developed music

Centuries passed. The glory of Greece declined. Rome rose to power. In 312 A.D. the Emperor Constantine decreed that Christianity should be the religion of the entire Roman Empire. From that time on, the lives of Europeans came increasingly under the influence of the Catholic Church. The Church not only owned and governed much of Europe but was also an important factor in the preservation of world culture.

Almost from its beginning the Church encouraged singing and music. About 575, under Pope Gregory the Great, for example, a school of church singing was started, and a system of musical education was begun. Monks and priests collected melodies and wrote hymns and Masses. Trained choirs developed in Rome and in other religious centers. The festivals of the year became great musical events.

Thus from 600 to 900 music became standardized throughout the Church in Europe. But except for the primitive organs practically no advance was made in the invention of instruments.

Slowly, however, another contribution to the development of music was made through the efforts of churchmen. Men gradually learned how to write down their music. During several hundred years after 900 the staff and other forms of musical notations were invented. The pitch of a note was indicated by its position on a series of horizontal lines and by the spaces between them. In the first attempts only a single line was used, the pitch being indicated by the position of notes above or below this line. After years had passed it was suggested that two lines and the spaces between, above, and below them be used. Still later other lines were added. Thus by 1500, after an interval of 600 years, the five-line staff of today had been developed. From this we see the slowness with which ideas were originated and developed in the Middle Ages. Today, because of the speed of communication, such a process might take place in a generation.

As the years passed there were other developments, both in music itself and in the writing of music. For example, about the year 1000 a Benedictine monk, Guido of Arezzo, named six of the parts of the scale that you use in singing and reading the staff today — ut, re, mi, fa, sol, la. It is also believed that he introduced the sign *F* to represent a clef. Other students developed the idea, and our modern treble and bass clefs resulted.

Two hundred years later (about 1190), in the work of Franco of Cologne, "measured music" — music written according to meter — was developed, and in the 1200's and 1300's students invented ways of representing half-notes, quarter-notes, and eighth-notes and also of showing sharps and flats. Thus knowledge of music-writing grew, and the foundation was laid upon which modern music could rise later.

In the late 1500's a true world genius of music appeared — Giovanni Pierluigi da Palestrina, commonly called Palestrina, from the little Italian town in which he grew up. A child musical prodigy, he was choir singer and cathedral organist while he was a mere boy. Later he composed beautiful Masses, undoubtedly the greatest music of that time and perhaps the greatest Masses of all time. He wrote, in all, nearly 100 Masses, in addition to much other church music. Seven Popes of the Church ruled and died while he lived out his long life.

It is clear, then, that the history of music, like that of science, language, and literature, is a story of long, slow evolution through thousands of years.

Outside the Church, bards and troubadours also contributed to the development of music

Turn back to figure 23 and recall the wandering bards and troubadours of feudal Europe. For about 400 years — from about 900 to 1300 — these entertainers of the nobility helped to promote secular, or nonreligious, music. There were many of these minstrels, and not all of them wandered from place to place. Hardly a castle but had its private bard, and larger courts employed several. The minstrels sang of the brave adventures and great deeds of the knights, often accompanying themselves with instruments such as the lyre and the harp. This form of entertainment became so popular that even young nobles learned to play and sing.

A vast library has been written about the development of this troubadour music. Although space is lacking to describe it adequately, at least one group of these secular musicians must be mentioned — namely, the Minnesingers of the German states, lyric poets of the twelfth and thirteenth centuries.

In the fourteenth, fifteenth, and sixteenth centuries the knightly Minnesingers were replaced by the Meistersingers. The Meistersingers were poets, singers, and musicians from the rising commercial groups of the cities and towns.

The art of minstrelsy introduced three things into music: new melodies were improvised, melodies were arranged in parts, and the knowledge of harmony was advanced.

Then, after 1500, came the Invention of Modern Instruments and the Development of the Orchestra

Thus by 1500 the foundation of modern music had been laid. At the very time when modern science began its spectacular development, music also began to emerge as a great modern art. By 1500 Europeans had composed many beautiful national and regional melodies and had developed an elaborate scheme of musical notation and ways of writing down complicated music. They had learned much about harmony. Singing in groups had been highly developed, and melodies were now arranged in parts.

The basis of the new movement in music after 1500 was the invention and perfection of new musical instruments. From the early single-stringed instruments the violin, the viola, the violoncello, and the bass viol were evolved. The wood-wind instruments — for example, the clarinet and the oboe — were developed. The clavichord and the harpsichord gradually evolved into the modern piano. A great array of horns and other brasses were perfected in England, France, and Germany. Many percussion instruments were improved.

Occasional references to crude bows have been found in the early history of India. Later, primitive bows were used by the Welsh for a three-stringed fiddle and by the Moors in Spain, even before 1000, for similar instruments. But the bows with which the new stringed instruments were played were the result of nearly 300 years of work between 1500 and 1800. The modern bow, as we know it, was perfected by François Tourte just before the outbreak of the French Revolution. Tourte made such excellent bows that since his time there has been little improvement upon them.

The forerunner of modern stringed instruments themselves was the "fiedel," which was used about 1100. It was known to traveling troubadours in France, Germany, and the British Isles.

The modern violin really developed in one little community, Cremona, Italy, between 1500 and 1700. Here a few families of talented craftsmen made wonderful violins. The Amati family, for example, made violins in Cremona for nearly 150 years. Stradivarius, the greatest creative craftsman of them all, was a pupil of one of the Amatis. So great did the fame of these instrument-makers of Cremona become that the royalty and nobility of all Europe sent them commissions.

In musical-instrument making we see the finest example of a handicraft which has lasted to our own times. Here is a skill that the machine has not touched and probably can never approach. The perfect violin can be made only by human hands and eyes, guided by the artistic understanding of the true craftsman. Each instrument is a unique thing, the product of a unique

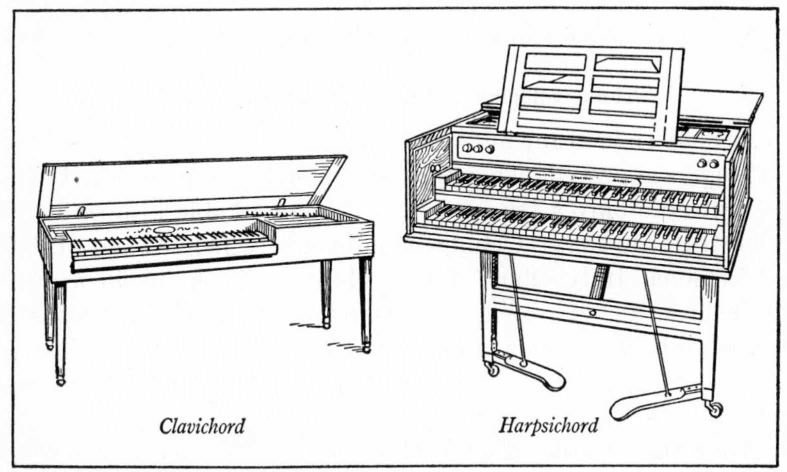

FIG. 169. The forerunners of the piano. What difference between these two instruments do you note? In what ways do they resemble the modern piano?

human personality. Each of various kinds of wood — maple, spruce, and ash — must be selected and treated with infinite care. The 60 different pieces must be put together in exactly the right way. To make a perfect violin takes time and painstaking care. In a long lifetime of work Stradivarius is said to have made not more than 1000 violins. Today each of those which are still in existence is reported to be worth $20,000 or more.

In the meantime other complicated musical instruments were developed, such as the piano. As we already know, the piano was evolved after 1500 from the clavichord and the harpsichord (see figure 169). The clavichord is believed to have grown from the monochord invented by Pythagoras. One can see how the box containing strings might slowly have become an instrument to be played by hitting keys. The harpsichord was shaped somewhat like our grand piano of today.

About 1710 an Italian, Cristofori, designed an instrument known as the pianoforte, in which the strings were struck by hammers operated by keys. This is the real beginning of the modern piano. From that time on, it was rapidly perfected, and became very popular. More and more it was used by musical geniuses. In the late 1700's and early 1800's great artists and composers on the piano appeared, such as Beethoven, Liszt, Schubert, Mendelssohn, Chopin, and Schumann, to name only a few.

The development of modern orchestral music

As modern instruments were perfected, talented composers and performers appeared. Then the modern orchestra came into being. We can note only a few names in the remarkable history of the orchestra. The first is Claudio Monteverde, who lived and worked in Cremona, Italy, about 1600. Monteverde, living in a great musical center and associating with renowned instrument-makers, composed brilliant orchestral music. He utilized about 40 instruments — the clavichord, lutes, violins, and other stringed instruments, as well as wood-wind instruments.

After Monteverde, at intervals of some years, various orchestra-leaders made variations in arrangement and in combinations of instruments and tones. Scarlatti, an Italian who lived until 1725, is remembered not only for his operas but because he first divided the violins into two groups, called first violins and second violins.

After 1700, however, most of the leaders who developed the orchestra lived in Germany. Among them were Johann Sebastian Bach (1685–1750), Georg Friedrich Händel (1685–1759), Franz Joseph Haydn (1732–1809), Wolfgang Amadeus Mozart (1756–1791), Ludwig van Beethoven (1770–1827), and Felix Mendelssohn (1809–1847). Each of these men contributed something new through astonishing orchestral compositions. Some, for example, emphasized the stringed instruments, as most of the earlier conductors had done. Others, such as Bach, made greater use of the wood-wind instruments. Händel used almost every instrument now known, even the organ and the harpsichord.

Fig. 170. Johann Sebastian Bach

A boy, scarcely in his teens, was waiting in the dark until the household should be in bed. When the last sound had died away, he crept silently toward a bookcase and, slipping his hand in, drew out a manuscript of music. Straining his eyes to see by the dim moonlight that filtered through the window, he copied from it the works of the great organists of his day. The boy was the musical genius Johann Sebastian Bach (1685–1750), whose brother, both teacher and guardian, was said to have forbidden him the use of the manuscript. At fifteen Johann became a chorister; at nineteen, an organist. He sometimes astonished and shocked the congregation by new harmonies. At twenty he wrote his first church cantata, "God is my King." At twenty-nine he was appointed chief concert master to the Duke of Weimar, and his career as a composer really began. Besides 190 church cantatas he wrote dozens of other musical compositions — concertos, sonatas, and preludes and fugues for the organ, clavier, and other instruments. Four of his sons became musicians. His triumph was complete when one of them was appointed court composer to Frederick the Great

Among the records of the household musicians of the archbishop-elector of Cologne was found the following: "Ludwig Beethoven, of good capacity, still young, of good, quiet behavior and poor." In contrast his father's record reads: "has a completely worn-out voice, has long been in service, is very poor, of fairly good behavior and married." Young Beethoven (1770–1827) entered the court orchestra when he was but fourteen years old, having begun his musical training at the age of five under his father, who was bad-tempered and frequently drunk. At thirteen he had already written three sonatas. When he was seventeen he visited Mozart, who, delighted by the boy's promise, gave him a few lessons. At 22 he moved to Vienna and for a time studied under Haydn; but, more important, he composed. By 1814 he had written many sonatas and the seventh of the symphonies which made him famous all over the musical world. His hearing began to fail, and by 1824 he could no longer hear the deafening applause which greeted him on the concert stage. He died while he was planning his tenth symphony

Fig. 171. Ludwig van Beethoven

Great advances toward the modern orchestra were made after 1800. Hector Berlioz, a Frenchman, and Richard Wagner, a German, made important contributions during this period.

The year 1813 may be remembered as the high-water mark of European music. Many composers whose names are famous today were living at this time. We find Beethoven, Weber, Meyerbeer, and Schubert in Germany; Rossini and Donizetti in Italy; Cherubini, Auber, Halévy, and Berlioz in France, to name only a few outstanding figures.

Then came Richard Wagner (1813–1883), the greatest orchestral master in all the history of music. Although he used the ideas of Berlioz and other composers, he also contributed much that was new. Around the great themes of the Minnesingers and the Meistersingers, around the Germanic folk epics of the *Nibelungenlied, Tristan and Isolde, Parsifal,* and others, he composed some of the world's greatest symphonic and operatic music.

Today there are few large cities of the modern world that do not have symphony orchestras. Through a long musical season, extending each year from November to April, the compositions of the musical geniuses we have named are played by talented musicians. These musicians are almost all Europeans; many are Germans and Italians. The genius of Germany and Italy has been especially important in the history of music and musical instruments.

Did the New Industrial Civilization contribute to this Rise of Beautiful Music?

In one sense the new industrial civilization did not contribute to the rise of music; in another it did contribute, although indirectly. On the one hand, music evolved as a great art independent of industrialism. Instrument-making, for example, is a handicraft almost untouched by power-driven machines. Although the instrument-maker uses modern improved tools, nevertheless his instrument is a handicraft product.

Similarly, almost to the present day composers have built up their music from ancient legends, from the world's great epics, poems, and plays, and from the natural beauty of nature. Indeed, the new power-driven machines, the new factory towns, and the new transportation and communication directly modified the art of music very little until 1900.

The new civilization made its great contribution indirectly. For one thing, a growing number of well-to-do upper-middle-class people of education and culture became patrons of the new music. Audiences grew larger. People demanded musicians and music-teachers. Long before 1900 most of the larger cities in Europe had organized local orchestras and choral societies, and the study of music was being introduced into the public schools of most of the Western nations. Furthermore, there can be little doubt that the development of music was inspired and stimulated very much indeed by the general advance in culture. Thus, indirectly, the new industrial civilization provided the setting for the new music.

We must remember that these famous musicians and composers lived in western Europe at the very time that the scientific and intellectual developments described in the earlier chapters of this book were taking place. The new machine civilization was being produced all about them. On every hand the new science was being discussed. It was impossible that they should not have been considerably influenced by the new ideas. The very facts that their music became more intricate and more intellectual and their use of instruments more complicated and skillful illustrate how the scientific and intellectual era of the past 200 years indirectly played an important part in the development of music.

In our day ultramodern music is developing in the new machine age

As we have seen, a new culture is now emerging in western-European countries. Each of the arts is changing sharply. Instead of copying the arts of other peoples or of other generations, artists in Europe are struggling to create original ways of expressing the new ways of living.

So it is not surprising that music, one of the most ancient of all arts, is becoming modern also. Music is now being created that is appropriate to the new industrial civilization.

Whereas the Germans and the Italians made the greatest contributions to music prior to 1870, the Russians and the French led in the development of the new modern music. Outstanding among the former were Tschaikowsky (1840–1893), Mili Balakirev (1837–1910), Modeste Moussorgsky (1839–1886), and Nikolay Rimski-Korsakov (1844–1908).

These modern Russians desired essentially to make the new Russian music express Russian life. Hence under Balakirev they composed their music around old Russian folk songs and melodies.

Rimski-Korsakov was at one time an admiral in the Russian navy. As a leader of naval bands he displayed great musical talent. Eventually he became a professor and composer of music, writing operas and symphonies around the folklore of the Russian people. Thus he succeeded in expressing in his music the characteristic rhythms and melancholy themes of the life of the Russian people.

Then came Alexander Scriabin (1871–1915) and Igor Stravinski (1882–). Scriabin was, and Stravinski is, even more modern than Rimski-Korsakov. These men and other modern musicians attempted and are attempting to reproduce the new sounds and tones of the industrial world as well as to dramatize the customs of the peasants in the villages and the workers in the cities. In doing so they have produced unique, mystic, and colorful music.

Similar experiments developed in France under the inspiration of Saint-Saëns (1835–1921), of César Franck (1822–1890), and of Maurice Ravel (1875–). New combinations of tones and harmony are being used in the effort to interpret the conditions of life in the new industrial environment. Note, for example, Arthur Honegger's "Pacific 231," an attempt to reproduce the sounds of an American locomotive hurtling through space at high speed.

This, then, is a short outline of the long story of music as it developed in Europe. By studying the slow evolution of music before 1500 one realizes the great achievements of the modern Europeans. It is clear that the European artists have produced beautiful and creative music which helps to make life in our hurrying, scientific age more worth while.

Europe's Contribution to the World's Architecture

In the buildings of a country, especially in the government buildings, libraries, museums, churches, and railway stations, we can study directly the artistic ability of a people. In the limited space at our command, therefore, let us make a quick survey of the architecture which Europe has given to the world.

The architecture — indeed, all the arts of a people — should be appropriate to their civilization

To judge the worth of a nation's architecture we must ask two very important questions.

First, are the habitations and public structures honest, original expressions of the way the people live? Do the buildings fit the true needs of the people and are they built on original designs by native artists? Or are they mere imitations of the architecture of some other country or of some other period of civilization?

For architecture to be truly appropriate to a civilization the architects must feel the spirit of the people and portray it in their buildings. Each people is unique. The Chinese people have produced a unique Chinese culture, and the Japanese a Japanese culture. Similarly, the Russians, the Germans, the French, the English, and the Spanish have produced unique cultures. Hence each nation should create an architecture appropriate to it alone. If the architects are merely imitators of other cultures, then the architectures of their countries will be found wanting.

A second question must be asked in judging the architecture of a people: Do the industrial buildings measure up satisfactorily to artistic standards of beauty? Are the various materials and parts truly appropriate to the design of the building and to the use to which that building is to be put?

We shall illustrate these two ways of judging a country's architecture in a brief study of three examples. The first is Greek architecture of more than 2000 years ago; the second is that of the Gothic cathedrals of the later Middle Ages; the third is the architecture of the industrial civilization that is predominant now in the Western world.

Three Examples of Creative Architecture in European History

1. More than 2000 years ago the Greeks developed one of the most original architectures in world history

As one reviews the architecture of ancient peoples — for example, the Aztec buildings (see figure 214), the Egyptian structures, and those of Assyria, Babylon, and the Near East — one

Fig. 172. A reconstruction of the Parthenon at Athens. (Courtesy of the Metropolitan Museum of Art)

finds occasional examples that measure up well by our simple standards. But when one comes to the Greeks, one is thrilled by many true masterpieces of building construction.

For example, study figure 172, a reproduction of the Parthenon, which is supposed to have been finished about 438 B.C. Here is a beautiful, simple building. Consider it in terms of the design and arrangement of two fundamental parts — the circular, tapering columns and the lintels laid across the top. Note how appropriately the columns are designed to hold up the massive roof and how *all* the structural parts are designed in proportion to one another. Note also the broad, easy approach to the building, the wide mounting steps, and the unified appearance of the whole structure. Even the decoration, which some critics find a little overdone, is essentially a real part of the building.

To understand the true beauty of this sort of building, contrast it with the building in figure 173. In the latter there is no single plan of design from the base to the roof; the whole structure is a mixed-up combination of several types of architecture. Note the hodgepodge of lines. Several kinds of arches are used on the second story, and differing proportions of window arrangement on the third. Superimposed on the whole is a conglomeration of ornament and design. Columns tacked on the outside plainly hold up nothing. Projecting balconies and curious designs of iron latticework are put on with no thought of symmetry.

What a contrast between these two buildings! How much more beautiful is the simple Greek plan! Indeed, for 2000 years these remarkable Greek buildings have been models of inspiration to the world. It is distressing to record, however, that most of the architects who came after the Greeks copied their designs indiscriminately instead of being inspired by them to create new buildings appropriate to their own times and to their own cultures.

2. The great Gothic cathedrals of the Middle Ages

For our second great example of creative architecture we must pass over 1000 years of the Middle Ages until we come to the Gothic cathedrals. No more appropriate buildings have ever been designed and constructed in perfect harmony of stone, brick, wood, and glass (see figures 49 and 50).

Lacking the steel and reënforced concrete which twentieth-century builders have at their command, the architects of the Middle Ages were forced to design new forms of construction before they could build high buildings. The two principal things which they designed to meet this need were the Gothic arch and the flying buttress. With the aid of this arch and the flying buttress to reënforce the massive walls, they were able to build to far greater heights than would otherwise have been possible.

But, besides the architects, other artists contributed to these cathedrals. Workers in glass, marble, and stone made stained-glass windows and sculptured ornaments appropriate to the buildings. Thus the Gothic cathedral at its best became a marvelous unity of massive strength and exquisite beauty of color and design.

Then, in the 1800's, came the new industrial civilization, but little creative architecture

We have no space in which to tell the struggle of men in the developing Western nations to produce characteristic styles of architecture. Each country — England, France, Germany, and Italy, for example — built houses for its families and larger structures for public uses. Each produced characteristic designs. Occasional examples of rare beauty in building can be found, but no great new form of architecture developed in all the period from about 1500 to about 1900.

FIG. 173. The Crédit Suisse, a bank built in Geneva, Switzerland, in the 1800's. (From Sheldon Cheney's *The New World Architecture*, published by Longmans, Green & Co.)

While industrialism swept onward through western Europe, architecture continued to be a mixture of designs copied from other buildings. This is plainly shown in figure 173. In England, France, and other European countries architects continued to combine various kinds of construction in making one building. They did not create structures which were in themselves simple, unified expressions of beauty and of the new civilization.

3. But in the 1900's a new creative architecture emerged

Then, just before 1900, a new school of architecture was born. A few great creative artists appeared who sensed what the Greeks and the medieval church-builders had achieved. They saw that the buildings of a people must honestly portray the life of that people. They realized that the designs must be original and appropriate to the ways in which buildings were to be used. They saw that each building must have unity and must not be a mixture of unrelated things thrown together. As a result they began to produce honest and creative architecture. A new world order had come, and at last a new world architecture arose appropriate to it.

Thus after 1900 a new architecture began to appear in Europe, especially in Germany. Note that simplicity of line was developing, as shown in figure 175, the Tietz Department Store, Düsseldorf, Germany, built in 1908. It lacks the tremendous height of our American skyscrapers, but there is an appropriateness, a simplicity, and a true unity that are utterly lacking in most of the buildings of the 1800's. So it was that even before the World War a new architecture was appearing in the Western world.

Fig. 174. The model for the new Crédit Suisse. (Maurice Turrettini, architect. From Sheldon Cheney's *The New World Architecture*, published by Longmans, Green & Co.)

Look at figures 173 and 174, which show the nineteenth-century Crédit Suisse building in Geneva, Switzerland, and the model for the new building. These figures show clearly the contrast between the two types of architecture — the one imitative, a mixture of many styles and designs, essentially an ugly thing; the other as simple and unified as a Greek temple.[1]

Let us turn now to a very brief review of the development of modern writing.

[1] No school should be without Sheldon Cheney's *New World Architecture* (Longmans, Green & Co., New York, 1930). This book stands alone in its assembly of examples of the modern architecture now developing in various Western countries.

Literature in Western Europe since 1700

1. *England's great contributions to modern literature.* The first really new contribution of Europeans to literature after 1700 was the novel. This form of writing, developed largely under the influence of English writers, was comparatively new to the world. It is true that short tales had been produced several hundred years before by Boccaccio and others, but the novel, as we know it, had not been developed.

Fig. 175. The Tietz Department Store, Düsseldorf, Germany. (Courtesy of the German Tourist Information Office)

Several authorities regard *Robinson Crusoe,* by Daniel Defoe (*ca.* 1661–1731), as the first real novel. This book obtained international and historic renown. It has been translated into most known languages and has been read by millions of young people throughout the world. Other authorities consider Samuel Richardson (1689–1761) to be "the father of the English novel." In 1740 appeared Richardson's *Pamela, or Virtue Rewarded*; in 1748, *Clarissa, or the History of a Young Lady.* Richardson, a typical moralist of his times, used the novel to teach how the passions "move at the command of virtue."

During the same decade there appeared an even greater writer of novels, Henry Fielding (1707–1754). In 1742, stimulated by Richardson's *Pamela,* he published *Joseph Andrews.* Then, in 1749, came a book which attained international renown — *The History of Tom Jones, a Foundling.* In this story of England in the middle of the eighteenth century we find the modern novel assuming shape.

In the early part of the nineteenth century appeared the novels of Jane Austen (1775–1817) and Sir Walter Scott (1771–1832). Jane Austen, in such novels as *Sense and Sensibility* and *Pride and Prejudice,* wrote simple stories which were a true reflection of English life. Sir Walter Scott, on the other hand, was the supreme writer of romances. Scott produced 32 novels, two thirds of which deal with Scottish scenes and themes. Many are historical, although very inaccurate from the standpoint of modern scientific scholarship. Among them are *Waverley* (1814), *Guy Mannering* (1815), *Rob Roy* (1817), and *Ivanhoe* (1819), which every schoolboy and schoolgirl knows. Scott certainly accomplished what he himself wanted to do. He said that he would be repaid if his

> scenes . . . have sufficient interest in them to assuage in one corner the pain of the body; in another to relieve anxiety of mind; in a third place to unwrinkle a brow bent with the furrows of daily toil; in another to fill the place of bad thoughts or to suggest better; in yet another to induce an idler to study the history of his country; [in brief] . . . . to furnish harmless amusement.

In the later 1800's came other important novelists. Charles Dickens (1812–1870) wrote such novels as the *Pickwick Papers, Oliver Twist, David Copperfield,* and *A Tale of Two Cities.* William Makepeace Thackeray (1811–1863) produced *Vanity Fair, Pendennis, The Newcomes,* and other novels. Famous among the women novelists were the sisters Charlotte Brontë (1816–1855) and Emily Brontë (1818–1848). Charlotte's masterpiece was *Jane Eyre,* in which for the first time the heroine of a novel was both homely and poor. Emily is remembered by *Wuthering Heights.* Mary Ann Evans (1819–1880), who wrote as "George Eliot," is known all over the world for such novels as *Adam Bede, Romola, Silas Marner,* and *Middlemarch.*

We must turn from the novel to less unique forms of literature that developed in England from 1700 to the end of the nineteenth century. Joseph Addison (1672–1719) and Richard Steele (1672–1729) wrote essays on the life and manners of the time in two newspapers called *The Tatler* and *The Spectator.*

Samuel Johnson (1709–1784), the outstanding literary figure of the eighteenth century, is remembered because of his striking personality rather than because of his literary work. Like Addison and Steele, Johnson wrote essays in a publication called *The Rambler*. Although Johnson is mentioned here as an essayist, it must be kept in mind that he wrote also poetry, a novel, and his famous *Dictionary*.

Three more really important essayists stand out in the remarkable literary group that developed in England in the 1800's: Thomas Carlyle (1795–1881), Thomas Macaulay (1800–1859), and John Ruskin (1819–1900). All three wrote critical essays

FIG. 176. Sir Walter Scott

FIG. 177. Thomas Carlyle

and history. Carlyle will live long in literature for his searching studies of the new industrial civilization and for his historical studies. Sometime you should read his *French Revolution*, *Sartor Resartus*, *Past and Present*, and *History of Frederick the Great*. Thomas Macaulay's *History of England* is a classic, as is John Ruskin's great work *Modern Painters*.

England produced also great poets. In the 1700's Alexander Pope (1688–1744), "one of the greatest versifiers of all ages," wrote his *Essay on Man*, and Thomas Gray wrote his "Elegy written in a Country Churchyard." A little later Robert Burns (1759–1796), the greatest of Scottish poets, wrote such well-known works as "Tam o' Shanter" and "The Cotter's Saturday Night."

Many of his poems have been set to music. Who does not know such songs as "John Anderson, My Jo" and "Auld Lang Syne"?

In the 1800's came several important poets. William Wordsworth (1770–1850) is famous for "Tintern Abbey" and "Intimations of Immortality." Samuel Taylor Coleridge (1772–1834) is known to every school child for his "Rime of the Ancient Mariner." William Blake (1757–1827) not only wrote poetry — for example, *Songs of Innocence* — but was also an engraver and a painter.

One of the figures in this period, interesting both for his poetry and for his personality, was George Gordon, Lord Byron (1788–1824). Byron's *Childe Harold's Pilgrimage* "lifted him into a dazzling fame in a single day." His long epic, *Don Juan*, is now equally famous.

Among the great singers of the world you must remember Percy Bysshe Shelley (1792–1822) and John Keats (1795–1821). They both made great contributions to English poetry — Shelley with "To a Skylark," "Adonais," and *Prometheus Unbound*, and Keats with "The Eve of St. Agnes," "Ode on a Grecian Urn," and *Endymion*, to mention only a few of their greatest poems.

Two other poets must be mentioned: Alfred Tennyson (1809–1892), whose *In Memoriam* and *Idylls of the King* are read in many high schools today, and another famous Victorian, Robert Browning (1812–1889), who is known for such poems (among others) as "The Pied Piper of Hamelin" and *The Ring and the Book*, and for such a play (really a dramatic poem) as *Pippa Passes*.

2. *Great French writers.* While Englishmen were making their contributions to poetry and prose, Frenchmen were doing likewise. We have already seen how Voltaire, Montesquieu, Rousseau, and Diderot helped to bring about the French Revolution.[1]

Then, in the early 1800's, came the two supreme novelists of France, Alexandre Dumas the Elder (1802–1870) and Victor Hugo (1802–1885).

If you consider Walter Scott, with his 30-odd novels, a mighty worker, what about Alexandre Dumas, with his reputed 300

[1] See Chapter VIII.

closely printed volumes! Although the writer of many plays, he is remembered especially for his historical novels and for such adventurous characters as D'Artagnan, in the famous *Three Musketeers*. Other well-known books by him are *Twenty Years After* and *The Count of Monte Cristo*.

Victor Hugo, the outstanding figure in the French literature of that period, was both poet and novelist. There has never been a greater French lyric poet than he. You probably know his novels better; for example, *Les Misérables*, *Notre-Dame de Paris*, and *Les Travailleurs de la Mer*.

Another French writer, Honoré de Balzac (1799–1850), planned a series of 150 novels to be known collectively as *The Human Comedy*. Although many were never written, he succeeded by prodigious work in producing a vast list. Many are widely read today; for example, *Le Père Goriot*, *La Peau de Chagrin*, *Le Curé de Tours*, and *Eugénie Grandet*.

One French woman of the 1800's achieved a place as a creative writer, — Amantine Lucile Aurore Dudevant (born Dupin) (1804–1876), who wrote under the pen name of "George Sand." Among her works are *Indiana* and *The Devil's Pool*.

3. *A great German, Johann Wolfgang Goethe (1749–1832)*. If the German people had produced no other great men of letters than this one—Goethe—they would have made an enduring contribution to the world's literature. There were, of course, others: Johann Christoph Friedrich von Schiller (1759–1805), poet and dramatist, author of *William Tell* and other great plays, and Gotthold Ephraim Lessing (1729–1781), writer of an essay, *Laokoon* (one of the most important books in the language), besides several plays. Even in so brief an account as this, one should not fail to mention the poet Heinrich Heine (1797–1856), whose beautiful lyrics have probably been more widely read abroad than any other German literary product of the nineteenth century.

But Goethe was, perhaps, the greatest mind of the nineteenth century. A great critic of his own age regarded him as "Europe's sagest head." Great he was, indeed. The most famous of his works is, of course, *Faust*, on which he wrote for 58 years. Another of his better-known works is *Wilhelm Meister*, the product of 52 years of work.

FIG. 178. Émile Zola

Early in October, 1902, more than 30,000 people in Paris followed the hearse containing the body of Émile Zola (1840–1902), critic, novelist, and defender of the downtrodden. In Paris, amid the most frightful poverty, Zola began to write. His work held little promise at first; but in 1867 his second novel, *Thérèse Raquin*, created a real stir in the literary world. Then he began his monumental cycle of twenty novels, in which more than 1200 characters appear, each based on painstaking observation of the places each of them "would inhabit, the air he would breathe, his daily life, down to the most trivial occupation." In 1894 Dreyfus, a young French officer accused of betraying his country, was sentenced to prison, and in 1898 Zola, convinced of his innocence, wrote a scathing denunciation of those who had withheld important information bearing on the case. For this Zola was put on trial and condemned. He fled to England, but was afterwards able to return. A few years later he died. His friend Maupassant asked: ". . . who fought more furiously for his ideas? Who attacked more violently what he believed to be unjust and false? Who triumphed more brilliantly, first over indifference and then the hesitant resistance of the vast public?"

The life of Johann Wolfgang von Goethe (1749–1832) had its real beginning in 1770, when he met Johann Herder, poet and philosopher. Through Herder he learned the meaning of Gothic architecture (which he already loved), was introduced to the works of Shakespeare, and was shown the beauty which lay in German folk songs. To Herder's influence and Goethe's love for the daughter of a village pastor we owe the early inspiration which made Goethe the greatest of the German poets. Exquisite lyrics began to flow from his pen, and in *Götz von Berlichingen*, his first important drama, Goethe introduced to the German stage the Shakespearean form of drama, which gained immediate popularity in Germany. From then on he wrote poetry, into which he put all his emotions, his experience, and the result of his thinking. In *Hermann und Dorothea* we have one of the most beautiful poems ever written, and in *Faust* a drama in poetry that has made his name immortal. His poetry is rich because of his interest in so many phases of life. He was a lawyer, he studied art and political economy, and he wrote a few important scientific works. We can say of him, as did Napoleon Bonaparte, "Here is a man"

FIG. 179. Johann Wolfgang von Goethe

How Drama became One of the Fine Arts

It is spring in Athens in the year 535 B. C. The whole population is moving toward the Acropolis, near which Pisistratus, who governs the city, has recently laid out a great new theater. Here the festival of the god Dionysus is to take place. Citizens, women, children, and slaves are all moving toward the great bowl which lies at the foot of the hill. This theater is not a building like the modern homes of the drama. It is a circle of earth, well tamped down, in which there is plenty of room for the participants to dance. Where the hill begins to slope upward, tiers of seats surrounding about two thirds of the circle have been placed to accommodate the audience.

For years these festivals of singing and dancing have taken place, but today something new is to be added. Thespis has written a drama which calls for a leader of the chorus and for an *actor* who will impersonate several characters. The audience is all agog with excitement.

The actor appears in the circle. He wears a different mask for each character he plays, and he and the leader of the chorus carry on the dialogue, which has been written in the form of poetry. This part of the program is very short, but the day has seen the first recorded actor and the first recorded drama. It is the birthday of a new art.

We have no record of Thespis's play. We merely know that it was a tragedy and that it must have appealed to the popular taste, for it was soon followed by others. Out of a host of these Greek dramatists the names of Æschylus, Sophocles, Euripides, and Aristophanes come down to us as writers of tragedies and comedies for the Dionysiac festivals. Aristophanes stands above all others as master of the classic comedy — Aristophanes, who dared to make fun of Socrates, the grave, dumpy philosopher, through an impersonation which showed the little man suspended in a basket between heaven and earth.

Under these Grecian dramatists tragedy and comedy began to take on plot, and they improved and modified the model which Thespis had given them. More actors were added, and the chorus became larger and better trained, though less important. The play itself began to deal less with the gods. Then the Greek theater spread to Rome, where it became even less religious in character.

During the early Christian Era the theater became so corrupt that the Catholic Church finally decided to suppress it. But the

FIG. 180. The performance of a religious play during the Middle Ages. The stage was part of a vehicle which carried the players and their properties from place to place. (From Thomas Sharp's *Dissertation on the Pageants or Dramatic Mysteries anciently performed at Coventry*, 1825)

spirit which made the festivals popular could not be suppressed. Wealthy lords attached actors to their households for entertainment, and the people still celebrated their festivals in dance. Finally the Church wisely permitted certain forms of drama — miracle plays and mystery plays based on stories from the Bible or on the lives of the early saints and martyrs. In medieval Europe even the churches and cathedrals in the cities were used as places in which to present the plays. Traveling troupes also acted these religious plays in the small towns, often using their carts as stages.

In Italy, at the beginning of the Renaissance in the 1300's, however, there was a revival of Greek and Roman plays, and new theaters were built on old Greco-Roman models. Thus the drama again found a permanent roof over its head. As kings, dukes, and lords became patrons of the art, stages, drop curtains, and scenery were added, and more attention was given to costumes. New playwrights appeared, and comedy became especially popular.

Into France, Spain, the "Germanies," and England the revived and renewed art of Italy spread. At first Italian companies were imported into these countries, but soon local companies began to be formed. The theater was slow in coming, however, and performances were often given in the tavern yards. When Elizabeth became queen of England in 1558, there was not a single theater in London, and by 1600 there was only one in Paris. Yet the next 50 years saw theaters springing up all over Europe.

Between the late 1500's and the end of the 1600's we find such names among the playwrights of Europe as the following: Cervantes and Lope de Vega in Spain; Corneille, Racine, and Jean Baptiste Poquelin (whom you already know under his stage name of "Molière") in France; and William Shakespeare, John Dryden, and Christopher Marlowe in England. Hundreds of others were writing for the European stage; but in these playwrights the drama of their day reached its height, and in Shakespeare it has never been surpassed.

Germany lagged behind the other important European countries in original drama as she did in government, but she was the first country outside England to recognize the worth of Shakespeare by making his plays a "national pastime." Gotthold Ephraim Lessing was Germany's first playwright of prominence, and Johann Wolfgang Goethe, who followed him, "remains even today the latest in the list of unquestioned world geniuses in the field of stage literature." Johann Christoph Friedrich von Schiller is best known for the last play he wrote, *William Tell.* Another of his better-known plays is the trilogy of *Wallenstein.*

In spite of one setback after another through the 1600's and 1700's, due to the Puritan influence and the general unrest in Europe, the theater, the drama, and acting continued to improve. Stages were now lighted by candles, and machinery for shifting scenery was introduced. The theater was roofed over, and the auditorium became horseshoe in shape. In Puritan England, however, actors were classed as vagabonds, and it was charged that the theater emptied the pews of churches and led to idleness, and even that it was the cause of the great plague! In 1642 the playhouses were all closed by law and were not opened again until after the Restoration.

By this time another change had taken place — women had entered the field of acting. Before this young boys had taken the female parts; but now we find, during the late 1600's and the 1700's, besides the names of such prominent male actors as David Garrick, Thomas Betterton, Colley Cibber, and Barton Booth, the names of Nell Gwyn, Peg Woffington, and Kitty Clive. In France, also, Adrienne Lecouvreur was "living" each part she played and was pleading for more sincerity, more naturalness, on the stage.

Until the late 1800's plays were largely of two kinds — sentimental comedy and heroic tragedy. Among the first class such plays as *She Stoops to Conquer*, by Oliver Goldsmith (1728–1774), and *The School for Scandal*, by Richard Brinsley Sheridan (1751–1816), have achieved lasting fame.

In the 1800's democracy was in the air. People were more concerned in experimenting with new forms of government than in experimenting with new forms of art. Until late in the century, therefore, we find no names comparable to those of the great dramatists who had "made" the theater. However, in most of the European capitals were theaters supported by the government. These theaters were overornamented; the stages were overcrowded with scenery and properties. Regal pomp prevailed. In order to compete with them, privately owned theaters followed their lead. The theater became a world of make-believe which had no relation to life itself.

After the middle of the 1800's, in many European countries, actors began to break down the rules set by earlier forms of acting and to bring realism into their art. In Italy there were Adelaide Ristori (1822–1906), Tommaso Salvini (1829–1915), and Eleonora Duse (1859–1924); in France, Rachel (1821–1858), Sarah Bernhardt (1845–1923), Benoît Coquelin (1841–1909), and Gabrielle Réjane (1857–1920); in England, Henry Irving (1838–1905) and Ellen Terry (1848–1928).

Dramatists, too, protested against "fictitious morals and fictitious good conduct, shedding fictitious glory on robbery, starvation, disease, crime, drink, war, cruelty, cupidity," and began to inject truth, as they saw it, into their plays.

Fig. 181. Sarah Bernhardt

The earliest of the great realists was Henrik Ibsen (1828–1906) of Norway. Following his lead were George Bernard Shaw (1856–) of England, Eugène Brieux (1858–) of France, Anton Chekhov (1860–1904) of Russia, and Arthur Schnitzler (1862–1931) of Austria. By this time much of the earlier artificiality had already been dropped; that is, plays were no longer written in poetic form, and Indian princes were not portrayed in the French costumes of the time of Louis XIV. But this was not enough. These dramatists felt that plays should be made out of life; that their characters must dress, speak, and act as they would in real life.

The fight for realism affected the theater itself. Showy, wasteful buildings began to give way to simpler, more honest expressions of architecture. Under such leaders of design as Adolphe Appia, Gordon Craig, and Max Reinhardt simplicity and beauty enhanced by perfect lighting of the stage began to accompany the production of plays.

And still another movement was put on foot. Groups of professional and amateur actors began to form all over Europe.

These groups upheld the pioneers of realism and simplicity and waged a war on the commercialized theater with productions so expensive that the common man could not patronize the drama.

In France, as early as 1887, André Antoine, a clerk in a gas company, pushed properties and scenery through the streets of Paris in a little handcart toward the garret which he had hired as a theater and which later became the famous Théâtre Libre. In the same city, before the World War, Jacques Copeau opened the Théâtre du Vieux Colombier and began to develop new methods of stagecraft, encouraging playwrights who were experimenting with the new techniques.

Led by France, Germany established the *Freihe Bühne* (Free Theater) and the *Volksbühne* (People's Theater). The latter is owned by the subscribers, and excellent plays can be seen for very little money.

In Russia, in 1895, the Moscow Art Theater was founded by Danchenko and Stanislavski to give expression to the thoughts of the younger generation of Russia — to their aims and their criticism of life. The founders said, "We declare war on all the conventionalities of the theater wherever they might occur — in the acting, the properties, the scenery, or the interpretation of the play." This declaration of war gave the world the plays of Chekhov, who, until then, had found no means of producing the kind of plays which he felt to be "true."

In Ireland, before the World War, the Irish Players were organized. Under their encouragement J. M. Synge wrote *Riders to the Sea* and *The Playboy of the Western World,* portraying the life of the Irish people and, through brilliant satire, pointing out their weaknesses.

In the suburbs of London other groups formed. At Barnes, for instance, a vacant moving-picture house was converted into a theater by Philip Ridgeway. Under the direction of Komisarjevsky of the Moscow Art Theater, with the simplest of properties, stage, and scenery, some of Chekhov's plays in translated form rivaled anything being played in England at the time.

Encouraged by these successes other "free" theaters are springing up all over Europe. Today the new movement is bringing about reforms in the art of the drama all over the world.

In this short sketch of the drama much has been omitted. We see, however, that the drama has a three-thousand-year history, that it has departed long since from its religious character, but that even today in Europe the play, the acting, the stage setting, the very theater itself, are still undergoing change. Perhaps in all Europe we may look toward Russia and Germany for the theater of the future — a real "art of the drama."

Painting and Sculpture

In Chapter VI we learned that from the 1200's through the 1600's the arts of Europe were slowly reborn. It was between these years that such masters as Giotto, Dürer, Rubens, Van Dyck, Rembrandt, El Greco, Velásquez, and Murillo gave the world new forms and new techniques in painting and sculpture.

During the 1700's and early 1800's few names were worthy of a place beside them. Spain, however, produced its Goya (1746–1828), who carried on the tradition of Velásquez. France produced its François Boucher (1703–1770) and Jean Greuze (1725–1805), who portrayed the artificial grace of French aristocratic life, and Jacques David (1748–1825), who painted epics of history in heroic style on great canvases — *Marat murdered in his Bath*, the *Coronation of Napoleon*, etc. In England the Puritan influence still found expression in Hogarth, in such moral tales on canvas as *The Rake's Progress* and *Marriage à la Mode*. In figure 89 we have already seen his portrayal of the political corruption of his day. But in Joseph Turner (1775–1851) we see again an experimentalist, trying new color effects, — catching rainbow colors to put into his skies, using mist to soften harsh outlines, — and in William Blake we see another — a mystic, translating poetry of depth and power onto canvas.

Only these last two had really freed themselves from the traditions. But the revolt which was making itself felt in the other arts was spreading to painting as well. Even sculpture, which was still working from classic models (Perseus, Venus, Cupid, Psyche), began to feel the need for expansion, for new expression, for truth — truth that would produce *emotion* through the eye of the beholder.

In France, Eugène Delacroix (1798–1863) combined a well-developed mind with artistic skill. Disdaining the somber colors used by his contemporaries, he flooded his canvases with light and bright colors and used his brain to give dramatic meaning to his great historical paintings. So different was his work from others that when he exhibited *The Massacre of Chios* a respected painter of the older school called it "The Massacre of Painting." Delacroix said, "I became the abomination of painting. . . . I was [therefore] enchanted with myself."

Other French revolutionaries, such as Honoré Daumier (1808–1879) and François Millet (1814–1875), breaking away from the classic school, found romance in the life of their time and their people. They, however, did not depart as far from the standard of their day as did a group of young artists who met frequently at one of the cafés in Paris to discuss their theories. The eldest of this group was Édouard Manet (1832–1883). Others were Hilaire Degas (1834–1917), Paul Cézanne (1839–1906), Claude Monet (1840–1926), Berthe Morisot (1840–1895), who is credited with being the most original painter of her sex, and Pierre Renoir (1841–1919). They were popularly dubbed Impressionists. Of them all only Monet was truly and solely an impressionist. He *suggested* a fleeting mood or scene on canvas, permitting the imagination to fill in the minute details. Monet boldly challenged the world of art to use its eyes. In essence he said: "The leaves of that small tree we *know* are green; but see how the shadow which the hill sheds upon them makes them *look* blue to us. Paint the leaves blue, therefore,— paint what you *see*."

Cézanne adopted the principle laid down by Monet, but he attained greater strength through almost primitive simplicity of design. To Monet and to Cézanne modern art owes a great debt.

Paul Gauguin (1848–1903) also turned to the primitive for his inspiration, but he carried his idea farther, even using primitive people and primitive surroundings in his pictures.

In our day Henri Matisse (1869–   ) horrified the world of art by the use of distortion in drawing to gain certain effects, and the Spaniard Pablo Picasso (1881–   ), the founder of cubism, created an equal sensation not so many years ago. In launching the new movement Picasso discarded the natural form of a thing and replaced it by a symbolic representation of what the thing stood for. For example, if the cubist wished to paint a bustling industrial city he might show a confused mass of conflicting lines and a maze of colors which seemed to whirl. Thus the spirit of a thing rather than the photographic representation of it is the aim of this late school.

FIG. 182. A painting by Matisse. Note particularly the face, where distortion has been used for effect

Many schools of painting have grown up in Europe since the turn of our century — naturalism, cubism, futurism, Dadaism, and others. Their final value cannot yet even be prophesied, but the experiments all illustrate a groping toward truth.

Sculpture too has witnessed changes since Auguste Rodin (1840–1917) broke away from the classicists of France and sought to give natural, unidealized form and simple mass treatment to his sculpture. Like European painting, European sculpture today is also groping for new expressions that will be strong, simple, and true, and out of it are coming all sorts of forms — forms still as close to the classical as figure 183 and as far from anything before produced as that shown in figure 184.

THE ART OF DANCING

The dance is far older than painting or sculpture, the theater or literature — older even than music. Through the story of the drama you already know the important part dancing played in the ancient days. Long after the drama had been established every tragedy ended with a dance. Dancing as an art owes much of its life to the theater and to opera.

The ballet — that is, the pantomimic dance which tells a story — is the highest form of the art. About 1900 every important European city in which opera was given had its own opera house

FIG. 183. This sculptured portrait of a woman shows the work of one modern school. It is so faithful to life that it is almost photographic. Is it not the face that interests you, rather than the woman's characteristics? (From a bronze by Charles Despiau. Courtesy of the Weyhe Gallery, New York)

FIG. 184. This sculptured portrait of a woman represents the work of another modern school. The artist is not trying to make a photographic likeness. He is trying to tell what he thinks the woman's characteristics are. (From a bronze by Pablo Picasso. Courtesy of the Weyhe Gallery, New York)

and its own school of ballet. In these schools young boys and girls entered at a very early age to receive their training. For instance, Anna Pavlova (1885–1930), whose grace and charm on the stage has perhaps never been surpassed, began her training at the Royal Opera House at Moscow when she was ten years of age.

By 1900 many conventions had grown up around the ballet. Dancers spent long and painful hours learning to dance on the tips of their toes. Clothes were tight and impeded free motion. Whatever was old was right; anything that was new was incorrect. Artificiality and bodily stiffness hampered every natural movement.

Then, in the first decade of the 1900's, an American woman appeared on the stage of Europe, — a woman with a theory of dancing so old that it was new. She was Isadora Duncan (1878–1927). She drew her inspiration from nature and from ancient Greece — from the movement of the wind, the birds, and the trees, and from the classic poses revealed by Grecian vases, where the body, freed of close-fitting clothes, assumed a natural grace. She had looked on all these, and she saw in them natural rhythms. She applied what she saw and produced a new classic form of dancing. The Russian ballet adopted some of her theories, and the blend of these two forms of dancing produced something which was finer than either of them had been. In Michel Fokine, Tamara Karsavina, and Anna Pavlova of the Russian ballet the new art was brought to perfection, and it spread rapidly to other countries of Europe.

Fig. 185. Anna Pavlova, whose dancing typified the best of the older school of Russian ballet

Other members of the Russian ballet, such as Vaslav Nijinsky, were influenced by Jacques Dalcroze. Dalcroze, a Swiss, worked out a theory of the harmony of mind and body — eurythmics. Dalcroze's ideas found their way to Germany, where a new school of dancing grew up under Rudolf von Laban. Von Laban inspired his pupils to creative effort, and from this work have come such unique interpretative dances as, for example, those given by Mary Wigman. In the meantime Isadora Duncan's sister, Elizabeth, carried on the dancer's ideas in a stimulating school for the dance which she established in Germany and Austria. The influence of this school has already spread to France, the United States, and other countries.

Still other dancers, like Harald Kreutzberg of the State Opera House in Berlin, see merit in both the older and newer schools. However, the stiff poses of the older ballet are gradually giving way to flowing movement in which the whole body is in rhythmic harmony.

FIG. 186. Isadora Duncan

Thus we have seen that while scientists and inventors were producing clever machines and changing Western civilization with them, and while other frontier thinkers were developing new experiments in government, sensitive musicians, architects, poets, novelists, painters, sculptors, and dancers were producing startling changes in their arts. There can be no doubt that in the fine arts, as well as in science, industry, and government, Europe made a great new contribution to the world.

INTERESTING READINGS FROM WHICH YOU CAN GET ADDITIONAL INFORMATION

AUSLANDER, JOSEPH, and HILL, FRANK ERNEST. The Winged Horse: the Story of Poets and Poetry. Doubleday, Doran & Company, Inc., Garden City, New York.

BAUER, MARION, and PEYSER, ETHEL. How Music Grew from Prehistoric Times to the Present Day. G. P. Putnam's Sons, New York.

BROWER, HARRIETTE MOORE. Story-Lives of Master Musicians. Frederick A. Stokes Company, New York.

CATHER, KATHERINE D. Boyhood Stories of Famous Men. The Century Co., New York. Includes Mozart, Chopin, Stradivarius, and Mendelssohn.

CATHER, KATHERINE D. Younger Days of Famous Writers. The Century Co., New York.

CHENEY, SHELDON. The New World Architecture. Longmans, Green & Co., New York. Very valuable.

CONWAY, E. A. and SIR W. M. The Book of Art for Young People. The Macmillan Company, New York.

LAPRADE, ERNEST. Alice in Orchestralia. Doubleday, Doran & Company, Inc., Garden City, New York. All about the modern symphony orchestra.

MACY, JOHN. The Story of the World's Literature. Horace Liveright, New York.

MARSHALL, HENRIETTA E. English Literature for Boys and Girls. Frederick A. Stokes Company, New York.

WHITCOMB, IDA PRENTICE. Young People's Story of Art. Dodd, Mead & Company, New York.

WHITCOMB, IDA PRENTICE. Young People's Story of Music. Dodd, Mead & Company, New York.

UNIT VIII

THE SPREAD OF EUROPEAN CIVILIZATION AROUND THE WORLD

THE SPREAD OF EUROPEAN CIVILIZATION AROUND THE WORLD

With Unit VIII we turn from the study of the changing governments and cultures of Europe to a similar study in Asia and other parts of the world. Between 1800 and the outbreak of the World War the industrial nations Europeanized the earth. They introduced their machines, railroads, telegraphs, and business methods into every continent. We have already learned how the economic life of people was changed by trade with England, France, Germany, and other countries. Now in Unit VIII we shall see how government and culture in general changed in these same regions as European modes of living were imposed upon them.

In Chapter XIX we shall sum up what we have already learned about the geography of Asia and the contrast between the several civilizations of Europe and the agricultural-handicraft civilizations of the Far East. This will prepare the way for the study of the changing cultures of China, Japan, and India.

In Chapter XX we shall witness the collapse of the world's oldest and largest civilization, that of China. In Chapter XXI we shall see the struggle for democracy in Japan which paralleled the astonishing industrialization of that country after 1870. In Chapter XXII we shall witness India's march toward self-government. Finally, in Chapter XXIII we shall note the sharp contrast between the way industrialism influenced Mexico and its effect upon the nations of the Far East.

CHAPTER XIX

THE WESTERN WORLD TURNS TOWARD ASIA

About 1500, while searching for an easy water route to Asia, western Europeans discovered America. Except for Mexico and Peru, where the Spanish conquerors were able to lay their hands upon fabulous quantities of gold and silver, this new continent at first had little attraction for the Europeans, whose imaginations still turned toward the wonderful Far Eastern countries of which Marco Polo had written. In the 1600's and 1700's, however, the colonization of America played an increasingly important part in the history of the leading European nations, and in the late 1700's Europe, already enriched and strengthened by the resources of the New World, entered upon the development of its modern industrial civilization.

During these three centuries the Portuguese, the Spaniards, the Dutch, the English, and the French had all attempted, with varying degrees of success, to carve out for themselves empires in the Far East, but in the 1800's European business men turned toward Asia with fresh energy. With their power-driven ships, their armies of commercial men, their new business methods, and their accumulated capital they "captured" Asia. They sold to the people of Asia great quantities of machine-made goods. They built factories, railroads, and telegraphs, opened up mines, and established banks. As a result several hundred million Asiatic people, although remaining politically independent, became "subjects" in the expanding empire of European business and contributed to the profits of European business men.

Today not merely the business men but all the people of the world are beginning to discover Asia. The headlines of our daily papers are filled with dramatic news from the other side of the world. Even the man on the street, in America and Europe, takes an interest in the latest revolution in China, in Gandhi's struggle for Indian freedom, and in Japan's activities in Manchuria.

Eastern Asia, the Home of Half the People of the World

Take a map of the world and put the point of a divider on Singapore. With a radius of 3500 miles swing an arc of about a

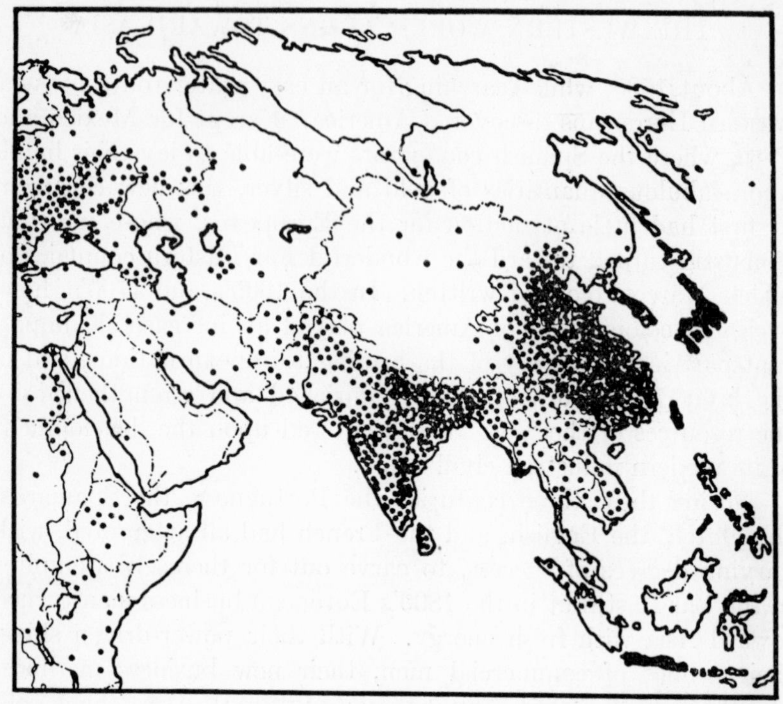

Fig. 187. Each dot represents the place where 10,000 people live. Note especially those areas which are so heavily populated that they must be shown as solid black

fourth of a circle, including Japan on the northeast and India on the northwest. Now draw the radii connecting the end points of the arc. Do you know what you have done? You have marked out a region in which live more than 850,000,000 people, nearly half the people of the entire world. Nowhere else on the earth can you find such a thickly populated region — not in Europe, nor in America, nor anywhere. In three countries alone — China, India, and Japan — there are more than 830,000,000 people. In the first two countries there are not less than 770,000,000 people, six times as many as in the United States.

South and east of these three countries are the Malay peoples, 100,000,000 strong, scattered over the mainland and countless islands. And far westward in the ancient crossroads of the world — the Near East — are five more Oriental countries: Persia with about 10,000,000 people, Turkey with 13,648,000, Irak with 2,850,000, Syria with 2,832,000, and Arabia with 7,000,000 — in round numbers approximately 1,000,000,000 human beings! This is Asia, the home of ancient man. Here a civilization rose and fell long before the industrialism of the West was created.

Western eyes turn again toward the East

Today the attention of educated Western peoples is directed to what is happening in Asia — in China, India, Japan, and in that great country that straddles both Europe and Asia — Russia. There, in that gigantic block of territory, new history is being made. There the governments and cultures are changing more drastically than anywhere else on the earth. In China today, even more radical changes in ways of living are taking place than in Russia. Indeed, the culture of half the people of the entire world is being uprooted.

Hence it is upon Asia (including Russia) that we must concentrate our study if we are to understand the changing modern world and America's relation to it.

Sharp Contrasts between the Civilizations of Western Europe and of Eastern Asia[1]

1. Contrasts in geography

In these books we have illustrated again and again the close relation between geographic factors and the civilization and culture of a people. What are the chief geographic factors? First are the climatic factors: the temperature, winds, and rainfall. Second are the topographic factors: the mountains and valleys and the "lay of the land." Third are the natural resources:

[1] At this point you might scan quickly pages 23–25 of this volume. See also Chapters V, XVIII–XXI, inclusive, and XXV and XXVI of *Changing Civilizations in the Modern World*. This present chapter merely summarizes significant ideas illustrated in the earlier study.

soil, forests, and other forms of vegetation, and deposits of minerals. Fourth is the character of the coast line: whether or not it is indented with bays and inlets which provide harbor facilities. Fifth is the shape of the land mass, the distances from the interior to the coast, and the natural facilities for transportation — for example, rivers and valleys. Sixth is the location on the earth's surface with respect to other centers of population and the developing trade routes of the world.

a. Contrasts in climate

Study carefully the colored map following page 56. Great Britain, Germany, and most of France — indeed, the greater part of Europe except Italy, Spain, Portugal, and the Balkan countries — lie north of 45 degrees north latitude. But the temperature of Europe is not so cold as we should expect from this fact. As you have already been reminded earlier in this book, the warm Gulf Stream from across the Atlantic courses along the northwestern coast of the continent. There are almost no high mountains in the entire distance from the British Isles across the central and northern parts of the continent. Hence westerly winds, blowing across the Gulf Stream and bringing warmth and moisture, penetrate far into the continent, moderating the temperature and giving Europe a rainfall of from 20 to 40 inches a year. Because Europe is, for the most part, a great plain, the population is rather uniformly distributed.

Now note on the map of figure 187 how humanity has crowded together along the coastal plain in Japan; in the valleys of the Yangtze, the Canton (or Chu), and the Hwang in China; and in the valleys of the Ganges and the Indus in India. Here the climate is warmer than it is in Europe, and the rainfall averages 60 inches or more. Much of Asia is not so fortunate. There are great stretches in which only from 10 to 20 inches of rain fall during the year, and other great stretches in which the rainfall is less than 10 inches. Do you think rainfall helps to account for the massing of the Asiatic population in the river valleys and along the coastal plains? Is there a direct connection between rainfall and food products?

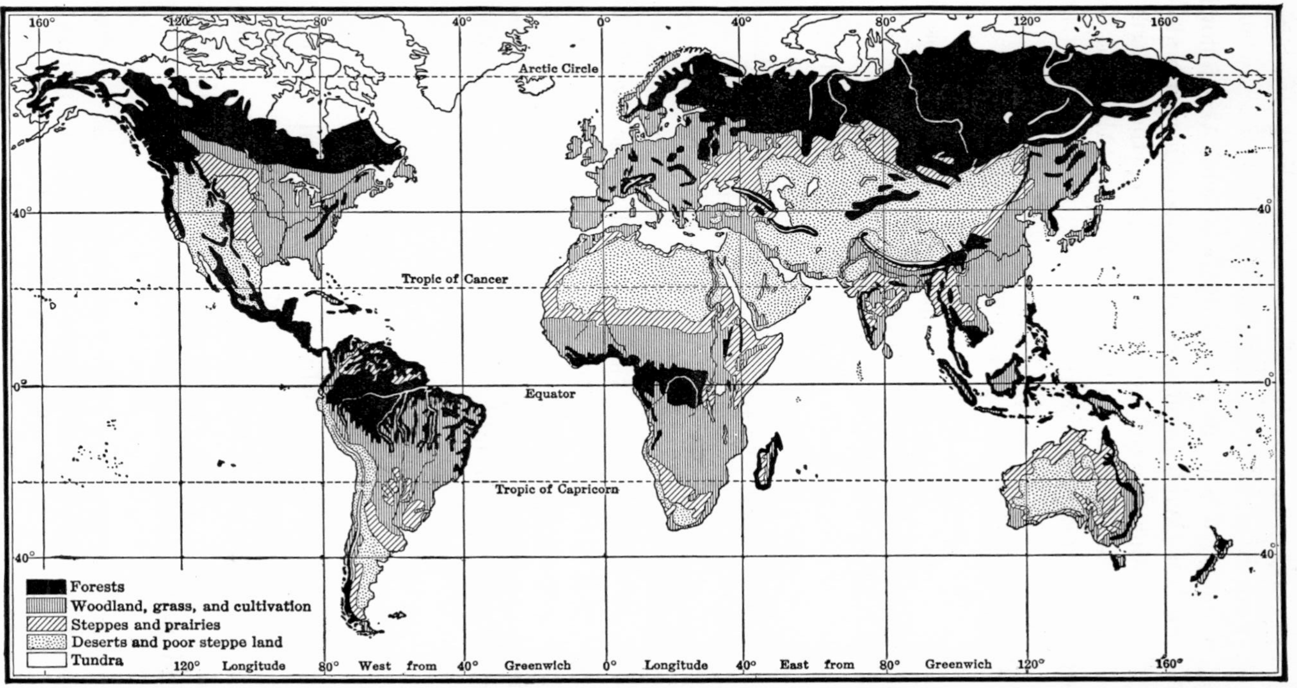

FIG. 188. With the help of the key in the lower left corner of the map you can contrast the areas of fertility in Asia and Europe. Note the large proportion of Europe which is especially fertile — the woodland, grass, and cultivation area

b. Sharp contrasts in topography

Now compare the colored maps of Europe and Asia following pages 56 and 520. We have already stated that there are almost no high mountains across the central and northern parts of Europe. With the exception of the great stony Alps and scattered lower mountains, this part of the continent is a vast level plain.

But how different is the topography of Asia! As you can see from the colored map of Asia, approximately half the continent consists of tremendous mountains and great plateaus. Note the vast plateau of Tibet, with an average of about 16,000 feet above sea level, and the broad, cold, arid deserts of Mongolia. Note the huge ranges of mountains — the Hindu Kush, the Altai, the Sayan, and, highest of all, on the northern boundary of India, the Himalayas. Here, then, is much waste land, so difficult to farm that only a few daring pioneers attempt it.

Compare the population map of figure 187 with the colored topographic map of Asia. Note the great concentrations of humanity on the broad, low coastal plains and in the river valleys and, in contrast, the sparse population of central Asia, where the mountains, plateaus, and deserts almost defy human habitation.

Differences in topography, then, accompany differences in climate, helping to determine where people live and how they live in the two separated parts of Eurasia.

c. Contrasts in natural resources

One of the great reasons why Europe produced the new industrial civilization was her vast natural resources. Especially important were the fertile soil and the great and easily accessible mineral resources — tremendous deposits of coal in the British Isles, in important centers in France, in Germany, and in southern Russia; and those of iron on the boundary between France and Germany, in Spain, and in Sweden. Here, in a territory approximately 2,660,000 square miles in area, is undoubtedly one of the greatest agricultural plains in the world — a garden spot of the earth. This land, well watered and warmed, produces not one kind of crop but a dozen or more, several of which are the basic foods of the modern world — wheat, potatoes, rye, the sugar beet, corn, etc.

Are there such natural resources in Asia? There are, indeed, large amounts of fertile land. For example, note the large acreage in the rich valleys of the Hwang, the Yangtze, and the Canton (Chu). But remember that, as compared with Europe, the waste lands of Asia are considerable (see figure 188), and the proportion of tall, rocky mountains, high, arid plateaus, and broad deserts is great. Moreover, in still further contrast with conditions in Europe, note the fact that even the rich valleys of Asia are subject to frequent and destructive floods. It is interesting to compare figures 187 and 188; for the map of world vegetation illustrates why the population of the agricultural continent of Asia is found closely concentrated in some places and why it is sparse in others.

Are there coal and iron? Estimates of the supplies in Asia vary greatly. European and American engineers have frequently made careful explorations of Asia, searching for deposits of minerals. The general belief among them is that there are fairly large deposits of both coal and iron, especially in China. Japan also has a moderate supply of coal, estimated at about 8,000,000,000 tons; but since she lacks iron she turns for it to Korea and to India.

There are other minerals in the Far East. In southern China are the world's largest deposits of antimony and very large deposits of tin. As you know, these are indispensable in the making of modern steel. Similarly with respect to tungsten, another ingredient of steel, China now produces more than any other country. Japan mines large amounts of copper, silver, sulphur, and gold.

Thus, although the mineral deposits of Asia are undoubtedly enormous in the aggregate, their inaccessibility and unfavorable distribution have prevented anything like the full use of these resources that has long been possible in Europe. The very fact that we do not know with any degree of accuracy how great the mineral deposits of Asia are shows clearly that, so far as *effective* natural resources are concerned, Asia is at a disadvantage in comparison with Europe.

d. The contrast in coast line

One of the reasons for the commercial supremacy of Europe is its low, well-indented coast line. Twelve of the 24 leading seaports of the world are on this coast. The Mediterranean Sea, with its branches the Adriatic, the Ægean, and the Black; the Baltic Sea, with its arms the gulfs of Bothnia, Finland, and Riga; the many navigable deltas and estuaries of "old" river valleys, — all these permit a vast volume of sea-borne traffic to penetrate far into the hinterland. No city of Europe is very far from the sea.

What about the coast of Asia? Only from the Yellow Sea around to India is it really well indented. Leaving the island empire of Japan out of account, it is here that the best Asiatic harbors for ocean-going ships are to be found — Tientsin, Shanghai, Hong Kong, Singapore, Rangoon, Calcutta, and Bombay. Outside of the limits just mentioned the coast is relatively unbroken and is characterized by narrow coastal plains. Even within these limits long stretches of land present no opening to the sea.

Europe, with less than one fourth the area of Asia, has a coast line one and a half times as long. In all the vast continent of Asia, including Japan, there are only five of the 24 great ports of the world.

e. The contrast in the ease by which warm-water oceans can be reached from the interior

Now compare the size and shape of the land masses of the two parts of Eurasia — Europe and Asia: Europe about 3,872,000 square miles; Asia about 17,000,000 square miles, more than four times as large!

But the difference in shape is more significant than that in size. Note the narrowness of Europe; not one point in the interior is more than 600 miles from a fairly warm sea. Furthermore, Europe is provided with the world's best arrangement of river valleys. Note on the colored map of Europe how the Danube runs east through central Europe into the Black Sea. In addition, the Rhine and the Rhône provide man with easy water transportation from the two sides of the Alps. One leads northward into the North Sea, the other southward into the Mediterranean. Note the lesser rivers — the Vistula, the Oder, the Elbe, the Weser, the Loire, the Garonne, and the Po. In huge European Russia there are the Dnieper, the Don, the Volga, and other broad rivers. In the great valleys of these rivers roads, canals, and railroads have been built. Thus no place in Europe is out of easy reach of the sea.

But what a contrast in Asia! Here is a huge land mass with most points in the interior 1500 to 2000 miles from a warm sea. To be sure, there are long, broad rivers on the coastal plains, — for example, the Hwang and the Yangtze; the Mekong, which feeds the plains of Indo-China and Siam; and the famous Ganges and the Indus, which water the great rice-raising regions of northern India. But two facts are to be noted: first, that these rivers are widely separated; second, that the lower reaches of some of the largest rivers are so choked with shifting sands that they do not afford entrance to ocean-going vessels. The rivers flowing north into the Arctic — the Ob, the Yenisei, and the Lena — suffer as commercial waterways because, for a large part of the year, they are blocked with ice.

From these facts it is clear that, especially when due account is taken of the difference in area, Europe and Asia are in sharp contrast as regards accessibility by sea. The vast central plains of Asia are out of reach of the warm-water oceans of the world — oceans on which sail the merchant ships of all nations.

f. The contrast in location with respect to other centers of population and to the world's trade routes

Finally we come to a most important contrast — namely, in location for world trade. The map of figure 8 shows that western Europe is in the very center of the trading world. Out from her ports radiate the great freight routes: first, to the ports of North America; second, through the Mediterranean; and third, to South America.

What about China, Japan, India, and the other parts of the Orient? They are far from these larger centers of world trade. They lie opposite the western coast of the United States and Canada, on which are only three large ports, and of Central and South America, which have few good harbors. Thus the trade of the broad Pacific cannot compare with that of the Atlantic and the Mediterranean, upon which Europe depends. It is true that the countries of Asia and the Pacific islands constitute a center of trade in themselves. However, this trade is insignificant in volume compared with that which crosses the Atlantic and passes through the Mediterranean.

2. The industrial civilization of Europe contrasted with the agricultural, handicraft civilization of Asia

So much for contrasts in what nature has provided for man in Europe and in Asia. We, of course, are more concerned with how man has taken advantage of the provisions of nature. Let us contrast the industrial civilization of western Europe with the agricultural, handicraft civilization of Asia.

1. *Man's use of power.* We have seen how men learned to make mechanical power in the Western world — to use giant steam and gas engines and electrically propelled motors. How different is the power that men still use in many parts of Asia!

There the tired muscles of human backs, arms, and legs provide the power which does the work for nearly 1,000,000,000 persons. Long hours of hard work, bodily fatigue, and short lives mark the story of work in the Eastern world. Hence the low standard of living revealed in the scarcity of goods, the humbleness and poverty of houses and furnishings, the lack of clothing, the almost complete absence of comforts and luxuries. First, then, is the contrast in power — mechanical power versus human-muscle power.

2. *Tools versus machines.* On the great agricultural plains of the Western world, giant gasoline tractors plant, cultivate, and harvest grain for its hungry millions. In huge factories powerful, clever machines lift, pound, heat, temper, weave, spin, and sew the goods of the Western world. Indeed, Europe is solving the problem of producing necessities, comforts, and luxuries cheaply and in huge quantities.

But in most parts of Asia the peasant grubs at the soil with the same crude instruments which his ancestors employed centuries ago. With such tools garments are made, buildings are erected, and roads are built by many of the Asiatic people.

3. *Transportation and communication.* In the industrial countries of the West, people and things are transported by rapid and efficient trains, boats, automobiles, motor cycles, electric cars, and elevators. Instantaneous electrical communication is established between distant centers, even with different continents.

In the nonindustrialized regions of Asia, however, men depend on primitive, natural means of transportation — on the wind-propelled sailboats along rivers and coasts, or on the wheelbarrow or "carrying-pole" in the towns and cities. In rural areas lumbering oxen slowly haul loads over almost impassable roads. The well-to-do still travel in elegantly ornamented sedan chairs, transported by the sweating muscles of human carriers.

4. *Handicraft production versus mass production.* In Europe huge quantities of things are made by standardized, power-driven machines, with men acting largely as starters and stoppers. Great corporations — with huge amounts of wealth invested in factories, mills, shops, office buildings, warehouses — are producing, in a complicated, interdependent way, more goods than the world ever dreamed of before.

In Asia, on the contrary, everything is produced on a small scale. Millions of Chinese, Indian, and Japanese peasants put in their rice plants one by one. Millions more do the multitude of things necessary for the production of silk. Everywhere human hands are making things. Chinese craftsmen produce carefully ornamented articles of pottery. Indian workers spend weeks on the embroidery of a single shawl. Cabinetmakers, carpenters, decorators of household furniture, and other craftsmen turn out their special articles. Every household is its own craft "factory," the family making most of its own tools and implements, cloth garments, and shoes.

In this unit on Asia we shall study only three countries — China, Japan, and India; but these three are the outstanding civilizations of the Orient.

INTERESTING READINGS FROM WHICH YOU CAN GET ADDITIONAL INFORMATION

Allen, Nellie B. Asia. Ginn and Company, Boston.

Bowman, Isaiah. The New World. World Book Company, Yonkers, New York.

Carpenter, Frank G. Asia. American Book Company, New York.

Chamberlain, James Franklin, and Arthur, Henry. Asia; a Supplementary Geography (The Continents and their People). The Macmillan Company, New York.

Huntington, Ellsworth. Asia. Rand McNally & Company, Chicago.

Miller, Olive Thorne. Little People of Asia. E. P. Dutton & Co., New York. Child life in Asia.

Whitbeck, Ray Hughes. Industrial Geography. American Book Company, New York.

CHAPTER XX

CHINA: THE BREAKDOWN OF A CULTURE

Chinese government was comparatively democratic during the centuries of one-man rule in Europe

Throughout this book we have been studying the long struggle of men for democratic government. Even today, as we have seen, the West is far from attaining its ideal.

However, during much of the time when Europeans were struggling, the Chinese people really had a kind of democracy. Indeed, the Chinese people had far more to say in the regulation of their affairs than did the people of Europe. Let us see how this was possible.

Old China: Many Independent Villages, not a National State

First we must note that the great mass of the Chinese people, 80 per cent or more, live not in cities but in thousands of small villages. The great coastal plain and the broad, fertile river valleys are literally dotted with these villages, often less than half a mile apart, and each of them, under the old imperial system, a tiny self-governing republic. Each tiny republic regulated its own local affairs — maintained its own school, settled the disputes between its people, and even, in most cases, tried and punished its own criminals. Like the manors of medieval Europe, the little village communities were, in economic matters, practically self-sufficient, and only a small portion of the products of their labor was carried off to the cities to be exchanged for "outside" commodities.

Thus China did not develop a national state. Although there was a single *written* language for the whole country, the people of each region *spoke* their own local dialect, all the important affairs of life were regulated by the village leaders, and the loyalty of the Chinese villager was concentrated upon his family and upon the village of which he was a member.

There was, of course, a Central Imperial Government

This is not to say that there was no central government in China. Centuries before the opening of the Christian Era the whole country had been united into an empire. On several occasions this empire had fallen into disorder and disunion, but since the middle of the thirteenth century it had remained united and practically unchanged except for two transfers of the imperial power.

At the head of this central government was the emperor. He was surrounded by a retinue of courtiers and assisted by the officials of a number of imperial "boards." Over the eighteen provinces, into which the empire was divided, were governors and provincial treasurers appointed by the emperor. The provinces, in turn, were divided into "prefectures," and these into districts, or *hsiens*, the "prefects" and the magistrates of the *hsiens* also being appointed by the emperor.

This pyramid of imperial governing officials had its foundation, then, in the magistrates who represented the emperor in the districts. Theoretically, therefore, these men were the real governors of the people. The magistrate decided what taxes each family should pay in support of the emperor's court and his officials. He collected the taxes. He was supposed also to police the community and to act as judge of the court. Actually, the only contact most of the people had with him was when he assessed and collected taxes.

Thus as far as *central* government was concerned, China was an empire. It was governed by one man — the emperor. In theory it was as absolute and "divine right" as any government of Europe. Actually, however, government in China had almost nothing to do with the emperor and his officials. It was local, not central, and was probably more democratic than that of any large country of the world.

The Families and the Guilds of the Communities really governed China

The supreme rôle of the family in China

To understand how the family really governed in China, we must realize the differences between families there and in the West. In the West the family consists merely of father, mother,

Fig. 189. So important a part does "family" play in the life of the Chinese, even today, that their religion is based upon ancestor worship. Should the living members of a family fail to do honor to their ancestors by regularly performing certain rites at the family graves or family temples, the Chinese believe misfortune would overtake them. This photograph shows a family temple. Note the coffin at the left

the children, and, occasionally, other relatives. Each generation tends to live by itself. This we call an individualistic way of living.

In China, however, the family includes all the relations of the father and the wives and children of the married sons: great-grandfather and great-grandmother, grandfather and grandmother, fathers and mothers, children, paternal uncles and their wives, and the unmarried paternal aunts. Frequently, because there are many children, these families are very large and are little communities in themselves. Some villages, indeed, consist of only one family; a majority of the villages have only two or three families.

Thus, in old China, most of the people in a village were related to one another. Furthermore, property — land, buildings, implements, animals — was owned by the family, not by the individual, as in Europe. Here, then, was a type of communism that was in operation for thousands of years. Furthermore, it was very different from the plan of western-European countries, in which each man had the right to own property.

The family was ruled by the eldest male, aided by the counsel of the other elder males. These elders decided everything for each individual member. They decided what his schooling should be and what occupation he should enter. They chose the wife for each young man, and the husband for each young woman. Individual choice was not permitted, for the mature judgment of the old men of the family was regarded as better than the personal desires of the young people.

In short, as all matters were settled within the family, there was very little need for central government as we know it today. Indeed, the representatives of the imperial central government really had little to do with the personal life of the Chinese.

In one respect, then, the government of the villages was indeed democratic. Everyone in each small group knew everyone else. Hence all "public" questions were settled through the most democratic discussions. Even in matters of legal dispute the imperial government had little occasion to act.

However, looking at the matter from the point of view of our Western ways of thinking, this may not seem like democracy. Perhaps you are thinking that it is a very autocratic way of living, since the individual has so very little independence. But there is another side of the matter. As one student of China says:

> What the individual loses in freedom of will he gains in protection. The collective resources of the family always stand behind him. If he is out of work he is lodged and fed, if he is ill he is taken care of, as a matter of right, not charity. . . . When he is old he must be taken care of by his children, who do so automatically, for he still has his place

in the home. There is poverty in China, bleak, bitter poverty, as everywhere in the East; but there is less of insecurity than in the richer, industrialized West.[1]

In the towns the guilds governed economic life

Although the vast majority of the Chinese people lived in villages and occupied themselves primarily with agriculture, some 20 per cent of the population dwelt in towns and cities, where they engaged in commerce or in various specialized industries. In the towns, as in the villages, the individual was governed, in all personal and social matters, by the family; but in the towns the control over his economic activities was exercised by trade guilds instead of by the village council. These corresponded fairly closely to the medieval guilds of Europe. There was a guild for every occupation, and practically every worker joined one.

These organizations governed the economic life of the country. For example, they set the prices for goods so that all would have at least a minimum of the available food, shelter, and clothing. All might nearly starve, but no one should be allowed to prosper while they did so. For in matters affecting human livelihood, China, unlike western Europe, did not believe in competition — each man for himself.

As a result, only in the more profitable merchant guilds of the larger towns and cities were there large profits and great inequalities in wealth, and it was more difficult for one individual to accumulate a fortune than in European industrial countries and in America.

The guilds also fixed wages, hours of work, and labor conditions. All these things were done through much more personal discussion by the members than was practiced in the competitive Western countries. One student of Chinese culture has given us a typical picture of how labor disputes were settled among the Chinese.

The writer witnessed [this] many years ago in the Chinese city adjoining the International Settlement at Shanghai. There was a wage dispute among the carpenters and a strike had been called. A meeting

[1] Nathaniel Peffer, *China: the Collapse of a Civilization*, p. 37. The John Day Company, New York, 1930.

had been summoned at the guild hall on the day that it was to go into effect. The hall seethed. The meeting opened, a bedlam. For a few minutes it settled to decorum, with appointed spokesmen presenting the case for each side. But the atmosphere was too overpowering, the Chinese habit of extracting the full histrionic value of every situation too irresistible. The speakers became rhetorical, then dramatic, then passionate. They were interrupted, not only by opponents, but by supporters, too full of words for restraint. Soon more than one was talking at a time, then many at a time. Both volume of noise and tensity of passion waxed to a crescendo. Nothing appeared to be left except physical violence, when suddenly servants entered bringing tea and cakes and sweetmeats. As suddenly the scene died down and was metamorphosed into an amicable, gossiping party. Tea things were cleared and the debate was resumed. It moved quickly again from decorum to passion, rose to crescendo, to the border of fracas; then when all hope seemed gone for any conclusion but catastrophe, certainly for a peaceful settlement, a compromise emerged and was accepted. The men were given a raise but less than they demanded.[1]

So it was that, outside of personal and family life, the guilds really governed the community, because they controlled the trade. Instead of laws passed by a council of representatives of the whole town or city, laws were made and enforced within the respective guilds. Economic disputes were settled within them, as personal disputes were settled within the family in the village. Westerners sometimes forget this, and maintain that there was no legal system in China. There was really a most effective one.

As representatives of the people of the towns the guilds also dealt with the officials of the imperial government. Thus the individual citizen had no direct relations with the latter.

We see that instead of being a nation in the Western sense, China was essentially a multitude of self-sufficient communities and groups. Practically everything needed to carry on life was produced within the local community.

Was there patriotism in China? loyalty to "country"? No; loyalty was to the family and to the guild — perhaps to the local

[1] Nathaniel Peffer, *China: the Collapse of a Civilization*, p. 28. The John Day Company, New York, 1930.

community. Little patriotic feeling could be experienced under such a way of living. It was difficult to make the people grasp the idea of China as a nation, as "my country."

Life under such conditions tended to be uniform. Each year was essentially like any other year. Customs were handed on

FIG. 190. The slums of China. As city populations grew in China thousands of poor people were crowded into ramshackle dwellings along the water front or into houseboats on bays, rivers, and canals. Most of these people lived in appalling poverty, among unpleasant odors, noise, and filth

from one generation to another practically unchanged. Furthermore, the people were incredibly poor. Food was hard to get and was of the simplest. Someone has described it as "rice and beans for breakfast, beans and rice for supper." Indeed, it was not much more extensive or varied than that. Comforts, few and far between, were almost unknown to the rank and file of the people. But, in spite of the poverty, government was more nearly democratic than in Western countries.

For thousands of years, in spite of foreign invasion, this old culture persevered

We are not sure just how long the Chinese people have lived in this family-guild way. Certainly it has been a long time.

In the larger towns and cities the Chinese achieved a very high level of civilization. Indeed, when Genghis Khan conquered northern China, and when his grandson Kublai Khan ruled the vast Asiatic empire, the civilization was distinctly higher than that of Europe. It was marked by fine architectural design, vast engineering construction, beautiful painting, sculpture, and carving, and fine handicraft.

Repeated invasions did little to change customs. In each case the Chinese, more numerous and slower to change, assimilated the invaders. This happened to the Mongols in the 1200's and to the Manchus in the 1600's. For about 250 years the latter ruled the millions of people without altering their habits or interests. Manchus, like Mongols before them, became "Chinese," although the Chinese, even in 1911, regarded them as foreigners.

Thus in the hundreds of thousands of Chinese villages, even in the larger towns and cities, Chinese culture went on much as in former centuries. Population grew and governors came and went, but customs and ways of living changed but little.

Then came the Traders and the Missionaries of Europe, pressing their Wares and their Ideas upon the Chinese

Then, for the first time in 4000 years, came invaders who had the power to change the culture of the people as well as to conquer their government. These were the Europeans — the British, the French, the Germans — and, later, the Americans.[1]

These came not only with warships and armies of well-equipped soldiers, but also with new ideas. They offered the isolated Chinese easier and more attractive ways of living. For example, they showed them cloth for garments made quickly and cheaply on machines, various new kinds of food, oil, lamps,

[1] A more detailed account can be read in Chapter XIX, "The Changing Chinese," in *Changing Civilizations in the Modern World.*

fine tools and implements, and engines running on tracks, and trains carrying huge numbers of people. More important still, they brought them new ideas of education and of religion, of health and of sanitation. Thus they did something that all previous invaders had failed to do: *they changed ways of living, and did not merely govern.*

This change did not come quickly. It took nearly 100 years. You probably know the story from your earlier studies. Let us recall it quickly.

In the 1600's and 1700's the British East India Company built up a valuable trade in India and succeeded in conquering about two thirds of the people. One of the richest prizes of trade which the company seized was a monopoly on the cultivation of poppies and the manufacture and sale of opium. Opium, as you probably know, is a vicious drug which undermines the health and mentality of those who contract the habit of using it.

Before 1800 few of the Chinese people used opium. But after that date the sale of the drug increased swiftly. Soon it constituted a real menace to the health of the people. As profits from this terrible business grew, the Chinese government made more and more determined efforts to check it.

The efforts of the Chinese authorities to check the opium trade resulted in stern measures against the British merchants, who were bringing to Chinese ports the greatest amount of the drug. The British government, regarding these measures as cruel and unjust, promptly took steps to defend its merchants. Two wars were fought, the first in 1840–1842 and the second in 1856–1860. Each time the British, with their powerful modern army and navy, made short work of the Chinese junks and small guns. After each of these wars the Chinese were compelled to surrender important rights to their conquerors. They handed over the island of Hong Kong, upon which the British have since built a great commercial city; they opened a number of their ports — Shanghai, Canton, Hankow, and others — to foreign trade and granted the British the right to establish at these places self-governing foreign settlements; they surrendered the right to levy a customs duty in excess of 5 per cent upon imports from foreign lands. Except for the cession of Hong Kong, all these rights and privileges were soon given to France, the United States, and other Western countries, which hastened to sign treaties with the defeated empire.

One concession demanded from China by the foreign powers was that foreigners who got into legal difficulties could have their cases tried in foreign courts. This amounted to a charge that Chinese law and judicial procedure could not be depended upon, which was naturally humiliating to the Chinese. There has been much trouble between them and the Europeans because of this fact.

Somewhat later the French established themselves in Indo-China, seizing territory and trading concessions as the British had done in China. By the 1860's they too were demanding privileges in China. At Shanghai, where a number of British and American merchants were residing on land that had been specially set apart for foreign residence, the French secured a special grant of land for themselves. These two areas gradually increased in size, and "foreign" Shanghai — the French Concession and the International Settlement — is now a great Western city in which life is more French, British, and American than Chinese.

As the years passed, more and more French, British, German, and American traders established themselves in the cities and towns of China. The sale of opium continued, and manufactures developed under the leadership of Western business men. Step by step China was opened up to the Western nations. The isolation of thousands of years was ended. The traders were changing the culture of the people as well as conquering the government.

There were also attacks from one of China's own Asiatic neighbors — Japan. Between 1860 and 1890 Japan swiftly transformed her industry and business, adopting the power-driven machines of industrial civilization. She built railroads and telegraphs, set up a great system of world trade, and developed a modern army and navy. Then, feeling strong enough to do so, she joined the Western powers in attacks upon the helpless Chinese. In 1894 she defeated China in a short war, forced the Chinese government to recognize the "independence" of Korea, took the island of Taiwan (better known as Formosa), and obtained a large indemnity.

Now, too, the Russian migration across Siberia had brought that empire up to the very doors of northern China. Russian emigrants penetrated into eastern Siberia, Mongolia, and Manchuria, finally taking the region of which the city of Vladivostok is the chief port.

As the powers established themselves within China, railways were built and operated under forced leases. The Russians built the Chinese Eastern Railway across Manchuria, shortening their Trans-Siberian Railway. Russia also obtained the Liaotung Peninsula and control of the cities of Dairen and Port Arthur. The Germans obtained control of the land about Kiaochow Bay, developed the seaport city of Tsingtao, and built railways through the province of Shantung. In the meantime Britain and France also forced China to grant them the right to build railways. These railways were nominally Chinese; but they were built with money borrowed from abroad, and the control of the railways was to remain in foreign hands until the loans were paid off.

In this way most of the important regions of China were practically under the control of one or more of the European powers before 1900.

Western missionaries also undermined the Chinese culture

It was not merely the construction of factories, railroads, and telegraphs and the introduction of new kinds of food, clothing, and conveniences that affected Chinese culture. Although these were important, there was another influence that affected it even more — the new education of the West. Increasing numbers of young Chinese were educated to a new way of living by missionaries of various churches sent into China from England, Germany, and other parts of Europe, and from America.

By a treaty made in 1860, missionaries were permitted to reside anywhere in China, to establish schools, churches, missions, and to educate Chinese in the Christian religion. This in itself was a revolutionary change, for up to that time foreigners could live only in certain places and could do only certain things. Furthermore, these missionaries were governed by the laws of their own countries, not by those of China. All these concessions gave the missionary freedom to spread propaganda which would radically change the most fundamental Chinese customs.

Soon mission schools were set up in various centers of China. Although not modern in the sense of the 1930's, they were revolutionary to the Chinese culture. Education in China had long consisted in studying the writings of the great Chinese poets, philosophers, and historians. The curriculum included little geography, no history of the world outside China, and none of

FIG. 191. Young Chinese, educated in the United States, on their way home

our modern scientific subjects. The mastery of the ancient classics, moreover, required many years; hence, although almost every little village had its own school, only a very small percentage of the Chinese people ever learned to do more than read a few simple characters.

The Chinese children really needed a modern school like your own, one that taught them reading, writing, and arithmetic, the history and geography of their own country and of other parts of the world, and the scientific knowledge which had begun its development in Europe during the 1600's. They needed to understand their own conditions, the real problems of their country, and the relation of the Far East to the West. They needed to be able to read and understand their own literature and help to create a new one.

But neither from their own schools nor from the Western mission schools did they obtain this kind of education. In the mission schools they were taught Western languages instead of their own. The American and British missionaries, for example, taught them to read and write English. They read English and American literature. They studied European and United States history. In short, instead of building a course of study to fit the civilization of China, the mission schools imposed upon the Chinese the curriculum of American and European schools.

In the 50 years after 1860, hundreds of thousands of young Chinese were educated in the ideas, ideals, and customs of the West. When they graduated from mission high schools they went either to mission colleges in China or to colleges in the United States, Europe, or Japan. By the time they were 25 most of these young people were imbued with Western culture and were determined to introduce it into China.

It was not merely in external things — such as clothing, hair cuts, diet, household furniture, and the like — that the young Chinese began to want to live in a different way. Their more fundamental customs also began to change; for example, their family life, their attitude toward women and children, and their guilds, their education, and their philosophy.

Thus Western Traders and Missionaries, supported by their Governments, broke down the Power of the Manchu Government and prepared the Way for Revolution

As the later decades of the nineteenth century passed, the younger native leaders determined to oust the Manchu rulers. The greatest leader among them all, Dr. Sun Yat-sen, says in his autobiography, "From 1885, that is, from the time of our defeat in the war with France, I set before myself the object of the overthrow of the . . . dynasty and the establishment of a Chinese republic on its ruins."

And later, describing how the foreign powers put down the

Boxer uprising of 1900 and got control of Peking (Peiping), he said: "All intelligent Chinese began to understand that China was on the brink of destruction. From this moment a new revolutionary wave began to grow up."

Revolution and the First Republic, 1911–1912

Grow up it did, indeed. In the 1890's, under the leadership of Dr. Sun Yat-sen and other Western-educated Chinese, revolutionary groups developed in various centers. So influential did they become that the imperial government took harsh measures. Sun Yat-sen himself was forced to flee from China, a price upon his head.

Fig. 192. Sun Yat-sen (1867–1925)

However, the spirit of revolution continued to grow. Dr. Sun Yat-sen and other leaders secretly traveled from place to place, organizing the revolution against the Manchu government. Sensing the impending danger, the government itself made "reforms." In 1905 the antiquated system of educational examinations was abolished. Year by year more modern schools were established; by 1910 nearly 1,600,000 children were attending these schools. It was in that year also that slavery was abolished.

During the same years commissions of political leaders went abroad to study government in Western countries. As early as 1906 the Manchu imperial officials promised a parliamentary government. Elections were held in 1909, a small, selected property-owning class being allowed to vote. In October, 1910, a national assembly met. The Throne promised to call a parliament in 1913 which should have certain powers over lawmaking.

But the revolutionary leaders would not wait. In October,

1911, a mutiny against the Manchus arose in Wuchang. Like wildfire the long-smoldering rebellion spread from city to city and from province to province. By December, fourteen of the eighteen provinces of China proper had declared against the Manchu rulers, who were deposed. On New Year's Day, 1912, Dr. Sun Yat-sen was elected first president of the Chinese Republic. He served, however, only two months, resigning in favor of the leading military general of China — Yuan Shih-kai. It was hoped that Yuan Shih-kai could bind together the many separated factions.

What a historic event this was! China, a multitude of isolated villages, proclaimed a republic and launched on a career of nation-building! Could it be done? Could this gigantic illiterate mass of humanity be welded into a modern nation? This question was in all thoughtful minds.

Fig. 193. A cartoon of three republics. What does the cartoon imply? (From the *North China Herald*, Shanghai)

Then followed Twenty Years of Turmoil

What were the tasks confronting Yuan Shih-kai, Sun Yat-sen, and their associates? Overwhelming ones indeed! In brief, they would have to set up a strong central government which should have (1) a well-disciplined and well-equipped army to keep order, to put down the bandits who were springing up in every quarter, and to keep rival military leaders in subjection; (2) a large staff of educated and loyal officials to represent the central government in the eighteen provinces and the smaller districts; (3) a uniform and sound system of currency and a way of raising money by fair taxation; (4) modern systems of roads, railroads, telegraphs, and postal service to bind the scattered villages and cities of the vast territory together into a loyal nation.

Finally, absolutely basic to the whole future building of a stable country, was the fifth necessity — the establishment of a nation-wide system of modern schools. Some way had to be found to construct school buildings, train teachers, and bring 99 per cent of the Chinese children into modern schools.

It was an overwhelming problem, indeed — surely not one that could be solved in a few years. Nevertheless Dr. Sun Yat-sen, General Yuan Shih-kai, and the other leaders heroically attempted the task.

A Nationalist Political Party — the Kuomintang — took the Leadership in the New Government

At the outbreak of the revolution, in 1911, no political organization prepared to cope with problems of government was in existence. Hastily Dr. Sun Yat-sen and his associates formed a "party"— the Kuomintang, or Nationalist party. To perfect such a complicated organization, however, requires many years of work; hence during the first ten years of the Kuomintang the leaders had no plan and no party machine.

So chaotic did government become that in 1913 Yuan Shih-kai dismissed the assembly of the party and attempted to rule China as a dictator, announcing a new "constitution" in 1914. During the next two years several rival war lords rose against him. These set up their own independent governments in different sections of the country, collecting taxes at will, quartering their armies on the people, looting property, and oppressing the inhabitants. Increasing numbers of young men turned bandits. Government completely broke down in many sections.

When Yuan Shih-kai died, in 1916, chaos increased. The country fell into indescribable disorder. From 1916 to 1926 civil war ruled China.

In the meantime the Kuomintang, under the leadership of Dr. Sun Yat-sen, launched one new provisional government after another from their headquarters in the southern city of Canton. Instead of being satisfied to govern merely the local district, establishing order in that region and gradually extending their control over a larger and larger area, Dr. Sun Yat-sen and the

Nationalist party attempted to govern all China. Under such conditions as existed in the country it was inevitable that they should fail.

Finally, in March, 1925, Dr. Sun Yat-sen died. Almost immediately he became a national hero. The Kuomintang launched a widespread national program based largely upon his book *Three Principles of the People* (*San Min Chu I*). These three principles were (1) democracy, (2) a better standard of living for the people, and (3) the recovery by China of the rights which have been granted to foreigners. For a few years this book of Dr. Sun Yat-sen's became the Bible of the Chinese revolutionaries.

The Nationalist Party finally became a Dictator Government, patterned after the Russian Communist Party

Shortly before the death of Dr. Sun Yat-sen the Russian Communist party entered the scene. Representatives of the Soviet government, led by Michael Borodin, flocked to China to spread their propaganda. Russian military officers helped to train the new Nationalist army, and Russian politicians helped the Kuomintang leaders to perfect a party organization. For a time many in the Western world were convinced that the Chinese would adopt a communistic form of society.

There was reason, indeed, for the belief. The new Kuomintang was patterned very closely after the Russian Communist party. No other parties were to be permitted in China. Government was to be frankly a party dictatorship.

Note how closely the Chinese party resembles the Russian model, which is shown in figure 224. There is a National Congress at the head, composed of delegates from the various districts of the country, elected every two years *by party members*. The real work, however, is done by the Central Executive Committee of 36 members. These, in turn, delegate their powers to a Standing Committee of from five to nine members. There is also a somewhat larger Central Political Council and a Central Supervisory Council. Thus the general organization of the party, as you can see, resembles the organization of the Russian Communist party.

That the National Government itself is a dictatorship of the

Kuomintang is shown by the fact that the Central Executive Committee appoints the Central State Council of the government. The chairman of this council is president of the National Government and commander in chief of the army and navy. There is also a Central Military Council and a Central Research Council. The members of these, too, usually belong to the party. Furthermore, every law proposed in the legislature must be approved by the leaders of the party before it can be passed. Thus

FIG. 194. Campaigning for the Nationalist party. It is a woman who is addressing the crowd. A generation ago such a sight would have been impossible, for women then took no part in public life

the Central Executive Committee — a little oligarchy of from five to nine men — is the real sovereign over the people, at least so long as its armies are in control.

The Nationalists say frankly that they propose to maintain their present dictatorship until 1935. They claim that only thus, under the existing conditions of turmoil, can a strong central government be established.

In the meantime, while central and county governments have been in turmoil, what about local government in the villages? Although the control of the family and its elders is weakening there, it has not yet been destroyed. These leaders continue to govern their little communities much as they did before. They are at the mercy, however, of raiding bandits and of the successive waves of advancing and retreating armies which have ravaged Chinese communities in many parts of China proper during the past twenty years.

Whether for Good or for Ill the Old Chinese Culture is Breaking Down

1. The Chinese are beginning to adopt industrialism

China, like Russia, like India, like other great sections of the world, is beginning to adopt European industrialism. In 1925 there were 400 electric-light and power plants in China. The larger cities had street-car and bus lines and were connected by the telegraph. By 1930 there were also more than 7000 miles of railroads and more than 1000 power-driven factories. Almost three fifths of all the factories are in the textile industry. In 1928 there were 120 cotton mills, with approximately 250,000 workers. Two thirds of them were owned by Chinese capitalists. Modern steel mills have also been built in several centers, and up-to-date shipyards are being developed.

These industries are, of course, concentrated near a few large cities. Almost half the cotton mills are near Shanghai, and many others are located in such cities as Tsingtao, Tientsin, Wusih, and Wuhan. Wuhan is a large industrial district on the Yangtze River and includes Hankow, Wuchang, and Hanyang.

Other industries are growing also. More flour is being manufactured, especially in Manchuria, near the grain-raising plains. Certain phases of silk-manufacturing are being carried on now by machines. Many match factories have also been built.

Thus China has already begun to adopt the West's industrial way of producing things. Only a small beginning has been made, of course; most of the villages are still untouched. But the change is really under way. After thousands of years of resistance to all foreign influence the Chinese are succumbing to the easier and more profitable ways of manufacturing and business characteristic of Western industrial countries.

As they do so they are building up a rich industrial capitalist class, as each of the Western countries has done. A new division of Chinese society is taking place. For example, bankers are rising to power. Since 1918 more than 200 banks organized on the pattern of Western banks have been formed. Unfortunately, many of these enterprises have been set up by political leaders, principally to enable them to carry on their schemes and make great profits. However, about one third of the banks are sound institutions. As in Europe, the bankers are playing a very important part in the new government.

2. The change in family life

While these industrial changes are occurring in the largest cities, another fundamental change is taking place in the family.

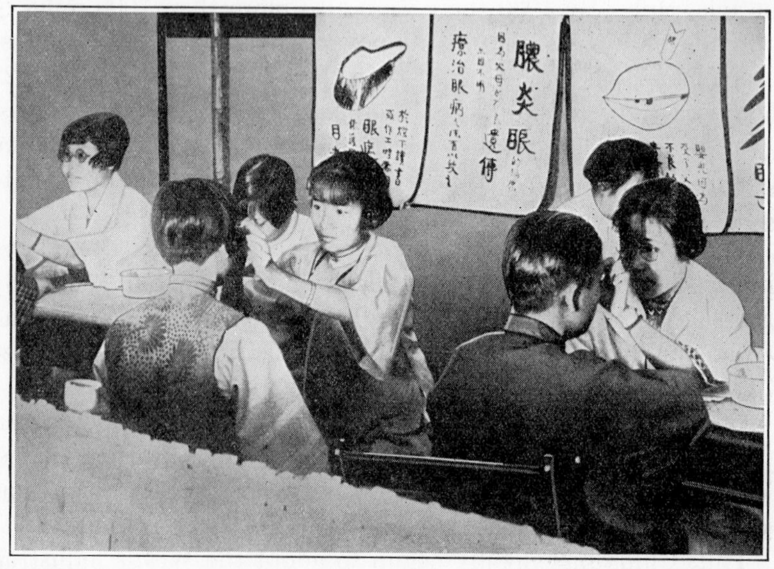

Fig. 195. An eye clinic conducted by the doctors and students of the women's medical college at Canton. This picture illustrates but one profession in which the young women of China engage today

Family life, influenced by European countries, is becoming individualized. Young men educated in Western schools are demanding the right to choose their own wives; young women are demanding the right to choose their own husbands. More important still, however, is the fact that the newly married couples insist on living alone in their own houses. They are breaking away from the old community home. Thus the control of the elders over the young people is breaking down, and it is difficult to perpetuate old ideas and customs.

In the second place, there is a radical transformation in the attitude of the Chinese women toward their part in the world. Young Chinese women are demanding homes of their own because it gives them personal independence. Instead of being a nobody in the home of her husband, the woman now becomes mistress of her own destiny and the leader of her children in her own home. Furthermore, women are entering the new occupations and are working outside the family. They are going to school, are learning to read and write, and are being educated in modern ideas.

3. The revolution in education

Under the influence of the West has come a new educational revolution. In the first place, there developed what is known as the "literary renaissance." This movement aimed to discard the classical language in which writing had been done for centuries and to substitute for it the common speech, or vernacular, generally used. In the vigorous controversy that developed between the older, conservative scholars and the younger, radical scholars, drastic changes were proposed that affected not only the language but the whole educational system.

As a result of the agitation of young educators a whole new curriculum is being introduced into the new schools which are springing up over the country. Dr. Sun Yat-sen's *Three Principles of the People* is now beginning to be taught in place of the old Confucian philosophy. Courses are given in modern Chinese and world history, in geography and current problems. The elementary subjects of reading, writing, arithmetic, and science are to be found in the new curriculum of the lower schools. In the meantime Chinese classical literature is practically ignored.

Note the swift rise in modern schools. In 1911 a minister of education of the Peking (Peiping) government stated that 52,000 modern schools had been set up, with 1,600,000 students in attendance. It was estimated in 1923 that there were more than

6,500,000 children in the new government schools. It is believed that today the number exceeds 10,000,000.

Another sign of the change in Chinese culture is the recognition of the need for universal education. At the time of the establishment of the first republic (1911), although statistics are unreliable, it is probable that 95 per cent of all the adults in China were unable to read and write. Imagine a population of

Fig. 196. Illustrating some of the work which is going on in Chinese higher education. Except for the fact that the occupants of the laboratory are Chinese, there is nothing in the picture to distinguish it from the chemical laboratories of American educational institutions

325,000,000 human beings, most of them totally unable to read and thus practically unable to keep in touch either with developments in their own country or with the world outside!

Recognizing this fact, brilliant young Chinese trained in Western schools set up a most important experiment known as "Mass Education," under the leadership of Y. C. James Yen. These leaders organized classes in Hunan province for the education of adults. They prepared textbooks written by means of a simplified alphabet of 1300 characters in place of the complicated and lengthy alphabet of several thousand characters. The rudimentary subjects of reading and writing and vocational and citizenship training appealed to the interests of the people of the community. Men and women of all classes enrolled, business men and leaders as well as peasants and craftsmen. Volunteer teachers offered their services. By 1924 the enrollment exceeded 150,000.

After several years of successful experiment the Mass Education Movement has concentrated in one county unit near Peiping. This unit provides a model which demonstrates to the 1834 other counties how adult education can be developed.

Thus it is that the Whole Chinese Culture is Changing

At last the barriers separating China from the West are breaking down. Every aspect of life is being changed. Factories are running machines; some of the old handicrafts are disappearing. Railways, smooth roads, telegraphs, even telephones and radios, are slowly tying separated regions together.

A national government is being set up, as yet no more than a dictatorship, but at least an attempt at a more national representation than the old empire of the Manchus provided.

But underneath all these external signs of change in civilization are the deeper changes in the culture of the people. A modern educational system is slowly taking shape, Western forms of family life are appearing, women are working at occupations outside the home, the control of the elder community leaders is weakening, and old philosophy and customs are disappearing.

No one can predict what will come in China in the next few years. But one thing is certain: the old China is disappearing, and a new one is taking its place. And no one can tell now whether this radical change is for better or for worse.

INTERESTING READINGS FROM WHICH YOU CAN GET ADDITIONAL INFORMATION

Chrisman, Arthur B. The Wind that wouldn't Blow: Stories of the Merry Middle Kingdom for Children and Myself. E. P. Dutton & Co., New York.

Franck, Harry A. Wandering in Northern China. The Century Co., New York. Excellent description of life in China.

Griffis, William Eliot. China's Story in Myth, Legend, Art, and Annals. Houghton Mifflin Company, Boston. A good brief history.

HEADLAND, ISAAC TAYLOR. The Chinese Boy and Girl. Fleming H. Revell Company, New York.

JOHNSTON, L. E., and FINNEMORE, JOHN. China and Japan (Peeps at Many Lands Series). The Macmillan Company, New York.

LEE, YAN PHOU. When I was a Boy in China (Children of Other Lands Books). Lothrop, Lee & Shepard Co., Boston.

MARSH, JAMES R. The Charm of the Middle Kingdom. Little, Brown and Company, Boston. A splendid book.

MORSE, EDWARD S. Glimpses of China and Chinese Homes. Little, Brown and Company, Boston.

SINGLETON, ESTHER. China. Dodd, Mead & Company, New York.

VAN BERGEN, ROBERT. The Story of China. American Book Company, New York.

CHAPTER XXI

THE STRUGGLE FOR DEMOCRACY IN JAPAN

Across the Yellow Sea, a day's sail from the east coast of China, the mountain-peaked islands of Japan extend 2500 miles along the coast of Asia. Here, in an area smaller than the American state of Texas, live more than 60,000,000 people.

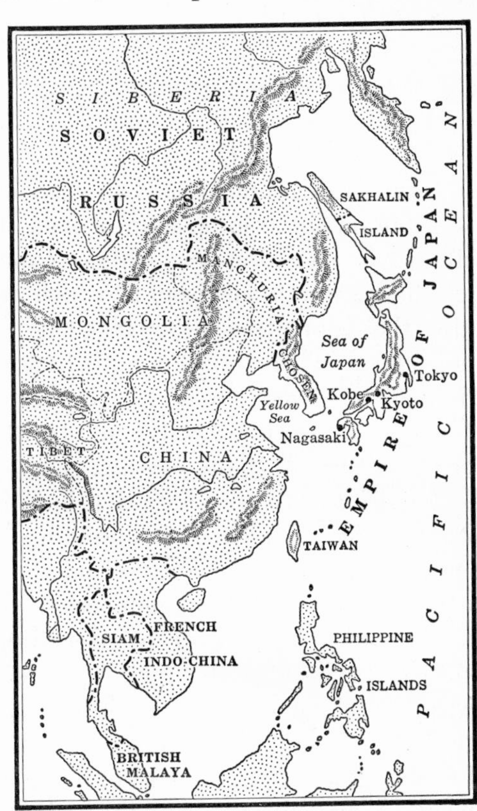

FIG. 197. Japan, the empire of mountainous islands near the mainland of Asia

In 1854 there were 30,000,000 Japanese people living enslaved under feudal nobles. They produced food, shelter, and clothing in the primitive ways of their remote ancestors. Fifty years later, in 1904, these same people, some 50,000,000 in number, were one of the world's leading industrial nations. They were engaging the armies of Russia in modern warfare and had built up a vast trading empire. Transportation by means of jinrikisha or kago was being replaced by modern express trains, airplanes, and automobiles. Little coastwise sailing ships were giving way to powerful motor-driven ocean liners plying the seven seas. This is one of the world's most astonishing transformations.

For 200 years the Japanese had tightly closed their doors against all Western trade. Then, in a period of little more than 75 years (1854–1930), they adopted power-driven machines, built railroads, erected factories, developed great corporations, opened up coal and iron mines, and built a world-wide system of trade. So swiftly did the transformation take place that it was almost incredible to other peoples. Only the development of Germany could at all compare to it.[1]

Japan and China: a review of sharp contrasts

Thus the story of changing government and changing culture in Japan is very different from that of China. It is different in every respect — in size of territory, in speed of industrialization, in form of government, and in ways of living.

Note on the colored map of Asia the difference in size of territory. Great, sprawling China is more than 25 times as large as the mountainous islands which make up Japan. Contrast also the population — 350,000,000 in "China proper" against 60,000,000 in Japan. But note that the 350,000,000 people live in 1,500,000 square miles in China, and the 60,000,000 in about 150,000 square miles in Japan. In which country are the people crowded together more closely?

Especially must we note that in China feudalism was abolished 2500 years ago, but that in Japan feudalism existed even to 1850. While the people of England and the United States were experimenting with industrial democracy the Japanese lived under a feudal system like that of the later Middle Ages in western Europe. On vast baronial estates they were controlled in the most exacting ways. Each person was born into a particular caste and could not rise above it through his own efforts. Thus a person could not win for himself a better standard of living and could not associate with people more cultured or educated than those belonging to the class into which he was born.

Peasants were not permitted to sell their land nor even to use their land for new kinds of agriculture. They were not al-

[1] If time permits you might read Chapters XX and XXI of *Changing Civilizations in the Modern World.*

lowed to move from one village to another without the permission of the government. They were restricted also even in little everyday affairs. What a man could wear was regulated; for example, silk was reserved for the so-called highest classes. The size of a man's house was fixed by law. It was even decided how much he could spend at festivals. Penalties for violation of decrees were severe, the death penalty being inflicted for trivial offenses.

Fig. 198. A Japanese feudal castle. Note the strong walls and the moat beside them. Many feudal castles of Europe were protected in this way

At the head of the Japanese feudal system was an officer called the Shogun, an official who had all the real power, whereas the emperor (or mikado) was a mere puppet. In 1603 the office of Shogun was bestowed upon the powerful Tokugawa family, which still held it when Japan was opened, in 1854, to intercourse with the outside world. During the entire period of the Tokugawa Shogunate the population of Japan remained practically stationary, as you can see by referring to figure 199; the Shoguns maintained peace throughout the country, and the farmers were able to work in the fields without fear of ravaging armies. Japan's agricultural resources were able to provide food for only about 30,000,000 people; when the population increased beyond that limit a famine occurred in some part of the empire and swept away hundreds of thousands by starvation.

Then came the Industrialization of Japan and the Appearance of her most Serious Problem

Then, after 1854, came the adoption of power-driven machinery. With astonishing rapidity the population increased. Note from figure 199 how it nearly doubled in a half-century. There were no famines. The standard of living rose. More children were born. The government definitely encouraged large families

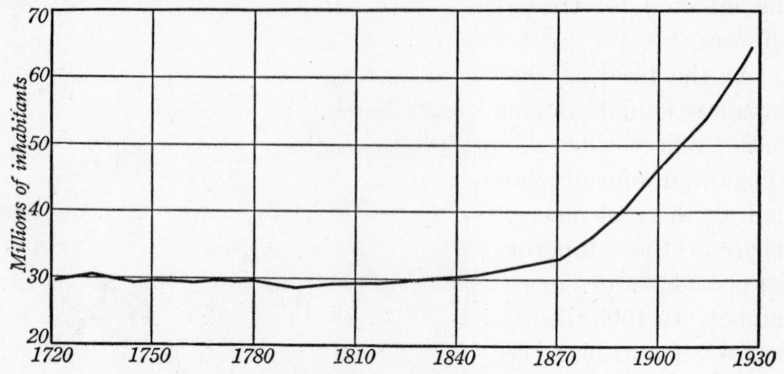

Fig. 199. The growth of Japanese population, 1721–1928

through widespread propaganda. As a result of all the new conditions the number of inhabitants in Japan is increasing now at the rate of practically 1,000,000 a year.

For a while the food supply increased, and the diet became more varied. As industrialization advanced, more and more people became educated. Farmers were taught how to make better use of their land; crops became larger. For example, the increase in rice production proportionately paralleled the increase in population. For a while all looked safe, and the prospect of Japan's becoming a great and prosperous nation seemed assured.

Then the same things happened in Japan that had taken place in other countries where machine manufacturing had been adopted. The machines lured people away from the farms. As factories sprang up cities grew more rapidly than ever before. Around the factories developed terrible slums, in which people lived under the most degrading conditions. Frazier Hunt has described one slum quarter of the new manufacturing port city of Kobe:

> . . . tiny crooked alleys, less than four feet wide, banked on both sides with narrow, wooden dog kennels, six by eight feet square and probably five feet high. Here twenty thousand outcasts live like homeless dogs; each human kennel crowded with squalling, quarreling creatures of filth and vermin, rotting with crime and tuberculosis and disease. Outcasts of all kinds — whites, blacks, Eurasians, Chinese — dregs of an old, old East.[1]

Thus the history of industrialism in Europe repeated itself in Asia. There were large cities, long hours of work for pitifully small wages, and miserable working and living conditions. And — most serious of all — there was overpopulation and the danger of starvation for millions of human beings.

In spite of gains in the food supply Japan is confronted by the very serious problem of overpopulation: 60,000,000 people are crowded together on little islands to a degree not equaled anywhere else in the world. In the industrial centers, where city factories are located, from 4000 to 5000 people are living per square mile. In fairly large areas around these there are districts where from 400 to 1000 people are living per square mile. On the whole there are in Japan today about 400 people to each square mile of cultivated area.

Japan, an Overpopulated Island Empire, is increasingly Dependent on the Outside World for Food

In several respects modern Japan is duplicating the history of modern England. First, it is a small island nation of limited territory. Second, it has adopted industrialism. Third, its population has multiplied at unprecedented speed. Fourth, it has attempted to build up an empire outside of its home territory. Fifth, it is experimenting with representative government.

From some of these characteristics came Japan's most serious problem; namely, the rapidly growing dependence upon the outside world for food. The entire Empire of Japan totals only 260,000 square miles, and Japan proper is only 147,000 square miles. The entire empire is less in size than our one state of

[1] Frazier Hunt, *The Rising Temper of the East*, p. 98. Copyrighted and published by The Bobbs-Merrill Company, Indianapolis, 1922. Used by special permission.

Texas. In this little area there live today more than 60,000,000 people where 75 years ago lived not much more than half that number. Furthermore, only one eighth of the land is level or fertile enough to produce food. Hence, if the Japanese ever again had to depend entirely upon their own food supply, they would have to produce it all from about 20,000 square miles of land.

During the past generation the Japanese people have steadily confronted the growing danger of starvation. A few handfuls of rice alone must even now suffice for the day's diet of many of the workers.

Japan has tried to solve her problem as England has tried to solve hers: first, by manufacturing and selling enough goods abroad to pay for food for her people; second, by encouraging emigration.

Consider Japan's attempt to build up foreign trade. As more and more of her people moved into the cities and turned to the manufacturing of goods, larger and larger quantities of these goods were sold to other countries. With the income from this trade, food and needed raw materials were bought abroad and were imported into Japan.

All is well in a little island manufacturing country so long as it can sell as much goods abroad as it buys. But *danger impends when its imports seriously exceed its exports.* That is what is happening now to England and what is happening to Japan also. Having turned to manufacturing as her chief resource, Japan now finds herself competing with England, France, Germany, the United States, India, southern Russia, and with other hitherto undeveloped regions which are also taking up manufacturing.

In recent years the foreign trade of Japan has grown to the sum of 4,000,000,000 yen ($2,000,000,000) annually. But the imports of food, iron, coal, oil, and other raw materials are increasing even more rapidly than the exports of manufactured goods.

Hence we see at once Japan's supreme problem — to provide food and goods enough for a rapidly growing population. Her leaders see very clearly that they must either reduce the population or increase the food supply. Since it will be almost impossible to increase the food supply substantially, some way must be found to reduce the population. Two ways are possible: (1) reduce the size of families; (2) encourage emigration.

Overpopulation and Empire-Building in Japan

Confronted by the danger of too many people, the Japanese government has followed the example of the Western industrial nations and has sought to obtain territory in other parts of the Far East. She too has adopted the militaristic tactics of empire-building. Note her attempts:

1875 Took the Ryukyu Islands.

1895 Defeated China and secured Taiwan (Formosa) and the Pescadores Islands.

1904–1905 Defeated Russia, secured certain economic rights formerly held by Russia in southern Manchuria, established a protectorate over Korea (Chosen), and recovered the southern half of the island of Sakhalin.

1910 Annexed Korea (Chosen).

1919 At the close of the World War received the German rights in Shantung[1] and at the same time got from China certain other rights which Germany had never had; and obtained a mandate over German islands in the Pacific.

This sums up briefly Japan's attempt to build an empire in the past 50 years. Altogether her possessions make up about 44 per cent of her entire small empire.

The government has done its best to encourage emigration to these new regions and other less-settled Japanese possessions, but without great success. Consider the attempt, for example, to get people to emigrate to the "Japanese Northland"— Hokkaido and other northern islands. Free land (12 to 24 acres per family) was given to families who would settle and homestead it. A fairly large number emigrated. Thus this northland of Japan is being settled by pioneer frontiersmen, much as the west of the United States was settled. Whereas the population in 1870 was a little under 60,000, in 1925 it was 2,500,000.

But, you exclaim, what are approximately 2,450,000 emigrants compared with a 30,000,000 increase in population in Japan? A

[1] Shantung was returned to China in 1922.

small portion indeed. Moreover, the entire northern islands could not accommodate more than the increase in population in Japan during two years alone.

Then there are other islands to which emigration has been encouraged; for example, the southern half of Sakhalin. But into this region also only a few thousand settlers are moving each year.

To the southward is Taiwan. The Japanese conquered the natives of this island and have done their best to get Japanese to emigrate there. But out of approximately 4,000,000 inhabitants in the large island only 5 per cent are Japanese. Furthermore, the entire number which the island could take in would be a small fraction of the Japanese population.

FIG. 200. Only a few thousand Japanese migrate to Manchuria yearly. Chinese, however, are settling in Manchuria at the rate of 1,000,000 a year. This picture shows a group of these Chinese immigrants waiting for the train that is to take them to their new home. (Courtesy of the South Manchuria Railway Company)

There is also the peninsula of Korea, or Chosen, which the Japanese annexed in 1910. The southern portion of this peninsula has about the same climate as much of Japan (see figure 197) and should be attractive to immigrants. Nevertheless, not more than 500,000 Japanese have moved there. Moreover, the region is already heavily populated.

Finally, there is the great region of Manchuria. In 1905, after her war with Russia, Japan secured a lease of the Liaotung region, in southern Manchuria, together with control over the South Manchuria Railway. Here the government urged the Japanese people to settle. At the end of the first quarter of a century of control, however, not over 10 per cent of the people in the Liaotung territory were Japanese; the remaining 90 per cent were Chinese. It is estimated that today there are about 250,000 Japanese out of a total population of 27,500,000 in Manchuria. Thus the entire Japanese population of Manchuria does not make up more than 1 per cent of the total. *In the meantime Chinese pioneers are moving north and are settling Manchuria at the rate of 1,000,000 a year!* Here is one of the greatest international sore spots of the world.

The Japanese government has also tried to encourage emigration to other countries, but with equally little success. Up to the time of their comparative exclusion from the United States in 1907, not more than from 10,000 to 15,000 Japanese were coming here each year. A few emigrants are now going to Brazil and to other regions of Latin America. However, almost as many Japanese return to Japan from other countries each year (approximately 15,000) as emigrate to those countries. In 1926 one official reported that only about 500,000 Japanese were residing in other countries.

This, then, is the dangerous situation of the Japanese today: too many people; growing dependence on the outside world for food: imports growing more rapidly than exports.

THE SWIFT CHANGE IN GOVERNMENT FROM FEUDALISM, IN 1850, TO EXPERIMENTS IN REPRESENTATIVE DEMOCRACY

The government of Japan, as well as its industry and population, has been transformed in the past half-century.[1] As late as 1867 Japan was still ruled by the Tokugawa Shogunate. But in that year the leaders of four southwestern feudal clans, jealous of the Tokugawa power, brought pressure to bear upon the ruling Shogun and forced him to surrender his administrative powers

[1] For the early history of Japan see *Changing Civilizations in the Modern World*, Chaps. XX, XXI.

into the hands of the emperor. This "restoration" of the imperial power was quickly followed by the abolition of the feudal system and by the establishment of a strong centralized administration controlled by the emperor — or rather by his advisers.

The Japanese, like the English, have retained their royal ruler because of sentiment and tradition. The sentiment and tradition surrounding the Japanese emperor, however, are incomparably stronger than those which maintain the British monarch on his throne. The national patriots in Japan maintain that for more than 2000 years a descendant of the original emperor, "Jimmu Tenno," has sat upon the throne. The people are taught that the original emperor was a direct descendant of the Sun Goddess. Thus a halo of reverence surrounds all emperors.

An oligarchy — the Elder Statesmen — controlled Japan after 1867

In 1867 the emperor, Mutsuhito, was a fifteen-year-old boy who had only recently ascended the throne. The real power in the new government was exercised not by the boy emperor, but by the small body of intimate advisers who surrounded him. These men all believed in the necessity of reform; and as the distinguishing name for the young emperor's reign they adopted the motto *Meiji*,— "enlightened government," — by which it was to be known.

Some of this little group of ardent reformers were members of the old court nobility; but most of them were men — usually young men — from the four southwestern clans of Satsuma, Chosun, Hizen, and Toso, which had forced the last Tokugawa Shogun to surrender his power. These men of the four clans — the so-called Sat-Cho-Hi-To combination — were "commoners," but they promptly received titles of nobility and became a bureaucratic oligarchy controlling the army, the navy, legislation, and the civil administration of the empire.

At first there was no intention of setting up a constitutional or parliamentary government, and for nearly a quarter of a century the people, even the well-to-do industrial class, had no voice in the government. However, the Charter Oath of the young emperor, in 1868, contained the following important passage: "Deliberative assemblies shall be established and all measures of government decided in accordance with public opinion."

"Public opinion" did not mean, of course, the opinion of the mass of the people, who at that time were illiterate and uninformed concerning public problems. It referred to the nobles. They wanted a deliberative assembly which would enable them to prevent oppression by the little oligarchy of Sat-Cho-Hi-To leaders. Such an assembly was established almost immediately, but after two sessions it was dismissed. In the next few years the little oligarchy of southwestern clansmen steadily increased their control over the government.

Between 1872 and 1881 two liberal leaders appeared in opposition to the oligarchy. In 1873 Itagaki left his position in the government and formed an independent political party. Nine years later Okuma did the same thing.

As a result of the agitation of these courageous democratic leaders and their followers, in the early 1880's they were promised that a constitution would be prepared. The government was to become more representative of the people — at least, of the well-to-do, propertied classes. Thus a beginning was made toward establishing a popular representative assembly in Japan.

One of the emperor's advisers, Prince Ito, made prolonged studies of Western governments, and with the help of his associates developed a written constitution based upon the Prussian model. This constitution, announced in 1889, was made secretly, Itagaki and Okuma and the more democratic groups not being consulted.

The plan of government provided by the constitution

On paper the constitution made the emperor supreme in power. Actually the power was left in the hands of the little group which, up to this time, had directed the affairs of the restored imperial government. The survivors of the group, who, nearly a quarter of a century earlier, had engineered the first Meiji reforms, now came to be known as the *Genro*, or "Elder Statesmen," and it was they who finally decided all important

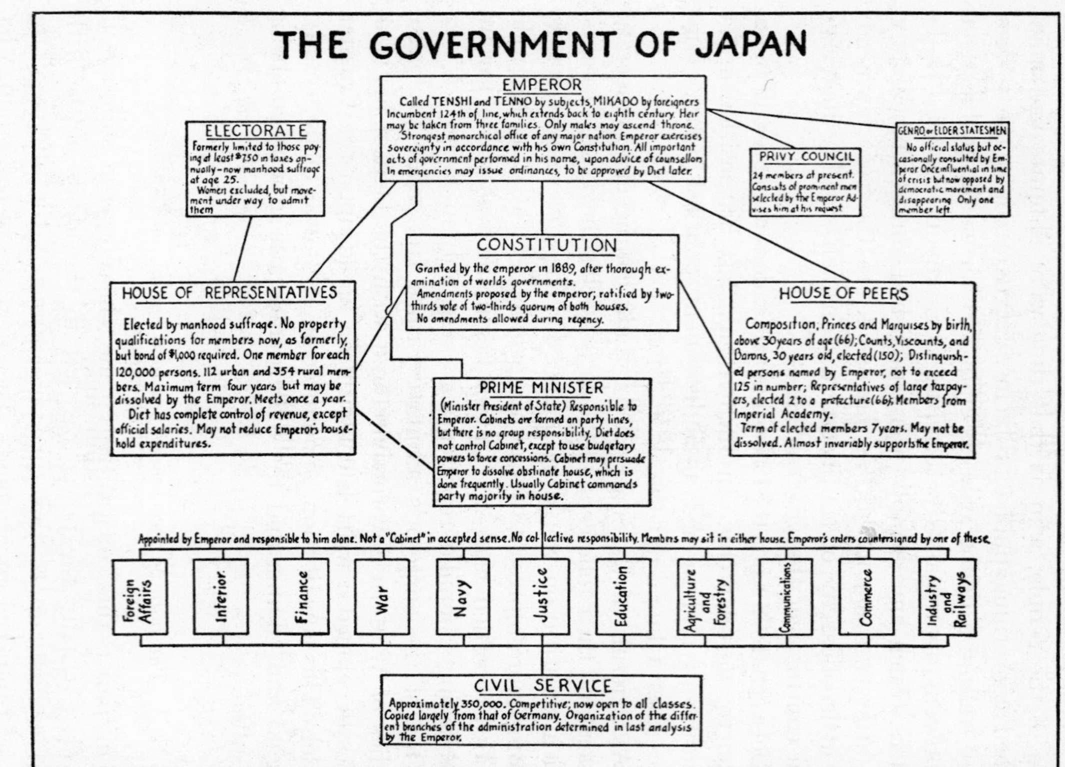

FIG. 201. (Prepared by Elmer D. Graper and James C. Charlesworth. Courtesy of *The Scholastic*)

questions of state. The government *appeared* to be representative. A legislature of two houses was provided: (1) a House of Peers, composed of "princes of the blood," titled nobles, a few representatives of the rising industrial and landed class, and others whom the government recognized as worthy of appointment by the emperor; (2) a House of Representatives, chosen at that time by all males who paid an annual tax of 15 yen ($7.50). Thus a House of Representatives was created, and moderately well-to-do persons were permitted to choose representatives in it. At least a step had been taken in the direction of representative government.

Nevertheless the actual power of the House of Representatives was very limited. This is illustrated by the fact that the cabinet, made up of the heads of government departments, was made responsible to the emperor (really to the Elder Statesmen) and not to the House of Representatives. Thus the Elder Statesmen could defeat any action of the House of Representatives without compelling the cabinet to resign. We must remember that in the English government and in other cabinet governments of Europe the cabinet must resign whenever its proposals are defeated in the popular assembly.

These characteristics of the new constitutional government formed in 1890 show us that, although feudalism had been wiped out, a small oligarchy of rich nobles really controlled the country. Something can be said for these Elder Statesmen. It was they who developed the new industries of Japan, the railroads, telegraphs, and power plants. It was they who built up the modern army and navy, who eventually succeeded in defeating China in the war of 1894–1895 and Russia in the war of 1904–1905. But it was also they who, in doing these costly things, created a condition of widespread poverty and nearly brought about the bankruptcy of the Japanese people.

As in Western Europe, so in Japan, Democracy advanced with the New Industrialism

We have seen that western-European countries became more and more democratic as industrial ways of living were adopted. This was true in England and in the United States after 1800, in France after 1825, and in Germany after 1850. It took place in Japan after 1890.

As the people crowded into the cities, educated radical leaders organized the labor movement in Japan as other workers had done in England, the United States, France, Germany, and other countries. Trade-unions were formed as they had been in western-European countries a half-century before, and became the centers of discussion. Among them was the *League for the Formation of Labor Unions*, organized in 1897, and the *Union of Railway Workers* in 1898.

Prominent among the leaders of the labor people was the "Gandhi of Japan," Toyohiko Kagawa of Kobe. Kagawa was educated at Princeton, in the United States. Returning to Japan he threw himself into the movement to help the factory workers of the great cities, secretly organizing the Federation of Labor for West Japan.

Soon this delicate semi-invalid was regarded as a saintly leader by the industrial workers of Japanese cities. People crowded the meetings at which he spoke so eloquently for "liberty and more rice." One American student described the attitude toward him:

> Crowding the doorways and filling the winding alley paths are hundreds of poor outcast children in filthy rags, whose eyes light up with happiness when they see Kagawa, this teacher of kindness, approach. For him it is always a triumphal march; shrill little voices herald his coming, while thin, hungry, half-clad little bodies scramble to hold his hand or even to touch his kimono. No Pied Piper ever had a more willing, joyful train.
>
> You follow him with real tears in your eyes . . . wan and undersized, smiling with warm brown eyes, preaching God; a young savior, walking among outcasts, murderers and broken lives of the lower depths, preaching a living, breathing Christianity.[1]

But no sooner did labor movements start than the Elder Statesmen and their police crushed them. For twelve years the harshest measures were taken to suppress what were called

[1] Frazier Hunt, *The Rising Temper of the East*, p. 98. Copyrighted and published by The Bobbs-Merrill Company, Indianapolis, 1922. Used by special permission.

"dangerous thoughts" against the government. Any proposal for more liberty for the masses and more food for their starving families was met by imprisonment and by other repressive measures. Spies worked their way into the labor organizations; other spies secretly watched liberal professors in the universities. Young students who organized movements to help the workers were dismissed from their universities and imprisoned, frequently without trial.

Gradually, however, a more liberal attitude was taken. In 1912 the Yuaikwai (Laborers' Friendly Society) was established. This expanded into a labor movement and developed into the General Federation of Japanese Labor of today. Thus, beginning as a social-welfare movement, this society finally became a widespread labor organization with a membership of more than 325,000 workers.

Democracy slowly advanced with the development of political parties

Gradually strong individuals appeared, and small independent-minded groups formed within the House of Representatives. As in various western-European countries, several parties appeared in addition to the two major parties. There are now nine political parties in existence. However, as in England and the United States, there are two major parties, the Seiyukwai and the Minseito, which control 90 per cent of the seats in the House of Representatives.

The Seiyukwai party controlled the government from 1927 to 1929; the Minseito party has controlled it since 1929. In the meantime, slowly but steadily, the Social-Democrats, the Labor-Farmer party, and the Local Proletarian party are electing representatives to the lower house. Thus the rise of labor in political life is to be seen in Japan as it was 50 years before in Western countries.

Then, too, the right to vote has been extended to more and more people. In 1900 the requirement of owning property on which an annual tax was paid was changed slightly, the tax being set at 10 yen. In 1920 it was reduced to 3 yen. At that time 3,000,000 men could qualify to vote. Then came still further agitation, and in 1925 a bill was passed which eliminated the property-owning qualification and gave the right to vote to all men over the age of 25. In the 1926 election 12,500,000 men were eligible to vote. Although there is also agitation for the enfranchisement of women, no action has yet been taken.

Paralleling this movement has been the swift increase in the number of public schools. In 1866 there were only about 240 schools in all Japan. Then came an announcement from the young emperor that "henceforward education shall be so diffused that there may not be a village with an ignorant family nor a family with an ignorant member." Education had become the concern of the government. Today elementary education is compulsory. In 1926 there were more than 11,000,000 children in school.

As a result illiteracy has been almost completely wiped out. It is estimated that less than 1 per cent of the Japanese people of school age and over are unable to read and write. A startling achievement, indeed, and one that has been attained in approximately half a century.

We see the general machinery of the representative government of our Western world working today in Japan. General elections are held at frequent intervals. Campaign rallies, political organizations, conventions, speeches, the use of the newspaper, the radio, the "movies"—practically every aspect of modern government is in action. This is, indeed, an experiment for Japan, one so recent that it is not yet possible to predict the outcome of it.

Is Japanese Culture changing with the Coming of Industrialism?

Throughout this book we have seen that the introduction of machine manufacturing has brought about changes in the culture of the people.

Japan is no exception. We have already noted some of the fundamental changes. As industrialism spread, population increased swiftly. People left the farms and went into the towns and cities to live, working in mines, factories, or stores.

Many Western customs were also adopted. For example, there were changes in dress, especially since the new machine industries demanded new kinds of clothing more appropriate to the work. More and more the Japanese kimono was replaced by the Western business suit for men, and the skirt and blouse for women. Figure 202 illustrates how far this tendency has gone in Tokyo.

FIG. 202. Baseball has almost become a national sport in Japan. Note the costumes worn by the assembly, and particularly that worn by the young woman who is cheer leader. Do they seem familiar to you?

Later, as Western motion pictures were introduced into Japan, more people could see for themselves how Europeans and Americans lived. In this way the "movies" played much the same rôle in Japan as they did in central and western Europe. Young Japanese girls, for example, began to demand that their hair be cut like that of American "movie" actresses. Motor cars, phonographs, and radios brought about marked changes in the customs of the people. Western sports were also introduced, and baseball, the national American sport, became the favorite outdoor game of the Japanese.

In modern times Japan has imitated the fine arts of industrial countries

Throughout her history Japan has imported her arts from other parts of the world more, perhaps, than any other important country. In architecture, for example, new building materials of steel, reënforced concrete, stone, and brick were introduced. Architects from the United States and European nations were invited

FIG. 203. After the earthquake of 1923 a new building program was begun in Tokyo. By 1931 the main business section was rebuilt in styles familiar to the Western world, and even skyscrapers will soon be completed in this and other Japanese cities

to Japan to erect buildings and to teach Japanese architects. In 1923 the great earthquake which destroyed much of Tokyo and all Yokohama proved the superior strength of the Western type of building construction. Since that time, therefore, the architectural characteristics of modern American buildings — especially of the new reënforced-concrete and steel construction — have generally grown in favor (see figure 203). The tendency now is to follow the models of Western architecture for public buildings and to keep the former Japanese styles for private dwelling houses.

The influence of the West in literature. Japanese literature was also greatly influenced by European and American literature. In the late 1800's the works of the leading English, French, German, and Russian authors were translated into Japanese. Translations were generally very "free," the translators attempting to use the Western material as a basis for creating something partially new which would be in keeping with Japanese culture.

Since the World War there has been another movement in Japanese literature. There has been more translation, with the modern Russians especially popular. Russian plays are translated, and acted in Japanese theaters.

Political writings, especially socialistic books and pamphlets, have achieved great popularity as the democratic movement has swept over Japan. It was estimated that in the year 1930 more than 200,000 copies of Karl Marx's *Das Kapital* were available in the islands.

Under the influence of the Western culture, native writers began to develop original types of Japanese literature. Among them were Kikuchi Kan and Kikuchi Yuho, who wrote Japanese "problem" novels. Today their place has been taken by Mrs. Ya yoi Nogami, whose novel *The Sea God Ship* is considered the best modern Japanese work. Another, Kurata Hyakuzo, is regarded as the outstanding dramatist of the Japanese theater. His play *The Priest and his Disciples* has been translated into English and is known even in the Western world.

There is also a widespread vogue of the cheap romantic novel, similar to the type sold by millions in the past generation in the United States and Europe.

The influence of European music. We have read about the wonderful contributions of western Europe, especially of Italy and Germany, to modern music. In the past 35 years this music has definitely begun to influence the Japanese. From the fifth century to the end of the twelfth century their music, like their other arts, was essentially borrowed from Korea and China. In the next 700 years, from about 1200 to about 1900, Japanese poets and musicians devised simple kinds of original music. Such music, however, did not reach the high point of development attained by western-European music.

In the year 1896 American and European phonographs began to make their appearance in Japan. At once they received a hearty welcome, and Western music began to have a great vogue. Even the Tokyo Academy of Music was influenced. Pianos, violins, and other modern instruments were purchased, and the young people of cultured homes were taught to play them. The

FIG. 204. Nothing is more typical today of the old culture of Japan than the gardens. Some of them may be only a few yards square; some are larger, like that shown in the photograph. All are retreats to which the Japanese go to refresh their eyes with a glimpse of Mother Earth

simple bamboo instruments and drums of the primitive Japanese, however, maintained their hold upon the less educated classes.

During the past few years even American jazz has begun to take some hold upon the Japanese people. The invention of the radio has led to the introduction of receiving sets in many centers. They increase the popularity of Western music.

A characteristic symbol of Japanese culture — the gardens. Around the world the Japanese are known for their lovely gardens, and the house of every moderately well-to-do family has one. "Garden," however, does not mean principally flower beds, as it does in America; it means, rather, the miniature reproduction of whole landscapes — for example, little mountains, grassy valleys, roadways, and miniature trees. In every garden one is practically sure to find a lovely pool with little islands, bridges, archways, and beautiful kinds of foliage. With loving care Japanese households tend their gardens and especially the trees. The present writer has seen trees which have been preserved in a family for more than 600 years.

Thus it is that Government and Culture are changing in Japan

Although we see that some of Japan's ancient culture still remains practically unchanged, this very brief glimpse of modern Japan has shown us problems that are similar to those of England and other Western countries, — problems arising from the swift advance of industrialism. More quickly than any people, except the present-day Russians, have the Japanese changed their ways of living. True to their old tradition of imitating other cultures, they have adopted the machines, the railroads, and the other paraphernalia of Western civilization, and they have built modern schools and have taught the people how to read and write. As cities have grown, organizations of the workers have developed and democratic ideas have spread. Feudalism and oligarchies have steadily given way to constitutional government; the political liberties, dear to Western peoples, are slowly being won. All men can vote; but women, as in some Western countries, are not yet allowed to do so. Constitutional representative government has been set up, but the rights of free speech, a free press, and fair trial are still frequently withheld from the mass of the people.

As in England, however, the central problems are overpopulation and lack of food. Japan must now face intense competition with other industrial nations. She must now expect increasing difficulty in selling abroad as much as she buys abroad.

INTERESTING READINGS FROM WHICH YOU CAN GET ADDITIONAL INFORMATION

FINNEMORE, JOHN. Japan (Peeps at History Series). The Macmillan Company, New York. An interesting account of Japanese history.

FRANCK, HARRY A. The Japanese Empire. F. A. Owen Publishing Company, Dansville, New York. Modes of living in Japan.

GAINES, RUTH. Treasure Flower, a Child of Japan (Little Schoolmates Series). E. P. Dutton & Co., New York.

GRIFFIS, WILLIAM E. Japan in History, Folklore, and Art. Houghton Mifflin Company, Boston.

HASKELL, HELEN E. O-Heart-San. L. C. Page & Company, Boston.

JOHNSTON, L. E., and FINNEMORE, John. China and Japan (Peeps at Many Lands Series). The Macmillan Company, New York.

KELMAN, J. H. Children of Japan. Fleming H. Revell Company, New York.

SHIOYA, SAKAE. When I was a Boy in Japan (Children of Other Lands Books). Lothrop, Lee & Shepard Co., Boston.

SUGIMOTO, ETSU INAGAKI. A Daughter of the Samurai. Doubleday, Doran & Company, Inc., Garden City, New York. Life in Japan.

TIETJENS, EUNICE S. Japan, Korea and Formosa (Burton Holmes Travel Series). Wheeler Publishing Co., Chicago. Description and travel.

VAN BERGEN, ROBERT. A Boy of Old Japan. Lothrop, Lee & Shepard Co., Boston.

VAN BERGEN, ROBERT. The Story of Japan. American Book Company, New York.

CHAPTER XXII

INDIA'S MARCH TOWARD SELF-GOVERNMENT

India: the third great center of changing Asiatic culture

Two of the three crowded centers of population in Asia — China and Japan — have passed before our eyes. We turn now to the third — India.

Every country or region that we have studied in this book presented new problems. Each country showed us different ways of living. Even in Europe we found that each people had developed a unique national personality. The cultures of England, France, Germany, and Russia were different from one another.

In Asia civilization and culture showed an even greater difference. Not only in external village and town life and in government were the Chinese and Japanese different: they were also unlike Europeans in philosophy, in outlook on life. Moreover, we found there two Asiatic civilizations different from each other.

And now we come to India, a region that is totally different from all the others — different in people, in social classes, in religion, in ways of living, in form of government, in history. More by its contrasts than by its similarities to other countries will India help us to understand the modern movement of changing governments and changing cultures.

Yet in one fundamental respect it is like all the others. The people want the same things — a secure and comfortable living, freedom to govern themselves, interesting recreations; in short, "life, liberty, and . . . happiness."

THE BACKGROUND

First let us recall briefly the physical facts about India which we have already learned. In this large peninsula of south-central Asia live approximately 320,000,000 brown-skinned, black-haired people. This land of India, separated from the rest of Asia on the north by the almost impassable Himalaya and Hindu Kush Mountains and surrounded by water on the other sides, is practically a subcontinent. Its territory covers 1,800,000 square miles — almost three fifths as much as the territory of the United States.

The land of India is unique in another respect. Alone of the large countries much of it is located in a semitropical climate.

Fig. 205. This photograph illustrates the standard of living of an agricultural group in southern India. Do you know any American families who possess so little?

Note on the colored map of Asia that it lies approximately between 10 degrees and 30 degrees north latitude. This tells us at once that, except in the mountainous regions, the heat is terrific throughout much of the year.

From June until October wet winds blow over the land, watering the rich soil and making possible the cultivation of rice. One third of all the farming land is devoted to rice. It is the rice crop that keeps the 320,000,000 people barely alive. When the weather is favorable the Indians manage to eke out a meager subsistence; but when drought and famine come, millions die. Indeed, India's entire history has been marked by famines. No numerous people on the earth have lived nearer to starvation than the brown-skinned peoples of India. Even today most of them live under conditions of poverty of which we in the United States have no conception.

FIG. 206. A cartoon which attempts to show that India is a conglomeration of political units, religions, and castes. Who is represented as the leader of this procession? (From *The Star*, London)

The Diversity of Life in India

We cannot understand the struggle of the people of India today to become an independent nation unless we comprehend their diversity. The Indian people cannot be classed as a nation, and certain conditions in India present grave difficulties in the way of their becoming one. They are separated from one another in political divisions; they speak many different languages; they are divided into rigid social classes and into hundreds of religious sects.

The different languages of India

Consider the language problem. In the census of 1921 it was estimated that the people spoke 220 separate Indian dialects. These could be grouped in some half-dozen chief languages, each almost completely different from the others. Two of them — Hindi and Bengali — were spoken by more than 145,000,000 people. Two other ancient tongues,— Tamil and Telugu,— which have come down to the present time in a great many diverse dialects, were spoken by approximately 36,000,000 people. As a result of a century and a half of British control about 2,500,000 Indians spoke English. And these numbers account for little more than half the people.

How, then, can a nation be developed in India? Without a common language it will be difficult, indeed. A common language is necessary if the culture of a people is a real measure of its interests, customs, and values. As you can see, the people of India are lacking in this respect.

Another factor making it difficult to unify the Indian people is illiteracy. Throughout India's history most of her people have been unable to read and write. In the census of 1921 it was estimated that 91 per cent of them were still illiterate.

Sharp divisions in religion

Differences in language are accompanied by differences in religion. According to the census of 1921 the religious membership of the people was as shown in Table XLII. Approximately two thirds of the people were Hindus, as were their ancestors 2000 years ago. One fifth were Mohammedans, the descendants of Mohammedan conquerors who invaded India during the 1200's. Twelve million still embraced the teachings of Buddha, who lived about 483 B.C. And as a result of 200 years of missionary work by Europeans about 5,000,000 — less than 2 per cent — were Christians. Furthermore, each of these major groups was divided into many sects, or subdivisions, each with its own set of creeds and practices.

TABLE XLII

Membership in the Chief Religious Groups of India, 1921

Hindu	217,000,000
Mohammedan	69,000,000
Buddhist	12,000,000
Animist	10,000,000
Christian	5,000,000
Sikh	3,000,000
Jain	1,000,000
Parsi	100,000

In general, however, Hindu beliefs are today held by the larger part of the population. These beliefs are ascribed to no particular leader. Thus Hinduism is unlike Christianity, which came from the religious teachings of Christ; Mohammedanism, which came from those of Mohammed; or Buddhism, which came from those of Buddha.

As a result it has no single creed to which, in its essentials, all its followers subscribe. Thus Hinduism is a changing, unfixed thing, totally unlike Christianity, which early developed a systematic written body of beliefs to which its believers have, with essentially slight deviations, subscribed.

The lack of unity illustrated in the caste system

Then there is the caste system, which divides these 217,000,000 people into classes so rigid that it is practically impossible for a person to change from one to another.

The caste system as it existed in 200 B.C. has been described in an earlier volume of the series.[1] Here we need only to understand that the great majority of the Indian people are born into castes, or social groups, in which they must live, marry, and die. The boundaries of the castes are largely determined on a basis of occupation; for example, sons who are born into a caste of traders or of tinkers become in time traders or tinkers also, and marry the daughters of traders or tinkers.

Fig. 207. One of the outcastes. By the outcastes only the most menial and unprofitable labor may be performed

But the system is even more complicated than that; for the castes are *subdivided*, and the subdivisions are also graded. The main point to remember is that the caste system of India divides the people into some 3000 or 4000 groups which must always differ from one another in their ways of living while the Hindu religion prevails. Does this help you to understand why the Indian people cannot be considered a nation?

Below the Hindus of caste are the "outcastes," or "untouchables." Today there are from 30,000,000 to 50,000,000 of these poor people. They can reside only in certain restricted places

[1] Harold Rugg, *Changing Civilizations in the Modern World*, p. 115. Ginn and Company, Boston, 1930.

and can draw water only from certain specified wells. So "low" are they in the estimation of the members of the castes that their bodies must not be touched. Not even must their shadows be allowed to fall upon one. If such a thing happens one must purge himself by going through elaborate rites and ceremonies.

This caste system is a way of living of which we in America can have little comprehension. Yet it is one of the conditions which we must try to understand if we are to sympathize with India's attempt to become a self-governing nation.

Government in India is also a mixed-up affair

Not only in race, language, religion, and social classes is India disunited; in government things are equally mixed up. India consists of a conglomeration of independent states — provinces ruled by Great Britain and hundreds of little principalities or estates ruled by feudal nobles. Furthermore, these are not grouped in well-bounded divisions: independent states are mixed in with British-ruled provinces and with other states.

Three Fourths of the Indians came to be governed by a Foreign Power — Great Britain

There were four steps by which Great Britain came to control three fourths of the Indian people and built up her empire. The first step was made by the English East India Company, which seized trade concessions in various centers. On December 31, 1599, the last day of the last year of the sixteenth century, Queen Elizabeth had signed the charter of this trading company.

For about 150 years the greater part of India was under the rule of the strong Mogul Empire, and the merchants of the English East India Company devoted themselves strictly to commercial activities. About the middle of the 1700's, however, the power of the Mogul rulers declined, and India once more broke up into a multitude of practically independent states. At this time India, like North America, was the scene of bitter rivalry between the English and the French; the East India Company of each nation strove by every possible means to secure special advantages and to exclude its rival from the profitable trade.

The end of the struggle came about 1760. The French were utterly defeated, and although they were permitted to retain a few trading posts, they ceased to exercise any real influence in the political affairs of India. The English company, on the other hand, now secured complete sovereignty over several large provinces and became the dominant power in the land. This was the second step.

Then came the third step. The East India Company maintained a great army in India and appointed English officials to rule over the people. Thus a business organization of one country ruled over tens of millions of human beings in a distant continent. Everything was done for the profit of the Company and nothing for the welfare of the people over whom it ruled. The Company's officials in India, moreover, seldom overlooked an opportunity to make war upon the independent Indian rulers for the purpose of bringing fresh territories under English control.

In 1857 the widespread discontent of the people under English rule led to a great mutiny of the Indian troops (sepoys) in the service of the Company. The revolt spread from province to province, and the British government was compelled to send a strong army to India for the purpose of restoring order. Parliament now decided that the task of governing India should no longer be intrusted to a commercial company. The fourth step was taken. The East India Company was dissolved, and India was brought directly under the rule of the British crown. Finally, in 1876, an act of Parliament conferred upon Queen Victoria the title of "Empress of India."

Even at the end of the period of "Company rule," when the territories of the East India Company were taken over by the British crown, there were many Indian states — some 30 of them fairly large and important — which had succeeded in maintaining their independence. All these states, however, had been compelled at one time or another to conclude treaties with the Company, granting it extensive commercial rights in their respective territories. When the British government, in 1858, took over all the rights of the East India Company, it also assumed all the rights which had been set up by these treaties. But the status of the sovereign Indian princes did not remain exactly the same.

Up to this time they had been "allies" of the Company; after this, although they still retained independence in matters relating to the domestic affairs of their respective states, they were regarded as "vassals" of the British crown. The British government, whenever it feels that one of these "independent" princes is not ruling wisely, can either compel him to accept a British adviser or, in extreme cases, put a more satisfactory ruler in his place.

India today is composed, therefore, of two main divisions: the Indian states, of which Mysore, Hyderabad, Kashmir, Baroda, and Gwalior are the most important, and British India, which is under the direct rule of the British government. In addition to these two main divisions, however, there are certain border states on the northern frontier which are still independent, but in which Great Britain has claimed the right to intervene whenever trouble arises. India is indeed a hodgepodge of "governments," as well as of languages, religions, and social castes.

Thus three fourths of the people of one of the oldest civilizations in the world were subjected to the control of a foreign nation.

How British India is Governed

British India consists of fifteen provinces, in which live 247,000,000 people. Nine of these provinces are so large in size and population that they can be compared to the outstanding countries of Europe. These are Assam, Bengal, Bihar and Orissa, Bombay, Burma, the Central Provinces and Berar, Madras, Punjab, and the United Provinces of Agra and Oudh. Each of these provinces is governed by a British governor and a council. There are also two smaller provinces and four other divisions which are governed by the central British administration.

The people of British India are governed partly from distant England and partly from Delhi, the seat of the central government. Foreign affairs and defense against outside enemies are controlled in England by the Secretary of State for India, who is also a member of the British cabinet and of Parliament. This secretary, like all other cabinet members, is responsible to the House of Commons.

To carry on the machinery of government, there is an India Office. The Council of India, numbering from eight to twelve persons, each serving for five years, assists the Secretary of State for India. For many years this council was made up entirely of Englishmen. Because of a growing demand for some degree of self-government, however, Indian members were appointed to

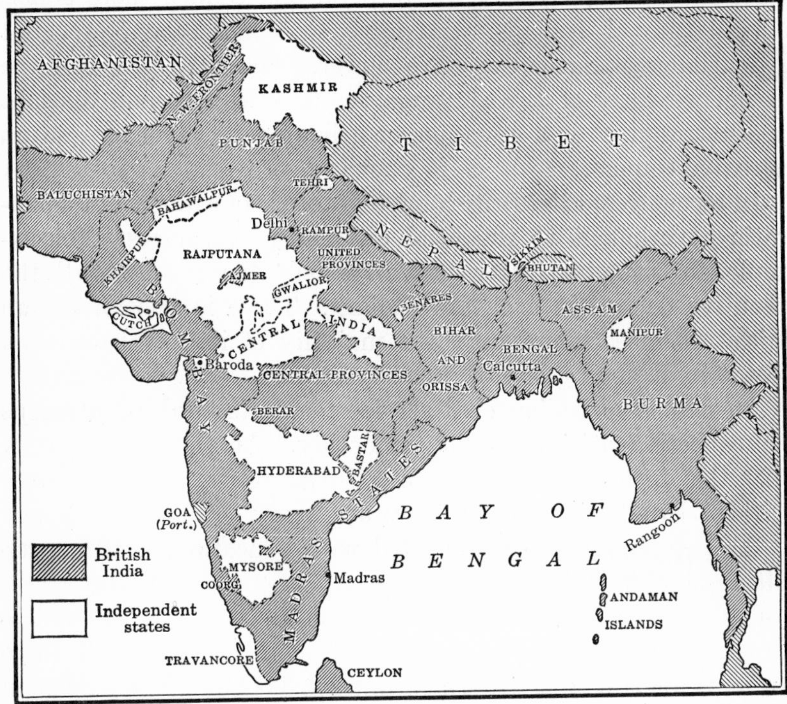

FIG. 208. This map illustrates India's political divisions. Note those areas which are governed by Great Britain. Note also the scattered native-ruled, or independent, states

the council in 1907. At the present time three of the members are Indians. There is also one other leading officer, the High Commissioner for India, first appointed in 1920. This officer is in charge of trade relations and is also the connecting official between the central government and the provincial governments.

Thus the 247,000,000 people of British India have very little to say about their foreign affairs or their national defense. Neither do they have much to say about their domestic affairs. These too are decided by the British. In India, at the head of the actual government, is the viceroy, or governor-general, appointed by the British crown usually for a term of five years. He is assisted by an executive council. Together they control the army, the lawmaking and the executive departments of the government, the courts, the police, and other civil services.

In addition to the governor-general and council there is also a legislature of Indians, who have some advisory power but no real lawmaking or executive power. And scattered over the fifteen provinces of British India are several thousand officials. In each province is a governor or a lieutenant governor and an executive council.

In recent years the British have granted some degree of democratic government to the local districts and villages. For example, in the nine larger provinces half the members of the executive council in each are Indians. There is also an Indian legislature in each province, the majority of its members being elected by a small group of property-owners.

An extensive Indian civil service maintains order and keeps the collective affairs running smoothly. At the beginning of 1929 this included 1261 persons, three fourths of whom were British. In addition to this there are many other services, such as the police and those connected with education, health, agriculture, and engineering.

Out of 5250 officials 3500 are British and 1750 are native Indians, but the chief executive positions in every one of these services are still held by Englishmen. The minor positions in the government, however, are filled by Indians.

The entire government machine consists of 1,500,000 Indians and 12,000 British. Thus fewer than 1 in 100 are British. Nevertheless this tiny minority rules India. How? By force. By the power of the British Empire, of British wealth, and of the British army and navy. In India itself the British-Indian army keeps the people under control. In 1930, of the 3365 officers in this army 3255 were British, while of the private soldiers 60,000 were British and 150,000 were Indians.

This, then, is the governing machinery by which little England succeeds in dominating a vast population.

What India owes to England

There are many fair-minded Englishmen who conscientiously believe that it is right for England to impose its government on the people of India. They point out that the Indians had never known peace before the English came, and that the princes were constantly quarreling among themselves. They maintain that England has kept law and order.

Furthermore, it cannot be denied that before the British came to India the people lived under conditions of degrading poverty, as bad as anything the world had ever known. Very few of them were able to read and write. They could not protect themselves against famine, pestilence, or plagues, or against attacks from invaders. As a result one disaster after another caused the death of millions.

Thus one group of British people has long maintained that in governing India they were really "lifting a backward race out of degradation." It cannot be doubted that there is something to support their contention. In certain regions the standard of living for the middle-class Indians has risen under the industrial ways of living introduced by the English.

Cotton, woolen, paper, and silk factories were built in the late 1800's. Jobs were given to an increasing number of people — at very meager wages, however. Sanitary water supplies were built in many communities, and disease-breeding centers were stamped out. Smooth, paved roads and railroads were constructed to join hitherto separated communities. Today, compared with all other parts of the Far East, India is well supplied with railroads. There are more railroads in India than in all the rest of Asia.

Thus physical improvements in some of the Indian provinces were made under British direction. To be sure, it should be added that the Indian people paid for them and that the Indian laborers who built industrial and other works received little more than starvation wages. British capital primarily developed these enterprises, and British industrialists made large profits from the vast trade of the Indian people.

The British established schools and educated leaders who later led India's march toward self-government

In 1835 a leading British official declared that "the great object of the British government ought to be the promotion of European literature and science among the natives of India." From that time on, British officials, who regarded Hindu civilization as degraded, developed a governmental system of Western education. In this there were (1) thousands of government schools, (2) many others established by local authorities, and (3) missionary schools. This school system, we must remember, was purely Western, and all work was done in English. In order to enter the Indian civil service young Indians were required to pass successfully through the various grades of these schools. As a result an increasing number of Indians learned English, tended to ignore their own native languages, and gradually became Westernized.

Many independent-minded men refused to permit their children to go to the British schools. Others, however, eagerly embraced the new education. As a result there were, in 1926, nearly 238,000 schools and colleges in India, with a total attendance of more than 10,000,000 children and youth. A large number, indeed! This was, in many ways, a startling advance in education. Yet we must remember that even today more than 90 per cent of all the people in India are unable to read and write.

After 1885, Educated Indians organized the Nationalist Movement for Self-Government

As education spread, history repeated itself in this third great center of Asiatic unrest. Never before recognized as a nation, the scattered Indian peoples began to work together in the hope of throwing off foreign rule and building a united India. Perhaps the best single date from which to mark the beginning of the Nationalist movement is the meeting of the first All-India National Congress in 1885. This was the first unified movement after decades of local revolt against British control in various centers.

The movement to wrest the control of government from the

British had two distinct phases: one, the violent, armed-force phase; the other, the passive "noncoöperation," or "civil disobedience," phase. The boycott of English goods was common to both phases.

The violent phase came first. In the northern region of the Dekkan, under the leadership of Bal Gangadhar Tilak, the people were inflamed to military revolt against their rulers. British officials and Indian subordinates who had accepted positions under the government were assassinated. Later, native newspapers fanned the flame of revolution. The people increasingly boycotted English goods, refusing to buy products made in British-owned factories. Riots occurred in and about Bombay.

The British government met these measures by equally violent ones. It stamped out freedom of speech. Leaders were arrested and imprisoned. In 1908 Tilak himself was sent to prison for six years.

In the meantime the All-India National Congress continued to meet each year, serving the cause of self-government in a more peaceful way. The Congress covered the various provinces of India, meeting first in one city and then in another. These meetings served as an important training school for the Indian leaders in self-government. More and more they came to think of India as a nation. Whereas in former centuries they had thought chiefly in terms of the needs of their local districts, provinces, and states, now the movement centered in a growing demand for national independence. "Home rule for India" became the slogan until 1914. Then, to the astonishment of most people, the Indians united with the British to help defeat Germany. They raised large sums of money and almost 1,450,000 men, of whom more than 940,000 actually served in the armies of the Allies, either in Europe or in the Near East.

It is certain, however, that the native Indian leaders expected England to reward them for their loyal aid and give them more self-government. Indeed, in 1917 the British government did promise vaguely to increase self-government. Once the war was over, however, a series of unwise acts by British officials stirred up Indian leaders more than ever against foreign control. Labor unions refused to work in various places. Riots broke out.

Then, on April 13, 1919, occurred a shocking incident which inflamed the Indian people against the British as had no other episode in 200 years. An assembly of unarmed Indians had met at Amritsar in a small courtyard entirely surrounded by high walls. The local British commander, General Dyer, had issued an order forbidding all public meetings. As soon as he heard of this assembly he led a body of troops to the spot and ordered his soldiers to open fire on the crowd. Three hundred and seventy-nine were killed and 1200 were wounded. An investigation made by a British commission condemned General Dyer and removed him from office. The House of Lords, however, passed a resolution defending him and helped to raise more than $100,000 for him.

Under a New Leader the People of India rose in an Astonishing Rebellion of Noncoöperation

Thereafter the rebellious Indian people were more closely bound together. Nine months later the All-India National Congress met in the city of the murders — Amritsar. At this congress appeared a great leader,— one of the most unusual figures in the world's history,— Mohandas Gandhi. Under him developed one of the strangest movements in the world — the mass civil-disobedience movement of millions of people.

Thus the Amritsar murders produced a national uprising, indeed, but one of an astonishing character. Instead of armed resistance, Gandhi preached and practiced passive resistance. Now millions of Indians disobeyed laws, edicts, and orders of the British government, but, though punished, refused to raise their hands in physical resistance.

Gandhi had had almost ideal preparation for this new leadership. The son of well-to-do Indian parents, he was educated in secondary schools in India. At the age of nineteen he went to London, studied at University College, and was admitted to the bar. Returning to Bombay, he began to practice law. In 1893 an Indian company sent him to South Africa to represent them among the Indian emigrants in that region. He found his people even more despised and oppressed by the British officials in South Africa than they were at home in India. They were doing the lowest kind of menial labor, were paid starvation wages, and were living generally under degrading conditions. Moreover, they were discriminated against politically.

Giving up his legal work, Gandhi devoted himself to the organization of his first campaign of noncoöperation. He taught his countrymen to refuse to take part in any way in the life of the community and of the province which refused them equality. For twenty years he worked heroically at the expense of his own health. He was constantly insulted by the rulers in South Africa; he was arrested and imprisoned. Nevertheless, whenever a crisis arose he helped England. For example, during the Boer War he organized Red Cross units and hospitals for the victims of the terrible plagues which developed in Johannesburg. At last, in 1914, the British government passed new laws giving the people many of the things for which Gandhi had fought. Soon after, he left South Africa and returned to India.

FIG. 209. Gandhi, the lawyer

Then, shortly after his return, came the Amritsar murders, the meeting of the All-India National Congress, and the acceptance of Gandhi as the unquestioned leader of the people in their campaign for *Swaraj* — self-government.

From that time the Indians fought their British rulers with Gandhi's tried weapon of nonviolent noncoöperation. Mohammedans as well as Hindus joined hands behind this humble, frail leader. For three years (1919–1922) millions of men and women turned to him for leadership and obeyed his program of civil disobedience.

His followers gave up their offices in the courts, the legislatures, and the other branches of the government. They withdrew their children from government schools. And, most important of all, they boycotted British goods. Gandhi himself led the way in trying to reëstablish the dying handicrafts of the people by adopting as a symbol the spinning wheel, on which he did a stated amount of work each day.

There were other important points in Gandhi's platform for an all-India campaign for self-government. Mohammedans and Hindus were to work together as citizens of the same country. Women were to be given all the rights and privileges of men. The millions of outcastes, or untouchables, were to be accepted everywhere by all Indians. And the sale of liquor was to be absolutely prohibited.

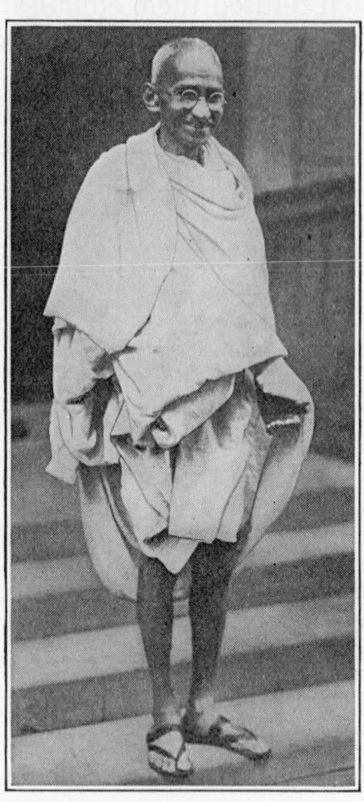

Fig. 210. Gandhi, the national leader

All this was to be secured by a great nation-wide campaign of love, not of hate. Furthermore, Gandhi practiced what he preached. It was not long before his followers were calling him "Mahatma," which means great-souled. By that name he is known today round the world.

Dissensions arose after 1922. In such a huge territory, with its hundreds of millions of people of diverse races, language groups, and provincial attitudes, it became increasingly difficult to discipline the people and to prevent violent outbursts.

Finally Gandhi was arrested, was tried for conspiracy against the government, and was sentenced to six years' imprisonment. In his absence many people gave up the noncoöperation plan and violent outbreaks occurred. Gandhi was released in 1924 after an operation for appendicitis, but on rejoining his followers it was noticed that he had lost much of his leadership. In 1925 he retired for a short time from active participation in the movement. During the next two years conditions became worse and worse.

Then in 1927 the Indian Statutory Commission was appointed.

This was known generally as the Simon Commission, because it was directed by Sir John Simon. It was formed to investigate conditions and to recommend a way by which British control over India could be continued to the satisfaction of Indian leaders. The Commission, however, was appointed entirely by the British and contained no Indian representative. Neither Gandhi nor any of the other real leaders of the Indian people were included. The Central Indian Committee, which was to assist the Commission, was also chosen by British interests.

Their report, issued in 1930, proposed a little more self-government than the Indians had had. There was to be a constitution; a Council of Greater India, composed of representatives of both the British Indian provinces and the independent Indian states; and a Central Legislature, members of which were to be elected by provincial councils. But the government was to be left in the hands of the governor-general-in-council, who was not responsible to the Central Legislature but to Great Britain.

At the appointment of the Commission indignation exploded throughout India, and a new revolt occurred. Mohammedans and Hindus joined hands, forgetting their differences in the need for common attack upon the foreign master. Gandhi came out of his retirement and at the All-India Congress of 1928 became the recognized leader of 300,000,000 people. Warning England that self-government must be given to India before January 1, 1930, Gandhi pledged that he would lead his people in another mass civil-disobedience movement. The British refused self-government, and Gandhi started anew his movement of noncoöperation.

Thousands of Indians violated British laws and were thrown into jail. It is estimated that even in 1931 more than 50,000 native Indians were still crowding the jails of India. In 1930 and 1931 important events followed one another swiftly. The government had by law assumed a monopoly over salt-making and required every Indian household to purchase its salt from government officials. In March, 1930, Gandhi openly violated the salt law by leading a march to the sea, where he deliberately made salt in violation of one of the most hated laws of the English. As a result of Gandhi's open violation he and his followers were again arrested and thrown into jail.

A few months later, however, Gandhi was released. Conferences were again begun between the Nationalists and the British. In March, 1931, Gandhi signed a truce with the British governor-general. The Indians agreed to suspend all their non-coöperative movements in return for promises of vastly increased measures of self-government. The boycott against British goods was to be stopped. Indians were to accept their responsibilities

Fig. 211. A parade of the Nationalists in 1930. Feeling against the British government ran so high that an effigy of British officialdom was shown and banners carrying taunting messages were displayed

in the carrying on of the government. The British, on their part, agreed to release Nationalist prisoners and to call a round-table conference to discuss the whole problem.

From that time on, the movement for a written constitution and a federal government for India advanced swiftly. Already, in the autumn of 1930, under the auspices of the Labor government, which had come into power in 1929, the first India Round-Table Conference had been held in London. The princes who governed the independent states indicated their willingness to join with the fifteen provinces of British India in an Indian federation under the general oversight of British officials.

In March, 1931, the All-India National Congress met again and ratified the truce that Gandhi had signed with the government. Gandhi himself had once more obtained complete leadership of the Nationalists in India. This is shown by the fact that he was appointed the representative of the All-India National Congress to the second Round-Table Conference, held in London in the autumn of 1931.

Thus the movement toward a federal government for India, with a large measure of home rule and a written constitution, was advanced far. The constitution proposed at this second conference would give India a vast measure of self-government. There would be a Federal Legislature, with a Senate and a House of Representatives. Members of the Senate would be elected indirectly, probably by provincial legislatures, and those of the House of Representatives would be elected by direct popular vote. There would also be a cabinet of ministers, as in the cabinet government of England, and a chief minister, probably the leader of the majority party, who would be named by the governor-general.

The governor-general would control foreign affairs and the defense of the country. The army, now largely officered by Englishmen, would be turned over rapidly to Indians, and a native training school would be set up.

Thus India at last is approaching Unity and Self-Government

A half-century of modern education, therefore, and a religious spirit are together achieving two goals that no amount of armed force was able to do. First, they are unifying the scattered Indian peoples and are increasing their understanding of one another. Thus, for the first time, the discordant states and principalities are tending to become a united nation.

Second, these two great forces of education and "soul-force," as Gandhi calls his spirit of passive nonresistance, are producing a better understanding with Great Britain, and progress toward self-government. Self-government of the type proposed, however, will not mean true government "of the people, by the people, for the people" of India. Some of them will still be governed by hereditary princes, and one-man governments will still be in force over more than 70,000,000 people. As for the 247,000,000 of British India, they will still be governed largely by appointed leaders; that is, the people themselves will not really elect the men who govern them.

This, no doubt, is inevitable in a nation which is still unenlightened. Democracy cannot advance far until education equips the mass of the people with understanding. Once they get self-government the construction of a great nation-wide system of schools is one of the next two steps before India's own leaders. The other is the improvement of India's standard of living so that every man, woman, and child in India shall be assured of food, shelter, and clothing.

INTERESTING READINGS FROM WHICH YOU CAN GET ADDITIONAL INFORMATION

BONSELS, WALDEMAR. An Indian Journey. Albert & Charles Boni, New York. A traveler describes life in India.

FINNEMORE, JOHN. Home Life in India (Peeps at Many Lands Series). The Macmillan Company, New York.

GILLIAT, EDWARD. Heroes of Modern India. J. B. Lippincott Company, Philadelphia. Stories of British statesmen, explorers, and military leaders in India.

HOWE, T. H. MANNERS. India (Peeps at History Series). The Macmillan Company, New York.

KIPLING, RUDYARD. Kim. Doubleday, Doran & Company, Inc., Garden City, New York. Gives a good picture of India.

MARSHALL, HENRIETTA E. Our Empire Story. Frederick A. Stokes Company, New York. Stories of India as well as of other parts of the British Empire.

MUKERJI, DHAN GOPAL. Caste and Outcaste. E. P. Dutton & Co., New York.

MUKERJI, DHAN GOPAL. Ghond the Hunter. E. P. Dutton & Co., New York. Life of the jungle villages.

MUKERJI, DHAN GOPAL. Jungle Beasts and Men. E. P. Dutton & Co., New York. Village and jungle life in India.

ROY, SATYANANDA. When I was a Boy in India (Children of Other Lands Books). Lothrop, Lee & Shepard Co., Boston.

STEEL, FLORA ANNIE. The Adventures of Akbar. Frederick A. Stokes Company, New York. A picture of life in India in the 1500's.

SURRIDGE, VICTOR. India (Romance of Empire Series). Thomas Nelson & Sons, New York.

CHAPTER XXIII

MEXICO: A CHANGELESS CULTURE

In one country — Mexico — the conquering march of European industrial civilization met a culture it could not change. It is true that for 400 years Europeans conquered and ruled the

FIG. 212. A typical Mexican farm. Note the barren mountains in the background, and the cactus — the sign of dry, sandy soil — in the foreground. The poorer Mexican people make their living on small farms like this

Mexican people. Yet even today most of the latter — 16,400,000 in number — continue to live in much the same way as did their ancestors before 1500 A. D. Here, next door to the United States, are simple people living their lives almost untouched by the modern civilization all about them.

There are hundreds of villages and towns in Mexico which have never had a wheeled vehicle of any kind. Men and women are still used as draft animals on the precipitous mountain paths. There are thousands of maize plots which have never known a metal plow. In hundreds of communities there is not a book, nor anyone who could read one.

The Mountain that is Mexico

There are several reasons why European ways of living have not been adopted in Mexico. One is topography. Another is

Fig. 213. Note in this map of Mexico how much of the land is mountainous. Does that imply easy means of communication? How would it affect culture?

the very large number of native "Mexicans" who were already living there when the Europeans came, — people with an ancient history and a highly developed civilization. And a third is the purpose of the conquering Europeans, which was to gain riches.

First, however, let us consider the "lay of the land." Mexico is one vast range of mountains, which forms part of the great mountain backbone of the two continents of North and South America. (See map, Fig. 213.) Starting in Alaska, these mountains spread out across the western third of the United States. But whereas the United States has a vast central plain of level land, Mexico is almost completely covered by mountains, which rise from the narrow, level plain on the Gulf of Mexico to great conelike peaks, some of which are more than 17,000 feet above sea level.

Here is a territory of 767,000 square miles,— about 490,000,000 acres, — one fourth as large as the United States. But of these 490,000,000 acres, 296,000,000, or three fifths, are rocky cliffs and deserts, practically useless for agriculture; 44,000,000 are in timber; 120,000,000 — one fourth — are used for pasture. Only 30,000,000 acres — about 6 per cent — are cultivated today. Experts have estimated that not more than 60,000,000 acres could be cultivated, even with modern irrigation. Thus today, although the Mexicans can grow food for their needs, they cannot maintain a very high standard of living.

The people live at a height of from 3500 to 6000 feet above sea level, in villages scattered through mountain valleys. They are almost isolated from one another and from the outside world. Two thirds of the villages of Mexico cannot be reached by wheeled carts, but only by walking or riding over burro trails. One fourth of them are connected with towns and cities by crude cart paths. Only one in 20 has railroad connections, and only one in 50 has smooth-surfaced automobile roads. Most of the Mexican people are isolated indeed!

A "violent country"

Mexico is frequently called a "violent country." Lying as it does in a semitropical region between 15 degrees and 30 degrees north latitude, its territory ranging from sea level to 17,000 feet, the temperature is like the topography — it has its ups and downs.

Its rainfall presents somewhat the same extremes. In some regions of Mexico there is as little as 25 inches of rainfall during the year; in others the rainfall reaches 100 inches. And rainfall is not distributed over the year as it is in moderate climates. For six months of the year, from June to October, there are almost daily showers — short in duration but violent in character. During the next six months, weeks upon weeks follow each other during which not a drop of rain comes to quench the thirsty earth.

In this Mountain Land Fine Ancient Civilizations Developed

How long ago the ancestors of the present Mexican people founded their civilization is a fact that is shrouded in mystery. We feel sure that it was several thousand years ago, and that several civilizations rose and fell there. Figures 214 and 215 give us hints of what those ancient civilizations must have been like.

Fig. 214. The Pyramid of the Sun. Note the stairway which is built from the base to the top. Note also the beauty and dignity in the design of the pyramid

What facts do we know about the early background of present Mexico? We know, first, that 2000 years ago very advanced peoples were living there. Even then, while the ancestors of present Europe were semi-nomad wanderers, hunting wild animals and grazing flocks, these "Mexicans" had discovered how to produce maize and other fundamental foods with which to support settled (civilized) ways of life. At the time of Christ theirs was a city civilization, probably as advanced as that of the countries around the Mediterranean Sea.

We know also that the people called Mayas were located in Guatemala about 2000 years ago. In the 600's A. D. they migrated northward and settled in the lowlands of the Yucatan

Peninsula. There they built their great stone cities, of which the ruins of at least 100 are still standing. The ruins of Chichen Itza, for example, cover several square miles, and archæologists state that they have not yet begun to uncover the whole city, most of which lies beneath a jungle-like mass of vegetation which has been accumulating for more than 1000 years.

How many people may have lived in this one Mayan city of Chichen Itza it is impossible to know; some guess the number

Fig. 215. Some of the sculptured detail work which is typical of the art of ancient Mexico

to be 100,000. And there are not less than 100 such communities. Does it not make one wonder whether our way of living is so much higher or more advanced than earlier ones?

Other examples of the high level of civilization which developed before the Europeans came

Although these ancient people lived almost entirely by agriculture, yet they also performed tremendous engineering feats. There were stone-paved roads, stone aqueducts, and stone bridges. Great forts dotted the mountain sides. The art of mining engineering was also developed to a high degree, vast amounts of silver, gold, and copper being taken from mines.

Single cut stones weighing 50 tons were dragged many miles for these great structures. With what implements the Mexican people could have cut such stones nobody knows.

Furthermore, these Mayan and Aztec people were not lacking in science. They had a well-developed system of measurement, and a number system which compares well with the Arabic, now used throughout the world. They had also a calendar that was more accurate than anything Europe had in 1500.

These ancient people wrote by means of hieroglyphics and made books of paper manufactured from local fibers. Professional historians recorded their history in painted sculpture and probably even in books. They used herbs to make medicines, and their medical men had developed an art of surgery, operating, for example, even upon the human skull and the eye.

By the 1500's handicraft had reached a high level, especially in gold and copper. The people wove lovely designs with cotton fibers and made straw matting. Their pottery has been regarded as equal to the best of the earlier civilizations of the world, and their minute carvings and feather work were unsurpassed.

In the 1500's Spanish *Conquistadores* subdued and looted the "Mexicans"

Then came the Europeans. In 1519, 100 years before the British began to drive the Indians back from the coasts of Massachusetts and Virginia or to take trading concessions in India, the Spanish began their conquest of Mexico.

In that year a band of 633 men — of whom fewer than 50 had either muskets or crossbows and only 16 had horses — landed on the coast of the Mayan territory. Cortes and his men frankly came seeking wealth. Many years before, in the Spanish colony of Hispaniola, Cortes had boldly stated his aim in coming to the new world: "I came to get gold; not to till the soil like a peasant."

Along the coast of Mexico, Cortes found Mayan tribes which he brought into subjection — sometimes by peaceful methods, sometimes through bloody battles. But the tales of a rich Aztec empire ruled by the Emperor Montezuma lured Cortes on. With

Mayan allies Cortes and his men marched on to the Aztec capital, which was situated where Mexico City is today. In spite of protests of friendship between the Aztec and Spanish chiefs, Cortes, convinced that Montezuma was secretly working against him, seized the Aztec emperor and held him prisoner in his own city. With most of his troops Cortes started back to the coast, leaving a small guard with Montezuma. He returned to the city to find it in turmoil, and his little band of defenders besieged by the natives. He called upon the prisoner-emperor to restore order. Montezuma, closely guarded by the Spaniards, pleaded with his people for peace. The answer was a volley of stones and darts directed at the Spaniards. The emperor was wounded and soon died.

The hostage for the safety of the Spaniards was now dead, and the hatred of the Aztecs knew no bounds. Cortes's 1300 men were no match for the many thousands of enraged Aztecs. He retreated to the coast for reënforcements. Then, returning, he besieged the capital city, cutting off its water supply. After horrible suffering the city fell to the Spaniards, and the Aztec Empire was conquered.

The treasure chests of Spain grew heavy with the gold taken from the native peoples. Viceroys and minor officials were appointed, and for 300 years Mexico was merely a colony of Spain.

But the villages in the higher mountain valleys had never really been conquered at all. Isolated and comparatively poor as they were, their Spanish conquerors paid little attention to them; and so they preserved their old primitive customs, raising maize and beans, cultivating the soil with their wooden plows, and making their articles of pottery, clothing, and metal trinkets. Occasionally they came down to the larger towns of the valleys to exchange their goods; but for the most part they lived on in their isolated villages, practically independent of the central government in the capital, Mexico City. Even today there are tribes of Mayas who speak not a single word of Spanish and who refuse to have the slightest communication with white people.

The Spanish conquest, then, was only a partial thing. The Spanish rule of 300 years affected primarily the people of the plateau and the coastal plain of the Gulf of Mexico.

Two Things the Spaniards imposed on the Mexicans

As in Asia, in Africa, and in the northern part of North America, so in Mexico, the Europeans who later came there to settle changed the civilization of the natives in two ways. First, they developed huge estates (haciendas) and practically enslaved about one fourth of the people. Second, they spread their religion — in this case the Catholic religion — among all the natives who came within their reach. To understand the mixture of cultures which is Mexico today, one must understand these two things.

1. Spanish landlords built up great estates, the haciendas, and practically enslaved the people

Today about one fourth of the cultivated land of Mexico is owned by descendants of the Spanish conquerors. About three fifths is controlled by native Mexicans who live in free and tribal villages, most of which lie in the higher mountain valleys. The Spaniards, however, took the best of the level plateau land.

Today most of the Spanish owners of great estates are really mestizos. In them flows a mixed blood — part Spanish and part native Mexican. Not more than 300,000 Spaniards settled in Mexico in 300 years, and few of these brought Spanish women with them. They intermarried with the native Mexicans (Aztecs, Mayas, and others), producing a mixed race, called mestizo.

To understand how the European has controlled the native Mexican and how he still controls him even today, we must understand the hacienda. It is essentially a great farm, owned by an *hacendado* — absentee landlord. (Although such estates vary in size, all are comparatively large.) A recent investigation of the land of the valley of Teotihuacan revealed that there were approximately 26,000 acres of cultivated land, with 8330 people living upon it. Of these persons 7907 owned absolutely no land. Seven persons, all either whites or mestizos, owned 23,000 acres, that is, nearly 90 per cent of the land; yet these seven owners all lived many miles away, in Mexico City.

When Porfirio Diaz made himself dictator of Mexico in 1876, he too, like the Spanish kings, granted enormous estates to his followers. For example, one person received 12,000,000 acres. Seven persons in one state owned 30,000,000 acres, two persons in another owned 5,000,000 acres, and one entire state was owned by only 32 persons.

Thus there grew up the great landed estate, the hacienda. Furthermore, because the people of the region depended upon the land for their livelihood, the landlord controlled the lives of the people themselves. Thus Mexican peonage developed.

Fig. 216. A small section of the grazing lands on a hacienda. For the most part the land in the broad, fertile valleys of Mexico belongs to a few wealthy owners

Of what is the hacienda itself composed? Of a fine manor house (seldom used by the owner), a village of peasant huts, vast fields, and a few general buildings. As one travels hour after hour through the broad plateau region, one sees huge fields of wheat or broad plains where great herds of cattle are grazing. Here and there are large stone or stucco buildings — manor houses of landlords. Near a manor house are large barns and stone silos, and the workers' houses. There is also a little church. The houses of the laborers are little more than one-room huts, of mud bricks, adobe, stone, stucco, or tile. Wood is rarely used.

On the hacienda the Indian inhabitants, in spite of recent labor laws, are practically serfs. They own no land, and they must work whatever hours the owner prescribes. They must produce their own food — corn and beans — and, in addition, everything needed by the owner, his immediate family, his foreman, his clerk, the school-teacher, cattle-herders, carpenters, mason, potters, blacksmith, weavers, and other workers.

Many of the haciendas lie too far distant from the markets for the native laborers to patronize these in purchasing supplies. On such haciendas, therefore, the owners set up stores and sell the natives goods at prices above those at which they could be purchased in the market. Money seldom changes hands in these transactions, for the wages of the laborers are credited to them against the supplies they buy. Because the prices of commodities are high and their wages pitifully small, because most of the laborers are ignorant of all but the simplest kind of arithmetic, and because of the temptation to overpurchase when buying on credit, they often discover too late that they have used up all their wage credits and are in debt to the owners of the haciendas. As these owners naturally will not let them leave until they have worked off their debts, the laborers' position is often not much above that of slaves.

Under the hacienda system Mexico remained primarily a feudal agricultural country. It used primitive methods and turned its back on scientific ways of farming and manufacturing. Under Spanish rule it also remained illiterate. At the outbreak of the rebellions which threw off the Spanish yoke in the 1820's, in a total population of 6,000,000 only 30,000 could read and write. Thus 99.5 per cent were illiterate. Moreover, almost no middle class of manufacturers, business men, engineers, lawyers, doctors, and teachers arose in Mexico as it did in each of the countries of western Europe and in the United States.

2. The Spaniards introduced their religion into Mexico

Acting on orders from the King of Spain the Spanish missionaries pushed with zeal the work of Christianizing the Indians, and as early as 1530 a bishopric was established in the colony. Franciscans, Augustinians, Dominicans, Jesuits, and secular priests arrived to preach the Gospel, and hundreds of thousands of the natives in the plateau and coastal regions were baptized.

In general every Mexican town had a plaza (central square), and along one side of it was built a church. Usually there was a school beside it, where manual arts as well as religion were taught the children. Hospitals were erected in many of the towns, and in 1535 the first college in the New World was established in Mexico City.

Thirty-nine years later in this city "there were about fifteen thousand Spaniards — *encomenderos* [agents], merchants, miners, and mechanics — and about one hundred and fifty thousand Indians. Besides the public buildings, the churches, and the monasteries, there were a university, a boys' and girls' high school, four hospitals, of which one was for Indians; in the Spanish quarter, well-built houses of wood, stone, and mason work."[1]

The temples of the Aztecs and other tribes had been the scenes of appalling human sacrifices, and these were speedily destroyed by the friars, who erected in their stead Christian churches. The present towering cathedral of Mexico City (see figure 217) stands near the site of the Aztec altar where flowed the blood of thousands of helpless captives sacrificed to the Aztec god.

By an agreement made with the Pope in 1508 the king of Spain nominated all the officials of the Church in the Spanish colonies. Frequently from the ranks of the archbishops and bishops the viceroys, or supreme rulers of the country, were selected. The Church in time became a large landowner, holding tens of thousands of natives as tenants under the strictest of rules. The large stone churches which today abound in Mexico were erected by native labor for which little or no wages were paid. At times, however, rich mine-owners erected massive churches at their own expense. The natives were frequently converted to Christianity and baptized in large groups. Without doubt many of them failed to grasp the truths of the Christian faith and the true meaning of its ritual.

The Spanish friars and monks brought with them from Spain seeds, trees, animals, and farm implements to develop agriculture in Mexico. They taught the natives to till the soil, to raise better crops, to breed domestic animals, to learn manual trades,

[1] Edward G. Bourne, *Spain in America*, p. 198. Harper & Brothers, New York.

and to build better houses. The missions everywhere in Mexico were scenes of great activity.

The Indians of Mexico, like the Indians of the north, often mixed harmless secular pleasures and activities with religious

FIG. 217. The cathedral in Mexico City. Near the place where this beautiful building stands today, another beautiful building stood hundreds of years ago. The earlier building was an Aztec temple

rites. That this is true even today in certain rural districts is shown by an American author who describes the "Tiger Dance," which he witnessed in a Mexican village in 1930:

It was performed in the courtyard of a hillside chapel by a group of Indians arrayed in masks and special costumes, to the music of drum and pipe played simultaneously by a single musician. For hours the pipe wove its primitive tune, the drum thumped its stirring, monotonous rhythm, and the dancers, surrounded by a dense ring of enchanted Indians, stamped out the long and involved story of the tiger hunt. (By tigers Mexicans mean jaguars; there are of course no genuine wild tigers in the Western Hemisphere.) At its conclusion, dancers and spectators filed into the chapel and listened to a priest perform mass, while little boys in the towers turned the great bells over and over. The mass finished, everybody repaired to the churchyard again, ate and drank at little booths which had sprung up like mushrooms, discharged fireworks, listened to the village band, gambled with grains of corn on pictures, and watched itinerant acrobats perform on bars and wires strung to the church wall itself. I tried with no success to picture such a scene in front of any Catholic church I had ever seen. Aztec dance, Roman mass, itinerant circus, all enacted in the same holy precincts.[1]

While there were, no doubt, lapses in the lives of some of the clergy, it is evident that for the most part they lived in accord with their solemn vows and gave themselves without stint to the welfare of the natives in their charge.

A Century of Struggle for Mexican Self-Government

For almost exactly 300 years Mexico was a colony of the Spanish Empire, ruled by governors sent out from Spain. Then a revolutionary movement swept over all Latin America, influenced by the earlier revolt of the American colonies from England and by the French Revolution. In the period from 1810 to 1826 practically all the Spanish and Portuguese dominions successfully revolted and established independent governments. Many of these became dictatorships — absolute one-man governments. Democratic government could hardly be expected in any region from Mexico to Argentina because of the lack of enlightenment among the people. Indeed, for 100 years Spanish-American political history is one long narrative of revolution and change in government.

In Mexico the upheaval was led by a priest who had been much influenced by the revolutionary doctrines of the French and Americans — Miguel Hidalgo y Costilla. The rebellion, which broke out in 1810, was short-lived. In 1811 the leaders were defeated and executed. However, another priest, José María Morelos-Pavón, carried on the revolt. In 1813 he issued a Declaration of Independence and drew up a draft of a constitution

[1] Stuart Chase, *Mexico: a Study of Two Americas*, pp. 99–100. By permission of The Macmillan Company, publishers, New York, 1931.

for the Republic of Mexico. In 1815 he too was captured and executed. Revolt continued, but without success, for six years.

Then, in 1821, Agustín de Iturbide successfully threw off the power of Spain and established a dictatorship under an Act of Independence of the Mexican Empire. From that time on for a century the history of Mexico was one revolution after another. In the 100 years from the establishment of the empire in 1821, there were no less than 75 revolutions (*between 1821 and 1876 there were 74 different governments*, many of which lasted only a few weeks or months). In that period the rule changed from one person and type of government to another — from emperor to dictator, to regent, to president, and then to provisional executive.

An interesting and important figure during this period was General Santa Anna, who succeeded in controlling the government of Mexico most of the time from 1834 to 1846. It was he who was defeated by the American pioneers when they settled the northern Mexican state of Texas. Gradually getting control of the entire state, the Americans declared Texas independent of Mexico and made that independence effective. The state was admitted into the Union in 1845. From 1836 until 1848 the Texas problem caused increasing difficulty between the United States and Mexico; open warfare came in 1846. American troops invaded Mexico from the north and from the coast, and in 1847 Mexico City was captured. Peace was concluded in 1848, when the huge territories of Upper California and New Mexico were ceded to the United States.

With the overthrow of Santa Anna a federal government followed from 1846 to 1853. Gradually, out of the chaos of revolutions, the country moved slowly toward a constitution and a republican form of government. In 1857 a constitution was actually adopted, only to be repudiated almost immediately as other rival governments ruled, each for a short period.

Then, in 1858, appeared Benito Juárez, president of the Republic — perhaps the greatest man of Mexican history. He is known as "the Liberator" or "the Abraham Lincoln of Mexico." It was Juárez who fought the growing control of the Church over the land of Mexico, and set up reforms designed to give the land back to the native peoples. His reforms, however, were held back by foreign interference in Mexican affairs. Juárez had no sooner taken office in 1861 than Great Britain, France, Austria, and other countries demanded the payment of large debts owed them by Mexico. British claims amounted to $70,000,000, and other European claims to $82,000,000 more.

France, taking advantage of the fact that the United States was involved in its great Civil War and was consequently not able to maintain the Monroe Doctrine, made Maximilian of Austria Emperor of Mexico, as you have already learned. For three years, supported by French troops, he retained the throne. Once the American Civil War was over, however, the United States in 1867 compelled the French to withdraw; Maximilian was soon captured by Juárez and was executed. Juárez then returned to power and was reelected president in 1867. Again he tried to improve the constitution in the interests of the Mexican people. Again the reforms led to more revolutions. He held on, however, until his death in 1872. From 1872 to 1876 there were more revolutions and more changes in government. Then, in 1876, began the astonishing dictatorship of General Porfirio Diaz.

FIG. 218. Benito Juárez (1806–1872)

Except for an interlude of four years, Diaz ruled continuously as president of Mexico for 34 years. He was a real dictator, maintaining order with an iron hand. Central authority was completely vested in him, and he enforced it by rigid military rule. Revolution ceased. Peace and quiet came to the country. Foreign capitalists came in and began to develop factories, dig oil wells, mine iron and coal, and, in a few urban centers, generally introduce industrial ways of living.

During his dictatorship Diaz accomplished the following constructive, modern things:

1. Built many miles of railroad.
2. Increased the production of silver fivefold and the production of gold 25 times.
3. Increased the exports and imports of Mexico tenfold.
4. Suppressed banditry and made Mexico a safe country.
5. Established a few free schools.
6. Developed modern ports at several places on the coast.
7. Erected public buildings.

But, on the other hand, Diaz subjected the mass of the people to one of the worst régimes in their history. Enormous concessions were granted to private capitalists from other countries. Native Mexicans were sold into slavery for a price. In the new factories inhuman hours of labor and working conditions and starvation wages were permitted. The communal life of the free villages was broken down.

Therefore it is difficult to say whether or not Diaz really improved the life of Mexico. Did external order, railroads, a few schools, and other aspects of modern industrialism compensate for the terrible conditions of life among the common people?

In 1911 Diaz was overthrown by Francisco Madero, and in 1913 Madero was murdered by General Huerta, a follower of Diaz. In the same year another leader, Carranza, overthrew Huerta. Two years later Carranza was recognized by the United States as President of Mexico.

In Carranza's rule an epoch-making event took place. The famous constitution was drawn up and was adopted in 1917. In this, frequently called one of the most advanced constitutions in the entire world, two provisions are worth remembering: the labor law and the land law.

The labor law makes eight hours the maximum limit of a day's work, with six hours a day the limit for youth over twelve years of age and under sixteen. It prohibits all overtime for women and children. It enforces one day's rest for every six days' work. It also calls for sanitary working conditions on plantations and in mines and factories. It provides for the creation of minimum-wage boards and requires that employers establish such things as schools, health agencies, markets, and playgrounds. These provisions were progressive indeed.

The land law declares that Mexican land belongs to Mexicans. Hence according to this law no one not a Mexican citizen can own land in Mexico. Villages can own land communally, but no stock companies or banks can do so. Haciendas were to be divided among the people, and the lands owned by the churches were taken by the government. Thus individual Mexicans living within the boundary of their country were favored instead of rich absentee landlords and foreigners.

Not all these provisions have been enforced, since revolutions continued to succeed one another after 1917; but some have been, and representative government in Mexico has advanced a little.

Five presidents have held office since 1917, two of whom were assassinated. But terms of office are slowly lengthening. Order is gradually being established, schools are being set up, and illiteracy is slowly being reduced.

How far, then, has democracy marched forward in Mexico?

As a result of 100 years of struggle for self-government, do the people of Mexico govern themselves? Let us see.

They have the *form* of democracy — a written constitution guaranteeing civil and political rights. Mexico is a federated republic of 28 states, one federal district, and two territories. The states, each of which largely governs itself, are bound together in a central government, as are the states of the United States. There are also a Chamber of Deputies and a Senate. The president is elected for a term of six years, and he appoints his own cabinet of seven secretaries, each at the head of a government department. The president and the members of both houses are elected through universal male suffrage. Thus it would appear that the country has moved far in the direction of democratic government.

Facts about the present population

Actually, however, most of the people are more or less uninterested in government. They live in their little isolated villages and carry on their own personal affairs without much interest in, or understanding of, national life.

Table XLIII shows that practically 10,000,000 people out of a total population of 16,400,000 live in free villages.[1] Only 13 per cent live in towns and cities.

TABLE XLIII

Distribution of Population in Mexico (Estimated, 1930)		
	Per Cent	Persons
Free villages	60	9,900,000
Hacienda villages	25	4,000,000
Mining villages	2	300,000
Towns and cities	13	2,200,000

Of the 13 per cent of the population, the 2,200,000 who live in towns and cities, approximately half — 968,000 according to the census of 1930 — live in the one federal district of Mexico City. The remainder are distributed in several fairly large cities, of which the most important follow, together with their populations:

Guadalajara	150,000	Tampico	80,000
Puebla	110,000	León	80,000
Monterrey	85,000	Vera Cruz	50,000
San Luis Potosí	85,000		

Furthermore, 96 per cent of all the people are either pure Indian or mestizo (mixed Indian and white). A large proportion of these people continue to speak their original native dialects only.

Indeed, after 400 years native Mexican blood is predominant in Mexico. Certainly less than 4 per cent of the people are regarded as pure Europeans. Furthermore, since few foreigners are coming in to settle, Mexico is becoming increasingly Mexican in population.

TABLE XLIV

Estimated Distribution of Population, 1930		
	Per Cent	Persons
Pure Indian or mestizo, about	96	15,700,000
Native white, about	3	500,000
Foreign, about	1	200,000

Then there is the further consideration that most of the Mexican people are still illiterate. Although many villages and towns now boast schoolhouses, 62 per cent of the people could not read or write in 1921. Nevertheless great advances toward enlightenment are being made. In 1928 there were about 1,250,000 pupils in schools and colleges.

[1] Tribal villages which were never conquered by the Spaniards. In these villages most land is not owned by the individual but by the community.

Is Mexico becoming Industrial?

Today there are fewer than 3000 manufacturing establishments in all Mexico, and these employ a total of approximately 100,000 workers. This number is less than that found in the one tiny American state of Rhode Island.

The leading industries among these few are textiles and boots and shoes. Textiles alone employ half of all the industrial workers. However, the total number is no more than can be found in two or three textile towns in the state of Massachusetts. The other industries which are carried on in machine-run factories are tobacco, paper, flour-milling, soap, brewing and distilling, and tanning. There is almost no steel-manufacturing.

Mexico has Vast Mineral Wealth

The world's largest single deposits of silver are in Mexico. It was these riches that first attracted the Spaniards and helped to finance Spain after 1500, during her century of decline. In the 400 years since the conquest of Mexico City in 1521, more than $5,000,000,000 worth of silver, or more than two thirds of the world's entire production, was mined in the Mexican mountains. Even today one third of the annual output of silver in the world is taken from there.

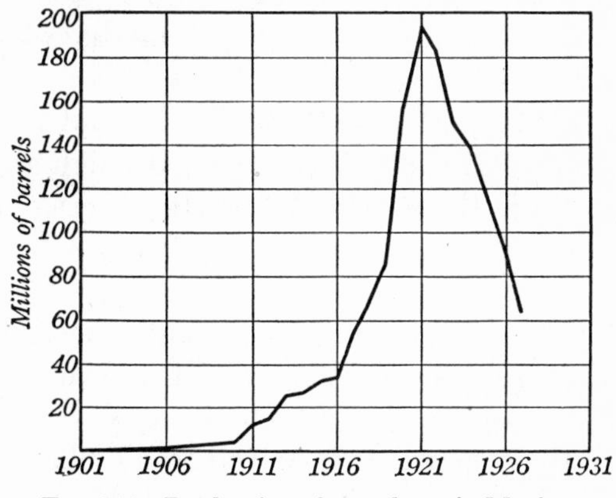

Fig. 219. Production of petroleum in Mexico, 1901–1927

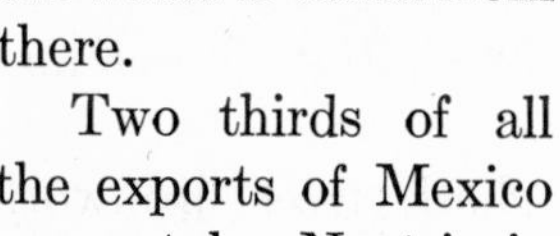

Two thirds of all the exports of Mexico are metals. Next in importance to silver is gold. Then, in turn, come lead, graphite, arsenic, mercury, antimony, tin, and tungsten.

But it is in oil that Mexico has been richest in recent years. Note in figure 219 the astonishing increase in the production of oil in Mexico after 1906.

In 1920 in one field alone — Naranjos — 90,000,000 barrels of oil were produced. But the development of Mexican mineral products has been largely left, until recently, in the hands of foreigners. Because of the national policy of "Mexico for the Mexicans," which the government incorporated in its national constitution of 1917, a provision secures to the government the mineral deposits beneath the soil. Some international difficulties have arisen because of this provision, and the oil industry has been very much affected. Whether the condition of the oil industry is due to the fact that the difficulties have not yet been solved in a manner satisfactory to the foreigners who have developed Mexico's resources or whether Mexico's oil supply is running low has not yet been satisfactorily determined. Since 1921 the production of oil has steadily declined.

The Village is the Center of Mexican Life

We see, then, that the Spaniard failed to make Europeans of the natives of Mexico. After 400 years Mexico is not industrialized; the very heart of Mexican life is still *village agriculture* and *village handicrafts*.

Sixty per cent of the arable land is still tilled by the natives who live in little villages. Although these villages vary in size, most of them are very small, averaging about 300 inhabitants each. Thus a village is made up of from 25 to 50 crudely built huts.

As in most primitive communities, the living quarters of these huts are crude and simple. There is usually a single room, in which men, women, babies, chickens, dogs, and pigs all live together. In the somewhat more well-to-do villages there are large buildings for the storing of corn and other foods, and separate barns and chicken houses for live stock.

The towns have central plazas, a few shade trees, ironwork band stands, and market places. A church, a few stores, the municipal hall, and possibly a little schoolhouse stand around the plaza. With the present movement for education in Mexico, schoolhouses are becoming more and more common, even in the little villages.

The culture of Mexico — primitive agriculture and handicraft

Thus the culture of our next-door neighbors, the Mexicans, is very different from our own highly interdependent industrialism. Here, except for the few cities, each one of the hundreds of little villages and towns is an almost self-sufficient region.

© Publishers' Photo Service

FIG. 220. A market scene at Guadalupe, Mexico

In these villages are no trains or telephones, no great corporations, no factory-made canned and bottled foods. Here are few middlemen and no banking systems; here is no hierarchy of wholesalers and retailers, no elaborate credit system — indeed, almost no money. Here, indeed, is a striking example of self-sufficient community life. Everything is made within the fields, villages, and central town of one little region.

Here, too, there are no business depressions, no hard times, no unemployment as we know it in industrial countries. It is true that people do not have large houses, fine asphalt streets, swift trains and airplanes, newspapers, magazines, books, museums, symphony orchestras, radios, "movies," or automobiles.

Only the few cities of Mexico have these, and the cities are not typical of the whole country. Even the towns of 3000 to 4000 people, largely Mexican in population, are practically self-sufficient.

Every Wednesday and Sunday morning is market day for the villagers. On these days they gather in the central town of the region, bringing their handicraft and agricultural wares for sale. In many of these village markets exchange is still by barter. What money is used is almost sure to be silver. The Mexican "cart-wheel" dollar, worth approximately 50 cents in United States money, is the standard medium of exchange.

What do they sell in these village markets? There are the staple foods — for example, corn, beans, squash, tomatoes, melons, oranges, chickens, eggs, milk, coffee, spices, and pastry. Possibly sugar, wheat, potatoes, onions, beets, lettuce, salt, and beer have been brought from near-by regions. Meat is on sale; but little is purchased, for these natives are essentially corn-and-bean-eaters, as their ancestors were 2000 years ago. Are hardware and various metal implements and tools for sale? Rarely, indeed. Except for the machete — a long, broad knife of which the natives make all sorts of uses — the native Mexican possesses few metal tools. He still makes his own farming implements. For example, his wooden plow is much the same crude instrument which men used 1000 years ago.

Are there no modern things at all in these Mexican homes? Yes, a few. Some of the more well-to-do homes boast sewing machines. Now and then one hears a phonograph and, very rarely, a radio. Also, in the more well-to-do communities, there are metal cooking utensils and glassware, plastered walls, and doors hung on hinges. In such homes the people sleep in raised beds, instead of on straw mats or in hammocks, as most Mexicans do. Furthermore, they have brick or stone floors instead of dirt floors.

However, the Mexican home most commonly found is still primitive. It continues to be of rough stone or adobe, with a single room, almost no windows, no glass, a floor of dirt, mats for sleeping, crude pots, grinding stones, and clay griddles for the cooking of the simple foods. How different from our homes, with their electric lights, gas stoves, vacuum cleaners, telephones, pianos, phonographs, and other comforts and luxuries!

In Mexico we have a Civilization that has Resisted Modern Industrial Ways of Living

Partly, then, because the mountains shut them in away from foreigners, partly because their foreign rulers themselves were not much interested in the new industrial ways of living, the characteristics of European civilization reveal themselves very little in Mexico. The culture has changed but little.

For 400 years the Spaniards and their descendants have lived in Mexico, ruling the descendants of the original natives, intermarrying with them, and producing a new race of people partly European and partly American. But after 400 years the native stock still predominates everywhere except in the few cities. In these cities live most of the mestizos and Europeans, and Spanish is spoken.

What about democracy? Has it advanced in Mexico? Yes; we have seen that some steps have been taken toward more representative government. Mexico is now, at least in form, a federated republic, with a written constitution which guarantees civil liberty and protects the common man. True, it is not completely enforced. However, it is plain that the first steps in the march toward democracy have been taken in Mexico.

INTERESTING READINGS FROM WHICH YOU CAN GET ADDITIONAL INFORMATION

Allen, Nellie B. North America. Ginn and Company, Boston. In this book is a very good account of Mexico.

Banks, Helen Ward. The Story of Mexico. Frederick A. Stokes Company, New York. The conquest of Mexico.

Chase, Stuart. Mexico: a Study of Two Americas. The Macmillan Company, New York. An interesting and valuable book.

Godoy, Mercedes. When I was a Girl in Mexico (Children of Other Lands Books). Lothrop, Lee & Shepard Company, Boston.

Janvier, Thomas A. Aztec Treasure-House. Harper & Brothers, New York. A search for ancient treasure in the mountains of Mexico.

Lang, Andrew (Editor). The Conquest of Montezuma's Empire. Longmans, Green & Co., New York.

Lang, Andrew (Editor). True Story Book. Longmans, Green & Co., New York. See pages 224–325.

Lanier, Henry Wysham. The Book of Bravery. Charles Scribner's Sons, New York. See Chapter XIII, which tells about Cortes in Mexico.

Rolt-Wheeler, Francis. The Aztec-Hunters. Lothrop, Lee & Shepard Company, Boston. Civilization in America before the days of Columbus.

UNIT IX

HOW THE MODERN WORLD IS GOVERNED

HOW THE MODERN WORLD IS GOVERNED

We need now to sum up what we have learned about the world's march toward democracy. We have seen how the four most powerful nations of Europe experimented in government: how three of them developed democratic, representative government and how the fourth, Russia, overthrew absolute autocracy, turned its back on democracy, and experimented with more socialistic kinds of government. We have also seen how these experiments in representative government influenced China, Japan, India, and Mexico.

Have other nations also been affected by this movement toward representative government? Or are the less powerful nations of the world still ruled by autocratic monarchs — rulers by hereditary right or by seizure of control? To a brief study of that problem we shall turn in Chapter XXIV. We shall learn to what extent one-man government still is practiced among the peoples of the earth. We shall learn what kinds of monarchies and aristocracies still exist. We shall note the epidemic of dictatorships which has swept over the world since the close of the World War.

CHAPTER XXIV

HOW THE MODERN WORLD IS GOVERNED

Nine governments have passed in review before our eyes — those of Great Britain, France, Germany, Russia, China, Japan, Mexico, India, and, from our earlier studies, the United States.

One conclusion comes to us immediately from the study of Table XLV. *The modern world has experimented with many new ways of governing.* A range of experiments indeed! And how different from 200 years ago, when almost all human beings on the earth were governed by absolute monarchs! Because we are living in a period of such rapid change, we must try to understand the significance of these chief experiments. At this point, therefore, let us try to see in a broad way how the world is governed. Figures 221 to 225 sum up the essential facts of the governments of Great Britain, France, Germany, Russia, and the United States. Can we make any generalizations about the governments of the other countries of the world on the basis of our study of these five governments?

These may seem too few upon which to base general conclusions. But we must remember that these are the five leading governments of the world. They control the destinies of some 900,000,000 human beings, or nearly half the population of the world. It is they, more than all others, who have developed the new industrial civilization.

From Absolute Monarchies toward Democratic Republics

In spite of what may seem to be confusion in the experiments in government today, one general historical trend of the past 200 years is perfectly clear, and that is that the one-man idea as represented by absolute monarchies, "divine right" kings, hereditary emperors, and autocratic Czars has passed out of existence

TABLE XLV. HOW THE WORLD IS GOVERNED[1]

Name of Country	Type of Government	When Present Government was Formed	Chief Executive Officers	National Legislature		Who can Vote [2]
				Upper House	Lower House	
1. Afghanistan	Constitutional monarchy	1922	King and cabinet	Legislative Assembly	State Assembly	No voting
2. Albania	Parliamentary monarchy	1928	King and prime minister	National Assembly		No voting
3. Argentina	Republic	1853	President	Senate	House of Deputies	All males 18 years and over
4. Australia	Self-governing dominion of the British Empire	1901	Governor-general (representative of king of England) and prime minister	Senate	House of Representatives	All adults
5. Austria	Federal republic	1918	President and ministry	First Chamber (advisory)	Assembly	All citizens 21 years and over
6. Belgium	Constitutional, hereditary monarchy	1831	King and prime minister	Senate	Chamber of Representatives	All males 21 years and over and some females
7. Bolivia	Republic	1825 (constitution dated 1880)	President and two vice presidents	Senate	Chamber of Deputies	All males 21 years and over
8. Brazil	Federal republic	1891	President	Senate	Chamber of Deputies	All males 21 years and over
9. Bulgaria	Kingdom	1908	King and premier	National Assembly (one chamber)		All adult males
10. Canada	Self-governing dominion of the British Empire	1867	Governor-general (representative of king of England) and premier	Senate	House of Commons	All adults 21 years and over
11. Chile	Republic	1810	President	Senate	Chamber of Deputies	All citizens 21 years and over
12. China	Republic	1912	President and council	Five councils: Executive, Legislative, Judicial, Examination, Control		Power of voting deferred
13. Colombia	Republic	1886	President and council of state	Senate	House of Representatives	All citizens

14. Costa Rica . .	Republic	1882	President	Chamber of Representatives (Constitutional Congress)		Adult males
15. Cuba	Republic	1901	President and cabinet	Senate	House of Representatives	All adults 21 years and over
16. Czechoslovakia	Republic	1918	President and prime minister	Senate	Chamber of Deputies	All citizens 21 years and over
17. Denmark . . .	Kingdom	First constitution, 1849	King	Senate	House of Commons	All adults 25 years and over
18. Dominican Republic . . .	Republic	1844	President and cabinet	Senate	Chamber of Deputies	All males over 18
19. Ecuador . . .	Republic	1830	President	Senate	Chamber of Deputies	All adults
20. Egypt	Hereditary monarchy	1922	King and prime minister	Senate	Chamber of Deputies	All adults
21. Estonia	Republic	1920	State and head ministers	State Assembly (one chamber)		All adults
22. Ethiopia . . .	Empire (monarchy)	Independence recognized, 1896	King	None		No voting
23. Finland	Republic	1919	President and prime minister	House of Representatives		All citizens 24 years and over
24. France	Republic	1875	President and prime minister	Senate	Chamber of Deputies	All males 21 years and over
25. Germany . . .	Republic	1918	President and chancellor	State Council (Reichsrat)	Reichstag	All adults 20 years and over

[1] A few countries and principalities have not been included in this list: Arabia, Bhutan, Danzig, Irak, Liechtenstein, Luxembourg, Monaco, Morocco, Nepal, San Marino, the Vatican City. Smaller divisions of the British Empire and of other empires have also been excluded.

[2] This column contains the general qualifications for voters for members of the national legislatures. Countries have varying limitations. Some, such as Bolivia, Brazil, Colombia, Chile, and Ecuador, exclude illiterates; others, such as Costa Rica, Italy, Bolivia, and Colombia, have certain property or income qualifications; others, such as Denmark, Japan, Great Britain, and the United States, have certain residence qualifications. Aliens, convicts, and lunatics are almost universally disqualified.

TABLE XLV. HOW THE WORLD IS GOVERNED (Continued)

Name of Country	Type of Government	When Present Government was Formed	Chief Executive Officers	National Legislature		Who can Vote
				Upper House	Lower House	
26. Great Britain and Northern Ireland	Constitutional, hereditary monarchy	Slowly evolving constitution, 1215, 1628, 1689, etc.	King and prime minister	House of Lords	House of Commons	All adults 21 years and over
27. Greece	Republic	1924	President and premier	Senate	Chamber	All adult males
28. Guatemala . .	Republic	1847	President and council of state	National Assembly (one chamber)		All males over 21; soldiers over 18
29. Haiti	Republic	1804	President (elected by the council of state)	Proposed organization of Senate and Chamber of Deputies		Power of voting deferred
30. Honduras . . .	Republic	1821; present constitution, 1924	President and cabinet	Congress of Deputies (one chamber)		All males 21 years and over; if married, 18 years
31. Hungary . . .	Constitutional monarchy	1920	Regent and prime minister	Upper House	Lower House	All males 24 years and over; females, 30 years and over
32. India (British) .	Empire under the British Crown	1876	Viceroy, representative of king of England	Council of State	Legislative Assembly	Voting restricted to specified males and a few females
33. Irish Free State	Self-governing dominion of the British Empire	1922	Governor-general (representative of king of England) and council	Senate	Chamber of Deputies	All adults 21 years and over
34. Italy	Kingdom	1860	King and prime minister	Senate	Chamber of Deputies	All males 21 years and over; if married, 18 years
35. Japan	Empire of limited royal power	Constitution dated 1889	Emperor	House of Peers	House of Representatives	All males 25 years and over
36. Latvia	Republic	1922	President (elected by parliament and prime minister)	Parliament (one chamber)		All adults 20 years and over

37. Liberia	Republic	1847	President and council	Senate	House of Representatives	Electors must be of Negro blood and owners of land
38. Lithuania . . .	Republic	Independence declared 1918	President and prime minister	Diet (one chamber)		All adults
39. Mexico	Federative republic	1917	President and council	Senate	Chamber of Deputies	All males 21 years and over; if married, 18 years
40. Netherlands . .	Constitutional, hereditary monarchy	1814	Sovereign	First Chamber	Second Chamber	All citizens 25 years and over
41. New Zealand .	Self-governing dominion of the British Empire	1852	Governor-general (representative of king of England)	Legislative Council	House of Representatives	All adult Europeans; every adult Maori resident
42. Nicaragua . .	Republic	1913	President	Senate	Chamber of Deputies	All adult males
43. Norway . . .	Constitutional, hereditary monarchy	First constitution, 1814	King and prime minister	Upper House	Lower House	All adults 23 years and over
44. Panama . . .	Republic	1903	President and cabinet	Chamber of Deputies		All adult males
45. Paraguay . . .	Republic	1870	President and ministry	Senate	Chamber of Deputies	All adult males
46. Persia	Constitutional, hereditary monarchy	1906	Shah and prime minister	National Assembly (one chamber)		All males 25 years and over
47. Peru	Republic	1824 (constitution dated 1920)	President	Senate	House of Representatives	All males over 21 years, or under 21 if married
48. Poland	Republic	Constitution adopted 1921	President and premier	Senate	Diet	All adults 21 years and over
49. Portugal . . .	Republic	1910	President and premier	Upper Chamber	National Council	All adult males
50. Rumania . . .	Constitutional monarchy	1861	King and prime minister	Senate	Chamber of Deputies	All adults 21 years and over

TABLE XLV. HOW THE WORLD IS GOVERNED (CONTINUED)

Name of Country	Type of Government	When Present Government was Formed	Chief Executive Officers	National Legislature		Who can Vote
				Upper House	Lower House	
51. Salvador . . .	Republic	Present constitution dated 1886	President and cabinet	Congress (one chamber)		All males 18 years and over
52. Siam	Kingdom	1895	King and council of state	Legislative Council (appointed by the crown)		No voting
53. Spain	Republic	1931	President	Chamber of Deputies (Cortes)		All adults
54. Sweden	Constitutional monarchy	1809	King and premier	First Chamber	Second Chamber	All adults 23 years and over
55. Switzerland . .	Republic	1874	Federal council and president of the confederation	Council of States	National Council	All adults 21 years and over
56. Turkey	Republic	1923	President and council	Grand National Assembly (one chamber)		Voting restricted to certain males
57. Union of South Africa . . .	Self-governing dominion of the British Empire	1909	Governor-general, representative of king of England	Senate	House of Assembly	Qualifications differ in various provinces
58. Union of Soviet Socialist Republics . . .	Republic	1917	Council of People's Commissars (dictatorship of workers' leaders)	All-Russian Congress of Soviets		Voting restricted to specified working classes
59. United States of America . . .	Republic	Constitution dated 1787	President and cabinet	Senate	House of Representatives	All adults 21 years and over
60. Uruguay . . .	Republic	1825 (new constitution in 1919)	President and national administrative council	Senate	Chamber of Representatives	All adults 18 years and over
61. Venezuela . . .	Federal republic	1830	President (elected by congress) and cabinet	Senate	Chamber of Deputies	All males 21 years and over
62. Yugoslavia . .	Kingdom	1929	King and prime minister	Senate	Chamber of Deputies	All adult males

in the greater part of the modern world. As it has done so, there has been a slow but steady advance toward government by a considerable proportion of the people.

The history of experiments in government is the story of the change from the one-man idea to the many-men idea. Abraham Lincoln's ideal of government of the people, by the people, and for the people has not yet been achieved in most countries of the world, but the trend of political affairs is definitely in that direction.

More than half the governments of the world are now democratic republics

If you will classify the kinds of government listed in Table XLV, you will find that of 62 governments there were, in 1931,

16 constitutional, limited, or democratic monarchies;
38 republics (including Russia);
6 dominions, or commonwealths (including India), 5 of which are essentially republics;
2 absolute monarchies (Ethiopia and Siam).

Note that absolute monarchy has disappeared from all but two states, — Ethiopia and Siam, — and these have only just begun to come under the democratizing influence of Western civilization.

In the Western world today not a single absolute, or divine-right, ruler remains. The few important ones that existed in 1914 at the outbreak of the World War were swept away in the epidemic of revolutions which spread over central and eastern Europe during the years of 1917, 1918, and 1919. The powerful empires of Germany, Austria-Hungary, and Russia, governing nearly 250,000,000 people, were broken up by popular insurrections. Republics were set up in their places. The German and Austrian emperors were exiled, and a Czar and all his immediate relatives were executed. Assemblies of one kind or another, representing large groups of people, took the place of the one-man governments. The name very generally given to each was *republic*.

But *republic* is almost a new name to us. What does it mean? The term *republic* may stand for different kinds of government to different people. To one leading American authority on government it means any state "in which the will of the state rests with more than one person."[1] Such a broad definition could include many kinds of government — aristocracies, oligarchies, and all sorts of democracies. It could include governments like that of Great Britain, which, although listed in our table as a constitutional, hereditary monarchy, is really a government of *many* people.

On the other hand, many authorities agree with Lord Macaulay that Great Britain is a "crowned republic," for the king has almost no governing power. He reigns, but he does not *rule*. Then, too, the term *republic* could certainly include the self-governing commonwealths and dominions of the British Empire — Canada, Australia, New Zealand, the Irish Free State, and the Union of South Africa. It might well include other democratic monarchies, such as Belgium and the Netherlands.

At any rate we can see that the term *republic* as generally used today can represent as widely differing governments as those of the United States, France, Germany, Russia, Austria, Mexico, and Poland.

The Important Fact is the Growing Democratic Character of Government

Regardless of what names we may give to the changing governments of the world, their increasing *democratic* character is clear. With each change in civilization *a larger proportion of all the people has shared in the government.* Turn back through the chapters of this book and scan again swiftly the story of the eight governments we have studied. One important fact you will note: there *has* been a slow but sure march away from absolute one-man or oligarchic rule *toward* democracy, the rule by larger and larger groups.

This trend has been brought about by the rise to economic power of new groups of people. Recall the story for England and the other countries. In England, after 1600, the smaller landowners and the merchants of the towns steadily acquired riches and, as they did so, took the ruling power away from the kings.

[1] James Wilford Garner, *Political Science and Government*, p. 254. American Book Company, New York, 1930.

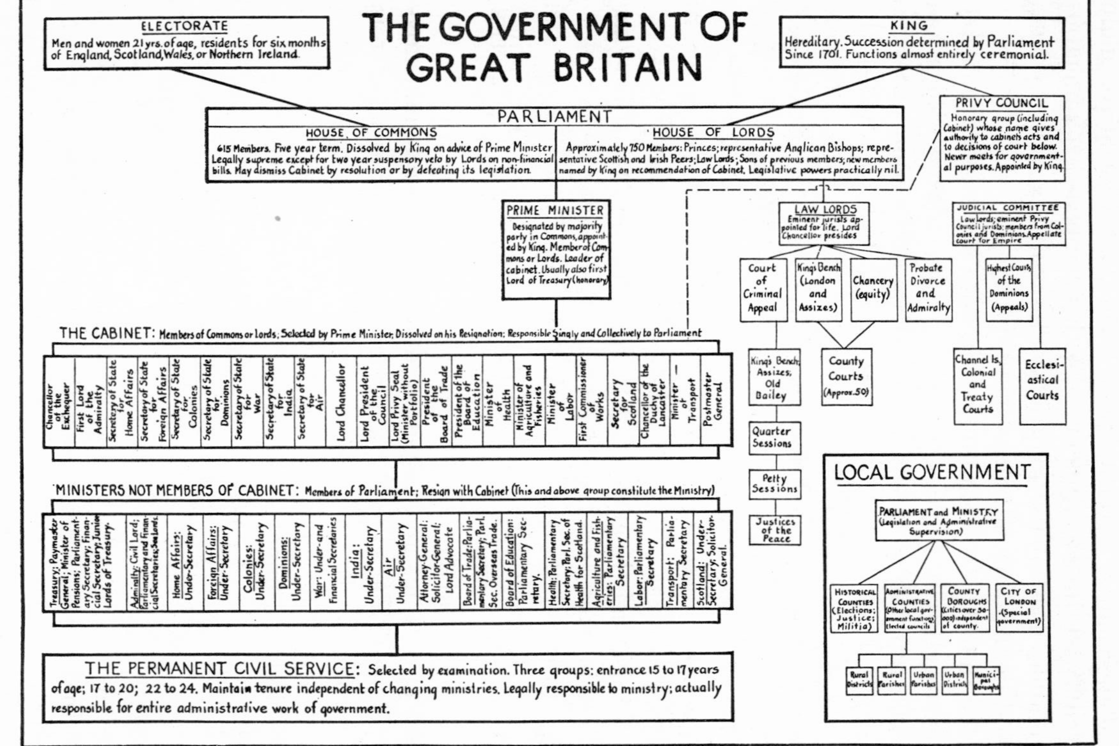

FIG. 221. NOTE. Figures 221–228 are from material prepared by Elmer D. Graper and James C. Charlesworth and are reproduced by permission of *The Scholastic*. Figures 226–228 are adapted

After 1800, with the development of the Industrial Revolution, a new class of well-to-do business men — manufacturers, bankers, and merchants — rose to power and played an increasingly important part in government. As this happened a numerous lower middle class amassed considerable wealth, acquired education, and demanded and got a share in government.

As the Industrial Revolution advanced, the mass of the people crowded together into cities, received more and more education, and began to think more about their share in government. They too demanded political rights, as well as the civil rights which the ruling classes were giving them. So by 1918 the right to vote and hold office in England had been given to all adult men and to women over 30 years of age. By 1920 times had changed so greatly that former miners and machinists, clerks and teachers, had become members of the House of Commons, even ministers in the British cabinet.

Thus, although England still had a king and a nobility, she had really become, in a high degree, a *representative democracy.*

The stories of the march toward democracy in France and Germany, although very different in many respects, were similar in one great outcome — namely, that by 1920 democratic governments by representatives of large groups of the people had been set up. Kings and emperors, dukes and counts, and many other people of the so-called upper classes were eliminated from the government. In their places were representatives of the new business men, of teachers, lawyers, doctors, and other professional people, of clerks, miners, mechanics, and other workers.

The Chief Kinds of Government

To clear up our thinking about this complicated mixture of ways of governing, let us define briefly the chief kinds of government. In doing so let us arrange them in order, from the *one-man* type to the *all-men* type. With these definitions in mind we can summarize more clearly the present status of government in the world. Because we have by now seen these governments developing and changing, very brief definitions will be sufficient.

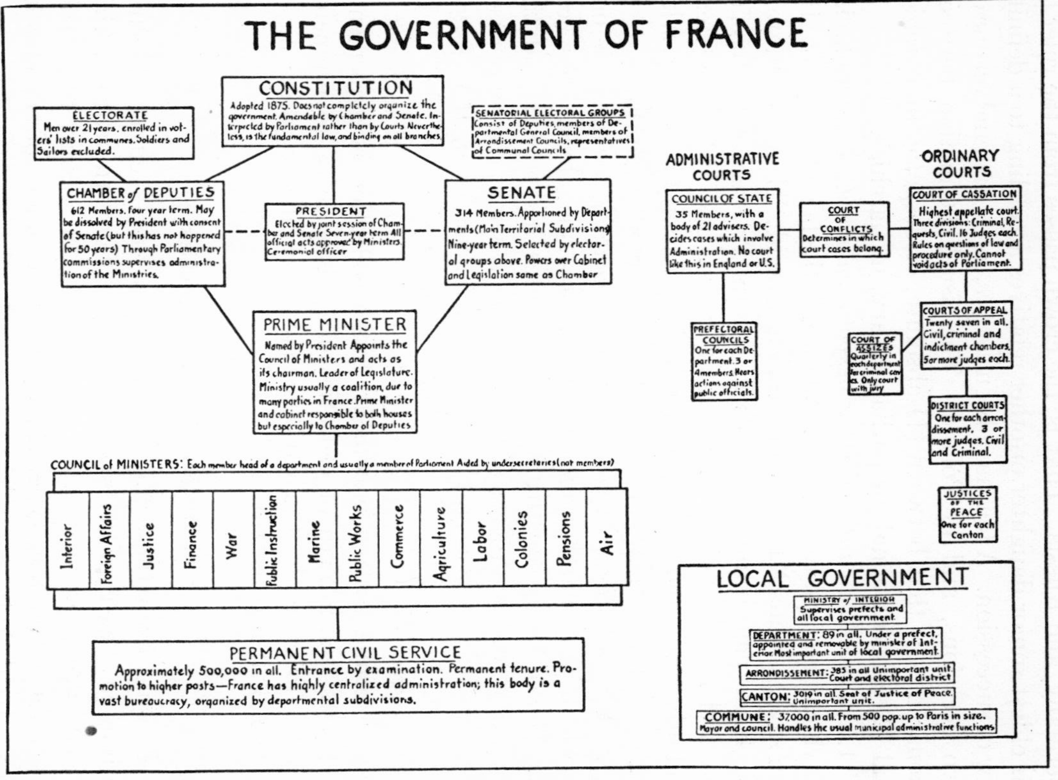
THE GOVERNMENT OF FRANCE
CONSTITUTION
Adopted 1875. Does not completely organize the government. Amendable by Chamber and Senate. Interpreted by Parliament rather than by Courts. Nevertheless, is the fundamental law, and binding on all branches
ELECTORATE
Men over 21 years, enrolled in voters' lists in communes. Soldiers and Sailors excluded.
SENATORIAL ELECTORAL GROUPS
Consist of Deputies, members of Departmental General Council, members of Arrondissement Councils, representatives of Communal Councils
CHAMBER of DEPUTIES
612 Members. Four year term. May be dissolved by President with consent of Senate (but this has not happened for 50 years) Through Parliamentary commissions supervises administration of the Ministries.
PRESIDENT
Elected by joint session of Chamber and Senate. Seven-year term. All official acts approved by Ministers. Ceremonial officer
SENATE
314 Members. Apportioned by Departments (Main Territorial Subdivisions) Nine-year term. Selected by electoral groups above. Powers over Cabinet and Legislation same as Chamber
PRIME MINISTER
Named by President. Appoints the Council of Ministers and acts as its chairman. Leader of Legislature. Ministry usually a coalition, due to many parties in France. Prime Minister and cabinet responsible to both houses but especially to Chamber of Deputies
COUNCIL of MINISTERS: Each member head of a department and usually a member of Parliament. Aided by undersecretaries (not members)
Interior
Foreign Affairs
Justice
Finance
War
Public Instruction
Marine
Public Works
Commerce
Agriculture
Labor
Colonies
Pensions
Air
PERMANENT CIVIL SERVICE
Approximately 500,000 in all. Entrance by examination. Permanent tenure. Promotion to higher posts—France has highly centralized administration; this body is a vast bureaucracy, organized by departmental subdivisions.
ADMINISTRATIVE COURTS
COUNCIL OF STATE
35 Members, with a body of 21 advisers. Decides cases which involve Administration. No court like this in England or U.S.
PREFECTORAL COUNCILS
One for each Department. 3 or 4 members. Hears actions against public officials.
COURT OF CONFLICTS
Determines in which court cases belong.
ORDINARY COURTS
COURT OF CASSATION
Highest appellate court. Three divisions: Criminal, Requests, Civil. 16 Judges each. Rules on questions of law and procedure only. Cannot void acts of Parliament.
COURTS OF APPEAL
Twenty seven in all. Civil, criminal and indictment chambers. 5 or more judges each.
COURT OF ASSIZES
Quarterly in each department for criminal cases. Only court with jury
DISTRICT COURTS
One for each arrondissement. 3 or more judges. Civil and Criminal.
JUSTICES OF THE PEACE
One for each Canton
LOCAL GOVERNMENT
MINISTRY of INTERIOR
Supervises prefects and all local government.
DEPARTMENT: 89 in all. Under a prefect, appointed and removable by minister of Interior. Most important unit of local government.
ARRONDISSEMENT: 385 in all Unimportant unit. Court and electoral district
CANTON: 3019 in all. Seat of Justice of Peace. Unimportant unit.
COMMUNE: 37,000 in all. From 500 pop. up to Paris in size. Mayor and council. Handles the usual municipal administrative functions

Fig. 222

1. Monarchies

Most monarchies have been *hereditary*, as in England, France, Germany, and Russia. That is, the crown passes from the ruler to his eldest son or daughter or other relatives according to a definite law of succession. A few have been *elective*, as in England on one or two occasions, and in Poland. The usual distinction between monarchies is that between (1) absolute, or despotic, monarchies and (2) constitutional, or parliamentary, monarchies.

1. *An absolute (unlimited), or despotic, monarchy* is a monarchy in which one man really rules. His will is the law of the land. He can say, as Louis XIV is reported to have said, "I am the State." We have seen examples of this in certain Prussian and Russian monarchs — Frederick the Great in Prussia and Peter the Great and other Romanovs in Russia. Such monarchies have now, with two exceptions, been eliminated from the modern world.

2. *A constitutional (limited), or parliamentary, monarchy* is one in which a monarch *reigns* but does not rule alone. His acts are *limited* by a constitution which states his powers and the powers of representatives of the people as a whole. In some cases the constitution is a single written document, as in the United States, in Germany, and in other recently formed republics. In other cases, notably in Great Britain, the constitution is not a single, formal written document, but a collection of agreements and laws, the growth of centuries of experience in government. Recall, for example, the various charters of liberty which make up the British constitution.

2. Aristocracies and oligarchies[1]

Passing from these forms of one-man rule — either absolute or limited — we consider next those forms of government in which a small group or class controls the state. In ancient times this was a most common type. Thus, the government of the Greeks was carried on by a small, aristocratic, well-to-do upper class.

The first governments in most of the American colonies — in Virginia, Massachusetts Bay, and the Carolinas — were illustra-

[1] Some authorities attempt to distinguish between these two types,— aristocracy and oligarchy,— but for our purposes it is not necessary to do so.

tions of this type of government. A few men governed the entire colony. There was no representative assembly. Theoretically this form of government is now nearly nonexistent on the earth; but, as we shall soon see, there is some reason for believing that actually many so-called democracies are oligarchies of one kind or another.

3. Democracies

If you ask the first ten people whom you meet what they mean by a "democratic government," do you think their answers will agree? They will probably not, for the term *democracy* has been used with many different meanings.

We can venture the opinion, however, that their answers will agree in one general respect. They will all insist that a democratic government is one in which a very large proportion of the people have a share in the government. It will be defined nearly always as a government of *many men* rather than as a government of *one man* or *few men*. But beyond that, definitions will differ widely.

Perhaps if we next distinguish various kinds of democracies it will be easier to define the idea more definitely. In the first place, democracies can be thought of as direct, or "pure," on the one hand, and indirect, or representative, on the other.

1. *Direct, or pure, democracies.* A pure democracy is one in which the people pass, execute, and interpret laws *directly*, in public assembly. Clear examples are found today in certain forms of local government. The New England town meeting is a good example.[1] Here the great majority of the citizens actually come together, discuss their problems, and decide them jointly. Each citizen registers his decision directly.

The outstanding examples of pure democracy in state government today are those of certain cantons in Switzerland. Today, as 1000 years ago, the territory and population of these cantons are both very small (something like an American township), and the people can come together in "open-air parliament" and decide public questions.

But a moment's thought will show us that the rapid growth

[1] See Volume V of this series, *An Introduction to Problems of American Culture*, Chap. X.

of population in the last century and the expansion of national territories have made the town-meeting type of government impracticable in most cities or states.

This form of government can be used only in *small localities*, in which the total number of electors is also small. Face-to-face meeting, public exchange of views, and the registering of judgments are essential.

How could the people of New York City, Chicago, or any other large modern city "come together," discuss their problems, and register public decisions? How, then, could the people of the United States, Great Britain, France, Germany, Russia, or any of the 60-odd governments today adopt the direct form of national government? Of course they could not.

2. *Indirect, or representative, democracies.* So, out of the necessities of the situation, modern peoples everywhere have devised one or another form of indirect, or representative, government. In this form the citizens choose representatives who, meeting for them in public assembly, discuss the problems of government of all the people and pass laws.

We have already seen how such a democratic public assembly grew up in England after 1200 and was known as the House of Commons. In the United States, after 1789, the same kind of body was known as the House of Representatives. In France, after 1814, such a body was called the Chamber of Deputies, and in Germany, after 1871, the Reichstag.

In almost all other modern countries today such a representative assembly acts in place of the whole body of citizens. Indeed, throughout all western Europe and the Americas one kind or another of representative government is employed.

Note, furthermore, that most of the so-called *monarchies* today are really representative democracies. Great Britain, Belgium, Denmark, Norway, Sweden, the Netherlands — all are constitutional, or limited, monarchies. Yet all are really *representative* democracies. Each has a constitution, restricting the powers of the king. Each has a legislative assembly to which is given the chief power to pass laws, levy taxes, declare war, make treaties, and do other things important to the lives of the people.

Thus we see that the general name given to a government —

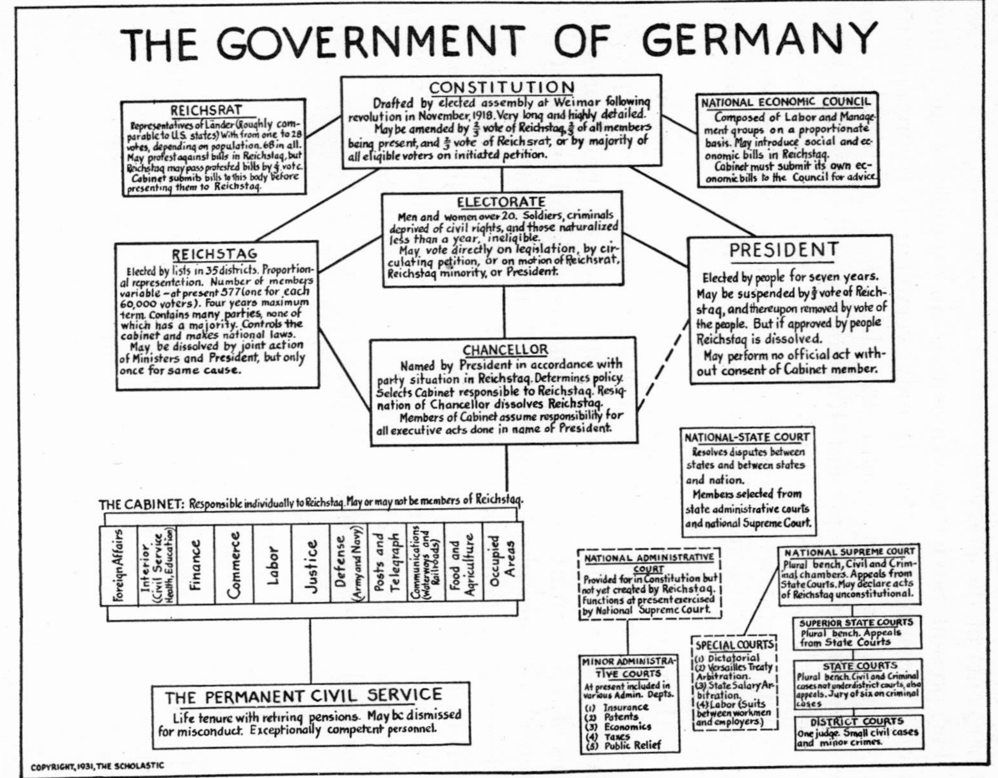

THE GOVERNMENT OF GERMANY
CONSTITUTION
Drafted by elected assembly at Weimar following revolution in November, 1918. Very long and highly detailed.
May be amended by 2/3 vote of Reichstag, 2/3 of all members being present, and 2/3 vote of Reichsrat, or by majority of all eligible voters on initiated petition.
REICHSRAT
Representatives of Länder (Roughly comparable to U.S. states) With from one to 28 votes, depending on population. 68 in all. May protest against bills in Reichstag, but Reichstag may pass protested bills by 2/3 vote.
Cabinet submits bills to this body before presenting them to Reichstag.
NATIONAL ECONOMIC COUNCIL
Composed of Labor and Management groups on a proportionate basis. May introduce social and economic bills in Reichstag.
Cabinet must submit its own economic bills to the Council for advice.
ELECTORATE
Men and women over 20. Soldiers, criminals deprived of civil rights, and those naturalized less than a year, ineligible.
May vote directly on legislation, by circulating petition, or on motion of Reichsrat, Reichstag minority, or President.
REICHSTAG
Elected by lists in 35 districts. Proportional representation. Number of members variable – at present 577 (one for each 60,000 voters). Four years maximum term. Contains many parties, none of which has a majority. Controls the cabinet and makes national laws.
May be dissolved by joint action of Ministers and President, but only once for same cause.
PRESIDENT
Elected by people for seven years.
May be suspended by 2/3 vote of Reichstag, and thereupon removed by vote of the people. But if approved by people Reichstag is dissolved.
May perform no official act without consent of Cabinet member.
CHANCELLOR
Named by President in accordance with party situation in Reichstag. Determines policy. Selects Cabinet responsible to Reichstag. Resignation of Chancellor dissolves Reichstag.
Members of Cabinet assume responsibility for all executive acts done in name of President.
NATIONAL-STATE COURT
Resolves disputes between states and between states and nation.
Members selected from state administrative courts and national Supreme Court.
THE CABINET: Responsible individually to Reichstag. May or may not be members of Reichstag.
Foreign Affairs
Interior (Civil Service Health, Education)
Finance
Commerce
Labor
Justice
Defense (Army and Navy)
Posts and Telegraph
Communications (Waterways and Railroads)
Food and Agriculture
Occupied Areas
THE PERMANENT CIVIL SERVICE
Life tenure with retiring pensions. May be dismissed for misconduct. Exceptionally competent personnel.
NATIONAL ADMINISTRATIVE COURT
Provided for in Constitution but not yet created by Reichstag. Functions at present exercised by National Supreme Court.
MINOR ADMINISTRATIVE COURTS
At present included in various Admin. Depts.
(1) Insurance
(2) Patents
(3) Economics
(4) Taxes
(5) Public Relief
SPECIAL COURTS
(1) Dictatorial
(2) Versailles Treaty Arbitration.
(3) State Salary Arbitration.
(4) Labor (Suits between workmen and employers.)
NATIONAL SUPREME COURT
Plural bench, Civil and Criminal chambers. Appeals from State Courts. May declare acts of Reichstag unconstitutional.
SUPERIOR STATE COURTS
Plural bench. Appeals from State Courts
STATE COURTS
Plural bench. Civil and Criminal cases not under district courts, also appeals. Jury of six on criminal cases
DISTRICT COURTS
One judge. Small civil cases and minor crimes.
COPYRIGHT, 1931, THE SCHOLASTIC

Fig. 223

be it republic, monarchy, commonwealth, or kingdom — is not the important thing. The really important question is, Does the government register the will of the people as a whole? Or, more definitely, Does it register the will of a majority (more than 50 per cent) of the people?

The present Soviet government is an example of an indirect form of government that is only very faintly representative. Notice from the chart of figure 224 the *indirect* and *unrepresentative* character of the present Russian government. The people themselves choose representatives who meet in local soviets. These representatives choose from their number other representatives who meet as a higher congress. They, in turn, choose others for a regional congress.

So the process continues until finally a small council of a score or so men govern the country. But they are not direct representatives of the people. At best they are no more than representatives of representatives of representatives of small groups of local interested people who belong to the Communist party.

From these examples we are reminded that representative government itself varies greatly. It may be (1) so direct that each citizen votes directly for presidents, senators, deputies, mayors, judges, what not; or (2) so indirect, as in present-day Russia, that it practically loses its representative character.

Most Representative Governments today are Parliamentary and have Two Houses

Following the example of England, the leading governments of the world have in recent times set up one form or another of parliamentary government. (See figures 221, 222, 223, and 225.) In the greater number of the chief representative governments of the world, laws are made by a twofold legislature. This is called a *bicameral* (two-chambered) government. There are only two instances of the *unicameral* (one-chambered) government among the more powerful governments of the world,— Spain and Russia.

This two-chambered scheme usually consists of a lower house, or popular assembly, elected directly by the citizens. This is given different names in different countries: House of Commons,

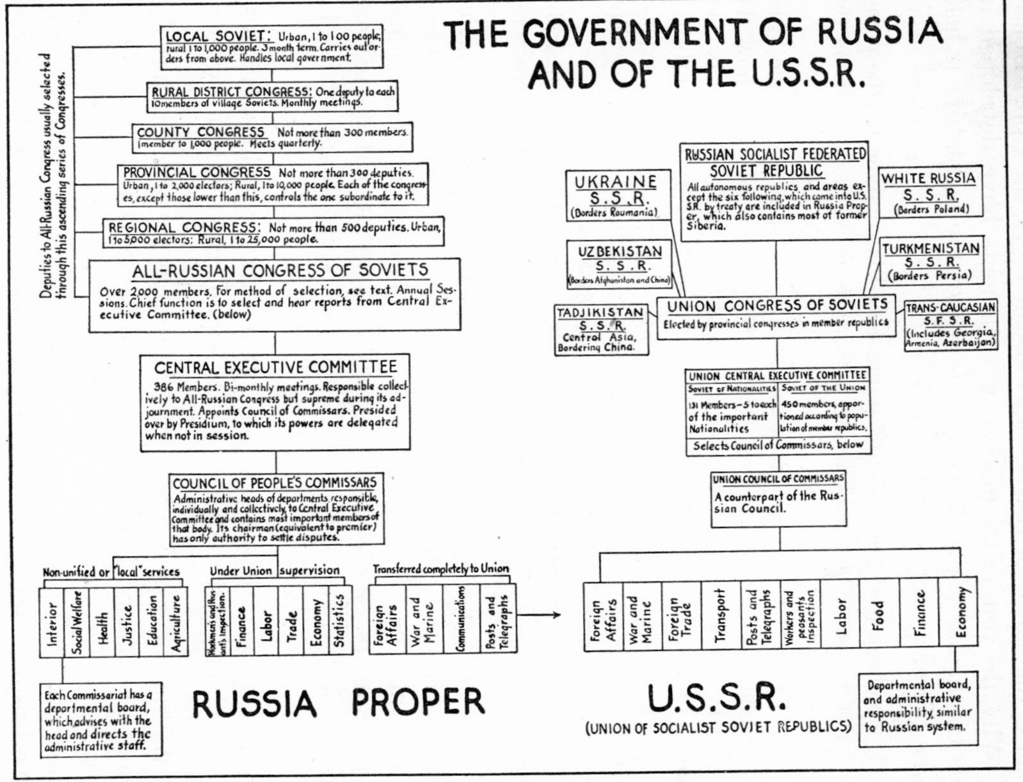
THE GOVERNMENT OF RUSSIA AND OF THE U.S.S.R.
Deputies to All-Russian Congress usually selected through this ascending series of Congresses.
LOCAL SOVIET: Urban, 1 to 100 people; rural 1 to 1,000 people. 3 month term. Carries out orders from above. Handles local government.
RURAL DISTRICT CONGRESS: One deputy to each 10 members of village Soviets. Monthly meetings.
COUNTY CONGRESS Not more than 300 members. 1 member to 1,000 people. Meets quarterly.
PROVINCIAL CONGRESS Not more than 300 deputies. Urban, 1 to 2,000 electors; Rural, 1 to 10,000 people. Each of the congresses, except those lower than this, controls the one subordinate to it.
REGIONAL CONGRESS: Not more than 500 deputies. Urban, 1 to 5,000 electors: Rural, 1 to 25,000 people.
ALL-RUSSIAN CONGRESS OF SOVIETS
Over 2,000 members. For method of selection, see text. Annual Sessions. Chief function is to select and hear reports from Central Executive Committee. (below)
CENTRAL EXECUTIVE COMMITTEE
386 Members. Bi-monthly meetings. Responsible collectively to All-Russian Congress but supreme during its adjournment. Appoints Council of Commissars. Presided over by Presidium, to which its powers are delegated when not in session.
COUNCIL OF PEOPLE'S COMMISSARS
Administrative heads of departments responsible, individually and collectively, to Central Executive Committee and contains most important members of that body. Its chairman (equivalent to premier) has only authority to settle disputes.
Non-unified or "local" services
Interior
Social Welfare
Health
Justice
Education
Agriculture
Under Union supervision
Workmen's and Peasant's Inspection.
Finance
Labor
Trade
Economy
Statistics
Transferred completely to Union
Foreign Affairs
War and Marine
Communications
Posts and Telegraphs
Each Commissariat has a departmental board, which advises with the head and directs the administrative staff.
RUSSIA PROPER
UKRAINE S.S.R. (Borders Roumania)
UZBEKISTAN S.S.R. (Borders Afghanistan and China)
TADJIKISTAN S.S.R. Central Asia, Bordering China.
RUSSIAN SOCIALIST FEDERATED SOVIET REPUBLIC
All autonomous republics and areas except the six following, which came into U.S.S.R. by treaty are included in Russia Proper, which also contains most of former Siberia.
WHITE RUSSIA S.S.R. (Borders Poland)
TURKMENISTAN S.S.R. (Borders Persia)
TRANS-CAUCASIAN S.F.S.R. (Includes Georgia, Armenia, Azerbaijan)
UNION CONGRESS OF SOVIETS
Elected by provincial congresses in member republics
UNION CENTRAL EXECUTIVE COMMITTEE
Soviet of Nationalities
131 Members—5 to each of the important Nationalities
Soviet of the Union
450 members, apportioned according to population of member republics.
Selects Council of Commissars, below
UNION COUNCIL OF COMMISSARS
A counterpart of the Russian Council.
Foreign Affairs
War and Marine
Foreign Trade
Transport
Posts and Telegraphs
Workers and peasants Inspection
Labor
Food
Finance
Economy
Departmental board, and administrative responsibility, similar to Russian system.
U.S.S.R.
(UNION OF SOCIALIST SOVIET REPUBLICS)

FIG. 224

House of Representatives, Chamber of Deputies, etc. There is also an upper house, elected generally by other representative bodies and not so directly a *popular* body. This is variously named: the Senate, the House of Lords, the House of Peers, the Upper House.

Why do you think modern governments have developed in this bicameral way? A second branch of the legislature is held to be necessary for several reasons:

1. To check hasty or rash and impassioned lawmaking by the popular lower house. The upper house is thus regarded as a check on the lower one.

2. To protect the people from the possible tyranny of a single legislating body. In the history of the United States we know how the Senate has delayed the passing of new legislation. The same has been true of the House of Lords in England. Although very frequently the second house has thereby retarded progress, in the long run experts believe that the security of the nation is greatly enhanced by requiring the concurrence of a second chamber in lawmaking.

3. To represent more fairly the various regions or units, such as the states of the United States, brought together under a federal government.

In the advance of democracy the tendency has been to restrict the powers of the upper chambers and to put the government chiefly into the hands of the lower, popular, directly representative chambers. We have already seen examples of that in Great Britain, in the curtailment of the powers of the House of Lords.

The Two Principal Types of Representative Government: (1) Cabinet (European); (2) Presidential (American)

Within the past century representative government has developed in Europe and in the Americas in two somewhat different ways. European countries have tended to follow England's example and organize what is known as cabinet government. Latin-American countries have tended to follow the United States and set up what is called presidential government. As we now study examples of the two, let us note three important differences between them.

First, the cabinet, as in Great Britain, France, and Germany, consists of a number of department heads, each of whom is gen-

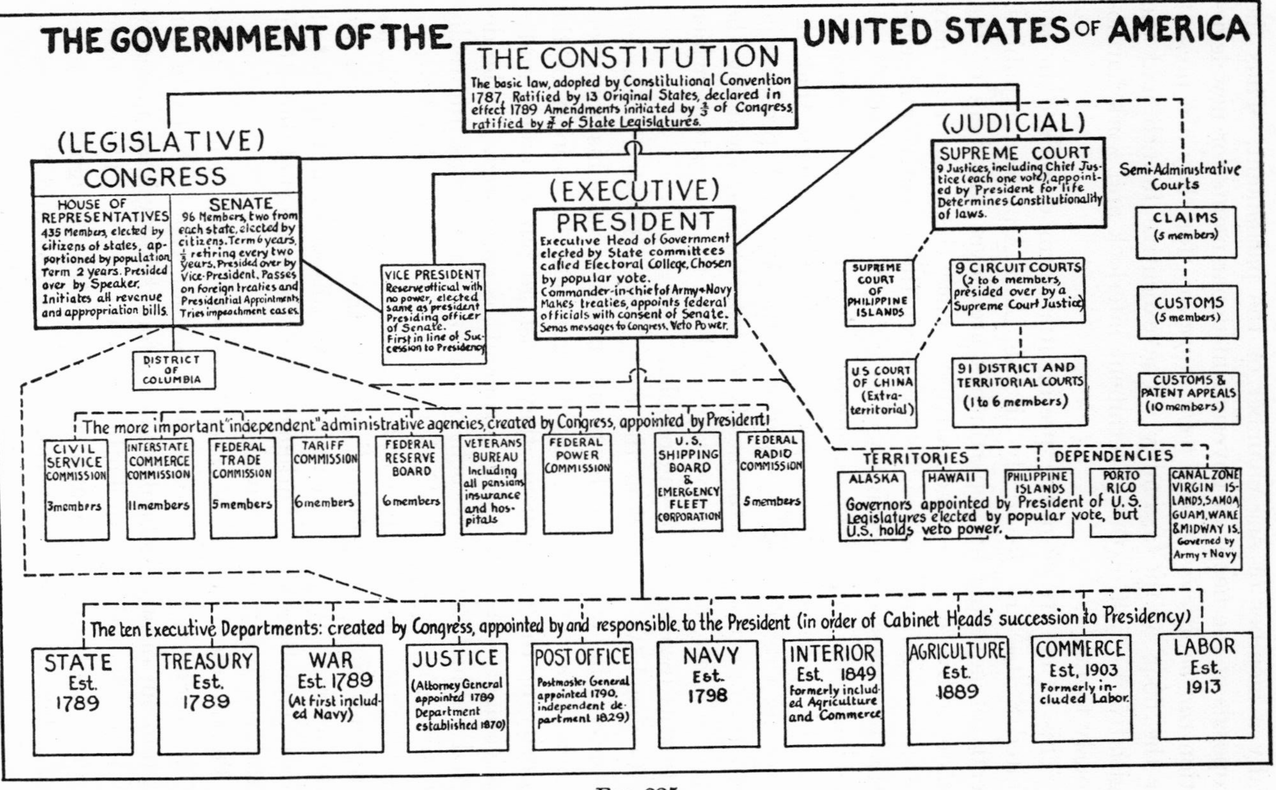
THE GOVERNMENT OF THE UNITED STATES OF AMERICA
THE CONSTITUTION
The basic law, adopted by Constitutional Convention 1787, Ratified by 13 Original States, declared in effect 1789 Amendments initiated by ⅔ of Congress ratified by ¾ of State Legislatures.
(LEGISLATIVE)
CONGRESS
HOUSE OF REPRESENTATIVES
435 Members, elected by citizens of states, apportioned by population Term 2 years. Presided over by Speaker. Initiates all revenue and appropriation bills.
SENATE
96 Members, two from each state, elected by citizens. Term 6 years, ⅓ retiring every two years. Presided over by Vice-President. Passes on foreign treaties and Presidential Appointments Tries impeachment cases.
DISTRICT OF COLUMBIA
(EXECUTIVE)
VICE PRESIDENT
Reserve official with no power, elected same as president Presiding officer of Senate. First in line of Succession to Presidency
PRESIDENT
Executive Head of Government elected by State committees called Electoral College, Chosen by popular vote. Commander-in-chief of Army+Navy Makes treaties, appoints federal officials with consent of Senate. Sends messages to Congress. Veto Power.
(JUDICIAL)
SUPREME COURT
9 Justices, including Chief Justice (each one vote), appointed by President for life Determines Constitutionality of laws.
SUPREME COURT OF PHILIPPINE ISLANDS
9 CIRCUIT COURTS
(2 to 6 members, presided over by a Supreme Court Justice)
US COURT OF CHINA (Extra-territorial)
91 DISTRICT AND TERRITORIAL COURTS
(1 to 6 members)
Semi-Administrative Courts
CLAIMS (5 members)
CUSTOMS (5 members)
CUSTOMS & PATENT APPEALS (10 members)
TERRITORIES
DEPENDENCIES
ALASKA
HAWAII
PHILIPPINE ISLANDS
PORTO RICO
CANAL ZONE VIRGIN ISLANDS, SAMOA GUAM, WAKE & MIDWAY IS. Governed by Army + Navy
Governors appointed by President of U.S. Legislatures elected by popular vote, but U.S. holds veto power.
The more important "independent" administrative agencies, created by Congress, appointed by President
CIVIL SERVICE COMMISSION 3 members
INTERSTATE COMMERCE COMMISSION 11 members
FEDERAL TRADE COMMISSION 5 members
TARIFF COMMISSION 6 members
FEDERAL RESERVE BOARD 6 members
VETERANS BUREAU Including all pensions insurance and hospitals
FEDERAL POWER COMMISSION
U.S. SHIPPING BOARD & EMERGENCY FLEET CORPORATION
FEDERAL RADIO COMMISSION 5 members
The ten Executive Departments: created by Congress, appointed by and responsible to the President (in order of Cabinet Heads' succession to Presidency)
STATE Est. 1789
TREASURY Est. 1789
WAR Est. 1789 (At first included Navy)
JUSTICE (Attorney General appointed 1789 Department established 1870)
POST OFFICE Postmaster General appointed 1790, independent department 1829)
NAVY Est. 1798
INTERIOR Est. 1849 Formerly included Agriculture and Commerce
AGRICULTURE Est. 1889
COMMERCE Est. 1903 Formerly included Labor.
LABOR Est. 1913

Fig. 225

erally a member of one chamber of the parliament. Thus the proposals of the heads of government departments for new legislation *can be discussed with them in person,* for they are present on the floor of the assembly. The executive branch and the legislative branch of the government interlock and work harmoniously together.

This is not true in the presidential form employed in the United States and in nearly all the Latin-American republics. Heads of government departments are never members of the senate or house of representatives; hence there are frequently misunderstandings and conflicts between the executive and legislative branches of government.

The second important difference has to do with the *responsibility of government to the people.* It is maintained that the European cabinet form is superior to the American presidential form because under it the heads of departments, including the *prime minister,* are directly responsible to the legislature, which in turn is responsible to the people.

As you have learned in the case of the British Parliament, whenever the cabinet — the prime minister and his ministers (heads of departments) — cannot command the support of the majority of the Parliament, they must go out of office, and a new cabinet (called a new government) is appointed. If the defeated cabinet members believe that their policies are really supported by a majority of all the voting citizens, then, instead of asking for a new cabinet to be appointed, they dissolve Parliament and "go to the country"; that is, they have a new countrywide election. If their adherents win at this election, they obtain a majority of the seats in Parliament, and the support of the cabinet in the near future is guaranteed.

The presidential system is very different. In the United States the president is elected for a term of four years. Nothing can put him out of office except his being found guilty in an impeachment for criminal or certain other specified actions. The president *appoints* his own cabinet and can ask for their resignation at his will. Thus for four-year periods the president and the heads of government departments are not responsible to the Congress and therefore to the people.

The third difference appears directly from this discussion of the other two. Cabinet government, it is maintained, is *responsive to the people*; presidential government is inflexible. A European cabinet goes out of office within a day or two from the time a proposal is defeated in Parliament. Thus the representatives of the people constantly keep their hands on government itself. Unless the members resign or are removed by the president, an American cabinet stays in office and does practically as it pleases, even if an overwhelming majority of the people turn against it. Not until its fixed term of office is completed is the cabinet disbanded. This kind of government, Europeans say, is rigid, — *not responsive to the people*, as government in a democracy should be.

Nearly All Modern Nations are governed by Political Parties

All the foregoing discussion of governments dealt with the theoretical form of government — the *paper* government. Behind the scenes, as we have found in our study of each of the chief countries, the real government is by *politicians, the leaders of political parties*. It is they who really control the government.

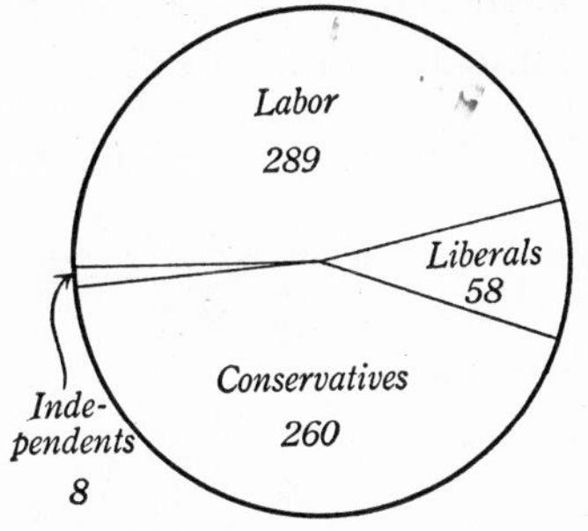

Fig. 226. The political division of the British House of Commons in 1931 and the number of representatives of each party

Now there are differences between countries as to the way in which political parties are employed. In the United States and in Great Britain the voters have tended to divide themselves chiefly between *two major parties*. In the United States there has rarely been a national election in which a third party has commanded a large proportion of the votes of the people. At one election after another either the Democratic or the Republican party (or parties corresponding to them, if not so named) has won.

So, too, in Great Britain. During the 1700's elections were divided between the Tories and the Whigs. In the middle 1800's, as these became, respectively, the Conservative and the Liberal party, the voters still continued to cast their lot with one or the other.

But gradually the workers of the trade-unions organized their own political party — the Labor party. This party eventually

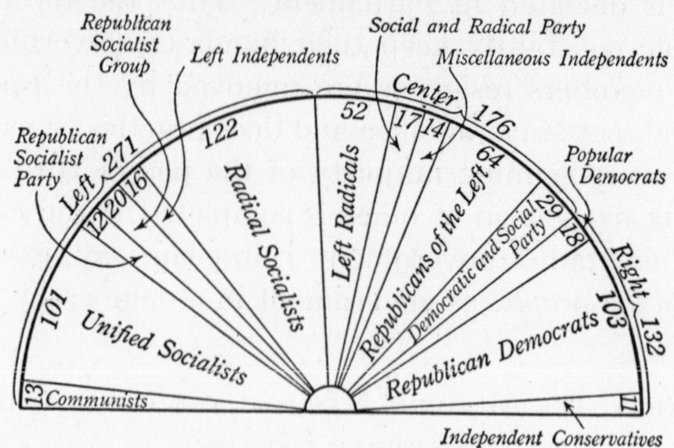

FIG. 227. The political division of the French Chamber of Deputies and the number of representatives of each party

gathered more and more people under its banner. By 1929 it almost commanded a majority in the House of Commons.[1] (See

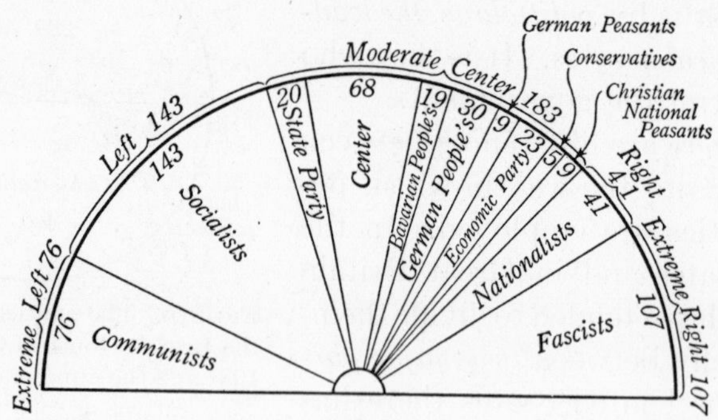

FIG. 228. The political division of the German Reichstag and the number of representatives of each party

figure 226.) As a rule, however, the two-party scheme of government has held, both in the United States and in Great Britain.

[1] In the election of October, 1931, the Labor party lost heavily. At that time the Labor vote was just over 6,500,000, while the Conservative vote was nearly 12,000,000, and the Liberal vote 2,000,000.

This is not true in France, Germany, and other European countries. Compare figures 227 and 228 with figure 226. Note the miscellaneous array of parties in France and Germany.

There are fourteen different parties in the French parliament, twelve different parties in the German Reichstag, and no one of them is able to command even a fourth of all the votes. In order to pass laws parties must form "coalition" governments, representing several of the larger parties.

One conclusion of importance can be drawn from the three graphs of figures 226, 227, and 228. This is that the essentially liberal parties, including the labor and the radical, or "left," parties have today achieved a very important place in each of the leading parliaments of Europe.

Since the World War an Epidemic of Dictatorships has spread around the World

Until now our review of how the world is governed points indubitably to the slow but steady advance toward more and more democracy. The one-man idea is steadily being displaced by the many-men idea.

If, however, we scrutinize carefully the actual governments behind the paper descriptions in Table XLV, we shall find facts that appear to upset our conclusions. Careful study of governments shows that there are today not less than fifteen dictators ruling arbitrarily more than 350,000,000 people; if China is included, the numbers become sixteen-odd and 750,000,000.

After 1916, in one country after another, strong, ambitious leaders at the head of well-disciplined troops overthrew the existing governments and installed themselves as sole autocratic rulers. They took various titles: Mussolini of Italy calls himself prime minister and secretary of the interior; Joseph Stalin of Russia is called secretary of the Communist party; Alexander I of Yugoslavia is king; Carmona of Portugal, Mustafa Kemal of Turkey, and others call themselves president. But they are practically all military dictators, ruling by the force of arms. Possibly not one is the choice of a majority of the citizens of his country. Thus in these sixteen countries democracy is indeed lacking.

DICTATORSHIP GOVERNMENTS IN 1931

In Europe	In Latin America	In Asia
Russia	Chile	Turkey
Italy	Peru	Persia
Poland	Bolivia	Afghanistan
Portugal	Venezuela	China (sectional dictators)
Yugoslavia	Cuba	
Hungary		
Greece		

Does this mean that one-man government has really come back? Has democracy's onward march been stopped? Many people have been asking these questions since the close of the World War. Let us study the movement for a moment to see its significance.

TABLE XLVI

Comparison of the Ability of the People to read and write in Democracies and in Dictatorships					
Per Cent of Recruits for the Army who were Illiterate					
Democracies			*Dictatorships*		
France	1870	22	Russia	1875	79
	1920	5		1920	60
Germany	1875	2	Italy	1870	57
	1920	0.3		1905	31

Scan carefully the foregoing list. Several very important generalizations occur to one at once.

First, only one of these dictatorships — Italy — is in a country where there has been much industrial development. Not a single advanced industrial country is on the list.

Second, although some of these countries are called by democratic names, none has ever tried representative democratic government on the scale on which it has been tried in the United States, Great Britain, France, or Germany.

Third, these dictatorships, with one or two exceptions, have been set up in countries that can be called in some degree backward; that is, the people themselves are comparatively poor, uneducated, and inexperienced in self-government. Note the sharp contrast, shown in Table XLVI, in the matter of illiteracy, between the people governed by the two leading dictatorships — Russia and Italy — and those of two of the leading representative democracies. Do not such facts suggest that dictatorships are much less likely to be adopted in countries in which the people have a considerable degree of education? As you have studied the world's march toward democracy, have you not noted the slow but sure increase in general education also? Have not the two — democracy and education — advanced hand in hand? There is no more important lesson to learn from modern history.

This, then, is the Way in which the Modern World is Governed

Summing up, then: First, in spite of a wave of post-war dictatorships, one important conclusion has been clearly illustrated; namely, the increasingly democratic character of government. All but a negligible few of the governments of the world are now democracies. Absolute autocratic government has nearly disappeared from the earth.

Second, many kinds of democracy are being experimented with in the modern world. Most of these, however, whatever their differences, are alike in that they are more or less of the representative type. As populations have become huge and have concentrated in cities, it has increasingly been made clear that pure, or direct, democracies cannot be carried on.

Third, in most countries of the world the people have obtained paper guaranties of their rights in written constitutions. To this extent there have been marked gains in both civil and political liberty. As for civil liberty, there are few countries, indeed, in which the right of free speech, a free press, free assembly, freedom of worship, and the right of petitioning the government and of receiving fair treatment in the courts are not now guaranteed in a constitution. And throughout the Western world there are few restrictions upon the right to vote. In most of the leading countries women as well as men, the colored as well as the white races, propertyless people as well as the more prosperous, have a share in government.

But there remain grave and baffling problems of government. The rise of dictatorships shows us that hundreds of millions of people have not yet advanced in education and general intelligence to the level which has been reached by the more developed industrial countries. In these one-man government still rules, and civil and political liberty does not exist.

Difficult problems also confront the advanced democracies. None is more important than that suggested by the question Are men really able to exercise the civil and political liberties which are guaranteed by their constitutions? Are they really free to criticize their government, to petition their government, to suggest new ways of governing? Does democratic government actually work as planned in the constitutions?

UNIT X

WORLD CONFLICT VERSUS WORLD ORGANIZATION

WORLD CONFLICT VERSUS WORLD ORGANIZATION

In conclusion we gather together the chief movements of our story of changing governments and changing cultures and strive to see clearly the insistent problems of the modern world. Our studies have taught us that a new world has been produced by the new ways of thinking that arose in western Europe after 1500. This new civilization has important achievements to its credit, but it has also debits on the ledger of history. These show themselves as pressing problems. As young American citizens it is our task to understand these problems and to aid in their solution.

In this concluding unit, therefore, we shall sum up the world's march toward democracy, its achievements and its problems. We shall ask frankly whether this new industrial civilization is a giant that cannot be controlled. We shall consider such serious problems as those of dictatorship in government, huge armies and navies, mass unemployment, international suspicion, revolt in Asia, and the like.

CHAPTER XXV

WORLD CONFLICT VERSUS WORLD ORGANIZATION

The world's march toward democracy has now been studied in nine great centers — the United States, Great Britain, France, Germany, Russia, China, Japan, India, and Latin America. We have witnessed the struggles of men of various races and nationalities to govern themselves and to win political and civil rights. We have studied the effect of the new industrial civilization on various phases of changing culture.

The study of these nine nations provides us with the facts needed to judge the changing governments and changing cultures of the world. More than 1,200,000,000 people — two thirds of the inhabitants of the earth — are living under these nine governments. The cultures of most of these countries are changing swiftly; some are being completely transformed. From them we can see the significant conditions and problems of our modern world.

We are now in a position, therefore, to gather together what we have learned — to inventory the achievements and the weaknesses of our new civilization.

The Achievements of European Industrial Civilization

Looking back at the thrilling struggle of the peoples of the world for a better way of living, we can see now the astonishing accomplishments of the scientific method of thought. In the 300 years since 1600 the new ways of thinking suggested by Roger Bacon, Francis Bacon, Copernicus, Galileo, Newton, and a host of other scientists have been applied to the world's problems by hundreds of clever and industrious workers. To the physical aspects of life especially they have applied the new method — to industry, to agriculture, to business, to government, to warfare. Each has been transformed, and totally new ways of living have been produced.

On the physical side the achievements of the new European civilization, now being adopted in every continent of the earth, are epoch-making. Note them briefly:

First, the world's highest standard of living — more food, more shelter, more clothing, more necessities, and more comforts and luxuries than the world has ever known before.

Second, longer life for hundreds of millions of human beings. People in industrial countries of the West, for example, live, on the average, about 56 years; those of undeveloped regions, such as the Far East, live only about half that long.

Third, shorter hours of labor than people have hitherto been compelled to work — eight to nine hours a day instead of twelve to fourteen hours a day.

Fourth, much fatigue and pain already eliminated from the world because of the machine production of food, shelter, and clothing.

Fifth, new "lively arts" — a great variety of activities for the increased leisure of the common man in the industrial nations.

Sixth, increased enlightenment and waning superstition. Knowledge is taking the place of myth and legend.

Seventh, world-shaking experiments in government. Already it is possible for a considerable proportion of the population of industrial countries to share in government. Paper guaranties (written constitutions) of civil liberties are carried into practice in many countries.

Eighth, human slavery — that is, the ownership of bodies — eliminated from modern civilizations.

Ninth, the beginnings of international coöperation.

Magnificent achievements, indeed! Clear evidence of the accomplishments of the new ways of thinking which the early modern scientists discovered and developed after 1500!

But there are debits on the ledger of this new civilization as well as credits. Let us confront them honestly and courageously.

A Fragile World Society of Interdependent Nations

One price the world has already had to pay for this new industrial civilization is the constant danger of its breakdown. One hundred and fifty years ago the countries of the world, although living at a low level, were fairly self-sufficient. Although few comforts, as we know them, were available to the mass of the people, at least the necessities of life could be produced within the boundaries of each country.

Then came the invention of power-driven machines, the building of factories, and the drift of people from the farms to the manufacturing cities. Self-sufficiency disappeared. In its place came fragile interdependence. Each industrial country became dependent on many others for food, for fuel, for raw materials, for markets.

In England, for example, the people multiplied threefold in a century. Eighty per cent left the farms to work in cities. As this happened England came to depend on the United States, Canada, Australia, Argentina, India, and other countries for food. Furthermore, she lacked important raw materials, such as raw cotton for her textile factories and iron for her steel mills. For these she also became dependent on other countries. She had to go to the United States, Egypt, and India for cotton; to Spain, Sweden, and Germany for iron. But to buy food and raw materials she had to have money. To get it she had to sell her surplus coal and her manufactured goods, and to do this she was again *dependent* — this time on other countries for markets.

These conditions, especially true of England, were reproduced on some scale in every other industrial country — the United States, France, Germany, Belgium, and Japan. Each one lacked certain foods or certain raw materials that it needed. These each one had to buy from other peoples. But to buy, each had to *sell* something so as to get the money with which to pay. Thus every country became dependent on other parts of the world for markets; that is, for places to sell their goods.

As this kind of *dependence* grew in the later 1800's, an intricate system of railways, motorized highways, steamship lines, telegraphs and telephones, banks, and wholesale and retail companies was developed to handle the trade of the world. But this merely increased the interdependence of peoples everywhere and created in industrial countries a dangerously fragile society.

The World War showed how fragile modern society had become. Many arteries of transportation, communication, and trade in Europe — railroads, highways, telegraph and telephone wires, canals, and rivers — crossed Germany or Austria-Hungary. These countries were now cut off from the rest of Europe, and a major tragedy occurred to 475,000,000 people. The trade of a whole continent collapsed. Cities declined in size. City dwellers fled on foot to the country, seeking food to keep body and soul together. Others starved and died by the hundred thousand.

The war presented an excellent object lesson of the fragile, interdependent character of the new industrial civilization.

Is this New Industrial Civilization a "Frankenstein" Giant that cannot be Controlled?

Startling events of the past twenty years put a pause to unquestioning admiration of the new civilization. In that time a gigantic World War has killed 26,000,000 people, has smashed the peace and the economic life of Europe, has aroused national hatreds and suspicion.

Although the world's most horrible war was fought by millions of youth in the hope that it would end war, it is clear to most students that the world has not yet been made safe for democracy. Conspicuous examples illustrate the truth of this statement:

1. One third of the people of the world are still ruled by the armed force of dictators. In nearly a score of countries government is still dominated by the one-man idea. In every continent some government has become as absolute as that of Louis XIV. Freedom of speech and other civil rights are denied in Russia, Italy, parts of Germany, China, India, Japan, and Latin America.
2. The world is "armed to the teeth." Instead of disarming at the close of the World War, the leading nations of both East and West have more men under arms today than in 1913. More is spent annually for armies and navies than was spent two decades ago.
3. The specter of mass unemployment confronts every industrial nation in the world. It was estimated that in 1931 not less than 15,000,000, and possibly 20,000,000, adult workers were walking the streets of their communities searching for jobs. Furthermore, new machines are constantly being produced, ousting more and more human beings from jobs. Technological unemployment again!
4. Suspicion rules Europe. Germany defaults her reparations. The

financial credit of England crashes. France and the United States gather into the vaults of their national banks three fifths of the entire gold supply of the world. The credit of every leading nation totters. Business men in various countries close their factories, declining to invest money or to order goods as long as the panicky condition of trade continues.

5. Asia is in revolt against the Westerner. Not only is there unrest in the score of Western countries, but also, in Asia, there is a gigantic uprising against European domination. Everywhere, from Japan to Egypt, the Orient is seething with revolt.

The Western world is indeed at a crossroads. Industrial civilization falters in its onward march toward mechanical conquest, bewildered by difficult human problems. At last Mr. Televox, the gigantic machine-man, seems to stand powerless. Thought is demanded, and he cannot think. He can only act. Are there leaders who can think their way out of the present tangle that he is leaving in his wake, and direct him to a saner adjustment of the balance between machinery and human needs?

Why has Industrial Civilization reached such a Condition?

We have spent a great deal of time in this course studying the history of changing civilizations and changing cultures in order that it may be possible for us to understand the baffling problems which confront us and how they were brought about.

Why has industrial civilization reached such a pass? Let us turn once more to England and show how the question can be answered by her history.

Our question answered by an example — England

The factors in England's development to 1914

In 1450 little England was on the edge of the known world, practically isolated from international trade, which then centered in the Mediterranean. By 1914 she had become industrial Great Britain, the very center of world trade and of an empire of 400,000,000 people. She was mistress of the seas, banker of the world's money, and dictator of the economic fortunes of many peoples. What factors brought this about?

Briefly summed up, there are six factors of central importance.

First, the long "head start" in the use of power-driven machinery. Newcomen, Savery, Kay, Hargreaves, Arkwright, Cartwright, to name only a few, were British men whose inventions made it possible to produce manufactured goods so much more cheaply and in so much greater quantity than they could be produced by the older handicraft industries that vast amounts of capital were accumulated through corporations. Thus it was Great Britain which, 50 years before France and 75 years before Germany, developed the standardized mass production of food, shelter, and clothing and laid the foundation for an enormous national wealth and a high standard of living.

Second, large coal deposits. The development outlined above was made possible in large part by England's fortunate possession of staggering amounts of coal — coal to run her growing factories, locomotives, and ocean-going steamships; coal to sell to other countries in payment for the vast amounts of food that they were sending to England in England's own ships.

Third, an early superiority in the control of sea trade. She was mistress of the seas because of the skill, experience, and courage of her island-born sailors.

Fourth, population multiplying threefold in a century. Large families meant many people ready to work. In 1815 the British Isles contained 15,000,000 people; today they contain 47,000,000.

Fifth, the building of large and rich colonies in the undeveloped continents of the world. As population grew, England's surplus sons emigrated in vast numbers and settled the dominions — Canada, Australia, New Zealand, South Africa. For a long time these chiefly agricultural lands provided much of the food needed by the people of the homeland. As we know, by 1900 the latter had almost all left their farms and gone to work in factories, shops, and stores in the cities.

Sixth, all these factors combined to produce the building of the world's greatest empire. Again the head start! Using her merchant marine, her navy, her manufactured goods, her enormous reserves of coal, England led the way in seizing so-called backward regions of Asia and Africa. There she sold her goods, there she acquired needed raw materials, and there much of her growing wealth was invested.

These, in brief, were the factors which by 1914 made England the center of world trade, the world's banker, rich beyond the dreams of any people.

The lack of national planning in England's development

All this was done essentially without planning for the future. England's leaders went on their way without regard for a rapidly changing world. They tried to carry on in the twentieth century by the same hand-to-mouth method of exploitation that was used in the nineteenth. But the world changed swiftly between 1870 and 1914.

First, rivals arose — especially the United States, France, and Germany — who caught up with Britain's lead in the use of machines. After the war they even outdistanced her in the production of iron and steel, of coal, of cotton and woolen textiles, and of other goods. In 1929 she sold only 80 per cent as much goods as in 1913. Today Great Britain sells one third less cotton, one fourth less coal, and nearly one half less iron and steel and textiles than before the war. As this happened mills stood idle, and thousands of people were left without work.

Second, the value of England's coal dwindled greatly. In Germany, France, America, and Russia vast stores of coal were mined and sold around the world. This took away much of England's trade. In addition the fuel for power-driven machinery was transformed. Oil and hydroelectric power began to supplant steam power produced by coal-burning engines. Steadily England sold less coal; steadily more coal-miners were thrown out of work.

Third, Germany and later the United States and other countries built up a rich world trade, cutting further into Britain's exports.

Fourth, population continued to grow, but new jobs became comparatively fewer. As bigger and cleverer machines were invented, more and more men were thrown out of work. Surplus population! Technological unemployment!

Fifth, until the war hundreds of thousands of Britishers emigrated annually to Canada, to Australia, to New Zealand, to South Africa, finding places on the undeveloped farms or in the growing factories of these colonies. Then came a drastic change. One by one the dominions restricted immigration. A crisis indeed! The British Isles over-populated, 1,000,000 unemployed even in times of prosperity, and no place to export the surplus labor!

Sixth, most of the colonies themselves became practically independent, home-ruled states within the British Commonwealth. No longer were they subordinate to little England. No longer could they be exploited.

Thus the nineteenth-century conditions which made Great Britain the leading world power have given place to new and less favorable twentieth-century conditions. How clear the gravity of the problem is when one sums it up! England vastly overpopulated, four out of five of her people in cities, a nation of shopkeepers dependent on the outside world for food, her foreign trade declining, her coal steadily declining in value, and unable to sell goods to her old customers, who now produce more and more themselves. Is it not clear that she confronts no mere temporary emergency?

Other industrial countries followed England's lead

On a somewhat smaller scale France, Germany, the United States, and Japan have assumed that they too could continue to manufacture machine-made goods and to sell them in the twentieth century in the same ways and to the same markets as they had done in the nineteenth century. But now they find that they cannot. They find that the hitherto agricultural regions — for example, Egypt, southern Russia, China, India, even the southern United States — all have their own factories, power plants, and corporations manufacturing cloth, steel, implements, and other goods. And so the time has come when the major industrial countries find that they must take careful account of the new conditions in the world and *plan together a way out.*

This is especially imperative because of the widespread unrest in Europe today.

What are the Chief Sources of Unrest in Europe Today?

In spite of the revolt in Asia and the changing movement of affairs in Latin America and Africa, the real center of unrest is in Europe. The entire continent is upset by the problems which have arisen since the World War. Some of these problems are economic, centering in the European nations' great losses of trade. Others are political, centering in the relation of Germany to other countries.

The economic sources of unrest

The first problem is due to the sharp change in the relation between Europe and the outside world with respect to agriculture, manufacturing, and trade. Before the World War European countries, especially Russia and Rumania, sold abroad approximately half the exported wheat of the entire world. In 1927 they exported less than 10 per cent. The United States, Canada, Argentina, and Australia, which exported only 50 per cent before the war, exported 90 per cent in 1927. The export sales of other foodstuffs have changed similarly; for example, in 1928 Czechoslovakia sold abroad 30 per cent less beet sugar than in 1925.

The condition of the coal industry is even worse. In the most prosperous years since the close of the war European countries have not sold abroad as much as they did in 1913. England, Germany, and other coal-producing countries are competing fiercely with one another at the same time that the United States is taking the coal trade away from all of them. And England is greatly dependent on her sale of coal to supply money with which to buy food.

A similar fight is under way between America and Europe in the sale of iron and steel goods, copper, tin, aluminum, and other metals absolutely necessary to industrial nations. All along the line nations are racing with one another for control of the markets of the world.

A political source of friction: "war guilt and reparations"

So much for a brief reference to the business causes of unrest in Europe. There are *political* difficulties which also separate the nations of Europe from one another. Indeed, the crucial world problems of today can be understood only by comprehending the sore spots that grew out of the treaty of peace which was imposed upon Germany by the victorious countries in the World War.

1. *The question of the war guilt of Germany*

Article 231 of the Treaty of Versailles contains the following sentence:

Germany accepts the responsibility of Germany and her Allies for causing all the loss and damage to which the Allied and Associated Governments and their nationals have been subjected as a consequence of the war imposed upon them by the aggression of Germany and her Allies.

Although the German leaders signed this, neither they nor their successors believed it. In one public utterance after another

FIG. 229. It seems as though the little tree in this cartoon is having a difficult time struggling for life. What does the cartoon tell you? (Cartoon by Herbert Johnson in the *Saturday Evening Post*. Reproduced by special permission)

German leaders have repeatedly asserted their belief that Germany did no more to cause the war than the other world powers.

Furthermore, an increasing number of students of government and history in other countries, after studying a multitude of new documents which have been published since 1917, have inclined toward this view. The war, they maintain, was the outcome of many factors which were produced by the development of the new industrial civilization. Among these were the increasingly keen competition between the European industrial countries for trade, raw materials, and colonial territories; the construction of great navies and armies by all; the secret military alliances between all of them; and the propaganda resorted to by the different countries, through which nationalistic loyalties were cemented and suspicion and hatred of other peoples were created. Scholars maintain that in this complex development Germany was little more guilty, if any more, than were the other powers — France, Great Britain, Russia, Austria-Hungary, and Italy. And it was the culmination of these things — not solely Germany's aggression — that brought on the war.

2. *Germany was forced to pay huge reparations and to give up valuable territories*

A chief source of unrest, therefore, is the increased resentment among the German people at being compelled to accept responsibility for war guilt. This is felt particularly in two ways. First, Germany resents being compelled to pay to France and her allies reparations totaling billions of dollars. The Germans insist that they cannot pay the huge reparations demanded of them and that it is not fair of their conquerors to expect them to do so.

Fig. 230. Germany and Austria-Hungary in 1918. Compare this map with figure 231

Second, Germany is bitter about the loss of much territory: Alsace-Lorraine to France, the eastern territory known as the "Polish Corridor" to Poland, other lands to Czechoslovakia and Poland, and all her colonies in Africa and Asia which are now mandatories of Great Britain and France.

In Alsace-Lorraine, which had been under German rule since 1871, large numbers of the people either are of German descent or have developed loyalty to Germany. These people are now ruled by a foreign government. Some of them speak German; some speak French. Naturally the German-speaking people resent the change which has been made. Indeed, the whole region is in a turmoil of animosity.

The "Polish Corridor" is an even greater source of friction between Germany and her neighbors. The Treaty of Versailles gave Poland direct access to the Baltic Sea by taking a considerable slice of territory, now commonly called the "Polish Corridor," from Germany and adding it to Poland. This separated the German district of East Prussia from the central, western, and southern parts of Germany. It also placed a large number of German subjects under the new Polish government. Many of the people in the "Corridor" resent being under a foreign government, and it appears impossible to have peace in north-central Europe until this question is settled to the real satisfaction of all concerned. France, in the meantime, holds the key to this problem, since Poland was set up as an independent state at her demand. Many authorities maintain that France can solve the difficulty by agreeing to a revision of the Treaty of Versailles which shall restore this land to Germany but shall also give Poland direct access to the Baltic Sea.

Until these problems are solved there can be no real peace in Europe.

Another political source of friction: the mixture of peoples in central Europe

At the Peace Conference in 1919 President Wilson and the Allied prime ministers tried to rearrange the frontiers between countries in central and eastern Europe so as to give independence to various small populations which spoke similar languages and felt that they belonged to the same racial groups. For example, out of territory belonging to Germany and Austria-Hungary the new state of Czechoslovakia was formed. Out of land belonging to Germany, Russia, and Austria-Hungary the independent republic of Poland was set up. Out of Serbia and lands belonging to Austria-Hungary and other Balkan territory the new national state of Yugoslavia was made. Thus Austria and Hungary were separated, and the territory of each was reduced approximately one half. The boundaries of Rumania, Greece, Armenia, Bulgaria, and Turkey were also rearranged.

Were the various minor groups of central and eastern Europe satisfied? Authorities agree that they were not and raise the serious question as to whether it is possible to satisfy them. As you have already learned, the racial and language groups of central and eastern Europe are completely mixed up. For example, one finds whole villages of light-haired German-speaking people in central Hungary or in Russia. Greeks, Turks, Armenians, and natives of other national groups all live together in the Balkans and in the Near East. Hundreds of thousands of Germans now live under Czechoslovakian, Austrian, Polish, and Hungarian rule.

Fig. 231. Germany and Austria today. Note the Polish Corridor, which cuts Germany in two

Altogether it is estimated that not less than 30,000,000 people of the 475,000,000 inhabitants of Europe are in these so-called "racial minorities." This mix-up is the result of several hundred years of the migration of people from one region to another, of the constant recurrence of wars, and of the frequent revisions of national frontiers. It is doubtful if any rearrangement of national boundaries can place each group under a government in which the people and their neighbors will be completely satisfied. Certainly this difficulty of the racial minorities is one of the chief sources of unrest in Europe.

The Imperative Need for International Coöperation and Control

Confronted by such conditions the leaders of the entire earth are baffled, uncertain what to do. They are asking, "Have the new industrial ways of living produced problems beyond the power of men's minds to solve?" Fearing disaster, the leaders of European countries have increasingly turned toward international coöperation and *planning* as the way out. Many of them are beginning to say frankly: "We are ruining the entire continent by this fierce race for trade, by these gigantic armies and navies which take so much of our people's hard-earned money. Let us join hands and form a 'Union.' Let us plan together how much

FIG. 232. These men were called "the Big Four" at the Peace Conference in 1919 because of the important parts they took. They are (from left to right) David Lloyd George of Great Britain, Vittorio Orlando of Italy, Georges Clemenceau of France, and Woodrow Wilson of the United States

food, fuel, and manufactured goods we need. Let us agree through frank discussion on how much each shall produce. Let us cease this constant warfare. Let us really try to find the road to permanent world peace."

It was with the idea in mind of the imperative need for international coöperation and control that Woodrow Wilson, president of the United States during the World War, went in person to the Peace Conference in 1919. And it was largely as a result of his unrelenting efforts that a great world organization — the League of Nations — was created in 1920 and was joined by 42 nations. Today 54 nations of the earth are members. Many leading Americans believe that a great danger came to the peace of the world when President Wilson's enemies in the United States Senate succeeded in keeping the United States out of the League. Today it is the only large and powerful nation standing aloof from the world organization.

One fact is clear: for the first time in all recorded history most of the nations of the world are seriously discussing together the problems of world organization. Two definite plans have already been proposed: (1) the League of Nations and (2) the United States of Europe. The former embraces the nations of the world; the latter, the countries of Europe. Let us see how much promise there is in each of these proposals.

Some Earlier Proposals to organize the World for Peace

The present-day movement for world organization is not new. Many similar proposals have been made during the past 150 years. In the 1780's Voltaire, whose pen exerted such a tremendous influence all over Europe, discussed the necessity of organizing the world to keep quarreling nations at peace. This critic of society hated war, calling it "the code of murder." He also said that wars were nothing but robbery. Likening Europe to a vast fair, in which many peoples were buying and selling from one another, he claimed that trade between nations must be free — not hampered by tariff barriers. Furthermore, he said that the continent of Europe must be organized. He made a practical proposal — namely, the establishment of a European Diet and the building up of an international code for settling disputes between countries.

Then, in 1795, came the publication of Immanuel Kant's *Eternal Peace*. Within a year the famous German philosopher's book achieved a large sale. In it he too set forth advanced views. He denounced all peace treaties which contained within them the seeds of new wars, and he urged the abolition of all standing armies. He said, "No independent state should be acquired by any other state in any way whatsoever, and no state should be allowed to use force to interfere in the affairs of another state."

He denied governments the right to contract national debts, because then the people of a nation are in the hands of those who control money. Finally, he said that no state should make war in such a way that confidence should be destroyed when the time came to make peace. Thus in Kant's suggestion that all nations renounce the right to go to war and organize a "State of Nations" we have the idea of a world federation.

In the next century several proposals for a European union were made. In 1848 the poet and statesman Lamartine, having written much about the reconciliation of races, issued his *Manifesto to Europe*, proclaiming that "war is nearly always a dictatorship. Soldiers forget institutions for men. Thrones tempt the ambitious; patriotism is dazzled by glory." He urged political leaders to understand that the "world . . . wishes to advance to brotherhood and peace."

Fig. 233. Immanuel Kant (1724–1804)

In 1869, at the International Peace Congress, another Frenchman, the famous novelist Victor Hugo, advocated a federal European republic. He said that the frontiers of Europe were making slaves of the people and of their leaders. "The first slavery is the frontier . . . wipe out the frontier, close down the customhouse, dismiss the soldier; in other words, be free, and peace will follow." At the Peace Congress he advocated setting up a United States of Europe.

In 1883 Jean Godin, who attempted to build an ideal community in France, presented suggestions for the way to world peace in a book on socialism. He demanded the setting up of a universal republic, the organization of international federations to bring about world peace and international laws and codes of arbitration. In his writing he urged nations to defend the peace of the world "by the joint action of all the federated powers." Then he said, "The constitution of the United States of Europe may, in a near future, inaugurate a definitive peace on the Continent."

Godin pointed to tariff barriers as one of the worst sore spots: "Large fortunes are built up in every country as the result of the disguised monopoly created by the customs [tariffs]." Thus, because of the greed of the privileged classes, the only way to solve the problem, he believed, was to wipe out the tariffs.

A Dream come True: the League of Nations

When the various peace treaties were signed in 1919, the yearning for a world union was put into practicable form. An actual League of Nations came into existence. A great catastrophe had opened the minds even of prime ministers, bound by the political practices of Europe, to the need for open coöperation. Twenty-four signed the preamble of the Covenant of the League, which reads:

> The High Contracting Parties
>
> In order to promote international coöperation and to achieve international peace and security
>
> by the acceptance of obligations not to resort to war,
>
> by the prescription of open, just, and honorable relations between nations,
>
> by the firm establishment of the understandings of international law as the actual rule of conduct among governments, and
>
> by the maintenance of justice and a scrupulous respect for all treaty obligations in the dealings of organized peoples with one another, Agree to this Covenant of the League of Nations.

Once launched, the League gripped the imaginations of peoples all over the earth, and soon 54 nations had joined hands in the attempt to effect a true world union. The United States and Soviet Russia stand out among those that do not belong. The list of countries whose governments are not willing to coöperate with the other governments of the world as members of the League includes the following names:

The United States	Turkey	Afghanistan	Nejd
Russia	Egypt	Brazil	Yemen
	Ecuador	Costa Rica	

Almost exactly half the countries in the League are in Europe, and almost half in Asia, Africa, and the Americas. It is truly a world organization.

To become a member of the League the applying government must agree (1) to settle all its disputes by arbitration, before either the Council of the League or some other arbitrating body; (2) to pay its share of the cost of running the League; (3) to send delegates to all meetings.

Allied to the League of Nations there are two other important international bodies; (1) the International Labor Organization, whose office is located at Geneva, and (2) the World Court, located at the Hague, Holland. These three great enterprises for world coöperation cost altogether only $5,000,000 a year. This is a mere pittance compared with the annual outlay of any one large country for armament. The expense is divided among the 54 countries in proportion to their population and wealth. Thus the larger powers together — Great Britain, France, Germany, Italy, and Japan — pay about one third of the total expense.

How the League of Nations is Organized

The League of Nations provides at last the practical working application of the dream of the social philosophers. There are three main divisions: (1) the Assembly, (2) the Council, and (3) the Secretariat. In addition there are allied bodies of experts and advisers. Chief among the expert bodies are three technical organizations: (1) Communications and Transit, (2) Health, and (3) Economic and Financial. There are also various advisory bodies; for example, the commissions on Mandates, on Intellectual Coöperation, on Opium, and on the Traffic in Women and the Protection of Children.

The Assembly, meeting annually in September at the League headquarters at Geneva, is composed of not more than three representatives from each member country and is the supreme legislative body. The Council, of fourteen members (with the British Empire, France, Germany, Italy, and Japan as permanent members), meets at least four times a year and is the real executive head. The Secretariat, composed of about 600 permanent, expert

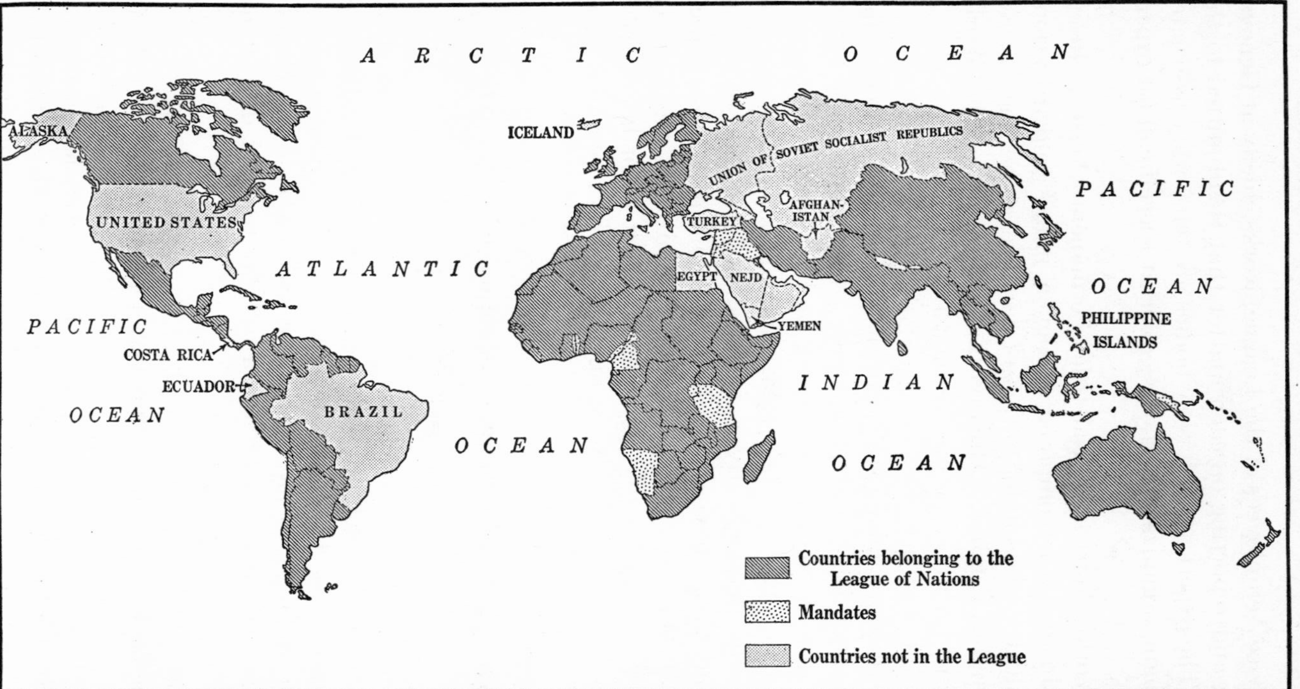

FIG. 234. This map illustrates the status of all the world with respect to the League of Nations. The darkest areas are the nations which, with their possessions, are members of the League. The dotted areas are the mandates, areas over which nation members have assumed a guardianship. They include weaker peoples which members of the League have promised to protect. The areas that are lightly shaded include those political bodies which hold no membership in the League of Nations

"civil service" employees of the League, works chiefly at Geneva, analyzing and reporting on each matter that is submitted to the League. The expert and advisory bodies are temporary associates of the League organization who assemble at special call for expert assistance.

The World Court — official title, Permanent Court of International Justice — is composed of eleven judges (aided by four deputy judges) chosen for terms of nine years by the League Council and Assembly. Already the judgments of the World Court, which are binding on the people concerned, have played an important part in international relations.

In the field of labor problems the International Labor Organization is an equally great influence. Its Geneva office makes studies and issues reports of pressing problems and conditions of labor in various parts of the world. Annual conferences are held, to which come representatives of capital, of labor, and of official departments and bureaus of various governments. Most important of all, the International Labor Organization has already succeeded in leading many countries to enact labor laws, based on its recommendations, concerning hours of labor and conditions of work.

What is the Nature of the League's Work?

1. It makes new international laws

Because of the interdependence of the modern world there is a great need for a definite body of international law. Without such a body of law the many disputes that arise between countries are more likely to have serious consequences. The League has already done a great service in interpreting and developing international law.

To improve the existing system of international communication in Europe, the League Assembly in 1922 voted appropriations authorizing a European railway conference to be held in 1923. As soon as this step was taken the permanent officials in the Transit Section of the Secretariat collected all available information in regard to the railway problem. The next step was to sound out railway experts throughout the Continent as to how the problems could best be solved. Finally a plan

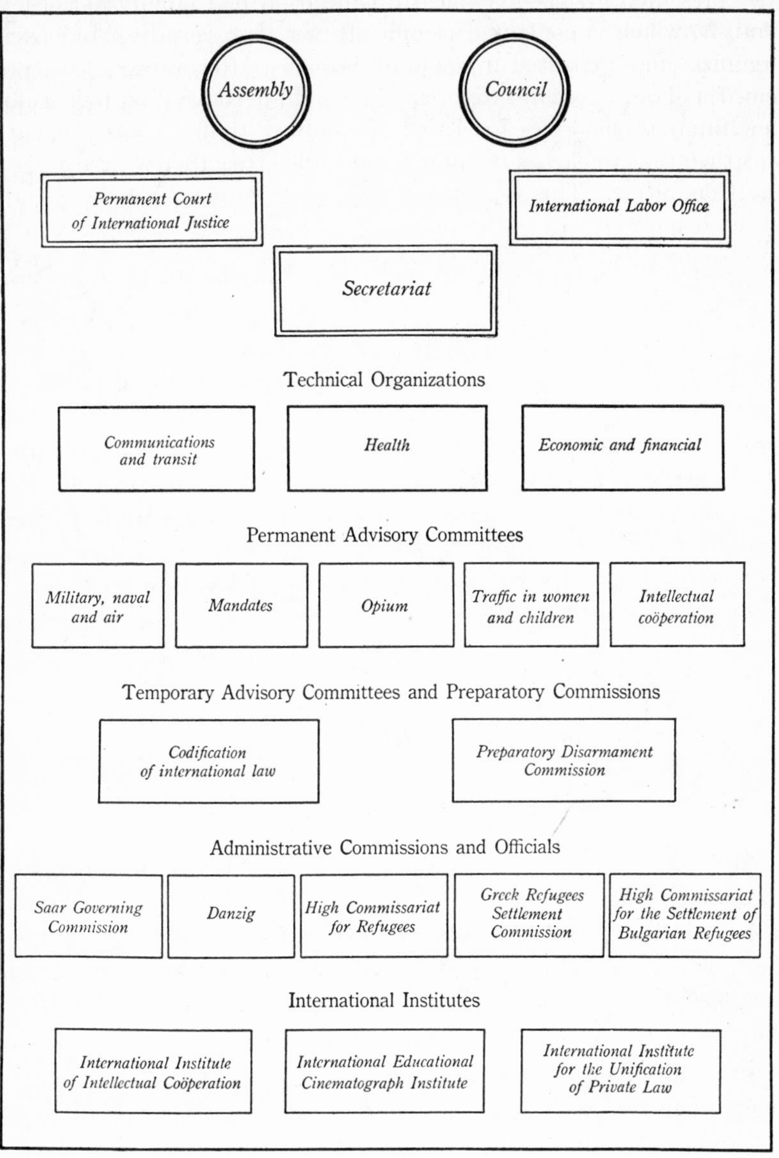

FIG. 235. A chart which illustrates the organization of the League of Nations. (From *The Aims and Organization of the League of Nations*, published by the Secretariat of the League of Nations)

was presented to the technical organization of Communications and Transit, which is composed of officials and representatives of business organizations interested in communications. After studying the problem, the Transit organization drew up a draft convention laying down new international rules for European railway traffic. This convention was then sent to each government concerned, together with a report of the Committee. This report and draft convention were then studied by each government as the basis for the diplomatic conference which the Council had in the meantime called. The governments therefore knew what the main proposals were to be and they had the opportunity of forming conclusions beforehand. In other words, the diplomatic conference was the last step in a carefully worked out process, in which the knowledge of experts and the negotiating ability of diplomats were combined.

Once a convention is signed, each government considers whether or not to ratify. Formerly many conventions went by default simply because of neglect. But if a government does not act upon a League convention within a reasonable length of time, the Council, Assembly or the Secretariat may make inquiries, and the League has been specially effective in this type of follow-up work. As a result of the creation of this League machinery — a machinery which is continuously in operation and necessarily complicated — the world may claim for the first time in its history that it has devised a method by which international problems may be intelligently solved.[1]

2. It settles disputes and prevents war

But the real test of the League is whether it has power to prevent countries from going to war. Does it have such power? It has, indeed, an elaborate machinery for preventing war. In the written agreement of the nations belonging to the League, Article XI states definitely that "any threat of war" is a matter of concern to the whole League, "and the League shall take any action that may be deemed wise and effectual to safeguard the peace of nations."

What action can the League take if a country threatens to make war on another? This can be answered best by considering an actual incident.

[1] Raymond Leslie Buell, *Europe: a History of Ten Years*, pp. 424–425. By permission of The Macmillan Company, publishers, New York, 1930.

How the League prevented war between Bulgaria and Greece in 1925

On October 19, 1925, a Greek soldier crossed the Bulgarian frontier, fired at a Bulgarian sentry, and was killed by the latter. Three days later the Greek government sent detachments of troops across the Bulgarian border. At this threat of war the Bulgarian minister of foreign affairs telegraphed to the League of Nations headquarters at Geneva, asking the League to intervene. The acting president of the Council telegraphed both the Greek and the Bulgarian government, reminding them that in signing Article XII of the Covenant of the League they had solemnly promised not to resort to war, and urging them to abstain from hostilities. Thus, first, the League's officers acted immediately to separate the contestants and prevent war.

FIG. 236. A cartoon which appeared in 1925 during the League's negotiations with Bulgaria and Greece. What does it illustrate? (From the Dallas *News*)

When the Council met, Greece was given 60 hours in which to evacuate Bulgarian territory, and military attachés of Great Britain, France, and Germany were sent to the place of hostilities to report on what was done. Eight hours before the end of the time limit the Council's orders were obeyed.

The Council then had an outside impartial study made of the facts in the controversy. When the report was made in December the Council ordered the Greek government to pay Bulgaria an indemnity. It was done, and the incident was closed.

This, then, is an example of the effective manner in which the League has actually succeeded in settling quarrels. From 1920 to 1928, inclusive, the League handled 24 disputes between countries, eight of which involved hostilities. In none of these eight instances did the disputing countries go to war. In the other cases the Council or its commissions were able to render valuable aid in bringing about peaceful settlement of the disputes. Thus it is beyond question that the League of Nations has already justified itself.

But we must note that not one of the 24 instances of dispute brought before the League concerned a major power within the League. Should the League encounter difficulties in settling disputes, as might conceivably happen in the case of major powers, other provisions have been made. For instance, under Article XVI *every one* of the other nations in the League is obligated to stop all personal, financial, and commercial intercourse with the warring powers at once. In short, practically the entire world — if it lived up to the terms of the Covenant which the governments of all 54 nations signed — would boycott the warring countries. They would be isolated and would soon be in danger, for today no country can live long to itself. All depend to some extent on the outside world. Not for long could they hold out against the refusal of the rest of the world to have dealings with them.

This, then, is the extent of the real power of the League to prevent war. It has no great superarmy or supernavy with which to police the world. It has merely the force of boycott. Even that depends upon the unanimity with which the member nations live up to the Covenant.

Indeed, at the present time there is very great lack of confidence in the power of the League to enforce peace between the big powers. Students of the problem remind us that all the leading nations have large navies and armies and that all have shown clearly an unwillingness to disarm. If they really believed in the power of the League to enforce world peace, would they not disarm?

In this connection most authorities point out that one of the most powerful factors weakening the League is the obstinate refusal of the United States Senate to permit the United States to join the League. In spite of widespread and increasing agitation among the people of the United States in favor of joining the League, the Senate has refused to do so. Furthermore, it must be admitted that the League is still definitely under the control of the countries that won the World War.

Nevertheless it is clear that the League of Nations has already been of great service to the cause of international coöperation. An organization has been developed by which nations can discuss and take action to improve the health of the world and the

FIG. 237. At the opening of a meeting of the Council of the League of Nations

conditions of labor, to regulate tariffs, and to develop international law and cultural relations between countries. Certainly much has been accomplished in a decade.

PRACTICAL PROPOSALS FOR A UNITED STATES OF EUROPE SINCE THE WORLD WAR

Besides the League of Nations, which is an organization of countries of the entire world, proposals have been made also for a union of the European nations. As we have seen, such proposals are not new; for many years leading thinkers have formulated different plans. But after the World War, increased impetus was given to them.

The most important plan was launched by a group of liberal students under the leadership of Count Richard M. Coudenhove-Kalergi, professor at the University of Vienna and president of the Pan-European Union. He and his group presented a definite proposal for a European organization for peace. They established branches in practically every European country, and issued regularly from France and Austria a magazine called *Paneurope.* In the United States the Foreign Policy Association and other groups held meetings, issued pamphlets, and otherwise supported the movement.

Twenty-seven European governments are now also discussing forming a United States of Europe

On May 17, 1930, Aristide Briand, foreign minister of France, submitted to the other 26 European governments represented in the League of Nations a preliminary proposal that the nations of Europe join together in a trading and political union — a so-called United States of Europe. This plan recognizes that the countries of Europe are thoroughly interdependent, even though they are free, independent political states. It proposes that an actual organization be set up to work out amicable business arrangements between the several countries. This organization would have a "European Conference," a Political Committee, and a Secretariat Service. It would protect the sovereignty of each nation and would work in close relationship with the League of Nations.

All the 26 other European governments to which the proposal was sent replied to it. All indicated their general interest in it, but most of the governments pointed out grave dangers. Chief among these was the danger that Europe herself would become organized against the other sections of the world and that great intercontinental disputes might arise which would be more destructive than any wars between separate nations. There were also many differences of opinion about the way such a plan should be worked out. For example, some nations believed Russia should be excluded from the union because of the great difference between her social and political organizations and those of other countries. However, this is another plan for international coöperation — the United States of Europe. It is impossible to predict how it would affect world peace. Most of its supporters, believing that the greatest sources of friction lie between the countries of Europe, regard it as a great step in the advance of the world toward permanent peace.

THE PROBLEMS SUMMED UP: ORGANIZING THE WORLD FOR SECURITY

It is clear, then, that our new industrial civilization has debits as well as credits on its ledger. And the debits bulk very, very large. Baffling problems that confront us demand solution. Problems of production of goods . . . problems of exports and imports . . . problems of tariff barriers between nations . . . problems of great armaments . . . problems of huge debts . . . problems of disputed boundaries between nations . . . problems of oppressed minor peoples. Difficult problems, indeed, confront the leaders of our new civilization.

But, authorities on international affairs tell us, these problems all reduce to one: How shall the world be organized to guarantee security? Every man, woman, and child on the earth wants security. Every government wants to guarantee security to its people. Back of France's demand for a large army and back of England's insistence upon the world's largest navy is this desire for security. Back of alliances between France and Germany's neighbors — Czechoslovakia, Poland, and Belgium, for example — is the desire for security. This desire is also back of the increasing tariff barriers which are being erected around every nation of the Western world.

We have already studied the most insistent problems which threaten the security of the world: the carrying on of our fragile interdependent scheme of trade; the planning of new international ways of trading to fit changing conditions; the question of war guilt and reparations, and of territories taken from Germany; and the mixed-up populations of European nations. But there are other problems equally pressing. In concluding our discussion we can do little more than enumerate them.

Costly armaments versus world disarmament

No issue concerning world security is more important than this one. What are the two alternatives? Either all the leading nations must arm to the teeth or all must lay down their arms. Most of them are now heavily armed. The result is a Europe that is in constant turmoil and that is now approaching bankruptcy and the wreck of her industrial civilization.

It is clear that the first alternative has been tried and has failed. Must not the world now resort to the other? Must it not scrap its great navies, armies, and fortifications, and in the future refuse to build more than enough to be thrown into a common pool as an international police force? So say many careful students of the problem.

© George Matthew Adams Service

FIG. 238. Through this cartoon the artist shows us that there is a strong feeling against the militaristic, or war, spirit. What else does the cartoon illustrate?

International control of natural resources

No problem is more serious today than that of the overproduction of goods, food, fuel, and raw materials. With modern power-driven machines the world now produces more goods than can be consumed. Furthermore, without scientific planning and control within each industrial country and without international planning and control for all countries, we shall continue to produce more goods than the world can use. Experts tell us that, as this happens, we shall periodically confront destructive hard times, in which millions of men, even tens of millions, will be thrown out of work and a vast number of human beings will come close to starvation.

These conditions can be averted only by international coöperation. Farseeing leaders are now suggesting that coal, oil, and other fuels, iron and other basic raw materials, should be controlled by a world economic council. Only by scientific planning of the amount produced in each country and distributed to various parts of the world can terrible future crises be avoided.

International control of world trade

If the production and distribution of the world's resources are planned and controlled by a world body, must not international trade be planned and controlled in the same manner? This is the query of leaders in world affairs. They raise the general question How can trade be carried on among nations with fair prices to business men and fair wages to workers?

Many difficult questions are involved in this great one. For example: What part is played by the sharp differences in standards of living in the various countries? What is the relation of these to wages, prices, and costs of production?

There is also the baffling problem of tariffs. Since the World War each of the principal countries of the world has erected tariffs against foreign goods. These are a constant cause of friction and a real source of danger to the peace of the world.

Should there not be an international body to study scientifically these problems of differing standards of living and of differing costs of production, prices, wages, and profits? Should not the determination of tariffs be decided by scientific study of the needs and the resources of the peoples of the world?

Difficult problems of the control of money and credit

No problem confronting the modern world needs international discussion and decision more urgently than that of the control of money and credit. After the World War the money of nearly every leading country shrank in value. This happened to the French franc, to the German mark, to the Italian lira, and even to the British pound. Furthermore, the gold supplies in the national treasuries of most of the countries of the world had dwindled to a dangerously low point when in the autumn of 1931 the vaults of the national treasuries of the United States and France together contained more than three fifths of the entire world's gold supply. Such a situation spells serious danger to money systems and to the trade of the world.

These conditions point to the imperative need for international bodies which will study scientifically how to distribute equitably the world's supply of precious metals and which will discover better ways of protecting world trade. Proposals are now being made for the organization of a world bank. Students are also questioning whether the world should continue to use the gold standard as the means by which the money systems of the world are guaranteed. One fact is clear: nations need a system which will guarantee credit to every individual, community, and nation that needs it and deserves it. Only through international co-operation and study can such a system be devised.

Important problems of changing culture

Throughout this book we have studied examples of the changing cultures of countries in which industrial ways of living have been adopted. Villages and towns long isolated from one another are becoming tied to the remotest corners of the world by instantaneous electrical communication. Automobiles, paved roads, swift trains, motion pictures, radios, and printed material — magazines, newspapers, and books — are transforming both outward ways of living and the inner attitudes of the people themselves. The habit of restlessness, the desire for bigger and better things, the artificial increase in wants, the speeding up of life, — all characteristics of the United States under the New Industrial Revolution, — are beginning to grip the people of Europe, even those of Asia. Some people in these other countries maintain that what is now taking place is "the Americanization of the earth."

At any rate it is clear that new cultures are evolving in most of the chief centers of the world. To study these changing cultures international bureaus should be established, and information concerning the changing ways of living should be given to schools all over the earth. The peoples of various nations should be encouraged to preserve the valuable things in their own cultures while adopting, at the same time, those aspects of the new industrialism which will contribute most to their well-being.

Permanent security and international understanding

The world's political leaders should at once make such agreements as will establish a feeling of real security. The people should be freed from the burdens of gigantic debts and armaments, and the credit of the leading industrial nations should be stabilized.

At best, however, the solution of these immediate problems will provide only temporary security. A more permanent basis must also be achieved. This can be done only by a world-wide program of education — education for adults as well as for children and youth. Permanent security can rest only upon true understanding; the peoples of the world must realize their common needs and interests and their absolute dependence upon one another.

Marked beginnings are already being made through the motion picture, the radio, and the daily newspaper. Through such mediums the people of each nation are recognizing the similarities between their ways of living and those of other peoples. Thus the basis for mutual understanding is being laid.

But more must be done. The schools of the 60-odd nations of the earth must consciously build tolerant understanding. In these schools are more than 100,000,000 children and youth, who should be given a sympathetic understanding of other peoples which is the very foundation of security. Through well-informed teachers, through rich libraries of reading materials, through motion pictures, and through music and the arts new attitudes of mutual respect and admiration must be developed. Then, when one believes in and understands his neighbor, one will feel secure with him.

INTERESTING READINGS FROM WHICH YOU CAN GET ADDITIONAL INFORMATION

Bowman, Isaiah. The New World. World Book Company, Yonkers, New York.

Davis, William Stearns. Europe since Waterloo. The Century Co., New York. See Part III, "Armageddon: the World War."

Dodd, William E. Woodrow Wilson and his Work. Doubleday, Doran & Company, Inc., Garden City, New York.

Ford, Henry J. Woodrow Wilson, the Man and his Work. D. Appleton and Company, New York.

GIBBONS, HERBERT ADAMS. Europe since 1918. The Century Co., New York.

GIBBONS, HERBERT ADAMS. The New Map of Asia. The Century Co., New York.

GIBBONS, HERBERT ADAMS. The New Map of Europe. The Century Co., New York.

PHELPS, EDITH M. (Compiler). A League of Nations. The H. W. Wilson Company, New York. A collection of articles on a League of Nations.

ROBINSON, JAMES HARVEY. The Ordeal of Civilization. Harper & Brothers, New York. See Chapters XXIX and XXX.

RUGG, HAROLD. Changing Civilizations in the Modern World. Ginn and Company, Boston. See Unit VIII, "Europe from 1914 until Today."

VAN LOON, HENDRIK. The Story of Mankind. Horace Liveright, New York. See pages 456–465.

APPENDIX

THE UNITED STATES OF AMERICA

The following is an extract from the American Declaration of Independence, 1776:

We hold these truths to be self-evident:— That all men are created equal; that they are endowed by their Creator with certain unalienable rights; that among these are life, liberty, and the pursuit of happiness. That, to secure these rights, governments are instituted among men, deriving their just powers from the consent of the governed.

We also give the first ten amendments to the Constitution of the United States. These amendments went into effect in 1791:

ARTICLE I

Congress shall make no law respecting an establishment of religion, or prohibiting the free exercise thereof; or abridging the freedom of speech, or of the press; or the right of the people peaceably to assemble, and to petition the government for redress of grievances.

ARTICLE II

A well-regulated militia being necessary to the security of a free State, the right of the people to keep and bear arms shall not be infringed.

ARTICLE III

No soldier shall, in time of peace, be quartered in any house, without the consent of the owner; nor in time of war but in a manner to be prescribed by law.

ARTICLE IV

The right of the people to be secure in their persons, houses, papers, and effects, against unreasonable searches and seizures, shall not be violated, and no warrants shall issue, but upon probable cause, supported by oath or affirmation, and particularly describing the place to be searched, and the persons or things to be seized.

ARTICLE V

No person shall be held to answer for a capital or otherwise infamous crime, unless on a presentment or indictment of a grand jury, except in cases arising in the land or naval forces, or in the militia, when in actual service in time of war or public danger; nor shall any person be subject for the same offence to be twice put in jeopardy of life or limb; nor shall be compelled in any criminal case to be a witness against himself, nor be deprived of life, liberty, or property, without due process of law; nor shall private property be taken for public use, without just compensation.

ARTICLE VI

In all criminal prosecutions the accused shall enjoy the right to a speedy and public trial, by an impartial jury of the State and district wherein the crime shall have been committed, which district shall have been previously ascertained by law, and to be informed of the nature and cause of the accusation; to be confronted with the witnesses against him; to have compulsory process for obtaining witnesses in his favor, and to have the assistance of counsel for his defense.

ARTICLE VII

In suits at common law, where the value in controversy shall exceed twenty dollars, the right of trial by jury shall be preserved, and no fact tried by a jury shall be otherwise reëxamined in any court of the United States than according to the rules of the common law.

ARTICLE VIII

Excessive bail shall not be required, nor excessive fines imposed, nor cruel and unusual punishments inflicted.

ARTICLE IX

The enumeration in the Constitution of certain rights shall not be construed to deny or disparage others retained by the people.

ARTICLE X

The powers not delegated to the United States by the Constitution, nor prohibited by it to the States, are reserved to the States respectively or to the people.

ENGLAND

Extracts from Magna Carta (1215):

JOHN, BY THE GRACE OF GOD, KING OF ENGLAND, LORD OF IRELAND, DUKE OF NORMANDY AND AQUITAINE, AND EARL OF ANJOU: To the Archbishops, Bishops, Abbots, Earls, Barons, Justiciaries, Foresters, Sheriffs, Reeves, Ministers, and all Bailiffs and others, his faithful subjects, Greeting. Know ye that We, in the presence of God, and for the health of Our soul, and the souls of Our ancestors and heirs, to the honour of God, and the exaltation of Holy Church, and amendment of Our Kingdom, by the advice of Our reverend Fathers, Stephen, Archbishop of Canterbury [and others] . . . have, in the first place, granted to God, and by this Our present Charter confirmed for Us and Our heirs for ever —

1. That the English Church shall be free and enjoy all her rights in their integrity and her liberties untouched. . . .

2. We have also granted to all the free men of Our Kingdom, for Us and Our heirs for ever, all the liberties underwritten, to have and to hold to them and their heirs of Us and Our heirs. . . .

12. No scutage or aid shall be imposed in Our kingdom unless by common council thereof, except to ransom Our person, make Our eldest son a knight, and once to marry Our eldest daughter, and for this a reasonable aid only shall be paid. So shall it be with regard to aids from the City of London.

13. And the City of London shall have all her ancient liberties and free customs, both by land and water. Moreover We will and grant that all other cities, boroughs, towns, and ports shall have all their liberties and free customs.

14. And for holding the common council of the kingdom concerning the assessment of aids other than in the three cases aforesaid or of scutage, We will cause to be summoned, severally by Our letters, the Archbishops, Bishops, Abbots, Earls, and great Barons; and in addition We will also cause to be summoned, generally, by Our sheriffs and bailiffs, all those who hold of Us in chief, to meet at a certain day, to wit, at the end of forty days, at least, and at a certain place; and in all letters of such summons We will explain the cause thereof, and the summons being thus made the business shall proceed on the day appointed, according to the advice of those who shall be present, notwithstanding that the whole number of persons summoned shall not have come. . . .

39. No freeman shall be taken, imprisoned, disseised, outlawed, banished, or in any way destroyed, nor will We proceed against or prosecute him except by lawful judgment of his peers or the law of the land.

40. To no one will We sell, to none will We deny or defer, right or justice.

The following are extracts from the Petition of Right, 1628:

The Petition exhibited to his Majesty by the Lords Spiritual and Temporal, and Commons, in this present Parliament assembled, concerning divers Rights and Liberties of the Subjects, with the King's Majesty's royal answer thereunto in full Parliament.

To the King's Most Excellent Majesty,

Humbly show unto our Sovereign Lord the King, the Lords Spiritual and Temporal, and Commons in Parliament assembled, that whereas it is declared and enacted by a statute made in the time of the reign of King Edward I, commonly called *Statutum de Tallagio non Concedendo*, that no tallage or aid shall be laid or levied by the king or his heirs in this realm, without the good will and assent of the archbishops, bishops, earls, barons, knights, burgesses, and other the freemen of the commonalty of this realm; and by authority of parliament holden in the five-and-twentieth year of the reign of King Edward III, it is declared and enacted, that from thenceforth no person should be compelled to make any loans to the king against his will, because such loans were against reason and the franchise of the land; and by other law of this realm it is provided, that none should be charged by any charge or imposition called a benevolence, nor by such like charge; by which statutes before mentioned, and other the good laws and statutes of this realm, your subjects have inherited this freedom, that they should not be compelled to contribute to any tax, tallage, aid, or other like charge not set by common consent, in Parliament. . . .

III. And whereas also by the statute called "The Great Charter of the Liberties of England," it is declared and enacted, that no freeman may be taken or imprisoned or be disseised of his freehold or liberties, or his free customs, or be outlawed or exiled, or in any manner destroyed, but by the lawful judgment of his peers, or by the law of the land.

IV. And in the eight-and-twentieth year of the reign of King Edward III, it was declared and enacted by authority of Parliament, that no man, of what estate or condition that he be, should be put out of his land or tenements, nor taken, nor imprisoned, nor disherited, nor put to death without being brought to answer by due process of law. . . .

X. They do therefore humbly pray your most excellent Majesty, that no man hereafter be compelled to make or yield any gift, loan, benevolence, tax, or such like charge, without common consent by act of Parliament . . . and that no freeman, in any such manner as is before mentioned, be imprisoned or detained. . . .

The Bill of Rights (1689), after enumerating the evil practices of government committed by the King and his ministers, makes the following declaration of rights:

And thereupon the said Lords Spiritual and Temporal, and Commons, pursuant to their respective letters and elections, being now assembled in a full and free representation of this nation, taking into their most serious consideration the best means for attaining the ends aforesaid, do in the first place (as their ancestors in like case have usually done), for the vindicating and asserting their ancient rights and liberties, declare:

1. That the pretended power of suspending of laws, or the execution of laws, by regal authority, without consent of parliament, is illegal.
2. That the pretended power of dispensing with laws, or the execution of laws, by regal authority, as it hath been assumed and exercised of late, is illegal.
3. That the commission for erecting the late Court of Commissioners for Ecclesiastical Causes, and all other commissions and courts of like nature, are illegal and pernicious.
4. That levying money for or to the use of the Crown, by pretence of prerogative, without grant of parliament, for longer time or in other manner than the same is or shall be granted, is illegal.
5. That it is the right of the subjects to petition the king, and all commitments and prosecutions for such petitioning are illegal.
6. That the raising or keeping a standing army within the kingdom in time of peace, unless it be with consent of parliament, is against law.
7. That the subjects which are Protestants may have arms for their defence suitable to their conditions, and as allowed by law.
8. That election of members of parliament ought to be free.
9. That the freedom of speech, and debates or proceedings in parliament, ought not to be impeached or questioned in any court or place out of parliament.
10. That excessive bail ought not to be required, nor excessive fines imposed, nor cruel and unusual punishments inflicted.
11. That jurors ought to be duly impaneled and returned, and jurors which pass upon men in trials for high treason ought to be freeholders.
12. That all grants and promises of fines and forfeitures of particular persons before conviction are illegal and void.
13. And that for redress of all grievances, and for the amending, strengthening, and preserving of the laws, parliament ought to be held frequently. . . .

FRANCE

After the French Revolution the following constitutions were adopted:

1. The Constitution of September 3, 1791: a limited monarchy, which fell with the King.
2. The Constitution of June 24, 1793: framed by the Jacobins for a republic.
3. The Constitution of August 22, 1795: a conservative reaction from the Jacobin Constitution; it reposed the executive power in a Directory of Five, and the legislative power in a Council of Five Hundred and a Council of Ancients.
4. The Constitution of December 13, 1799: under this the Directory of Five assumed autocratic powers; in this Directory Napoleon ultimately obtained the supreme executive authority.

5. The Constitution of May 18, 1804: under this the Consulate was replaced with the Empire, and Napoleon assumed the title of Emperor.

6. The Constitutional Bourbon Charter of June 4, 1814, when the Bourbons were restored, with Louis XVIII as king: under it a parliamentary system was established.

7. The Constitution of August 14, 1830: this reëstablished constitutional monarchy in France.

8. The Constitution of November 4, 1848: the Republic restored; this conferred universal [male] suffrage, created a single-chamber government, forced the separation of powers, and appointed a president elected by universal [male] suffrage for a period of four years.

9. The Constitution of November 7, 1852: the Empire reëstablished; Louis Napoleon assumed the title of Emperor.

10. The Constitution of May 1, 1870: actually a new imperial constitution, submitted as such to a vote of the people and confirmed by that vote.

11. The Constitution of September 4, 1870: creating a provisional government, which gave way in February, 1871, to the National Assembly.[1]

The following is an extract from the Declaration of the Rights of Man made by the National Assembly of France, August, 1791:

Men are born and continue equal in respect of their rights.

The end of political society is the preservation of the natural and imprescriptible rights of man. These rights are liberty, property, security, and resistance to oppression.

The principle of all sovereignty resides essentially in the nation. No body, no individual, can exert any authority which is not expressly derived from it.

All citizens have a right to concur personally, or through their representatives, in making the law. Being equal in its eyes, then, they are all equally admissible to all dignities, posts, and public employments.

No one ought to be molested on account of his opinions, even his religious opinions.

THE COMMUNIST MANIFESTO (1847)

In *The Communist Manifesto* of 1847 Karl Marx and Friedrich Engels reviewed the historical development of the struggle between various social classes and stated the fundamental principles upon which communists would try to socialize government in the future. The *Manifesto* itself is long, totaling, in the printed edition from which these extracts are taken, 44 pages. It is difficult, if not impossible, to select a few paragraphs which shall represent adequately the entire *Manifesto*. We give herewith, however, ten fundamental changes in economic, political, and social life which the authors maintain must come in the socialization of collective life.

1. Expropriation of landed property and the use of land rents to defray State expenditure.
2. A vigorously graduated income tax.

[1] Adapted from *Select Constitutions of the World*, pp. 385–386. Prepared for presentation to Dail Eireann, by Order of the Irish Provisional Government. Messrs. Eason and Son, Ltd., Dublin, 1922.

3. Abolition of the right of inheritance.

4. Confiscation of the property of all *émigrés* and rebels.

5. Centralisation of credit in the hands of the State by means of a national bank with State capital and an exclusive monopoly.

6. Centralisation of the means of transport in the hands of the State.

7. Increase of national factories and means of production, cultivation of uncultivated land, and improvement of cultivated land in accordance with a general plan.

8. Universal and equal obligation to work; organisation of industrial armies, especially for agriculture.

9. Agriculture and urban industry to work hand-in-hand in such a way as, by degrees, to obliterate the distinction between town and country.

10. Public and free education of all children. Abolition of factory work for children in its present form. Education and material production to be combined.[1]

CHINA

Sun Yat-sen's *Fundamentals of National Reconstruction* (there are 25 articles altogether. Only the first four are given here):

I. The National Government shall reconstruct the Republic of China upon the basis of the revolutionary principles known as the *San Min Chu I* ("The Three Principles of the People") and the Five-Power Constitution.

II. The first principle of reconstruction is that of popular livelihood or the promotion of general welfare. In order to meet the most urgent needs of the people for food, clothing, shelter, and communication with one another, the Government shall coöperate with the people in the improvement of agriculture so that all may have sufficient food, in the development of the textile industry so that all may have sufficient clothing, in the building of houses on a large scale so that all may have comfortable homes, and in the building and improvement of roads and waterways so that all may conveniently travel and transport their goods.

III. The next principle of reconstruction is democracy. In order that the people may be fitted for participation in government, the Government shall instruct them in the exercise of their rights of voting for public officers, and of initiative, referendum, and recall.

IV. The third principle of reconstruction is nationalism. The Government shall protect the racial minorities within the country and assist them so that they may become able to exercise their rights of self-determination and self-government. It shall also resist oppression from foreign powers and at the same time shall revise the treaties with the powers so as to secure national independence and equality with all nations.[2]

[1] *The Communist Manifesto of Karl Marx and Friedrich Engels*, pp. 52–53. International Publishers, New York, 1930.

[2] Arthur N. Holcombe, *The Chinese Revolution*, p. 352. Harvard University Press, Cambridge, Massachusetts, 1931.

MEXICO

Extracts from the Political Constitution of the United States of Mexico. Adopted on January 31, 1917, amending that of January 5, 1857:

... Article 27. The ownership of lands and waters comprised within the limits of the national territory is vested originally in the Nation, which has had, and has, the right to transmit title thereof to private persons, thereby constituting private property. ...

... Legal capacity to acquire ownership of lands and waters of the Nation shall be governed by the following provisions:

I.—Only Mexicans by birth or naturalisation and Mexican companies have the right to acquire authority over lands, waters, and their appurtenances, or to obtain concessions to develop mines, waters or mineral fuels in the Republic of Mexico. The Nation may grant the same right to foreigners, provided they agree before the Department of Foreign Affairs to be considered Mexicans in respect to such property, and accordingly not to invoke the protection of their Governments in respect to the same, under penalty, in case of breach, of forfeiture to the Nation of property so acquired. Within a zone of 100 kilometres from the frontiers, and of 50 kilometres from the sea coast, no foreigner shall under any conditions acquire direct authority over lands and waters.

II.—The religious institutions known as churches, irrespective of creed, shall in no case have legal capacity to acquire, hold, or administer real property or loans made on such real property; all such real property or loans as may be at present held by the said religious institutions, either on their own behalf or through third parties, shall vest in the Nation, and anyone may give information as to property so held. ... Places of public worship are the property of the Nation, as represented by the Federal Government, which shall determine which of them may continue to be devoted to this purpose. Episcopal residences, rectories, seminaries, asylums or collegiate establishments of religious institutions, convents or any other buildings built or designed for the administration, propaganda, or teaching of the tenets of any religious creed shall forthwith vest, as of full right, directly in the Nation, to be used exclusively for the public services of the Federation or of the States, within their respective jurisdictions. ...

OF LABOUR AND SOCIAL WELFARE

... Article 123. The Congress and the State Legislatures shall make laws relative to labour with due regard for the needs of each region, and in conformity with the following principles, and these principles and laws shall govern the labour of skilled and unskilled workmen, employees, domestic servants and artisans, and in general every contract of labour.

I.— Eight hours shall be the maximum limit of a day's work.

II.— The maximum limit of night work shall be seven hours. Unhealthy and dangerous occupations are forbidden to all women and to children under sixteen years of age. Night work in factories is likewise forbidden to women and to children under sixteen years of age; nor shall they be employed in commercial establishments after ten o'clock at night.

III.— The maximum limit of a day's work for children over twelve and under sixteen years of age shall be six hours. The work of children under twelve years of age shall not be made the subject of a contract.

IV.— Every workman shall enjoy at least one day's rest for every six days' work. . . .

VI.— The minimum wage to be received by a workman shall be that considered sufficient, according to the conditions prevailing in the respective region of the country, to satisfy the normal needs of the life of the workman, his education and his lawful pleasures, considering him as the head of a family. In all agricultural, commercial, manufacturing or mining enterprises the workman shall have the right to participate in the profits in the manner fixed in Clause IX of this Article.[1]

[1] *Select Constitutions of the World*, pp. 248–249, 282–283. Prepared for presentation to Dail Eireann, by Order of the Irish Provisional Government. Messrs. Eason and Son, Ltd., Dublin, 1922.

RUSSIA

The Constitution (Fundamental Law) of the Russian Socialist Federal Soviet Republic. Adopted by the Fifth All-Russian Congress of Soviets, at the Session of July 10, 1918:

PART I

Declaration of Rights of the Labouring and Exploited Masses

Chapter I

1. Russia is declared a Republic of Soviets of Workers', Soldiers' and Peasants' Deputies. All central and local authority is vested in these Soviets.

2. The Russian Soviet Republic is established on the basis of a free union of free nations, as a federation of national Soviet Republics.

Chapter II

3. With the fundamental aim of suppressing all exploitation of man by man, of abolishing forever the division of society into classes, of ruthlessly suppressing all exploiters, of bringing about the Socialist organisation of society, and of establishing the triumph of Socialism in all countries, the Third All-Russian Congress of Soviets further decrees:

a. In order to establish the socialisation of land, private ownership of land is abolished; all land is declared national property, and is handed over to the workers, without compensation, on the basis of an equitable division, carrying with it the right of use only.

b. All forests, underground mineral wealth, and waters of national importance, all live stock and appurtenances, together with all model farms and agricultural concerns, are declared public property. . . .

PART II

General Principles of the Constitution of the Russian Socialist Federal Soviet Republic

Chapter V

. . . 13. To ensure for the workers genuine liberty of conscience, the Church is separated from the State and the school from the Church; and freedom of religious and anti-religious propaganda is assured to every citizen.

14. To ensure for the workers effective liberty of opinion, the Russian Socialist Federal Soviet Republic puts an end to the dependence of the press upon capital; transfers to the working class and to the peasants all the technical and material resources necessary for the publication of newspapers, pamphlets, books, and other printed matter; and guarantees their unobstructed circulation throughout the country.

15. To ensure for the workers complete freedom of meeting, the Russian Socialist Federal Soviet Republic, recognising the right of its citizens freely to organise meetings, processions, and so on, places at the disposal of the workers and peasants all premises convenient for public gatherings, together with lighting, heating, and furniture. . . .

17. To ensure for the workers effective access to education the Russian Socialist Federal Soviet Republic sets before itself the task of providing for the workers and poorer peasants a complete, universal, and free education.

18. The Russian Socialist Federal Soviet Republic proclaims it the duty of all citizens to work, on the principle "He that does not work, neither shall he eat." . . .

22. The Russian Socialist Federal Soviet Republic, recognising the equality of all citizens before the law, irrespective of race or nationality, declares it contrary to the fundamental laws of the Republic to institute or tolerate privileges, or any prerogative whatsoever, founded on such grounds, or to repress national minorities, or in any way to limit their rights.

23. In the general interest of the working class, the Russian Socialist Federal Soviet Republic deprives individuals and sections of the community of any privileges which may be used by them to the detriment of the Socialist revolution. . . .

GERMANY

Extracts from the Constitution of the German Commonwealth of August 11, 1919:

The German people, united in every branch and inspired by the determination to renew and establish its realm in freedom and justice, to be of service to the cause of peace at home and abroad, and to further social progress, has given itself this Constitution. . . .

FUNDAMENTAL RIGHTS AND DUTIES OF GERMANS

Section I. The Individual

Article 109. All Germans are equal before the law.
Men and women have fundamentally the same civic rights and duties.

Public legal privileges or disadvantages of birth or rank shall be abolished. Titles of nobility shall be simply a part of the name, and may no longer be conferred. . . .

Article 114. Personal liberty is inviolable. No encroachment on or deprivation of personal liberty by any public authority is permissible except in virtue of a law.

Persons who have been deprived of their liberty shall be informed — at the latest on the following day — by what authority and on what grounds the deprivation of liberty has been ordered; opportunity shall be given them without delay to make legal complaint against such deprivation.

Article 115. The residence of every German is an inviolable sanctuary for him; exceptions are admissible only in virtue of laws.

Article 116. No punishment may be inflicted for any action unless the action was designated by law as punishable, before it was committed.

Article 117. The secrecy of correspondence and of the postal, telegraph, and telephone services, is inviolable. Exceptions may be permitted only by law of the Reich.

Article 118. Every German has the right, within the limits of general laws, to express his opinion freely, by word of mouth, writing, printed matter, or picture, or in any other manner. This right must not be affected by any conditions of his work or appointment, and no one is permitted to injure him on account of his making use of such rights.

No censorship shall be enforced, but restrictive regulations may be introduced by law in reference to cinematograph entertainments. Legal measures are also admissible for the purpose of combating bad and obscene literature, as well as for the protection of youth in public exhibitions and performances.[1]

[1] *Select Constitutions of the World*, pp. 179, 197–199. Prepared for presentation to Dail Eireann, by Order of the Irish Provisional Government. Messrs. Eason and Son, Ltd., Dublin, 1922.

INDEX

Page numbers in italics refer to maps